A COLLECTION OF UPPER SOUTH CAROLINA

GENEALOGICAL and FAMILY RECORDS

Volume II

D1265104

Editor:
James E. Wooley

Please direct all correspondence and orders to:

www.southernhistoricalpress.com
or
SOUTHERN HISTORICAL PRESS, Inc.
PO BOX 1267
375 West Broad Street
Greenville, SC   29601
southernhistoricalpress@gmail.com

ISBN #0-89308-210-4

Printed in the United States of America

PREFACE

This is the second volume in a proposed series of titles on
Upper South Carolina genealogical and family records and it is
hoped that they will provide considerable source material for
those people whose research efforts have been stymied in that
area of Upper S.C. formerly known as Old 96 District.

These records are taken from the vast files of the late Pauline
Young of Liberty, S.C., probably the most well-known genealogist
in Upper South Carolina. Her most widely known book "Abstracts of
Old Ninety-Six and Abbeville District, S.C." is still the "bible"
for people doing research in this area.

The files from which this volume is taken were given to the
Publisher in 1968 and they were loose sheets that filled some three
file cabinet drawers. At the same time an equal number, if not a
larger number, of similar typed papers were sold to the Ladson
Library in Vidalia, Georgia. This private library has now been
given to the city of Vidalia and is probably the largest genealogical library in Georgia with the exception of the Georgia State
Department of Archives and History, Mr. John E. Ladson, Jr.'s
private collection of books numbering over 40,000 volumes.

Mr. James E. Wooley of Asheville, N.C., and his wife Vivian
have been doing personal genealogical research for thirty or more
years and in recent years came to be good friends with the Publisher. As a result of the Publisher mentioning these records
to Mr. Wooley and asking if he would be interested in working on
these miscellaneous family papers from Miss Young's files, Mr.
Wooley agreed to see what he might do to make them available to
the public in book form.

Originally, we had hoped that we might be able to abstract and
condense these papers down from their original length. However,
the more involved he became the more Mr. Wooley realized that
Miss Young had already condensed them from the originals, so that,
in effect, there was little that could be done to shorten them.

In order to try and present as balanced a set of data and
records as possible, it was decided to provide more data on those
letters of the alphabet from which more surnames began, i.e.,
A, B, C, J, M, S, W, etc., in Volume I; and for those letters
like I, Q, O, Z, etc., to include families beginning in letters
similar to these in other volumes. Hence, for instance, in this
Volume II the reader will note that there are Surnames beginning
with all letters, even I and Q, etc., and such will be the case
for all future volumes. Volume III will be out by some time
around December 1981.

At some future date these private family files belonging to the
Publisher will be given to a repository for cataloging and for use
by the public. At this point it is not definite which Library
will benefit from these records, but most likely the new Ladson
Memorial Library in Vidalia, Georgia, so that the complete Pauline
Young collection can be available in one place.

June 1981
The Rev. Silas Emmett Lucas,Jr.
Publisher

ABNEY, JAMES M. Box 2 Pack 48. Probate Judge Office. Edgefield, S. C. Paid 13 Sept. 1848 James M. Abney in full of the estate, both real and personal $2,385.87. Paid 23 Dec. 1846 Susan Abney for making clothes $2.00. Paid 30 Dec. 1845 Lewis Sample for six months board for ward and one month for horse $40.00. Paid 20 Dec. 1842 Joel Abney tuition $16.00. Received 7 Dec. 1834 of Wm. T. Abney admr. of John R. Abney decd. for the share of James M. Abney of said estate $1,451.41.

ABNEY, JOEL Box 2 Pack 35. Probate Judge Office. Edgefield, S. C. Will dated 3 Feb. 1816. Proven 22 Feb. 1816. Wife Elizabeth Abney, executrix Chn. Narcissa Abney, Elimina Abney, Elijah P. Abney, Mark M. Abney, Charlotte E. Abney, Azariah S. D. Abney. Wit. Azariah Abney, Wm. Coleman, W. D. Boatman. Inv. made 29 Feb. 1816 by Wm. Hill, John Inlow, Urbane Nicholson. 1817 paid Lark Abney admr. $1,353.93 1/4.

ABNEY, JOEL Box 1 Pack 8. Probate Judge Office. Edgefield, S. C. Est. admr. 3 Sept. 1838 by William Mobley, Richard Coleman, Michael Watson, who are bound unto the Ordinary in the sum of $8,000.00. 15 Sept. 1838 this is to certify that I Martha Abney the wife of Joel Abney decd. have assigned all my right of admr. in the est. of above decd. to Wm. Mobley. Signed: Martha X Abney. Paid 4 Oct. 1852 John Abney in full his share $1,394.87. Paid 7 April 1853 J. L. Walton and N. E. A. Walton in full $1421.35. Paid 19 Dec. 1856 John P. Abney Admr. of Mathew A. Abney decd. in full $1,648.16. Paid 21 Sept. 1857 Joel Abney in full his share $1,712.58. Inv. made 12 Sept. 1836 by Wm. Boadan, E. P. Abney, Mark Black. Sale made on 13 Dec. 1838, buyers: Wiley Clery, Patsey Abney, George Hueit, Mark Black, Dennis McCarty, Richard Coleman, Wm. Strother, John H. Smith, N. W. Clary, E. P. Abney, Thomas Carson, Aza Abney, William Mobley.

ABNEY, JOHN Box 2 Pack 38. Probate Judge Office. Edgefield, S. C. Est. admr. 1 Dec. 1823 by John Chapman, James Bell, Peterson Borroum who are bound unto the Ordinary in the sum of $12,000.00. Agatha Abney was the wife. Paid James Ramage 14 Feb. 1828 bal. of note $167.45. Paid 13 Aug. 1828 Wm. Griffith his wife share $92.94. Paid 13 Aug. 1828 Matthew Abney his share $92.94. Paid 13 Aug. Wm. Bladon his wife share $92.94. Paid 13 Aug. Jos. Griffith in part of Agathas Abney share $30.00. Paid 1 Dec. 1829 Cadaway and Agatha Clark the portions to which they are entitled $100.00.

ABNEY, JOHN R. Box 1 Pack 24. Probate Judge Office. Edgefield, S. C. Est. admr. 17 Mar. 1829 by Wm. T. Abney, Mastin Abney, Leroy Brown who are bound unto the Ordinary in the sum of $6,000.00. I relinquish all my claim as an Admr. of the est. of my husband, John R. Abney decd. Signed Alesey Abney, Dated 20 Feb. 1829. Inv. made 17 March 1829 by Tuliver Towler, Edw. Clark, James Maynard, Thomas Scurry, Sr. Paid on 20 June 1831 the est. of Walter Abney Sr. the amount of purchased of the said est. of John R. Abney decd. $369.63. Rec. 1 Feb. 1831 of Simeon Abney $9.00. Paid 6 Sept. 1831 Lewis Sample and wife widow in part of share $595.56 1/2. Paid 31 Dec. 1829 to the est. of Mary Abney $100.00. Rec. of Est. of Walter Abney $6.12 1/2.

ABNEY, LARK Box 2 Pack 40. Probate Judge Office. Edgefield, S. C. Will dated 6 May 1822. Executrix wife Martha Abney. Wit: Jesse Blocker, Eben Hammond, Barkley M. Blocker. Proven 1 Oct. 1822. Lark Abney was in the State of Alabama. Bequeath to his chn. Elizabeth Lark Abney, Claricy Jane Abney, Dabney Parner(?) Abney, and his wife Martha, thirteen slaves and two tracts of land in Edgefield Dist., S. C. One tract on Mountain Creek on Cane Creek Road the other tract known as the Hamilton tract on Sleepy Creek containing 80 acres. Received from his father and guardian of my brothers Henry Madison Abney, Jonathan Abney, Ira Abney, minors.

ABNEY, MARY   Box 1 Pack 23.   Probate Judge Office.   Edgefield,
S. C. Est. admr. 2 Nov. 1829 by Wm. T. Abney, Leroy Brown, Mastin
Abney who are bound unto the Ordinary in the sum of $1500.00. Cit.
Pub. at Chestnut Hill Meeting house 24 Oct. 1827. Personally appeared
before me John Chapman, Wm. T. Abney securities of Mrs. Mary Abney
surviving Admr. of Walter Abney decd. their being duly sworn on their
oath dispose that they have just reason to apprehend and do convey
themselves in danger of being injured by continuance of such. Signed
John Chapman, Wm. T. Abney. Dated 20 July 1829. received 5 March
1832 by cash of Mastin Abney $85.50. Rec. by cash of Simeon Abney
$85.50. Rec. by cash of Edw. Clark gdn. $85.50. Inv. made 10 Nov.
1829 by James Maynard, Edward Clark, Thomas Ross.

ABNEY, MASTON   Box 1 Pack 18.   Probate Judge Office.   Edgefield,
S. C. Est. admr. 10 Feb. 1835 by Simeon Abney, Wm. Abney, Sr.,
Oliver Towles who are bound unto the Ordinary in the sum of $600.00.
Inv. made 14 Feb. 1835 by Wm. T. Abney, Edward Clark, James Maynard.
Sale held 27 Feb. 1835. Buyers: James Maynard, Lewis Sample, Simon
Abney, Benjamin Richardson, David Payne, Wm. Abney, Jr., W. T. Abney,
Wm. Scurey, Jesse Attaway, Edward Clark, Sampson Christy, Hazel Cul-
breath, John Brown, Thomas Scurry, Jr., Saml. Strum, Cadaway Clark,
Thomas Christan, Saml. Deloach, Walter W. Brown, Simeon Dean, Benjamin
Grigsby, Larkin G. Carter, Benjamin Broadaway, Wm. Harmon, John H.
Allen.

ABNEY, PAUL   Box 2 Pack 33.   Probate Judge Office, Edgefield,
S. C. Will dated 24 Oct. 1819. Executors John Chapman, John Abney.
Wit: John Chapman, Agatha Abney, Sophia Chapman. I give unto my son
John Abney five negroes (not named) and to my dtrs. Jane Barnes,
Martha Peterson, Mary Bates, Tabitha Hicks, and Elizabeth Black each
$100.00. My dtr. Elizabeth Black I give property by a direct line
running through the land nearby. They shall live there rent free
until Paul Abney Peterson their son is 21 yrs. old. Paid on 19 April
1826 Edw. I. Hicks $12.37 1/2. Paid 1825 James Barnes balance of
legacy $36.00. Paid 4 Aug. 1826 Peter Black his share $14.67. Inv.
made 13 Jan. 1821 by Zachariah Abney, John Inlow, M. W. Coleman and
Daniel Berry.

ABNEY, SIMEON   Box 1 Pack 19.   Probate Judge Office.   Edgefield,
S. C. Est. admr. 5 Feb. 1838 by William Abney, Thomas Scurry, John
Chappell who are bound unto the Ordinary in the sum of $1200.00.
Cit. Pub. at and before the congregation at Chestnut Ridge on 11 Mar.
1837. Inv. made by David Payne, Robert Maxwell, Cadaway Clark. Paid
the widow Sophia Abney her part $684.25. Paid Master Abney his part
$758.02. Paid William T. Abney admr. of Mastia Abney the balance of
account due from Simeon est. to Mastins $758.02.

ABNEY, SUSAN   Box 2 Pack 43.   Probate Judge Office.   Edgefield,
S. C. Est. admr. 16 Jan. 1832 by Lewis Sample, Tolever Towles, Edw.
Clark who are bound unto the Ordinary in the sum of $2,000.00. Cit.
Pub. at Chestnut Meeting House, 25 Dec. 1831. Received 9 Sept. 1834
from Wm. P. Abney admr. of the est. of John R. Abney decd. $967.61.

ABNEY, WALTER   Box 1 Pack 26.   Probate Judge Office.   Edgefield,
S. C. Will dated 8 Dec. 1827, Executors Thomas Christian, John R.
Abney. Wit: John Chapman, Michael Deloach, Abjah(?) Abney. I give
to my dtr. Arathuisa Brown 100 acres of land. Also to my dtr. R.
Abney 175 acres of land. I give to my son Mastin Abney 175 acres of
land. I give to my son William Abney 175 acres land I give to my son
Simeon Abney 175 acres of land, on south west of my son John R. Abney
land. Est. admr. 31 Dec. 1827 by John R. Abney, Murry Abney, John
Chapman, and Wm. T. Abney who are bound unto the Ordinary in the sum
of $3,500.00. Cit. Pub at Chestnut Hill, 25 July 1829. Sale made 21
Jan. 1828. Buyers: Leroy Brown, Wm. Colbreth, Mastin Abney, Murry
Abney, Jesse Colbreth, George Dean. Michael Deloach, John Kelly,
Benjamin Philpott, Wm. Turner, John Abney Sr., Charity Johnson. Paid
21 Jan. 1829 Absalom T. Abney on proven account $2.75. Paid Mastin
Abney in full on account $77.84. Paid 27 Jan. 1829, Wm. B. Abney
book account $15.25.

ABNEY, WALTER, Jr.   Box 1 Pack 28.   Probate Judge Office, Edgefield, S. C. Est. admr. 8 Nov. 1830 by Absalom T. Abney, Edw. Clark, Wm. T. Abney who are bound unto the Ordinary in the sum of $1,800.00. Inv. made 27 Nov. 1830 by Wm. Culbreath, John Culbreath, Edw. Culbreath. Rec. 30 Jan. 1832 of Simeon Abney $25.00. Paid 6 Feb. 1831 John Abney his share of est. $327.75. Paid 25 Dec. 1839 Benjamin F. Jones in full for the dist. share of Robert Blythe and wife Frances which amount said Jones is authorized to receive as per power of attorney from said Blythe. $67.00

ABNEY, WILLIAM Box 2 Pack 50.   Probate Judge Office. Edgefield, S. C. I Barshaba Abney the wife of Wm. Abney decd. do hereby certify unto all whom it may concern that I relinquish my right of Admr. over to my brother Sampson Pope. Wit my hand this 25 Aug. 1811. Est. admr. 13 Aug. 1811 by Sampson Pope, Stanmore Butler and Jeremiah Hatcher who are bound unto the Ordinary in the sum of $4,000.00. Cit. Pub. at Chestnut Hill Meeting House, 10 Aug. 1811. Paid boarding and clothing Susannah, Ellen, Barahaba and Charlotte Abney. For the years 1817-18-19. He owned three slaves (not named). Paid 27 April 1814 debt and cost of suit brought against Phillip Hazwl (?) and Wm. Abney decd. $13.00

ABNEY, WILLIAM, Sr.   Box 1 Pack 22.   Probate Judge Office, Edge-field, S. C. Est. admr. 6 Feb. 1832 by David Mack, John Abney, Saml. Christian who are bound unto the Ordinary in the sum of $600.00. Inv. made 11 Feb. 1832 by Isaac Herring, Jacob Holtenwanger, Allen Christian. Cit. pub. at Chestnut Hill Meeting house. Paid 15 Jan. 1833 John Abney $7.00. Paid 24 April 1834 A. T. Abney $5.00. Paid 1 March 1834 Hiram Abney $37.18 3/4.

ABNEY, WILLIAM T.   Box 1 Pack 21.   Probate Judge Office. Edge-field, S. C. Est. admr. 6 Feb. 1837 by Richard Coleman, Wm. Strother and Simeon Christie who are bound unto the Ordinary in the sum of $24,000.00. Cit. Pub. at Good Hope Church on 28 Jan. 1837, and at Mayold Field muster ground on 4 Feb. 1837. Received 8 Mar. 1837 of Azariah Abney $63.56 1/4. Received 13 Dec. of Wm. Abney $4.50. Paid on 25 Nov. 1839 Ira Culbreath for tuition for the yrs. 1838-39 for Henderson Abney, Mary Abney, Susan Abney, and Lucian Abney. Paid 10 Jan. 1840 David Patton his wife share of the est. $3,735.97. Paid on 26 Dec. 1838 R. H. Coleman for Mary E. Abney $6.43 3/4.

ABNEY, ZACHARIAH Box 1 Pack 11.   Probate Judge Office. Edgefield, S. C. Est. admr. 23 Feb. 1838 by Thomas W. Pope, Y. J. Harrington, John S. Carville who are bound unto the Ordinary in the sum of $30,000. Inv. made 6 March 1838 by Bannett Perry, Aza Abney, Richard Coleman, James Maynard, Light P. Abney, and Wilson Abney the two only heirs. Upon application of Thomas Pope, Admr. ordered that the admr. sell at Newberry Court House on the first Monday in Jan. next a negro man named Sam belonging to the est. of decd. under credit until 25 Dec. 1829, dated 22 Nov. 1838 signed O. Towles. Paid 9 March 1847 Wilson Abney in full $172.08. Paid 27 Oct. Zachariah $15.00. Paid 9 March L. N. Abney part of legacy $1,000.00. Paid 4 Feb. L. N. Abney part of legacy $100.00 by Tabithea Abney the widow. Paid 17 Jan. 1839 James L. Gilder in part of his wife Melinda share $500.00, paid 16 Jan. Thompson Cappock in part of his wife Lucenda share $500.00, paid 19 Jan. J. K. Schumpert in part of his wife Harriett share $500.00, paid 18 Jan. Benjamin T. Abney in part of his share $1308.45. Paid 12 Jan. Wm. C. Gilder in part of his wife Luthuis share $1300. Paid 25 Dec. 1838 Martha in part of her share, receipt is confirmed by her husband $57.00. Paid 7 Aug. 1843 A. H. Coleman in full of his wife Minerva share $71.59. Paid 27 Dec. 1838 George Huiet intestate subscription for building Bethany Church $20.00, same date paid George Huiet the amount collected by intestate for said church from Benj. Corley, James Tampkins, Griffin Rutherford, and Edward Coleman $9.00. Sale held 8 March 1838, buyers; Benjamin T. Abney, Tabitha Abney, Azariah Abney, Miss Martha Abney, Miss Minerva Abney, Thomas Berry, Z. S. Pipps, John Chapman, Sazon(?) Coppock, Benj. Corley, W. Curbreath[?], Lewis Crary, Guijnano Sanders, Richard Coleman, George Huiet, Thomas Y. Logan, Livingston Daniel, George Long, David Mack, Donald Mangum,

Abney, Zachariah - Continued. John Mangum, Dennis McCarty, Robert McCarty, Robert Marchant, Lewis Sampler, J. K. Schumpert, John Scurry, John Summers, Jacob Smith, Arthur Webb, Caleb Willis, Daniel Wheeler, Elias Walton.

ACKER, PETER No. Ref. Greenville Court House. Greenville, S. C. To Susannah Acker, the widow, Halbert Acker, Alexander Acker, William Mattison and wife Elizabeth, Joel M. Townsend & Mary his wife, Allen McDavid & Teresa his wife, Jesse McGee and Lucinda his wife, Peter N. Acker, Joel M. Acker, Joshua S. Acker, and the heirs of Frances Hammond decd. Being legal heirs and representatives of Peter Acker decd. who died intestate. You are required to be present at the Court of Ordinary in Greenville Dist. on the first Monday in August in 1834 to show cause if any why the real estate of Peter Acker decd. should not be divided or sold. Land in Greenville Dist. on Saluda River, adj. land of Harrison Clark and others containing 200 acres. Dated 2 June 1834. Signed Jno. Watson, O. G. D., Joel Townsend and Mary were made guardian of Frances Hammond heirs, and Joel Acker and Joshua S. Acker. The heirs of Frances Hammond who lived in Georgia, viz: Teresa C. Hammond, Christopher C. Hammond, Julian F. Hammond, Wm. H. Hammond, Susanna Hammond, Mary C. Hammond.

ADAMS, CHARLES Box 1 Pack 4. Probate Judge Office. Edgefield, S. C. Will dated 17 June 1824, recorded 21 May 1837. I leave the plantation where I now live containing 239 acres to be hers (name not given) and for her use during her natural life. The balance of my property to be divided in 7 equal parts between my dtr. Fanney & Elizabeth and Nancy and my sons William, Wiley also to Maryann and Sally. I leave to my loving wife Sally Adams as a guardian to manage the legacy bequeath by this will to my dtr. Fanny Bartlet, so she may benefit during her natural life, then to pass to her chn. if she sould not have chn. then return to her brothers and sisters. Wit: John Mayes, Jr. Paid 8 Dec. 1835 Wiley T. Adams in part his share $400.00. Paid 1 Nov. 1828. Simeon Deen his share $109.61. Paid 11 July 1829 John Still in part $129.25. Paid 17 April 1837 William Deen his share in right of his wife $4.50. Date of sale not given. Buyers Sarah Adams, Simeon Deen, John Dorn, Sr., John Dorn, Jr., Robert Bryon, James Clark, M. E. Berry, Thos. Youngblood, Wm. Buckalew, Ezekiel Crabtree, Wiley Thompson, John Faulkner, Henry Adams, R. W. Smith, Gibson Collins, Mark Nobles, W. T. Hubbard, Frederick Williams, John Matthews, Stephen C. Terry, Lewis Clark, John May, Goody McManus, Robert Smith.

ADAM, DRURY Box 2 Pack 31. Probate Judge Office. Edgefield, S. C. Will dated 1814. Executors wife Sarah Adams, Jonathan Devore, Daniel Roper. Wit: Roger M. Williams, Benj. Hargrove, I give to my son James F. Adams one small tract of land lying cross the Martin Town road. The remaining property to be divided between my four children. James F., Mary Devore, Aggie Bird, Elizabeth Roper. I give to my step children, Benj. Roper and Polly Roper the tract of land known as the walnut hill tract. I give to my son Abraham Adams the tract of land cornering on Niles land. I give to Sarah Adams my wife the plantation whereon I now live with ten negroes. (Not named) At the death of my wife son John Adams shall have the land whereon I now live. Will proved 26 May 1851. Sale made 15 July 1815. Buyers: John C. Garrett, Thomas H. Howle, John Jones, Hillary Collier, Robert Lang, Sr., David Quarles, Mrs. Sarah Adams, Chas. Hammond, Daniel Roper, Jos. Mealing, Edw. Martin, Jonathan Devore.

ADAMS, DRURY Box 1 Pack 1. Probate Judge Office, Edgefield, S. C. Est. admr. 27 Oct. 1834 by John Adams, Benjamin Roper, N. Sampson who are bound unto the Ordinary in the sum of $15,000. Inv. made 19 Nov. 1834 by George Getzen, Sampson Sullivan, C. B. Limbecker for the amount of $6746.00. Cit. published at Antioch Church 23 Oct. 1834. Settlement made 12 Dec. 1836. Roper L. Glauton share $322.92, Martha S. Adams share $1,956.38. 26 Dec. 1835 C. S. Adams share $1,956.38. 5 Feb. 1836 Drury S. Adams share $1,956.38. 20 Jan. 1836 share paid Mary Glauton $161.46. 8 Jan. 1836 share paid Benjamin Roper share $161.46.

ADAMS, JOHN   Pack 500.   Clerk of Court Office.   Abbeville, S. C.
Deed from Basdell Darby to John Adams both of Abbeville Dist.   Dated
23 Oct. 1822.   In consideration of $1220.00.. have granted, sold,
bargained and released unto John Adams all that tract of land containing 225 acres.   Originally granted unto Robert Norras, Jur., also
part of a grant to John Foster, decd.   Bounded by John Foster land,
Thos. Osburn land, and E. C. Morgan land, lying on Frazars Creek
waters of Norris Creek, waters of Long Cane Creek.   Wit: Sam L. Watt,
Thos. McMillion.   Signed Basdell Darby.   On the 15 March 1823 Martha
Darby the wife of Basdell Darby did release and renounce and relinquish her dower on the above land before John Devlin, J.P.   On 15 Oct.
1838 in the State of Miss. Pontotoc County personally appear before me
Benjamin D. Anderson, J. P., Samuel L. Watt one of the subscribing
witness, who swore he saw Basdell Darby sign the within deed.

ADAMS, JOHN   Pack 499.   Clerk of Court Office.   Abbeville, S. C.
We Joseph Hall Sanders, Wm. Springle and Frances his wife, Marcus D.
Moore and Catharine his wife, heirs, and Rebecca Sanders the widow and
relict of Joseph Sanders decd. to John Adams of Abbeville Dist.
Dated 3 March 1831.   In consideration of $605.00 have granted, sold
bargain and released unto John Adams all that tract belonging to the
late Joseph Sanders decd. containing 193 acres in Abbeville Dist. on
McCords Creek and Long Cane.   Adj. land of James Wardlaw, Mrs.
Tennent and Wm. P. Paul.   Wit: A. Bowie, D. Lesly.   Signed Joseph
H. Sanders, William Springle, Frances Springle, M. D. Moore, Catharine
Moore.   Proved on oath of David Lesly before Jno. F. Livingston, Clk.
Power of attorney from Frances Springle and Catharine Moore both of
the State of Alabama, Marengo County, did appear before R. R. Moore
and Daniel T. Fitchett, Commissioners and being privately and seper-
ately examined did renounce, release and relinquish all their right
of interest and inheritance on the real estate of Joseph Sanders decd.
Dated 11 Nov. 1831.

ADAMS, JOHN SR.   Box 2 Pack 39.   Probate Judge Office.   Edge-
field, S. C.   Will dated 11 Oct. 1822.   Executors son James Adams,
Wm. H. Adams.   Wit: James M. Harrison, Wm. H. Buffington, Edw.
Harrison.   Inv. made 22 Nov. 1822 by John Anderson, Jonathan Glanton,
Covington Hardy.   To wife Sarah Adams, son Wm. H. Adams I give 100
acres.   I give to Bartholomew S. Adams all my interest in the mill
on Hard Labor Creek.   I give to Elizabeth Tompkins, Mary Statesworth,
Susannah Tompkins and Rebecah Halloway $50.00 each.   I give to my son
James Adams, John Adams, Wm. H. Adams and Sarah Gibson the remainder
of my est. and eight slaves. (Not named).

ADAMS, THOMAS   Box 2 Pack 51.   Probate Judge Office.   Edgefield,
S. C.   Will dated 9 July 1809.   Proven 13 Oct. 1809.   Wife Elizabeth
Adams.   Children are: Wright, Hiram, Talbert, Joseph, Lucintha.
Executors wife Elizabeth, Samuel Nicholson, Jesse Blocker.   Wit:
Abner Blocker, Theophilus Nicholson, David Nicholson.   Paid 21 Feb.
1820 for boarding and clothing Joseph and Syntha Adams while going to
school nine months $10.00.   Received Dec. 1817 of Solomon Adams $20.00.
Paid 22 May 1821 Wright Adams $300.00.

ADAMS, WILLIAM   Box 1 Pack 14.   Probate Judge Office.   Edgefield,
S. C.   Will dated 5 Feb. 1842.   Proven 6 June 1842.   Executor son
William Adams.   Wit: Robert Bryan Sr., William May, Levi N. Churchill.
Signed Wm. X Adams.   Give to sons, James, Levi, Aaron and Charles
Adams land at value of $150.00 each.   Rest of estate to be divided
between my 10 chn.   I give to Patsey $100.00 Paid 29 Oct. 1842 Mary
Henson in full her share $580.94.   Paid 29 Oct. Wm. Lang in full share
$580.94.   Paid 29 Oct. Wm. N. Stuart in full his share $580.94.   Paid
29 Oct. Martha Lang in full her share $100.00.   Paid 29 Oct. Aaron
Adams in full his share $580.94.   Paid 29 Oct. Charles Adams in full
his share $580.94.   Paid 4 March Levi Adams in full his share $580.94.
Paid James Adams in full his share $580.94.   Paid Milly Trotter in
full her share $580.94.   Paid 17 Nov. Daniel Adams in full his share
$580.94.   Inv. made 16 July 1842 by Elisha Stevens, David Butler,
Martin X Coon.   Sale held 24 Oct. 1842.   Byrs; John W. May, Johnson
Lowry, Edmund Brown, J. W. Matthew, James Glaze, Saml. Webb, John W.

Adams, William - Continued. Smith, John Culbreath, Milly Trotter, Henry Adams, Lewis May, Stanford May, Mary Croker, Mary Trotter, William Adams, John Bryan, Robert D. Brian, Wm. Walton, George Reaves, Daniel Rogers, Terry C. Martin, Dan Hollaway, Elisha Stephens, John Eliza, John Hollewager, Aaron C. Dean, John Christie, James Richardson, Gidean Turner, Phillip Hazle, Elihu Payne, L. N. Churchill, Alford May, J. W. Coleman, David Butler, Martin Wit, Wm. Stuard, Lewis Adams, Wm. Lang, Thomas Powers, Levi Adams.

ADDISON, JOSEPH R.   Box 2 Pack 52.   Probate Judge Office.   Edgefield, S. C. Will dated 27 Aug. 1832.   Proved 24 April 1835.   Wit: Samuel B. Marsh, George A. Addison, A. B. Addison.   I give to my dtr. Eliza that I had by my first wife one third and furniture.   I here mention the reason that I have not made her share equal to my children by my last wife, that is because her grand father Phil A. Thurmond who raised her has promised to provide for her and do much better by her than I shall be able to do for the chn. of my last wife.   I desire to give to my beloved wife Matilda Addison the following during her natural life 3 slaves.   Her children, Martha Ann Addison, Mary Ann Addison, Whitfield B. Addison, Allen Addison and John Addison.

ADDISON, JOHN   Box 1 Pack 3.   Probate Judge Office.   Edgefield, S. C. Will dated 14 Dec. 1827 of John Addison, Sr. give to his youngest son James Madison Addison the sum of $300.00.   It is my desire that the balance of my est. be equal divided between the balance of my chn. Joseph B. Addison, Patsy Howard, Harriett Martin, Benjamin Addison, Tresa Addison, John A. Addison, Samuel Addison and David Addison.   Executors, Joseph R. & Benjamin Addison.   Wit: Edw. E. Ford, Sampson H. Butler, A. B. Addison.   Signed: John Addison.   Will approved 17 Jan. 1829 by John Simkins, Esq.   Ord. on 5 Mar. 1832 paid Sarah Addison for the maintenance of James Addison a minor $43.75. Memorandum of amount of property given by John Addison to his chn. Joseph R. Addison $512.00.   Patsy wife of B. A. Howard $452.00. Harriett wife of George Martin $424.00.   Benjamin Addison $617.00. Sale of est. made 5 Feb. 1829.   Buyers: John Colter, George Martin, Henry Mims, Matt. Martin, Matthew Martin, Joseph Addison, A. B. Addison, Dr. Mims, E. I. Youngblood, John Matthews, B. Mims, Benjamin Addison, Samuel Williams, Bate Howard, Elum Buckhelter, Robert Glover, William Briant, Joseph Brunson, Henry Huffman, Jesse Briant, Daniel Mayes, Mrs. Baty, John Harrison, N. Cristmass, John Stirow, Daniel Huff, George Getzson, B. Harrison, William Moss, W. Blalock, William Robertson, William B. Mayes, Ben Tillman, John Hinton, Dr. But, Robert Cockrum, John Rion, Elizabeth Mims, Robert Wates.

ADERHOLD, CONRAD   Book C Page 165.   Clerk of Court Office. Anderson, S. C. Deed from Conrad Aderhold to Thomas Goss both of Pendleton Dist.   Dated 25 Nov. 1795.   In consideration of 30 pds. sterling paid by Thomas Goss hath granted, sold, bargained and released a tract of land being in Washington Dist. lying on the South side of Rices Creek waters of 12 mile river, containing 100 acres being part of the tract granted to William Henderson on 5 June 1786.   Wit: Nathaniel Henderson, William Coun[?].   Signed Jn. Conrad Aderhold.

ADERHOLD, CONROD   Book B Page 152.   Clerk of Court Office. Anderson, S. C. Deed from William Henderson to Conrod Aderhold both of Pendleton Dist.   Dated 11 Feb. 1793.   In consideration of thirty six pounds current money paid by said Aderhold, have granted, sold, bargained and released all that plantation lying on Rices Creek of 12 Mile River containing 243 acres, being part of an original grant of 450 to said William Henderson on 5 June 1786.   Wit: Isaac Miller, John Glenn.   Signed: William Henderson.   Proven on oath of Isaac Miller before Elijah Browne, J.P. on the 12 April 1793.   Recorded 16 April 1793.

ADERHOLD, JOHN C.   Book O Page 332.   Clerk of Court Office. Anderson, S. C. Deed from John C. Aderhold of State of Georgia, Franklin Co. to David McCollum of Pendleton Dist., S. C.   Dated 22 Feb. 1819.   In consideration of $600.00 paid by said David McCollum

Aderhold, John C. - Continued hath granted, sold, release and
bargained all that tract of land lying and being in Pendleton Dist. on
Rices Creek near the Cedar Rock. Adj. land of Benton Freeman, Barnett's,
Duke's line. Containing 400 acres. Wit: Robert Verner, Sam. G.
Earle. Signed: John C. Aderhold. Proven on oath of Robert Varner
before George Varner, J.P. on the 22 Feb. 1819.

ADERHOLD, JOHN C. Book K Page 254. Clerk of Court Office.
Anderson, S. C. Deed from Abraham Duke, blacksmith to John C. Ader-
hold, taylor, both of Pendleton Dist. Dated 26 Jan. 1810. In con-
sideration of $20.00 paid by John C. Aderhold have granted, sold,
bargained and released, all that tract of land containing 60 acres.
No water course given. Wit: Thomas W. Saterfield, Lewis Gillstrap.
Signed: Abraham Duke. Proven on oath of Thomas W. Satterfield before
Wm. Jameson, J.P. on the 27 Jan. 1810. Recorded 22 Oct. 1810.

ADERHOLD, JOHN CONRAD Book I Page 85. Clerk of Court Office.
Anderson, S. C. Deed from Abraham Duke, blacksmith to John Conrad
Aderhold, taylor, both of Pendleton Dist. Dated 13 Nov. 1800. In
consideration of forty two eagles, eight dollars, dismes, seven cents
and one mil ($428.17 & 1 mil.) paid by John Conrad Aderhold have
granted, sold, bargained, and released all that tract of land, con-
taining 200 acres (no water course given). Wit: Isaac Miller, Robert
Glenn. Signed: Abraham Duke. Proven on oath of Isaac Miller before
David Murphree J.P. on the 15 Feb. 1805. On the 27 April 1805,
Rosannah Duke the wife of Abraham Duke and freely and voluntarily
released and relinquish her dower to the above land before James
Wardlaw, J.Q. Recorded 26 Oct. 1807

ADERHOLT, JOHN CONROD Book C Page 356. Clerk of Court Office.
Anderson, S. C. We Martha Henderson widow of late William Henderson
decd. and Nathaniel Henderson her son to John Conrod Aderhold, taylor.
All of Pendleton Dist. In consideration of $25.50 paid by Aderhold
have granted, bargained, sold and released all that tract of land
containing 100 acres lying on a branch of 12 River (now known as Rices
Creek) granted unto William Henderson 5 June 1786. Dated 10 June
1797. Wit: Abraham Duke, Margaret X Henderson, Jane Henderson.
Signed: Martha X Henderson and Nathaniel Henderson. Proven on oath
of Abraham Duke before John Wilson J.P. on the 10 Aug. 1797.

AGNEW, SAMUEL Pack 3363. Clerk of Court Office. Abbeville,
S. C. Abbeville Dist. In Equity to the Honr. Chancellors, your
oratrix Malinda Agnew is the widow of Samuel Agnew late of this dist.
now decd. who died about the 20 July 1844 intestate, leaving nine
children to wit: Enoch Agnew, Elizabeth the wife of Ebenezer E.
Pressly, James W. Agnew, Samuel Agnew, William Agnew, Joseph Agnew,
all over the age of twenty one. Washington Agnew, Alfred Agnew,
Melinda Jane Agnew under the age of twenty one. At the time of his
death he was seized and possessed with three tracts of land to wit.
The home tract whereon he died on Long Cane, containing 400 acres.
Adj. land of James Agnew Senr., Thomas Hawthorn. Tract #2 The mill
tract containing 370 acres, also on Long Cane bounded by Toliver
Johnson, James Blain. Tract #3. The Andrew Agnew tract, also on
Long Cane Creek, containing 270 acres, bounded by James Agnew, Enoch
Agnew and Thomas Hawthorn. The estate was admor. are Enoch Agnew and
James W. Agnew. Your oratrix has heard that all debts are paid and
that they have some assets in their hands. Your oratrix is now
desirous of having a partition of the land, and her share in severality
assigned to her. Filed 29 May 1845.

AKERMAN, JACOB Box 2 Pack 36. Probate Judge Office. Edgefield,
S. C. (Also written Ekerman) Know that I Christina Ekerman, wife of
Jacob Akerman, decd. do agree for James Smyly to admr. est. Wit:
Martin Cooke this 25 Mar. 1820. Est. admr. 1820 by James Smyly, John
Coates, Conrad Lowry who are bound unto the Ordinary in the sum of
$3,000.00. Paid 30 Nov. 1823 John Brisco and wife $8.69. Paid 2 May
1831 Jesse Smith and wife legacy $17.53. Cit. Pub. at Stephens Creek
on 2 April 1820.

ALLEN, ARON Box 1 Pack 6. Probate Judge Office. Edgefield, S. C.
Will dated 16 Oct. 1823. Proven 10 Nov. 1823. I do bequeath to
Bethany Kirkland 3 negroes and their increase (not named). I bequeath
to Benjamin Frazier 1 mulatto man named Jim and two noted of hand of
$600.00 each upon Turner Crookes. I bequeath to my father and mother
my horse and my sulkey. I give to William Frazier my silver watch
now in possession of Theophulus Hill. I bequeath to Benjamin Frazier,
Susan Willis, Enoch Phillis, negroes, Mira, Lewis, Henry and Simon
also a negro boy named Will given to me by my grandfather named Will.
Wit: A. B. McWortes, Edward Garret, Mack Melton. Signed A. Allen.
Sale held 22 Dec. 1823, buyers: Jesse Betty, Benjamin Frazier, Young
Allen, Noah Deese, John Hendricks, Crecy Murphy, E. W. Gill, Jesse
McClendon, John Cloud, Daniel Coleman, Major Coker, Crisppin [?] Davis,
Benjamin Tillman, John Patterson, Edmund Harrison, Whitfield Brooks,
John Henry, D. Bird, Stephen Stillman, Michael Melton, A. B. Addison,
H. W. Lowe, Major Crooker.

ALMAN, ARON Box 2 Pack 44. Probate Judge Office. Edgefield,
S. C. Est. admr. 5 May 1834 by Derick Holsonbake, Robert Holsonbake,
Jesse Williams who are bound unto the Ordinary in the sum of $1,000.00.
Received 5 Aug. 1834 of Mary Alman admr. of Hezekial Alman decd. share
of Aaron $271.50. Received 8 Dec. of J. Richardson share of Aaron
Allen of the real estate $68.10. Received from sale of land in
Lexington Co. $5.31.

ALMON, HEZIKIAH Box 1 Pack 25. Probate Judge Office. Edgefield,
S. C. Est. admr. 8 Oct. 1823 by Murry Almon, Solomon Almon, Moses
Holstrum, Lewis Almon who are bound unto the Ordinary in the sum of
$8,000.00. Inv. made 24 Oct. 1823 by Thos. Wynn, Saml. Redrick,
Benj. Evans. On 1 Aug. 1834 sett. made and find due to Aron Almon
$244.39. Paid 31 Dec. 1825 Thomas Claxton and wife $225.62 1/2.
Paid Charles N. Suton and wife $225.62 1/2. Paid William Almon
$225.62 1/2. Paid Holston Almon $225.62 1/2. Paid Derick Holsonback
$225.62 1/2. Paid Hezekiah Almon $225.62 1/2. Paid Solomon Almon.
Paid Aron Almon $30.00.

ALMON, WILLIS Box 1 Pack 16. Probate Judge Office. Edgefield
S. C. Est. admr. 2 Jan. 1826 by Holsom Almon, John Murrick, Derrick
Holsonback and Thomas Loveless who are bound unto the Ordinary in the
sum of $1,000.00. I do hereby assign over my right of Admr. on this
date of my son Willis Almon decd. to my son Hogan Almon. Sign
Mary Almon. Paid 8 Dec. 1834 Moses Almon. Paid 29 Dec. 1828 Thomas
Claxton $19.00. Paid Derrick Holsomback $19.00. Paid Lewillen,
Simon and Hezekiah Almon each $19.00. Paid Charles M. Sutton $19.00.
Paid Mary and William Almon each $19.00.

AMES, NATHAN C. Box 2 Pack 42. Probate Judge Office. Edgefield,
S. C. Est. admr. 3 Nov. 1813 by Jonathan Fox, Robert Brooks, Joel
Hill who are bound unto the Ordinary in the sum of $1,000.00. Cit.
read 3 Oct. 1813 at Swamp Meeting House. Cit. Pub. at Quals Meeting
House. Inv. made 9 Dec. 1813 by Thomas W. Morton, Richard Quarles,
Moses Tullis.

ANDERSON, ALLEN Box 1 Pack 13. Probate Judge Office. Edgefield,
S. C. Will dated 6 Jan. 1828, Executors his three sons George, James
and Allen Anderson. Wit: John R. Vartee, George Anderson, Covington
Hardy. Signed Allen X Anderson wife Mary Anderson. House and
plantation on which I now reside containing 100 acres given to my two
grand dtrs. Mary and Susannas Quarles. Inv. made 10 Dec. 1842 by
Silas Lanier, Jonathan Taylor and Albert Morgan had 37 slaves (names
not given). Sale held 5 Jan. 1843. Buyers: Allen Anderson, James
Mann, Hadley Cooper, Charles Hammond, Sterling Quarles, Goodman Roper,
Samuel Getzen, Charles Garrett, Wiley Glover, George Anderson, W. L.
Gerty, Edward Morse, Wm. W. Day, Seth Butler, Joseph Morse, John
Rainsford, John P. Mays, T. R. Anderson, Benj. Roper, David Mealing,
James Curry, John H. Cosby, Joel Curry, John B. Glover, G. W. Harrigal,
George Mathis, Edward S. Mays.

ANDERSON, COLBERT Box 105 Pack 2567. Probate Judge Office.
Abbeville, S. C. Ninety Six Dist. I Colbert Anderson being of sound
and perfect mind and memory, etc. First I desire my just debts be
paid. I give to my son James Anderson 150 acres, joining my own
plantation. I give to my son John Anderson one half of the tract
willed to myself, my brother James Anderson, my brother Stephen
Anderson, containing 350 acres on Landon Wilsons Creek. I give to
my daughter Jane Anderson 200 acres on half way swamp and 100 acres on
Charles Town Road. I give to my son Colbert Anderson my present
dwelling plantation containing 100 acres also my still. I give to my
beloved wife Mary one negro wench named Jane also my household furniture, stock of all kinds, all bonds, notes of hand and accounts for
her support and the children till they come of age. I appoint my son
James and my beloved wife executors. Dated 20 Nov. 1782. Wit:
William X Mathis, Elizabeth X McCrae, Molley Mathis. Signed: Colbert
Anderson. Proved on oath of William Mathis, 29 Nov. 1785.

ANDERSON, E. A. Box 2 Pack 54. Probate Judge Office. Edgefield,
S. C. Paid 1 Jan. 1839 Mrs. A. Anderson (mother) for clothing and
supplies, Miss Ann with $18.38 for her share of same $96.00. Received
15 Oct. 1838 of James Terry Esq. Comm. of Equity the first installment
due as a legatee on the land $432.94. Received 19 Dec. 1838 of Mrs.
A. Anderson admr. of est. of George Anderson, decd. has full receipt
given her until a final sett. is made $2,525.00. Paid Edmund J.
Miller in full for his share of E. A. Anderson now Miller of the real
and personal est. of her father George Anderson, Sr. decd. as per
receipt $3,792.60. Guardianship bond made 1 Jan. 1838 by Benjamin R.
Tillman, Thomas R. Anderson and John P. Mays in the sum of $10,000.00.
Guardian named Benjamin R. Tillman.

ANDERSON, ELIZA ANN Box 2 Pack 55. Probate Judge Office. Edge-
field, S. C. Est. admr. made 3 Feb. 1813 by Thomas Purves, Thomas
Anderson, James Spann who are bound unto the Ordinary in the sum of
$3,000.00. Inv. made 6 Feb. 1813 by John Ross, Andrew Bates and
Richard Eskridge.

ANDERSON, GEORGE No Ref. Pendleton Dist. Anderson Court House.
Anderson, S. C. Will of George Anderson. Dated 18 July 1807. First
I will all my just debts be paid. I give to my loving wife Molley
Anderson the plantation whereon I now live containing 125 acres, also
all household furniture and working tools, also some negroes during
her natural life to work and help school the children. Son David
Anderson to have what he has. Also daughter Margret Burnside to have
what she has. To son James Anderson to have what he has. Also
William Anderson to have what he has. Judey to have the balance of
the price of the land that I gave her. To son John Anderson I give
him a piece of land lying down the creek from this plantation, also a
negro named Harry, one sorrel colt and saddle. Also I leave to my
daughter Polley Anderson a negro girl named Anikey, also a good mare
and saddle and bridle, also half of the Meeting House Tract of land.
To my daughter Sally the other half of the Meeting House Tract of
land, also a negro girl named Seley when she comes to years of discretion have one horse and saddle and bridle. Also to my son Dixon
Anderson a negro boy named Gilbert, also I leave him $250.00 to school
him. I make my son Davis L. and my wife Molley Anderson, with my
brother Lewis Saxon my lawful executors. Wit: Lewis Sherrill, John
Dickson, James Dickson. Signed: George Anderson. Will proved on
oath of Lewis Sherrill on the 4 July 1808 before John Harris, O.P.D.

ANDERSON, GEORGE Box 1 Pack 9. Probate Judge Office. Edgefield,
S. C. Est. admr. 17 Feb. 1834 by John B. Cobington, John H. Fair,
Beverly N. Rogers who are bound unto the Ordinary in the sum of
$2,000.00. Cit. Pub. 2 Feb. 1834 M. Hamburg. Inv. made 12 Mar. 1834
by B. R. Tillman, G. Henderson Sr., Lewis Curry. Sale made 10 April
1834. Buyers: Wiley Glover, James Bann, Dr. Ayre, Mrs. Anderson,
Jane B. Covington, John W. Fair, A. Anderson Jr., Boling Wheller,
John Roper, Albert Ranbo[?].

ANDERSON, GEORGE L. Box 1 Pack 2. Probate Judge Office.
Edgefield, S. C. Est. admr. 19 Mar. 1830 by William Webb, John
Roundtree, E. B. Hibbler who are bound unto the Ordinary in the sum of
$2,000. Personally appeared before me John M. Anderson, Harriett
Anderson and Driziller Anderson who being duly sworn made solemn
oath that all the above stated property is our own right and property
and that it does not belong to the estate of George L. Anderson decd.
was no part of the same. Sworn to me this 20 April 1830. Thomas W.
Morton, J. Q. Signed: John H. Anderson, Drisilla L. Anderson, Harriett
X Anderson. Inventory made of the est. 20 Mar. 1830. Beverly Burton,
Daniel W. Brooks, Peter Quattlebaum. William Webb, Admr.

ANDERSON, GEORGE L. Box 2 Pack 47. Probate Judge Office.
Edgefield, S. C. Guardinship bond dated 1 Jan. 1838 by John P. Mayes,
Benjamin R. Tillman, Thos. R. Anderson in the amount of $10,000.00.
John P. Mayes is guardian of Geo. L. Anderson. Paid 6 May 1839 Geo.
J. Anderson in full for his dist. share of personal est. of Geo.
Anderson decd. $850.27.

ANDERSON, JAMES Box 1 Pack 30. Probate Judge Office. Edgefield,
S. C. Est. admr. 3 May 1827 by Nancy Anderson, Tully F. Sullivan,
James Tatom who are bound unto the Ordinary in the sum of $3,000.00.
Cit. read at a company muster at Hamburg 14 April 1827. Show that
George J. Anderson is a minor over 15 yrs. of age desire that John P.
Mays be his gdn. 1 Jan. 1838. Inv. made 3 May 1828 by J. Richardson,
Keith F. Williams, Haley Johnson.

ANDERSON, JAMES Box 1 Pack 5. Probate Judge Office. Edgefield,
S. C. Est. admr. 14 Nov. 1832 by William Andrews, John McGeheen,
Semion Christie, who are bound unto the Ordinary in the sum of $1500.00.
Know all men by these presence that we Luke Mathis, Gillam Sales,
Bartholomew Jordan and Thomas Efort, Owen all of Abbeville Dist., S.C.
are bound to William Andrews of Edgefield Dist., S. C. in the sum of
$1,000.00 to be paid to said William Andrews his certain attorney and
admr., heirs or exr. the 14 Nov. 1832 in account with William Anderson
admr. Paid my expenses in gold and returning from Charleston two trips
to collect the money from the bank $38.00 personally appeared before
me William Holloway, Sr., Calib Holloway, Sr. after being duly sworn
says that Luke Mathis and Parmetia Sale are half brothers and sister to
James Anderson who formerly lived near Cambridge, S. C. and formerly
in Charleston Dist. near Goose Creek and that Luke Mathis and Parmetis
Sale are the only or nearest relatives and heirs that they know of
that are living unless there should be some of John Anderson chn.
living and that if any of said John Anderson chn. are living they do
not live in this State. Dated 29 Oct. 1832.. by A. B. Addison.
Signed: William Holloway and Calib Holloway, Sr.

ANDERSON, MARY Box 3 Pack 45. Probate Judge Office. Edgefield,
S. C. Est. admr. 15 Feb. 1830 by James Adams, Jefferson Richardson,
Fredrick W. Timmerson who are bound unto the Ordinary in the sum of
$400.00. Cit. pub at Good Hope, 31 Jan. 1830. Paid 8 Sept. 1830
Thomas Anderson the only heir of the est. $24.25.

ANDERSON, PATIENCE Box 1 Pack 7. Probate Judge Office. Edgefield, S. C. Est. admr. 6 April 1838 by Elijah Watson, Artemus Watson,
Burrell Boatwright who are bound unto the Ordinary in the sum of
$8,000.00. Inv. made 12 April 1838 by T. Watson, A. Watson, B. Boat-
wright. Expend of the est. 17 Dec. 1838 paid IRA Scott and Mary Scott
in full for their share of the est. $302.46. Paid 9 Jan. 1839 Mary
Perry her full share $906.87 1/2. Paid 11 Jan. 1839 Robert Willis
in full his share $906.87 1/2. Paid 11 Jan. 1839 Jesse Rouse in full
his share $302.28. Paid 1 April 1839 N. W. Perry his share $302.28.
Sale held on 20 April 1828. Buyers: Elijah Watson, William Mobley,
Robert Willis, Sr., Joshua Warren, John Roberts, Richard Howard, Roy
Perry, N. Watson, P. Williams, Wheaton Jones, Warren Kirkland, James
Clark, Staumore Watson, Thomas Roden, Abram Rutland, Stephen Senterfit,
Lewis Tallow, Samuel Barker, Artemus Watson.

Ardis, Abraham - Continued. intermarried. Abram Ardis late was
of Beach Island, Edgefield Dist. Paid 18 Oct. 1844 Matthias Ardis
for board of S. M. Ardis from 1 Jan. 1840 to 1 Jan. 1841, $170.00.
Paid 1 Nov. 1844 W. L. Mayson and S. Mayson in full for their share
$7,026.78. Paid 6 Jan. 1842 James L. Gardner for Lucien A. Ardis
$275.00. Cit. Pub. at the Presbyterian Church, 10 Dec. 1837.

ARDIS, JOHN Box 1 Pack 15. Probate Judge Office. Edgefield,
S. C. Est. admr. 3 Dec. 1838 by Milledge Galphin and Matthias Ardis
and Darson Atkinson who are bound unto the Ordinary in the sum of
$30,000.00, M. Gilphin guardian of Anne J. Ardis and John G. Key
the husband of said Anne J. Ardis. John Ardis died about the year
1825. Paid 1 Jan. 1842 C. W. Ardis expenses to and from Savannah, Ga.
$40.00. Paid John S. Ardis on return from West $40.00. Paid 8 Jan.
Mary J. Ardis $48.39. Inv. made 31 Dec. 1838 on 14 slaves (not named)
made by Stephen Wesson, ___ Reddrick, John Coker.

ARDIS, JOHN Box 1 Pack 17. Probate Judge Office. Edgefield,
S. C. (No will date given.) Will was approved 30 Dec. 1825. I give
and bequeath all my property both real and personal to my chn. John
Safford, Anne J., Christopher W., and Mary Terry Ardis, as soon as
they attain the age of 21 or marry. I appoint my brothers Matthias,
Abram Ardis, Milledge Galphin, and Casper Nail my executors and
guardians of my chn. Wit: Casper Nail, Jr., R.S. Nail. Signed:
John Ardis. Paid Jan. 1838 John and Christopher Ardis to defray
expenses at Furman institution $595.37 1/2. Paid 31 1834 David Ardis
decree in Equity $804.07. Cit. Pub. at Union Church, Barnwell Dist.
on the 29 Nov. 1825. Est. admr. 19 Dec. 1825 by Matthias Ardis,
Abram Ardis, Casper Nail, David Ardis and Dawson Adkinson who are
bound unto the Ordinary in the sum of $20,000.00. Inv. made 31 Dec.
1825 by Henry Starr and Briton M. Ware on 17 slaves.

ARDIS, SARAH R.N. Box 1 Pack 20. Probate Judge Office. Edge-
field, S. C. Est. admr. 6 June 1836 by Saml. Clarke, Henry Y. Ardis,
John Sturzenegger and Undrick Redrick who are bound unto the Ordinary
in the sum of $8,000.00. Cit. pub at Philadelphia Church 6 May 1836.
Cit. read at Beech Island, 18 May 1836. V. Mattis Ardis, Ulbrick
Reddrick, and David Ardis having been called upon by William Samuel
Clarke and Mrs. Murray A. Mills to value the property of Sarah R.
Ardis decd. which she inherited from the est. of her husband Geo.
Bender decd. To Wm. Saml. Clarke 160 acres of swamp, bounded on by
own land and the Savannah River value at $8.00 per acre and sale on
14 slaves. To Mrs. M. A. Mills, one tract called Goose Pond, bounded
by land of Mrs. Prior, Cyrus Prior Miller, and Galphin containing 81
acres value at $7.50 per acre. One tract known as Zubly tract bounded
by her own land, the Mayers and Foster land containing 34 1/2 acres
value at total $320.00. Another tract on Savannah River known as the
Harris Varn tract, containing 200 acres value at $7.50 per acre total
of $1500.00.

ARRINGTON, BURREL Box 1 Pack 29. Probate Judge Office. Edgefield, S. C. Est. Admr. 24 Oct. 1817 by Charity Arrington, John
Edison, Moses Holstum who are bound unto the Ordinary in the sum of
$10,000.00. Cit. read 28 Sept. 1817 at Cardis Divine Worship. Left
to widow and 5 chn. Inv. made 21 Oct. 1817 by Richmond Watson, Thomas
X Cates, Richard (R) Howard, Sr.

ASBIL, AARON Box 2 Pack 41. Probate Judge Office. Edgefield,
S. C. This is to certify that I do relinquish my claim of writ as
admr. on the estate of Aaron Asbil to my son John Asbil. This 21
July 1814. Signed Ann Asbil. Est. admr. 26 Aug. 1814 by John Asbil,
John Loveless, Stephen Frederick, John Simkins who are bound unto the
Ordinary in the sum of $4,000.00. Paid 15 Oct. 1814 Josiah Todd in
part of his legacy $20.00. Paid Chas. Williamson his share $31.50.
Paid Nathaniel Burton $22.75. Paid Edw. W. Browning $21.50. Paid
Louis Absil $400.00. Paid Elisha Absil $133.00. Paid Jarvis Absil
$91.50. (Sometimes spelling - Absell)

AVON (ARON or AARON), JACOB Box 2 Pack 53. Probate Judge Office.
Edgefield, S. C. Est. admr. 20 Jan. 1806 by Thomas West, Thomas Black,
Sampson Pope, who are bound unto the Ordinary in the sum of $1,000.00.
Paid 23 March 1807 for boarding Tally Aaron dtr. of Jacob Aron from
March 1807 to March 1808 $15.00.

BAKER, CHRISTOPHER Deed Book C. Elbert Co. Elberton, Ga.
This indenture made 14 Aug. 1793 between Christopher Baker of State
of N.C. Cabarrus Co. and Jesse Baker of State of Georgia, Elbert Co.
In consideration of 60 pds. sterling in hand paid by Jesse Baker. Doth
grant, sold, bargain and release all that tract of land of 200 acres
lying in Elbert Co., Ga. lying on South West of Falling Creek, bounded
by William Blakes, South by Jane Mitchel. Wit: James McCleskey, John
Baker, Isabella McCleskey. Christopher Baker. On the 14 Aug. 1793
Agness Baker the wife of Christopher Baker did relinquish her dower to
the above land, before James McCleskey, J.P. Recorded 2 May 1795.

BARKER, JESSE Box 2 Pack 63. Probate Judge Office. Edgefield,
S. C. Letter dated 28 August 1857 from Fredonia, Ala. F. Durisoe,
Esq. Dar Sir: Enclosed you will find the receipt for you from R. H.
Porter and Margaret A. Porter signed by J. D. Porter for them. Please
inform me by return amil if it is satisfactory. If you prefer a
receipt over their signatures for your protection enclose one for
me and I will forward it to them for them to sign. I took the receipt
with me to Tuskegee to have it enclosed with the check to them, J. D.
Porter said to me as they had written to him to receipt their money
that he felt that he was authorized to sign for them, which he did.
Though as above stated if you desire a receipt signed with their own
hands, enclose one to me and it shall be attended to with as little
delay as possible on my part. Yours Truly, J. P. Barker. (Jesse
Barker Will) Dated 2 Nov. 1835. Wit: Ansel Talbert, Sr., Gilbert
Temmand, B. G. Talbert. I give to my son James Barker the sum of
$100.00 when he comes to the age of 21 yrs. To my loving wife Spelia
Barker this payment at this time and should she be delivered of a
living child either male or female they shall have the sum of $100.00
when they have arrived at the age of 21 yrs. Executors brothers
James P. Barker, John Barker.

BATES, DAVID Box 2 Pack 57. Probate Judge Office. Edgefield,
S. C. To John Simpkins Esq. Sir you will oblige by granting letter
of Admr. on the Estate of my decd. husband David Bates to my brother
John W. Lee as I wish him to have the entire management of the Estate.
I therefore relinquish to him my right to the Admr. Signed: Sarah
Bates. Dated 26 May 1818. Est. Admr. 3 June 1818 by John W. Lee,
Sampson Pope, Matthias Jones and Sampson Butler in the amount of
$8,000.00. On the 25 May Sarah Bates & John Lee applied for letter of
admr.

BARNARD, ELIJAH Pack 11 Clerk of Court Office. Anderson, S. C.
Deed from Elijah Barnard to Daniel Duncan both of Pendleton Dist.
Dated 10 April 1821. In consideration of $200.00 paid by said Duncan
hath granted, sold, bargain and released all that tract of land lying
on the main fork of Georges Creek waters of Saluda River. Containing
111 1/2 acres. Wit: William McCollum, Joel Jones. Signed: Elijah
X Barnard. Proved on oath of William McCollum before Joseph Grisham,
N.P. & J.Q.

BARNETT, DAVID Deed Book T Page 424-425. Mesne Conveyance,
Greenville, S. C. We David Barnett & Lucinda his wife to Abner B.
Dunahoo all of Greenville, Dist. Dated 10 March 1836. In consideration of $30.00 paid by said Dunahoo have granted, sold bargained and
release all my interest in a tract of land containing sixteen and
two third acres whereon Runnell Dill now lives, as my share in the
real estate of David Dunahoo decd. Wit: Joseph McMillon,
James M. Bailey. Signed: David Barnett. On 2 Jan. 1840 Lucinda
the wife of David Barnett relinquish her dower on the above land, before
Hardy J. Gilreath J.P. Lucinda X Dunahoo. (Written this way on deed.)

BARNETT, DAVID, SR. No Ref. Greenville Dist., S. C. David Barnett Sr. died in 1837, children Mary Barnett married Isaac Taylor, William, John and James Barnett went to McMinn, Tenn. Agness Barnett married Terry Couch and went to Hall Co., Ga. Priscilla Barnett married Thomas Crawford and went to McMinn, Tenn. Margaret Barnett married Elisha White and went to McMinn, Tenn. Narcissa Barnett married James Magness and went to Izard Co., Ark. Thomas, Lemuel and David Barnett were living in S. C. at the time of their fathers death.

BEATY, WILLIAM Pack 11. Clerk of Court. Anderson, S. C. Pendleton Dist. Deed from William Beaty to Sanford Vandiver both of said Dist. In consideration $200.00. William Beaty hath granted, sold, bargain, and released two tracts of land. One tract of 102 acres lying on both sides of Neels Creek, being part of a tract granted unto Hugh Wornock on the 6 April 1786. Tract conveyed from Andrew Wornock heir of Hugh Wornock decd. to Joseph Wornock from him to Stephen Willis. The other tract of 20 acres part of a grant to Hugh Wornock dated 5 Jan. 1789. Conveyed from Andrew Wornock to John Wornock, from him to William Brown. Wit: W. Brown, James Allen. Signed: Wm. Beaty. Deed dated 9 Nov. 1805. Proved on oath of W. Brown, before E. Brown J.Q. on the 21 Nov. 1805. On the 2 Nov. 1805 Elenor Beaty the wife of William Beaty renounce, release and relinquish her dower on the above tract of land, before Elijah Brown, J.Q.

BELL, ARCHY Bundle 113 #15. Probate Judge Office. Sumter, S.C. I Archy Bell being weak but of sound mind and memory. Dated 4 Oct. 1839. I will to my beloved wife Margaret Bell the plantation whereon I now live being 275 acres during her natural life or widowhood, then to be equal divided between my five children viz: Benjamin Sumter Bell, Margaret Louisa Bell, Ezekial Dixon Bell, Hugh McCallum Bell and Columbus Campbell Bell. I also will to my beloved wife two cows and calves, two feather beds, one horse, enough to keep the family for one year. Teh balance of my property including my negro boy Simus to be sold and pay my just debts and remainder to be equally divided between my beloved children viz: John Bell, Celey Amoson, Harriott Bell, Martha Bell, William Wesley Bell and James Bell. I appoint John Dixon and James McCallum my executors. Wit: W. H. Magee, William Copeland, James D. Jenkins. Signed: Archy Bell. Recorded 22 Oct. 1839.

BELTON, JONATHAN Vol. 11, page 157. Probate Judge Office. Charleston, S. C. I my wife shoudl be with child or have one within nine months after my death, in that case I make it my whole and sole heir of everything both real and personal allowing my wife her maintenance as my executors shall see sit. I also give to my wife my two negroes named Caty and Mintey during her widowhood, in case said child should not come to the year of maturity, then it shall come to my brother Robert eldest son. I appoint James Parsons, Esq. Attorney at law in Charleston, Mr. David Chaney, Mr. Robert Belton, at the Wateree and Mrs. Henrietta Belton during her widowhood. Dated 2 Nov. 1766. Wit: Joikim[?] Hartstom. Proved by Virtue of a didimus by Lord Charles Montague on 24 Aug. 1767. Also in open court the 9 Jan. 1768.

BELTON, PETER Vol. 4 Page 111. Probate Judge Office. Charleston, S. C. I, Peter Belton, of Colleton County being of sound mind and memory. I do give order and bequeath and dispose of ye same to my beloved wife Margaret Belton all such temporal estate of goods and chattels and lands. I do make and appoint my wife sole executrix. I have set my hand at Charles Town this 15 Jan. 1735. In the ninth year of the reign of our Sovereign Lord George the Second. Wit: Rowland Sargeant, Edward Soull, Geo. Beamish. Signed: Peter Belton. Recorded 8 Jan. 1738. By the Honr. William Bull, Esq. President and Ordinary of this Province.

BENNETT, HOLLY B. Apt. 9 File 654. Probate Judge Office. Greenville, S. C. State of Ala., Cherokee County. Power of Attorney. We the heirs of Samuel Stiles late of Greenville Dist., S. C. John Chapman and his wife Narsissa, Johnson Vandiver and his wife Lucy Rier,

Bennett, Holly B. - Continued. Moses H. Bennett, Sarah A. Bennett, and Matilda C. Bennett who are twenty one years of age and each of us are heirs of Holly B. Bennett decd. We make and constitute William J. Bennett of Jefferson County State of Ala. our true and lawful attorney to receive and receipt for our share from the estate of Samuel Stiles decd. and the estate of Celia Stiles decd. both of Greenville Dist., S. C. Dated 19 Sept. 1859. Signed: Matilda C. X Bennett, Johnson Vandiver and Lucy R. Vandiver, Sarah X Bennett, Moses H. Bennett, John Chapman and Narcissa X Chapman. State of Alabama, Jefferson County. We the heirs of Holly B. Bennett one of the heirs of Samuel Stiles late of Greenville Dist., S. C. John Chapman and his wife Narsissa, Johnson Vandiver and his wife Lucy Rier, Moses H. Bennett, Sarah A. Bennett, and Mitilda C. Bennett, Isaac Newberry and his wife Jane, and heirs of Nancy Langston decd. dtr. of said Holly B. Bennett who are entitled to the share of their mother Nancy Langston. John A. Conner and his wife Elizabeth. We make and constitute William J. Bennett of Jefferson County, Ala. our true and lawful attorney to receive and receipt for our share of the estate of Samuel Stiles decd. and Celia Stiles decd. both of Greenville Dist., S. C. These heirs recd. $795.46 as being the heir of Holly B. Bennett who was entitled to one share of Samuel Stiles est. Dated 7 Oct. 1859.

BERRY, RICHARD Box 3 Pack 62. Probate Judge Office. Edgefield, S. C. Est. admr. 25 June 1838 by Shurley Cook, Jeremiah Cook and James Sheppard who are bound unto the Ordinary in the sum of $20,000.00. Cit. pub. 10 June 1838 at Stevens Fork. Pub. 17 June 1838 at Gilgal. Pub. at Mountain Creek 24 June 1838. Paid 30 Oct. 1839 Jane Berry for board and schooling Julia, Emely, Edny, Richard, Marja, Nancy, Sarah and Jane Berry for the years 1839 $240.00

BICKETT, JOHN Pack 3352. Bill of Account. Clerk of Court Office. Abbeville, S. C. To the Honr. the Judge of the Court of Equity. Your orator John Young and your oratrix Mary Young his wife. That John Bickett late of Abbeville Dist. died in the year 1803 or 1804 intestate, seized and possessed with considerable real and personal property. Leaving the widow Nancy Bickett and chn. Jenny Bickett, Mary Bickett and another who died an infant soon after the death of intestate. Nancy the widow, admr. on the estate in the same year that he died, and had about seven hundred dollars and other property, and that Nancy died the same year as her husband intestate. That one Joseph Creswell Senr. took into his own hands the estate of both John and Nancy Bickett estate, with all money, notes and accounts, real and personal property. That your orator intermarried with your oratrix Mary Bickett in July 1816. The real estate was on Long Cane Creek containing 120 acres, which has been rented out each year. That said Joseph Creswell Senr. has not paid any support to the minors and has refused to give an account to your orator or oratrix. If it pleases your Honor to grant a writ of subpoena to the said Joseph Creswell Senr. to personally appear before this Court and answer the premises and to attend to other orders. Filed 12 April 1820.

BOWIE, WESLEY Pack 38. Probate Judge Office. Anderson, S. C. Will dated 13 Sept. 1839. I Wesley Bowie being low in health but of sound mind and memory. The tract of land whereon I now live containing 136 acres with two mules, one wagon, stock of all kinds, smith tools, all household property, also crop in the field, and any other property I may possess one half to my Livona. The other half to my brother William Bowie to care and support my mother Catherine Bowie as long as she may live. I appoint my brother William Bowie executor. Wit: Jno. W. Connor, David Martin, D. J. Tucker. Signed: Wesley X Bowis. Proven on oath of David Martin before John Martin, Esq. O.A.D. on the 7 Oct. 1839.

BOWIE, CHARLES Pack 38 Probate Judge Office. Anderson, S. C. Will dated 22 Oct. 1836. I Charles Bowie being of sound and disposing mind. I give to my son Wesley Bowie the tract of land whereon I now live, containing 136 acres, also my horse named Rock, my smith-tools, and plantation tools. For the support of me and my wife Catherine during the remainder of our natural life to such necessaries

Bowie, Charles - Continued. as either of us may need to our old age, also ten dollars in pocket money to find me a horse if the one I now have should die. I give to my son Charles in trust my little tract of land containing 50 acres to the use and benefit of Mary C. and John T. McColough the children of my dtr. Catherine to share and share alike, or the trustee may sell if they think best, or allow my dtr. Catherine to live on said land to raise and school her children. All my household and kitchen furniture to my wife Catherine during her natural life and at her decease to be sold and money equally divided between my dtrs. Nancey, Catherine, Mary and Jane to share and share alike. To my grandson John M. White son of my dtr. Nancey, I give my colt and the increase if any, to his brothers and sisters equally. My sons William and Charles has previously received their share, also my dtr. Sarah. I appoint my sons William and Charles executors. Wit: E. B. Gibert, Peter Gibert, A. Hunter. Signed: Charles Bowie. Proven on oath of Peter Gibert before John Martin Esq. O. A. D. on the 7 Oct. 1839.

BOWMAN, WILLIAM Box 105 Pack 2652. Probate Judge Office. Abbeville, S. C. Will dated 4 Nov. 1789. I William Bowman of Abbeville Dist. being sick and weak, but of usual mind and memory, first I leave to my grand sons William Bowman and Samuel Moore Wardlaw all that tract of land where I have formerly lived and if my daughter in law Jean Bowman may choose to go there to live, she is to have the benefit of said plantation until my grandson come of age. If either of my grandsons die the other to possess the whole. The remainder of my estate after paying my just debts to be equally divided amongest my children and grandchildren at the discretion of my executors. I appoint my friend Samuel Reid, John Wardlaw Junr. and Hugh Wardlaw executors. Wit: Samuel Agnew, Alexander Reid, George Reid. Signed: Wm. Bowman.

BOYD, ALEXANDER Page 34-35, #19. Chester Courthouse, Chester, S. C. Petition to the Honr. Elihu Hall Bay: The humble petition of Alexander Boyd, sheweth that your petitioner was born in the Kingdom of Ireland, a subject to the King of Great Britain and that it is his bona fide intention to become a citizen of the United States of America, that he has previous to this time resided at least five years within the limits and under the jurisdiction of the United States and one year at least under this State. Your petitioner there for prays your Honor that he may be made a citizen according to the form of the act of congress in that case made and privided. And your petitioner will ever pray. Alexander Boyd. 2 day April 1806. Be it so E. H. Bay. South Carolina, Chester District. We Andrew Crawford and Jas. Kennedy, certify that Alexander Boyd who now petitions to be made a citizen has resided within the limits and under the jurisdiction of the United States at least five years previous to this time and at least one year within the limits and jurisdiction of this Sate and during that time has behaved and demeaned himself as a man of a good moral character attached to the principles of the continuation of the United States and will dispose to the good order and happiness of the same. 2 day April 1806. Andrew Crawford and Jas. Kennedy.

BOYD, JANE Case 13 File 567. York County Courthouse, York, S.C. I Jane Boyd of York Dist. being very sick and weak in body but of perfect mind and memory, etc. I give to my dtr. Mary one negro girl named Violet. I give to my dtr. Margaret one negro boy named Sam. I also give to my dtr. Margaret my young sorrel horse. I direct that my negro boy John with all other property be sold and all my just debts paid, the balance to be divided between my dtrs. Jincy and Permilia and my grandson Andrew N. Smith. I appoint my friend John Glenn and Rufus J. Boyd executors. Dated 26 Oct. 1847. Wit: Wm. H. Johnston, T. M. Boyd, John A. Laney. Signed: Jane X Boyd. Probated 28 Nov. 1849.

BOYD, HUGH Apt. 1 File 72. Probate Judge Office. Greenville, S. C. I Hugh Boyd of Greenville Dist. being weak in body but of sound mind and memory. After my just debts are paid I give and demise unto Alexander Thompson of the State and dist. aforesaid all that I have. I allow and constitute William Morrow my executor. Dated 25 Jan. 1826.

Boyd, Hugh - Continued. Wit: James Morton, John Wasson, William Morrow. Signed: T. Hugh Boyd. Proven on oath of William Morrow before Spartan Goodlett, O.G.D. on the 5 June 1826.

BOYD, JOHN No Ref. Given. Abbeville, S. C. Est. admr. 12 Sept. 1836 by William Campbell, Joseph Hughey, Thomas J. Foster who are bound unto the Ordinary in the sum of $2,000.00. Cit. Pub. at Mt. Moriah Meeting House on the 28 Aug. 1836 by N. W. Hodges. Est. appraised on the 16 Sept. 1836 by Edmond Cobb, Elijah Teague, Ephraim Davis, Charles Calhoun. Settlement was made 7 Dec. 1838 with Wm. Campbell admr. Hugh Boyd, William Boyd, John Boyd who were of the State. Elenor Boyd, Ebenezer Boyd, A. P. Boyd, Hannah Boyd, Jane Boyd by their written consent, Robert Boyd chose William Boyd as his guardian, Adam Boyd chose Hugh Boyd as his guardian. Sale was held 12 Oct. 1836 buyers are: George Paul, Elender Boyd, John Hinton, H. B. Campbell, Robert Anderson, Peter Rykard, E. Boyd, Hugh Boyd, Jefferson Jenkins, Samuel Jenkins, John R. Campbell, E. Davis, John Henderson, John Buchanan, Henry Riley, Wilkison Motes, John Thompson, James Partlow, John Hughey, William Blake.

BOYD, JOHN Book B Page 10. Probate Judge Office. Union, S. C. I John Boyd of Union Dist. being very weak and sick in body, but of perfect mind and memory, etc. After paying my just debts, I give to my wife Jane my beloved wife all my land situate in said dist. and State on Brushy Creek for her life time and at her death to be divided between my two sons Josh Boyd and Abram Kesler equally according to quantity and quality and Kesler is to live on the place until the division take place. Also I give to my wife my servant Nancy during her life time and at her death to have her freedom, provided that she has two children, and the youngest one to be one year old when she is to be free. I give to my son Nathan Boyd one dollar. I give to my son David Boyd one dollar. I give to my dtr. Elizabeth Frederick one dollar. I give to my son Samuel Boyd two horses and cows that he now possess, and my two young servants Dan & Lucy with my household and table furniture. My stock of horses, cattle, hogs to be sold and my wife to have her third and the remainder to be equally divided between John, Joseph, Samuel, Nancy Kesler and Jane Wiggans and my crop also to be sold. I appoint my wife Jane Boyd executrix and Samuel Boyd executor. Dated 28 Oct. 1815. Wit: J. T. McJunkin, A. McJunkin, Joseph McDanal junr. Signed John X Boyd. Proved on oath of the three witnesses before William Rice, Ord. on the 6 Nov. 1815.

BOYD, JOHN Box 5 Pack 91. Probate Judge Office. Abbeville, S. C. Est. admr. 22 Nov. 1833 by William Brooks, James Boyd, John L. Boyd as admor. and John Gray, Henry Brooks and Archibald McMullan securities who are bound unto Moses Taggart, Ord. in the sum of $30,000.00. Cit. Pub. at Penial[?] Meeting House. Sale of personal estate held on 18 Dec. 1833, buyers: A. Giles, Dr. Lockhart, J. Yarbrough, John Gray, A. McMullin, A. Gillespie, J. C. Martain, J. Richey, Wm. Yarbrough, M. Chiles, Robert Richey, S. Linton, A. Russell, James Herron, E. Tilman, Dr. Tennent, Robert McMullin, James Dunn, J. P. Johnston, Hm. Prince, A. Hunter, B. Cheatham, J. Duglass, Wm. Gains, Dr. McAlister, Wm. Baker, Wm. McCord. Estate received from notes and accounts, James B. Herrins, James Boyd, John Richey, Milton Chiles, John C. Martins, Thomas C. Tinsley, A. Hunter, Andrew Gillespie, Senr., John Asbel, John Gray, James Purdays, Mrs. Nancy Martins, Mrs. Mary Crawford, Edward Tillmans, Ezekiel Beams, James B. Herrens, Doctor Lockharts, Andrew Edwards, Alexander Spence, Sydney Linton, Wm. Gains, Wm. P. McCords, B. M. Cheatham, Isreal P. Johnston, Robert M. Davises, Alexander Russell, H. M. Prince, John Yarbrough, Moses Yarbrough, David R. McCalisters, John McNeels. Paid: Wm. McDow, John L. Boyd, Wm. Brooks, Samuel B. Thompsons, James Bowie, Josiah Patterson, Thomas S. Spierin, Doctor Tennent, Henry Brooks, James Hueys, James Boyd, James Murray for Frances Boyd, Andrew Giles, James S. Wilson for Frances Boyd, William Thompson (no heirs given). John L. Boyd, widow was in Court of Equity on 15 Oct. 1856 for a partition of the real estate, which was lying on Little River in Abbeville Dist., adj. land of Hon. David Lewis Wardlaw, Barnett M. Cheatham, Frances Marion Brooks, Charles T. Haskell containing 1400 acres. Two heirs are named

Boyd, John - Continued. Josephine Boyd, age nine; Sarah Ann Boyd, age six. The widow not named on the half of a page that is in the notes.

BOYD, JOSEPH Case 9 File 361. York County Courthouse. York, S. C. Will dated 23 Jan. 1822. I Joseph Boyd of York Dist. being in my perfect senses and memory and in a common state of health etc. I will to my wife Sarah Boyd the plantation whereon I now live, also three negroes named hones Jim, Falls and Dianh[?] during her natural life, the negroes not to be removed from the State without leave of my executors. I will to my dtr. Maryan Mannon ten dollars. I will to my son James Lee Boyd two negroes boys Jep and Sandee also $150.00 in cash. I will to my four youngest dtr. Sally Jinny Clark, Eliza, Livena and Peggy all the remaining part of my real and personal estate, to be equally divided between them. Real property to remain in the hands of my executors until they marry or become of age. Also each to get one negro. I will my wife Sary Boyd one third part of my household and kitchen furniture, also third of all stock. I appoint my son James Lee Boyd and Robert Mannor my executors. Wit: Jno. Ellis, Thomas Clark. Signed: Jos. Boyd, Probated 4 June 1822.

BOYD, ROBERT Box 1 #2. Probate Judge Office. Pickens, S. C. Admr. bond of Elijah Cannon and Robert Boyd who are bound unto James H. Dendy, Ord. in the sum of $2,000.00. Dated 23 Jan. 1829. Wit: Thomas Boyd and William Boyd. Letter of admr. was granted unto Elijah Cannon for the est. of Robert Boyd Junr. decd. dated 26 Jan. 1829. Sale was held 19 Feb. 1829 buyers: Mary Boyd, widow, John Bowen, Alige Cannon, John Prince, Benjamin Hagwood, Robert Blessinggame, Abraham Lasley, Absolem Howard, Henry Griffin, Joseph Young. Notes due the estate as of 2 May 1829, James Cary, Samuel McCollum, John Chapman, Benton Freeman, William L. Keith, John S. Edwards, Reden Freeman, David Danol, John H. Roe, Richard Roe, John Jones, Riley Smith, Reason Julen, William Lesley, Morgan Darnol, Abel Hill, William Bray, William Phillips, John Knight, Lewis Barret, Esley Hunt, Alexander Clark, Peter Corben, Aron Cantrel, John Crain, Rasher Bruse, Enoch Hood, Thomas Rakley, James Satterfield, Mary Barret, Peter Rolen, Chesley Davis, Jeremiar Eliot, Allen Braseal, Edward Prince, Robert Hood, Reuben MacClanihan, Elijah Cannon, James Blakeley, Absalom Reas, Joseph A. Fields, Strete Singleton, Enoch Hollingsworth, John Bowen, Thomas Edmunson, Aron Cantrel, Benjamin Day, Wm. Barretts, Charles Davis, Wm. Bray, Peter Roland. The petition of Moses Smith Junr. to the Honr. James H. Dendy, Ord. that he is the husband of the late widow of Robert Boyd Junr. late of this Dsit. therefore he is desirous of being appointed gdn. of the infant boy child John H. Boyd. Dated 5 April 1830.

BOYD, THOMAS #35. Clerk of Court Office. (Basement) Pickens, S. C. I do certify for Thomas Boyd a tract of land containing 327 acres (surveyed for him 8 Nov. 1791). ___ Dist. of 96 on waters of 18 Mile Creek a branch of Keowee River, bounded by Henry Norton and Henderson lands and John Boyd land. Dated 25 Sept. 1792. Signed: Robert McCann, Dept. Survr.

BOYD, ROBERT Box 9 Pack 175. Probate Judge Office. Abbeville, S. C. I Robert Boyd being of sound mind and memory, etc. First I give to my beloved wife Mary Boyd 200 acres of land and improvement, during her widowhood. I give to my son Robert Boyd 200 acres of land with improvement over by the Cold Spring. I give to my dtr. Agnes Boyd 100 acres of land with improvement formerly belonging to Hugh Calhoun. I give to my wife Mary one bay mare. I give to my son Robert Boyd one mare and colt. I give to my dtr. Agnes Boyd one mare colt. I give to my son William Boyd three dollars. I appoint my friend William Hays and Patrick McMaster executors. Dated 21 June 1779. Wit: Robert Boyd, Patrick McMaster. Signed: Robert (R B his mark) Boyd. Proved on oath of Robert Boyd before Jno. Ewing Calhoun on 20 April 1782.

BOYD, THOMAS SR. Case 4 File 50. York County Courthouse. York, S. C. I Thomas Boyd Sr. of York Dist. being of sound mind and memory and good health. Do this day the 10 Nov. 1834 make this my last will and testament. I will to my beloved wife Elizabeth Boyd during her natural life the house and the tract of land whereon I now live, adj. lands of James Boyd, Samuel Smith, William Boyd, Robert Boyd, Aquilla Dyson (with the exception of the priviledge to be hereafter mentioned to my dtr. Nancy Smith on said land.) Also I give to my wife during her natural life negroes viz: Virgil, Bacchus, Amanda, Mitchel and Melinda, also my household and kitchen furniture, all stock, horses, cattle, hogs, farming gear and tools, also all corn, wheat, cotton and crops of every description. My wife is to pay all my just debts. I will to my son John Boyd my wearing apparel, having given him heretofore all that I allow him. I will to my dtr. Nancy Smith the priviledge of living in the house wherein she now lives on my land, to have use of the spring, and firewood, etc. and as much land as she and her chn. can cultivate, convenient and adjacent to her house. This priviledge to continue as long as she lives separate from her husband Wm. Smith and no longer. I allow her mother to furnish her yearly ten dollars worth of provision during her mothers life, which I allow to be continued by my son Bennet Franklin Boyd so long as he becomes possessed of my land after the death of his mother during the life of said Nancy or her separation from her husband. I have given to my son Thomas Jefferson Boyd all that I allow him. I have given to my son Robert Boyd all that I allow him, but it is my desire that at the time of my youngest child is twenty-one years old, and if my wife is dead or at her death. That he take my negro boy Virgil at the valued price and pay over to my executors for the use of my dtrs. here after mentioned. To my son James Boyd I have given him all I allow. To my son William Boyd I have given him all I allow, but I desire him to take my negro boy Bacchus when my youngest child is at the age of twenty-one and if my wife is deceased, if at her demise to Pay over to my executors his value for the use of my dtrs. here after mentioned. To my son Bennet Franklin Boyd at the death of his mother the plantation where I now live subject to the incumbrances of my daughter Nancy, and that my five daughters to have ahome while they are single, also after the death of his mother, I allow him my negro boy Mitchel and my cupboard and clock. I will to my five dtrs. viz: Jane, Elizabeth, Mary, Rachel and Louisa each to have a bed and furniture, a horse, worth fifty dollars, a saddle and bridle, and a spinning wheel. I also allow the last named five dtrs. an equal division of the negroes Virgil and Bucchus also Amanda and Melinda at the time of my wife death, or the youngest child is twenty-one years old. I allow my threashing machine to my son William. I appoint my wife executrix and my son John Boyd executor. Wit: Wm. Moore, John McGill, John Glenn, Wm. Campbell. Signed: Thomas Boyd. Probated 7 May 1838.

BOYD, WILLIAM Box 5 Pack 86. Probate Judge Office. Abbeville, S. C. Will dated 20 May 1801. I William Boyd Senr. of Abbeville Dist. being in a low state of health but of sound and disposing mind and memory. First I will my just debts just debts and funeral expenses be paid. I give 200 acres in the State of Georgia to be equally divided between my sons James, William, Robert and John. I give the plantation whereon I now live to be equally divided between my sons Joseph and Samuel. I will my daughter Margaret be maintained out of my estate while she lives. My will is that my dtr. Mary shall have the choice of my two colts when she choose to make it. My family is to stay together unless they refuse to take the council of my son James, in which case I authories him to bind them out to some trade at his descretion. When one of my chn. come of age, they shall have a part of my est. but not injure the raising the others chn. none is to take a bed except Mary. When the youngest become of age the estate to be divided between my chn. viz: James, William, Mary, Robert, John, Joseph and Samuel. I appoint my son James and my friend John Glasgo Junr. my executors. Wit: Flm. Bates, P. McCarter, Josiah Patterson. Signed: William X Boyd. Recorded 2 Sept. 1803. Bond for the exor. was made by James Boyd and John Glasgow on the 13 Dec. 1802. Sale of the personal est. was held (no date given) buyers, John Lord, James Boyd, John Waddle, Robert Glasgow, Thomas Morrow, William Norris.

BOYSE, ALEXANDER Box 2 #49. Probate Judge Office. Anderson,
S. C. Will dated, 14 Jan. 1806. I Alexander Boyse of Pendleton Dist.
being weak in body but of sound and perfect mind and memory, etc.
First I direct my just debts be paid. I give to my beloved wife Jane
Boyse a liberal support off the land where she now lives, and cattle
as she deem necessary, with household furniture, also a negro woman
called Dinah. I Give to my dtr. Jane McCluskey one cow and calf. I
give to my son William Boyse a bay mare, saddle and bridle. I give to
my son John Boyse all the land I possess on the South side of Hurricane
Creek. I give to my son Maclen Boyse all the land on the North side
of Hurricane Creek. Except the land lying East side of the springs
branch adj. land of Joshua Smith which I direct to be sold, also 190
acres known as the Dorses old place on Beaver Dam Creek which I also
direct to be sold. I also give to my son Maclan a sorrell mare called
Starling. I give to my sons Alexander and George Thompson Boyse the
tract of land whereone I now live, to be equally divided between them,
except my youngest son Thompson shall have the part whereon the
buildings are. I give to son Alexander one colt called fox and s
saddle. I give to my son Thompson Boyse my large bay mare. I give to
my dtr. Agness Boyse a bay mare called bounce, one feather bed and
furniture and one cow and calf, also a saddle. The balance of my
estate to be sold and pay my just debts for the schooling of my sons
Alexander and Thompson Boyse. I appoint John Cochran Esq. and my son
William Boyse Executors. Wit: Wm. Hunter, John Y. Mozley, Wm. Brown.
Signed: A. Boyse. Proven on oath of Doctr. Wm. Hunter and Capt. Wm.
Brown before John Harris O.P.D. on the 3 Feb. 1806. Est. appraised on
1 March 1806 by David Murphree, William Brown, Joshua Dyer. Sale held
on 21 March 1806 Buyers: Moses Hunt, Wm. Boyse, Elisha Kirksey,
Andrew Davis, Mecklin Boyse, John Cockram, Aaron Murphree, Abram Horton,
Jno. Holland, Amos Ladd, Jacob Lewis, Hugh Porter, Solomon Murphree,
Wm. Chapman, Daniel Murphree, Wm. Brown, Miss Dinah Murphree, Samuel
Reed, Sergent Griffin, John Gardner, Henry Gardner, Elnathan Davis,
Edward Norton, Moses Murphree, John Chapman, Jay Kirksey, Isaiah
Kirksey, Wm. Wilson, Danial Duram, John Oliver, Widow Boyse, Buckner
Smith, Joshey Smith, Zachary Smith, John Wiggonton, Thomas Adams, Wm.
Avret.

BROOKS, CHRISTOPHER Box 8 Pack 139. Probate Judge Office.
Abbeville, S.C. I Christopher Brooks now in a low state of health
but of sound mind. I have given to my son Henry Brooks 113 acres of
land, one horse and saddle, one feather bed and furniture, and one
cow and calf. I give him one negro man named John. I have given to
my son Wm. Brooks one horse and saddle, one cow and calf, one feather
bed and furniture, one set of blacksmith tools. I now give him one
negro woman named Nance. I have given to my dtr. Sally Wilson 10
acres of land, one feather bed and furniture, one cupboard, one set of
smithtools, one loom, one rifle. I now give her one negro woman
named Mary, never to be sold or hired out. I have given to my dtr.
Polly Prince one beast and saddle, one loom, one sow and shotes, one
feather bed and furniture. I now give her one negro woman named
Phebe. I give to my dtr. Betsy one negro woman named Annike. I give
to my dtr. Nancy one negro woman named Fanny, I give Betsy and Nancy
an equal portion with the others. All above named negroes, with old
Jenna and Nancy, all stock, tools and household and kitchen furniture,
with my books with my wife Sarah Brooks during her widowhood or life.
At her death negro Jenna to be set free. I give five dollars to the
use of furin missoons [foreign missions] by the hands of brother
Jesse Mercer. I appoint Wm. Brooks, Sarah Brooks and Henry Brooks to
execute this will. Dated 15 Sept. 1819. Wit: Wm. H. Caldwell,
William Lesly Jr., Jane Caldwell. Signed: Christopher Brooks.
Proved on oath of Col. William H. Caldwell before Moses Taggart Ord.
on the 1 April 1820. Legatees paid Henry and William Brooks, Joseph
Willson, Silvanis Prince, Paten Price, Edward S. Prince. Buyers at
sale viz: Henry Brooks, Edward Prince, Elizabeth Brooks, John Boid,
Silvanus Prince, Wm. Brooks, Christian Barns, Wm. H. Caldwell, Wm.
Davis, Daniel Jones, Sarah Brooks widow, Wm. Kirkpatrick, John
Gillespie.

BROOKS, GEORGE Apt. 1 File 51. Probate Judge Office. Greenville, S. C. I, George Brooks being weak of body but of a sound mind. I give to my wife Sarah Brooks all my lands, stock, tools, household and kitchen furniture and all things I may possess, during her natural life or widowhood save so much to pay my just debts. But in case my wife should marry again then all my est. both real and personal to be sold to the highest bidder on twelve months credit and divided as; my wife to have twenty dollars and the balance equally divided between my chn. Polly Blackmon, Thomas Brooks, Samuel Brooks, George Brooks, John Brooks, Elizabeth Baker, Joseph Brooks, Moses Brooks, David Brooks and Leah Fletcher, or their children in their stead. In case my wife should not marry again then at her death the property to be disposed as above directed. I appoint my friend John W. Hansell and David Brooks executor. Dated 3 Feb. 1824. Wit: William Bridges, William Earnest, Lucy X Bridges. Probated 19 Sept. 1825.

BROOKS, SARAH R. Box 7 Pack 117. Probate Judge Office. Abbeville, S. C. I, Sarah Brooks, widow being in a sick and low condition but of sound mind and disposing memory. I give to my beloved daughter Sarah Amanda Brooks the whole of my estate real and personal of every description. It is my desire that my negroes continue this year and work on the plantation of my son Thomas's hands as we have agreed to do so. My executor enter into writing to that effect in order to secure my half of the crop. I hope the difference in the circumstances of my children will be a sufficient apology to my son Thomas A. Saunders for not leaving him any part of my estate. I appoint Thomas Livingston, Esq. my sole executor. Dated 20 Feb. 1826. Wit: A. Hunter, Wm. McCaw, Mary A. Fraser. Signed: Sarah R. X Brooks. Proved on oath of Mary A. Fraser before Moses Taggart O.A.D. on the 28 Feb. 1826. An inventory was made 31 March 1826, by A. Hunter, Jno. Powers Senr., Wm. M. Johnson. One negro named Haney is listed.

BRADLEY, ABRAHAM Apt. 1 File 39. Probate Judge Office. Greenville, S. C. I Abraham Bradley of Greenville Dist. make this my last will. I give unto my wife my land and house as long as she lives, after her death, I give said land unto my son Isaac Bradley and my dtr. Betsey Benson. My dtr. Judy Bradley to have the place she is now living on as long as she thinks proper. I also give to my wife one negro girl named Clary and a child in all the rest of my estate. After her death the property to be sold and the money equally divided with all my chn. but George Bradley and Judy Bradley and their chn. is to have their part equally divided with them. I appoint my son A. Q. Bradley to be executor. Dated 11 Oct. 1823. Wit: David Armstrong, Ameley X Holt. Signed: Abraham Bradley. Probated 17 Nov. 1823.

BRADLEY, EARL D. Box 178 #11. Probate Judge Office. Pickens, S. C. On 10 Nov. 1882 W. A. Lesley, B. F. Lesley are bound unto Olin L. Durant, Ord. in the sum of $400.00. W. A. Lesley gdn. for Earl D. Bradley a minor under 21 yrs. heir of Joel Bradley decd.

BRADLEY, ELIZABETH Deed book C-2 Page 195. Clerk of Court Office. Pickens, S. C. For and in consideration of the sum of $100 and for the further consideration that the divorce suit now pending between Joel Bradley and my self be discontinued. I have this day relinquished all my titles and interest in or for the premises conveyed to Earle D. Bradley by the Joel Bradley, etc. Dated 27 Feb. 1875. Before R. E. Holcombe, J.P. Signed: Elizabeth X Bradley. Recorded 23 June 1876 and examined by S. D. Keith, C.C.

BRADLEY, JOEL Pack 961 Apt. 91. Probate Judge Office. Pickens, S. C. Whereas we D. F. Bradley, J. E. Boggs, W. T. McFall are bound unto Olin L. Durant, Ord. in the sum of $2,000. Bond dated 29 June 1881. Est. was appraised by Elias E. Mauldin, W. H. H. Arial, W. J. Smith. Sale was held on 4 Aug. 1881. On 1 March 1883 D. W. Bradley made his settlement with $3.28 over after paying funeral expenses, medical bills, Judge of Probate Fees.

BRADLEY, JOEL Deed Book C-2 Page 100. Clerk of Court Office.
Pickens, S. C. I Joel Bradley of Pickens County in consideration of
the natural love and affection I have for my son Earle D. Bradley
and desirous to provide for him before my death, and in consideration
of five dollars to be paid by said Earle D. Bradley I have granted,
sold, bargained and release all that parcel of land on Goldens Creek
adj. land of William Smith, Milton Rogers, Allen Mauldin containing
223 acres. This being the land whereon I now live, and composed of
several small tracts, #1. 100 acres bought from James McCollum on
23 March 1831. #2 45 acres bought from John E. Smith on the 12 Nov.
1829. #3. 50 acres bought from Thomas Henderson 20 Sept. 1837. #4.
78 1/2 acres bought from Benjamin Hagood on the 28 Jan. 1846. Dated
17 Feb. 1875. Wit: Alonzo M. Folger, R. A. Child. Signed: Joel
Bradley. On the 27 Feb. 1875 Elizabeth Bradley the wife of Joel
Bradley did release and relinquish her dower on the above land, before
R. E. Holcombe, J.P. Signed: Elizabeth X Bradley. Recorded 24 Jan.
1876.

BRADLEY, PATRICK Box 7 Pack 113. Probate Judge Office. Abbeville, S. C. I Patrick Bradley of Abbeville Dist. being of sound
mind etc. To my two dtrs. who live with me viz: Isabella and Mary,
I give the plantation on which I now live containing 100 acres, and
my wish that they reside on the place, and if one should die without
heir my wish is that the whole shall go to the survivor. I also
leave to them jointly the best horse, a cow and calf, my household
and kitchen furniture, all corn, wheat, fodder in the barn, etc. The
reaminder of my property to be sold at public sale, and after paying
my just debts, I wish the proceeds to be equally divided between all
my chn. I appoint my sons John and Archibald Bradley executors.
Dated 13 Oct. 1828. Wit: John McComb, Alexander Laughlin, Robert
McComb. Signed: Patrick X Bradley. Will proved on oath of Alexander
Laughlin before Moses Taggart Ord. on the 29 Jan. 1831. Buyers at
sale. Isabella Bradley, P. Gibson, A. Bradley, A. Laughland, John
Bradley, Thomas Chriswell, G. B. Crawford, D. McClain, Josiah McGaw,
Andrew Weed, Samuel Wideman, Doctor Whitten, James McFarland, Thomas
Lindsy, Matthew Shanks, George McFarland.

BRANNON FAMILY Tombstone Inscriptions, taken from Lindsey
Cemetery, 2 miles south of Due West, S. C.
William T. Brannon, born 8 Nov. 1823, died 27 Sept. 1857
Mrs. Anne Brannon, born 31 July 1796, died 20 March 1867

BRANDON, CHRISTOPHER Book F Page 412. Mense Conveyance Office,
Greenville, S. C. I, Christopher Brandon of Union Dist. in consideration of the sum of $65.00 to be paid by Joseph Tankersly of Greenville
Dist. have granted, sold, bargained and release a certain tract of
land on the Reedy fork a branch of the Middle fork of Saluda River.
Containing 180 acres. Dated 30 Dec. 1800. Wit: James Brandon,
William X Tankersley. Signed: Christopher Brandon. Proved on oath
of William Tankersley on the 24 April 1801 before H. McVay, J.P.
recorded 16 March 1802.

BRANDON, CHRISTOPHER Box 33 Pack 19. Probate Judge Office.
Union, S. C. I Christopher Brandon being old and weak in body but of
sound and disposing mind and memory. I want all my just debts paid
out of any money I may leave at my death. I give to my son Christopher
Brandon one negro man named Jack in trust for my beloved wife Sarah
Brandon, said negro to be in the nature of a body servant for my wife,
and after the death of my wife said negro to be sold and money divided
between all my chn. I give to my dtr. Elizabeth the wife of John
Forbes one negro woman named Hannah and her son named Francis. To my
dtr. Mary the wife of Turner Bentley having heretofor received her
full share of my est. I have nothing more to give her, except as
herein after excepted. I give to my dtr. Rebecca Brandon one negro
man named Leonard, one negro woman named Sarah and her two chn. named
Molly and Miller and one negro girl named Mariller, one horse valued
at seventy five dollars, two cows and calves, and I give her one third
part of all my household and kitchen furniture, and I give her my
walnut bureau. I have heretofor given to my dtr. Ann wife of John

Brandon, Christopher - Continued.   Roundtree what I consider her
share of my estate, and I give her no more except as herein excepted.
I give to my dtr. Jane Roberson a negro woman named Rachell and her
chn. named Simpson, Cornelia, Wright, Abram, also I give her Mary and
Sam.   I also give her a horse valued at seventy five dollars and one
third part of my household and kitchen furniture. I also give her two
cows and calves and one bureau with twenty five dollars. I give to my
son Jesse the sum of $600.00 on condition that he applies for it
within the time of two years after my death, if he does not apply
then the sum to be equally divided among all my chn., share and share
alike.   I give to my son Christopher Brandon all the rest of my estate
both real and personal, he being bound to find his mother a home and
all necessaries of life until her death. I appoint my son Christopher
Brandon executor. Dated 4 Sept. 1846. Wit: D. Wallace, Giles Sharp,
Wm. A. H. Bevill. Signed: Christopher X Brandon. Proven on oath of
Wm. A. H. Bevill on the 5 Jan. 1847 before J. J. Pratt Ord.
An inventory of the estate was held 23 Feb. 1847 by J. E. Ming, Wm.
A. H. Bevill, Dabny Becknell. Negroes listed as Jack, Charles, George,
Tom, Frank, Leonard, Sam, Hannah Holly and three chn. Albert, Leroy,
Tailor, Mary, Rachael and five chn. Simpson, Cornelia, Right, Abram,
July. Sarah and three chn. Milly, Miller and an infant babe. Old
negro woman named Milly worth nothing. The following is a list of
accounts due Christopher Brandon decd., Thomas Harris, John Long,
Charles Freman, Wm. Mitchell, J. B. Porter, Oney Oneal, Mathias Harris,
Rickison Lipsey, Rardon Bevell.
Brandon buried in Union Cemetery, Union, S. C. (In the town part)
Isabella Brandon, born 21 Nov. 1821, died 20 Feb. 1865
James K. Brandon, born 15 Aug. 1810, died 11 Feb. 1859
Mary A. Brandon, wife of H. S. Beaty, born 1 Nov. 1846, died 5 Sept.
1880.

   BRANDON, GENERAL THOMAS   Box 4 Pack 51.   Probate Judge Office.
Union, S. C.   I Thomas Brandon General a citizen of the United States
and living in Union Co., S. C. at this time, being sick in body but
of sound memory, etc. First I will my just debts be paid and to my
loving wife Rebecka Brandon. I give all the property that was bequeath
to her by her late husband George Harland to her and her heirs forever. I give to my three sons Thomas, William and James Brandon all
my estate real and personal of whatever kind. All my negroes and stock
to remain on my plantation till my son James come to the age of twenty
one, at that time an equal division to be made among my three sons.
It is further my will that George Brandon son of my brother John of
Browns Creek and George Young of Duncans Creek to be my sole executors.
Dated 14 Dec. 1801. Test: it is my will that my loving wife Rebekah
live on my plantation during her natural life. Wit: Arthur Brandon,
Miles X Summer, Jesse Howard. Signed: Thos. Brandon. I Thomas
Brandon of Union Dist. being in perfect sense and memory do direct
this added to my last will and testament. After the arrival of my son
to the age of twenty one, I direct my executors to raise out of my
estate in the most convenient way they may think proper fifty pounds
current money and divide the same equally between my five dtrs. viz:
Mary, Jane, Elizabeth, Martha, Anna and each to have a feather bed
and furniture. Dated 2 Feb. 1802. Wit: John Sanders, Joseph Hughes,
John Savage. Signed: Thos. Brandon. Recorded 8 March 1802.
Negroes listed in the inventory are: Man Mingo, man Toby, boy Ben,
Woman Ailse and Jim, girl Hannah, girl Jane, boy John, boy Minga.

   BRANDON, GEORGE WASHINGTON Family, born 20 Oct. 1808, Greenville
or Spartanburg County. Was the son of John Brandon and Diana Scott.
He married 6 Oct. 1831 to Keziah Fawler, she was born 19 June 1815
Gibson Co., Indiana. Chn. #1. Thomas Jefferson, born 20 Aug. 1832 in
Henry Co., Tenn. m. Mary Margaret Cherry. #2. David L., born 17 Dec.
1833 in Henry Co., Tenn. #3. John L., born 20 Jan. 1835. in Henry
Co., Tenn. #4. Elizabeth Jane, born 18 Mar. 1836 in Henry Co., Tenn.,
m. Jochua [?] Davis. #5. Welford Woodruff, born 16 July 1838 in
Henry Co., Tenn, m. Margarett Wilcox. #6. Mary Caroline, born 17
Dec. 1839 in Henry Co., Tenn., m. Elihu Hiatt. #7. Martha Francis
born 27 Feb. 1842 in Henry Co., Tenn., m. Elihu Hiatt, 5 Apr. 1861.
#8. Rebecca Ann born 11 Aug. 1844 in Hancock Co., Ill. m. Francis

Brandon, George Washington - Continued. Wilcox. #9. Elaline
Mallsa born 27 Jan. 1846 in Hancock Co., Ill. #10. Diana Abigail
born 19 June 1848 Cauncil Bluff, Iowa M. Jacob Wane Hendrickson. #11
Moroni born 27 Dec. 1852 in Cauncil Bluff, Iowa.

BRANDON, JOHN Box 7 Pack 34. Probate Judge Office. Union, S. C.
Admr. bond. George Brandon admr. Christopher Brandon, Benjamin B.
Kennedy who are bound unto William Rice, Ord. in the sum of $300.00.
Dated 12 Feb. 1814. Paid George Brandon, Junr. for two days service
appraising and crying the affects of said est. Paid William Sharp for
one day service appraising the effects of said decd. $1.00. Paid the
Ordinary $9.07. Paid John W. Mayfield $76.00. Paid James Steen
$76.00. Paid Samuel Gordon $76.00. Paid Green Sorrels $38.00. Paid
Samuel Armstrong $38.00. Total amount paid $317.07. Proved in Court
of Ord. 22 Feb. 1819. Sale of the decd. held on 2 March 1814. Buyers,
George Brandon, John Jolley, James Ming, Elias Mitchel, Rickison Lipsey,
Hezakiah Porter, Hencock Porter, Benjamin Kennedy, Giles Fawcet, Jesse
Hix, Thomas Kennedy, Richard L. Wilkerson, Joseph Howard, George
Vance, Christopher Brandon, William Eves, James Gage, Richard Humphres.

BRANDON, JOHN Deed Book E, Page 302. Mesne Conveyance Office.
Greenville, S. C. I John Brandon of Union Co. for and in consideration
of $200 paid by James Brandon of County aforesaid, have granted, sold
bargained, and released a tract of land lying on the middle fork of
Saluda River, containing 140 acres. Dated 10 Dec. 1798. Wit:
Christopher Brandon, George Brandon. Signed: John Brandon. On 21
Dec. 1798 Mary Brandon the wife of John Brandon did freely relinquish
her right of dower to the within deed. Before Wm. Kennedy. Signed:
Mary X Brandon. Proved on oath of Christopher Brandon before George
Salmon Esq. on the 23 July 1799.

BRANDON, JOHN Deed book D, page 506. Mesne Conveyance Office.
Greenville, S. C. I John Brandon of Union Co. for and in consideration
of $50.00. paid by George Brandon of said State and County have
granted, sold, bargained and released a tract of land on the middle
fork of Saluda River, containing 240 acres. Dated 15 Dec. 1797. Wit:
Christopher Brandon, James Brandon. Signed: John Brandon. On 21
Dec. 1797 Mary Brandon the wife of John Brandon did freely relinquish
all her right to dower on the within deed. Before Wm. Kennedy.
Signed: Mary X Brandon. Proved on oath of Christopher Brandon before
William Kennedy Esq. on the 27 March 1798.

BRANDON, JOHN Deed Book F, page 171. Mesne Conveyance Office.
Greenville, S. C. I John Brandon of Union County, for in consideration of $10.00 me paid by Jeremiah Nisbett of Greenville County, have
granted sold, bargained and released a tract of land containing 100
acres lying on a branch of devils fork a branch of the middle fork
of Saluda River. Dated 25 March 1799. Wit: Christopher Brandon,
James Brandon. Signed: John Brandon. Proved on oath of Christopher
Brandon before Robert Cook, Esq. on the 11 March 1807.

BRANDON, JOHN Deed Book D Page 408. Mesne Conveyance Office.
Greenville, S. C. I John Brandon of Union County for and in consid-
eration of $50.00 to me paid by Christopher Brandon of Greenville
County have granted, sold, bargained and released 150 acres lying on
both sides of the middle fork of Saluda River. adj. land on Jeremiah
Nisbetts. Dated 18 March 1797. Wit: James Brandon, John Brandon.
Signed: John Brandon. Proved on oath of James Brandon before John
Tubb Esq. on the 15 June 1797.

BRAMBLETT, MARY Box 1 #12. In Equity. Probate Judge Office.
Pickens, S. C. On 30 Jan. 1854 Mary Bramblett mother of James Quilla
Robinson wanted Lewis Bramblett to be guardian. Had interest in
father est. Vincent Robinson decd. of Laurens, S. C. Melinda C.
Robinson a minor over 14 yrs. wanted Lewis Bramblett of Pickens Dist.
to be her gdn. dtr. of Vincent Robinson decd. of Laurens Dist.

BRANDON, THOMAS ESQ. Deed Book A Page 320. Mesne Conveyance Office. Greenville, S. C. This indenture made 23 May 1788 between Thomas Brandon Esq. of Union County and Lemuel James Alston Esq. of Greenville County. For and in consideration of two shillings sterling money, paid by Lemuel James Alston hath granted, sold, and released all that tract of land containing 400 acres, living in Greenville Co. on both sides of Reedy River, including Richard Paris' plantation with his mill seat on said river. Wit: Zach. Bullock, John Lindsey, Samuel Earle. Signed: Thomas Brandon.

BRANDON, WILLIAM Deed Book B, page 104. Probate Judge Office. Greenville, S. C. This indenture made the 23 Dec. 1788, between William Brandon of Union Co. and Jeremiah Stokes of Greenville Co. Whereas by a grant bearing date 15 Oct. 1784 granted unto William Brandon a tract of land of 640 acres in 96 Dist. on the West of the old Indian boundary line, on both sides of Reedy River. In considera- tion of L100 lawful money of the State, have granted, sold, bargain, and released the tract of 640 acres with all houses, gardens, orchards etc. Wit: Thomas Brandon, Elisha Green. Signed: William (B) Brandon. Proved on oath of Elisha Green in open Court. Dated 16 Nov. 1789.

BRANYON, REUBEN Pack 340. Clerk of Court Office. Abbeville, S. C. Abbeville Dist. To the Honr. Chancellors: Your oratrix Polly Ann Branyon sheweth that she is the widow of the late Reuben Branyon who departed this life __ day of Dec. 1857 leaving as his sole heirs your oratrix his widow, and Nancy A. Branyon his dtr. by a first marriage who is about ten years of age. At the time of his death Reuben Branyon was possessed with two tracts of land, one in Abbe- ville Dist. Adj. land of Hugh Orince, Elias Kay, Roger Williams, Major Jas. H. Cunningham containing 260 acres. The second tract in Anderson Dist. containing 110 acres lying on Weems Creek, waters of Big Generstee Creek, adj. land of Thomas Dean, Jos. McCarley, George Stewart, and Z. Gentry. Your oratrix further states that the two tract of land are not occupied and are wholly profitless, your oratrix prays for a partition or a sale for partition. Filed 9 Sept. 1858.

BRANYON, THOMAS W. Was born about 1800. Son of James Branyon, married Eliza. Davis who was born ca. 1812, children: Davis Branyon born ca. 1842 married Nariza C. Armstrong, born 19 July 1847, died 7 Jan. 1915 a dtr. of Andrew B. Armstrong and Nerisa Pearman, chn: James, Cowan, Nell, Lura Branyon. John Montgomery G. Branyon b. 23 Sept. 1816, D. 9 Jan. 1866 and is buried at Little Rock Cemetery, S.C. He m. Rosannah Kay b. 28 Dec. 1824, d. 17 Dec. 1899 a dtr. of John Kay. Chn: Reuben Oliver Branyon, b. 14 Apr. 1851 son of John M. G. Branyon and Rosannah Kay m. Missiour[?] Ann Pruitt, b. 28 Mar. 1852, d. 9 June 1911. Reuben O. Branyon died 1 Mar. 1922, Chn. Luther C. Branyon b. 21 Aug. 1870, Lewis R. Branyon b. 11 May 1873, James O. Branyon b. 26 Sept. 1874, Lislie K. Branyon B. 1 Oct. 1877, Rosa M. Branyon b. 30 Jan. 1880, Maud Belle Branyon b. 10 Feb. 1882, Allie Lea Branyon b. 21 Apr. 1884, d. 21 Nov. 1910, Julia Pearl Branyon b. 26 May 1886, Winnie Mabrie Branyon b. 12 July 1888, Gupsie M. Crea b. 21 Sept. 1890, Brainerd Cambresis Branyon b. 20 July 1892, Oliver Pruitt Branyon b. 1 July 1894, Harold Branyon b. 29 Mar. 1897. James L. Branyon son of John G. Branyon and Rosannah Kay b. 1857 died 1930 is buried at Little River Cemetery, married Anna M. Walker b. 1864, died 1900 buried at Little River Cemetery. Anna M. Walker was a dtr. of Margaret E. Armstrong and William Walker their chn. Zebelia Branyon, Indicott Branyon, Corine Branyon, Endora Branyon, Lewton Branyon, Homer Branyon, Daisy Branyon, Bonnie Branyon, Lucille Branyon, Ruth[?] Branyon... Reuben Branyon son of Joseph (married twice). 1. Louvenia Naomi Shirley, #2. Polly Ann Sherley, dtrs. of Nathaniel Sherley and Nancy Grubbs, Their children Nancy Alkansa Branyon b. 5 Aug. 1849 d. 14 May 1908, M. G. W. Milford. Lawrence Branyon, died young..

BREAZEALE, SAMUEL P. Book A Page 234. Probate Judge Office. Pickens, S. C. On 4 Oct. 1858 Samuel P. Breazeale and his wife Sarah Ann were heirs of Nathaniel Duncan decd. of Pickens Dist.

BREWER, ELIZABETH Box 46 #506. Probate Judge Office. Pickens, S. C. Elizabeth Brewer mention in the will of D. T. Holland decd. of Pickens Dist. in 1857 was probably his sister

BREWER, JAMES Box 49 #539. Probate Judge Office. Pickens, S. C. I James Brewer being in a low state of health yet of a sound and disposing mind and memory. First I desire a sufficient amount of my property be sold to pay all my just debts. I then will to my beloved wife Elizabeth Brewer all remainder, both real and personal during her natural life or widowhood. In the event she should be married again I desire and direct that the property both real and personal, household and kitchen furniture be sold and an equal division be made between my wife and my children herein named, Cornelia Elizabeth, Mary Susanna, Joseph Ganniwell, William Taylor, I appoint my wife Elizabeth my lawful executrix. Dated 8 Nov. 1858. Wit: M. L. Davis, C. B. Janes, William Janes. Signed: James Brewer. Proven 28 Feb. 1859.

BREWER, MARGARET Pack 653 #3. Clerk of Court Office. Pickens, S. C. Margaret Brewer single woman of Pickens Dist. charges Jasper Crenshaw as being the father of a male bastard child born to her on the 14 May 1858.

BREWER, MARY Pack 231. Clerk of Court Office. Abbeville, S. C. In Equity: To the Honr. the Chancellors, The petition of Levi Pressly a citizen of Louisiana, parish of DeSota sheweth that his mother Mary Brewer in 1850 was sent to the lunatic asylum of S. C. by the Commissioners of the poor for Abbeville Dist. and has been an inmate ever since. Your petitioner thought his mother was dead. One James Ray the brother of your petitioner mother, about the year 1843 died in the State of Texas without heirs other then brothers or sisters, who are as follows, Silas Ray, Jane Ray, Nancy McClelland, Sarah Weems and the Mary Brewer. The estate of James Ray decd. consist almost entirely of wild lands scattered over the State and a few cattle. Sarah Weems intestate sister admr. upon the est. until her death, then her son William Weems who claims the whole and refuse to account to the other heirs. Your petitioner in the year 1858 in his own behalf and others heirs instituted suit in Brogonia County, Texas against sd. William Weems to the surprise of your petitioner he found to be a fact his mother is alive, and has traveled to visit his afflicted mother, and your petitioner prays that he may be appointed his mother committee to represent his mother interest in her brother est. Filed 9 June 1859.

BRIDGES, LUCY ANN Apt. 1 File 66. Probate Judge Office. Greenville, S. C. I Lucy Ann Bridges being in my usual state of health and of sound mind and memory. Dated 9 Dec. 1836. I give to my dtr. Mahaley one feather bed and furniture. I give to my son Jeremiah one feather bed and furniture. I give to my dtr. Sarah one feather bed and furniture. I appoint James Bridges and James Goodlett executors. Wit: James Goodlett, Ann Goodlett, Eliza G. Goodlett. Signed: Lucy Ann X Bridges. Probated 13 Feb. 1837.

BRIDGES, SARAH Box 2 Pack 64. Probate Judge Office. Edgefield, S. C. Will dated 8 June 1820. Proved 12 March 1827. Wit: Robert Johns, Benjamin A. Stevens, Matthew Stevens. Dtr. Polly Lowry. I do give to Edwin Bridges so of Polly Lowry $15.00. Children: Stevens Bridges, Patience Rhoads, and Roday Lascitor. Executors, son, Steven Bridges and Issac Lascitor. Paid 28 March 1828 John Lowry $115.00. The exr. is entitled to one half balance to be divided between four. Paid 19 May 1834 Raidford Rhodes share of est. $17.00. Paid 7 Sept. 1833 Collins Rhodes $16.70. Paid 25 May 1830 Rollin Rhodes $16.71.

BRIDGES, THOMAS Deed Book B, Page 138. Mesne Conveyance, Greenville, S. C. This indenture made between Thomas Bridges and Overton Goodman both of Greenville Dist. Dated 10 Nov. 1789. In and by a certain grant dated 21 Jan. 1785 did grant unto Isham Foster a tract of land containing 200 acres, lying in 96 Dist. Greenville Co. on both sides of Ready River near Parises mountain west of the antient?

Bridges, Thomas - Continued. In consideration of Ł96 said Thomas Bridges have granted, sold, bargain and released the said tract of land with all out houses. Proven before Lemuel J. Alston Esq. by and on the oath of Harden Kemp. Recorded 15 March 1790.

BRIGGS, JOHN Box 5 #88. Probate Judge Office. Abbeville, S. C. Abbeville Dist. by John Thomas Junr. Esq. Ord. To Robert Hannah, Jas. Montgomery, Jos. Greer and John Owens these are to authorize and empower you or any three of your to repair to all places within this State as you shall be directed unto by Elizabeth Briggs administratrix of John Briggs late of this Dist. Dated 6 Juen 1783. Signed: John Thomas Junr. Ord. (in the inventory is this line) the estate of William Cox desesed d.r to the estate of John Briggs desesed in sterling money Ł31 0 0. Signed: John Owens, Joseph Greer

BRIGGS, MINOR Box 1 #11. In Equity. Probate Judge Office. Pickens, S. C. On 30 Aug. 1842 Alexr. S. Briggs, H. T. Arnold, E. Alexander are bound to Miles M. Norton Clk. of Equity in the sum of $16,000. Alexr. S. Briggs made gdn. of Henry C. and Myra L. Briggs minors under 21 yrs. Capt. Alexr. S. Briggs was a brother to said minors. Chn. of Robert H. Briggs, decd.

BRIGGS, ROBERT Pack 238 In Equity, Clerk of Court Office, Pickens, S. C. Jane Arnold late widow of Robert Briggs decd. and her present husband ___ Arnold and Elizabeth Watson dtr. of sd. Robert Briggs and over 21 yrs. old, Elijah Watson her husband and Harriet T. Grisham dtr. of sd. Robert Briggs and John O. Grisham her husband, and A. S. Briggs son of Robert Briggs, states their father departed this life some years ago intestate leaving considerable property in sd. Dist. That Jane Arnold and William Holcombe took out letter of admr. on the personal property. That Robert Briggs left the following chn. who are minors, viz: Henry C. Briggs, Myra L. Briggs, A. S. Briggs, Elizabeth Watson and Harriet Grisham. Filed 18 Jan. 1840. Recd. 11 Nov. 1842 $200 in part of the share of my ward Myra L. Briggs. Signed: A. S. Briggs, dgn. Recd. 24 Dec. 1842 Alexr. S. Briggs recd. $292.23 for the share of his ward Myra L. Briggs. Owned five tracts of land sold #2 and #3 to Revd. H. T. Arnold, #4 to William Holcombe, #5 to Elijah Watson, #6 to Readin Freeman.

BRIGGS, ROBERT H. Deed Book A-1 Page 26. Clerk of Court Office. Pickens, S. C. I Frances Mauldin of Pendleton Dist. to Robert H. Briggs of same Dist. in consideration of $92.50 paid by sd. Briggs have granted, sold, bargained and release all that tract of land containing 125 acres lying on Wolf Creek waters of 12 Mile River, being a tract of land whereon Thomas Christain now lives, conveyed to me by William Guest. Dated 14 March 1827. Wit: Benjamin Willson, Thomas X Christain, Saml. E. Mauldin. Signed: Francis X Mauldin. Proved on oath of Samuel E. Mauldin before Edward Norton, J.P. on 9 Aug. 1828. Recorded the 5 Jan. 1829.

BRIGGS, ROBERT H. Box 7 #87. Probate Judge Office. Pickens, S. C. Est. admr. 2 May 1836 by Jane L. Briggs, widow, Wm. Holcombe, Bailey Barton, Benjamin Hagood, Elijah Watson, Jr. who are bound unto James H. Dendy, Ord. in the sum of $30,000.00. Cit. Pub. at New Hope Church. Expenses: 1 Jan. 1841 A. S. Briggs recd. $2,768.40 of est. On 11 Jan. 1839 John O. Grisham recd. $2,314.00. in part due to his wife Harriet from estate. On 1 Jan. 1841 John O. Grisham recd. of Mrs. Jane L. Arnold nee Briggs admr. of said est. $114.00 due his wife Harriet T. Grisham.

BRIMER, BENJAMIN Box 2 #53. Probate Judge Office. Anderson, S. C. Will dated 13 June 1803. I Benjamin Brimer being sick of body but of perfect mind. First I give my wife Rebecka Brimer all my moveable property goods and chattles according to the intent here of and no man to interfere. The property to be divided at the decd. of my wife as I third part of Jery Brimer 1 third part ot Nancy Maus, 1 third part to Betsy Lenard. I likewise give unto Caty Gaber fifty dollars. I likewise give unto Rebacke Brimer the child of Samuel Brimer decd. five Ł sterling. I likewise will unto the under named

Brimer, Benjamin - Continued. persons five shillings a piece,
William Brimer, Polly Henry,, Jas. Brimer. I Likewise do desire Wm.
Lennard to see to the business given under my hand this day and tear
above written. Wit: J. L. Brook, Jonathan Watson. Signed: Ben. X
Brimer. Proved on oath of Jonathan Watson before John Harris, O.P.D.
on the 30 Sept. 1803. Cit. pub. at the Roberts Congregation on 26
Sept. 1803. Whereas Rebecca Brimer and Joseph Brimer made suit to me
to grant him a letter of admr. of the est. and effects of Benjamin
Brimer late of Pendleton Dist. Given under my hand and seal this 19
Sept. 1803. Signed: John Harris, O.P.D. Pendleton Dist. To the
Ordinary of sd. Dist. Your petitioner Rebecka Davis formerly the widow
of Benjamin Brimer decd. prays that the property left me by sd. Brimer
will you order the executor to sell the same and allow me one third
part to support on instead of the whole. Dated 28 Oct. 1803. Signed:
Van Davis and Rebecka Davis. An inventory was made on 15 Oct. 1803 by
Alexander Stevenson, Samuel Dean, John Adam Miller. Sale was held on
11-12 Nov. 1803. Buyers: Van Davis, George Stevenson, William Bennet,
Lewis Shamley, Zadek Shamley, William Smith, Fleming Waters, William
Leonard, Edward McCollister, William McCleskey, Abrim Sanders, Joseph
Brimer, Jesse Brown, John Hillis, John Heter, John Thomas, Davis Tate,
Elisha Herrin, Daniel Edwards, Ephraim Herrin, Cooper Bennet, Archibal
Shelton, Agnes Martin, William McGrigger, Andrew Hanah, Adam Files,
James Brice, John Brice, George Chamble, William Wilson, Samson Tippen,
John Waters, John Hays, David Tate, Henry Ledbetter, Joseph Land, Junr.,
James Morrow, John Carrck, Nancy Moss, William Burns, Richard Specks,
Jonathan Watson, Jesse McMullin, James Blague,

   BRISON, SUSAN Pack 213 #4. Clerk of Court Office. Pickens,
S. C. On 18 March 1842 Susan Brison a single woman was ordered to
appear in Court and give evidence as to who the father was of her
bastard child William Brison.

   BROUGH, THOMAS No Ref. or County, only one page the middle of
the will. No date. ...and bequeath to my second son Thomas Jefferson.
I will my three slaves Sookey, Dephne and Jonas to be keep during my
wife natural life or widowhood of my wife Eveline on the home portion
of land, and their service under her direction, to support her and my
two dtr. and son during their minority, viz; Frances Ann, Louisa
Eveline and William Henry, Louisa Eveline and William Henry to have
one year schooling. At the death or end of my wife widowhood the said
slaves to be sold, the three youngest chn. to get $200 each, with the
remainder divided between my six chn. viz; Jane Elizabeth Humphries,
John Flemming, Thomas Jefferson, Frances Ann, Louisa Eveline and
William Henry. I also give my negro Eugenia to my dtr. Frances Ann and
my negro Amanda to my dtr. Louisa Eveline. All household and kitchen
furniture, stock, cattle, horses, farm tools etc. to my wife, for her
support and the minor chn. I appoint my neighbor J. W. Jones and my
son John Flemming Brough executor to his my last.

   BROUGHTON, WILLIBOUGH Box 2 #74. Probate Judge Office. Anderson,
S. C. I Willibough Broughton of Pendleton Dist. being weak in body
but of sound mind and memory. After my just debts are paid, I be-
questh to my wife Joanna all that tract of land that I now live on
containing 107 acres during her life time and after her death I allow
the tract to be divided between Federick Johnston my son-in-law and
Elijah Smith, Federick Johnston step-son it to be equally divided
between them. I bequeath to my eldest dtr. Catharine Holkom $1.50.
I bequeath to Jessee Broughtons heirs $1.50. I bequeath to Job
Broughton $1.50. I bequeath to my youngest dtr. Winifret Davis $1.50.
I bequeath unto my wife Joanna all my live stock, also the rest and
residue of my goods and chattles. I appoint my wife Joanna, Federick
Johnston and James Garvin my executors and executrix. Dated 28 Oct.
1804. Wit: Thos. Garvin, Jas. Garvin. Signed: Willibough X
Broughton. Proved on oath of Thomas Garvin before John Harris on the
5th Nov. 1804. An inventory was made 17 Nov. 1804 by Thomas Garvin,
Bazel Smith, Ezekiah Lisenbeath.

   BROWN, DAVID Box 1 #37. Probate Judge Office. Anderson, S. C.
I David Brown of Pendleton Dist. being sick and weak in body but of
perfect mind and memory, etc. I allow my just debts and funeral

Brown, David - Continued. expenses be paid. I give to my wife
Jean, one bed and clothing, the plantation whereon she now lives
during her widowhood, at her decease the said plantation to avert to
my two sons John and Joseph. The two sons are to care for their
mother, and work the land and see that she never wants in sickness or
health, if the two sons see not cause to perform, then the land to
-hall avert to any one of my son that will perform. I give to my dtr.
Jean one bedding of clothes, also to my dtr. Elizabeth one bedding of
cloaths. At the decease of my wife the personal est. to be sold and
equally divided between all my chn. (not named). I appoint my wife
Jean executrix and my brother Joseph Brown executor. Dated 7 June
1796. Wit: John Reid, William Brice, William X Reid. Signed:
David Brown. Proved in open Court 26 June 1797 on oath of John Reid.

BROWN, JAMES Box 1 #31. Probate Judge Office. Anderson, S. C.
Est. of James Brown Sr. admr. 2 March 1830 by George R. Brown, James
Telford, and Ephraim Mayfield who are bound unto John Harris Ord.
in the sum of $8,000. Sale held 1 April 1830, Buyers, John Leach,
Nancy Brown, John Avary, G. R. Brown, James Telford, John B. Anderson,
Henry Gambrell, James Harkens, Andrew Brock, Jacob Adams, Young
Castlebury, Grant A. Mmr[?], Martin Phillips, Wm. Mattison, Elisha
Kelly, Robert Telford, Jno. Towns, Wm. White, John T. Broyles, Tobias
Smith. Est. paid Wm. F. Clinkscales, Esq. Wm. Telford, Samuel
Williams, Nancy Brown, Johnson Day, John Poor, H. Acker, C. Orr,
Benj. Stanton, G. A. Brown, Dated 2 March 1835.

BROWN, JOANNA Pack 9 Clerk of Court Office. Anderson, S. C.
Whereas I Joanna Brown of Pendleton Dist. since the separation of
myself and my husband Col. John Brown. I have been dependant on and
a charge of Aaron Nalley and his family. Colonal Brown having taken
up with another woman and left the State. Not being able to provide
for myself save the labor of one negro man named Bob. I therefore
agree and contract with Aaron Nalley to care for me in sickness and
health and commit my body to the earth in a christian burial, I give
him and his wife all I possess of furniture and wearing clothes, my
negro man Bob. Wit: Jacob Bowyer, James Booker. Signed: Joanna
X Brown. Aaron Nalley. Dated 14 June 1824. Proven on oath of Jacob
Bowyer and James Booker before J. Douthit, J.Q. on same date. Certified on 25 Oct. 1826.

BROWN, JOHN IRVIN Box 1 #15. In equity, Probate Judge Office.
Pickens, S. C. To the Honr. the Chancellors: The petition of Oliver
M. Doyle suing for himself and other such creditors as shall come.
Your petitioner sheweth that John I. Brown is indebted to him in the
sum of $9.37 1/2 with interest by note under seal, and another sum
of $3.25 for medical service and medicines, by open account. On the
15 May 1857 Rebecca Brown the wife of said John I. Brown died intestate, being entitled to a distributive share of the real estate of
Allen Black which at that time had not been partitioned. That she
left an infant son William Allen Brown and her husband, John I. Brown
as her heirs. Since her death on __ day of August 1857 the said
William Allen Brown died aged about three months, leaving neither
brother nor sister only the father. That the real estate of Allen
Black was sold by Wm. J. Parson, Esq. on twelve months credit of one
year. That said John I. Brown removed to the State of Texas or
California and has no property in this State that may be attached.
Your petitioner prays that the said distributive share of the real
estate of Allen Black to which John I. Brown in entitled be attached
to pay to his creditors. Filed 22 Dec. 1858. The real estate of
Allen Black was sold 3 May 1858 viz; tract #1 to Robert Powell, tract
#2 to Jane Black, tract #3 to Wm. Black. E. Hugh and J. R. Hunnicutt
are the admor. of Allen Black Est. This was signed by Rebecca X
Black and E. Hughs.

BROWN, JOSEPH Box 2 #79. Probate Judge Office. Anderson, S. C.
On 28 May 1838 Daniel Brown applied for letter of admr. upon the est.
of Joseph Brown decd. Cit. pub. at Anderson Church. Est. admr. 4
June 1838 by Daniel Brown, William Acker and Robert Brown who are
bound unto John Harris, Ord. in the sum of $2,000. On 11 April 1844 a

Brown, Joseph - Continued. summons in partition to Mary Ann
Brown, widow, Susan Brown, Eliab Brown, Nancy E. Brown, John Jos. Brown
and Samuel Brown legal heirs of Joseph Brown who died intestate. You
are required to appear at a Court in Anderson Court house on the 3 May
1844 to show why the real estate of Joseph Brown decd. should not be
divided. Land lying on Beaver Dam Creek, adj. lands of Herbert
Hammond, Elisha Lewis, Mary Ann Brown the widow to have one third, the
other two thirds divided between the chn. Mary Ann Brown accept the
appointment of guardinship ad litem of her chn. who were minors.

BROWN, ROBERT Box 2 #67. Probate Judge Office. Anderson, S. C.
Est. admr. 19 Dec. 1803 by Elizabeth Brown, John Parker, Elijah Major
who are bound unto John Harris Ord. in the sum of $2,000.00. The
sale was held no names of who bought or the date given. Thomas
Willingham was clerk of sale.

BROWN, WILLIAM Box 2 #41. Probate Judge Office. Anderson, S. C.
(Only part of this will in the notes, no date). I William Brown of
Pendleton Dist. being very sick and weak in body but of perfect mind
and memory. I will my just debts and funeral expenses be paid. The
Manner Plantation or tract of land whereon I now live shall belong to
my wife Hannah Brown during her life or till she pleases to give it
up, then it shall belong to William Brown son of Alexander Brown. I
will that my wife Hannah peaceably possess all the negroes which I now
possess during her life, she shall dispose of them as she sees cause.
I also will to my wife all my household and moveable effects together
with all debts due and accounts due me.

BROWNLEE, JOHN Box 5 Pack 87. Probate Judge Office. Abbeville,
S. C. Will dated 25 Feb. 1802. I John Brownlee of 96 Dist. Abbeville
County being weak in body, but of sound mind and memory. I give to
my wife Alley Brownlee two negroes namely Susanna and Harry together
with all stock, tool and household furniture during her life, after
her death to be equally divided between my son Joseph Brownlee and my
dtr. Nancy Richey. I give at my death my wagon and gear, and all shop
tools. I give to my dtr. Nancy after my death $200 made up with what
her husband now has in his hands. I give to my grandson Joseph Richey
at my death what money I lent him, also my big Bible. I give to my
son Joseph at my death $356 in lieu of the land sold Doctor Thomas
Taylor and after the death of my wife, the two negroes are to be free
in case Harry is twenty one years old, otherwise to be keep in the
hands of my son Joseph till that time. I also give the sd. two negroes
113 acres of land lying on Turkey Creek, to be sold by my sd. son, the
land to be bought convenient to him with the purchase thereof and for
him to conduct and manage for sd. two negroes. I appoint my wife
Alley Brownlee, my son Joseph Brownlee and George Brownlee, Senr.
executrix and executors. Wit: Samuel Anderson, Joseph Brownlee.
Signed: John Brownlee. Appraisment was made 15 July 1802... by John
Weatherall, Robert Swain, John Hodges.

BRUCE, CHARLES Box 8 #99. Probate Judge Office. Pickens, S. C.
Est. admr. 8 March 1838 by James M. Bruce of Georgia, Robert Bruce,
Geo. C. Cleveland who are bound unto James H. Dendy Ord. in the sum
of $1600.00. Charles Bruce was late of the State of Georgia. Robert
Bruce was of Franklin County, Ga. Cit. mention that Charles Bruce
was son of Robart Bruce of Ga. who died in Alabama. Legatee, J. M.
Bruce, Robert Stribling, Jesse Thompson. In 1838 paid D. S. Bruce
$30.75.

BRUCE, J. FRANK Box 123 #7. Probate Judge Office. Pickens,
S. C. Est. admr. 22 Nov. 1893 by Mrs. Alice M. Bruce, H. Earle Russell,
A. G. Wyatt, A. W. Folger who are bound unto J. B. Newberry, Ord. in
the sum of $700.00. Died 5 Nov. 1893... left a widow and a step-son.
A mother Sarah Bruce, Brother W. B. Bruce, Sisters, Alpha Elliot,
Emma Whelchel.. Sarah Bruce, W. B. Bruce, and Alpha Elliot were of
Dixon, Ga., Emma Whelchel was of Dalonega, Ga. Alice M. Bruce was
the mother of H. Earle Russell.

BRUCE, JAMES Book A Page 9. Probate Judge Office. Pickens, S. C. Personally appeared Horatio Bruce who being duly sworn saith that the tract of land containing 201 acres belonging to the estate of James Bruce decd. lying on Wolf Creek is not worth $1000 and it would be in his opinion best advantage for the legatee to sell the same. Dated 3 June 1833. Heirs: Stephen Adams in right of his wife Patience, Nancy Bruce and Heirs of Wm. Bruce. decd. Heirs of Burt Moore in right of his wife, heirs of James Bruce and wife Priscilla, Henry Wolf in right of his wife Rebecca, John Bruce, George Bruce, Daniel Bruce, Sarah Bruce.

BRUCE, JAMES Box 1 #13. In Equity. Probate Judge Office. Pickens, S. C. State of Ala., County of Benton, I Rebecca Wolf, having full confidence in the honesty and inegrity of John N. Swords of same State and County. Do hereby appoint him my true and lawful attorney to use my name, etc. to receive and receipt from the executors of the estate of James Bruce decd. of old Pendleton Dist. now Pickens and Anderson Dists. Dated 24 June 1842. Wit: J. W. Ledbetter, J.P. Signed: Rebeca X Wolf.

BRUCE, JAMES Box 1 #13. In Equity. Probate Judge Office. Pickens, S. C. Est. admr. 21 March 1837 by Joseph A. Field, John Gilstrap, Jr., Joseph League who are bound unto James H. Dendy, Ord. in the sum of $1,000.00. On 31 Aug. 1841 Adonejah Edwards of Cobb Co., Ga. appointed James Bruce of Cherokee Co., Ga. his attorney to collect his part of James Bruce, Sr. est. of Pickens Co., S. C. Said James Bruce was late of Habersham Co., Ga. On 2 June 1840 George Bruce of Lumpkin Co., Ga. appointed his brother Daniel Bruce of Cobb Co., Ga. his attorney to receive from his father est. On 28 Jan. 1842 Abraham Bruce of Union Co., Ga. appointed Edly Hood of the same place his attorney to collect his part of the est. In Sept. 1839 Nancy Bruce of DeKalb Co., Ga. appointed Daniel Bruce her attorney, to collect her part as a legatee by being the widow of Wm. Bruce who was a son of James Bruce, Sr. of Pendleton Co., S. C. On 17 May 1841 Ruthy Watson of Forsythe Co., Ga. appointed James Bruce of Macon Co., Ga. (Must be Bibb Co.) to collect her part of the est. of Jas. Bruce, Sr. est. . (Loose papers.) On 15 Dec. 1833 Stephen Adams asked Mr. Dendy, Ord. to pay Wm. Adams of Pickens Co., S. C. his claim for traveling expenses for James Bruce decd. Paid $24.50 in full (Loose Papers). Recd. 25 Aug. 1841 of James Dendy, Ord. $7.75 my claim of the real est. of James Bruce, Sr. an inheritance descended to me a son of James Bruce, Jr. late of Georgia decd. and in full for the claim of James Eaton, John Eaton, Wm. Eaton, Ruthy Watson, and Adonejah Edwards each of whom married dtrs. of my father vizt. (Jas. Bruce, Jr.) and are legally entitled as such and in this estimate is included the share of my mother decd. and who I hereby certify is dead. On 11 Feb. 1843 John Bruce recd. share of $51.00 of real est. of his father James Bruce decd. Recd. of W. D. Steele, Ord. $1891 my share of what is due to Stephen Adams from real est. of James Bruce decd. this 7 Dec. 1846. On 7 Feb. 1842 Edy Hood recd. $4.00 in full for the claim of Abraham B. Bruce grandson of James Bruce, Sr. and son of James Bruce, Jr. decd. On 31 Oct. 1839 George O. Bruce son of James Bruce decd. and grandson of James Bruce Sr. decd. formerly resident of Pickens Dist. states that his father is dead and has left a widow Priscilla and 11 children including himself viz, Jonathan Bruce, James Bruce, Rutha Watson widow, John Eaton and wife Rebecca, Abraham Bruce, Aquilla Bruce, Wm. Eaton and wife Sarah, Daniel A. Bruce, Adonejah Edwards and wife Patience.

BRUCE, JOHN Apt. 1 File 70. Probate Judge Office. Greenville, S. C. I desire a settlement of the Estate of John Bruce decd. Please give the lawful notice. The following are the heirs: 1. G. T. Hughes and wife. 2. A. S. Burns and wife Hulda, Alabama. 3. Wesley Bruce, Mississippi. 4. Heirs of Robert Bruce decd. of Greenville, S. C. viz.; Wm. A. Austin and wife, Thomas Halbert and wife resides out of State, John Bruce, Robert Bruce both of Greenville, S. C. 5. Heirs of Mrs. J. B. Jennings decd. resides in Alabama. Signed: Tho. P. Brockman. Dated 26 Jan. 1859. Power of Attorney to Abram S. Burnes, State of Alabama, Calhoun County. I Mahulda Burns of said State and

Bruce, John - Continued. County the wife of Abram S. Burns have
constituted and appointed my husband Abram Burns my true and lawful
attorney, to use my name, act in my place, to receive and receipt from
the admr. exect[?] Ord. or anyone having money or chattles, due me
from the est. of John Bruce decd. of Greenville, S. C. Dated 7 April
1859. Attest. Joseph M. Roberts. Signed: Mahulda X Burns. Power
of attorney to John B. Jennings. State of Alabama, County of Calhoun.
That we William Jennings, Polly Jennings, John Jennings, Thomas
Jennings, David Jennings, Banister Jennings, Nancy Jennings, Jackson
Jennings, Henry Jennings, Leander Jennings of the County of Calhoun,
State of Alabama have this day constituted and appointed in my stead
put and depute our father John B. Jennings our true and lawful attorney
and agent for us. To receive and receipt from any admr. exect. or
Court, money or goods due us from the est. of John Bruce decd. Dated
7 April 1859.

BRUCE, JOHN & JANE Pack 31 #7. Clerk of Court Office, Pickens,
S. C. (Basement). We John Bruce and Jane Bruce his wife of McMinn
County, Tenn. late of S. C. In consideration of $1200 in hand paid
by Major James McKinney of Pendleton Dist., S. C. have sold, bargained
and released all that tract of land containing 226 3/4 acres in
Pendleton Dist. on the North Fork of Little River. It being the same
tract granted unto Jane Peteat now the wife of John Bruce on the 2
April 1821, now occupied by James McKinney, Jr. Dated 13 Aug. 1823.
Wit: William Grisham, Reuben Grisham. Signed: John Bruce and Jane
X Bruce. On the 19 Aug. 1823 Jane Bruce appeared before Jacob Capehart,
J.Q. and renounced and relinquished her dower on the above land.

BRUCE, JOHN & JANE Pack 296. Clerk of Court Office. Pickens,
S. C. We John Bruce and Jane Bruce of Pendleton Dist. are firmly
bound unto James McKinney of same Dist. in the sum of $2,400. We bind
ourselves, heirs, executors unto said James McKinney if we fail in
performing the condition under written to make or cause to be made a
good and lawful right and title to a tract of land in Pendleton Dist.
lying on North Fork of Little River, adj. lands of Martins Reserve
containing 226 3/4 acres, then the above obligation to be void.
Dated 22 Jan. 1821. Wit: John McKinney, William Bruce. Signed:
John Bruce and Jane X Bruce.

BRUTON, DAVID SR. No Ref. Probate Judge Office. Spartanburg,
S. C. I, David Bruton Sr., of Spartanburg Dist. being infirm in body
but of sound mind and memory, etc. First I will to my wife Susannah
Bruton to have and enjoy that part of the plantation whereon I now
live containing 27 acres, with all crops, household furniture, tools,
stock, cattle, horses, hogs during her natural life. I give to my
eldest son George Bruton one feather bed which was his mothers in her
lifetime. I will that my negro man Isaac with 50 acres of land that
the title was made to me by Daniel Bragg, with my riding horse, saddle
and bridle to be sold, and money arising to pay my just debts, and my
wife to have ten dollars, with my son in law John Williams to have one
shilling if he should apply for any part of my est. he has received
what I consider to be his part. The remainder to be divided between
my six sons viz; George Bruton, Jonas Bruton, Enoch Bruton, David
Bruton, Isaac Bruton, Philip Bruton. I appoint my sons Jonas and
Philip Bruton and William Tippins executors. Dated 17 March 1815.
Wit: Go. Brewton, John Brewton, Nancy Brewton, JOel Brewton. Signed:
David Bruton.

BRUTON, SUSANNAH No Ref. Spartanburg Courthouse. Spartanburg,
S. C. I Susannah Bruton being of sound and disposing mind and understanding; I give to my great grand daughter Susannah E. B. Cockram,
the tract of land whereon I now live, containing 70 acres, also all my
personal estate of what ever kind in trust for the following uses and
purpose. For the sole and seperate use of her mother Celia Cockram
during her natural life free from and without the control of her
husband Jacob Cockram and after her death of the said Celia, for the
use and benefit of the said Susannah E. B. Cockram her heirs and
assigns for ever. I appoint my great granddaughter Susannah E. B.
Cockram executrix. Dated 23 April 1835. Wit: C. P. Woodruff, H. P.
Woodruff, Thos. Woodruff. Signed: Susannah X Bruton.

BRYANT, FAMILY BIBLE   Now in possession of Mr. Ervin Agustus
Bryant of Liberty, S. C.   (No date in notes as when copied.)
William Hardy Bryant was born 4 March 1859 in Anderson County, near
Piedmont.   Sallie E. Bryant was born 27 Oct. 1858, wife of William
Hardy Bryant.   Children: Mattie Rebecca Bryant was born 2 Oct. 1879
in Anderson Co., S. C.; Newton Oscar Bryant was born 8 July 1882 in
Anderson Co., S. C.; Ervin Augustus Bryant was born 22 Sept. 1885 in
Anderson Co., S. C.; Annie Idell Bryant was born 4 March 1889 in
Anderson Co., S. C.; Homar Eugene Bryant was born 29 Jan. 1892 in
Anderson Co., S.C.; Fannie May Bryant was born 7 June 1895 in Anderson
Co., S.C. Williae Irene Bryant was born 23 June 1898 in Anderson Co.,
S.C.; James Terrell Bryant was born 12 Aug. 1903 in Oconee Co., S.C.;
Ethel E. Moss sister of Alvin Moss was born 15 Oct. 1908; Alvin Moss
nephew of said Ervin Augustus Bryant was born 27 Aug. 1906; William
Bryant grandfather of said Ervin Augustus Bryant was married to
Clara C. Bryant the 23 Dec. 1852. William Bryant father of said Ervin
Augustus Bryant was married to Sarah Elizabeth Sheriff the 2 July 1878.
Mattie Rebecca Bryant died 19 Oct. 1880 in Anderson Co., S.C.
Newton Oscar Bryant died 19 Sept. 1884 in Anderson Co., S.C.
Clara C. Bryant died 17 Feb. 1897 in Anderson Co., S.C. Ethel E. Moss
sister of Alvin Moss was born 15 Oct. 1908.

BRYCE, JAMES R. G.   Box 1 #31.   Probate Judge Office. Pickens,
S. C.   On 7 Jan. 1852 Jonathan R. Cleveland, A. J. Lowery, Wm. O.
Dleveland are bound unto W. D. Steele, Ord. in the sum of $250.00.
Jonathan R. Cleveland made gdn. of James R. G. Bryce a minor under 21
yrs.

BRYCE, THOMAS   Box 16 #206.   Probate Judge Office. Pickens, S.C.
Est. admr. 9 July 1847 by Alexander Bryce, W. L. Keith who are bound
unto Wm. D. Steele, Ord. in the sum of $600.00. On 5 Nov. 1849 heirs
were to appear in Court to show why the real estate of the said decd.
lying on Coneross Creek adj. land of Col. J. C. Kilpatrick, containing
230 acres should not be sold. The heirs were: Jane the wife of Wm.
Hays. Jas. R. G. Bryce, Elizabeth the wife of Jonathan R. Cleveland.
On 3rd or 5th Nov. Jas. R. G. Bryce a minor over 14 yrs. wanted to
appoint Yancy White his gdn.

BRYSON, JOHN   Box 2 #46.   Probate Judge Office. Anderson, S.C.
Est. admr. ____ 1824 by Penuel Price, Isaac Long, Fenton Hall who are
bound unto John Harris, Ord. in the sum of $3,000 Cit. Pub. at Rockey
River Meeting House by James Crowther M.G. Sale of est. was held 23
March 1824. Buyers are: Penuel Price, Zachariah Gentry, William
Latham, Lent Hall, Fenton Hall, William McKee, James Cosper, David
Steel, John Herrin, William Keown, Rachel McCullough, Ephraim Hampton,
Robert Milford, Moody Gentry, Hugh McKay, William Nichols, Thomas
Townly, William Simpson, Andrew Cunningham, John Stevenson, William
Beaty, Hugh Carithers, Andrew Brownlee, James Shererd, Archibald
McMahan, Spencer Wiles, William Allen, James Henderson, James Jones,
Charles Stark, Esq., Jacob Braselton, Samuel D. McCullough, Rachel
McCullough Junior, David Gillespie, Elisha Brown, John Scott, James
Cooper, Stephen Downs, Alexander Gray, Gideon H. Johnson, Ephraim
Allen, Ephraim Hampton, William McCarley, Luke Hamilton. Signed:
William McKay, Clerk.

BUCHANAN, ROBERT   Box 4 Pack 74.   Probate Judge Office. Abbeville,
S. C.   I Robert Buchanan of Abbeville Dist. being of sound mind and
memory, but weak in body, etc. I give to my three grand children,
namely Robert B. Buchanan, James W. Buchanan, and Mary C. Buchanan
the lawful heirs of my son James Buchanan decd. the following my negro
woman named Emily and her child Augustus, and one negro girl Suffrona
to them and their heirs forever, the property to remain in the hands of
the executors free of interest until the youngest son arrives to the
age of twenty one. I give to my son William Buchanan four negroes
Namely, Mary and her three chn. Milly, Mary, and Asburry. I give to
my son Robert E. Buchanan three negroes, namely Rusilla, Alick and Sam.
I give to my son Francis A. Buchanan three negroes namely, Frank,
Burgess and Alcy. I give to my granddaughter Jane Logan, one negro
named Amanda, said Amanda to remain in the hand of my dtr. Mary Logan

Buchanan, Robert - Continued. until my grand dtr. become of age or marry. I give to my dtr. Mary Logan $1000 to be paid three yrs. after my death. All other property both real and personal with the exception of two colts and my negro woman Eliza. The property which the home of James Buchanan widow and their chn. not to be sold, during her life or widowhood. My negro Eliza to remain under the special care and charge of my son Francis as long as she lives, she to have my milk cow. I hold in my hand sixty dollars belonging to Snelson four chn. which I authorized my executors to lay out for them as they need it, in such a manner as will be equal amongst said negroes. I appoint my sons William, Robert and Francis Buchanan executors. Dated 8 Oct. 1838. Wit: John Matthews, John Irwin, W. B. Arnold. Signed: Robert Buchanan. Proven on oath of John Matthews and John Irwin on the 1 Nov. 1838. Inventory was made 5 Dec. 1838 by G. Apelton, John Roman, Stanly Crews. Listed are two negroes, Belinda and Winny. By 13 Oct. 1845 Robert Buchanan was dead and his wife Elizabeth was executrix. Robert had given his father est. admr. a note for $1131.00. It was agreed that said note be given to chn. of Jas. Buchanan decd.

BUCKHALTER, JEREMIAH Deed Book 32 Page 271. Probate Judge Office. Edgefield, S. C. Deed from Jeremiah Buckhalter to Thomas Chapel both of Edgefield, Dist. Dated 31 Jan. 1815. In consideration of $100.00 paid in hand, have granted sold, bargain and released a tract of land containing 50 acres lying on little Stephen Creek on the North side, adj. land of widow Camelsons land, Peter Ouytzs line. Wit: Abraham Stevens, James X Morris. Signed: Jeremiah Buckhalter. Proven on oath of Abraham Steven before James Adams, J.P. on 13 May 1815.

BUCKHUSTER, JOEL R. Book B Page 99. Probate Judge Office, Pickens, S. C. On 7 May 1866 Joel R. Buckhuster of Pickens Dist. is mentioned as being the husband of Nancy M. Albertson a dtr. of Samuel Albertson Senr. decd. of Pickens Dist.

BUFFINGTON, EZEKIEL Deed Book B-1 Page 116. Clerk of Court Office. Pickens, S. C. We Ezekiel Buffington and Ellis Harling to Oburn Buffington, dated __ July 1797. In consideration of ₤150 have granted, sold, bargained and released unto Oburn Buffington all that part of the tract of land lying North side of Cain Creek, leaving a part on the South side of about 25 acres the whole containing about 567 acres on Cain Creek waters of Keowee River, granted to Ezekiel Buffington and Ellis Harlin on the 5 March 1792. Wit: John Beazley, William Beazley. Signed: Ezekiel Buffington and Ellis Harlin. Proved on oath of William Beazley before Benjamin Bryan J.P. of Hall County, Georgia on the 27 Nov. 1826. Recorded 28 Dec. 1831 by W. L. Keith, Clk. Pickens, S. C.

BULL, JOHN #31. Clerk of Court Office. Abbeville, S. C. Abbeville, S. C. In Chancery. To the Honr. the Chancellors: Your orator and your oratrixes Andrew Burnet and E. Ann Dent formerly E. Ann Horry and Mary L. Allen formerly Mary L. Horry sheweth that on the 6 Feb. 1855 John Bull died intestate leaving three large and valuable cotton plantation in said Dist. and 97 slaves, with other personalty of great value. That W. P. Noble and Sarah Bull the widow too kout[?] a letter of admr. from the ordinary office and assumed possession of both real and personal property. John Bull left no father nor mother, brother or sister or lineal descendants of any kind, but left a widow Sarah Bull and three first cousins being the next of kin, who are your orator and oratrixes. The widow Sarah Bull was born in Ireland and is therefore, subject of the Queen, having never been naturalized according to the laws of the U.S. is therefore incapable of inheriting any portion of the said estate.. (no more genealogical information in papers). Filed 8 June 1855.

BULLWINKLE, CLAUS Pack 74. In Equity. Clerk of Court Office. Pickens, S. C. Claus Bullwinkle died the 7 May 1851. Owned a tract of land in Pickens, Dist. containing 208 acres and two lots in Wallhalla. Left a widow Catherine Dorothea Bullwinkle and one child Nicholas George Bullwinkle a minor under the age of 14 yrs. Filed 2 July 1853

BURGESS, WILLIAM SENR. Abstracted from a copy of the original.
Probate Judge Office. Abbeville, S. C. Dated 15 May 1775. I William
Burgess Senr. of 96 Dist. being in perfect memory and sense etc. I
will all my just debts and funeral expenses be met and paid. I
appoint my loved wife Olive and my friend John Evans executor. I
leave my wife the plantation whereon I now live, with all stock, tools,
household furniture during her life. And after her death the 100
acres with another 100 acres joining on the East, purchased of Clark,
I give and bequeath to my sons John, James, Jacob Burgess to be
equally divided between them. The moveable property, belonging to my
wife at her death to be divided between my younger chn. Delilah,
John, Elizabeth, James, Jacob, Jemima and Sarah Burgess. Except my
home which I bequeath to my son Jacob Burgess. I bequeath to my son
Joseph one shilling. I bequeath to my son William Junr. and my dtr.
Roda Williams one shilling. Fifty acres of land to be sold to pay
debts after my wife death, the remainder to be divided between Delilah,
John, Elizabeth, James, Jacob, Jemima and Sarah Burgess. Wit: John
Evans, William Evans, Sarah Evans. Signed: William Burgess. Proved
on oath of Sarah Evans before William Moore, J.P. on the 1 July 1783.
On 25 June 1783 William Rucks applied for a letter of admr. before John
Thomas, Ord. of 96 Dist.

BURKE, JOHN BREWSTER (Loose papers in basement). Clerk of Court
Office. Anderson, S.C. In the May term of General Court of Pendleton
Dist. That John Brewster Burke was born in Nottinghamshire in the
Kingdom of Great Britian, that he is twenty six years old and was born
under the allegiance of the King of Great Britian that he emigrated
to the United States, arrived in New York City on the 18Oct. 1820.
By profession and calling a school master and he intends to make his
residence in Pendleton Dist.. Dated 29 March 1825.

BURNETT, HEZEKIAH Box 2 Pack 56. Probate Judge Office. Edge-
field, S. C. Will dated 1 Feb. 1825. Wit: Isaac Herring, Edw.
Osborn, Felic Rogers. Exrs. Pleasant Burnett, and my son John Burnett.
Wife Elizabeth Burnett. Prov. 28 Mar. 1825. Paid 19 July 1834 Daniel
Butler dist. $7.56 1/4. Paid Willis Burnett $8.00. Paid 28 Jan. 1835
Martin Carter $43.00. Sold to Sarah Burnett three head of cattle on
25 Dec. 1832 for $24.00. Paid 29 Jan. 1824 John Burnett note and
interest $36.55 1/2.

BURNETT, ELIZABETH Box 2 Pack 61. Probate Judge Office. Edgefield, S. C. Will dated 31 Jan. 1820. Proved 8 Aug. 1820. Wit:
Wiley Berry, Hezekiah Burnett, Solomon Nobles. My executor to pay all
my just debts from the money that remains in Captain Lark Abney's hands.
Dtr. Ceilia Frances, dtr. Martha Pennington. 3 youngest children.
Martin Burnett, Marium Burnett and Elizabeth Lark Burnett. Executors
brother Martin Cook, James Harrison, Edmund Belcher.

BURNS, ALLEN Pack 603 #108. Land Warrant. Clerk of Court Office.
Pickens, S. C. To any lawful surveyor you are authorized to lay out
unto Allen Burns a tract of land not exceeding ten thousand acres.
Dated 6 Feb. 1854, executed 15 Feb. 1854. Certified 21 Feb. 1854.
Signed: W. L. Keith, Clerk P.D.

BURNS, REVD. LAIRD Apt. 1 File 67. Probate Judge Office.
Greenville, S. C. I, Laird Burns of Greenville Dist. being in a low
state of health but of sound mind and judgment. First all my lawful
debts be paid, and all the rest of my estate both real and personal
to remain in the hand of my wife Nancy Burns during her natural life or
widowhood. At her death or intermarriage the est. to be given to my
executors for use of my chn. All my younger children to have schooling
near to equal to the elder ones. If any of my negroes get ungovern-
able I empower my executors to sell them. If my executors think best
to sell and move, I empower them to do so. I wish all my chn. to
share alike. I appoint my wife Nancy executrix, and my two sons John
Burns, Philip Burns, Daniel Ford and Elhanon W. Dumas Executor. Dated
13 Nov. 1820. Wit: James Hiett, Wade Staton, Hudson Berry. Signed:
Laird Burns. Proved on oath of James Hiett and Hudson Berry before
Spartan Goodlett, O.G.D. Dated 1 Jan. 1821.

BURNETT, WILEY Pack 335. Clerk of Court Office. Abbeville,
S. C. In Equity, to the Honr. the Chancellors: Your oratrix Jane
Burnett the wife of Wiley Burnett, by Isaac Kennedy her father and
next friend. Your oratrix in the month of November 1851 in the Dist.
of Abbeville intermarried with the said Wiley Burnett who was a resident of Edgefield Dist. at the time, she was a widow with three chn.
She was the owner of a small tract of land given her by her father.
Her husband was at the time of marriage without property so far as she
knows. Within the first year of their marriage she interceding for a
negro whom he was punishing ceased whipping the negro and whipped your
oratrix. He has whipped her several times with a hickory, leaving
marks on her body. He has charged her with infidelity to her marriage
obligation, and accused her of stealing his money. He had avowed his
intention to leave her deserted and penniless, take her property with
him. He has sold some personalty with a view of removing, has taken
a part away, to wit. three negroes. At the time of marriage she had
seven slaves all belonging to your oratrix, the others are the increase,
viz. Junia about 18 yrs, Jim about 16 yrs., Bill about 13 yrs.,
Martin about 11 yrs., Orange about 9 yrs., Mary about 6 yrs., and an
infant Henry about 3 yrs. The above property worth about $5,500.00.
Filed 15 Dec. 1858.

BURROW, HENRY Box 1 #30. Probate Judge Office. Anderson, S. C.
I, Henry Burrow of Anderson Dist. being well in health and of sound
and disposing mind and memory, etc. First I desire my executors to
pay all my just debts and funeral expenses. I give to my beloved wife
Amy the following property, three negroes namely Isaac, Lila, and
Wilson, four head of horses, two mules, one waggon, and riding chair,
all my ready money, notes, and book accounts, household and kitchen
furniture, live stock, set of black smith tools, one rifle gun, two
shot guns, one brass pistol. I give to Nancy Langston, one negro
named Steven, one sorrel mule, all other property I have already given
her, and $100 in ready money. I give to my dtr. Rebecca Holliday one
negro girl named Chainy, and $100 in ready money, with all other
property I have given her. I give to my dtr. Amy Gray one negro named
Dolley, one waggon, one still, and $100 in ready money, with all other
property I have already given her. I give to my son Henry Burrow one
negro girl named Mary, $100 in ready money, with all other property
I have already given him. I give to my son Lewis Burrow, three
negroes namely Sam, Jefferson, and Clary, $100 in ready money with all
other property I have already given him. I give to my son Thomas
Burrow, four negroes namely Levi, Jack, Roda, Toney and 250 acres of
land where I now live at his mother death, and $100 in ready money, and
a young colt. I give to my dtr. Tabitha Burrow five negroes namely,
Jinny, Darky, Emely, Atrer and Anthony with $100 in ready money. I
give to my son William Burrow, two dollars in ready money, with all
other property I have already given him. I give to my son Green
Burrow $2.00 in ready money, with all other property I have already
given him. I give to my dtr. Susanna Gibson $2.00 in ready money with
all other property I have already given her. I give to my dtr. Mary
Harris $2.00 in ready money, with all other property I have already
given her. I give to my son Joel Burrow $2.00 in ready money, with
all other property I have already given him. It is my desire that my
negro man named Isaac that I will to my wife be free at the death of
my wife. I appoint Wm. Burrow my executrix. Dated 12 Oct. 1829. Wit:
Lewis Sherrill, Joseph Mahon, I. C. Anderson. Signed: Henry Burrow.
Proved on oath of I. C. Anderson before John Harris, O.A.D. on the 21
Dec. 1829.

BURROWS, GEORGE Deed Book A Page 1. Probate Judge Office.
Williamsburg, S. C. We Arthur Burrow and Henry Capell minor of
Sumpter Dist. in consideration of $1100 to us paid by George Burrows
of Williamsburg have granted, sold, bargained and release all that
parcel consisting of two tracts lying on Turkey Creek in Williamsburg
County, one tract granted to Alexander Swinton and contains 300 acres,
the other tract granted to John and Joseph McGrea contained in the
original grant 900 acres. The one half of this tract being 450 acres,
making the whole 750 acres, said tracts joins each other. Adj. land
of Alex. Nesbit, Stewart Dickey Esq. William Burrows, and John and

Burrows, George - Continued. Deed Book A, Page 1. Probate Judge
Office. Williamsburg, S. C. We Arthur Burrow and Henry Capell minor
of Sumpter Dist. in consideration of $1100 to us paid by George
Burrows of Williamsburg have granted, sold, bargained and released all
that parcel consisting of two tracts lying on Turkey Creek in Williamsburg County, one tract granted to Alexander Swinton and contains 300
acres, the other tract granted to John and Joseph McGrea contained in
the original grant 900 acres. The one half of this tract being 450
acres, making the whole 750 acres, said tracts joins each other. Adj.
land of Alex. Nesbit, Stewart Dickey Esq., William Burrows, and John
and Joseph McGrea. Dated 1 Jan. 1806. Wit: James McKnight, Tared
Nelson, William Scott. Signed: Arthur Burrows and Henry Capell.
Mary Burrows wife of Arthur Burrows did renounce and relinquish all
right of dower to the above land before John Perry J.Q. on the 11 Feb.
1806.

BURT, FRANCIS ESQ. Pack 69. Clerk of Court Office. Pickens,
S. C. I Francis Burt of Pickens Dist. in consideration of $1,000 in
hand paid me by Joseph Grisham of Falls in the same Dist. have granted,
sold, bargained, released all that plantation whereon I now live,
joining land laid off in lots in the town of Pickens. Adj. land I sold
to John Burdine Colhouns, Andrew Kellys land, being the land I bought
from James Robertson. Also the land I sold to bury the criminals.
This tract contain about 120 acres. Dated 27 Sept. 1836. Wit:
Pleasant Alexander, Robert Knox, Miles M. Norton. Signed: Francis
Burt. On 27 Sept. 1836 George Ann Burt relinquished her dower
on the land. Before Miles M. Norton, N.P. Recorded 2 Dec. 1836.

BURTON, JOSIAH Pack 6 Clerk of Court Office. Anderson, S. C.
We Josiah Burton and Marry Burton of Abbeville Dist. to Charles Duncan
of Pendleton Dist. Dated 27 Feb. 1800. In consideration of $120.00
paid by said Charles Duncan have granted, sold, bargained and released
a tract of land containing 200 acres in 96 Dist. on waters of Chagess
Creek, and Tooglow River. Adj. land of the Indian Boundary Line, others
sides vacant. Wit: Samuel Henson, Archabald Shaw. Signed: Josiah
Burton and Marry X Burton. Proved the 21 Feb. 1800 by Samuel X
Henson before Ebenezer Miller, J.P. Recorded Book E, Page 240 the 10
April 1800.

BURTON, THOMAS Deed Book C. Elbert Co., Ga. Elberton, Ga.
This indenture made 23 April 1795, between Thomas Burton, Jr. and Ann
his wife and Henry Burton both of Elbert Co., Ga. In consideration of
50 pds. sterling to him in hand paid. Thomas Burton, Jr. and wife Ann
hath granted, sold, bargained and released in fee simple all that tract
of land in Elbert Co., lying North East of Coleman land, and South by
James Easters land, on all other sides by Thomas Burton, Jr. land,
whereon Henry Burton now lives. Containing 200 acres. Wit: W.
Hatcher, Evan Ragland, J.P. Signed: Thomas Burton, Jr. and Ann
Burton. Reg. 28 July 1795.

BUSH, ISAAC Box 2 Pack 58. Probate Judge Office. Edgefield,
S. C. Will dated 18 Mar. 1836. Exr. Thomas Deloach. Wit: Harwood
Burt, John Gormillion, Harmon Gallman. Proved 23 May 1836. Wife Sally
Bush. Owned 5 slaves. Dtr. Sarah Deloach, Dtr. Pherbe Ward, dtr.
Susan Watson, dtr. Elizabeth Whitlock. Gr. Chn. Issac Slaten and Sarah
Slaten. 2 Jan. 1847 paid Elizabeth Whitlock in part of her share
$125.00. Paid 5 Jan. 1846 H. and Susan Winn in full of their share
of the est. $677.52. Paid 24 Jan. 1846 Mary Swearing in full of her
share $677.52. Paid 30 Jan. R. Ward trustee of Issac Slaten in full
of his share $169.38. Paid 2 Feb. 1836 John Swearing in full his
share $169.38. Inv. made 28 May 1836 by Marshall Lott, Robert Kinney,
J. Cogburn. Left five legatees each share is $1,899.92. Richard Ward
share is $1,899.92. Paid 7 Jan. 1837 R. Ward in full of his share
$1,852.44. Susan Watson in full of her share $1,852.44. Paid 10 Jan.
1837 John Whitlock in full of his share $926.22. Paid Isaac and
Sarah Staton in full for their share $926.22.

BUSH, WILLIAM Box 2 Pack 59. Probate Judge Office. Edgefield,
S. C. Will dated 18 July 1837. Proven 25 Sept. 1837. Exr. Elizabeth

Bush, William - Continued. Bush. Wit: John Gormillion, Harmon Gallman, Jesse Gormillion. Son Wm. Burgess Bush. Dtr. Lucretin Williams, dtr. Lucinda Randall, dtr. Harriet Bush, dtr. Syntha Bush, dtr. Sarah Bush, dtr. Talitha Bush, dtr. Mary Bush, dtr. Addeline Bush, son Wm. Burgess Bush. Owned eight slaves. Paid 8 Oct. 1838 Henry Howard, Harriet Howard the amt. left in said will $40.00. Paid 6 Jan. 1838 John Autrey in full for his wife Tillithia Atrey $40.00. Paid 9 Feb. 1854 John Randall $49.45. Paid 24 July Arthur Lott $49.45. Paid 24 July T. H. Williams $49.45. Paid 25 March Addeline Bush $49.45. Paid 25 March W. B. Bush $49.45. Paid 25 March Henry Howard $49.45. Paid 3 Feb. B. Bledsoe $49.45. Paid 5 Jan. 1842 Arthur and Sarah Lott his wife amt. left them $40.00. Paid 10 Feb. 1824 Frank Butler $1,734.00.

BUSBY, HENRY Box 2 #48. Probate Judge Office. Anderson, S. C. Est. admr. the 3 Oct. 1836 by Rebecca Busby, James Gilmer who are bound unto John Harris, Ord. in the sum of $300. Signed: Rebecca X Busby and James Gilmer. Cit. was pub. at Roberts, S.C. 2 Oct. 1836 by Benjamin D. DePre. Recd. 20 Jan. 1841 of Mrs. Rebecca Busby the admr. of the est. of Henry Busby decd. in cash for our part of the est. of sd. Henry Busby. Signed: David Y. Griffin and Martha X Griffin. Wit: William Richardson.

BUTLER, GEORGE Box 2 Pack 60. Probate Judge Office. Edgefield, S. C. Est. admr. 19 Nov. 1821 by William Butler, Frank Butler, Allen B. Addison who are bound unto the Ordinary in the sum of $25,000.00.

BUTLER, JAMIMAH Apt. 1 File 40. Probate Judge Office. Greenville, S. C. On 14 Sept. 1837 Col. Thomas P. Brockman applied for a letter of admr. on the estate of Jamimah Butler decd. of Greenville Dist. Cit. was mailed to T. P. Brockman at Soneville P.O., Greenville, S. C.

CAIN, JAMES Box 21 Pack 486. Probate Judge Office. Abbeville, S. C. I, James Cain Senr. of Granville County being weak and very sick, but of perfect mind and memory thanks be to God. First I will and desire that my just and lawful debts be paid being lawfully proven. I give to my wife Frances Cain during her natural life or widowhood my maner house, one feather bed and furniture, four milk cows and kitchen furniture. I give to my son William Cain one shilling sterling. I give to my son James Cain one shilling sterling. I give to my dtr. Frances Norrell one shilling sterling. I give to my dtr. Hannah Caudle one shilling sterling. I give to my dtr. Peggy Cain one shilling sterling. I give to my son Randel Cain my Maner house and plantation containing 100 acres and two feather beds and furniture, two iron potts and hooks, one large and others small four head horses, my sorrel riding horse, five head of cows. If my son Randel die before he come the age of twenty one, the land to be equally divided between my sons William and James Cain. I appoint John Cowen and George Walton my executors. Dated 21 Aug. 1777. Wit: Jno. Cowan, George Walton. Signed: James FC Cain. 96 Dist. a Dedimus to me directed by John Thomas Esq. Will proven on oath of Jno. Cowan on the 27 Oct. 1783 before Robert Anderson, J.P. By John Thomas Jr., Esq. to Robert Patterson, Daniel Walker, Rivers Banks, John Travis. All or any three of you are authorized and impowered to view and appraise the goods and chattels of James Cain decd. Dated 12 Nov. 1783.

CALANAHAN, EDWARD Book 1 Page 162. Clerk of Court Office. Pickens, S. C. On 15 Dec. 1855 he owned 210 acres on Crooked Creek waters of Little River adj. land of Thomas Dodd est. William Steele and others. Heirs Sarah L. Calanahan, Willie Carver and wife Harriet.

CALDWELL, ___ Pack 3366. Clerk of Court Office. Abbeville, S. C. Abbeville Dist. To the Honr. Henry W. Desaussure, Theodore Gaillard, Thomas Waters, Waddy Thompson, W. D. James judges of the Court of Equity. Your orator and oratrix Alexander Stewart and Peggy his wife sheweth that ___ Caldwell departed this life intestate

Caldwell, ____ - Continued. possessed with considerable real estate, consisting of a tract of 330 acres bounded by land of Samuel Young, Joel Lipscomb on Quarter Creek, waters of Saluda River. Your oratrix Peggy his widow has now intermarried with your orator Alexander Stewart, and the following chn. William Caldwell, Alexander Caldwell, Sibby Wilson the wife of Drury Wilson, Elizabeth Caldwell, Margaret Caldwell, Edmond Caldwell, James Caldwell, John Caldwell, Jesse Caldwell, Belinda Caldwell, Sarah Caldwell. Your Oratrix prays for a partition of the real estate. Filed 14 Feb. 1820.

CALDWELL, BELINDA Pack 3350. Clerk of Court Office. Abbeville, S. C. Abbeville Dist. To the Honr. the Chancellors: Your oratrix Belinda Caldwell sheweth that on the day in June 1826 Hugh Porter was appointed by this Court guardian of the person and property of your Oratrix. That as your oratrix is informed and verily believes that Hugh Porter received from the estate of her decd. father John Caldwell several large sums of money, which with the interest is in his hands, that the expenditures has been very small. That the said Hugh Porter has refuses to account with your oratrix, etc. May it please your Honors to grant unto your oratrix the writ of subpona to be directed to said Porter requiring him to answer this bill agreeable to law. Filed 4 April 1839. On 11 May 1845 Belinda Caldwell wrote her attorney to stop the suit against Hugh Porter her gdn. as she was living with him at this time. And to leave the money with him. On the 1 April 1844 William Caldwell wrote Belenda Caldwell attorney that the case was settled, and he was agreeable with him for her to remain in his hands.

CALHOUN, JOHN Box 21 Pack 466. Probate Judge Office. Abbeville, S. C. Inventory made 24 Feb. 1826 by James Calhoun, Richard H. Lester, and Christopher Conner. Sale made 7 March 1826. Named John Reid and John L. Calhoun was the admrs.

CALHOUN, WILLIAM H. Pack 501. Clerk of Court Office. Abbeville, S. C. I William Calhoun of the County of Pontotoc in the State of Mississippi, have appointed Jno. H. Willson of Abbeville Dist. in the State of S. C. my true and lawfully attorney to use my name, to ask, sue demand receive and receipt, especially of selling a certain tract of land known as the Cabbin lands. Dated the 20 Jan. 1858. Wit: F. Richman, Samuel C. Gill. Signed: W. Henry Calhoun.

CAMP, OLIVER G. Apt. 2 File 93. Probate Judge Office. Greenville, S. C. I, Oliver G. Camp of Greenville Dist. being low and weak in health, but of a sound disposing mind. First I will that my executors to pay all my debts and funeral charges from the whole of my estate if need be, the blanace to my wife Narissa Camp during her life for the support and education of my chn. and after her death or marriage to be equally divided between my chn. viz. Leonidas M. Camp, Sary Ann Camp, Thomas Lorans Camp, Aaron Chisterfield Camp, or such as may be living. I appoint my wife Narcissa Camp and David Hamrick executrix and executor. Dated 10 June 1840. Wit: James Mays, Henry L. Cross, S. Goodlett. Signed: O. G. Camp. Proven 27 July 1840.

CAMPBELL, WILLIAM Box 14 #602. Probate Judge Office. York, S. C. Est. admr. 15 Aug. 1836 by Elizabeth Campbell, Wiley Reeves, Wm. T. Hart who are bound unto the Ordinary in the sum of $25,000.00. Cit. pub. at the Cross Road congregation mention that Wm. Campbell was of the Indian Land. Heirs Thomas Campbell, Rosanna Brown, John Campbell, Alexander Campbell, Mary Sillerman, the heirs of Betsy Buchanan, the heirs of Samuel Campbell and Jane Black say 8 in all. On 25 Feb. 1842 Revd. Archibald Whyte in right of his wife Elizabeth (alias) Campbell admr. of Wm. Campbell. John Sillerman married Mary. Rosannah married Wm. Brown, A. T. Black married Jane.

CAMPBELL, SAMUEL Case 14 #599. Probate Judge Office. York, S. C. Est. admr. 3 May 1830 by William Campbell, John Silleman and Thomas Campbell who are bound unto Benjamin Chambers Ord. in the sum of $12,000.00. Paid Elizabeth J. Campbell $53.06. Paid Mary L. Campbell $48.54. Paid the widow E. R. Campbell $1204.17. Paid Hugh W. Campbell $53.06.

40

CAMPBELL, ELIZABETH Box 14 #601. Probate Judge Office. York,
S. C. Est. admr. 13 Feb. 1837 by John Campbell, Isaac McFaddin, Esq.
James Dunlap who are bound unto Benjamin Chambers, Ord. in the sum of
$25,000.00. On 7 Feb. 1837 Joseph White applied for letter of admr.
Left three chn. John Campbell gdn. of Hugh W., E. J., and M. S.
Campbell. Cit. Pub. at Unity Church.

CAMPBELL, JAMES Will Book 3 Page 139. Probate Judge Office.
York, S. C. I James Campbell of York Dist. being of feeable health
but of sound mind and memory. I will to my son Thomas Campbell the
plantation whereon he now live. I will to my son Robert the plantation
whereon I now live, also my negro by Aaron, my wagon and sorrel horse,
black smith tools and farming tools. I will to my sons Elias and James
and to my dtr. Mary Sutton each twenty dollars and to my granddaughter
Elizabeth Campbell fifty dollars. I will to my dtr.Jane my negro boy
Stephen and that she have her maintenance from the plantation willed to
son Robert. The remainder of my property to be equally divided between
my son Robert and dtr. Jane. I appoint my sons Thomas and Robert
executors. Dated 20 May 1841. Wit: John S. Moore, H. F. Adickes,
S. R. Moore. Signed: James Campbell. Recorded in the year A.D. 1841.

CANNON, HENRY Pension No. S. 8187. Served in Virginia. Spartan-
burg Dist., S. C. He was born 11 April 1752 in Stafford County,
Virginia. Served under Capt. McClanahan lived in Culpepper Co. when
he volunteered. Served at Norfolk, discharged 1776 at Old Jamestown,
Va. served 13 mo. Mentioned Ellis Cannon, a clergyman. Lived in
Greenville Dist. for 22 yrs. moving there in 1781 or 1784.

CANTRELL, MICAJAH Pack 297 #3. Clerk of Court Office. Pickens,
S. C. A letter from Nancy Cantrell to her husband Micagger Cantrell
who is in prison for mistreating his family, she said, that she would
take him back if treat her and the children as he aught [sic] "and
promis not to beat me and my dear children again and more than all
that you must promis to forsake your way of doing and leave off keeping
company with this vile set that has brought you and me to what we are."
Dated 2 March 1854. Signed: Nancy Catherine Cantrell. To W. L.
Keith, "If you are willing and satisfied for me to be released agreeable to my wife request, I will take her home and treat her and her
children well and live with them in peace from this time and quit all
bad company." Dated 2 March 1854. Wit: A. B. Grant. Signed:
Micagger Cantrell.

CARLILE, JAMES #222. Clerk of Court Office. Abbeville, S. C.
I James Carlile of Abbeville Dist. In consideration of $100 paid me
by Isaac Carlile of same Dist. have granted, sold, bargained and
released all that tract of land containing 75 acres in said Dist. adj.
land of Mordecai Shackelford on the South and John Carlile on the North.
Dated 5 Sept. 1838. Wit: R. E. Carlile, T. W. Boles. Signed: James
Carlile senr. Proved on oath of Robert E. Carlile before Wm. C.
Cozby, J.P. on the 6 Sept. 1838. Recorded 6 June 1842.

CARLILE, JAMES #222. Clerk of Court Office. Abbeville, S. C.
I James Carlile of Abbeville Dist. do hereby give and grant unto the
widow and orphans of Robert Carlile decd. 100 acres, lying on the upper
end of my plantation adj. land of George Patterson and Hugh Maxwell.
Dated 6 July 1840. Wit: John Carlile, Ethel T. Carlile. Signed:
James Carlile. Proved on oath of Ethel Carlile, before Wm. C.
Cozby, Magr. on the 3 June 1842. Recorded on the 6 June 1842 in Book
16 Page 189. (This must be one of the Deed books that was burned in
the fire, P.Y.)

CARNE, THOMAS WM. Box 8 #100. Probate Judge Office. Pickens,
S. C. I Thomas William Carne, being of sound and disposing mind and
memory, but weak in body, etc. I give to my wife Elizabeth Carne my
plantation on which I live on the waters of Cane Creek my three negroes
named: Jack, Betty and boy William. Also my stock, cattle, hogs, and
household furniture, and all notes and interest that I hold, One on
Benjamin David DePre for $550 and one on Benson and Sloan of $100, for
her comfort and support during her lifetime, after her death to be

Carne, Thomas Wm. - Continued. divided between my children equally (no named). I appoint my wife Elizabeth Carne executrix. Dated 8 Sept. 1838. Wit: Frances Jenkins, Anderson Jenkins and Cornelius P. DuPre. Signed: Thomas Wm. Carne. Proven 8 Oct. 1838.

CARRILL, ELIZABETH Pack 287 $22. Clerk of Court Office. Pickens, S. C. In 1857 Elizabeth Carrill was mentioned as being the wife of Benjamin Carrill of Pickens Dist.

CARROLL, LUCINDA Pack 289 #41. Clerk of Court Office. Pickens, S. C. Lucinda Carroll mentioned as the wife of John Carroll in 1860.

CARROLL, LEWIS Pack 382 #21. Clerk of Court Office. Pickens, S. C. On the examination of Ellen Marshal a single woman before me J. W. Singleton one of the Magistrates on this 4 Sept. 1860. Saith that on the 6 Nov. 1854 Ellen Marshal was delivered of a girl child with blue eyes and yellow hair and that Lewis Carroll did get her with child, and that she has no other bastard child. Signed: Elen X Marshal.

CARTER, WILLIAM Vol 22 Pack 156. Probate Judge Office. Charleston, S. C. I William Carter of the province of South Carolina, do make this my last will etc. My mind and will is that my estate be kept together until my sister arrives to the age of eighteen excepting on girl named Celia which I give her immediately after my dec. To my beloved sister Elizabeth I give at the age of twenty one or marriage, provided she marries to the approbation of my executors, the free use and enjoyment of the profits arising from my slaves for and during her life, and at her demise I give my said slaves to such issue as she may leave at time of her death. In case of no heirs, I give my said slaves to my relation Hepworth and James Carter of Georgia. Except 1000 L currant to be paid into the hand of my friend Wm. Skirving, Esq. to be placed on interest for his son William Skirving, to be paid him with the interest at the age of twenty one. My will that after the demise of my sister and such issue as she may leave, that 500 L be laid by and devoted by executors to the education of Charles Chamberlain a minor son of Hubbard Chamberlain. I appoint my friends Wm. Skirving, Esq., Thos. Hutchinson, Philip Smith and Peter Leger, Esq. executors. Dated 19 June 1776. Signed: William Carter. Wit: Benjamin Perriman, William Bowler. Proved before Charles Lining Esq. O.C.T.D. 5 July 1787.

CENTER, NATHAN Apt. 14 Pack 471. Probate Judge Office. Camden, S. C. I Nathan Center, being weak and low in health but of a perfect mind thanks be to God, etc. I give to my beloved wife Martha Center on negro girl named Tantzey and her increase for ever. I give to my dtr. Elizabeth Center one negro girl named Rouk and her increase for ever. Also I will that my dtr. Elizabeth Center should have three young negro wenches bought from the first money raised after my debts are paid, with their increase for ever. I give to my son Nathan Center one negro boy named Dick to him for ever. I give to my son John Center one negro boy named Sam son of Sarah, to him forever. I give to my son William Center one negro boy named Ephrim to him forever. I will to my beloved wife during her natural life, the house and plantation with one fifth part of the remainder of my est. The other four fifth to be divided between them. I give all my land to be divided among them as they come of age equally by my executors. I appoint Thomas Taylor, James Taylor and William Howell, Senr., my executors. Dated 21 Dec. 1782. Wit: Solomon Peters, Elizabeth Jackson, Lucy Howell. Signed: N. Center. Proved 26 Jan. 1783.

CHAMBERLAIN, ROBERT Box 24 Pack 558. Probate Judge Office. Abbeville, S. C. Inventory made 17 May 1845 by Obadiah Campbell, Alexander Oliver, Michael Kennedy, Alex. McAlister. Margaret Chamberlain was the widow. Amount paid to the following children. Wm. Chamberlain one horse $50.00. Alexander Chamberlain one horse $25.00. James Chamberlain one horse $25.00. To dtr. Caroline Bowen bed and furniture $8.00.

CHALMERS, MARTHA   Box 24 Pack 556.   Probate Judge Office.   Abbeville, S. C.   I Martha Chalmers now of Abbeville Dist. do make this
my last and testament.   First I direct my just debts be paid.   I give,
devise and bequeath my whole estate both real and personal unto Thomas
Parker now of this Dist. to his heirs, executors, admr. and assigns
in trust to and for the following uses and purposes, that is to say,
in trust during the life time of my sister Sarah Wilson widow.   She is
to possess, have the profits, receive the dividends or interest of any
stock or notes, etc.   At her death her two chn. are to have the same
possession, they are nieces Martha Wilson and Anna Maria Wilson.
Dated 21 April 1824.   Wit: Richard B. Carter, Stephen Lee, Washington
Langford.   Signed: Martha Chalmers.   Inventory made 30 Aug. 1832 by
Wm. A. Bull, Nathl. Harris, W. P. Noble.

CHAMBERS, STEPHEN   Box 21 Pack 465.   Probate Judge Office.   Abbeville, S. C.   Admr. bond Abbeville Dist.   We John Sanders, John
Brannon and Joseph Sanders are bound unto A. Hamilton Ord. in the sum
of $5,000.   Dated 15 April 1809.   Estate appraised 4 May 1809 by Joseph
Sanders, John Brannon, Robert Henderson.

CHANDLER, HENRY F.   Pack 5 (Basement)   Clerk of Court Office.
Pickens, S. C.   Henry F. Chandler married Frances Harbin a dtr. of
Thomas W. Harbin decd.   When the equity records of T. W. Harbin was
filed 24 March 1855 mention that the Chandlers as living in Georgia.

CHANDLER, MATTHEW & MARY   Pack 4-A.   Clerk of Court Office.
Pickens, S.C.   We Matthew Chandler and Mary his wife of the County of
Granville, State of North Carolina do hereby nominate, constitute and
appoint our trusty son Daniel H. Chandler of the same County and State
our true and lawful agent and attorney for the following prupose.
Whereas Abraham Crenshaw late of Pendleton Dist. the father of Mary
Chandler died about the 8 March 1807.   Leaving a will, he devised a
certain tract of land on which he resided of about 900 acres to be
divided equally between his twelve chn. subject to the lifetime of his
widow Nancy Crenshaw, who was alive when heard from some three or four
years ago.   Now our attorney to ask, demand and take possession of
our portion or interest in case the widow is dead, or sell, dispose
of our part or interest, etc.   Dated 16 Nov. 1835.   Wit: James H.
Strut, Joel Chandler.   Signed: Matthew Chandler and Mary X Chandler.
Person County, N.C. Matthew Chandler and Mary his wife appeared before
me William Norwood, Judge of the Superior Court.   Did privately
examine, and seperately apart from her husband, touching her execution
of the Power of Attorney and saith that she freely and of her own
accord signed same.   Dated 16 Nov. 1835.   On 12 Dec. 1835 received of
Nathan Boon Comm. in Equity for Pickens Dist. in the est. of Abraham
Crenshaw decd. the sum of $26.00 which is the full of Matthew Chandler
and his wife Mary.   Wit: Pleasant Alexander.   Signed: Daniel Chandler.

CHAPMAN, REBECCA   Pack 52 #2.   Clerk of Court Office.   Pickens,
S. C.   I Rebecca Chapman the widow of James Chapman decd. for and in
consideration of $450.00 to me paid by Benjamin Chapman of same Dist.
have sold, bargain, and relinquish all my rights, claim and interest
in and for all the land and tenements of my late husband James Chapman,
decd.   It being and consisting of one third part thereof.   Dated 29
Nov. 1837.   Wit: F. N. Garvin, Daniel J. Chapman.   Signed: Rebecca
X Chapman.   Proved on oath of F. N. Garvin before J. A. Evatt Mag. P.D.
on the 31 Aug. 1841.

CHASTAIN, ABNER   Box 10 #131.   Probate Judge Office.   Pickens,
S. C.   Est. admr. 1 Nov. 1841 by John A. Chastain, James M., William
L., G. W. Keith who are bound unto James H. Dendy, Ord. in the sum of
$1,000.   Cit. Pub. at Bethlehem Church.   John A. is a son, William
received a share, Temperance was the widow, Lucinda, Tilman R., Alford-
more Cleveland, Anson Monroe, Nancy Eviline Chastain minors heirs of
Abner Chastain decd.

CHASTAIN, EDWARD   Box 92 #972.   Probate Judge Office.   I, Edward
Chastain, being of sound mind and memory.   First I desire my just debts
be paid.   I give to my beloved wife Mileyann Chastain all my real and

Chastain, Edward - Continued. personal estate during her natural life and at her death, I desire my son John Chastain and my dtr. Mary Emelissa Chastain have the home plantation. I desire that my dtr. Susan Roper to have the tract of land known as the big bottom or mountain tract. At my wife death if any of my personal estate remain, I desire it to be equally divided between my son John and my dtr. Mary Emelissa Chastain. I appoint my son John Chastain sole executor. dated 10 Aug. 1867. Wit: G. M. Lynch, J. T. Burdine, M. R. Chastain, T. R. Price. Signed: Edward X Chastain. Proven 15 Aug. 1867.

CHASTAIN, JOHN Box 13 #174. Probate Judge Office. Pickens, S.C. On 6 Jan. 1845 letter of admr. was granted to Littleton Akins. Left a widow Jemima Chastain and five chn. On 17 Jan. 1848 paid James and Martha Allen share $32.00. Paid Friendly Chastain and wife share $32.00. Paid William Adams and wife Rebecca share $32.00. (one place James Allen wife name is Elizabeth). Recd. from Edward Chastain on old acct. $3.00. Recd. of Maxwell Chastain on old acct. $19.00. On 30 April 1847 John C., Samuel D., James, Matilda, Nancy Allen, Ervin Simmons of Habersham Co., Ga. appointed Nolen L. Meroney their attorney to receive their part of the est. of John Chastain decd. of Pickens Dist., S. C. Cit. Pub. at Bethlehem Church.

CHASTAIN, JOHN Box 89 #943. Probate Judge Office. Pickens, S.C. Est. admr. 20 Aug. 1883 by Mary M. Chastain, widow, James M. Stewart, William R. Price who are bound unto J. H. Newton, Ord. in the sum of $492.00.

CHASTAIN, MAXWELL Box 91 #966. Probate Judge Office. Pickens, S. C. I Maxwell Chastain being weak in body but of sound mind. I desire my just debts be paid. I give to my chn. as following, unto Little Chastain $100. Unto Peter R. Chastain's heirs $100. Unto John D. Chastain son of John Henry $100. Unto Sarah M. Stewart $200. Unto Mary Looper $200. All the rest of my personal estate I give to my wife Malinda Chastain to have and hold during her natural life, at her death to be equally divided between my son Littleton Chastain, heirs of Peter R. Chastain, heirs of John D. Chastain, John Henry, Mary M. Looper and Sarah M. Stewart. I desire that Abner B. and John J. Chastain to receive nothing of my personal estate as they have all ready receive their share. I appoint Abner B. and John J. Chastain sole executors. Dated 15 Aug. 1883. Wit: G. M. Lynch, John L. Gravley, J. J. Chastain. Signed: M. Chastain. Filed 8 Oct. 1883.

CHASTAIN, MINORS Box 5 #99. Probate Judge Office. Pickens, S. C. On 14 March 1846 W. L. Keith, P. Alexander are bound to Wm. D. Steele, Ord. in the sum of $381.34. W. L. Keith made gdn. of Tilmon R., Lucinda, Alfred M., Anson M., and Nancy E. Chastain minor under 21 yrs. Heirs of Abner Chastain.

CHASTAIN, MINORS Box 149 #10. Probate Judge Office. Pickens, S. C. On 8 May 1874 John A. Chastain, John Masters are bound to J. H. Philpot, Ord. in the sum of $200. John A. Chastain, gdn. for W. P., Susan, Martha L., Abner, Nelson, Roland, John, Joseph, William Chastain minors under 21 yrs. Mary Chastain widow of Wm. Chastain decd. shews that her son Wm. Chastain is a minor. Appointed John Chastain his uncle his gdn. Sarah Chastain, widow of Tilmon Chastain decd. chn. were John L., Joseph T. Chastain. Temperance their grandmother.

CHASTAIN, TEMPERANCE Box 102 #1066. Probate Judge Office. Pickens, S. C. She died 25 March 1871. On 18 April 1871, heirs: Nancy Evaline Burgess, Lucinda, Abner D., John B., Mary M., Martha L., William and Washington Pierce heirs of Tilmon Chastain, decd. Abner, Nelson Rowland, John L., Joseph Tilmon Chastain, the heirs of Cleveland Chastain, decd. also a son of intestate viz; Nancy R. L. J. Chastain, Rachael L. Chastain who resides in Transylvania Co., N.C. Owned 400 acres on Garracks Creek waters of Oolenoy River, adj. land of James M. Keith, Van S. Jones and others.

CHEATHAM, BARTLETT M.   Pack 37 Clerk of Court Office. Abbeville,
S. C. Abbeville Dist. In Equity. To the Honr. the Chancellors:
Your oratrix Sarah E. Cheatham widow and relict of Bartlett Cheatham
decd. planter, departed this life in the 18 Sept. 1859 leaving a paper
purporting to be the last will and testament of which John T.
Cheatham, one of the defendants to this bill, and William Jasper
Cheatham who was killed in 1863 were named executors.   Soon after the
death of Bartlett M. Cheatham, probate in solom form of the said paper
was required of the interested parties, in the course of time caused by
the late war, the incidents of issue (three words not plain) was
joined and tried in the Court of Common pleasat [?] March 1857 and
resulted in that the said paper was not the last will and testament
of Bartlett M. Cheatham.   Whereupon letter of admr. were granted by
the Ord. of Abbeville, Dist. to your oratrix and John L. Cheatham.
The estate of the testator was large in both real and personal. The
real estate was the home place on Calhoun Creek waters of Little River
in a total of 1605 acres, bounded by land of Andrew Gillespie, William
H. Brough, Thomas C. Perrin and others. Bartlett M. Cheatham left
as heirs and distributes viz: Mary M., wife of Dr. James W. Thomas,
Susan Ann wife of John James Gray, Robert Joseph Cheatham, James
Hayne Cheatham, Preston Augustus Cheatham, James Bartlett Seigler,
together with James Hayne and Preston Augustus was at the time of his
death and the three still are minors.   James Bartlett Seigler the first
one a son of Permelia a pre-deceased daughter who had intermarried
with Tandy Seigler. Susan Ann wife of John James Gray departed this
life since the death of her said father to wit. 14 Jan. 1867.
Leaving as heirs and distributees, her husband John James Gray, Sarah
Jane and James Edwin Gray. There is a trust fund held by Bartlett
M. Cheatham decd. for the use of Mrs. Jane Simpson and which the said
John and William Jasper Cheatham were unable to pay on for want of a
fit person to receive and receipt of said debt. Your oratrix will ever
pray. Filed 7 June 1867.

CHEATHAM, PETER Pack 405. Clerk of Court Office. Abbeville,
S. C. Abbeville Dist. In Equity. To the Honr. the Chancellors:
Your orators and oratrixes sheweth that Peter Cheatham departed this
life in the latter part of the year 1840. Leaving a will in full
force, that your orator John R. Cheatham and James Gillam were appointed
executors. The said will was on the 23 Nov. 1840 admitted to probate
in this Dist. and said James Gillam alone qualified as executor thereof, and took upon himself the sole execution of said will, and possessed
himself of the whole estate both real and personal. The testator
at his death owned a large estate consisting of a valuable tract of
land containing about 350 acres, personal est. amounting to about
six or seven thousand dollars, besides notes, accounts and cash on hand.
The testator in his last will devised his whole est. after payment of
his debts, to his wife and children equally divided between them,
charging some chn. with articles of property given to them in his life
time as part of their share. Legatees: Elizabeth Cheatham the widow,
Chn: Lucy Cheatham, James Cheatham, Elizabeth Dodson (widow), Susan
Cheatham, Agnes Cheatham, John R. Cheatham, Sophronia Cheatham who
has since the death of her father married William Wagner, Frances
Henderson the wife of Dayson Henderson, who resides in the State of
Georgia. Jackson Cheatham who died since the death of testator and
left a widow and three chn. viz; Sarah Ann Cheatham the widow, Westley
Cheatham, Nancy Cheatham, Elizabeth Cheatham. Calvin Cheatham the
youngest son of testator and now a minor, resides in Abbeville Dist.
Filed 6 Oct. 1849.

CHEESBOROUGH, JOHN W. Deed Book 1 Page 60. Clerk of Court Office.
Pickens, S. C. We John W. Cheesborough and Cathrine LaBruce, executor
and exectrix of the last will of Joseph P. LaBruce decd. of the city
of Charleston, by William Choice of Greenville, our attorney and John
H. Goodlett and Richard Goodlett both of Greenville Dist. in consideration of the sum of $2500.00 in hand paid by Col. John Easley of Pickens
Dist. Have granted, sold, conveyed and released two tracts of land,
first being on Georges Creek waters of Saluda River, being the same
tract that James O. Lewis conveyed by deed the 25 Sept. 1826 to said
Joseph P. LaBruce in his life time John H. Goodlett and Richard

Cheesborough, John W. - Continued. Goodlett and contains 400 acres. The second tract adj. the first being on Georges Creek, containing 150 acres, being the tract conveyed by Tandy Walker by deed dated 25 Sept. 1826 to said Joseph P. BaBruce[?], John H. Goodlett and Richard Goodlett. Conveyed to them by Jesse P. Lewis. Know as the tract conveyed from Joab Mauldin to Little Berry Roberts for the same land. Dated, 24 Feb. 1831. Wit: Jeremiah Cleveland, John Machen. Signed: John W. Cheesborough Exor., Catharine LaBruce, Extrx. William Choice Atty. John H. Goodlett, Richard Goodlett. Proven on oath of Capt. Jeremiah Cleveland before Jeremiah Cleave the subscribing Justice. This 1 March 1831. I William Choice, J.Q. did this day examine Sarah Catharine Goodlett the wife of John H. Goodlett and Ann Goodlett the wife of Richard Goodlett and they renounce and relinquish all claim of dower to the above land. Dated 1 March 1831. Recorded 22 Aug. 1831.

CHILD, IDA Box 150 #10. Probate Judge Office. Pickens Dist. S. C. On 13 Jan. 1875 Robert R. Child is bound unto J. H. Philpot, Prd. in the sum of $100.00 guardian of Ida Child a minor under 21 yrs. Grand dtr. of Charity Williams. On 6 Jan. 1875 Eliza. Williams, widow of Thomas Williams decd. shews that her chn. W. B., J. F., Earnest C. Williams are minor under 14 yrs. entitled to share from their grand mother est. Charity Williams.

CHILDRESS, JESSE Box 94 #994. Probate Judge Office. Pickens, S. C. Est. admr. 21 Oct. 1884 by Martha Emma Childress, widow T. P. Looper, G. F. Robinson who are bound unto J. H. Newton, Ord. in the sum of $675.00. Died 31 Aug. 1884. Paid 31 Jan. 1885 Charles Childress $8.00. Recd. 20 Nov. 1884 from Marshall Childress $30.45. From R. E. Childress $20.93. M. O. Childress $6.50.

CHILDRESS, JOHN A. Box 38-55, #434-603. Probate Judge Office. Pickens, S. C. On 9 Jan. 1856 W. Berry Childress applied for letter of admr. on the est. of John Childress decd. He owned 150 acres of land on Saluda River and 12 mile Creek. Adj. land of John Findley, Levi Wimpy and others. Heirs: William B. Childress, Sarah Childress, John H. Childress, Abraham O. Childress, Mary M. Childress, Anderson M. Childress, Laurissa J. Childress, Bethany C. Childress, the heirs of Nicey Gantt, who husband was Redin Gantt, Chn. Caroline Gantt, John Gantt, Wm. Gantt, Alexander Gantt. Land was sold on the first Monday in Feb. which was the 6 Feb. 1860 to B. J. Williams. With William Fendley, John W. Singleton as security, in the sum of $910.00. By 1861 F. C. Gantt had married a Kennemore and Laurissa Childress had married Bailey A. Cooper.

CHILDRESS, L. E. Pack 216 #22. Clerk of Court Office. Pickens, S. C. On 20 Oct. 1894 L. E. Childress made oath that he had been arrested for the killing of Will Lathem in Pickens Co., S. C. That H. O. Bowen is a material witness to his defense that said Bowen intends and is going to the State of Texas before the next term of court.

CHILDRESS, OBEDIAH W. Box 90 #950. Probate Judge Office. Pickens, S. C. Est. admr. 12 Nov. 1866 by Reese, W. T. Bowen, John M. Field who are bound unto W. E. Holcombe, Ord. in the sum of $800.00. Heirs: The widow Emily Childress, John T., Lucinda, Nancy, Perry Childress. Paid on 17 April 1868 for caring body to Clear Springs in Greenville Dist. $10.00. Paid 20 Jan. 1874 Nancy E. Baldwin in full $2.95. Paid 15 Dec. 1885 Edward N. Childress share $31.68. Paid 31 May 1870 James Childress $20.00.

CHILDRESS, ROBERT Box 3 #112. Probate Judge Office. Anderson, S. C. Est. admr. 25 June 1799 by Mary Childers, William Bates, Hugh Patrick who are bound unto the Judge of Ord. of Pendleton Dist. in the sum of $1,000.00. On 10 July 1797 Robert Childress gave Jacob Holland a mortgage on 200 acres of land lying below the mouth of Big Beaver Dam, including the mill and plantation for $214.50. The same sum to be paid unto said Jacob Hollon on or before the 25 Dec. 1798, then the bill of sale or deed to be void or to remain in full force. Wit:

Childress, Robert - Continued. Moses Guest, Hugh Patrick.
Signed: Robert Childress. The est. was appraised on 12 Aug. 1799 by
Jacob Holland, William Guest, Aquiller Green.

CHILDRESS, W. B. Box 127 #9. Probate Judge Office. Pickens,
S. C. Est. admr. 20 Aug. 1897 by Charles, J. T. Childress, D. A.
Allgood, Warren Boyd who are bound unto J. B. Newberry, Ord. in the
sum of $300.00. Died 24 July 1897. Heirs: Charles, J. T., B. S.,
J. M., R. S. Childress and the minors of M. O. Childress decd., Elvira
Holcombe, R. J. Jamison, Lucy Henson, Etta Porter, Lola Stephens and
the widow.

CHILES, NIMROD Pack 3359. Clerk of Court Office. Abbeville,
S. C. Abbeville Dist. In Equity. To the Honr. the Chancellors:
Your orator and oratrix John Presley and wife Farr, Reubin Golding and
his wife Susana, William Stewart and his wife Eliza. and that the
youngest child will be fifteen yrs. old next May, she Lucinda has
intermarried with one Lewis Ball. Filed 14 Feb. 1820.

CHILES, NIMROD No. ref. Probate Judge Office. Abbeville, S. C.
I Nimrod Chiles of Abbeville Dist. being of sound mind and memory,
etc. I leave to my present wife Elizabeth Chiles during her natural
life or widowhood, provided she pay all my just debts, bring up, cloth
and educate all my children while under her care. For which I leave
all my property, and no charge to be brought against my chn. when they
receive their portions for clothing or schooling. Should my wife
marry again, I give during her natural life only part of my plantation
or tract whereon I now live. Start at James Maysons decd. line on the
upper side, and run thence up to my spring branch a direct line till
it strikes Walter Chiles land on the South, and one third of my
personal property, and after her death to be equally divided between
all my children. When the youngest child become the age of fiteen
yrs. old a division may be made. Chn: Ferr, Susan (Lurana) Eliza and
Lucinda. I appoint my wife Elizabeth executrix and my friend Walter
Chiles and Archey Mayson executors. Dated 7 May 1805. Proves 10
April 1819. Wit: John Mayson, Robert Cox, John Chiles. Signed:
Nimrod Chiles.

CHILES, REUBEN Box 21 Pack 468. Probate Judge Office. Abbeville, S. C. I Reuben Chiles in a low state of health but perfectly
in my mind and sences. I give to my wife Fanney during her natural
life the plantation whereon I now live including 535 acres, with all
appertenances there unto, and after her death the tract of land I give
to my son Reuben his heirs for ever. I give to my son Thomas the mill
and the adj. land of 648 acres. I give to my dtr. Moriah 390 of land
including Dorrisold field with land adj. I give unto my child that my
wife is pregnant with at this time all the balance of my land bought
from Robert Morrison and others. I give to my wife during her natural
life negroes Fill, Abrilla, Alley and Mary and all the balance of my
negroes to be equally divided amongest my chn. when they marry or
come of age. I give to my wife all stock, cattle, etc. and household
and kitchen furniture, and after her death to be divided between all
my chn. I ordain my wife Fanny and son Thomaa and brother John and
William my executors, Dated 3 March 1808. Wit: Joseph Herst, John
Wallace, John Chiles. Signed: Reuben Chiles. Recorded 2 Sept. 1808.
Inventory made 20 Sept. 1808 by John Pressly, Phillip Stiefle, Saml.
Perrin.

CHILES, WILLIAM Box 20 Pack 429. Probate Judge Office. Abbeville, S. C. I William Chiles of Abbeville Dist. being old and weak
but perfect in mind and memory, etc. First that my burial be left to
the discretion of my chn. and that all my just debts be paid. I do
hereby ratify and confirm all the gifts that I have already given to
my children which is in their possession. I give to my son John part
of a tract of land of 400 acres granted to Patrick Gipson, lines given,
except a small part down by Reubin Chiles Mill Pond. Also to my son
John 70 acres, bounded by Reubin Chiles land formerly held by Wm.
Smith. I give to my son William the plantation or tract whereon I
now live containing several tracts agreeable to a plat by Abner Perrin

Chiles, William - Continued. DS of 355 acres, I also give to my
son William two negroes named Moses and Dafney, also one feather bed
and furniture. The remainder to be equally divided between my children
to wit: Reubin, Thomas, John, William, Elizabeth, Sally, Eunice,
The land I ga-e to son Thomas is not as valuable as the others, there-
for, I direct that he shall be paid 39 ₺ sterling from the estate. I
appoint my four sons Reubin, Thomas, John and William executors.
Dated 4 May 1804. Wit: James Adamson, Robert Jones, John White.
Signed: William Chiles, Senr.

CLANAHAN, ROBERT SENR. Box 3 #21. Probate Judge Office. Pickens,
S. C. Est. admr. 1 Feb. 1830 by Joseph Grisham, Esq. merchant, James
Gains, Wm. Oliver who are bound unto James H. Dendy, Ord. in the sum
of $80.00. To a judgement, principle, interest and cost in a case,
Joseph Grisham vs. Robert, Mary Calanahan in Pendleton Dist. for $60.00.

CLANTON, CHARLES Will Book A, Page 19-20. Probate Judge Office,
Union, S. C. I Charles Clanton, of Union County, Pinckney Dist., S.C.
Being weak in body but of sound memory and judgment. This 15 Nov.
1793. I will and require that all my just debts be paid and bequeath
to my well beloved wife (not named) her maintainance during her natural
life on the plantation which she now lives upon, and one feather bed
with furniture. I will to my two sons Sian Clanton and Stephen Clanton
each one feather bed with furniture. The two sons to divide the
plantation after the death of wife. Land on thicketty Creek. I
appoint my son Sian Clanton and James Petty my executors. Wit:
Absolom Petty, James Thompson, Millington Ledbetter. Signed: Charles
X Clanton.

CLARDY, MARIAH Box 16 #205. Probate Judge Office. Pickens,
S. C. Mariah Clardy was a daughter of Jonabad Gaines of Pickens Dist.

CLARDY, LANGSWORTH Book A. Page 32. Probate Judge Office.
Pickens, S. C. George D. Clardy, applicant, viz: John B. Clardy and
Andrew N. Clardy defendants. For a division or sale of a tract of
436 acres of land former residence of their decd. father Langsworth
Clardy, lying on Buck Creek, waters of Saluda River. George Dilworth
the uncle of these legatees desire a division of the land, and they
have appointed James Latham, Joshua Burtz, John Bowen to divide said
land. Filed 21 Aug. 1837. Signed: George D X Clardy. J. H. Dendy,
Ord. commission the above named men to divide said land. Division made
on the 28 Aug. 1837.

CLARK, JOHN (In same box and pack as above.) Probate Judge
Office. Abbeville, S. C. The est. of John Clark was admr. 8 Nov.
1803 by Sarah Clark, Abraham Hadden, William Beck who are bound unto
Andrew Hamilton, Ord. of Abbeville, Dist. In the sum of $5,000.
Signed: Sarah X Clark, Abraham Haddon, Wm. Beck.

CLARK, JOHN Box 106 Pack 2706. Probate Judge Office. Abbeville,
S. C. I, John Clark, of Abbeville Dist. being of sound and disposing
mind and memory. To John Clark Scott son of William Scott of Abbeville Dist. I give the following negroes and their increase to wit:
Sally, Lucinda, Archey, Alexander, Sarah, Mary, Harriet, Thomas,
Martha, Jane, Eliza and Katharine. Also the tract of land whereon I
now live containing 273 acres, to have and hold said negroes and land
forever. Unless he should die without legal male issue, in that case
I give the negroes and land to his next oldest brother of full blood
that may then be alive or afterwards come into existence. To my worthy
friends Joshua DuBose and Thomas Cunningham, I give in trust my two
old negroes Jesse and Jinny to be taken special care of and supported
as herein after provided. I wish the whole of the above negroes
named and bequeath to John C. Scott be keep together on the same tract
of land by my executors until said John C. Scott arrives at the age of
twenty one or his brother. With the profit from the plantation, with
the cash on hand, notes and accounts to pay my debts and funeral
expenses and support the two said negroes Jesse and Jinny and the
comfort and support of the others negroes named above. I wish a bed
and bedstead and furniture be given to old woman Jinny, and the whole

Clark, John - Continued. of the other furniture give to the other
negroes, except my clock and a sorrel named Florid. To my sister
Nancy Clark, I give her one sorrel mare named Floria and my clock
forever and the sum of $1,000 for and during the term of her natural
life, to be put on interest for her. I give to my sister Hannah
Goodman, I give the like sum during her life time, put on interest
for her. I will that my negroes Jack and his wife and son Washington,
also negro man Andrew, William and Charles be sold on twelve months
credit (those having wives not to be sold from them and also having
regard to good master). The money arising from sale applyied to pay
my two sisters legacies, the balance of the money I give to Celia and
Esther C. Boyd dtr. of John Boyd decd. late of Fairfield Dist. share
and share alike. The unexpended part of the legacies if any of my two
sisters Hannah and Nancy. I give to Katharine Wilson, Joseph Wilson,
Samuel Wilson and James Wilson, sons and dtr. of James Wilson decd.
late of Abbeville Dist. I appoint Joshua DuBose and Thomas Cunningham
executor. Dated __ 1839. Wit: A. Houston, J. L. Bouchillon Senr.,
Robert T. Jennings. Signed: John Clark. In a settlement with the
Wilson heirs on 12 Sept. 1850. Katharine Hanway formerly Katharine
Wilson who died leaving a husband and two children. In the settlement
with Celia D. Boyd who has married George Leitner by the 14 Jan. 1848.
George Leitner of Fairfield Dist. gave a power of attorney to Dr.
Thomas R. Center of Richmond Dist. to collect and receipt for a legacy
to Celia D. Boyd by will of John Clark decd. Dated 10 Jan. 1848.

CLARK, WILLIAM Pack 6 Clerk of Court Office. Anderson, S. C.
I William Clark of Pendleton Dist. for and in consideration of $100.00
to me paid by Samuel Nelson of same place, have granted, sold, bar-
gained and released all that tract of land on the head of Little
Toxaway Creek. Originally granted to my self the 3 March 1806, con-
taining 80 acres. Dated 23 Jan. 1823. Wit: Abel X Honey, Robert
Stribling. Signed: Wm. Clark. Proved on oath of Abel Honey before
John T. Humphreys, J.P. on the 25 Jan. 1823. Recorded 31 March 1823.

CLARKSON, WILLIAM Box 4 #137. Probate Judge Office. Anderson,
S. C. I William Clarkson Junr. of Charleston, S. C. being weak in body
but of sound memory and understanding etc. First in addition to what
my dearly beloved wife Esther Susannah Clarkson will receive by her
right of dower. I give her all my household furniture of every
description whatsoever. The rest and residue of my estate both real
and personal, I give to be equally divided among all my children,
whether already born or hereafter to be born that shall attain the
age of twenty one yrs. if male. If female the said age or date of
marriage. I appoint my friend Lewis Cisles executor and my wife
Esther Susannah Clarkson executrix. Dated 20 March 1815. Wit: Peter
Dubois, Thomas W. Carne, Elizabeth Carne, John D. Carne, Cornelius L.
Dupre, Mary Dupre. Signed: Wm. Clarkson. Codicil. "The household
furniture given and bequeath to my wife in the forgoing will, I give
and bequeath upon her decease, equally to all my then surviving children,
and I nominate, constitute and appoint my dear cousin William Clarkson,
Senr. in addition to the said Esther Susannah, executor of this my
last will and testament.." Dated 16 Dec. 1823. William Clarkson Junr.
executrix paid Elam Sharpe for a coffin in Feb. 1824 $12.00.

CLAY, S. H. Pack 501. Clerk of Court Office. Abbeville, S.C.
State of Florida, County of Sumter. I S. H. Clay do hereby appoint
my mother Elizabeth Clay of Abbeville Dist. S. C. my true and lawful
attorney to ask, sue, demand, receive and receipt the sum of $557.08
being now in possession of W. H. Parker, Commissioner in Equity for
Abbeville Dist. The sum being an inheritance from my fathers est.
Dated 8 Oct. 1860. Wit: W. C. Williams, J. E. Williams. Signed:
S. H. Clay.

CLAY, JOHN Pack 13. Equity Records. Clerk of Court Office.
Abbeville, S. C. John Clay of Abbeville Dist. died in Jan. 1855.
Owned a tract of land called the homestead tract, containing 170 acres
bounded by land of Josiah Wells, and the estate of Samuel S. Baker
and others. The Wilson tract containing 140 acres, bounded by land of
J. W. Jones, Est. of S. S. Baker, Josiah Wells and others. At the time

Clay, John - Continued. of his death he left a widow, Elizabeth
Clay and the following children. viz; Shadrick Clay, James Clay, H.
Washington Clay, Elisha Clay, William A. Clay, Mary Speed the wife of
Samuel D. Speed, Moses S. Clay and grandchildren William Wells,
Lucretia Wells, Martha E. Wells, Catharine Wells, minors under 21
yrs. of age and children of a decd. dtr. Sarah Wells who had married
Josiah Wells and died before her father. The widow prays for a division
of the real estate. James T. Robinson of Willington, Abbeville Dist.
Surveyed the land for the division. Filed in Equity the 25 May 1855.

CLYDE, MINORS Box 2 #30. In Equity. Clerk of Court Office.
Pickens, S. C. On 20 March 1866 Samuel C. Clyde, Bradwell Day, Wm.
A. Lesley are bound unto Robert A. Thompson, Clk. of Equity. in the
sum of $4800.00 S. C. Clyde gdn. for Wm. A. Clyde, Leonard K. Clyde
minors under 21 yrs., S. C. Clyde their brother. Paid 9 April 1868
L. K. Clyde for 1 yr. tuition at Wifford College $72.00 Paid Mrs. A.
Walker for 12 months board $216.00.

CLYDE, THOMAS M. Pack 231 $6. Clerk of Court Office. Pickens,
S. C. On 18 March 1867 Samuel C. Clyde guardian recd $561.52 for the
shares of William A. Clyde and Leonard K. Clyde from the real estate of
Thomas M. and Harriet L. Clyde decd. Samuel C. Clyde recd. $280.76
as his share from said est. W. A. Alexander and Lavinia M. Alexander
recd. their share from the estate $280.76. I Sallie C. Clyde of
Anderson Dist. in consideration of $200.00 to me paid by Joseph B.
Clyde, Edgar W. Clyde, William A. Alexander and Lavinia M., Thomas J.
Clyde, Samuel C. Clyde, William A. Clyde and Leonard K. Clyde (heirs
at law of Harriet Clyde decd.) of said State, except Alexander and wife
of the State of Georgia. Have granted, sold, bargained and set over
to the heirs of Harriet Clyde, decd. all my right, title and interest
in the real estate of Thomas M. Clyde, decd. by reason of my being
heir at law, or distributee of my late husband Charles E. Clyde decd.
Dated 7 March 1866. Wit: J. A. Cobb, W. A. Lesley. Signed: Sallie
C. Clyde. The estate of Thomas M. Clyde was admr. 1 Sept. 1863 by
Thomas J. Clyde, John Burdine, Rucker N. Mauldin and Wm. A. Lesly.

CLECKLY, DAVID F. Pack 14, Equity Records. Clerk of Court
Office. Abbeville, S. C. David F. Cleckly of Abbeville Dist. died
intestate in Aug. 1852. Left a widow Elizabeth A. Cleckly and six
chn. viz: Rufus Cleckly, William J. Cleckly, Alonza Cleckly, Addison
Cleckly, Irvin Cleckly, Johnson Cleckly all of whom except Rufus
are minors. At time of his death he owned a tract of land containing
600 acres on waters of Little River bounded by land of Jonathan
Johnson, Banister Allen, William Smith, Jacob Martin and others. On
13 Nov. 1852 Giden J. Johnson was appointed guardian Rufus Cleckly
age 25, William J. Cleckly age 17, Alonzo Cleckly age 8, Addison Cleckly
age 6, Irvin Cleckly age 4, Johnson Cleckly age 1 1/2.

CLEMENT, REUBEN Book H, Page 193-194. Clerk of Court Office.
Anderson, S. C. This indenture made 6 April 1795. Between Reuben
Clement of Pendleton Dist. and Joel Brazeal of same dist. In consideration of 30 ₺ in hand paid by Joel Breazeal hath bargained, sold,
aocfirmed[?] and released all that tract of land containing 331 acres
in Pendleton Dist. lying on Rockey Creek waters of Rocky River. Being
part of 412 acres granted unto Reuben Clements on the 7 Jan. 1792.
Wit: James Clements, David Collier, William Murphree. Signed:
Reuben Clements. Reuben Clements came before John Willson, J.Q. for
Pendleton Dist. and did acknowledge that he did sign, seal and deliver
the within deed unto Joel Brazeal. That the within subscribing witnesses are all left this country. Dated 12 March 1805. Recorded same date.

CLEVELAND, JOSEPH Apt. 1 File 27. Probate Judge Office. Greenville, S.C. On 24 Feb. 1824 Gen. John Blessingame of Greenville Dist.
advanced property to his following children. Among them was Joseph
Cleveland was mentioned.

CLYDE, CAROLINE J. Book B, Page 44. Probate Judge Office.
Pickens, S. C. On 12 Jan. 1860 Caroline J. Clyde wife of Joseph B.
Clyde was formerly the widow of Bailey A. Barton decd. of Pickens Dist.

CLARDY, JOHN Pack 402 #4. Clerk of Court Office. Pickens,
S. C. Rebecca A. Clardy was the wife of John Clardy, John L. Clardy
was his son. On one occasion Henry Williams had been employed by
them one summer and while there did steal bacon, etc. from the said
John Clardy.

CLAYTON, JOHN (Book not given). Page 113. Probate Judge Office.
Pickens, S. C. In the Court of Ordinary: The petition of Hannah
Clayton, sheweth that John Clayton departed this life leaving tracts of
land undisposed of viz: one town lot in Pickens Village, held jointly
with F. N. Garvin, another tract containing 120 acres on Little River,
corn house creek. Another tract containing 280 known as the Gregory
tract lying on Gregorys Creek. John Clayton decd. left the widow
and seven children: 1. Sarah Ann the wife of Charles Allen. 2. John
Thomas Clayton who resides in Miss. 3. Mary Elizabeth wife of James
Young. 4. Margaret a minor. 5. Jesse Madison a minor. 6. Robert
Carter a minor. 7. Stephen Garrison a minor. Your petitioner prays
that the real estate may be disposed of according to rules of this
Court. Filed 22 May 1849. Signed: Hannah Clayton.

CLINKSCALES, FRANCIS SR. Pack 140. Probate Judge Office.
Anderson, S. C. I Francis Clinkscales Senr. of Anderson Dist. being
of sound and disposing mind and memory, but weak in body, etc. First
I desire that all my real and personal property be sold after my
decease. Out of the money arising there from, all my just debts and
funeral expenses be paid, the sum of money to be divided between my
nine children viz; Whereas I have given to my children in my life
time the sum annexed to their name. To my dtr. Katharine Campbell
decd. $180.00. To my dtr. Priscilla Clement $125.00. To my dtr. Jane
B. Orr $105.00. To my son William F. Clinkscales $268.00. To my son
John Clinkscales $265.00. To my son Levi Clinkscales $265.00. To my
son Francis B. Clinkscales $268.00. To my dtr. Elizabeth Kay $130.00.
To my dtr. Polly Kay decd. $75.00. Each child is to have an equal
amount with my sons William and Francis before the estate is divided.
Then all to share alike, the decd. dtrs. heirs are to get their mother
share. Son William to be guardian of the chn. of Katharine Campbell
chn. Son Francis to be gdn. of Polly Kay chn. I appoint my son William
and Francis Clinkscales as executors. Dated 18 Nov. 1831. Wit: S. D.
Kay, Daniel Mattison, Aaron Davis. Signed: Francis Clinkscales Senr.

CLINKSCALES, FRANCIS B. Pack 308-A. Clerk of Court Office.
Abbeville, S. C. I Frances B. Clinkscales being advanced in life but
of sound and disposing mind and memory, etc. First I will my just
debts and funeral expenses and expenses setting up my estate be paid
by my executors. I give unto my beloved wife Barbary D. Clinkscales
for and during her natural life or widowhood and jointly with my son
William V. Clinkscales all that plantation upon which I now live known
as the home tract together with all that part of of Linton tract,
that is situate eastwardly of a line at the road opposite the gin
house of James Crawford, running along the fence line to the old field
on A. J. Clinkscales and myself. To be occupied jointly by my wife
and son till her death or marriage then, I give to my son in fee
simple the said plantation forever. I give to my wife during her
natural life negroes viz: Frank and his wife Eliza and their two chn.,
at the division of my property negroes May and his wife Curda and their
two chn. to be sold at public outcry, money to be divided equal
between William V. Clinkscales and the other half among my other chn.
and grandchildren. Wife to get her selection of my horses, buggy, a
wagon, one year supply of provision for herself and family, $400 to be
paid her, stock, hogs, sheep, two beds and furniture etc. My negro
Cyrus and his wife Mary, may choose which of my children shall be
their owner. The Power tract of land to be William V. Clinkscales in
fee simple the appraised value if he chooses. Heirs Louisa Jane wife
of L. D. Merriman, George B., Albert J., Mary C. wife of John M.
Hamilton, James W., William V. Clinkscales Sarah decd. wife of John
Cowan. John B. was dead when will was made 1857. I appoint my sons
George B. Clinkscales, James W. Clinkscales executors. Dated 21
Aug. 1857. Wit: J. J. Cunningham, James W. Black, James A. Black.
Signed: F. B. Clinkscales.

CLINKSCALES, DR. FRANCIS   Pack 357.   Clerk of Court Office.
Abbeville, S. C.   Your orator Reuben Clinkscales sheweth that his
brother Dr. Francis Clinkscales departed this life on the 27 June last
on one of the battle fields before Richmond intestate leaving con-
siderable real and personal estate (but neither father or mother wife
or child) which is subject to distribution among his brothers to wit:
John F., William, James, Lewis C., Addison and your orator, his sister
Essie Ellis, wife of Christopher Ellis, the chn. of deceased brother
Abner to wit: John B. Alkanza who has intermarried with A. G. Cook,
Esse who has intermarried with Saml. Wharton, James L., Reuben P.,
Sarah F., Wm. A., Laurence S., and Milton B., and the chn. of his late
sister Mary C. Robinson, who had intermarried with Hugh Robinson to
wit: John A., James, Jasper, Lawrence, Mary Jane and Essie all whom
are minors under the age of 21 yrs.   A letter of admr. have been
granted by Wm. Hill, Ord. on the personal effects to John F. Clinkscales and William Clinkscales.   Which is more than sufficient to pay
all debts.   The real estate lying on Little River and Hodskin Creek
contains 600 acres bounded by land of Joseph F. Burton, Wm. Clinkscales, Addison Clinkscales, Bennett McAdams, Reuben Clinkscales and
James B. McWhorter it being land purchased from the heirs of John
Clinkscales decd. and from Polly Houston and is subject to partition
among the heirs at law.   Filed 20 Aug. 1862.

CLINKSCALES, GEORGE B.   Pack 308-A.   Clerk of Court Office.
Abbeville, S. C.   I George Clinkscales of Abbeville Dist. being sick
in body, but of sound mind and memory, do make this my last will and
testament.   First I will my debts be paid.   I will to my beloved wife
Eliza A. Clinkscales shall remain in possession of all my estate both
real and personal, and raise and educate my children and support my
surviving family.   In case my wife death or marriage all property to
be sold and money arising to be divided between my chn.   As each child
shall attain the age of twenty one he or she shall receive negroes
and other property in proportion to that I have already given to my
dtrs.   Mrs. Martha A. Prince and Mrs. Barbara A. Clement and my dtr.
Sarah J. Clinkscales, to the latter I have given Negroes Phillisand
her three chn. ranging from five to one yrs. and girl Dinah about ten
yrs. old.   I my son Francis William Clinkscales survive the present
war to him the following negroes: Henry, Mack, Haney and Gracy the
dtr. of Rose.   Should he not survive the property to be kept for his
child till he comes of the age of twenty one.   My executrix and
executors shall be guardian of my minor children.   I appoint my wife
executrix and son Frances W. and son in law Washington L. Prince
executors.   Dated 21 May 1864.   Wit: J. J. Cunningham, James W. Black,
J. B. Kay.

CLINKSCALES, JAMES W.   State of Texas County of Fort Bend.   Filed
18 May 1868.   I James Wesley Clinkscales of the State of Texas County
of Fort Bend, being of sound and disposing mind and memory, but weak
in body.   I will that my just debts and funeral expenses be paid.   I
will that all my property both real and personal be sold by my executors here after named, except two negroes viz: Lige a boy about 14
yrs. old and Lucy a girl sixteen yrs. old.   I will to my sister Louisa
Jane Merriman the two negroes, and my executors to retain in his hands
for her use and benefit five thousand dollars.   I will to my niece
Rowena Elizabeth Merriman eight thousand dollars.   I will to my nephew
Frank Clinkscales Merriman eight thousand dollars.   I will to my
niece Eleanor Brownlle Merriman eight thousand dollars.   I hereby
appoint Lewis D. Merriman guardian of the above named children being
the lawful heirs of Lewis D. Merriman and Loisa Jane Merriman.   The
balance of my estate be equally divided between my brothers and sisters
or their lawful representatives viz: The surviving chn. of my sister
Sarah Cowan.   The surviving chn. of my brother Albert J. Clinkscales
and my sister Mary C. Hamilton.   I will to my half brother William V.
Clinkscales my gold watch.   I appoint Lewis D. Merriman my executor.
Dated 15 March 1862.   Wit: J. Adams, J. H. Boozer, D. N. Boozer.
Signed: J. W. Clinkscales.   Proven in open court by Jack Adams on the
27 Dec. 1865.   On the 29 Jan. 1866 came the petition of W. D. Mitchell
stating on or about 9 Dec. 1865 it came to his knowledge that said
descendent left a last will which is on file in this Court.   That one

Clinkscales, James W. - Continued. Lewis D. Merriman is named executor thereof and said executor is a non resident of this State, and prays that the will be probated and that he be permitted to carry on the admr. etc. etc. and that W. D. Mitchell be authorized and directed to carry on said admr. under said order until executor may qualify. Recorded 5 March 1866 W. Andrus, Clk.

COBB, REV. JOHN From a paper in the notes of Miss Youngs. Rev. John Cobb was born in Halifax Co., Va. In 1833 he was 74 years old. died in Pickens Dist. in 1841. Married Frances Smith, 27 Aug. 1786 in Spartanburg Dist., S. C. Children of John and Frances Cobb, Rowland Born 20 May 1796, in Pickens Dist., S. C. Died before 1887 in Ladonia, Fannin County, Texas. Married Mary Ann Morgan, 18 March 1817, Mary Ann born 7 June 1803, died 1887 in Ladonia, Fannin County, Texas. The second child of John married A Whitmire.. #3 Martha married a Coffee. #4 Verlinda married a Norton. A dtr. married a Wallis. #6. John married __.

COBB, RANSOM Apt. 2 File 95. Probate Judge Office. Greenville, S. C. I Ransom Cobb of Greenville Dist. being low and uncertainty of this life but being of sound mind. I desire my executors to collect and pay the debts of my estate and to have full control of the same. I give to my wife Matilda T. Cobb the whole of my estate both real and personal during her natural life time or widowhood. In case she marry she to share equally with my children. I desire that my wife do raise and educate my children viz: Helin Mariah Cobb, William T. Cobb, Frances Emily Cobb, James Humphrey Cobb, Judith Caroline Cobb. And at time of marriage or of full age each to get one negro and other property as my wife thinks proper to spare. I appoint Humphrey Cobb, Josiah F. Cobb and George Seaborn my executors. Dated 28 Oct. 1835. Wit: M. M. Johnson, L. Cobb, M. C. G. Johnson. Signed: Ransom Cobb. Probated 9 Nov. 1835.

COCHRAM, JOHN Apt. 2 File 96. Probate Judge Office. Greenville, S. C. I John Cochram of Greenville Dist. being afflicted by the hand of God, etc. After my just debts are paid. I give unto my loving wife Nancey Cochram one half of the tract of land whereon I now live containing 102 acres, also one bed and furniture, also half of my stock of cattle, hogs, sheep and half of my kitchen furniture and one cupboard during her life or widowhood. I give to my dtr. Lucy Cochram one half of my land whereon I now live, also the other half at my wife death, also one bed and kitchen furniture, half of my stock of cattle, hogs, sheep. I also have one negro named Tom and one mare and colt to be sold and after paying my debts to be equally divided between all my chn. viz: Peggy Cochram, Nancey Waldrop, Matthew Cochram, Bidey Herrel. I appoint George Russell, Milton Ponder, Lemuel C. Page. Signed: John X. Cochram. Probated 12 Oct. 1829.

COFFEE, ELIZABETH Box 11 #138. Probate Judge Office. Pickens, S. C. Elizabeth Coffee wife of Edward Coffee was probably a daughter of James Nevill whose will was proven in 1842. He bequeathed to them a negro girl named Minerva.

COFFEE, JESSE Pack 11. Clerk of Court Office. Anderson, S. C. This indenture made 19 Sept. 1795 between Jesse Coffee of Pendleton Dist. and John Davis of the same Dist. for and in consideration of 30₺ paid by John Davis have granted, sold, bargained and released a tract of land lying on Toogolo River containing 140 acres. The land that Thomas Standage now lives on. Wit: Benj. Cleveland, Wm. Cleveland. Signed: Jessey X Coffee. Proved on oath of Benjamin Cleveland before B. Earle, Clk. on the 30 June 1796.

COLEY, ELIZABETH Book A-1, Page 25. Clerk of Court. Pickens, S. C. Pendleton District, Pickens County. I Elizabeth Coley wife of John Coley decd. for and in consideration of $16.50 in hand paid, I bargain, sell and release unto John Garrett of State and Dist. aforesaid my part or third of a tract or parcel of land containing 200 acres, lying on waters of Crook Creek property of John Coley decd. Dated 15 Nov. 1828. Wit: David Morgan, Morgan Colly. Signed:

Coley, Elizabeth - Continued. Elizabeth X Coley. Proved on oath
of David Morgan before William L. Keith, Co.C the 30 Dec. 1828.

COLHOUN, ALEXANDER Pack 2 (basement) Clerk of Court Office.
Anderson, S. C. The State of South Carolina, Pendleton Dist. To the
Honor. the associate Judge of the said State. The humble petition of
Alexander Colhoun (word) of the county Tyrone in the Kingdom of Ireland
sheweth that your petitioner has been resident in the United States of
America 18 yrs. and the whole time within this district. That your
petitioner is attached to the principles of the United States constitution and government and is desirous of becoming a citizen of the
said U.S. Your petitioner therefore prays your Honor that you would be
pleased to admit him to the rights and privileges of citizenship and
as in duty bound he will ever pray. Alexdr. Colhoun. We do certify
that we have known Alexander Colhoun for nine years. That he has
resided within the jurisdiction of this State for that time. That he
is a man of good moral charactor, etc. Dated 27 Oct. 1813. Signed:
Newman Moore, Samuel Cherry, John McFall, David Sloan, Benjamin Dickson,
John McMillian.

COLLINS, ELIJAH Pack 634 #176. Clerk of Court Office. Pickens,
S. C. On 16 Jan. 1845 Elijah Collings appointed a constable of Pickens
Dist.

COLLINS, THOMAS Pack 646 #7. Clerk of Court Office. Pickens,
S. C. On 13 April 1861 John Daniels of Pickens Dist. had a right
title and claim in the undivided real estate of Thomas Collins decd.
lying on Toxaway Creek waters of Chauga, containing 300 or 400 acres.

COLLONS, SUKEY Box 106 Pack 2733. Probate Judge Office. Abbe-
ville, S. C. Ninety Six Dist. I Sukey Collons the daughter of Joseph
Collons being in sound and perfect memory, etc. I give and bequeath
unto my loving mother Luse Collons my four hundred acres of land on
Thickety Creek. I appoint my loving mother Lucy Colings and William
Burton my lawful executors. Dated 14 Feb. 1784. Wit: James Johnson,
William Burton Junr., Phebe X Burton. Signed: Sukey X Collons.
Proven on oath of James Johnson before Bartlett Satterwhite, J.P.
on the 6 June 1784.

COLSON, JOHN Box 3 #85. Probate Judge Office. Anderson, S. C.
Est. admr. 24 Dec. 1827 by William Simpson, Benjamin Dickson who are
bound unto John Harris, Ord. in the sum of $200.00. Sale of est. was
held the 10 Jan. 1828 for a total of $19.41. No other inf.

CONNER, JAMES OLIVER Pack 363 A & B. Clerk of Court. Abbeville, S. C. Abbeville Dist. In Equity: To the Honr. the Chancellors:
Your orator and oratrix, Thomas R. Cochran and Mary L. his wife
sheweth that in the month of July 1854 James Oliver Conner of said
Dist. departed this life leaving as his only heirs and distributees
his widow Mary L. and an infant son Oliver Admr. of his est. was granted
by the ordinary to Alexander P. Conner the brother of the intestate
and James B. Crawford the brother of the widow. The admor has sold
the personal estate and still have charge of same. The sale was due on
the 6 Dec. 1855 and we believe the debts of the estate have been paid.
On the 14 Feb. 1856 a decree was ordered against Alexander P. Conner
and J. B. Crawford admor. by William Hill Esq. Ordinary in favor of
Andrew J. Conner a brother of one of the admr. for the sum of $572.29.
James O. Conner in his lifetime was the gdn by appointment of the
ordinary of his minor brother Andrew J. Conner, the decree is for money
alleged to be due him as the ward. Your oratrix Mary L. was present
in the life time of said James Oliver Conner when he and his ward
Andrew J. Conner then recently arrived of age, had a full statement
of their accounts as gdn. The settlement was made at the house of the
James L. Conner. Your oratrix and her brother James B. Crawford were
both present and witnessed this settlement. Part of the settlement
was the negro named Joe who is still in the possession of Andrew J.
Conner. Proof of the payment by one of the witness James B. Crawford
was not considered by the Court admissible testimony. Filed 25 April
1856.

COOK, WILLIAM Pack 603 #64. Land Warrant. Clerk of Court Office. Pickens, S.C. By W. L. Keith, Clerk. To any lawful surveyor you are authorized to lay out unto William Cook a tract of land not exceeding ten thousand acres. Given under my hand and seal 10 Jan. 1856. Signed: W. L. Keith, Clk.

COOK, SOPHRONIA Box 24 Pack 355. Probate Judge Office. Abbeville, S. C. A petition for guardianship: To David Lesly Ord. the petition of Sophronia Cook sheweth that she is a minor of the age of choice, and entitled to a small legacy under the will of Elizabeth Irwin decd. to her mother Mary Cook now decd. That the legacy of Elizabeth Irwin was to be equally divided and the chn. of Mary Cook taking one half. Your petitioner prays that her brother Frederick Cook be appointed her gdn. etc. to receive and manage her estate above and as in duty bound will ever pray. Filed 14 Jan. 1845. Sophr. Cook.

COOPER, THOMAS Pack 84. Probate Judge Office. Anderson, S.C. I Thomas Cooper being weak in body but of a sound mind and wishing to privide for my wife Elizabeth Cooper. I give to my wife Elizabeth my land and all household and kitchen furniture, all stock of cattle and hogs and sheep. One wagon and two horses, tools. All my ready money, notes of hand now due or will be due, all open accounts to remain and belong to her for her support during her natural life. At her decease if any remains it is to be equally divided amongst my three children viz: John Cooper, James Cooper, and Jo Hannah Perry. I bequeath to my son John my set of blacksmith tools also my shot gun. I give to my son James my rifle gun at my decease. I also give to William Rea the son of my wife Elizabeth after her decease one feather bed and furniture. My sons John and James Cooper my executors. Dated 2 April 1821. Wit: John Edmondson, William Singleton. Signed: Thomas T. Cooper. No recording date.

CORBIN, JAMES D. Box 73 #776. Probate Judge Office. Pickens, S. C. Est. admr. 21 Dec. 1863 by Benjamin Nicholson, John Price, Elijah E. Alexander who are bound unto W. E. Holcomb, Ord. in the sum of $4,000.00. Left a widow and three chn. Paid Frances E. Corbin gdn. for William B. F., Sarah M., and Frances M. Corbin.

CORBIN, JARRETT G. Box 5 #77. Probate Judge Office. Pickens, S. C. On 11 Jan. 1860 Joseph J. G. Hightower, Robert Powell, W. W. Leathers are bound unto W. E. Holcomb, Ord. in the sum of $1200.00. On 3 Oct. 1859 Joseph J. G. Hightower gdn. for Jarret G., Calvin B., Amanda C. Corbin minors under 12 yrs. 3 Oct. 1850 Rosa Corbin states that the minors were heirs of Alexr. Corbin, decd. and have funds due them in Georgia from est. of Alexr. Corbin decd.

CORBIN, PETER Book A Page 57. Probate Judge Office. Pickens, S. C. Whereas John O. Grisham and F. N. Garvin sayth that the tract of land containing 273 acres lying on North fork of Georges Creek, adj. land of Richard Burdine, Simeon Wade is not worth one thousand dollars and think it best for the parties interested that it be sold. James Mansell states that he has purchased six of the legatees claims on said land. Per: Peter Corbin will his widow to have plantation during her life time, she is now decd. Heirs: Samuel Corbin, John Corbin, Judy Corbin, Heirs of William Corbin, Sarah Corbin, Elijah Corbin, David Corbin, Elizabeth Corbin, Jesse Corbin and James Corbin. Filed 1 July 1844.

COSBY, JAMES Will Book. Page 600. Probate Judge Office. Columbia, S. C. I James Cosby of Richland Co. being of sound disposing mind and memory, but weak in body, etc. First after my death I desire and instruct my executors give my body a decent burial, and all my just debts be paid out the first money which may come in. I will all my estate both real and personal, my notes, accounts and debts due me to my wife Sarah Cosby for and during the term of her natural life and after her death to be held in trust by my executor for the use and benefit of my adopted son George Cosby. If my adopted son George Cosby shall arrive at the age of twenty one and my wife be living at

Cosby, James - Continued. the time of his maturity, my executors
shall set aside $10,000 to be held by them for the sole use and benefit
of my adopted son George Cosby and not subject for his debts or contracts. I appoint my wife Sarah Cosby and my friend John H. Pearson
Executrix and executor. This 30 May 1864. Wit: W. W. Andrews, Wm. C.
Bishop, L. M. Caldwell. Signed: James Cosby. Proved this 7 June 1864.
on oath of W. W. Andrews and Sarah Cosby and John H. Parson before
Jacob Bell, Ord. Filed 7 June 1864.

COSBY, ROBERT Deed Book D, Page 48. Elberton, Georgia. This
indenture made 4 April 1797. Between Robert Cosby, Sheriff of Elbert
Co., and Timothy Saxton of same place. Whereas an execution or fieri
facias (an execution to be levied on the goods of a debtor) from the
Superior Court against John Johnson at the suit of John Milliam for
the sum of $49.00. The said Robert Cosby, Sheriff was commanded of
the goods and chattels and land, tenaments of said John Johnson to
cause to be made the sum of money aforesaid. A tract of land containing 200 acres was sold to Timothy Saxton for the sum of $61.00. Wit:
Jon. M. Whitney, M. Woods, J.P. Signed: Robert Cosby, seal.
Registered 4 April 1797.

COUCH, JAMES W. Book A Page 246. Probate Judge Office. Pickens,
S. C. On 6 June 1859 James W. Couch, decd. owned 223 acres of land
originally granted to Samuel Maverick decd. on a branch of Little
George Creek waters of Saluda River, adj. land of William Benson decd.
Joel Ellison and others. Heirs: His widow Cyntha J. Hendricks nee
Cynthia J. Couch, Matilda F. Couch, William Hamilton the gdn. of
Matilda F. Couch a minor.

COUCH, JOHN Pack 52 #7. Clerk of Court Office. Pickens, S. C.
Dated 6 Dec. 1843, this is to certify that I William Barrett do testify
that John Couch was clear of any misdemeanor in a fracas which took
place on 14 Feb. 1841 in company with James Boyd and Frederick Magaha
and the above named John Couch, Jr. I John Couch have paid the said
Barrett $25.00 in witness whereof I set my hand and seal. Signed:
Wm. Barrett. Wit: Jas. L. Howard, L. R. Perry, Wm. Pilgrim, McElroy
Jamison. For assault and battery on Wm. Barrett committed the 22 May
1842 by beating and abusing him and by biting of his right ear. John
Couch was cleared. Larrence R. Perry and Saml. Nicolas were State
witness. On the 4 Oct. 1843 James Boyd was tried and convicted and
fined $25.00 for an assault, Riot and Battery.

COUCH, JOHN Pack 218 #4. Clerk of Court Office. Pickens, S.C.
Pickens Dist. in Equity: To the Honr. the Chancellors: Your oratrix
Mary Ann Couch of said Dist. sheweth that her late husband John Couch
departed this life in the year 1857 intestate. That he was possessed
with two tracts of land in this Dist. One known as the home place
lying on Bruchy Creek containing 450 acres adj. land of Thomas Montgomery, Samuel Cruikshank and others. One other tract on Brushy
Creek containing 483 acres adj. land of Thomas Montgomery, Joel Ellison
and others. That said land is subject to distribution amongst his
heirs to wit: The widow Mary Couch, Robert Couch, Margaret the wife of
Henry Hendrix, William Couch, Mary A. wife of Spencer Stegall, Sidney
Couch, Dorcas D. wife of William M. Jamison, John A. Couch, Ellender
Baker decd. who was the wife of Wm. Baker decd. and lived in Louisana
about 1854. Melinda Orr the wife of Alexander Orr. Filed 3 Sept. 1860.

COUCH, TERRY Apt. 1 File 22. Probate Judge Office. Greenville,
S. C. On 7 Aug. 1837 Terry Couch and his wife Agnes of Hall County, Ga.
were heirs of a David Barnett Sr. decd. of Greenville Dist., S. C. whose
estate was admr. in 1837.

COUCH, WILLIAM Book C-2 Page 551. Clerk of Court Office. Pickens
S. C. I William Couch of Pickens County. In consideration of $120.00
to me paid by Lemuel A. Perry of same Dist. have granted, sold, bargained and released unto Lemuel A. Perry two lots in the town of Easley,
S. C. Lots #11 and 14 each containing 3/4 of an acre. Lying on the
South of the Air Line Railway. Adj. land of H. M. Ellison on the East
and Doct. Glazener on the West. Dated 3 Feb. 1874. Wit: Olin L.

Couch, William - Continued. Durant, P. D. Cureton. Signed:
William Couch. Proved on oath of P. D. Cureton before R. E. Holcomb,
N.P. on the 3 Feb. 1874. On this 21 Feb. 1874 came Eliza Couch the
wife of William Couch and freely released and relinquish unto Lemuel
A. Perry all rights and interest or claim of dower.

COVINGTON, RICHARD Pack 236. Clerk of Court Office. Abbeville,
S. C. I Richard Covington of Abbeville Dist. being of sound and disposing mind memory and understanding etc. I direct that my just debts
and funeral expenses be paid out of the money as I may have at my
death. To my natural son Josephus Langdon I give, devise, and bequeath the plantation now in my own occupation which I purchased from
James Crawford decd. containing about 230 acres, bounded by George
Miller, W. McAlister, Doctor Lockhart and Mrs. Crawford, with all tools
and live stock and negroes; Nanny and her two chn. Charles and Millie
and the present and future issue of Mill, also Cinda and her chn.
Milly and Melissa and my girl Jane, man Eliza Jackson. To my nephew
Edmund Covington son of my brother William Covington, I give negroes
Lewis, Joe, Isham and Sally. Also my saddle horse, watch, and my
stud. But if he fail or neglect to execute the trust herein after
imposed on him in relation to my mulatto girl Mima and her son Alfred
this devise shall be void. To my neice Emily the wife of Morgan
McMorris I give her my negro girl Nancy and Frances and my man Creswell
and boys Sam and Levi. If she die without issue then the same to go
to my brother William. To my nephew Benjamin R. Covington I give my
mulatta boy Reuben and my horse nuffifier. To my nephew Charles
Covington son of Wm. I give my negro boy Davy and my horse ned bichut.
To my nephew James, son of Wm., I give my negro boy Smart and my
Crusader Colt. To my nephew Samuel Watt, son of Wm., I give my negro
Henry and my filley Queen Adalaide. I give to my nephew William son
of Wm., my negro girl Olive, and director Filley. To the infant child
(nane not known) of my brother William, I give my negro girl Lucy and
the first colt of my horse Ann Reid shall hereafter have.
To my little friend Andrew William Bowie son of Alexander Bowie, I give
the colt lately fouled by my mare Ann Reid in 1833. To Taictus
Johnston the eldest son of Gideon H. Johnson decd., I give the sum of
$100 to him forever. I give devise and bequeath to my nephew Edmund
Covington and his heirs forever under the trust and stipulation herein
after set forth, my mulatto girl Mima and her child Alfred, that is to
say in trust, that the said Edmund Covington will and shall procure and
provide for the said Mima and Alfred a tract of fifty acres of land
worth three hundred dollars per acre and cause to be vested thereon a
comfortable log cabin for their residence, and permit them to live
there and have and enjoy all the profits of their own labor during
their natural lives and that he will protect them as far as can from
injury or imposition. (No more of the will in notes.) Abbeville
Dist. In Equity: To the Honr. the Chancellors: Your orator Margan
McMorris and Oratrix Emily C. McMorris the wife sheweth that Richard
Covington late of this Dist. died about the 12 Jan. 1836 after having
duly made his will and testament with a codicil dated 11 Jan. 1836 to
wit. It is my will I do hereby give and bequeath all the residue of
my estate of what nature or kind soever to my brother William Covington
and his chn. to be shared equally between them. Under this clause a
certain tract of land containing about 1500 acres lying on Kerr Creek
and Alexander Creek waters of Little River, bounded by Mrs. McCaw,
William Smith, James Wardlaw, EdwardTilman, the same whereon the said
Richard Covington resided. At the time said codicil was made William
Covington had children living to wit: Edmund M. Covington, Emily C.
the wife of Margan McMorris, Richard B., Charles W., James B. M.,
Augustus W., William Covington, the last named five are minors,
residing in Columbus in Lowndes County, Miss. and their father has
been named their guardian by the probate court of that County. By the
said Codicil Richard Covington named Capt. James Baskin the executor.
Filed: 27 Sept. 1836.

COWAN FAMILY Tombstone inscriptions taken from "Lindsay Cemetery"
2 miles South of Due West, Abbeville County, S. C.
Lewis R. Cowan, born 6 May 1848, died 23 Oct. 1854.
Balnnd W. [written like this] born 4 Oct. 1837, died 23 Oct. 1854.

Cowan Family - Continued.
John Cowan, born 16 May 1806, died 27 Dec. 1874.
Sarah B. Cowan, wife of John Cowan, born 9 Nov. 1811, died 6 March 1852.
Isaac B. Cowan son of John & Sarah Cowan, born 2 Nov. 1830, died
16 Oct. 1846
Martha Cowan, born 14 June 1839, died __ Sept. 1840
Infant son of John Cowan, born 9 Aug. __, died the 27, 1860
Annie R. Cowan, dtr. of John, born 11 March __, died 11 Oct. 1864
Jane Cowan, born 31 Jan. 1771, died 11 March 1859.
Col. Isaac Cowan, died 25 Dec. 1831, age 67 yrs.
Laney Elizabeth dtr. of Jane Cowan, born 8 April 1828, died 6 Oct. 1829

COWAN, FRANCIS Apt. 2 File 83. Probate Judge Office. Greenville,
S. C. On 7 Sept. 1828 Jesse Patty withdrew his claim as administrator
to the est. of Francis Cowan decd. and on 6 Oct. 1828 Mary Cowan
became the admr. At his death he left a widow and three chn., but no
names given. On 13 June 1831 mentioned that Mary Cowan now Mary
Thomason was married in 1827 or 1828. Anna Cowan, James Cowan and
John Thomason etc. bought at the sale of the estate.

COWAN, JOHN Box 106 Pack 1749. Probate Judge Office. Abbeville,
S. C. I John Cowan of Abbeville Dist. being very weak in body, but of
perfect mind and memory. I leave and bequeath to my mother Ann Cowan
all of my household furniture and all the beds, and as many cattle as
she wants for her support. I leave to my brother William Cowan my
plantation whereon I now live containing 150 acres, also my three
negroes, Smart, Hary, Kate, also one half of the crop on the ground, and
one half of the hogs. My brother William is to give sufficient support
to my mother during her life. When my brother William dies, I leave
my negro man Smart to my brother Isaac Cowan, and he is to raise and
support my two negroes Hary and Kate to the age of twenty one, then
allow to be given to my brother Williams two children, Harry to William
Cowan and Kate to Ann Cowan. I also give to my brother Isaac one half
of the crop now on the ground and one half of the hogs. I leave to my
brother in law David Hawthorn $100 now in his hands. I order and allow
all the remainder and residue of my estate to be sold and equally
divided between my brother Isaac Cowan, William Cowan, my brother-in-
law Samuel Snoddy, my brother in law William Brownlee. I appoint
Isaac Cowan, William Cowan, and John Shannon my executors. Dated 18
Sept. 1804. Wit: James Lindsey, Joseph Lindsey, Samuel X Lindsey.
Signed: John Cowan.

COWDRESS, GEORGE Box 21 Pack 464. Probate Judge Office.
Abbeville, S. C. Adrm. Bond, Abbeville Dist. We, Elizabeth Cowdress,
John Thomson, Samuel Saxon and Thomas Lee Junr. are bound unto Andrew
Hamilton, Ord. in the sum of $1500. Dated 6 Jan. 1808. Estate
appraised 12 Jan. 1808 by Samuel Saxon, Isaac Davis, Thomas Lee Senr.,
Sale made 16 Jan. 1808 Buyers: Allen Glover, Benjamin Saxon, Frances
Sutherland, Drury Breazeale, Saml. Saxon, Caleb Jenning, John Thompson,
Lazarus Covin Junr., Thomas Lee, Benjamin Carrel, James Carrel,
Richard Stricklin, Peter Covine, Andrew Lee, James Boyse, Peter Culle-
beau, Peter Gibert, Delany Carrel.

COX, MARGARET Box 21 Pack 467. Probate Judge Office. Abbeville,
S. C. Admr. Bond, Abbeville Dist. We James Young, Robert Young,
and Alexander Adams are bound unto Moses Taggart Senr. Ord. in the sum
of $3,000. Dated 11 Feb. 1822. Inventory made 11 March 1822 by
Thomas Edwards, Alexr. Sample, Robert Young. She was the widow of
the late William Cox.

COX, WILLIAM #108. Probate Judge Office. Anderson, S. C.
The est. of William Cox was admr. 1 Sept. 1828 by Nancy Cox, Edward
Cox Junr. Edward Cox Senr. and Gideon Willbanks, all of Pendleton Dist.
who are bound unto John Harris, Ord. in the sum of $3,000. In same
file William Cox, John Cox, Edward Cox and Jonathan Skelton recd. $60
from their father last will settled 1 April 1817. In same file a will
of a William Cox of Pendleton Dist. First pay all debts as soon as
money come in. I give to my wife Mary Cox her support during her
natural life. I give unto William Bolen Cox and John Wesley Cox the

Cox, William - Continued. plantation where I now live, to be
equally divided between them. The rest of my property to be equally
divided between my chn. except Garner Brooks, I leave him nothing but
his son William Temson Brooks I leave an equal share with the rest of
the last mentioned children. I appoint Richard Madden and Isaac
Steat my executors. Dated 16 April 1821. Wit: Thomas Jones,
Ezekiel Madden, Thomas Wiley. Signed: William X Cox.

CRAIG, LAWRENCE C. Pack 94. In.Equity, Clerk of Court Office.
Pickens, S. C. Will - I Lawrence C. Craig of Pickens Dist. being of
sound mind and disposing memory, etc. I desire that all my just debts
be paid by my executors as soon as practicable. I will to Sarah E.
Craig the wife of W. N. Craig my negro girl Susan and her increase, If
said Sarah should die after W. N. Craig and without issue, then the
said negro to go to my father and mother. All rest and residue of my
estate both real and personal, I will to my father and mother, the one
that survives the other to hold and enjoy the property. At the death
of my father and mother the property to be equally divided between my
brothers and sisters. I will that my father and mother if both or
either of them survive me, shall take my friend Thomas R. Brackenridge, and give him a comfortable support during his natural life. I
appoint my father Robert Craig and my friend James E. Hagood executors.
Dated 13 Dec. 1862. Wit: E. E. Alexander, W. E. Holcomb, Wm. A. X
Evatt. Signed: L. C. Craig. Proved on oath of W. E. Holcomb, Ord.
one of the witness on the 19 Oct. 1864. Lawrence C. Craig died in
Oct. 1864 unmarried. Left his father and mother Robert and Rachel
Craig, and the following brothers and sisters, Martha C. Griffin wife
of Thomas Griffin, William T. Craig, John C. Craig, Arthur R. Craig,
Esther M. Craig, Laura Baker, widow, Sarah E. Craig, Josephine E.
Craig. All of age except Josephine who is 18 yrs. of age. He owned
land in Pickens Dist. known as the Howard Lands containing 800 acres,
adj. land of John Howard, Jeremiah Looper, another tract on the cedar
rock containing 35 acres, and stock in L. C. Craig and Co. Filed 28
April 1868 for partition of the land.

CRAFTON, JOSEPH AND WIFE No Ref. Edgefield, S. C. I Joseph
Crafton and Lucinda G. Crafton my wife do in our own right as heirs
and distributees of the est. of Daniel Barksdale decd. also heirs of
Susannah Barksdale decd. wife of said Daniel. In consideration of
$800 to us in hand paid released and forever claim unto Thomas Meri-
wether all claims and demands that we may have on said land. Dated
7 Jan. 1817. Test: Wm. Thomas. Signed Joseph Crafton and Lucy
Green Crafton. Proved on oath of Wm. Thomas before A. Edmunds, J.P. on
the 11 March 1817. Recorded same date.

CRAIG, LAWRENCE COATSWORTH Pack 87 In Equity, Clerk of Court
Office. Pickens, S. C. Lawrence Coatsworth Craig of Pickens Dist.
states that Elliott M. Keith about the 21 March 1857 was indebted to
him in the sum of $300. He made and executed a deed for two tracts of
land on Keowee River, known as the Merritt tract and the Pleasant
Alexander tract, both containing 360 acres. L. C. Craig was the
sheriff and E. M. Keith was an attorney at law. Dated and filed 26
May 1860.

CRAWFORD, ELIZABETH Pack 257. In Equity. Clerk of Court Office.
Abbeville, S. C. Abbeville Dist. To the Honr. the Judges of the
Court of Equity; Your Orator Benjamin H. Saxon, sayth that sometime
in the year 1807 Elizabeth Crawford made and executed her last will and
testament, which she devised to her two grandsons James C. Crawford
and John M. Crawford in equal shares to be divided between them, when
they arrive at the age of twenty one yrs. a tract of land on which she
resided containing 114 acres, bound on East by Thomas Brough, on South
by land of John Moore, on West by Little River, on North by land of
John McKelvey and John Wilson decd. The said James C. Crawford died
intestate, unmarried and without issue shortly after his grandmother,
leaving a mother Rhoda Crawford, a sister Rhoda Crawford and two
brothers John M., and Ebenezer Crawford. The brothers and sister at
time of his death being minors, but now of full age. Your orator
purchased from John M. Crawford his interest in said land, also on 18

Crawford, Elizabeth - Continued. Sept. 1822 purchased from Ebenezer Crawford and Isham Medford who had intermarried with Rhoda the sister of the decd. James C. Crawford their share. On the same day Ebenezer and Isham produced a power of Attorney authorizing them to convey Rhoda Crawford (the mother) share. Your orator gave notes for some of the land, and very soon afterwards they were transferred by the payee and your orator has been compelled to pay them, and Ebenezer Crawford and Isham Medford still hold the deed of Rhoda Crawford. Your orator sheweth that the parties live out of this State and your orator is remindless save in this honorable Court. Filed 2 Dec. 1824.

CRAYTON, MARY Apt. 8 File 545. Probate Judge Office. Greenville, S. C. I Mary Crayton widow of late Samuel Crayton decd. being low in health and body but of sound disposing mind and memory. I give to my dearly beloved little dtr. Mary Jane Crayton, one bed and furniture, all my silver plates and glasses etc. If she have a taste for music my executors to purchase a piano for her. To my little son Thomas Crayton $150 to be laid out to purchase a gold watch when he arrives at the age of twenty one, to made him equal with his brother Baylis to whom his father gave a watch of that value. To my dear beloved son Baylis F. Crayton one bureau forever. I desire that my sister Mrs. Elizabeth Sloan to take charge of my dtr. and direct her education. I appoint my sister Mrs. Elizabeth Sloan and William Choice Junr. executrix and executor. Dated 27 March 1831. Wit: M. F. Lewis, J. Cleveland, W. Hornbuckle. Signed: Mary T. Crayton. Proved 9 May 1831.

CRAYTON, SAMUEL Apt. 2 File 89. Probate Judge Office. Greenville, S. C. I Samuel Crayton of Greenville Dist. being of sound mind and disposing memory. First I will that my executors pay my just debts. I desire my executors sell two tracts of land lying in Greenville Dist. one containing 113 acres purchased by me at sheriff's sale, the other lies on Enoree adj. land of Street Thruston, containing 60 acres also purchased at sheriff's sale. I have five shares purchased from five heirs of Mathew Wynne decd. in the tract, whereon Mrs. Susannah Wynne now lives which is to be divided at her death, I authorize my executors to bid on others shares before Mrs. Wynne death. I f the above tract of land be purchased by my executors, this tract with my plantation lying on waters of George's Creek be rented out from year to year till a partition shall be made among my heirs. My negro Clara and her trhee children, Kitty, Tilda and Jackson shall remain with my mother during her life free of charge for her assistance and support, and at her death to return to my estate and made part of it. My wife Mary Crayton be permitted to have as many negroes as she think necessary, also all the stock of horses, cattle, hogs, household and kitchen furniture as she deem necessary for her support and maintenance. She may live and occupy my house and lot in the town of Greenville during her natural life or widowhood. It is my will that my three chn. Bayles F., Mary Jane, and Thomas Crayton be educated out of the estate before any partition is made, and I desire that Baylis I. Earle, Esq. direct the manner in which my son shall be educated and in case of his death Baylis I. Earle then William Choice Esq. shall direct. I give to my son Baylis F. Crayton my gold watch to be keep by his mother till he is the age of twenty one. My wife to have a one forth share of my estate with my chn. the other three parts. I appoint my wife Mary Crayton executrix and Baylis I. Earle and William Choice Esq. executors. Dated 15 Nov. 1828. Wit: P. E. Duncan, I. McDaniel, James M. Lewis. Samuel Crayton. A codicil was added on the 22 March 1829 directing the executors to sell the negroes except the ones at his mother's and may sell the whole or part of the land, and put the money on interest for the family. Wit: M. F. Lewis, J. M. Lewis, P. E. Duncan. Probated 5 May 1829.

CRAYTON, THOMAS Apt. 2 File 87. Probate Judge Office. Greenville, S. C. I Thomas Crayton of Greenville Dist. being weak of body but of perfect mind and disposing memory. I give to my two chn. William L. Crayton and Eliza Crayton five negroes to wit: Middleton, Milly, Curtis, Abb and Henry and their increase to be divided when

Crayton, Thomas - Continued. they become of age or marry, to remain in possession of my wife Mary Crayton for the sole benefit of her and the chn. I give to my wife all my stock of cows, three cows and calves and horses, tools, household and kitchen furniture to raise and educate my chn. I authorize my executors to sell the land on Hencoop Creek in Pendleton Dist. of about 100 acres, I bought from Azle D. Harris, the title to be made to Thomas Haze upon him paying $150 by next Christmas, Also the other tract on Hencoop Creek be by my executors, it containing 150 acres. The plantation whereon I now live, on the waters of Little River I allow my wife to live and raise my chn. I have a negro boy named Washington in the hands of Hiram Biggerstaff of Kentucky and a mare, saddle and bridle. Which were sent there to meet a note of three hundred dollars or a little more. I am willing for the said property to settle the debt. I give the house and lot in Greenville to my two chn. William and Eliza., to be leased or rented for their use. I wish that my executor may have my business of my store carried on until my brother Samuel Crayton time is up at Sherman & Co. I widh my executors to settle with James Duncan est. from the papers will be found in my possession. I appoint Conrod Hacklaman, Hezikiah Rice, Alexander Sloan my executor. Dated 29 April 1815. Wit: Jeremiah Cleveland, Hugh Robinson, James Robinson. Probated 23 June 1824. Exps. Paid 21 May 1834, Mary Crayton and William L. Crayton both of McDonongh, Henry Co., Ga. $500 each.

CRENSHAW, JESSE Pack 181 #28. Clerk of Court Office. Pickens, S. C. To the Board of County Commissioners: The undersigned most respectfully petition your board for a license to retail spiritous at his house in said County from the 12 Feb. 1869 to the 1 May 1869. Dated 23 March 1869. We the undersigned recommend Jesse Crenshaw as a fit and suitable person to retail spiritous liquors. Signed: B. F. Morgan, John Julien, Wm. M. Jones.

CRESWELL, ELIHU Box 4 #42. Probate Judge Office. Pickens Dist., S. C. Est. admr. 30 Aug. 1833 by James, Robert, Sarah Creswell and Albert Waller who are bound unto James H. Dendy, Ord. in the sum of $30,000.00. Elihu the father of James, Robert Creswell. Inv. made 11 Oct. 1833 mention that he had 32 slaves. Recd. cash 20 Nov. 1833 from E. Crewswell Jr. for hire of negroes in Georgia $194.00. Paid 10 Jan. 1835 for John Creswell necessaries $40.00 Had five chn. no names given. Buyers at sale: Sarah, Henry H. Creswell, John Quarles, James McKinney, Senr., Adam Hill, John Sharo, James Laurence, William Cobb, John Elihu, James Creswell.

CRESWELL, THOMAS Pack 9. In Equity. Clerk of Court Office. Abbeville, S. C. On 28 April 1856. Thomas Creswell mentioned as the husband of Mary Spence a str. of James Spence Sr. decd. of Abbeville Dist. Jacob Creswell husband of Peggy Spence another dtr. John Creswell husband of Ann Spence a dtr. of James Spence Jr. decd.

CREW, MOSES W. Box 124 #15. Probate Judge Office. Pickens, S. C. I M. W. Crew being of sound mind and disposing memory. First I desire my executors to pay my just debts and funeral expenses. I give to my daughter in law wife of my decd. son John P. Crew, Catharine Crew, now (Cannon) twenty acres of land lying on the South side of the branch running through my farm, adj. land of Duncans line, adj. myself, Sarah Craigs Col. It being all the land I own on the South side of the branch. It is agreed between me and Catharine Cannon that she will take care of me in my old age, feed, clothe and give me such medical attention as I may need, etc. I appoint my son Willie J. Crew as executor. Dated 4 May 1895. Wit: J. T. Youngblood. B. D. Stewart, J. M. Stewart. Signed: M. W. Crew. Died: 2 June 1895. Filed 21 Oct. 1895.

CREWS, JOHN P. Box 119 #9. Probate Judge Office. Pickens, S.C. Est. admr. 14 May 1891 by Moses W. Crew, Baylus Arter, Jesse Arter who are bound unto J. B. Newberry, Ord. in the sum of $60.00. He died 14 April 1891. Moses W. Crew his father.

CRISWELL, DAVID Deed Book A, page 6. Elberton, Georgia. Wilkes County, Georgia. This indenture made this 21 Feb. 1791 between David Criswell of Wilkes Co., Ga. and Thomas Brown of Elbert Co., Ga. By virtue of special authority given to him by John Wattson bearing date 4 Oct. 1790. For and in consideration of 50₤ paid by Thomas Brown hath granted, sold, bargained and released all the tract of land being in Elbert Co., Ga. bounded by Powers land and James Alfords. Wit: Geo. Walker, W. Williamson. Signed: D. Criswell. Proved in open Court on the 24 Feb. 1791. Matthew Tollet, Clk.

CROSBY, ABNER Box 2 Pack 13. Probate Judge Office. Pickens, S. C. Est. admr. 2 Feb. 1829 by Col. Robert Anderson, Richard Harris who are bound unto James H. Dendy Ord. in the sum of $3,000. Bond witnesses Thomas B. Reid, Elijah Cannon. Annanias Tilletson deed of conveyance of a tract of land now belonging to estate of Abner Crosby containing 202 1/2 acres lying in Carroll Co., Ga. Sale held 27 Feb. 1829: Buyers: Mrs. Frances Crosby, Annanias Tilletson, William Frazier, Richard Harris, Thomas Patterson, Randolph Lee, Alexander Bryce, Samuel Thomas, John Brown, Jr., James O. Lewis, Reuben Hix. Cit. Pub. at Rock Springs Church on 3 Jan. 1836.

CROSBY, ABNER Pack 60 In Equity, Basement, Clerk of Court Office. Pickens, S. C. Andrew Alexander and his wife Mary E. Alexander sheweth that Abner Crosby the father of said Mary E. Alexander died in 1835 intestate, leaving a considerable real and personal estate to be distributed amongst his heirs at law. That Benjamin D. Dupree took out letter of admr. that afterwards about the 11 Oct. 1837 that Samuel Moseley took out letter of guardianship of the estate of Mary E. Alexander then Mary E. Crosby a minor. That during the year 1846 Andrew and Mary E. Alexander intermarried. Filed 17 April 1847. Samuel Moseley states that Mary E. Alexander is now in her 17th year. On 26 Aug. 1846 Andrew Alexander and Mary appointed Absalom Hyde their attorney to receive their part of said estate.

CROSBY, MINORS Box 4 #103. In Equity. Clerk of Court Office. Pickens, S. C. On 16 Aug. 1837 Leonard Towers, Thomas J. Humphreys, E. B. Benson are bound to Nathan Boon, Esq. C. in E in the sum of $2400.00. Leonard Towers gd. of Atilla Crosby, Frances Jane Crosby minor chn. of Abner Crosby decd. On 11 Oct. 1837 Samuel Moseley, James H. Dendy, Smith White are bound to Nathan Boon, Esq. C. in E. in the sum of $1200.00. Samuel Moseley gdn. of Mary Elizabeth Crosby minor child of Abner Crosby decd. Frances Crosby their mother.

CROSBY, WILLIAM SENR. Pack 22 In Equity. Clerk of Court Office. Anderson, S. C. PendletonDist. To the honr. the judges of the Court of Equity. Your orator James Crosby and your orator and oratrix Luke Hubbard and Jane his wife. Sheweth that William Crosby Senr. late of this Dist. departed this life leaving Nancy Crosby and John Crosby, William Crosby, John Huntley and Nancy his wife late Nancy Crosby, Samuel Crosby, Levi Crosby, Abner Crosby all defendants hereto his heirs with James Crosby, Jane the wife of Luke Hubbard, William Crosby Senr. was possessed with real estate consisting of about 214 acres lying on Conneross Creek waters of Seneca River, adj. land of Abner Crosby, and others.

CROW, ISAAC Book A Page 114. Probate Judge Office. Spartanburg, S. C. I Isaac Crow of Spartanburg Dist. being weak in health and body, but of a sound mind and memory. I give to my beloved wife on half of that tract of land that I now live on (lines given) during her natural life, also I give my wife one negro woman Sarah, to have said for her life time, also one bed and furniture and all her wearing appareal and a large trunk. I give to my dtr. Hannah one tract of land lying on Tiger River being the tract I bought from Edward Hooper containing 132 1/2 acres, also one negro by name Bob. I give to my dtr. Hannah son John one tract of land lying on Jameses Creek, being the tract I bought from William Chambler and Thomson Chambler and Isaac Crow the son of James the said land to be left for the executors to manage as they think best for the boys. I give to my son Samuel Crow and his wife Rebeckah Crow his wife and the heirs of her body one

Crow, Isaac - Continued. one negro man named Jack. I give to
Samuel Crow one negro girl named Marak. I give to James Crow son of
Samuel Crow one negro boy named John. I give to Elizabeth Crow dtr. of
Samuel Crow one negro boy named Allin. I give to Samuel Crow Jr. son
of Samuel Crow Senr. one negro boy named Lewis. I give to Sarah Crow
the other half of the tract of land whereon I now live, also one tract
lying on the Tiger River being the tract I bought from James Beard. I
give to Benjamin Crow, son of Samuel Crow 100 acres of land on the
waters of James Creek, being the tract I bought from Misaja Lindsay
and the heirs of the widow McClunkin. I want 100 acres taken off the
upper end of said tract, land adj. Chasneys land and Wm. Posey. I
give to Samuel Crow son of Isaac Crow Senr. all the tract of land that
I give to Benjamin Crow son of Samuel Crow. Any property not bequeath
in the foregoing will to be equally divided between the following my
wife and legatees Hannah Langston, Samuel Crow, Isaac Crow. I appoint
Joseph Barnet, Samuel Woodruff, Esq. executors. Dated 28 May 1817.
Wit: Joseph Barnett, Samuel Woodruff Senr., Easter X Shurley.
Recorded 22 Oct. 1817.

CROWTHER, JAMES No. ref. given only the last page. From Abbeville, S. C. One tract of 100 acres on Johnsons Creek waters of Little
River, bounded by land of Conrad Wakefield, Michael McGehee. The home
tract lying on Rockey River containing about 135 acres, bounded by
Robert Boyd, Robert Stuckey. The Knoght tract on Rockey River containing about __ acres bounded by Robert Hill, William Crowther. His
heirs at law and distributees your orator John Crowther, Hannah Crothers,
Sarah Alewine, Mary Boyd, Elizabeth the wife of Alexander C. Bowen. The
admr. of the est. has been committed to your orator William Crowther.
Filed 27 Jan. 1863. N. B. Since the filing of this bill Alexander C.
Bowen has died. John Crowther and Alexr. C. Bowen resides beyond the
limit of this State.

CROZIER, JAMES Box 24 Pack 557. Probate Judge Office. Abbeville, S. C. I James Crozier do leave and bequeath unto my wife and
two chn. that is to say Samuel Crozier and Agnes Crozier all my estate.
The property to be divided into three equal parts, wife to get a share
during her widowhood or life time. The chn. part is forever. Son
Samuel to get two tracts of land with one hundred acres in each. If
wife remains a widow she to enjoy and live on the plantation. I
appoint Wm. Reightly and Thomas Croazier my executors. Dated 27 May
1778. Wit: William Davis, Andrew Crozier. Signed: James Crozier.

CRUIKSHANKS, DANIEL Vol. 41 Page 698. Probate Judge Office.
Charleston, S. C. I Daniel Cruikshanks of Charleston, S. C. being sick
in health, but of sound mind and memory. First I direct my just debts
be paid with funeral expenses. I give to my wife Jane Cruikshanks her
heirs and assignes forever, all my house and lot number 22 on Queen
Street in which I now reside with all furniture etc. etc. and I
further give to my wife my slave Chloe and her son George, Fanny and
her dtr. Ann, Charity and her son Toby. I also give to my wife during
her natural life an annuity of three hundred dollars a year, payable
quarterly of seventy five dollars each, hereinafter devised to my son
Samuel Cruikshanks. I further give to my dear wife during her natural
life my negro Betty, her dtr. Dinah and her son John. At the death of
my wife I give said negroes to my granddaughter Jane Miller Ferguson
and Sarah Ann Ferguson to be equally divided between them. I give to
my son Samuel, my house and lot at the North West corner of East Bay
and Elliott Streets, with the three tenements on Elliott, subject to
the payment of said annuity of $300 payable quarterly payments unto
his mother during her life. I give to my dtr. Jane Cruikshanks Gordon
the wife of Alexander Gordon, merchant, all my house and lot number 61
on East Bay Street to her and for sole use. I give to my grandchildren the issue of my decd. dtr. Mary Ferguson namely, Jane Miller
Ferguson, John Ross Ferguson, James Hugh Ferguson, William Ferguson,
Sarah Anne Ferguson their heirs and assigns forever all my house and
lot number 51 State Street and my negro man George Brown to them and
their heirs forever. I appoint my wife Jane Cruikshanks executrix and
my son in law Alexander Gordon and my son Samuel Cruikshanks executors.
Dated the 17 Feb. 1834. Wit: John C. Miller, James Duncan, A. Williams

Cruickshanks, Daniel - Continued. Signed: Daniel Cruickshanks. Proven before Thomas Lehre O.C.T.D. on the 6 Jan. 1838 at the same time qualified Alexander Gordon and Samuel Cruickshanks execrs.

CRUICKSHANKS, MARY Vol. 46 Page __. Probate Judge Office. Charleston, S. C. I Mary Cruickshanks of Charleston being a widow with sound and disposing mind and memory. I direct my just debts and funeral expenses be fully paid. I give the house and lot which I now occupy being on the West side of Coming Street known as number 63, also all my silver plates and half of my furniture to John Mood Senr., Robert W. Burnham, James Tupper in trust for the sole and separate use and benefit of my dtr. Mary Elizabeth Vanwinkle for and during her natural life, free from the debts, control of her present husband or any future husband. I also give and bequeath the house and lot on the East side of Coming Streets a few doors above Calhoun formerly boundary street, conveyed to me by deed of Carolina M. Tresott on the 27 Feb. 1844, also one half of my furniture to John Mood Senr., Robert W. Burham and James Tupper in trust for the sole use and benefit of my grand daughter Frances Mary Thompson for and during her natural life. All stock, bonds, other lands, houses to be in trust for the dtr. and gr. dtr. with all interest, rent, profits to be equal divided. I give the sum of $500 to the Methodist Church at the corner of Calhoun Street known as Bethel Church. If my grand dtr. die without heir the executors to be divided the residue into six equal parts, one part to my neice Margaret Elizabeth Minus and her two dtrs. now living to share and share alike. One other part to my neice Sarah Applebee dtr. of Stephen Minus to her and her heirs forever. One other part to the chn. of my nephew Richard Minus share and share alike. One other part to the children of Caroline Bunch decd. dtr. of my niece Margaret Elizabeth Minus. The other part to the chn. of my niece Betsey Harley to share and share alike. The remaining part to Savage Minus to his heirs forever. Dated 7 Oct. 1851. Wit: A. E. Vacetti, William Pettigrew, John De Bow. Signed: Mary Crukshanks. Proved before George Buist, Esq. O.C.D. 16 Jan. 1854.

CRUICKSHANKS, WILLIAM Vol. 40 Page 124. Probate Judge Office. Charleston, S. C. I William Cruikshanks of Charleston Dist. being of sound and disposing mind and memory, etc. I will and direct that my funeral expenses and all other debts be fully paid. I give and devise the house and lot which I now occupy in King Street next to the corner of John Street, with all my personal property to the sole use and enjoyment of my wife Mary Cruickshanks during her natural life. After her death, I devise said house and lot with all personal property to Charles Moison and Campbell Douglas to them their execr. and admr. in trust never the less to and for this special purpose, that they pay over to my dtr. Mary E. Thompson the wife of Henry Thompson (taking her receipt for their payment) all the proceeds or interest arising out or become due on this said real and personal estate. This said real and personal est. nor interest or proceeds there from be subject to the control or liable to her present husband or any future husband which she may have, and after her death I devise the whole est. to her lawful issue to them and theirs for ever. I bequeath also unto my wife Mary Cruickshanks one half of the proceeds arising from the rest and residue of my real est. to be paid over to her regularly during her natural life and for her own use. After her death, I devise the said half unto Charles Moison and Campbell Douglass to them in trust for the use and benefit of my dtr. Mary E. Thompson the wife of Henry Thompson, with the same control as the first. The other half I bequeath to my wife Mary and Charles Moison in trust for my dtr. Mary E. Thompson, under the same control as the other, if my dtr. die leaving no lawful issue, I devise one third of the real estate to her present husband Henry Thompson and his heirs forever. One dollar I give to my brother Daniel Cruickshanks. The rest and residue of said est. I devise unto Elspeth Duncan and her children, unto my decd. brother James Cruickshanks widow and chn., unto my brother John Cruickshanks and his chn. and to my brother Alexander Cruickshanks and his chn. all of whom are now residing in Scotland in Europe, to be equally divided among the whole of them. I appoint my wife Mary Cruickshanks executrix and Charles Moison executor. Dated 17 Aug.

Cruikshanks, William - Continued. 1829. Signed: Wm. Cruick-shanks. Wit: T. W. Johnson, Donald McIntosh, John Phillips. Proved before Thomas Lehre Junr. O.C.T.D. on the 3 Nov. 1834 and at the same time qualified Mrs. Mary Cruickshanks Executrix (T.L.) "On the twenty third day of November 1868 granted administration with annexed to Robert Oliver of Spartanburg County Minister of the Gospel." Recorded in Will Book H. 1834-1839.

CUMMINS, C. W. Box 128 #8. Probate Judge Office. Pickens, S.C. On 16 June 1897 letter of admr. was granted to J. M. Stewart. Cummins died 31 May 1897. L. E. Cummins was his wife.

CURTIS, NAAMAN Pack 31 #4. In Equity, In Basement. Clerk of Court Office, Pickens, S. C. Naaman Curtis died in 1829 in Pickens Dist. Owned three tracts of land. One lying on the West side of Keo-wee River at Cravens Ford, originally granted to Honr. John F. Grenike and Robert Cravens containing 613 acres. Another tract on East side of Keowee River at Cravens Ford containing 725 acres whereon Naaman Curtis lately lived, adj. land to Tarleton Lewis and others. Another tract granted to Naaman Curtis on six mile creek containing 100 acres, bounded by land of Henry Gassaway, John Green, James Beatty. Left a widow Milly Curtis and chn. viz: William Curtis, Cosby the wife of William W. Gassaway, Lucinda Curtis, Milly Curtis, Naaman Curtis, Elizabeth Curtis, Sarah Ann Curtis, Martha Matilda and Frances Ann who are chn. of John Curtis decd. On 5 Oct. 1829 Milly Curtis states that she has three minor chn. under 14 yrs. of age viz; Naaman now in his 14 yr. Elizabeth and Sarah Ann Curtis who wanted Col. Joseph Grisham to be their guardian. Lucinda who was over 14 wanted David Sloan Esq. to be her gdn. Milly wanted Enoch B. Benson Esq. to be her gdn. On 5 Oct. 1829 Nathan Boon sheweth that Frances Ann and Martha Matilda Curtis the chn. of John Curtis decd. are entitled to a share of the est. of Naaman Curtis decd. These chn. are the chn. of his daughter and are under 14 yrs. Nathan Boon made gdn. of said chn.

DAVIS, ALEXANDER Deed Book A Page 18. Clerk of Court Office, Abbeville, S. C. A citizen grant of 200 acres, lying on both sides of Broadway Creek, a branch of Great Rockey Creek, and bounded on West by land laid out for John McCollister. Surveyed by David Hopkins D.S. on the 25 May 1784. Recorded this 5 June 1784. Robert Anderson, C.L.

DAVIS, BENJAMIN No ref. Probate Judge Office. Elbert County, Georgia. I Benjamin Davis being sick but of perfect memory. I give to my beloved dtr. Ann Morning Davis a feather bed and furniture that she generally lyes on, one black horse named Jack. I give to my beloved dtr. Mary Davis thirty dollars cash. I give to my beloved dtr. Elizabeth Davis the feather bed I generally lie upon with all furniture and one butter pot, a hemp hackle, a loom with all the gear. I give to my beloved son Benjamin Davis the land I now own, with the house, one sorrel horse, one cow and calf, should Benjamin die without heir his property to go to his sister Elizabeth. When the chn. break up the house or part, the stock, cattle, hogs, household and personal property to be sold and equally divided amongest all my chn. With the land and house rented, and the rent go to support my beloved son Benjamin Davis. I appoint William John Jones, Senr. and John Davis my executor Dated 2 Sept. 1796. Wit: Gibson Jarrell, Simeon Jarrell, Elijah Jarrell. Signed: Benjamin Davis. Recorded th 24 July 1794??

DAVIS, HENRY H. Apt. 2 File 120. Probate Judge Office. Green-ville, S. C. Will dated 9 Oct. 1839. Probated 4 Nov. 1839. Wife Evelina W. Davis. Exor. Father-in-law William Thruston. Wit: Je-se Hammett, Polly Davis, Henry Davis.

DAVIS, JESSE & ZELPHA Pack 9. Clerk of Court Office. Anderson, S. C. We, Jesse Davis and Zilpha Davis in consideration of $362.80 to us paid by George Tippen all of Pendleton Dist. have granted, bargained, sold and release a tract of land containing 134 acres, lying on a branch of Beaver Creek. being part of a tract granted to Mark

Davis, Jesse & Zelpha - Continued. Bird the 7 Nov. 1791. Dated
13 Jan. 1836. Wit: George Stevenson, James Stevenson. Signed:
Jesse Davis and Zilpah X Davis. Also with this deed. Anderson Dist.
"Know all men by these presents that we Ephraim Cannon and Mary Cannon
have recey a certain tract of land which we have soaled to George
Tippen and we take it for all our part of Jesse Davis and Zelpah
Davis's land now and hear after this they 30 Jan. 1836. Wit:
James Stevenson, George Stevenson. Signed: Em. Cannon and Mary X
Cannon."

DAVIS, JOHN Pack 428. Clerk of Court Office. Abbeville, S. C.
I John Davis of Abbeville Dist. being of sound and disposing mind and
memory. I desire my just debts and funeral expenses be paid. I give
to my wife Ursla Davis the whole of my estate both real and personal
during her life time or widowhood. At death or marriage of my wife, I
devise all my property both real and personal to be sold, and a division be made between my sons and dtrs. and my granddaughter Lucinda
Tucker, and each accounting by bringing into hotch pot the advancement
made by me, to them, so each child may be equal. The share of my granddaughter Lucinda Tucker I bequeath $627 in trust, held by Edward Davis,
John Davis and Winston H. Davis for said Lucinda for and during her
life. The share of my dtr. Lucy Hadden, the wife of Wilson Hadden (the
same amount to same trustees). My dtr. Mandeline, the wife of Elias
Kay nee the wife of Theodore Baker, by whom she had two chn. to wit.
John T. Baker and Theodore Baker minors now living. I desire that if
my dtr. Mandeline should die she share be divided into two equal shares,
one share to the above named chn. The other half to any chn. be her
present Husband Elias Kay. The advancement to each child which are to
brought into hotch pot and accounted for, will be found in a book kept
by myself and in my own handwriting. I appoint Edward Davis and John
Davis my sons executors. Dated 6 Sept. 1853. Wit: Elias Earle,
V. D. Fant, P. S. Vandiver. Signed: John Davis. In Equity. To the
Honr. the Chancellors: Your oratrix Lucinda Tate wife of Wm. M. Tate
by her next friend William Clinkscales, that about five years ago John
Davis departed this life leaving both real and personal property.
Your oratrix is the grand daughter of said John Davis and in right of
her mother Pursulla or Permella Tucker decd. That she is entitled to
the sum of about $1,080.00. and further states that Edward Davis
executor of John Davis will is about to remove to the State of Florida
and she is about to remove from this State. Other heirs are: Emma
Powers wife of Jesse Powers in Florida, Lizzy Davis also in Florida but
a minor, Wilson Hadden in Florida, Sarah Williams wife of Rogers
Williams, Lycena Deal and husband Shadrack Deal and Eliza the wife of
Milton Deal were also heirs. Filed 7 Jan. 1868.

DAVIS, JONATHAN No ref. Clerk of Court Office. Anderson, S.C.
I Jonathan Davis of Pendleton Dist. in consideration of $80.00 paid to
me in hand by John Dickson of same dist. have granted, sold, bargained,
and released all that tract of land containing 160 acres, lying on
East side of six Mile Creek waters of Keowee River. Adj. lands of John
and Edward Burrows, Perkins line, Grants line, Swifts line. This being
the plantation where Edward Burrows formerly lived on the Keowee Road.
Being part of a tract originally granted to John Burrows. Dated 3
Sept. 1816. Wit: Thos. Garvin, John Brownlow. Signed: Jonathan
Davis. Recorded on the 6 Jan. 1817 and proved on oath of Thomas Garvin
before John T. Lewis Clerk of Court.

DAVIS, NANCY Box 25 Pack 580. Probate Judge Office. Abbeville,
S. C. Admr. bond, we Robert Davis, Moses Davis, William H. Caldwell
and John Baskin are bound to Moses Taggart, Ord. in the sum of $8,000.
Dated 18 Sept. 1823. Cit. pub. at Rockey River Church, 7 Sept. 1823.
Inventory made 1 Oct. 1823 by Wm. Buford, Saml. Scott, John Ellington.
Sale held 15 Oct. 1823. Buyers: Robert Davis, Moses Davis, Jane
Davis, Saml. Scott, Eliza Davis, Sarah Davis, James Davis, John C.
Harris, Arch. Scott Sr., Wm. Wauldgridge, G Cornet, R. Boyd.

DAVIS, R. M. Pack 413. Clerk of Court Office. Abbeville, S. C.
I, R. M. Davis, of Abbeville Dist. being of sound mind and memory. I
give to my wife Catharine Jane Davis in fee simple as follows: My

Davis, R. M. - Continued. negroes, Aron, Rose, George, Marta, Little Joe, Leah and Ted. The homestead where I now live, including the following tracts, the Casper tract, the Degernet Tract, Kenedy tract, and the Harris tract. The whole consisting of about 640 acres. Less the tan yard of about 2 1/2 acres excepted. My carriage and horses Mary, Henry and Tom and harness, likewise one buggy and road wagon, as many cattle, hogs, sheep as my executor think proper. With corn, wheat, flour for one year. I give my wife $500 in cash. I give my wife all my household and kitchen furniture as she may need, giving the dtrs. as they marry what they may need. After my wife portion of slaves are taken, I desire my executors to lot into five lots, one for each child, I have viz: Bannister Andrew, Matilda Mildridge, Mary Elizabeth, Hester Ann, Susan Louisa, each child shall draw its lot. Any other property not disposed of shall be sold and pay my just debts. (The last part of the will not in notes.)

DAVIS, REBECCA Pack 439 #17. Clerk of Court Office. Pickens, S. C. Be it remembered that on the 1 Oct. 1838 William Gilbert and Amos Gilbert both of this Dist. came before me Jesse S. McGee, J.P. and acknowledge themselves to owe the State the sum of $257.16 to be levyed on their goods and chattles, lands and tenements to the use of the poor etc. The condition of the above bond, whereas William Gilbert upon due examination and proof hath been adjudged to be the father of a male bastard child of which Rebecca Davis of said Dist. at the house of said William Gilbert was lately delivered. Now the said William Gilbert shall pay or cause to be paid on the first day of May next the sum of $21.43 and a like sum on the same day every year thereafter until the said child shall arrive at the age of twelve years.

DAVIS, ROBERT Box 26 Pack 586. Probate Judge Office. Abbeville, S. C. Bond only, we Martha Davis, Isreal Davis, Ezekial Calhoun and Robert Davis are bound unto Andrew Hamilton, Ord. in the sum of $10,000. Dated 7 Oct. 1801. Signed: Martha X Davis, Isreal Davis, Ezekiel Calhoun, Robert Davis.

DAVIS, WILLIAM Book A Page 18. Clerk of Court Office. Abbeville, S. C. A citizen grant of 200 acres lying on Great Rockey Creek a branch of Savannah River, surveyed by David Hopkins D.S. on the 26 May 1784. Recorded this 5 June 1784. Robert Anderson, C.L.

DAVIS, ZERAH Apt. 2 File 119. Probate Judge Office. Greenville, S. C. I Zerah Davis of Greenville Dist. being weak in body but of sound mind and memory. I desire that Jesse Hammett and his wife Nancy shall take my chn. Mary E. Davis, Susan E. Davis, and William H. Davis, raise them and to give them a good common education and have management of them until full age. It is my desire that my negro woman Dolly go with my three chn. to aid and assist in raising and attending them, when my chn. come of full age, my negro Dolly with her increase be equally divided between the three chn. My negro Dicy and her increase to be sold if advisable by my executors, before the chn. become of full age, if not sold to be divided between them. If said Dicy is sold then my negro man Moses to be sold also, if not sold they all to be hired out together. My negro man Notty and Mary with her four chn. named Ben, Bob, Frank, and Reuben to be sold. I give to each of my chn. one bedstead bed and furniture. I give to my brother H. H. Davis, my wearing apparel. The rest of my estate of every nature and kind be sold on one and two years credit and the money arising from sale be put on interest after my debts are paid, said money to be divided between the chn. when of age. I appoint my brother Henry H. Davis, and William Thruston executors. Dated 9 Feb. 1838. Wit: Nathan Davis, William Wheeler. Signed: Zerah Davis. Probated 6 Mar. 1838. Est. appraised the 29 March 1838 by Thomas Roe, Martin Hunt, and James Farr. Sale held on 29 March 1838, Buyers: John Benson, Thomas Roe, R. Marston, James West, John Shcokley, Henry Davis, Wm. Wheeler, Leroy Green, Moses Fenley, James Farr, Wm. Thurston, Green Bradley, Hiram Bradley, Mary Benson, George Evans, Silas Benson, James Young, Jeremiah Phillips, Henry Mosley, Jessey Hammett, Ted Bradley, Wm. Shelton, Esly Hunt, Tomy Keeler, John Harris, D. Henning, T. Ridings, Peter Hawkins, Street Thurston, A. Bridges, Hamilton Young, Wm. West, Andrew Bridges,

Davis, Zerah - Continued. Heugh Bradley, John Ward, Wm. Gibson, Aaron Kemp, Thomas Springfield, Tom Rector, Daniel Wheaton, Moses Fenley, Robert Cox, E. S. Irvin, Williford Jonson, Tyre Ridings, Dr. Wm. Robinson, Hewlett Hunt. In the 1841 account to the Ordinary, Wm. Thurston was executor and in the 1842 account Jesse Foster was gdn. for a portion of the chn.

DACUS, NATHANIEL SENR. Apt. 2 File 140. Probate Judge Office. Greenville, S. C. I Nathaniel Dacus Senr. of Greenville Dist. being in a low state of health, but of sound mind and memory. I will unto my loving wife Elizabeth Dacus during her natural life my plantation whereon I now live, also the following negroes, Nappy, Magor, Ritter, Liza, and her two chn. Silvia and Merida. Also enough feed for the year, my sorrel mare called Shiney and the yellow mare, two cows and calves as she may choose. With household and kitchen furniture, at her death to be sold and equally divided between all my children. I will to my son John A. Dacus my young sorrel horse to be delivered at my death. The remainder of my real and personal property to be sold and my just debts paid, and the balance equally divided between all my chn. (No extr. named). Dated 15 Nov. 1831. Andrew McCrary, Elizabeth Austin, Wm. L. M. Austin. Signed: Nathaniel X Dacus. Probated 30 March 1835.

DACUS, WILLIAM Apt. 2 File 141. Probate Judge Office. Greenville, S. C. I William Dacus Senr. of Greenville Dist. being of sound mind and memory, but advanced in age, and feeble health. I give to my grand children, the chn. of my decd. son Pascal Dacus the following negroes, Lancaster, Creecy, Andrew, Mary, Sarah, Peggy, Isham, Tom, Caroline, Little Mary, Frances, and Elias to be euqally divided between them after my death. I give to my dtr. Polly Cureton the following negroes, Cloe, Ritter, Jack, Randal, Daniel, Gilbert, Clarissa, Eliza, Ben, Hammett, Martha and John to her and her heirs at my death. I give to my grand son William Dacus, Junr. the whole of my household and kitchen furniture in fee simple at my death. I give to each of my grand sons a horse, and should there be any other left after they are all supplied. They are to be equally divided amongst my grandchn. I give to my grand chn. share and share alike the whole of my stock, after my death, meaning by this clause cattle, hogs, sheep, etc. If I live until my present crop is planted, the plantation to remain as is till crop is gathered, then the whole crop I give to my grand son William Dacus Junr. I will my farming utensils may be equally divided at my death between my dtr. Polly Cureton and the chn. of my late son Pascal Dacus. I appoint my son in law John Cureton executor. Dated 15 Feb. 1839. Wit: Tandy Walker, Wm. T. Dacus, Isaac West. Signed: William Dacus. Probated 15 July 1839.

DANIEL, WILLIAM AND NANCY Deed Book A, Page 30. Clerk of Court Office. Elberton, Ga. This indenture made 14 Jan. 1791 between William and Nancy Daniel and Nathan Childs all of Elbert Co., Ga. In consideration of £300 sterling, paid by said Nathan Childs have bargained, sold and release a tract of land on the South side of Beaverdam Creek, containing 550 acres. Adj. land of Wiley Davis, Walker Richardson, Robert Middleton, Thomas Burton, Walter Nunnelee, Womack Blankingship and James Madkin. Wit: John Patterson, William Arnold, Reuben Allen. Signed: William Daniel and Nancy X Daniel. Proven 24 Jan. 1791 by William and Nancy Daniel before Reuben Allen, J.P. Reg. 17 Aug. 1791.

DARBY, ZADOCK Case 16 File 670. Probate Judge Office. York, S. C. I Zadock Darby of York Dist. being in perfect health, of sound and disposing mind and memory. I give to my wife Mary Darby one half of the plantation whereon I now live, and at her death to my grand son Zadock D. Smith to have and hold forever, also to my wife my negro man Simon and his wife Fanny and their two chn. Garland and Sarah and my negro boy Jim. Also including horses, cattle, hogs, sheep and household and kitchen furniture and the crop on my farm. My wife to pay all debts. I will to my dtrs. Delilah Darby alias Delilah Gingles the plantation whereon she now lives during her life time and at her death to be equally divided between her children. Two hundred dollars

Darby, Zadock - Continued. from the estate to be placed in the hands of my executors and by them put intrust--the interest to be paid annually to said Delilah Gingles. I give unto my dtr. Jane Darby alias Jane Smith the other half of the plantation I now live on during her life time and at her death to my grand son Zadock Smith to have and hold forever. Also to my dtr. Jane Smith my negroes Frederick, Charity, and her youngest child not yet named and John, Hamilton. I appoint my beloved wife Mary Darby, William Campbell of York Co., S.C. and Isaac Price of Mecklinburg Co., N.C. My executors. Dated 27 July 1824. Wit: David Johnson, John Glen, Franklin Glen. Signed: Zadock Darby. Probated 6 Nov. 1824. Recorded in will book G page 150.

DARRACH, HUGH Apt. 2 File 138. Probate Judge Office. Greenville, S. C. I Hugh Darrach of Greenville, S. C. being in tolerable state of health but of perfect mind and memory, etc. I give to my son David Darrach one dollar and one hand saw. I give to my dtr. Rosey Morrow one dollars. I give to my dtr. Nancy Morrow one dollar. I give to my dtr. Jinny Hanady one dollar. I give to my two dtrs. Ester and Peggy all my plantation and lands together with all stock and property of every kind whatsoever. I appoint Samuel Pedan and David Pedan executors. Dated 5 March 1809. Wit: David Peden, Anthony Savage, Bennett Parish. Signed: Hugh Darrach. Probated 3 June 1811.

DART, THOMAS LYNCH No ref. Probate Judge Office. Anderson, S.C. I Thomas Lynch Dart of Anderson Dist. being of sound and disposing mind and memory and understanding. First I will my just debts be paid. I give to my beloved wife Mary Louisa Dart and her chn. viz: Isaac Mott, Elizabeth Martin, Arabella Ann Rend, Mary Louisa, George Ann, Henrietta, and Catharine Barnwell Dart, all my estate both real and personal, viz: a negro named Richard, a negro named Cora and her chn. viz: Amos, Fanny, Ben, Lucinda, and Franklin and the issue of the females. I give to my wife Mary Louisa and the above named chn. my tract of land lying on Garvens Creek in Adnerson Dist. with all stock, cattle, horses, tools, household and kitchen furniture. I give to my son Isaac Mott Dart my gold watch and trinkets belonging thereto, also my wearing apparerel. I appoint my wife Mary Louisa Dart executrix and C. C. Pinckney and C. L. Gailliard executors. Dated 2 May 1835. Wit: Thomas L. Reese, Wm. T. Potter, Wm. Sanders. Signed: Thomas L. Dart. Proved on oath of Thomas L. Reese before John Harris, Ord. A.D. on the 26 June 1835.

DAUGHERTY, WILLIAM Apt. 2 File 122. Probate Judge Office. Greenville, S. C. Will dated Aug. 1839. Probated 29 Oct. 1839. Sons William and Benjamin Daugherty Exors. Wife Lucy Daugherty, Moses McCrary. Wit: William Goldsmith, Joel League Senr., William Howard.

DAVIDSON, JOHN Pack 7. Clerk of Court Office. Anderson, S. C. I John Davidson of Pendleton Dist. Where as I am indebted unto Elijah Davidson in the sum of $1500.00 of lawfull money. Said Elijah Davidson and Frederic Davidson stand jointly and severaly engaged for me in several bonds or obligations for several sum of money. To better satisfaction and payment of said sum have granted, sold, bargain all manner of goods, chattles, debts, and monies, as well as real and personal property, etc. Dated 23 Oct. 1820. Wit: John ___, William Knox. Signed: John Davidson. Reg. on oath of John ___, before Joseph Grisham N.P. and J.Q. on the 28 March 1821.

DAVIDSON, WILLIAM Will Book 1740-1747. Page 255. Probate Judge Office. Charleston, S.C. I William Davidson of Dorchester in Berkley County, S. C. a Practitioner in Physick [sic] being in good health and in my right mind, etc. I give to my brothers George, John and Robert Davidson and my sister Christian the sum of ten pounds sterling each as a legacy and to my loving mother the sum of fifteen pounds sterling. I leave to my brother Alexander Davidson all my clothes, books, papers. All other worldly goods I give to my brothers James and Alexander. I appoint James Michie Esq. and Capt. John McKenzie merchant both of Charleston as executors. Dated 12 March 1744. Wit: Ch. Shepheard, Murry, Robert Lammond. Signed: Will Davidson. Proved before John Glen, Esq. 21 Oct. 1745 also same time qualified John McKenzie, James Michie executors. Recorded 22 Oct. 1745.

DAWSON, JOSEPH #2. Clerk of Court Office. Pickens, S. C.
The Court of Common Pleas and general sessions. To the Honr. Edward
Frost. The Petition of Samuel Baker Dawson age 32 yrs. occupation a
farmer, sheweth that he was born in Maidstone Kent England. He arrived
in the United States to wit. Charleston, S. C. on the 2 Feb. 1846. That
on the 4 April 1848 he before the Clerk of said Court declared on oath
his intention to become a citizen of the U.S. We the subscribers do
hereby certify that we have known Samuel Baker Dawson for five years,
etc. etc. W. G. Caradine, O. H. P. Fant, E. E. Alexander, P. Alexander,
Allen R. Elliott, James Lawrence, James Young, T. C. McGee.

DAWSON, JOSEPH #L Label 1. Clerk of Court Office. Pickens,
S. C. The Court of General Sessions and Common Pleas. I W. L. Keith
Clerk of the Court with Honr. Edward Frost one of the law Judges of
the State presiding. That on __ day of Nov. 1851 Joseph Dawson a
native of Lynne Regis Dorselshire England by occupation a farmer, made
application to be made a citizen of the United States, he having com-
piled with all the conditions and requirements of the acts of congress
in such cases. Dawson was 55 yrs. old.

DAY, BENJAMIN Real Estate Book A, Page 80. Probate Judge Office.
Pickens, S. C. The undersign, Jane E. Day widow of Benjamin Day, Jr.
decd. petition your Court to have the real estate of said decd. consisting of 160 acres on the waters of Goldens Creek, adj. land of John
Ariall, William Odell, Elihu Griffin sold or divided for which I will
ever pray. Dated 28 Nov. 1846. Jane E. Day had one child a minor
Jacob L. Day, with John Gearin gdn. ad litem.

DAY, MANSFIELD Box 26 Pack 583. Probate Judge Office. Abbeville,
S. C. Admr. bond made by Willis Holms, Thomas Goodman and Joseph
Talbert who are bound unto Moses Taggart, Ord. in the sum of $5,000.
Dated 5 Jan. 1824. Est. appraises 24 Jan. 1824 by Garland Chiles,
Joseph Talbert, Robert Cheatham. Cit. pub. at Mount Garrison Meeting
in Cambridge (Ninety Six), S. C. Buyers at sale John R. Day, Jacob
Cauly, Leroy Day, Wm. Hill, Wm. Webb, James Criswell, John D. Williams,
Littleton Myrick, Willis Holloway.

DEAN, SAMUEL Pack 173. Probate Judge Office. Anderson, S. C.
I Samuel Dean of Pendleton Dist. being weak in body of of sound and
disposing mind and memory. I give to my beloved wife Gwenna Dean one
third part of my real and personal estate during her natural life, and
at her decease to return to my heirs, she to have the disposing of one
negro out of her third. I give to my sons Aaron Dean and Moses Dean
all my tract of land containing 130 acres, whereon Moses Dean now lives.
The rest of my estate to be divided between my heirs as follows, Thomas
Dean, Miriam McGregor, Joseph Dean, Samuel Dean, Mary Millhouse, and
the heirs of my son John Dean decd. as follows Obediah Dean, Elizabeth,
Matason, Samuel, Rhoda and Joseph these six chn. to receive their
fathers legacy, and my son Richard and Griffith and Moses whereas I
sold property to Joseph Dean and now hold note of $600 payable to the
heirs of my son John. I will that said note stand. I appoint my sons
Thomas and Griffith Dean as my executors. Dated 22 May 1826. Wit:
W. McGregor, Aaron Dean, Elizabeth T. Dean. Signed: Samuel Dean.
"I decline the execution of the will and protest against the probate
of the same, because all the witnesses are legatees and interested.
This 25 Sept. 1826." Signed: Samuel Dean. "On examination of Capt.
William McGregor one of the witnesses upon being sworn declares that
all the witnesses to the within will are interested and this will is
disallowed. Dated: 25 Sept. 1826." Signed: John Harris, P.P.D.

DEBRUHL, STEPHEN Pack 368 Clerk of Court Office. Abbeville,
S. C. In Equity: To the chancellors of the State. Your oratrix Susan
E. DeBruhl the widow of Stephen DeBruhl late of this Dist. Your
oratrix father James Cammer late of Richland Dist. during his lifetime
made a deed of gift bearing date 3 Feb. 1842. For natural love did
grant, bargain, sell and release unto his daughter Susan E. DeBruhl a
house and lot in the town of Columbia, containing one forth of an acres,
bounded by land of G. M. Thomson, M. Shelton, on the East and the
Presbyterian Church lot on the West and by Marion St. To have and hold

DeBruhl, Stephen - Continued. said lot during her natural life, and at her death to her children forever, share and share alike. Your oratrix sheweth that her husband Stephen DeBruhl departed this life in Nov. 1855, intestate leaving your oratrix and four chn. to wit: Susan C. DeBruhl, age over twenty one, Stephen C. DeBruhl, age over twenty one, Marion F. DeBruhl, age about ten years, Marshall P. DeBruhl, age about six yrs. As defendants to the bill of complaint. Having only a small estate of real and personal, which has been sold according to law. That since her husband death, she has rented the house and lot, that she is willing for the house and lot to stand good for deed on lot in town of Abbeville, S. C. Filed: 15 March 1858.

DEETON, BURRELL Deed Book M, Page 447. Clerk of Court Office. Anderson, S. C. Pendleton Dist. I Moses Pickens in consideration of ₤20 to me paid by Burrell Deeton have granted, bargained, sold and released all that tract of land containing 105 acres first granted unto Moses Pickens, lying in Pendleton Dist. on waters of Coneross Creek. Dated 1 Jan. 1798. Wit: John Harper, Nicholas Clark. Signed: Moses Pickens. Proved on oath of John Harper before James Starritt, J.P. on the 9 Nov. 1805. Recorded 4 Dec. 1815.

DEETON, WILLIAM Deed Book M, Page 447. Clerk of Court Office. Anderson, S. C. Pendleton Dist. I William Watkins in consideration of ₤25 13 shillings and four pence to me paid by William Deeton have granted, sell, release all that plantation of land containing 100 acres being part of a tract of 231 acres, first granted to Moses Pickens. Now in possession of Wm. Deeton. Dated 4 Oct. 1799. Wit: John Harper and Elizabeth X Harper. Proved on oath of John Harper before James Starritt, J.P. on the 9 Nov. 1805. Recorded the 4 Dec. 1815.

DENCH, JOHN C. Pack 3. Clerk of Court Office. Anderson, S.C. (Basement). Pendleton Dist. To the Honorable the Court of Common Pleas and now sitting in Pendleton Dist. Courthouse March term 1817. The humble petition of John C. Dench, a native of Cambridge in the Kingdom of Great Britian, who arrived in the U.S. about the last day of Nov. 1807. That your petitioner is attached to the government, constitution and laws and is desirous of becoming a citizen of the same. He therefore prays that the Court to accept this as a notice. John C. Dench swear to support, preserve, protect and defend the constitution of the U.S. and renounce and abjure all allegiance to any power but the U.S. Dated 25 March 1817. We certify that we have known John C. Dench for fifteen years, and that he is of good moral man, etc. Signed: T. W. Symms, George Lewis, David Cherry, Samuel Cherry, A. Lawhon, and Joseph Grisham who have known him for eleven years. (another paper) Dench was 43 years old in 1820, and that he arrived in the city of Charleston, S. C. He took the allegiance of fidelity again on 29 Oct. 1823.. before John S. Lewis, Clerk of Court.

DEVALL, MICHAEL Pack 3202. Clerk of Court Office. Abbeville, S. C. In Equity: To the Honr. Hugh Rutledge, William James, Waddy Thompason, Theodaore Gaillard, Henry Williams Dessesure, Judge of the Court of Equity. Your oratrix Harriett Devall, late Harriet Brown widow of the third part, by her next friend and brother John Parson, of the first part, and Michael Devall of the second part, all of Abbeville Dist. That on or about 1 Nov. 1808 your oratrix intermarried with the said Michael Devall, that previous to her marriage a marriage settlement was made and executed by Michael Devall in favor of your oratrix. Witnesseth that for and in consideration of a marriage shortly intended to be had and solemnized between Michael Devall and Harriet Brown, and to this end that a competent maintenance may be said and provided for the said Harriet Brown in case the marriage shall take place. The said Michael Devall hath granted, bargained, sold into John Parson one half of the plantation whereon he now lives, containing now about 260 acres, lying on the South side of Long Cane Creek. With John Parson having the right to choose his half of said land. Negroes to be divided are: Molly, Billy and Catherine the chn. of said Molly, Pompey and Milley. All the household and kitchen furniture and half of the stock with the use of negro Charles until Catherine and Ann Devall shall become of

71

Devall, Michael - Continued.   age.   Yet nevertheless in full
trust and confidence that if the intended marriage shall be solomnized
that John Parson shall permit Michael Devall to continue to enjoy the
profits from said land, during the term of his natural life.   And at
his death said John Parson shall hold same in trust for the Harriett
Brown during her natural life.   And after her death John Parson shall
hold same in trust for her two chn. and their heirs forever (these chn.
not named).   But if Devall shall survive said Harriet Brown then the
said estate to be held immediately in trust for the said chn. and their
heirs forever.   Your oratrix sheweth unto your Honors that in a very
few weeks after the marriage to Michael Devall, his two sons Samuel
and Jacob Devall appeared highly dissatisfied with the marriage settlement above recited.   They did wantonly and cruelly interfere between
your oratrix and said Michael Devall and used every means in their power
to urge and instigate the Michael to ill treat, abuse and slander your
oratrix.   The said Michael Devall directed his son Jacob M. Devall to
compel your oratrix to forsake and leave his home, and that Jacob being
thus directed by his father to turn your oratrix out of doors, forbid
her to enter the house at the resique of her life, presenting at same
time to her breast a loaded pistol and bitterly swearing that it was
his intention to kill her if she entered the house.   Said Michael
Devall on 13 Dec. 1808 forwarn all persons from trading with his wife,
this being done by written notice.   Filed 10 March 1809.   In another
case in Equity, Uel Hill Vs. Michael Devall dated 20 March 1806.   One
of Devall son had married a dtr. of Uel Hill and said Hill gave to his
dtr. a negro named Charles to be her property during her natural life
and at her death to be the property of her two chn. Hill's dtr. name
was Elizabeth Devall nee Hill.   Her two chn. were Anna Devall and
Catharine Devall.   Elizabeth was the name of Michael Devall first wife

DEVENPORT, JOSEPH Apt. 2 File 127.   Probate Judge Office.   Green-
ville, S. C.   Will dated 11 April 1804.   Probated 4 March 1805.   Wife
Margaret Devenport.   Chn. James Devenport, Robert Devenport, John
Devenport, Joseph Devenport, Sarah Devenport, Francis Devenport, Levina
Devenport, Buesy Devenport, Polly Devenport.   "Will that my stud
horse be conveyed to Capt. John Foyd of Newberry Dist."   Exors, wife
Margaret Devenport, Hudson Berry.   Wit: Jesse Kirby, William Devenport,
Sarah Sawer.

DICKINSON, JOSEPH B.   Box 26 Pack 593.   Probate Judge Office.
Abbeville, S. C.   Admr. bond.   We Elizabeth C. Dickinson, Billups
Gayle and James Spann who are bound unto Talo. Livingston, Ord. in the
sum of $10,000.   Dated 1 March 1816.   Inventory made 4 April 1816 by
Thomas M. Devenport, John McKellar, Walter Chiles.   Sale held 6 April
1816.   Buyers, Elizabeth C. Dickinson, J. M. White, John Frank,
Billuops Gayle, Wm. Swift, John McKellar Junr., D. Cunningham, J. C.
Lewis, Thos. Cobb, Joseph Wardlaw, Thos. M. Devenport, John Ganes,
Joseph Cason, Robert Chatham, Isaac Heard Junr., Josiah Cason, Jonathan
Swift, Edmund Stallsworth, Benjamin Hatter, A. Pool, John Stott,
Willis Mayson, William Ware, David Cunningham.

DICKEY, HENRY Pack 4 (Basement).   Clerk of Court Office.   Anderson, S. C.   To the Honourable the Court of General Sessions of the pleas
and now setting at Pendleton Court House, October Term 1820.   The
humble petition of Henry Dickey a native of Antrim County in Ireland in
the Kingdom of Great Britain who arrived in the U.S. on the 18 Jan.
1805.   A farmer, and is 28 yrs. of age.   And tend to reside in the said
Dist.   That your petitioner is attached to the government, constitution and laws is desirous of becoming a citizen of the same.   He
therefore prays the Court to accept this as a notice.   Dated 25 Oct.
1820.   Signed: Henry Dickey.

DICKSON, SAMUEL H.   Pack 9.   Clerk of Court Office.   Anderson,
S. C.   This indenture made 31 Jan. 1794 between Samuel H. Dickson
and Joseph Smith both of Pendleton Dist.   In consideration of five
shillings paid by said Joseph Smith, have bargained, sold and released
a tract of land containing 331 acres in said Dist. lying on 12 Mile
River, waters of Savannah River.   With all houses, barnes, orchards,
etc.   (This is a lease and release).   Wit: Hugh Dickson, James

Dickson, Samuel H. - Continued. Dickson, Samuel Clowney. Signed: Saml. H. Dickson. Proved on oath of Hugh Dickson before Michael Dickson, J.Q. on the 7 Aug. 1799.

DILBONE, HENRY Box 26 Pack 595. Probate Judge Office. Abbeville, S. C. Admr. bond. We John Hearst, Joseph Hearst and William Hearst are bound unto Talo. Livingston, Ord. in the sum of $2,000. Dated 1 Oct. 1817. Letter of admr. granted to John Hearst on the 28 Sept. 1817. Inventory made 17 Oct. 1817 by Philip Stiefel, John Holloway, Harmon P. Cosper, Peter X Rampy. Sale held 18 Oct. 1817. Buyers, Peter Rampy, Joseph Hearst, John Hearst, Saml. Perrin, Larkin Cason, Philip Stiefhell, Wm. R. Nelson, Harmon P. Cosper, Anny Clem, Onan Elison, David Rush, Nicholas Rampy, David Rush, Mary Hanie, Mary Hanie, John Stiephel, James Tutt, John Laner, Jacob Langly, Nicholas Rampy, Harmon P. Cosper, Henry Huffman, Margaret P. Sullivan, Samuel Gauliher, Stephen Mantzs, Lott Ethridge, Mrs. Clark, Chemp Wilborn, John Dorris, David Hamilton, Wm. Goodman, Richard Smyth, Henry Timerman, John Dilbone, Anderson Wilborn, Joseph Thornton, Elizabeth Dorris, Burgis Pitman, Thomas Chiles, Ritchard Welborn, James Russell, Julis Dean, Syth Robison, Robert Perrin, Joseph Rabourn, Wm. Thomas, Wm. R. Nelson, Henry Hose, Ruben Pierce, Samuel Perrin, John Adams, Jessey Ragin, Dr. Saml. Pressly, Thomas Downey, James McClain, John Wilson, Kincheon Adcason[?], James Lishman. Notes due the est. John Dilbone, Samuel Moushett, Annis Clem and Jonathan Adamson.

DILL, JOHN Apt. 2 File 135. Probate Judge Office. Greenville, S. C. I John Dill of Greenville Dist. being old and frail in body but of a perfect mind and memory, etc. I give to my loving granddaughter Peggy Randolf one feather bed and furniture and a one year old heifer. I give to my well beloved wife Mary Ann Dill all the blance of my estate at her disposal while a widow and at her death or marriage to be equally divided among all my children. I appoint my son Renuls Dills and George Mitch executors. Dated 7 March 1807. Wit: Reubin Barrett, David Barrett. Signed: John X Dill. Probated 30 Sept. 1809.

DILL, STEPHEN Apt. 2 File 123. Probate Judge Office. Greenville, S. C. I Stephen Dill of Greenville Dist. being very sick and weak but of perfect senses and memory. I bequeath unto my wife Polly Dill my tract of land containing 150 acres during her lifetime and I bequeath unto her all my ready money, also stock hogs, cattle, mare sheep, and two feather beds with clothing. Also I bequeath unto her a negro boy named Mops her lifetime and my negro woman named Mint her lifetime and at her decease she is to live with them that treat her best. I bequeath unto my son Charles one hundred dollars out of the est. I bequeath unto my son Ezeas $125 from my est. I will that my son Jefferson to have $100 from my est. I will that my dtr. Frankey Henson $100 out of my est. I will to my dtr. Polly Henson $100 out of my est. After the above named three sons and two dtr. the amount that they to be equal with the rest. I bequeath unto my son George one negro boy named Rubin, also one clay bank colt. I bequeath unto my son Benjamin F. Dill one negro named Zed, also one horse colt. The two above named sons have already received their part or portion of my estate and all rest of my property to be divided between the rest of my chn. I appoint my wife Polly Dill and my son Elvah Dill my executrix and executor. Dated 18 Feb. 1839. Wit: Bumel I. Stewart, T. Jefferson Dill, B. F. Dill. Signed: Stephen X Dill.

DIXON, STARLING Box 26 Pack 581. Probate Judge Office. Abbeville, S. C. Admr. bond, We William Pettigrew, James N. Dickson and Oswell Houston are bound to Moses Taggart, Ord. in the sum of $3,000. Dated 12 Jan. 1827. Cit. pub. at Lebanon Church 7 Jan. 1827. Inventory made 31 Jan. 1827 by G. M. Morrow, James Morrow, John Cheves. Sale held 1 Feb. 1827. Buyers: Hannah Dixon, Ellis Dixon, Maryann Dixon, O. Houston, James Dixon, Nathl. Cameron, Alexr. Foster, John McFarland, James Morrow, James Alexander, John McDonald.

DOBBS, JESSE Box 25 Pack 579. Probate Judge Office. Abbeville, S. C. I Jesse Dobbs of Abbeville Dist. being very sick and weak in body, but of perfect mind and memory. First I give to Elizabeth my

Dobbs, Jesse - Continued. beloved wife my real estate and Silvey and Jim Parmer and little Jim and Easter and all my goods and chattles till my son Elijah come to the age of twenty one years of age. Harray to be hired out to the highest bidder till Elijah come of age, the money to be equally divided amongest my chn. as they come of age or marry. I appoint my wife Elizabeth executrix. Dated 2 Nov. 1819. Wit: Louisa Collier, Edward W. Collier, Moses Tullis. Signed: Jess Dobbs. Some items were sold on 4 Dec. 1819. Another sale on 6 Feb. 1834. Named E. H. Dobbs, Polly Dobbs, E. Dobbs, Saml. Wideman, Mary Dobbs, Susan Dobbs.

DOBBS, JOHN SENR. Book C. Clerk of Court Office. Elberton, Ga. This indenture made 1 Feb. 1794 between John Dobbs, Senr. and Jacob Skelton both of Elbert Co., Ga. In consideration of the sum of Ł25 sterling, hath bargain, sold and confirmed unto Jacob Skelton a tract of land lying on water of Cedar Creek, originally granted to Gabrill Smith, containing 75 acres. Wit: William W. Skelton, Moses Haynes, J.P. Signed: John X Dobb. Reg. 14 May 1795.

DONALD, JANE Box 131 Pack 1793. Probate Judge Office. Abbeville, S. C. I Jane Donald of Abbeville Dist. being of sound mind, memory and understanding but some what advanced in age, etc. I will that all my just debts be paid. I will that my negro Antony and his wife Dicy to have the priviledge of choosing whom they desire to live with and serve, and whom they choose their value to be divided among my heirs that is Rachel Teague, decd. heirs of her body, the heirs of James Atkins, decd. John Adams, Abram Liles, David Atkins, Francis Atkins, Joseph Atkins, Thomas Atkins and Teresa Lipford and the remainder of my property I allow to be sold, except the household furniture, I will to my two dtrs. Jane Lite and Teresa Lipford. The rest to be sold and pay my debts and funeral expenses. I appoint my son Joseph Atkins my executor. Dated 14 Sept. 1853. Wit: Lewis Smith, Bartw. Jordon, Thomas Jordon. Signed: Jane X Donald. To William Hill Esq. Ordinary of Abbeville Dist. The petition of Francis Atkins sheweth that Mrs. Jane Donald departed this life leaving a will and appointed her son Joseph Atkins as her executor. The said Joseph Atkins lives in the State of Georgia and it will be very inconvenient for him arising from the distance from his home. He thought proper to relinquish his right to administer. Now your petitioner prays that admr. with the will annexed of the est. be granted to him, etc. etc. Dated 9 Jan. 1854. Signed: Francis Atkins. He was made admr. A power of attorney from Thomas Atkins of Rush Co., Ind. dated 13 June 1856 to Mr. W. C. Davis of Abbeville Court House, his true and lawful attorney to receive and receipt for same. Benton County, Ala. Sept. 25, 1856. "Recd. of W. C. Davis a check on Charleston for $328.28 being the amount due my-self, H. B. Johnson and wife, O. D. Whiteside and wife, Elijah Teague and Robert J. Teague from the personal estate of Jane Donald lately decd. of Abbeville Dist. The said check is drawn payable to W. C. Davis but endorsed by him and made payable to the undersigned, for the benefit after behalf of myself and other brothers and sisters. Signed: Abner A. Teague." In another paper H. R. Johnston wife name is Luranah Johnston. O. D. Whiteside wife name is Sarah J. Whiteside.

DONALD, JOHN Box 26 Pack 603. Probate Judge Office. Abbeville Dist. We John A. Donald, Joel Lippford and Duey Lippford who are bound unto Moses Taggart, Ord. in the sum of $6,000. Dated 17 June 1831. Inventory made 6 Dec. 1831 by West Donald, Charles Sprulle, Deuy E. Lippford, Sale buyers: John A. Donald, James A. Gray, Elisha Lyon, Hugh McCormick, Robert D. Gray, West Donald, Alexander Donald, Wm. Reynolds, John Crisswell, A. Thompson, A. McGill. Expend 4 Feb. 1833. Cash paid Jane Donald $25.00.

DONALDSON, MATHEW Box 27 Pack 634. Probate Judge Office. Abbeville, S. C. I Mathew Donaldson of Abbeville Dist., S. C. a wheel wright, being weak in body but of sound mind and memory. I will that my just debts be paid out of the money due me. I give to my wife Jennet during her natural life all my estate both real and personal for her use and benefit. At the death of my wife, I will and desire my negro Jean and her two chn. Derry and Charlotte should be free. Also

74

Donaldson, Mathew - Continued. after the death of my wife my estate both real and personal be divided into two equal parts. One part I give to my wife to will or dispose of as she may wish. One half of the other half to be equally divided between my neice Jean Campbell wife of Robert Campbell and the other half to my nephew Andrew Cowan and Mathew Cowan all living in the Kingdome of Ireland. I will to my wife all the money which may be collected from the debts due me, after paying my debts. No more of the will in the notes.

DOUGLASS, JOHN Box 26 Pack 585. Probate Judge Office. Abbeville, S. C. Admr. bond, We Sarah Douglass, Jno. Wardlaw and Andrew McAllister are bound to Abbeville Court in the sum of ₺1000. Dated 6 April 1790. Inventory made 8 May 1790 by Jas. Wardlaw, John Irwin, Samuel X Youngblood. Sale held 5 July 1790, Buyers: Sarah Douglass, Joseph Bowin, Nancy Duncan, James Campbell, John Calhoun, John Logan, Sr., David Thomas, Wm. Heard Sr., David Steel, Andrew McAllister, Wm. Duncan, Wm. Brown, Jr., Nancy Campbell, Wm. Chambers.

DOUGLASS, WILLIAM Box 30 Pack 667. Probate Judge Office. Abbeville, S. C. Inventory made 11 Dec. 1841 by James L. Partlow, Joseph Wardlaw, Wm. Cochran, and John R. Tarrant. Sale held 14 Dec. 1841 buyers: James Douglass, Mary Douglass, John R. Tarrant, James Anderson, Augustus Griffin, John Douglass, James Pert, James Partlow, A. Arnold, L. J. White, Charles Cunningham, James Waites, T. L. Coleman, Larkin Griffin, E. Anderson, James L. Mayson, Thomas J. Henderson, Francis Arnold, Hardy Clark, John Holland, Martin Hacket, Wm. Prater, Wm. A. Douglass, Lewis Busby. Paid 1 Feb. 1843 James Anderson $378.66. James Pert $411.00. James Douglass $397.36. John Douglass $231.71. Wm. A. Douglass $413.68. James L. Mayson $400.00. James Waites $400.00. Paid 27 March 1843 Mrs. Mary Douglass $659.59. Mrs. Nancy Wardlaw $400.00.

DOWNES, RICHARD JUNR. Vol. 14 Page 246. Probate Judge Office. Charleston, S. C. I Richard Downes being sick in body but of sound mind and memory. I will my just debts and funeral expenses be paid by my executors. I give devise unto my mother Joyce Downes of Bishop Castle in Shropshire in the Kingdom of England, all my real and personal estate I shall die within the Kingdom of Great Britain. I give devise unto my dear uncle Richard Downes of Charles Town (legacy not named) to hold to his heirs etc. I appoint my said uncle Richard Downes and my uncle Richard Thomas of Shropshire in the Kingdom of England my executors. Dated: 10 Jan. 1768. Wit: James Hunt, John Thompson, Joseph Oliver, Cato Ash, Evan Jonas, Andrew Slann. Signed: Richard Downes Junr. Proven before Governor in the Court of Ordinary, 22 May 1772.

DOWNEY, JOHN. No ref. given. Probate Judge Office. Abbeville, S. C. I John Downey being in usual health and of a sound and disposing mind and memory. I will and desire that all my just debts and funeral expenses be paid. I give to my wife Sarah Downey all my estate both real and personal, that I now have or may have, to her and her heirs forever to be disposed of as she may think proper. I appoint my friend John Burton and Alexander C. Hamilton executors. Dated 15 May 1826. Wit: John Douglass, E. S. Davis, Thos. Snierin. Signed: John Downey. "A settlement of the estate of John Downey decd. was this day the 12 May 1835 made in the Ordinary Office, setting for the particularly the acting and doing of A. C. Hamilton decd. as derived from his books, in his own handwriting and exhibits by James S. Wilson admr. and in the presence of Sarah Downey the widow and sole legatee of her husband estate." Inv. made 9 Nov. 1827. Sale held 12-13 Dec. 1827. Buyers: Alexr. Bowie, Esq., John Wilson, Wm. Gilkeyson, Robt. Morrah, A. C. Hamilton, John Burton, David Roberson, Donald Douglass, Charles Dendy, James Burnett, David Lesley, Moses Taggart, James Moore, Saml. Branch, Henry Norell, Thos. Keown, Robt. Richey, Wm. Morrison, John Richardson, Wm. Russell, Wm. Butler, Isaiah Curry, James McIlwain, John McCord, Jr., Patrick Noble, John Johnson, Robt. Gilmer, Jas. Lockridge, Andrew Moatz, John Allen, Saml. Roberson, Alexr. Martin, Wm. Lomax, Esq., Capt. Wm. Smith, Henry Ruff, Wm. Paul.

DOWNY, TONY H. #5. Clerk of Court Office. Abbeville, S. C.
Office of the Court of General Sessions and Common Pleas; before me
Martin G. Zeigler, clerk, personally appeared Tony H. Downy a native
of Germany about twenty one years of age. After duly sworn according
to law, declares that it is bona fide his intention to become a citizen of the U.S., and renounce forever all allegiance to every foreign
power, etc. filed 5 March 1877.

DOWNEY, RICHARD Box 26 Pack 584. Probate Judge Office. Abbeville, S. C. Admr. Bond, We Martha Downey, widow of Richard Downey
decd. James Foster, Senr., and Adam Hill are bound the court in Abbeville in the sum of ₤500. Dated 10 June 1794. Cit. was read at a
public meeting at David Cannedays on Mountain Creek the 30 May 1794
by Jas. Foster Senr., Saml. Foster, Senr., James Chalmers, Enos
Crawford and John Devlin were ordered to appraise the est.

DOWTIN, THOMAS P. #125. Clerk of Court Office. Abbeville,
S. C. I Thomas P. Dowtin of Abbeville Dist. being of sound mind and
memory, but weak in body. I give to my wife that tract of land known
as the Cook place, containing 105 acres, also 50 acres of wood land of
the home place, commencing at the North corner of the Cook running
that line to Mrs. Margaret Wideman, thence along smake road for enough
to take in 50 acres. I also give a negro girl Elenans known as
Frances, one bed and furniture, also she is to have $2,000.00
in cash. I have given to my son John S. Dowtin two thousand dollars.
I have given to my dtr. Mary Ann Sprowl two thousand. I have given to
my dtr. Drusillah Ray nineteen hundred dollars. My son James C.
Dowtin must have $2,000 to be equal to the above named children, before
they get any more. I have given to my dtr. Mildred W. Wideman fifteen
hundred dollars, she must have five hundred more to be equal with
the rest. I give my son Thomas A. Dowtin must have two thousand dollars to be equal. I give to my dtr. Nancy L. Dowtin must have twenty
one hundred dollars to be equal. Also my son David Dowtin must have
two thousand and three hundred dollars to be equal. Also I give my dtr.
Katharen three hundred dollars more, it being all that she is to have
of my estate. I desire that my wife and the four chn. that is with me
viz; James C., Thomas A., Nancy L., and David Dowtin have dressing
necessary for them, also provisions of all kind for their support
until after the sale. My cotton be picked, gined and sold to pay my
just debts. The land whereon I now live to be sold on credit of one
or two years and all negroes consisting of about thirty eight including
men, women, and children. The stock of cattle, hogs, horses, sheep,
crop, gin, blacksmith tools, to be sold on twelve months credit. I
desire that Henry D. Ray who married my dtr. Drusillah get one hundred
dollars more to make him equal. At the Cook place my wife must have
a garden built and the house repaired, a cross fence to be built and
about four acres of wheat be sowed for my wife. I desire that my sons
James C., Thomas A., and David Dowtin get their est. of age of nineteen yrs. of age, and Nancy L., to get her when she marry. I appoint
M. O. McCaslan, John S. Dowtin executors. Dated 22 Sept. 1854. Wit:
J. A. Gibert, Jas. W. Child, R. A. F. McCaslan. Signed: Thomas P.
Dowtin. In Equity: To the Chancellors of the State. Your orator
sheweth unto your Honr. that Mildred W. Wideman the wife of W. H.
Wideman by James C. Dowtin her next friend as follows. That in the
year 1854 Mildred W. Wideman intermarried with William H. Wideman of
this dist. Both she and her husband being very young. Soon after the
marriage her husband removed with her to the State of Miss. where she
lived with him until the latter part of the year namely 1855. Whilst
in Miss. family disagreements arose between her husband and herself
which have resulted in their living apart, with no probability of their
living again in the conjugal relation. That the said W. H. Wideman
being now without the limits of this State. There has been no child
of this marriage nor is there any probability of such event. Filed
18 Feb. 1856.

DOWTON, KETURAH Box 30 Pack 661. Probate Judge Office. Abbeville, S. C. We Thomas P. Dowton, Oliver McCaslan and Alexander Mc-
Caslan are bound unto David Lesly, Ord. in the sum of $2,000. Dated
1 Jan. 1845. The petition of Thomas P. Dowton sheweth that his daughter

Dowton, Keturah - Continued. Katurah Dowton departed this life
intestate, having neither wife or chn. or linial decendant, but a
father your pet, and brothers and sisters of the whole, as well as of
the half blood. The father taking a child part with the whole blood.
Your petitioner further states that he was the gdn. of the est. of the
said decd. dtr. who was a minor and that her est. consists of money.
Your petitioner prays that a citation be issued and published. Dated
19 Dec. 1844. Signed: Thomas P. Dowton. In the settlement of 21
Jan. 1845 her net est. was $1211.28. Thomas P. Dowton being gdn. of
John, Drusilla Dowton and Mary Ann the wife of Elihu Spruill, all
distributees of Keturah Dowton decd. Each recd. $302.82.

DORRIS, WILLIAM Box 26 Pack 604. Probate Judge Office. Abbeville, S. C. I William Dorris of Abbeville Dist. being of sound and
disposing mind and memory, but weak in body. I will to my wife one bay
mare and saddle, one cow, one bed and furniture to her and her heirs
forever. I will to my dtr. Catherine one half of the tract of land
lying in Edgefield Dist. taking in a part of the Rushes old field and
$30 when the money is collected from the sale. I will to my dtr.
Margaret the other half of the tract of land and $30 when the money
is collected from the sale. I will to my son William one mare, saddle
and bridle which he now claims, one cow and calf, sow and pigs, one
plow and gear. I will to my son John the property already given him.
I will to my grandson William Gable one heifer. I will to my granddaughter Mary Ethridge one heifer which is now called hers. I will to
my stepson Henry Merk one colt when my mare foals, one black heifer
and one sow shoat. I desire the balance of my est. be sold and funeral
expenses paid and any just debts paid. Then my wife to have one third
in place of dower the rest to be equally divided between my sons and
dtrs. Dated Samuel Perrin, Samuel Caldwell, Hugh Moseley. Signed:
William Dorris. Sons William and John Dorris and friend Moses Thomson
executors. Est. appraised 28 Oct. 1818 by Wm. Chiles, Robert Kay,
Robert Perrin, Philip Stiefel. Sale buyers: Beverly Burton, James
Stiefel, Wm. Walker, John Zimmerman, Henry Zimmerman, Samuel Zimmerman,
Joshua Bell, Jacob Gable, Thomas W. Chiles, Wm. Thomas, Senr., Philip
Stiefel, James Russell, Hugh Moseley, Henry Shelnut, Susan Brisky,
John Rabourn, John Little, Joseph Thornton, Benj. McGill, Moses Thomp-
son, Samuel Prrin, Wm. Chiles, John Dorris, Wm. Dorris.

DOZIER, RICHARD M. Apt. 2 File 126. Probate Judge Office.
Greenville, S. C. Will dated 1829. Probated 26 Nov. 1832. Chn. Lukey
Dozier, Mary Dozier, Leonard Dozier, Richard Dozier, Billups Dozier,
John Dozier, Ann Ramsay, Jocie Gale. Owned four tracts of land in
Edgefield Dist. bought of Dr. Bulger, Gen'l W. Butler, Thomas Scott,
Thomas Davis. Bought land in Greenville from William Wickliffe.
Exors Leonard Dozier, Richard Dozier, Lukey Dozier. Wit: Henrietta
Johnson, William B. Johnson, Theodore Gourdin.

DRENNAN, CHARLES No Ref. Probate Judge Office. Abbeville, S.C.
Admr. bond. We Wm. T. Drennan, Thomas Dickson and William McCaslan
are bound unto Moses Taggart, Ord. in the sum of $5,000. Dated 27 Nov.
1835. Cit. pub. at Hopewell Church 22 Nov. 1835. Inventory made 27
Jan. 1836 by Wm. McCaslin, John Bradley, Josiah McGaw. Sale date not
given, buyers: James Cochran, John Conner, Wm. Bradford, Jas. Glasgow,
Wm. T. Drennan, Thos. Cowan, Joseph Drennan, James Shanks, Mathew
Brown, John Foster, Silas Cooper, Rody McKenney, Giles Burdit, Thomas
Thompson, David Holder, Robt. McKinney, David Cowan, Peter Downey, James
Gordon, Saml. Atkins.

DRENNAN, JOSEPH Pack 366. Clerk of Court Office. Abbeville,
S. C. Abbeville Dist. To the Honr. the Chancellors: Your orators and
oratrixs, George W. and wife Mary Ann McKinney and William O. and
wife Elizabeth McKinney. Sheweth that about seventeen or eighteen
years ago Joseph Drennan departed this life intestate, seized and
possessed with a tract of land lying in said dist. on Bold Branch,
waters of Long Cane Creek. Containing about 145 acres. Bounded by
lands of George Zaner, Mary Bently, William W. Belcher, and on which
Phebe Drennan now lives. That said Joseph Drennan left the widow
Phebe Drennan and Mary Ann, Elizabeth your oratrixs, and Martha J.

Drennan, Joseph - Continued. Drennan a minor about twenty yrs. old, Joseph J. Drennan a minor about nineteen yrs. of age, Nancy Drennan a minor who died since unmarried. John Kennedy was admr. of the estate, dated 3 April 1836, by Moses Taggart, Ord. of Abbeville Dist. A final settlement was made on the 9 Feb. 1847 in the Ordinary Office by Isaac Kennedy admr. of the estate of John Kennedy. Filed 7 Oct. 1854. (part of this court case is missing from the notes.) There is a release of dower on some land, Elizabeth Young renounce, release and forever relinquish unto the within named Charles Drennan his heirs and assigns all her interest and estate, all her right, claim of dower of in and to all singular the premises within mentioned. Before Patrick Gibson, J.Q. Dated 15 Feb. 1830. Signed: Elizabeth Young.

DRENNON, ROBERT Pack 304. In Equity. Clerk of Court Office. Abbeville, S. C. Abbeville Dist. To the Honr. the Chancellors. Your orators, John W. Drennon, Oscar N. Drennon, R. Lewis Drennon sheweth that Robert Drennon died intestate leaving considerable personal and real estate and leaving distributees and heirs at law, his widow Mary Drennon and chn.: Mary L. Drennon, Elizabeth L. Drennon, Martha Arabella Drennon, Rebecca Jane Drennon, the last two minors. Your oratrix the widow Mary Drennon took out letter of admr. upon the personal est. and your orators believe that the personal est. was more than sufficient to pay all debts. The deceased owned at his death a tract of land containing 270 acres in Abbeville Dist. on Long Cane bounded by Johnathan Jordan, Wm. Lyon, Terry or Henry? Purdy, James J. Devlin. The deceased also owned a house and lot in the village of Due West, S.C. containing about four acres, where the widow Mrs. Mary Drennon now resides, bounded by land of R. E. Sharp, land of est. of John Brownlee and John Mathis. Your orators are desirous that the tract of land with the house and lot be sold or partitioned to the parties in interest according to their legal rights. Filed 5 Nov. 1863.

DRENNAN, THOMAS Pack 9. Probate Judge Office. Anderson, S. C. I Thomas Drennan of Pendleton Dist. in consideration of $205.00. Paid me by Washington J. Gambrell of same Dist. have granted, sold, released a tract of land containing 153 acres, being part of a tract granted unto William Bell on 5 Aug. 1799. Lying on a branch of Rock Creek, waters of Rockey River. Dated 16 Sept. 1825. Wit: Matthew Gambrell, Isreal W. Greene. Signed: Thomas Drennan. I John George one of the J.Q. of said Dist. to all whom it may concern that Martha Drennan the wife of Thomas Drennan renounce, release and relinquish all interest of dower in the said land. Dated 26 Dec. 1824. Proved on oath of Matthew Gambrell before John T. Lewis, C.C. and J.Q. this 26 July 1826.

DRENNAN, WILLIAM Box 30 Pack 663. Probate Judge Office. Abbeville, S. C. Admr. bond. We Robert Drennan, James J. Devlin and Robert Devlin are bound unto David Lesly, Ord. in the sum of $6,000. Dated 13 Jan. 1845. Appraisement made 28 Jan. 1845 by Bartow Jordon, Jonathan Jordon, Robert F. Nealy, William Sanders, J. J. Devlin. Sale held 4 March 1846. Buyers: Geo. Marshall, Wm. Sanders, Uriah Colvin, Robert Drennan, John R. Martin, Dr. Pressly, Jonathan Jordon, A. Donald, D. Atkins, Daniel Hadden, Lewis Rich, Robert F. Nealy, W. Robinson. Received 4 March 1846 of Robert Drennan admr. $456.75 being in full of John D. Upson and Rachel C. G. Upson distributee share of the est. of William Drennan decd. est. received by Marcus Upson guardian. A power of attorney from Wolcox[?] County, Ala. I Mary Robinson of said county and State, have this day appointed William H. Drennan (of Holmes County, Miss.) my legal and lawful agent to transact any business in my name in the State of S.C. and to receive and receipt and settle any matter of the property of my father est. William Drennan decd. Dated 1 May 1845. Signed: Mary Robinson. In the settlement made 26 May 1845. Present Robert Drennan, admr. Wm. H. Drennan from Holmes Co., Miss. for himself and hold power of attorney from his sister Mary Robinson dtr. of Wm. Drennan decd. and widow of B. Robinson, who died before settlement, James Drennan, Eliza Jane who intermarried with Marcus Upson and who died before intestate having two chn. John D., R. E. J. Upson who are entitled to the whole estate real and personal of said decd. mother. William Drennan died Dec. 1844.

DRUMMOND, DANIEL Pack 2. Clerk of Court Office. Anderson, S.C.
Pendleton Dist. To the Honr. the associate Judges of said State. The
humble petition of Daniel Drummond a native of the County of Antrim in
the Kingdom of Ireland, sheweth that he has resided in the U.S. fifteen
years and the whole time within this State. Your petitioner is desirous
of becoming a citizen of this U.S. Therefore your petitioner prays
that you would admit him to the rights and privileges of citizenship.
We do certify that we have known Danl. Drummond for five yrs. and that
he is a man of good moral charactor. Signed: John T. Lewis, Patrick
Norris, John McFalls, James Todd, Newman Moore, John Bryce, J.P.,
E. Herrin, J.P., Nathan McAlister, Andrew McAlister. Dated 26 Oct.
1813. When he renounce and adjure all allegiance and fiedlity to every
foreign power, his name is given as David Drummond. Dated 26 Oct.
1813. Signed: David Drummond.

DRUMMONS, JAMES Box 20 #148. Probate Judge Office. Pickens,
S. C. I James Drummons being and lying in a low state of health tho
of sound mind and memory, etc. I give to my wife Letteann Drummons
all my real estate not already disposed of including the house and farm
where we now live together with all stock, with a brown mare called
Jiney, now in possession of Christopher Whisenant, with all household
and kitchen furniture to hold the above property during her natural
life. At her death my granddaughter Lettyann Liles the wife of Joseph
Liles who is now living with us to have one feather bed and clothing
and farm tools of every description. The rest of my property to be
sold and equally divided my decd. dtr. Nancey Whisenant. I appoint
my friends Wm. B. Davis and William Cape executors. Dated: 6 Feb.
1847. Wit: Harvey Davis, Edw. Hughs. Signed: James X Drummons.
Proven 29 March 1847.

DUNCAN, GEORGE Box 30 Pack 665. Probate Judge Office. Abbeville,
S. C. We, Elizabeth Duncan, William Loaner, William Duncan are bound
unto David Lesly, Ord. in the sum of $600. Elizabeth Duncan made gdn.
of her minor chn. Dated 25 Sept. 1844. The petition of Elizabeth
Duncan sheweth that her husband George Duncan died a few yrs. since
leaving his widow and four infant chn. Viz: John, Polly, William and
Margaret Duncan. Each child recd. $27.63. Which was used to pay for
the home place.

DUNCAN, JESSE Apt. 2 File 125. Probate Judge Office. Greenville,
S. C. On 2 Jan. 1809 Mary Duncan the admr. Paid on 6 Dec. 1808 George
Duncan $49.00, Jesse Duncan $49.00, Mary Duncan $49.00. Paid in 1802
James Duncan 11-13-4, paid 9 Jan. 1804 Allen Moore, legatee (amount not
given), paid June 1804 Elish Moore legatee 14-9-7, in 1799 paid John
Duncan 5-6-8.

DUNCAN, JOHN Apt. 2 File 134. Probate Judge Office. Greenville,
S. C. On 6 Jan. 1816 Elizabeth Duncan applied for letter of admr.
left a widow and two chn. No names given. On 1 March 1817 James
Duncan and Rebecca Duncan minors under 14 yrs. On 1 March Elizabeth
Duncan recd. of the U.S. the balance of pay as a soldier $67.35.

DUNCAN, SALLY Apt. 2 File 124. Probate Judge Office. Greenville,
S. C. Will dated 11 Nov. 1826. Probated 1 Jan. 1827. Heirs William
Elbert Duncan, Sion Turner Duncan, Lisey Duncan, Nancy Duncan, William
Neal, Stephen Neale, mother, Sally Duncan. Exors. Nathaniel Dacus,
Stephen Neal. Wit: Blackmon Ligon, Elizabeth Turner, William Duncan.

DUNCAN, WILLIAM Pack 6. Clerk of Court Office. Anderson, S.C.
Pendleton Dist. I William Duncan Senr. in consideration of $140.00
paid me by John Davis, have bargain, sold and released a tract of land
in said Dist. containing 212 acres lying on hencoop creek waters of
Rockey River, it being part of a tract granted to William Benneson on
21 Jan. 1790. Adj. land of John Maxwell, Josiah Burton and his own
line. Dated 25 March 1817. Wit: Thos. Grayton, C. Orr. Signed:
William Burton. Proved on oath of Christopher Orr before James Brock,
J.P. on the 12 April 1817. I Wm. F. Clinkscales one of the Justices
of the Quorum, do certify unto all it may concern that Nancy Duncan
the wife of William Duncan did renounce, release and relinquish all

Duncan, William - Continued. her interest in said land, this
17 Nov. 1822. Signed: Nancy X Duncan.

DUNN, JOHN Box 30 Pack 666. Probate Judge Office. Abbeville,
S. C. I John Dunn of Abbeville Dist. do make this my last will and
testament, I desire my just debts and funeral expenses be paid. I
give to my wife Jane C. Dunn all my est. of every kind. I give to my
neices Ally Ann, Jane, Margaret and Elizabeth J. Dunn chn. of my
brother James Dunn $100 each. I appoint John Weir executor. Dated
1 Sept. 1841. Wit: Wm. Dunn, Joseph Lyon, Thomas Thomson. Signed:
John Dunn. Est. appraised 29 Sept. 1841 by Joseph Eakin, Robert
Richey, Senr., Joseph Lyon.

DUNNEHOO, DAVID Apt. 2 File 118. Probate Judge Office. Green-
ville, S. C. On 22 Feb. 1823 Sarah Dunnehoo relinquish her right of
Admr. on estate of her husband David Dunnehoo decd. and wanted her
brother-in-law John Dunnehoo to be admr. On 7 Oct. 1839 Wesley
Phillips purchased all Runnell Dills Jr. right which he had in right
of his wife Sarah Dill, the widow of David Dunnehoo. Owned land on
South Tyger River. Heirs, widow, Sarah Dill, Patsy the wife of
William Morgan, Lucinda the wife of David Barnett, William Dunnehoo,
Abner Dunnehoo, John Dunnehoo, Whitfield Dunnehoo.

DURHAM, J. G. Equity #26. Clerk of Court Office. Pickens,
S. C. (Basement). I J. G. Durham in consideration of $50.00 to me
paid by Silas Stone do grant bargain, sell, release all that tract of
land in said Dist. on East side of Six Mile Creek (Amount not given).
adj. land of Keith's, John Howard, William Johnson. Dated 27 Feb.
1856. Wit: Wellington Ree, Thomas S. Ree. Signed: J. G. Durham.
Proved on oath of T. S. Ree before Thos. Dillard, M.P.D. on the 2
March 1857.

DURHAM, JOHN Will Book G, Page 315. Probate Judge Office.
York, S.C. I John Durham of York Dist. being of sound and disposing
mind and memory. I will and devise to my son George G. Durham, my
dwelling house with 300 acres of land surrounding and adjacent thereto
to be laid off by Geo. G. Durham, wheresoever he may choose. I will
to my dtr. Elizabeth Durham the tract of land purchased by me from
Alexander Eakin containing about 65 acres. Also I will to her 100
acres in addition to the above to be chosen by her from land not herein
before devised. I will to Hugh Currence 100 acres of land to be laid
off to him from my land adj. the line of his land and shall be so
allotted and surveyed as to extend the whole distance along his line
which adjoin to my line. The remainder of my property shall be laid
off into lots which shall be convenient for sale and for that purpose
I appoint my friends David Watson, Duncan McCollum, William Berry to
make such division.. (no more of will in the notes.)

DUVALL, MICHAEL Box 27 Pack 622. Probate Judge Office. Abbe-
ville, S. C. Admr. bond, We Elizabeth Devall, Hel[?] Hill, Edward
W. Collier are bound unto Andrew Hamilton, Ord. in the sum of $10,000.
Dated 17 Jan. 1803. Est. appraised by James Foster, Andrew Crozier,
John Patterson, and John Wallace made on 30 Jan. 1803. Negroes listed
Sarah and her two chn. Jane and Rebeca, Cumbogh. Grace and Hannah and
Sarah.." Omitted appraising of Lucy and her increase by reason of
old Mrs. Cathareen Devall having a claim for her life time, to said
property, Lucy and Charles her child." Signed: Elizabeth Devall.
Sale held on 1 March 1803. Elizabeth Duvall, Mathew Goodwin, George
Crawford, Shepperd Grosse, Samuel Devall, Amos Shepperd, Thomas Benton,
Ezekiel Adeer, John Wallace, Thomas McBride, Turner Mohead, Joseph
Barksdale, John McCuller, John Tolbert, James Hughs, Edward Collier,
Josiah Patterson, Macklin Devall, Joshua Hill, William Gray.

DYER, SAMUEL Apt. 2 File 136. Probate Judge Office. Greenville,
S. C. Will dated 22 July 1824. Probated 20 Nov. 1824. Wife Elizabeth
Dyer. Chn. mention, no name given, executor wife, Elizabeth Dyer.
Brother, Thomas Dyer. Wit: Martin Carter, Jacob Lenderman.

EAKIN, MINORS Pack 418. Clerk of Court Office. Abbeville, S.C. On 28 May 1852 Thomas Eakins was guardian of Jane Eakins a minor about 15 yrs. who had intermarried with George W. Barnes. On 14 July 1847 recd. of admr. of James Eakins personally $529.55. Was also guardian of Elizabeth S. Eakins who had become the wife of Thomas P. Hamilton. Dated 7 Dec. 1866. On 15 Jan. 1859 was also gdn. of George W. Eakins who has now come of age. Also gdn. of John Eakins a minor on 23 Jan. 1850 recd. from exors of James Eakins Senr. $119.35. In 1852 John Eakins was in Miss, Kemp Co. with his uncle William W. Eakins.

EARLE, GEORGE WASHINGTON Apt. 2 File 143. Probate Judge Office. Greenville, S. C. Will dated 7 Nov. 1821. Proved 4 Dec. 1821. Dtr. Sarah Caroline Earle, son Elias Drayton Earle, owned land on French Broad, N.C. also in Rutherford, N.C. on Pacolet on Enoree and Tyger, also on Vaughans Creek a branch of Pacolet I bought of Will Banks, also my interest in land belonging to my father est. lying on Big Forked Deer River in Tenn." Exors wife Elizabeth Earle, son, Elias Drayton Earle, brother in law Samuel G. Earle. Wit: Jeremiah Cleveland, John Robinson, B. Earle Jr., John McClanihaw.

EARLY, PATRICK Pack 185. Probate Judge Office. Anderson, S.C. I Patrick Early of Pendleton Dist. being of sound and disposing mind and memory, but weak in body etc, I give to my eldest dtr. Mary white ten shillings at my decease. I give to my eldest son James Early ten shilling at my decease. I give to my youngest dtr. one cow and calf and ten shillings at my decease. I give all my land which I now live on unto my beloved wife Pheby during her natural life, and at her decease, I give said land to my youngest son Eanoch Early. If my wife and my son should covnant and agree to sell said land, I agree for my wife to have one third of the proceeds and my son two thirds. I give to my wife all moveable estate, during her natural life and at her death, I give to my dtr. Lettice Early the same at her mother's death. I appoint Moses Haynes Senr. and my wife Phebe Executors. Dated 10 June 1798. Wit: Hugh Simpson, Thomas Seals or Scals. Signed: Patrick X Early. Proven on oath of Hugh Simpson before John Verner, J.P. on the 19 Sept. 1799.

EDGAR, JOHN Box 31 Pack 696. Probate Judge Office. Abbeville, S. C. I John Edgar of Abbeville Dist. being of sound mind and memory, etc. I give unto my beloved wife Judeth Edgar all that tract of land whereon I now live, containing 75 acres, being part of the tract granted unto John Edgar, Senr. The rest and residue of my personal estate, goods and chattles of every kind and nature, I give to my dear wife Judeth Edgar, to have and hold during her natural life, or dispose of in her life as she think proper. I appoint my wife executrix. Dated 17 July 1823. Wit: Wm. Robinson, John Goldin. Signed John Edgar Junr. Inventory made 15 March 1819 by John Guthrie, Peter Hemmenger, W. W. McElhenney.

EDWARDS, DAVID Pack 258. Clerk of Court Office. Abbeville, S.C. Abbeville Dist. In Equity: To the Honr. the Chancellors, Your orator and oratrix Matthew Campbell and Rebecca his wife sheweth that in March 1840, David Edwards, late of Abbeville Dist. died intestate leaving a widow, Sarah Edwards and six children to wit., Rebecca your oratrix who intermarried with Mathew Campbell, James Edwards, Mary Edwards, Thomas Edwards, David Edwards, John Edwards heirs surviving, Thomas Edwards, David Edwards and John Edwards are now minors, the last named under 14 yrs. the other two over 14 yrs. At time of his death David Edwards possessed two tracts of land, one tract contained 213 acres, bounded by land of Thomas Riley, Henry Boozer, James Jonas, Thomas Wier. (No more of this suit in notes.)

EDWARDS, JOHN Apt. 3 File 155. Probate Judge Office. Greenville, S. C. Will dated 29 Sept. 1799. Proven 16 March 1801. Wife Henrietta Edwards, Chn. Sarah Edwards, William Edwards, Elizabeth Bridwell, Mary Bruce, Joseph Edwards, John Edwards, Exors. Thomas Edwards, Pleasant Hudson. Wit: Mary Ann Edwards, Thomas Edwards.

ELGIN, ANN Box 31 Pack 686. Probate Judge Office. Abbeville,
S. C. I Ann Elgin of Abbeville Dist. being well and in perfect mind
and memory. I give and devise my plantation whereon I now live, which
I got from Stephen Northcutt, containing 200 acres and adj. land run
in my name, I give to my three dtrs. Catharine Elgin, Ann Elgin,
Elizabeth Elgin to be equally divided between them, with my dtr.
Catharine to have her choice when divided. All the remainder of my
estate to be divided between my said dtrs. Dated 25 July 1791. Wit:
Adm. Cr. Jones, Mary X Jones, Adam Crain Jones Junr. Signed: Ann
Elgin. Recorded 11 Nov. 1794. Inv. made 14 April 1795 by Benj.
Mattison, Capt. Reuben Nash, Abner Nash..." We hereby inform the Hon-
ourable Court of Abbeville that we the legatees appoint Robert Elgin
to Admr. on the will of Ann Elgin decd." Signed: Catharine, Ann,
Elizabeth Elgin..

ELLINGTON, JOHN Box 31 Pack 694. Probate Judge Office. Abbeville, S. C. Admr. bond. We Bedy Ellington, John C. Caldwell, James
Murray, James Caldwell and David Lesly are bound unto Moses Taggart,
Ord. in the sum of $20,000. Dated 5 July 1820. Cit. Pub. at Upper
Long Cane, 27 Jan. 1828. Inventory made 14 Feb. 1828 by James, Elijah
Hunt, John Smith. Another admr. bond was made in the same amount with
the same persons except Jacob Martin in the place of James Murry. Sale
held, buyers, Bedy Ellington, Silas Glover, Jas. A. Moore, Jno. Win-
field, John Smyth, Jno. G. Caldwell, Arch. Scott, Rolen Grant, B. H.
Moseley, Edw. S. Murry, Joseph Scott, Francis Thornton, James Hunt,
T. Hamilton, W. W. Bowman, Wm. Covington, Francis Y. Baskin, Uriah
Barron, John Allen. Paid cash April 1830 Joel Lipford part of what
was coming to him $100. Paid cash John Speer per Mary Ellington
$16.37 1/2 Paid cash 7 Jan. 1831 A. Malden his wife legacy $233.00.

ELLIS, JOHN E. Pack 331. Clerk of Court Office. Abbeville, S.C.
Abbeville Dist. To the Honr. the Chancellors: Your oratrix Elizabeth
Ellis sheweth that John E. Ellis the husband of your oratrix departed
this life on the 16 May 1859 intestate possessed with considerable real
and personal est. leaving as heirs and distributees your oratrix the
widow and fifteen chn. viz: The chn. of one decd. son to wit; Matilda
the wife of Turner G. Davis, Polly the wife of Zachariah Hadden, Louanna
the wife of James Strawhorn, Elizabeth Ellis, Christopher Ellis, John
E. Ellis, Joseph N. Ellis, Robert M. Ellis, Ebenzer P. Ellis, Benjamin
F. Ellis, William T. Ellis, Mimminger M. Ellis, Amaziah R. Ellis,
Luther T. Ellis and Permelia S. Ellis the last four are minors, also
four minor chn. of Augustus E. Ellis decd. viz; John Calvin, James
Lucien, Mahala Elizabeth and Savannah Paratine Ellis. Christopher
and Ebenezer Ellis are the admr. and have enough to pay all debts, which
is small. John E. Ellis had two tracts of land at time of his death,
one the home place consisting of 800 acres lying on Chickasaw Creek,
waters of Little River, bounded by land of Robert Ellis, Joseph Ellis,
William Ellis and Robert Pratt. The second tract known as the
Groggy Springs place containing about 700 acres, lying on Jobs Creek,
waters of Long Cane, bounded by land of William Stevenson, Peter Henry,
John Cowan and others. Your oratrix will ever pray. Filed 25 May
1859. On another paper the age of the minors are given, Elizabeth of
age, John Calvin are 10 yrs., James Lucien 8 years, Mahala Elizabeth
6 years, Savannah Paratine age 4 years, Memminger M. age 18 years,
Amaziah R. age 17 years, Luther T. age 16 years, Permelia S. 14 yrs.
On the 2 Jan. 1859 Joseph N. Ellis lived at Acquilla P.O. Franklin
Co., Ga.

ELLIS, ROBERT No ref. Probate Judge Office. Abbeville, S. C.
Abbeville Dist. The petition of John L. and Robert Ellis executor of
Robert Ellis decd. sheweth that their father departed this life many
years ago and left the est. real and personal to be managed and kept
by his widow Margaret Ellis and at her death to be sold by his executors.
The petition sheweth that their mother departed this life lately, they
pray for a warrant of appraisment and an order for the sale of the
personal est. (No date given, other est. on this page are dated 1828
and 1825.)

ELLIS, TOMBSTONE INSCRIPTIONS. Bethelem Church Cemetery, located about 3 miles from Pickens, S.C. on the road to Liberty.
Gideon Ellis was born in North Carolina 27 Feb. 1786, died 30 Nov. 1859. He joined the Methodist Episcopal Church in his 17th year. He was a local preacher for about 30 yrs. previous to his death.
Lucy Ellis wife of Gideon Ellis born 22 Sept. 1786, died 24 June 1855.
Reuben Ellis departed this life in the 25th year of his life. No dates given.

ENGLISH, DANIEL Pack 420. Clerk of Court Office. Abbeville, S. C. Abbeville Dist. In Equity. To the Honr. the Chancellors, Your orator and your oratrixs, George W. Dooley and his wife Besheba and Elizabeth the widow. Sheweth that Daniel English died in Nov. 1853 the husband of your oratrix Elizabeth, leaving at will, he gave among other things the whole of his est. to your oratrix for life and at her death to her chn. Your oratrix took charge and has endeavored to manage the same, with John Sentell, who is the qualified executor of the said will. But your orator is about seventy years of age and harm in one ankle, weak and infirm and unable to keep up the establishment, she cannot live by herself and the property is going to ruin. Therefore, your oratrix desire an order to sell the whole property, with the interest being paid to your oratrix and the corpus to be over to the children. The said property consists of a tract of about 289 acres with five negroes viz: Abram, Chany, Hampton, Huldah and Wesly. The children of said Elizabeth are: Sarah the wife of William Hardin, Lucinda the wife of Hiram Jay, David Jackson English, Elizabeth the wife of Reuben Morris, Frances the wife of John Sentell, Amanda the wife of Benjamin F. Spikes, and Behaheba the wife of George W. Dooley and Rosely the wife of Thomas W. Aiton. Filed 28 Feb. 1860. Amanda Spikes resides in Cass Co., Ga.

ENGLISH, JANE Box 31 Pack 695. Probate Judge Office. Abbeville, S. C. Abbeville, S.C. I Jane English in a low condition and not knowing the day of my death, etc. I will to Nancy Kenedy the whole of my kitchen furniture, also pne half price of the plantation whereon I now live, and if she pleases she may have the half where the house now stands, also the whole of my stock of cattle, hogs, sheep with other out of doors articles. Nancy Kenedy shall take care of my dtr. Mary in decency while she lives, and if she become a charge my other chn. shall assist in helping Nancy Support Mary by giving five dollars a year a piece. I bequeath to my son James B. English my house Bible and Psalm book. I bequeàth to my son Andrew English my feather bed with part of the furniture. The other half of the price of my land be divided between my children. I will to Jane Alexdr. shall have the whole of my wearing apparel. I will and bequeath that my executors make a present to Nancy Young one plane frock patron for a remembrance of me. I appoint James English, John H. Armstrong and Andrew English my executors. Dated 13 March 1825. Wit: James B. English, John H. Armstrong, Hugh P. English. Signed: Jane X English. Inv. made 14 Oct. 1826 by Samuel A. Wilson, Robert Spence, Wm. E. Kennedy. Sale held 27 Oct. 1826. Buyers, Wm. E. Kennedy, John H. Armstrong, Alexander Spence, James Alexander, Simeon Bonham, Hugh P. English, Nancy Kennedy, John Kennedy, Jos. Williams, Andrew English, Cornelius Gillespie, John Clay, Thos. Guffen. Paid 30 Jan. 1830, James English $7.82, paid Andrew English $7.82, paid James Alexander $7.82, paid William McGaws share of Hannah $12.75, Daniel Gillespie share $7.82, Ann Kenedy $7.82, Nancy Kenedy $46.92.

EVANS, THOMAS 437. Clerk of Court Office. Abbeville, S.C. Abbeville Dist. In Equity: To the Honr. the Chancellors, Your orator James Evans of Rockingham County, N.C. Sheweth that Thomas Evans the son of your some years ago, at least ten years, intermarried with Elizabeth Hooper the dtr. of Elizabeth Hooper a widow and grand dtr. of Robert Pollard decd. all of this Dist. After living with said Elizabeth the said Thomas Evans died leaving his relict, but no child nor linpal descendant, only your orator his father and brothers and sisters. Thomas Evans died on the 4 Sept. 1848. About the year 1859 Elizabeth intermarried with Benjamin Y. Gold man. Whereas at time of his death Evans was not possessed of any real estate, of his personalty

Evans, Thomas - Continued. the admr. was committed by the
ordinary to Samuel Y. Hooper. By the last will of Robert Pollard
devises the residue of his est. not willed should after a time be sold
and the proceeds divided between four of his children of whom said
Elizabeth Hooper was one. This partition was of your orator believes
was carried out by the executors of Robert Pollards est. Some six
years ago about 1840 your orator is informed the children of Elizabeth
Hooper widow, the dtr. of Robert Pollard who first intermarried with
Samuel Young and then with Hooper, the father of Elizabeth Goldman,
with the consent of Elizabeth Hooper divided among themselves personal
est. which was in possession of their father. At time of this
partition the said Thomas Hooper received in right of his wife Elizabeth certain slave among them one named Antony, after having them in
their possession some time Elizabeth Hooper and Thomas Evans exchanged
all except for a certain slave named Eliza, who at or before the
exchange hath two chn. born to her, named Huldah, and Joicy and continued in possession of them till death. Filed 24 Sept. 1849.

EYMERIE, JOHN Box 31 Pack 685. Probate Judge Office. Abbeville,
S. C. I John Eymerie of Hillsbourough Township in 96 Dist. planter,
being of sound mind and memory and body. First pay all my debt truly
and faithfully paid. The real and personal property if any over, it to
be conveyed to my dear brother John and my sister Henrie Eymerie who
married to Peter Chany to be equally shared. I was married to Angelica
(or) Elizabet Baor the dtr. of Adam Baor of Hardlabor in this Dist.
She without reason and provacation whatsoever hath eloped from my bed
and boarding, and associated herself with one vagabond, to rob me of
all my effects and carried them off, being discovered, have tried to
rob and kill to get my small estate after death, I dissonne her for my
wife and exclude her from all my estate, except I do give her one shilling sterling or seven shilling current to be paid to her in six
months time after my death. I have named Mr. Peter Moragne of Long
Cane in 96 Dist. and Mr. Francis Gros. of Charleston, formerly tavern
keeper, to whom I give the sum of fifty ₤ currency or seven ₤ sterling
as executors. Dated 10 Feb. 1781. Wit: Pierre Guearineau, John Bert,
James Cowan. Signed: J. Eymerie. Recorded 13 Sept. 1798. Sale date
not given, Buyers: Thomas Gray, Joseph Barksdale, Peter Gillebau,
Peter Moragne, Peter Gibert, John Bicket, Andra Gillebeau, George
McFarlin, Charles Bright, Drury Breazeale, David Boyse, Jeremeyer
Rogers, Lewis Baylard, Allin Bagly, John Paterson.

FEEMSTER, JAMES No ref. or County given, only the middle page of
a will. I will to my two single dtr. Mary and Nancy Feemster in kind
as much as will be equal with my two married dtrs. viz: Prudence Brown
and Lettitia Gaston. I give to my dtr. Jane Leach three hundred
dollars to be placed at interest for her until called for by her. I
give to my four dtrs. Prudence Brown, Lettitia Gaston, Mary Feemster
and Nancy Feemster each the sum of seven hundred dollars and after the
legacies are paid, the balance of my property to be equally divided
among Prudence Brown, Lettitia Gaston, William Feemster, Joseph Feemster
James B. Feemster and Mary and Nancy Feemster share and share alike.
I order and ordain that old Mariah be comfortably maintained out of my
est. and in the next place as it has been under me and my family that
little motherless child Caroline which has been nursed by my dtr. Mary
Feemster should and ought of right to belong to her the said Mary
Feemster. As the black persons belonging to me have been long in the
family, it would appear harshness for force them contrary to their
desires to leave the family. Therefore I will and ordain that where
any or all of them wish and make choice to live with any of my chn.
That said negro or negroes shall be appraised with other personal
property in making division to the child or children. I will that
sufficient sum to maintain Mariah during her life time be given to my
dtrs. Mary and Nancy Feemster. I appoint William, Joseph and James B.
Feemster sole executors.

FLEMING, JAMES Box 35 Pack 768. Probate Judge Office. Abbeville,
S. C. Abbeville Dist. Admr. bond. We Thomas P. Martin, Jacob Martin,

Fleming, James - Continued. George Miller are bound unto Moses
Taggart, Esq. Ord. in the sum of $1,000.00. Bond date 5 June 1822.
Whereas Thomas P. Martin has made suit to me for a letter of admr. on
the estate and effects of James Fleming decd. Granted the 10 May 1822.
Cit. pub. at Long Cane. 13 May 1822 by Wm. H. Barr.

FOORD, RICHARD Box 35 Pack 770. Probate Judge Office. Abbeville,
S. C. I, Richard Foord Senr. of Abbeville Dist. being in a low state
of health, but in my perfect senses and of a sound mind. I give to my
beloved wife Elizabeth Foord all my household furniture and stock of
every kind during her life and at her death, I will to Rebekah Hollond
one dollar to my dtr. Sally Ann Nelson one dollar, to my dtr. Fanny
Foord one dollar, to my dtr. Elizabeth Tims one dollar, to my son Barrat
Foord one dollar, to my son Samuel Foord, one dollar, to my son Richard
Foord one dollar. After these are paid the remainder of my est. to be
divided between my dtr. Mosey Foord and my dtr. Milly Foord. Dated
___, 1808. N.B. I do appoint Elizabeth Foord and my son Samuel Foord
my executors. Signed: Richard X Foord Senr. Wit: Sarah X Brooks,
Christopher Brooks, Milly X Foord. Recorded 28 Sept. 1810. Inventory
made 22 Nov. 1810 by Christopher Brooks, Wm. White, Andrew Galaspy.

FOOSHEE, CHARLES B. Pack 343. Clerk of Court Office. Abbeville,
S. C. Abbeville Dist. To the Honr. the Chancellors: Your orator and
oratrix Joel Fooshee and his wife Mary and your oratrix Sarah Fooshee
widow. That on the 13th instant (13 Jan. 1850) that Charles B. Fooshee
of this Dist. departed this life intestate leaving his only heirs your
oratrix Sarah the widow and five living chn. Mary the wife of Joel
Fooshee, James Fooshee, Washington Fooshee, Casen Fooshee and Rebecca
Ann Fooshee and Martha who dies before the intestate leaving an infant
son John Fooshee who is still living. The said Charles Fooshee was
possessed with the following land, the home place containing about 460
acres lying on Wilson Creek waters of Saluda River. adj. land of N.
McCants, Esq., Griffin Golding and Winston Davis. Another tract called
the Mill Place, containing about 200 acres lying on Cornacres Creek,
waters of Saluda River, adj. land of Thomas B. Boyd, Nathan Calhoun,
and others, another tract called the old place containing about 200
acres adj. the last tract. Your orator and oratrixs has been informed
that the personal est. will pay all debts on the est. Filed 26 Jan.
1850.

FOREMAN, GEORGE Box 107, Pack 2810. Probate Judge Office.
Abbeville, S. C. I George Foreman of Edgefield, being infirm in body
but of perfect mind and memory. I give to my beloved wife Charity
Foreman the plantation and land whereon I now live, with two negroes,
Patt and Joe during her natural life. I also give unto Charity one
feather bed and furniture and an equal part with my chn. that are now
living. I give unto the lawful heir and heirs of my son Jacob Foreman
decd. all the land which I formerly resigned unto Jacob in Cracker Neck
on Savannah River. I give unto the lawful heirs of my son George
Forman decd. the sum of seven shillings sterlings to be levyed out of
my est. I give unto my five dtrs. namely, Mary, Sarah, Martha, Judah,
and Nancy Forman the sum of ten pounds sterling to each. The rever-
sion of my estate both real and personal to be equally divided amongest
all my chn. that are now living to wit: Isaac, Verly, Olive, Zilpah,
Mary, Sarah, Martha, Judah and Nancy. The land and items lent to my
wife, during her life time, at her death to be equally divided between
the aforenamed chn. I appoint my son Isaac Forman executor and my dtr.
Mary Forman executrix. Dated 20 May 1786. Wit: Jonathan Gouldsbrough,
Benjamin Harvy, Athanathan Thomass. Signed: George Forman. Inventory
made 13 Jan. 1787 by Benjamin Ryan, Jr., Nathan White, Gasper Gallman.

FOREST, JEREMIAH Apt 3, File 160. Probate Judge Office.
Greenville, S. C. Will dated 16 Aug. 1829. Probated 28 Sept. 1829.
Wife Julia Forrest. "Desire proceeds arising from sale be given unto
James Maderson Branon. Should he die before 21 yrs. of age, desire
that Jim Trammel shall have it." Exor. wife, Julia Forest. Wit:
Wilson Barton, Jefferson Barton, Joseph Barton.

FOSTER, ALEXANDER Pack 358. Deed of Land. Clerk of Court
Office. Abbeville, S. C. I Alexander Foster of Abbeville Dist. in
consideration of $285.00 paid me by Basdail Darby, have granted, sold,
bargained and released a tract of land containing sixty one acres,
being part of a grant of 350 acres originally granted to Samuel Foster
Senr. lying on Norrises Creek bounded by land of Basdail Darby, Nathaniel
Cammorns, Samuel Foster, S. S. and John Foster. Dated 19 March 1822.
Wit: James Foster, Samuel Foster. Signed: Alexander Foster.

FOSTER, JOHN Apt. 3 File 159. Probate Judge Office. Greenville,
S. C. I John Foster of Greenville County and Dist. of 96. Carpenter,
being weak in body yet of a sound and perfect memory. I will that all
my just devts be paid. I give to my loving wife three negroes, Sam,
Cole and Lill with stock and household goods, at her decease to be
equally divided among the chn. I give to my dtr. Mary Hendley one
negro girl named Silvia which she has now in her possession. I give to
my son John Crow Foster one negro named Cain, with two tracts of land
I bought of John Hambleton and Robert Ramsey containing 246 acres to
be equally divided between said John and his brother George Singleton
Foster. I give to my son George Singleton Foster one negro named
Sheriff. I give to my son Josiah Foster one negro named Carolina. I
give to my son James Hacket Foster one negro named Limbrick. I give to
my dtr. Nancy one negro named Sall. I give to my son Robert Singleton
Foster two negroes named Kitt and Sawyer. I give to my dtr. Frances
fifty acres of land at the lower end of the plantation whereon I now
live. I give to my sons James Hacket and Robert Singleton and my dtr.
Nancy the plantation whereon I now live, containing 300 acres with
forty acres being part of a tract I sold unto Josiah Smith. My debts
to be collected and the to be laid out in young negroes for the use of
the chn. I appoint my sons John Crow Foster and George Singleton
Foster executors. Dated 9 Oct. 1787. Wit: Rich. Thompson, Dave
Hidden and John X Rabun. John Foster.

FOSTER, SAMUEL SENR. Esq. Pack 381. Clerk of Court Office.
Abbeville, S.C. Whereas Saml. Foster Senr. Esq. decd. departed this
life intestate and whereas the heirs and representatives have entered
into a bond and instrument authorizing John Foster and John English to
sell and dispose of the real and personal est. of said decd. and make
distribution of same. We John Foster and John English in consideration
of $91.50 paid us by James Stuart have granted, bargained, sold and
release a tract of land containing 61 acres, being part of a tract
granted originally to Saml. Foster, lying on Norris' Creek, bounded by
land of Toliver Livingston, Wm. Covey, Jane Foster. Dated 5 Sept.
1814. Wit: Andq. Crawford, John Foster. Signed: John Foster and
John English. Proved on oath of John Foster before John Foster, J.P.
on 5 Sept. 1814.

FOSTER, SAMUEL SENR. Esq. Pack 358. Clerk of Court Office.
Abbeville, S. C. Whereas Saml. Foster Senr. Esq. decd. departed this
life without leaving a will, the heirs representatives have mutually
agreed and entered into a bond or instrument authorizing John Foster to
sell and dispose of the est. both real and personal and make distribution of the same. I John Foster in consideration of $230.00 paid me
by John English, have granted bargained, sold and release a tract of
land containing 95 acres, being part of a tract containing 350 originally granted to Saml. Foster on waters of Norris' Creek bounded by
land of Robert Norris, James McConnel, David Pressly. Dated 11 Aug.
1810. Wit: Alexr. Porter, Lyddal Gordon. Signed: John Foster.
Proved on oath of Revd. Alexdr. Porter before H. Morrah. Dated 7 Jan.
1811.

FORD, MAJOR JOHN Apt. File 158. Probate Judge Office. Greenville, S. C. Will dated 15 Oct. 1795. Recorded 29 April 1796. Wife
Ann Ford. Chn: William Ford, Isaac Ford, Leah Ford, Tressia Ford,
Linna Ford, Arasmus Ford, Levi Ford. "give unto Stacy Sibley." Owned
land adj. Thomas Rowlands land a lapsed from William Flippo. Owned
land in Spartan County on waters of Fair Forest. Also on both sides
of Terry's Creek waters of Greer River granted to Joseph Terry. Also
in Union County on both sides of Enoree River. In Greenville Co. on

Ford, Major John - Continued. both sides of Hensons Creek. Also land leading from Merritts Mill to Butlars on Green River that alapsed from James Leak. Exors: Wife Ann Ford, George Salmon. Wit: John Motlow, Elizabeth Salmon, Armond Gipson. Thomas Edwards states he was married to Leah Ford, 22 Nov. 1824.

FOWLER, ARCHIBALD Apt. 3 File 161. Probate Judge Office. Greenville, S. C. Will dated 22 Feb. 1839. Probated 1 June 1840. Wife Edy Fowler. Children, Jessey Pike decd., West I. Fowler, Mary Evans, Leah Mahaffey, Rachel Pike, Louisa Miller, Luna Pool, John W. Fowler, Lovey Waldrop, Alexander W. Fowler. Sit: Lyn Walker, Thomas I. Dean, Isaac Walker.

FOSTER, JAMES Box 36 Pack 783. Probate Judge Office. Abbeville, S. C. Abbeville Dist. We James H. Foster, Archibald Kennedy, James Lesly who are bound unto David Lesly Esq. Ord. in the sum of $4,000. Bond dated 6 Jan. 1845. The petition of James H. Foster sheweth that his father James Foster departed this life intestate leaving a widow and other chn. Dated 20 Dec. 1844. The inventory was made in Jan. 1845. Sale date not given, Buyers are James H. Foster, Mary Foster, Major Cochran, J. I. Kennedy, G. J. Camron, S. Jordan, W. H. Robinson, David McLain, A. Kennedy. Recd. of James H. Foster admr. of James Foster decd. $736.00 in full for James B. Foster and Thomas H. Foster minor heirs of John G. Foster decd. son of said James Foster decd. Signed: William A. Pinkerton gdn. of said minors, dated 1851. Recd. $736.43 being in full money coming to me as legatee of said est. Signed: A. P. Lesly. Recd. 1 Jan. 1849. from Nancy C. Foster $92.65. Recd. 1851 $49.42 in full of our share of said decd. Signed: James Lessly, J. P. Kennedy.

FOSTER, JOHN EDWARD Pack 359. Clerk of Court Office. Abbeville, S. C. Abbeville Dist. In Equity to the Honr. the Chancellors: Your oratrix Jane B. Foster by her next friend David J. Wardlaw sheweth that she is the wife of John E. Foster. She intermarried with said Foster about twenty two years and has borne him eleven children, six of whom are living, two dtr. have married and have establishments of their own, the other four are unmarried, viz; Robert about fifteen, Mary Caroline about ten, John Edward about six, Jane B. about four. For many years they had a happy marriage, but for the last four or five years he has not treated me kindly and has become the victim of intoxicating drink, when drunk he is violent and cruel and he seems to have become so far destracted as to have lost all sense of the proprieties of life as well as the feeling for his family, etc. Filed 5 April 1859.

FRANKLIN, ASA Box 35 Pack 765. Probate Judge Office. Abbeville, S. C. Abbeville Dist. Admr. bond. We William Barmore, Joseph Richey, James Franklin who are bound unto Moses Taggart, Esq. Ord. in the sum of $10,000.00. Bond dated 2 Nov. 1835. Whereas William Barmore made suit to me for letter of admr. on the goods and chattels of Asa Franklin decd. Dated 23 Sept. 1835. Cit. Pub. at Greenville Church the first sabbath in Oct. 1835. Inventory made the 30 Dec. 1835. Negroes named are: Jane and Willie, Hirom, Jack, Pompy, George, Hagar, Polly and child, Sary. Made by James Dodson, Alexander X Norris, Joseph Richey. Sale buyers, James Franklin, William Franklin, Robert Seright, Benjamin Jones, James Seright, Ezekiel Raser, Joseph McKowen, Aaron Drumman, A. C. Hawthorn, Isac Agnew, John Donald, William R. Swain, Joseph Kennan. Notes due the est. one on Thomas Howthorn Senr., Seburn, A. C. Jones Junr.

FRANKLIN, JAMES Box 35 Pack 767. Probate Judge Office. Abbeville, S. C. Abbeville Dist. We Stanley Crews, Larkin Griffin and Downs Calhoun who are bound unto Moses Taggart, Esq. Ord. in the sum of $10,000.00. Bond dated 4 Oct. 1836. Stanley Crews was made Admr. the 13 Sept. 1836. The inventory was made the 17 Dec. 1836, Negroes named are: boy Alford, woman Miley, woman Aggy, man Dick, girl Patty, girl Ginny Ann, girl Fillis, Jim and Annica, one woman Sudy and child, appraisers, William A. Moore, David W. McAnts, G. Apelton. Sale held 20 Dec. 1836. Buyers are: S. Franklin, Joel Smith, Willerson Besly,

Franklin, James - Continued. Robert Warters, Amos Roberts, John
Dunn, Wm. Smith, John Holt, James Calvert, David McCants, John Romans,
Nathan Calhoun, Jesse Calvert, Philips Wates, Sarah Franklin, John
Mathis, Robert Jones, Downs Calhoun, Franklin Bowie, Wm. H. Moore,
Thomas Greah, Zachriur Carwile, Joseph M. Patterson, Elias Huskerson,
Gabrel Hodges, James Moore, Duke Good, William Willson, Thomas Great,
John Mathis, James Willson. To Susan Franklin and Stanley Crews
guardian for Benjamin Franklin and William W. Franklin heirs of the
est. of James Franklin decd. You are required to appear at Abbeville
C.H. on 10 Dec. 1839 to show cause why the real estate of said decease
lying on waters of Saluda River, containing 406 acres, bounded by land
of Joel Smith, Wm. A. Moore, Robert Y. Jones, Edward Lipford, Eliza
Adams, and James Smith should not be sold or divided. Final settlement made 21 Dec. 1840. Present Stanley Cruse admr. and gdn. of
Benjamin Franklin a minor aged about ten yrs. Benjamin F. Sloan gdn.
of Eliza Ann and William W. Franklin. The widow Susan Franklin was
notified, but did not attend. "Deduct on a/c of demands of
Alexander W. King and Elizabeth A. King of whom James Franklin was
guardian."

FRANKLIN, WILLIAM Box 2 #37. In Equity. Clerk of Court Office.
No County given in notes. On 18 July 1838 Benj. F. Sloan, W. H. D.
Gaillard are bound unto W. H. Harrison in the sum of $3600.00. Benj.
F. Sloan gdn. for Elisa Franklin dtr. of William Franklin a minor
over 12 yrs. (Same Pack) Oct. 1835 Benj. F. Sloan gdn. for Benj. F.
Sloan, Susan A. Sloan, minors chn. of Capt. David Sloan.

FRAZIER, CHARITY Box 145 Pack 4102. Probate Judge Office.
Abbeville, S. C. I Charity Frazier of Abbeville Dist. in pursuance of
the power given me by my the last will of my decd. husband James
Frazier. I give to my dtr. Lucretia Devlin the negro boy Washington
son of Clara and Caroline the dtr. of Violet for the life of said dtr.
Lucretia at her death said slaves to belong in equal shares or parts
to Tallulah H. Frazier, Antoniette Frazier, Sarah C. Frazier my grand
dtrs. I also give to my dtr. Lucretia Devlin my bed and bedstead and
clothing belonging to it. I give to my grand dtr. Tallulah H. Frazier
the negroes Augustus, Eliza and John Lewis. I give to my grand dtr.
Antoinette Frazier the young negroes Julia, Oliver and Henry. I give
to my grand dtr. Sarah C. Frazier the young negroes Louisa, Martha,
Rebecca and Hiram. I give unto my nephew John F. Livingston in trust
for my son James W. Frazier the following negroes, Clara, Anne, Peter,
John, Charlotte, Anthony, and Violet. At the death of my son James
W. Frazier said negroes to be free from said trust and given in equal
shares between my grand dtrs. Tallulah H., Antoinette and Sarah C.
Frazier. I give to Charity Elizabeth and Mary Jane infant dtrs. of
Martha B. Lites from the profits left me the sum of $200. I give from
the profits left me $200 unto Allen S. Walker. Any amount left after
paying the said legacies shall become part of the trust to my son
James W. Frazier. I appoint Thomas Thomson and C. H. Allen the execu-
tors. Dated 16 May 1846. Wit: S. S. Marshall, Lewis Smith, Bartw.
Jordon. Signed: Charity X Frazier. A Codicil added but not dated,
gives the negroes to Martha Lites and her husband John Lites until
their dtrs. become of age. In another codicil states that V. Antoinette
Frazier is dead and her share to be given to Charles Bingley a son of
Clara. On a petition of James Frazier sheweth that his mother Mrs.
Charity Frazier departed this life in 1853, and the two executors
named refused to qualify as such. Therefore your petitioner prays
for a letter of admr. Signed: 25 Aug. 1857. Same granted.

FRAZIER. DAVID Box 107 Pack 2805. Probate Judge Office. Abbeville, S. C. Abbeville Dist. Admr. bond, We John Frazier, John Gray,
John Leary who are bound unto the Judge of Abbeville Co. Court. in
the sum of $2,000.00. Dated 13 Sept. 1797. Whereas John Frazier hath
applied to this Court for a letter of Admr. on the goods and chattels
of David Frazier decd. this 13 Aug. 1797 James Wardlaw D.C.C. "Certified by me Samuel Douthit Preacher of the Gospel have red this
publication to my congregation this 2d of Sept. 1797" [sic]. The
inventory and appraisement was made 16 Sept. 1797 by Andrew Gray,
Thomas Keown, John Gray. Sale held 3 Oct. 1797. Buyers: Andrew Paul,

Frazier, David - Continued. John Frazier, John Henderson, Doctor
B. Haworth, Thomas Keown, John Gray, David Pressley, Erchd. Douglass,
Henry Timmerman, Grehory Codle, James Anderson, Phill Foster, Wm.
Brightman, John Leaney, John Anderson, Arthur Morrow, Simon Beard,
James Smith.

FULTON, THOMAS No Ref. Clerk of Court Office. Abbeville, S. C.
(First page in this suit not in notes, will part of case). Abbeville
Dist. I Thomas Fulton being weak in body but sound mind and understanding. I desire that all my real and personal property be sold by
my executors. If not enough money on hand at my death to pay my debts,
use whatever needed from the sale to pay off. After paying my debts,
I give to my wife Sarah Ann one third of the proceeds of the sale of
my real estate, this is in lieu of her dower in my real property. All
the balance to be equally divided between my ch., Richard B. Fulton,
Amanda M. Ingram, Eliza A. Fulton, Jane Augusta Fulton, Frances C.
Fulton, Lenora B. Fulton, Anna Adelia Fulton, Jordon W. Fulton, share
and share alike and to my two grandsons Samuel J. Fulton and John C.
Fulton chn. of my decd. son Benjamin H. Fulton who is to have their
father's share. I appoint my friend Robert H. Wardlaw and Thomas B.
Dendy executors. Dated 10 July 1848. Signed: Thomas Fulton. Wit:
Thos. Thomson, W. Aug. Lee, R. A. Fair. Other inf. Thomas Fulton died
in the year 1856 and that Thomas B. Dendy one of the executor died
before the testator. Your orator charges that the execution against
Richard B. Fulton are unsatisfied, no part thereof having been paid,
and that Richard B. Fulton resides beyong the limits of this State.
Filed 12 March 1858.

GAINES, MARGARET #472. In Equity. Clerk of Court Office.
Abbeville, S. C. Abbeville Dist. I Margaret Gaines being of sound
and disposing mind but in feeble health. Whereas Dr. F. Branch by a
deed dated 7 Oct. 1848, conveyed to my brother Andrew Wilson a negro
girl named Clarissa and her son Tom in trust for my sole use for life,
with power to dispose of the said slaves by will at my death. Whereas
said Clarissa has since had Sally and Henry. I desire my executors
to sell the said negroes, and from the proceeds after paying my just
debts. I give to my nephew Samuel Wilson son of my brother John
Wilson the sum of eight hundred dollars. To my nieces Sarah Kennedy,
Lucinda Margan and Eliza Ann Wilson I give on hundred dollars each. I
give to my nephew Andrew Wilson son of my brother Andw. Wilson the
boy Tom to him forever. I appoint John H. Wilson Esq. executor. Dated
23 Aug. 1856. Wit: W. M. Hadden, J. W. Livingston, John A. Wier.
Signed: Margret Gaines. Deed, Abbeville Dist. I Franklin Branch
in consideration of $336.09 to me paid by Andrew Wilson of the State
of Miss., Rankin County, the next friend of Mrs. Margaret Gaines of
Abbeville Dist. For the sole use of Margret Gaines, not subject to
debts of her husband or future husband. Subject to her disposal at
her death by will. This 7 Oct. 1848. Wit: Samuel Reid. Signed:
Franklin Branch.

GAINS, DAVID Box 39 Pack 849. Probate Judge Office. Abbeville,
S. C. Admr. bond: We Larkin Reynolds, James Goudey and James Watson
are bound unto Andrew Hamilton Esq. Ord. in the sum of $5,000. Dated
6 March 1804. Whereas Larkin Reynolds has applied for me to letter of
admr. on the good and chattels of David Gaines decd. as highest
creditor. This 6 Feb. 1804. Cit. pub. 19 Feb. 1804 by Arthur Williams.
Appriment made by John Ball, L. Pulliam, Henry X Johnson. Sale held
26 March 1804, buyers, James Gaines, Peggy Gaines, Doctor Meriwether,
Benjmain Cochran, Richard Gaines, Wm. Gaines, Patty Nichols,
Matterson, Jno. Richardson, Jno. Meriwether, Pleasant Wright. The
sale list was signed by Richard Gaines. In another place "By Margret
Gains, receipt for sundries. By Mary Gains and others cost in a suite
at law. By John Ball suite at law. By Peggy Gains for her part of
the land.."

GAINS, EDMOND Box 40 Pack 871. Probate Judge Office. Abbeville,
S. C. I Edmond Gaines of Newberry Dist. being in perfect sense and

Gains, Edmond - Continued. memory. I lend to my wife Susannah
Gaines the use of all my estate both real and personal during her
widowhood for her support, maintenance and education of my children
during their minority. At the death of my wife, my estate shall be
equally divided between my children, if any be decease, their heirs if
any shall take the part of the parent. I will and desire that my
honored father Henry Gaines and my two brothers Richard and Henry Mayo
Gaines shall make such division among my said children as shall appear
most just to them. I appoint my honored father Henry Gaines and my
two brothers Richard and Henry Mayo Gaines executors. Dated 18 May
1802. Wit: Larkin Gaines, Richard Gaines, Robert Gaines. Signed:
Edmond Gaines. Proved on oath of Robert Gaines before Talo.
Livingston O.A.D. on this 21 Jan. 1809. An inventory was made 23 Nov.
1809 by Edward McGraw, Wm. (A) Arnold, Jordon Mosley. Negroes named
Jim, George, Frank, Delpha, Cloe and child, Fanny and three small
children. Admr. bond. We Suckey Gaines, Richard Gaines, Henry Gaines
and William Ware Esq. all of Abbeville Dist. are bound unto Andrew
Hamilton Esq. Ord. in the sum of $10,000. Dated 1 Nov. 1809. To
Richard Gaines Senr. and Suckey Gaines (now Perret) and also Perry
Perret who intermarried with Suckey Gaines. Whereas Robert Gaines
has applied to me for a citation to the admr. and admrx. of the est.
of Edmond Gaines, You are to appear before me on the 20 Jan. next to
show cause why the est. of Edmond Gaines can not be settled. Dated
this 13 Dec. 1828. Moses Taggart Ord. Abbeville Dist.

GAINS, WILLIAM Box 40 Pack 887. Probate Judge Office. Abbeville, S. C. I William Gains of Abbeville Dist. being in a low state
of heath, but perfectly in my mind and senses. It is my desire that
my executors sell my brown horse and grey mare, and the money put on
interest till the death of my wife. The ballance of my property to
be keep together as long as my wife lives, and my children to be keep
together and raised until they come of age. At the death of my wife
I desire all my property be sold and the money divided between all my
children (not named). I appoint my wife executrix and James Gains
and John Merriwether executors. Dated 30 March 1804. Wit: Dabney
Puckett, James Puckett. Signed: William X Gaines. Recorded 13 April
1804. Inventory made 17 April 1804 by Joseph Merriwether, Dabney
Puckett, James Johnson.

GARDNER, JOHN Book 5 Page 149. Probate Judge Office. Charleston,
S. C. This 19 July 1742. I John Gardner, Indian Trade, being in
perfect health of body mind and memory thanks be to God. I leave my
whole and sole estate both real and personal to my beloved wife Rachel
Gardner her heirs executors assigns for ever, that is after my just
debts are paid. I give to my beloved cousin John Nelson one mare
called Allen and her colt and one horse called Chukusaw. I do appoint
my wife Rachel Gardner my executrix. Wit: James Maxwel, John Durent,
Sam. Bright. Signed: John Gardner. Proved this will was proved
before George Haige, Esq. by virtue of a Dedimus issued the 14 Mar.
1744 and on the 23 July 1745. Recorded 6 Aug. 1745.

GARNER, LEWIS Box 40 Pack 870. Probate Judge Office. Abbeville,
S. C. We John Garner, William Nibbs and Robert Marsh are bound unto
Taliaferro Livingston, Esq. Ord. in the sum of ten thousand dollars,
lawful money of this State. Dated 22 May 1816. Condition to admr.
all the goods and chattels of Lewis Garner decd. Whereas John Garner
hath made suit to me to grant him letter of admr. on the est. of Lewis
Garner of Cambridge (Ninety Six) of this Dist. Dated 22 Feb. 1816.
Published 2 March and third and last time by Richard M. Todd, M.G.
The inventory of Garner is that of a merchant, made by John Mayson,
Jno. McBride, Jno. Whellar.

GAMBLE, SAMUEL Box 41 Pack 934. Probate Judge Office.
Abbeville, S. C. I Samuel Gamble of Abbeville Dist. being weak in
body but of sound mind and memory. I give to my well beloved wife
Jane Gamble the plantation with all improvements thereon, whereon I
now live to occupied by her and the family as long as she remains my
widow, and not longer. I also leave in her care all my moveable
property for her support and her chn. Except I give to Harris Jones

Gamble, Samuel - Continued. one young sorral mare with whatever
he already has. If my wife thinks proper she may divide my moveable
property with my dtrs. that now lives with me. To my eldest son John
I give him 125 acres of land on which I now live, at the expiration
of his mother widowhood. Dated 19 Oct. 1800. (no more of this will
found in the notes).

GANT, WILLIAM Box 40 Pack 876. Probate Judge Office. Abbeville,
S. C. I William Gant, of Abbeville Dist. (two lines torn into). I
will to my son in law Jacob Lollar my plantation whereon I now live,
and I also allow Jacob Loller one half of the meat I now have. I
appoint my two sons Frederic and Cador executors to my estate to sell
my personal property and pay my just debts (a line torn). I give to
my son Frederic $56. I give to my son Cador $56. To my son Britain
$56. To my son John $56. To my dtr. Levina $56. To my dtr. Sally
$28. To my dtr. Nancy $28. To my dtr. Aimy $10. To my son Tyre $10.
If my estate is more than the above amount, the balance to be equal
divided between the last named chn. Dated 1 May 1809. Wit: William
Shirley, William Burton, James P. Conner. Signed: William Gant,
Recorded 6 May 1809. Appraisement was made 25 May 1809. By William
Burton, Andrew Jones, Stephen Durrum.

GANTT, FREDERICK Box 39 Pack 866. Probate Judge Office. Abbeville, S. C. I Frederick Gantt, being weak in body but of sound mind
and memory. I will as much of my property to be sold as shall pay
my just debts. I will that all my other property to my wife (not
named) as long as she live and my land to my two sons John and James
Atteson at her decease. Dated 5 May 1814. Wit: Cador Gantt, Frs.
Cunnungham, Benjamin Griffin. Signed: Frederick Gantt. N.B. I do
appoint my wife Elizabeth and my brother Cador Gantt executors. Will
proved on oath of Benjamin Griffin, before Talo. Livingston, O.A.D.
on the 2 Jan. 1815. Inventory made 24 Feb. 1815.

GASTON, ALEXANDER Box 41 Pack 910. Probate Judge Office. Abbeville, S. C. Guardinship bond, We Andrew Mantz, Hamilton Hill and
Samuel L. Hill are bound unto Moses Taggart, Ord. in the sum of
$10,000. Dated 1 Feb. 1836. Whereas Moses Taggart, Ord. has this day
granted a letter of guardinship to Andrew Mantz on the person and
personal est. of Alexander Gaston a minor. He shall make a yearly
account to the ordinary for all sum of money, books, and things which
shall come into his hands. Signed: Andrew Mantz, Hamilton Hill,
Samuel Hill.

GASTON, ELIZABETH Apt. 3 File 209. Probate Judge Office. Green-
ville, S. C. Will dated 29 Oct. 1824. Probated 1 Jan. 1825. Brother
David Pendens, three youngest chn. Ellin Peden, Andy Peden, David
Peden. Niece, Mary Peden. "Allow John Stenhouse, Gaston Grace,
Gaston Terry." Exros: Anthony Savage, James Morton. Wit: Jabez
Terry, Asbury Terry, Anthony Savage.

GEE, JOHN Box 40 Pack 888. Probate Judge Office. Abbeville,
S. C. Abbeville Dist. Admr. bond, We John Hearst, John McComb and
John Pressly are bound unto Moses Taggart, Ord. in the sum of $2,000.
Dated 3 July 1826. Inventory made 22 July 1826 by Jonathan Arnold,
John Chiles, Samuel Mouchet. Sale held 22 July 1826 buyers:
Jonathan Arnold, George Moushett, John Chiles, Samuel Perrin, Esq.,
Jos. Drinkwater, Samuel Bradford, Sam Goff, John Hearst, Eve Moushett.
Recd. 14 March 1827, James Puckett for land sold by Robert Gee, Atty.
to said Puckett.

GASTON, JANE & JOHN Box 41 Pack 909. Probate Judge Office.
Abbeville, S. C. Guardinship bond: We John Norwood, William Lyon
and Charles Dendy all of Abbeville Dist. are bound unto Moses Taggart,
Ord. in the sum of $3,000. Dated 16 Sept. 1837. Whereas this day
Moses Taggart, Ord. has granted a letter of guardinship to John Norwood
on the personal estate of Miss Jane Gaston and John Gaston minors.
(parents not named).

GEORGE, DAVID Box 39 Pack 835. Probate Judge Office. Abbeville,
S. C. 96 Dist. Admr. bond. We Rebeca George, William George, James
Hogans and David Hutson are bound unto John Ewing Calhoun, Ord. in the
sum of 14 thousand pounds money. Dated 14 Nov. 1782. Estate was
appraised 22 Nov. 1782 by William Hill, John Gorman, George Ashford.
Rebeca George was of Tagger River in 96 Dist. and was the widow..

GEORGE, JOHN Pack 3 (basement). Clerk of Court Office. Anderson,
S. C. Petition for naturalization. Pendleton Dist. To the Honor.
the Associate Judge; The humble petition of John George a native of
the County of Antrim, in the kingdom of Ireland. Arrived in Charleston,
S. C. in the year 1791. That your petitioner is attached to the
principles of the U.S. and is desirous of becoming a citizen thereof.
Your petitioner will ever pray. We do certify that we have known John
George since the year 1791 and has resided in this State since that
time. That he is of good moral character etic. Signed: Geo. Bowie,
Pat Norris, Thomas Farrar, David Sloan, Robert Anderson. Dated 1 Nov.
1806. John George being duly sworn in open Court, that he doth
absolutely and entirely renounce and abjure allegiance and fidelity
to every foreign power, etc. Dated 1 Nov. 1806 M. Hammond, D. Clerk.

GENRY, WILLIAM D. Box 40 Pack 889. Probate Judge Office.
Abbeville, S. C. Abbeville Dist. Admr. bond. We Gen. Edmund Ware,
William Kyle, J. W. Taggart are bound unto Moses Taggart, Ord. in the
sum of $2,000. Dated 17 Jan. 1829. Appraisement made 5 Feb. 1829 by
Wm. Pyles, John Mattison, Augusta Maddox. Slae held 5 May 1829
buyers, Barzella G. Jay, Augusta Maddox, Elizabeth Genry, Joshua
Cullins, William Pyles, Thomas Norwood.

GENT, JESSE Pack 390. Clerk of Court Office. Abbeville, S.C.
Abbeville Dist. In Equity, To the Honr. the Chancellors: Your orator
and oratrix Benjamin Mattison and his wife Jane, and Sally Gent, some
of the heirs of Jesse Gent. Sheweth that about the 14 Sept. 1849
Jesse Gent departed this life intestate. At time of his death he
was possessed with two tracts of land, one lying on Broad Mouth and
Turkey Creek waters of Saluda River, containing 800 acres, bounded by
on East by George Mattison, South by William Long, West by Jane
Webster and North by John Smith. The other tract of about 150 acres
lying on Broad Mouth Creek waters of Saluda River, bounded by George
Mattison and John Smith, Jesse Gent left as his only heirs your
oratrix Sally Gent, Jane Mattison another sister, Daniel Gent a
brother, and the children and grand children of a deceased sister
Elizabeth Nash the wife of George Nash. Elizabeth Nash died many years
ago leaving seven children: Nancy wife of T. Hagewood, Sally wife of
John Airs, John, Cooper, Milton, Jesse, Peggy now the wife of David
Hornesby, Polly now wife of Samuel Truss, Mahala now the wife of
Warren Truss. Nancy died before intestate Jesse Gent, leaving five
chn. Robert Mansfield and the names of the others unknown. Sally Nash
who intermarried with John Airs died before the intestate, leaving seven
chn. names unknown. The admr. named by David Lesley, Ord. to G. M.
Mattison and W. P. Martin, Esq. Filed 2 Nov. 1849. On another paper
mentioned that Sally Gent, Jane Mattison wife of Benjamin were of
Benton County, Ala. Elizabeth wife of George Nash of Mississippi died
before Jesse Gent. Also Daniel Gent, John Nash, Cooper Nash, Milton
Nash, Jesse Nash, David Hornesby and Peggy his wife and Warren Truss
and Mahala his wife, Samuel Truss and Polly his wife all reside beyond
the State.

GENT, JESSE Pack 18. Clerk of Court Office. Abbeville, S. C.
Abbeville Dist. In Equity, to the Honr. the Chancellors: Your
orators William P. Martin and Gabriel M. Mattison sheweth that Jesse
Gent died about the 14 Sept. 1849, intestate. The admr. on the est.
was granted to your orators on the first day of Oct. 1849. Your
orators further sheweth that Daniel Gent a brother of Jesse Gent decd.
one of the distributees of his estate, at the sale of the personal
property, purchased largely, the amount of his purchase were charged
against him on the sale bill of the estate. Now your orators find that
the distributive share of said Daniel Gent in the personal estate, will
not pay his indebtedness to the estate. Your orators on the 2 Oct.

Gent, Jesse - Continued. 1850, they instituted in the Court of
Common Pleas action against Daniel Gent, and succeeded in recovering
a verdict in the sum of $203.00, besides cost of suit. That the said
Daniel Gent pending the action and before judgment was abtained
secretly and without the knowledge of your orators left the country,
talking with him all the property of every nature or kind. Your orators
sheweth that the real estate was sold by the commissioners in the year
1850, the sale amounted to near three thousand dollars, with one half
in cash and the balance in two years. Therefore, your orators has
did receive one half of the said Daniel Gent indebtness. Filed 15 Nov.
1852. There was a warrant issued for the arrest of Daniel Gent in
Taladega County, Ala. Where he was last seen.

GENT, JOHN Box 38 Pack 816. Probate Judge Office. Abbeville,
S. C. Admr. bond, We James Hunt, David Lesley and John Gray who
are bound unto Moses Taggart, Ord. in the sum of $1000. Dated 13 Nov.
1826. Inventory was held 30 Nov. 1826 by Ro. Smith, Jonathan Johnson,
Bannister Allen. Negroes named boy Daniel, Girl Angy. Sale held
1 Dec. 1826 buyers: Mordecai Shackleford, Banister Allen, Robert
Smith, Elijah Hunt, Joseph Scott, Roland Grant, Elijah Kimble, Wm. P.
Raiford, Milton Pascal, John McNeil, Wm. Keown, Lucy Gent, Thomas
Sanders, Freeman Wiley, Susan Bozeman, Sanford C. Clark, John M. Porter,
Wm. L. Crawford, Jacob Martin, Wm. Ward, E. Hunt, Abram Bell, Austin
Scuddy, David Robertson.

GIBERT, CAPT. JOHN LEWIS Box 38 Pack 820. Probate Judge Office.
Abbeville, S. C. Admr. bond, We Jane Gibert, Peter B. Moregne, John
Moragne and Edward Collier all of Abbeville Dist. are bound unto Moses
Taggart, Esq. Ord. in the sum of $12,000. Dated 22 Dec. 1825. Whereas
Jane Gibert and Peter B. Moragne have made suit to me to grant them
letter of Admr. on est. of John Lewis Gibert decd. this 25 Nov. 1825.
An appraisement was made 9 Jan. 1826 by Edwd Collier, Isaac Moragne,
Arthur Slaughter, M. G. Williams. Negroes named, Ned a carpenter, Guy,
Stephen, Redman, Maryann, George, Jessy, Samuel, Ned, Liza, Malinda,
Louzan, Rose, Abisba, Harriet and Sam. Sale held 10 Jan. 1826.
Buyers: Jacob Bellotte, Jane Huese, Reubin L. Mabry, Thomas Harris,
Philip Leroy, Senr., Joseph Gibert, John David, John Moragne, John
Bouchillon, Isaac Bouchillon, John Furgason, Elijah Legard, James
Huese, Thomass Morrow, William Truit, Edward Collier Senr. On 29
Dec. 1835 Peter B. Moragne and Jane Gibert admor and admrx. and Benja-
min E. Gibert, Susan E. Gibert, William J. and his wife Drusilla E.
Huston agree to settle debts against the est. An order to sell the
land was issued 19 March 1836, at this time John Gideon Gibert,
Carolina Jane Gibert, and Harriet Adeline are minors.

GIBERT, PETER Box 39 Pack 830. Probate Judge Office. Abbeville,
S. C. I Peter Gibert, being weak in body but of sound mind and memory
and understanding. I give to my son Stephen Gibert the tract of land
on which he now lives on Long Cane, also 600 acres on waters of
Savannah River, part of three tracts, one granted to Ebenezer Pettigrue,
one to Peter Gibert Junr., one to Peter Gibert Senr. I give to my son
Lewis Gibert the mill tract containing 300 acres, I purchased from John
E. Calhoun and also another tract containing 80 acres which I purchased
from Andrew Bowdan. I give to my wife Elizabeth Guname Gibert all the
rest of my estate both real and personal during her life time or remain
my widow, in case of the marriage of either of my dtrs. Mary Harriet
or Susan Gibert, I wish my wife to give her or them so marring as much
as she may feel to dispose of. In case of death or marriage of my
wife, I wish my estate be divided, except wheat I have given to
Stephen and Lewis, equally between my sons Clement, Joseph B., and
Elijah Gibert and dtrs. Lucy, Mary, Harriot Susan Gibert, and my dtr.
Elizabeth C. Lee, late Elizabeth C. Gibert. I give to my dtr. Elizabeth one negro girl. I appoint my sons Lewis and Joseph B. Gibert and
my wife Elizabeth B. Gibert executor and executrix. Dated 8 June 1815.
Wit: Peter B. Rogers, Susanne David, M. X. Covin. Signed: P. Gibert.
Proven on oath of Peter B. Rogers before Talo. Livingston, Ord. this
3 July 1815. An appraisement was held on 24 July 1815 by R. Watkins,
James Collier, Jean Bouchillon. In this paper Peter Gibert is listed
as Esq. Negroes named, Phillis and Banna, Moses, Charles, Harry,

Gibert, Peter - Continued. Hannah and child Ephraim, Peggy and child Nancy, Rachel, Kitty, Robin, Charlotte, Nepos, Tim, Violet

GIBSON, ROBERT Box 39 Pack 829. Probate Judge Office. Abbeville, S. C. I Robert Gibson, being in a weak state of body but of sound mind, memory and understanding. I will that my just debts be paid. I give unto my beloved wife during her life one negro named Herrod and two children, one named Lenard the other named Steven, also one gray horse and riding chair. Also two beds and all the furniture that she brought with her when we married. The above named negroes at death of my wife be given to my son John Gibson. I will to my dtr. Mary McCain $250 to be paid out of money arising from the sale of my property. I give to my son John Gibson one negro man named Mingo and Cambo. I give to my dtr. Elizabeth Taggart one negro woman named Fan. I give to my dtr. Jane Con one negro woman named Cate and her child named Rose. I give to my dtr. Prudence $600 to be paid her for the price of negro Tom. The remainder of my property be sold and the money left after paying my debts, be equally divided between all my children. I appoint my son John Gibson and David Taggart my son in law executors. Dated 23 Jan. 1816. Wit: Samuel Foster Senr., Samuel C. Foster. Signed: Robert Gibson. Proved on oath of Samuel C. Foster, before Talo. Livingston, O.A.D. on the 27 Jan. 1816. The inventory was made the 13 Feb. 1816. Negroes named, Mingo, Cumbo, Rose, Lean, Stephen, Hariot, Fan, Date. Inventory made by Moody Burt, Wm. Hall, Adino Griffin. Sale held 15 Feb. 1816. Buyers, John Gibson, James Conn, Mary Gibson, David Taggart, John Smith, George Conn, Samuel C. Foster, Samuel McWherns, James Johnson, Alexander R. Gray, William Stuart, Robert Hearst, Joseph Conn, Sharlot Keller, Benjamin Foster, Thomas Mealy, Samuel Spence, James Jones, Andrew McGill, Alexander Lesly, John Baird, Dr. S. Marshall, Nancy Pain, William H. Glover, Joshua Teague, John Calhoon, Ely Dodgin, James Patterson, Daniel Foster, Robert Hearst, Thomas Davis, Daniel Foshee, Samuel Cummins, James Watson, James Christian. Notes due the decease. Adino Griffin due $600, James Hinton due $10, Benjamin Goodman due $37.50, John Houston due $109, John Burt due $8, Joseph Conn due $130, John Hearst due $100, Adino Griffin due $75, George B. Allen due $7.

GIBSON, SAMUEL Box 39 Pack 834. Probate Judge Office. Abbeville, S. C. 96 Dist. Admr. bond. We Mary Gibson, Joseph Dawson, William Carson are bound unto John Ewing Calhoun Ord. in the sum of 14 thousand pounds money, dated 21 Sept. 1782. Estate appraised 2 Nov. 1782 by Joseph Dawson, William Moore, William Carson. Mary Gibson lived on Hardlabor Creek in Abbeville, Dist. Sale held 12 Dec. 1782, buyers, Mary Gibson, Thomas Carson, John Hearst, Samuel Bell.

GILES, JOHN Will Book A, Page 50. Probate Judge Office. Elberton, Ga. I John Giles of Elbert Co., Ga. being weak in body but of perfect mind and memory. First I will my just debts be paid. To my dear and loving wife I give one horse and one mare, two cows and calves, the house whereon I now live and the plantation on which it stands, to have and hold during her natural life. All the rest of my property of what nature or kind soever be equally divided between my children (not named) and my will is that my grand child Jonathan Gray have an equal share of my property with my children. My negro fellow Daniel I give to my dear wife for the term of her natural life. At the death of my wife, my plantation and other property to be sold and an equal division between the surviving children, except my dtr. the wife of Jerimiah Wells must have fifteen pounds deducted, as they have before received this sum. I appoint my wife executrix and William J. Hobby executor. This 12 April 1794. Wit: Andrew Elliet, John X McNeel, Sam M. Thomson. Signed: John Giles, Recorded the will of the late John Giles. 28 July 1794.

GILES, JOSIAH P. Pack 361. Clerk of Court Office. Abbeville, S. C. Abbeville Dist. In Equity. To the Honr. the Chancellors: Your oratrix Sarah C. Giles of this Dist. sheweth that on or about the ___ day of June 1855 her husband Josiah P. Giles late of this Dist, departed this life, possessed with a tract of land lying on Rockey River containing 375 acres, bounded by land of George R. McCalla,

Giles, Josiah P. - Continued. John M. Mosely, Sugar Johnson and others. Leaving your oratrix the widow and chn. Eliza Ann Giles, James M. Giles, Mary Sue Giles, the oldest of whom is only about nine yrs. old. The admr. of the est. was granted to Hamilton T. Miller, the brother of your oratrix by William Hill, Ord. The personal est. more than paid all debts, and a settlement is on file in the Ordinary Office. Your oratrix believes and submits that it would be to the advantage of the parties interested, that a partition be made of the tract of land. Filed 17 April 1857.

GILES, MARY Box 40 Pack 891. Probate Judge Office. Abbeville, S. C. Abbeville Dist. Admr. bond. We James S. Baskin, John Baskin, and James F. Cook are bound unto Moses Taggart, Ord. in the sum of $3,000. Dated 17 April 1835. Cit. Pub. at Glover Chapel. Appraisement made 28 April 1835 by Oeville Tatam, William Ward, and Sugar Johnson. Settlement made 6 June 1845. Present the Admrs. Elihu Beard absent. Parties in interest. John Baskin and Jane his wife. Francis Young desd. John Young, Samuel Young, David and Susannah Carr both desd. Martha Mitchell desd. Her heirs, Isabella MGilld[?] desd. Mary Giles wife of William Giles died without children leaving as her heirs, her husband William Giles, who takes over half the estate and her brothers and sisters having the balance. She was the dtr. of Francis Young.

GILES, ROBERT Box 38 Pack 826. Probate Judge Office. Abbeville, S. C. I Robert Giles, being weak in body, but of sound mind and disposing judgment. First I desire that all my just debts are paid that my estate both real and personal be equally divided between my wife not named and two children (Sally and Peggy). I appoint Andrew Giles my executor. Dated 27 March 1817. Wit: Samuel Pressly, William Giles. Signed: Robert Giles. The estate was appraised the 1 July 1817, by James X McClain, Allen Glover, William Giles.

GILL, DANIEL Box 39 Pack 828. Probate Judge Office. Abbeville, S. C. I Daniel Gill of Rockey River Congregation in Abbeville Dist. being in health of body and of sound mind, memory and understanding. I give to my son John one dollar. To my dtr. Fanney one dollar. My will and desire is that all my real and personal estate be sold, and after paying my debts and expenses, the balance be equally divided between my wife Susanah Gill and my four last chn. My wife Susanah to have one fifth, my son Peter one fifth, my son Ezekiel one fifth, my dtr. Sarah one fifth, my dtr. Polley one fifth. I appoint Samuel Linton, John Coldwell, Esq., Thomas Franklin executors. Dated 5 Dec. 1800. Wit: John Baskin, William Bole. Signed: Daniel Gill. Recorded 11 June 1802. The real estate of Daniel Gill decd. was 279 sold by John Gill executor to Milton Paschall for $1515 in Aug. 1803. John Gill was gdn. for Ezekiel Gill minor. The executor paid to John Cowen part of widow legacy. In another place John Cowen is one of the legatee. Paid 1804 Sarah Slaughter her legacy. An inventory was made 17 July 1802 by James Caldwell, John Baskin, Wm. Kerr. Negroes named Jack, Isaac, Dick, Cloey, Jenney, Suckey, Jane.

GILLEBEAU, ANDREW Box 40 Pack 892. Probate Judge Office. Abbeville, S. C. I Andrew Gillebeau of Abbeville Dist. being weak in body but of perfect mind and memory. First I will and demise that all my debts be paid by my executor. I will to my wife Jean Guilbeau all my estate both real and personal during her natural life. I will to my dtr. Susannah Beaushalon forty dollars. I will to Eliser Guilbeau supposed to be the dtr. of James Guilbeau begotten by Liddy Bellot seventy dollars. I will to my son James Guilbeau one dollar. I will to my son Peter Guilbeau all the balance of my estate. I appoint my son Peter Guilbeau executor. Dated 18 Feb. 1806. Wit: Charles Hathorn, Eleseraur X Cavin, Peter Cavin. Signed: Andrew X Guilbeau. Proved on oath of Peter Cavin before Talo. Livingston Ord. on the 21 Feb. 1815.

GILLESPIE, MATTHEW Box 40 Pack 880. Probate Judge Office. Abbeville, S. C. Admr. bond, We Frances Gillespie, widow, James Gillespie, Wm. McCleskey Senr. are bound unto the judges of Abbeville

Gillespie, Matthew - Continued. Dist. in the sum of £1000
sterling. Dated 25 March 1793. Whereas Frances Gillespie hath applied
to this Court for letter of Admr. on the good and chattles of Matthew
Gillespie late of this Dist. as next of kin. Dated 12 Nov. 1792.
Cit. Pub. at Rockey River 16 Dec. 1792. An inventory was made 1 May
1793 by John Patterson, Aaron Steel, John Caldwell.

GILLISON, JAMES No ref. Clerk of Court Office. Anderson, S. C.
I James Gillison in consideration of £30 paid me by Abraham Elledge,
both of Pendleton Dist. Have granted, sold, bargained and released
all that tract of land lying on Twenty Six Mile Creek, containing 90
acres being part of a tract granted to said James Gillison on 3 Dec.
1787 containing 888 acres. Bounded by land of John E. Calhoun, Dick-
sons land, Elledges land. (No more of this deed in notes.)

GILLISPIE, JAMES Box 40 Pack 882. Probate Judge Office. Abbeville, S. C. Abbeville Dist. Admr. bond. We Elizabeth Gillespie
(widow), Lowry Gillespie, Andrew Pickens and John Harris of Flatwoods,
planters are bound unto the Judge of Abbeville County Court in the sum
of £1000 sterling. Dated 10 Nov. 1795. Cit. Pub. at Rockey River
Church. Est. appraised 5 Dec. 1795 by James Caldwell, Joseph Lemaster,
Andrew Pickens. Sale held 10 Dec. 1795, buyers, John Robeson, Abraham
Pickens, Gabriel Pickens, Lowry Gillispie, Jonathan Pickens, Margaret
Gillispie, widow, Joseph Vernon, Stuard Baskin, Capt. Linton, David
Gillispie, John Allison, Phanny Gillispie, John Moore, John McNeil,
Thomas Wilson, John Campbell, Harris Jones, Cary Evens, Lewis Howlin,
Nehemiah Vernon, Mason Izard, Patrick Cain, Wm. Walker, Robert Smith,
Wm. Love, Francis Cummins, Wm. Dunlap, Samuel Green, Francis Drinkard,
Robt. Dennomm, Francis Sutherland, Hugh Baskin, Wm. Harris, Wm.
Gillispie.

GILMER, JAMES Box 38 Pack 814. Probate Judge Office. Abbeville,
S. C. Admr. bond, We Samuel Gilmer, Robert Gilmer and William
McClinton are bound unto Moses Taggart, Ord. in the sum of $2,000.
Dated 17 Feb. 1820. In the bond his name is James Gilmer Senr. An
inventory was made 23 Feb. 1820 by Matt Wilson, Patrick Johnston, Wm.
Lesly. Sale held 17 March 1820, buyers, Samuel Gilmor, William
McClinton, James Cobb, Wm. Lesly, Samuel Murry, Mrs. Gilmor, Robert
Gilmor, Joseph Gibbons, Edward Phar, Joseph Lesly, James Russell,
George Miller.

GLASGOW, JAMES Pack 431 A & B. Clerk of Court Office. Abbeville,
S. C. I James Glasgow, being of sound mind and memory, but weak in
body. I give to my two youngest children, Sarah and James my land
consisting of 160 acres to be equally divided between them, also one
bed a piece. I desire that the rest of my property be sold and monies
arising there from, to pay my just debts and funeral expenses if any
over to be divided between the two above named chn. I have given the
rest of my children, their full share of my est. namely, Thomas
Glasgow, Mary McClellan, Jane Burdit and Nancy Hunter. I appoint
Moses McCaslam executor. Dated 12 Feb. 1847. Wit: James F. Mabry,
James Cason, A. N. Darracott. Signed: James Glasgow. Abbeville Dist.
In Equity, to the Honr. the Chancellors. Your orator James N. Glasgow
of this Dist. a minor under the age of twenty one, by John Hunter of
Abbeville Dist. his next friend. That your orator father departed this
life in the year 1848 testate, which was proved in this Court and
Moses McCaslan as executor. Your orator's father gave his sister
Sarah E. and himself a tract of land, bounded by land of Thomas P.
Dowton, William W. Belcher and others to be divided equally between
them. That in the year 1850 his sister intermarried with one Robert
McKinney. The said Robert McKinney and his wife Sarah partition this
Court in 1851 for a division of said land. Your orator then fifteen
years of age and living in the State of Kentucky. On the same day
Robert McKenney made a motion that Moses McCaslan be appointed guardian
ad litem of your orator. Four commissioners namely, James McCaslan,
John Wideman, Thomas P. Dowton, and Robert McComb, who returned their
writ of partition, that the said land could not be fairly and impar-
tially divided, and that the land was of the value of $8 per acre. The
said Robert McKenney was not satisfied with the return. He demanded

Glasgow, James - Continued. that the said land be sold at public out cry to the highest bidder. That said Robert McKenny departed this life in Feb. 1853, leaving the widow and two sons Robert Alexander McKinney and William Henry McKinney. Filed 27 April 1854.

GLASGOW, JOHN Pack 817. Clerk of Court Office. Abbeville, S.C. Abbeville Dist. I John Glasgow in consideration of $800 paid by James Glasgow both of Abbeville Dist. have granted, bargained, sold and release, all that tract of land, containing 150 acres. Bounded by land of James Glasgow, George Roberts, Thomas P. Dowden and Oliver McCasland. Dated 20 Oct. 1835. Wit: John W. Foster, Robert McComb. Signed: John Glasgow. Proved on oath of John W. Foster before John Kennedy, J.P. on the 21 Jan. 1827.

GLASGOW, JOHN D. Box 41 Pack 933. Probate Judge Office. Abbeville, S. C. Abbeville Dist. In Equity. The petition of Archibald Kennedy sheweth that John Glasgow departed this life, having made and executed his last will and the same was proved and recorded in the Ordinary Office on the 23 Oct. 1843, and R. A. Martin as exor. After his debts are paid he willed the remainder of his estate both real and personal to his widow, Elizabeth A. Glasgow to her and her heirs forever, except 166 acres of land on Bowel Branch which he will to his sister Jane McCallister during her life time and at her death to said Elizabeth A. Glasgow. Your petitioner further states that since making said will and shortly before the death of the testator then was born a child John D. Glasgow. Your petitioner is advised to entitled to the same provisions as is made for posthumorus children and is entitled to at least a moiety of the general bequeat if not two thirds. An application to the Court of Ordinary to sell the tract of 227 acres, the widow consents to this and whatever her child inheritance maybe. The child full name John David Glasgow. Archibald Kennedy was made guardian of child on 1 Jan. 1845. With James H. Foster and James Lessly as security.

GLOVER, ALLEN Box 38 Pack 808. Probate Judge Office. Abbeville, S. C. Admr. bond: We Silas Glover and Benjamin McGaw, admr. and Wm. Giles, Mathew Brown are bound unto Moses Taggart, Esq. Ord. in the sum of $600. Dated this 6 Dec. 1823. Whereas Silas Glover and Benjamin McGaw has made suit to me for letter of admr. on the goods and chattels of Allen Glover decd. This 22 Nov. 1823. An appraisement was made 22 Dec. 1823 by James McBride, William Giles, Archibald Kidd. Sale was held 23 Dec. 1823. Buyers, Silas Glover, Benjamin McGaw, William Weed, James McBride, William Robinson, William Mantz, Henry Robinson, Isaac Lassety, Saml. Coleman, Ludia Glover, Jno. Wardlaw, Saml. Cowen, Francis Pitman, S. B. Robinson, John Presley, Archibald Kid, J. C. Cowey, Jas. Cason, Jacob Giles, Wm. Drenan, Lydia Glover, Revd. John T. Pressly, Thomas McBride, Josiah McGaw, Wiat Taylor, Daniel Wideman, Thomas Cresswell, Young Reagan, Baily Reagan, Mathew Brown, David Robertson, Wm. Drenan, John Kenedy, George McFarlin, Elias Gibson, Timothey Russel.

GLOVER, JANE Box 39 Pack 837. Probate Judge Office. Abbeville, S. C. I Jan Glover of Abbeville Dist. being sick and weak in body, but of perfect mind and memory. I will and desire that all my just debts be paid out of my estate. I give the whole of my estate both real and personal, after payments of my debts unto my two beloved sons John Caldwell and James H. Caldwell to be equally divided between them. They are to give to my beloved grand son John Bowman when he arrives at the age of twenty one, a horse worth sixty dollars. I appoint my son John and James H. Caldwell my executors. Dated 19 July 1822. Wit: Jno. Lipscomb, Stephen Witt, Hugh Wardlaw. Signed: Jane Glover. Est. appraised by James Patterson, John Burton, William H. Glanton. Sale held 7 Dec. 1822. Buyers: Abraham Thornton, Elijah Teague, Stephen Witt, John Lipscomb, Allen Glover, John B. Burton, James H. Caldwell, Nathaniel Cobb, John Coldwell, Thomas Eakin, John Gibson, Wm. H. Glanton, Alexander Jorden, Jarrot H. Glover, John Wardlaw, John Ravlin, Joseph Jay, Wm. N. Sanders, John V. Reynolds.

GLOVER, JOHN Book C. Clerk of Court Office. Elberton, Ga.
This indenture made 16 Jan. 1794, between John Glover and Ellender
his wife, and James Certain, all of Elbert Co., Ga. In consideration
of one hundred Ŀ sterling, have granted, bargained, sold and delivered
part of six hundred acres in said county, granted to John Glover on
the 24 Nov. 1786. Being the mill and one hundred acres including.
Bounded by John Wilkins, John Brown and Joseph Huddlestons land. Wit:
James Bell, J.P., Wm. Rogers. Signed: John X Glover and Ellender X
Glover. Registered 1 May 1795.

GODFREY, BENJAMIN Vol. 46 Page 107. Probate Judge Office.
Charleston, S. C. I Benjamin Godfrey Being of sound mind and disposing
memory. I desire that my executors pay all my just bets of whatsoever
nature. I will and direct my executors to set aside $600 and pay the
interest annually to the support and expenses of James Parker, Thomas
Parker and Harriet Parker, children of Harriet Parker Senr. and as each
arrives at the age of twenty one, pay him or her two hundred dollars
from the first amount, also I give 200 acres on the South end of the
tract bought by me from Enos Easterling to them and their heirs forever.
I give to my son Benjamin D. Godfrey, the two tracts I bought from the
est. of James Bradham with the saw and grist mills thereon, containing
in the two tracts 650 acres, also I give to my son six negroes to wit:
Cash, Plenty, Mary, Robert, Bella, Caesar. I give to my son John
Godfrey formerly of Alabama, but whose present residence is unknown to
me, if alive the sum of six hundred dollars. All other property in
my possession at my death, I give to my chn. James W. Godfrey, Leonora
V. Godfrey, and Charlotte R. Godfrey to be equally divided between
them. I appoint James W. Godfrey, Henry B. Godfrey, Albert C. Godfrey,
and Elias Weatherford executors. Dated 13 Aug. 1851. Wit: Chester
S. Coe, William Mellard, John I. Singletemy. Signed: B. Godfrey.
Proved before M. T. Mendenhall, Esq. O.C.D. the 30 June 1852 at same
time qualified Elias Weatherford as executor and on 17 June 1853
qualified James W. Godfrey as executor before George Buist O.C.D.

GOFF, ANN Pack 361. Clerk of Court Office. Abbeville, S. C.
Abbeville Dist. To the Honr. the Chancellors: Your orator John H.
Wilson sheweth that the 17 March 1849 Ann Goff died intestate leaving
her father Samuel Goff and her brother David C. Goff distributees.
Your orator applied for and obtained letter of admr. upon the estate
the 5 Feb. 1852. Your orator cannot find that the intestate left any
personal estate, though he has discovered that the decease was indebted
at time of his death to wit: To your orator $300 with interest from
14 Feb. 1848, also to Charles Dendy of about $170 and interest, also
a debt to Thomas E. Owens of about $70 with interest, another to
Franklin Branch of five dollars and interest. The deceased Ann Goff
died seized of some real estate to wit, one lot in the village of
Abbeville containing one acre and a quarter, bounded by land of
Charles Dendy and Doct. S. Branch, and one the North East by Main
Street, formerly owned by Eli Holliday, also one other lot containing
one acre adj. the Methodist Church lot and land of Doct. S. Branch.
Filed 11 June 1852. On another paper, Anderson Dist. 3 June 1852.
"I hereby constitute my son David Goff my agent in regard to all my
interest in the estate of my dtr. Ann Ware Goff, authorizing him to
account the service of all write and process at law or in Equity
relating to said estate." Signed Samuel Goff.

GOFF, AUGUSTUS Box 40 Pack 890. Probate Judge Office. Abbeville, S. C. Abbeville Dist. Admr. bond. We Samuel Goff, Thomas
Jackson and Robert Cochran are bound unto Moses Taggart, Ord. in the
sum of $2,000. Dated 2 Feb. 1838.

GOLDING, RICHARD Box 41 Pack 928. Probate Judge Office. Abbeville, S. C. Abbeville Dist. Admr. bond, We Reuben G. Golding,
Charles B. Fooshee and Harris Y. Gillam who are bound unto David
Lesly, Ord. in the sum of $4,000.00. Dated 2 Nov. 1842. To David
Lesly, Ord. whereas R. A. G. Golding of this dist. decd. being a minor
and leaving a considerable personal estate consisting of some negroes
and the rest in money. The estate being liable to waste and abuse
your petitioner therefore prays for a letter of admr. Being a brother

Golding, Richard - Continued. of said decd. and at the request of the others relations he be made admr. Dated 15 Oct. 1842. Est. appraised 31 Dec. 1842 by William Eddins, C. B. Fooshee, Larkin Carter. Recd. 12 April 1844 from R. G. Golding admr. of R. A. G. Golding decd. as per settlement foregoing my one half of the estate of R. A. G. Golding decd. in right of my wife Louvena who was the mother of the decd. in full of and I do further consent that the other half say $285.80 do remain in hands of R. G. Golding the admr. subject to the disposal and control of my wife Louvenia. Signed: Wiley D. Mounce. Recd. 25 June 1845 of Reuben Golding formerly the guardian and at present the admr. of R. A. G. Golding decd. minor $617.90 in full of the said est. my distributive share. Signed: Nimrod C. Golding of Lousiana. Others who recd. a share, R. G. Golding, John M. Golding.

GOLDING, WILLIAM Box 39 Pack 839. Probate Judge Office. Abbeville, S. C. I William Golding of 96 Dist. being at this time in reasonable health and sound memory. I give to my son John Golding the plantation I now live on continaing 150, also one tract lying between said land and land of Col. James Williams mill containing 146 acres. One feather bed and furniture, also five negroes, Doll, Lucy, Jack, Harry and Hannah. I give to my son Reuben Golding one tract of land that I purchased of James Daniel containing 300 acres lying on Little River, adj. the land I now live on, also one feather bed and furniture. With three negroes, George, Joe, Cate. I give to my son Anthony Golding one tract of land containing 200 acres, which I purchased of Capt. John Caldwell lying and joining the land I now live on, to the North East. Also one negro named Jacob. I give to my son Richard Golding one negro boy Lankistor. I give to my dtr. Mary Leonard four negroes, Callamy, Ben, Milley, Lett. I give to my son William Golding two negroes, Wagoner and Lucy. I give to my dtr. Milley Griffin one negro Jene. I give to my dtr. Sarah Foster one negro Nan. I give to my dtr. Elizabeth Tinsley one negro Jane. I give to my son Robert Golding one negro, Nan, and one named Poss. I give to my dtr. Mary Leonard one feather bed and furniture. All rest and remainder of my stock, cattle, tools, wagons of every kind to be equally divided between my two sons John and Reuben Golding. I appoint my two sons John and Reuben Golding executors. Dated 4 Sept. 1777. Wit: James Griffin, Laughlin Leonard, Peggey X Golding. Signed: William Golding. Proved on oath of Peggey Golding before Pat. Calhoun, Surrogate on this 23 Sept. 1782. An inventory was made (no date given) by Thos. Hallum, Alexr. Oliver, Jonathan Clark. negroes named, Man Ivy, man Moses.

GOODLETT, JOHN H. Apt. 3 File 143. Probate Judge Office. Greenville, S. C. Will dated 2 Aug. 1831. Probated 28 Nov. 1831. Wife mentioned no name give. Children: Robert Y. H. Goodlett, William C. Goodlett. Wit: W. Thompson, Jr., W. M. Goodlett, Richard Young, A. B. Cook.

GOWDY, WILLIAM A. Box 38 Pack 825. Probate Judge Office. Abbeville, S. C. Admr. bond, We Thomas Gillespie, David Gillespie and Nathan M. Strickland are bound unto Moses Taggart Esq. Ord. in the sum of three thousand dollars. Dated 18 Oct. 1819. An inventory made 29 Feb. 1820 by Joseph Groves, John C. Oliver, N. M. Strickland, William Grantt.

GRACE, JOEL E. Apt. 3 File 193. Probate Judge Office. Greenville, S. C. I Joel Grace of Greenville Dist. being in a low state of Health, but of sound mind and memory. After my just debts are paid, my desire that all my estate both real and personal remain in the hands of my beloved wife Elizabeth Grace during her natural life or widowhood. If she marry, I give her a child part, or in case of death my estate to be divided between my chn. James H., Grace, Sophramia Grace, Matilda Grace and should I have another child, it is to share with the others. I appoint my wife executrix and Micajah Berry executor. Dated 14 Aug. 1813. Wit: Thomas Hamilton, Charles Tony, Hudson Berry. Signed: Joel Grace. Probated 6 Sept. 1813.

GRACE, JOEL E. Apt. 3 File 193. Probate Judge Office. Greenville, S. C. Will dated 14 Aug. 1813. Probated 6 Sept. 1813. Wife Elizabeth Grace. Children: James H. Grace, Sophramia Grace, Matilda Grace. Exors: Wife, Elizabeth Grace, Micajah Berry. Wit: Thomas Hamilton, Charles Tony, Hudson Berry.

GRAHAM, MINORS No. Ref. Clerk of Court Office. Abbeville, S.C. James Graham was made guardian of his two chn. Sela M. and Valentine, they being heirs at law of V. Young Junr. decd. coming to the wife of your petitioner James Graham, his wife now being dead. Graham gave his bond in Abbeville, S. C. for the sum due his chn. He removed his children and himself without the limit of this State. (No date shown only part of this suit in notes). Another bond: State of Miss. County of Itawamba, dated 6 March 1848 James Graham was made gdn. of Culy Ann? and Valentine minors and heirs at law of Valentine Young decd.

GRAHAM, WILLIAM Box 41 Pack 932. Probate Judge Office. Abbeville, S. C. To Mr. Lesly: I want a citation for to admr. on the estate of Wm. Graham Junr. decd. he died in Abbeville, but his property is in Laurens Dist. Co. Irby says I must get a citation from Abbeville for admr. and one from Ordinary in Laurens for appraisement and the sale. If I can get your citation, I will have it read on the 15 Jan. 1845. This letter dated 26 D-c. 1844. Signed: Jno. Smith. The admr. bond granted 11 Jan. 1845 to John Smith of Laurens Dist. with John White, John Taggart of Abbeville Dist. as being security in the sum of $500. Appraisement was made 31 Jan. 1845 by Wm. Graves, A. C. Jones, Henry Pitts. Sale held 5 Feb. 1845 buyers: John Smith, Polly Graham, Henry Pitts, James Graham. Recd. 5 March 1845 of John Smith admr. of Wm. Graham decd. $33.66 in full my portion. Signed: J. G. Traynham. Recd. 5 Mar. 1845 from John Smith admr. of Wm. Graham decd. my portion for coffin $1294. Signed: Albert M. Grahm.

GRAY, ELIZABETH Box 39 Pack 836. Probate Judge Office. Abbeville, S. C. An inventory of the estate as made by Thomas E. Owen, John Tennent, Wm. P. Paul, this 16 April 1840. Negroes named, Titus, Jane and child William, Edmond, Cato, Lucinda. Sale held 17 April 1840. Buyers: James McCree, John E. Williams, John A. Hamilton, Philip Hughey, John H. Armstrong, Andrew Kennedy, John R. McCord, Lewis J. Miller, James S. Wilson, Wm. H. Alexander, John Tennent, John Martin, Richard Hill, J. Kingsmoore, Hugh Armstrong, Johnson Ramsey, Miss Fulton, Wm. P. Paul, James J. Devlin, George W. Pressly, Thomas J. Douglass, Jackson Paul, Franklin Branch, James J. Gilmer, Wm. Gaines, George Lomax, Benjamin McFarlin, John Adams, George Martin. Notes due est. Edmond Keelin $6.87, Zachariah Gray $11.00. Johnson Ramsey $20.00, Dr. Isaac Branch $14.87. (Note on the back of each paper the name Agnes D. Gray is written on the front pages Elizabeth Gray is written.)

GRAY, GEORGE J. Pack 4 (Basement) Clerk of Court Office. Anderson, S. C. Petition for naturalization. Pendleton Dist. The petition sheweth that George J. Gray was born in Balk. Somersetshire in the Kingdom of Great Britain. That he is twenty seven years old. That he arrived in the city of Boston in the month of Oct. 1818. That he is by profession a physician and intends to make his residence in Pendleton Dist., S. C. Dated 25 Oct. 1826. Wit: John T. Lewis. Pendleton Dist., S. C. I George J. Gray do solemnly swear that it is my bona fide intention to become a citizen of the U.S. and renounce for ever all allegiance and fidelity to any foreign power. Signed: G. J. Gray this 25 Oct. 1826.

GRAY, JAMES Box 38 Pack 821. Probate Judge Office. Abbeville, S. C. I James Gray of Abbeville Dist. being weak in body of disposing mind and memory. I will that all my personal and real property be sold agreeable to law and after my lawful debts and burying charges is paid. I will that the money be divided into two equal lots, I will my dtr. Anne Beatty have one half of the money and my bed and kitchen furniture and family bible. I will that my son George Gray have one half of the second part. I will that my son William Gray have the other half. I will that my dtr. Margaret Gilmore be paid fifty dollars out of the part, I willed to Anne Beatty. I will that

Gray, James - Continued. my son James Gray be paid twenty five
dollars to be paid out of the last part willed to George and William
Gray. I will that my grand children, Elizabeth Gray, William Gray,
Mary Gray, Margaret Gray, Sarah Gray and Thos. Gray be paid by my
executors five hundred dollars taken from the whole and cause it to
be put on interest until these chn. come of age, and to receive the
principal and interest. I will that my dtr. in law Saray Gray wife of
Thomas Gray decd. be paid one dollar out of the whole. I appoint my
grand sons James Beatty and Thomas Beatty executors. Dated 12 Feb.
1821. Wit: William Bond, Henry Wideman, John Beatty. Signed: James
Gray. Proved on oath of William Bond, Henry Wideman, John Beatty
before Moses Taggart, Ord. on the 9 June 1821. An inventory was made
by A. Wideman, William Bond, John Beatty on the 15 June 1821. Negroes
named, John, Sally, Bill, Rachel, Joshua. Note on Joseph Mosely.
Sale held 11 Oct. 1821. Buyers; Robert McCaslin, Henry Hufman, David
Taylor, John Young, Alexander McKiney, John Harris, Edward Carter,
Robert Patterson, James Beatty, Peter Leroy, William Bonds, Samuel
Wideman, Joshua Willis, Thomas Beatty, Robert McComb, James Finley,
John Weed, George McFarland, John Beatty, Rhuben Mayberry, James
Taggart, Richard W. Calla, James Cain, Archibald Bradley, Isiah Trotter,
Peter King, Robert Paterson, Thomas Criswell, Abner Campbell, Willis
Palmer, David Blackwell, Joseph Liles, Edmond Atchison, Henry Wideman,
Ann Beatty, Samuel Barren.

GRAY, JAMES & MARY Deed Book A, Page 6. Clerk of Court Office.
Elberton, Ga. We James and Mary Gray of Wilkes Co, Ga. In considera-
tion of Ł current money, paid me in hand by Thomas Lovelady, have
granted, bargained, sold and released all that tract of land lying
in Elbert County, Ga. Containing 380 acres, bounded by land of
Bradfords, Johnsons, Thomas and Robert Burk, and Brannen. Granted
originally to James Gray by Edward Telfair Govr. the 12 July 1790.
Dated this 18 Oct. 1790. Wit: William Leach, Robert Ross. Signed:
James and Mary Gray. Proved before Jno. Cunningham, J.P. on the 7
March 1791.

GRAY, MARY Box 38 Pack 822. Probate Judge Office. Abbeville,
S. C. Admr. bond, We Alexander Gray, James Gray and James Weems, Esq.
all of this Dist. are bound unto Moses Taggart, Esq. Ord. in the sum
of $20,000. Dated 26 May 1827. An inventory was made 11 June 1827
by Bartw. Jordan, Abraham X Lites, Jonathan Jordan, Malon Morgan, Jas.
Atkins. One negro named man Mico. Notes due est. Andrew McGill and
A. D. Gray for $124.43 paid on from time to time leaving a balance
of $4.39. Andrew McGill and J. D. Gray for $50.

GRAY, MARY A. Pack 310. Clerk of Court Office. Abbeville, S.C.
Abbeville Dist. In Equity. To the Honr. the Chancellors: Your
petitioner Mary A. Gray sheweth that she is the mother of William
Gray, son of the late Thomas R. Gray, decd., a minor under the age of
choice to wit about thirteen years old. Said minor is entitled to
a share of the real and personal est. of his father amounting to about
four thousand dollars, owing to his minority he is unable to manage.
Your petitioner prays that she may be appointed guardian. Filed 13
June 1854.

GRAY, "MINORS" Box 41 Pack 907. Probate Judge Office. Abbeville, S. C. Guardinship bond, We Elizabeth Gray, James C. Wharton
and James S. Wilson are bound unto Moses Taggart, Ord. in the sum of
five thousand dollars, dated this 13 Nov. 1835. Whereas Elizabeth
Gray gdn. of the person and personal est. of Margret M. and Agnes D.
Gray minors. Elizabeth Gray is the widow of James A. Gray and the
mother of his eight children, two are minors, twins.

GRAY, "MINORS" Box 41 Pack 908. Probate Judge Office. Abbe-
ville, S. C. Guardianship bond, We Sealy Walker, West Donald and
James Donald are bound unto Moses Taggart, Ord. in the sum of $7,000.
Dated 14, 1825 Sealy Walker gdn. of the person and personal est. of
Robert Douglas Gray a minor over the age of 14 yrs. shall carefully
and handsomely bring up the said minor during his minority and nonage.

GRAY, "MINORS" Box 41 Pack 906. Probate Judge Office. Abbeville, S. C. Guardinship bond, We Alexander D. Gray, Fenton Hall and William Tucker are bound unto Moses Taggart, Ord. in the sum of $1,000. Dated 12 Dec. 1835. Whereas Alexander D. Gray gdn. of Zachariah Gray and Nancy Augustine Gray during their minority, he shall carefully and handsomely bring up said chn.

GRAY, THOMAS Pack 3354. Clerk of Court Office. Abbeville, S.C. Abbeville Dist. To the Honr. the Judges of the Court of Equity. Your oratrix Sarah Gray of Abbeville Dist. Sheweth that Thomas Gray late of this Dist. died intestate, leaving your oratrix his widow and relict and five children all of whom are minors, to wit: Elizabeth, Mary, Margaret and Sarah Gray (only four named). That the said Thomas Gray was possessed of in fee, a plantation on Long Cane Creek, waters of Savannah River. Bounded by land of James Gray, Thomas Creswell, Edward Collier and James Goodwin. Your oratrix is entitled to one third part, and the children the other two thirds, the said minors are in their tender years and cannot consent to a division, but Eliza- beth William, Mary, Margaret and Sarah with their guardian can make a true and perfect answer. May it please your honor to grant a writ of subpoena to be directed to said defendants. Filed 11 June 1821.

GRAY, THOMAS Box 37 Pack 799. Probate Judge Office. Abbeville, S. C. Admr. bond W. Sarah Gray, Robert McCaslan, Adam Wideman and John Harris are bound unto Moses Taggart, Senr. Esq. Ord. in the sum of $8,000. Dated this 10 Feb. 1821. Whereas Sarah Gray and Robert McCaslin have made suit to me to grant letter of Admr. on est. of Thomas Gray decd. This 3 Feb. 1821. Cit: pub. this 4 Feb. 1821 by R. L. Edwards. An inventory was made the 13 Feb. 1821. by A. Wideman, John Harris, George X Roberts and James Beatty. Negroes named Squire, woman and two children, Ebb, Charles, Sam, Philiss, Alphey...

GRAY, THOS. Pack 409. Clerk of Court Office. Abbeville, S.C. In 1822 James T. Taggart was the guardian of Elizabeth, William, Mary, Margaret, and Sarah Gray minors. Children of Thomas Gray decd. Paid 27 June 1831 J. Wideman and Elizabeth his wife. Paid 133 Abner D. White and wife (not named). Paid in 1837 A. J. Dunn who married a Gray. In 1835 paid James S. Hussey or Hassey who married a Gray.

GRAY, WILLIAM Box 39 Pack 867. Probate Judge Office. Abbeville, S. C. I William Gray of Abbeville Dist. planter, being weak in body but of sound mind, memory and understanding. I give to my wife Rosannah one third of the tract of land on which I now live, and land adj. it containing about 545 acres. For her use and benefit of my wife during her natural life, and support of my minor chn. At the death of my wife, I will the aforesaid land to my two sons William and James to be divided between equally. The negroes to remain on my premises until my youngest child arrives at the age of eighteen, or marries. At which time I wish them to be appraised and equally divided amongst my dtrs., except two, which I will to my wife at her own choice during her natural life, or widowhood. The remainder of my personal estate be divided as follows: after my chn. Arthur, William, James, Rebecca and Anne receives a horse, saddle, bridle, one cow, ewe, sow, one feather bed and furniture as they come of age or marry. I appoint Majr. Andrew Weed, Col. Joseph Hutton and John Gray, Senr. executors. Dated 2 Dec. 1809. Wit: William Baldy, John Culbertson, Alice Baldy, Signed: William Gray. Proven on oath of Alice Baldy before Solomon Knight, J.P. of Beaufort Dist., S. C. on this 28 Oct. 1814. Inventory made on 15 Nov. 1814 by Patrick Calhoun, Robert McComb, ___? negroes named, Philis, Bob, Nell, Rose, Clarrissa, Milley, Sarah. Notes due the est. Mathew Brewer $1.70, Saml. Adams $1.93, Starling Dixon $2.06, Benjamin Finney $3.18, Archd. McLean $690. Found in another box. Jim... Paid 8 July 1815 to Arthur Gray legatee, one horse, saddle and bridle, also one cow, ewe, sow, bed and furniture. Paid 8 July 1815, Wm. Gray legatee, one horse, saddle and bridle, also one cow, one ewe and sow. Paid 8 July 1815, James Gray legatee, one horse, saddle and bridle, also one cow, ewe, sow and bed and furniture. Paid 13 Sept. 1817 Saml. Spence one negro as legacy agreeable to the will of the decd. Paid 13 Sept. 1817 Robert Pettigrew,

Gray, William - Continued.   legatee $351.66 1/2.   Paid
Robt. Davis, legatee $351.66 1/2.   Paid 13 Sept. 1817 Reuben Roberts,
legatee $351.66 1/2.   Paid William Sims, legatee $351.66 1/2.   Paid
James Craig, legatee $351.66 1/2.   Paid Reuben Roberts, one horse,
saddle and bridle, bed and furniture and cow and ewe, sow $120.00.
Paid William Sims, one horse, saddle and bridle, bed and furniture,
sow, ewe, as ___.   Dated 6 April 1818 signed: Andw. Weed, Extor.

GRAY, WILLIAM Box 40 Pack 869.   Probate Judge Office.   Abbeville,
S. C.   Admr. bond, We Jesse Gray, John Cochran, and James Cochran are
bound unto Talo. Livingston, Ord. in the sum of $2,000.   Dated 1 June
1818.   Whereas Jesse Gray has made suit to me for letter of admr. on
the est. and effects of Wm. Gray decd.   This 27 April 1818.   Cit.
Pub. at Smyrna Church, 3 May 1818 by H. Dickson V.D.M.   An inventory
was made 16 June 1818 by Benjn. Adams, Samuel Thompson, John H. Spruce.
Negroes named Boy Bill, boy Sam.   Buyers at sale are: Malon Morgan,
William Adams, William Gray, Jinney Gray, John Gray, Asa Burt, James
Gray.

GRAY, WILLIAM "MINORS" No ref. Probate Judge Office.   Abbeville,
S. C.   (This bond may be in same pack as above).   Guardianship bond,
We George Cochran, Jacob Thornton and Adam Cole all of Abbeville, Dist.
are bound unto Moses Taggart, Ord. in the sum of $1,000.   Dated 3 Dec.
1828.   Whereas George Cochran gdn. of the person and personal est. of
William A., John G., Martha Ann and James A. Gray minors under the age
of 14 yrs.

GREER, JOSEPH Box 40 Pack 886.   Probate Judge Office.   Abbeville,
S. C.   96 Dist. Admr. bond.   We Thomas Murphey, Robert Neel, Isaac
Mathews, Benjamin Killgore are bound unto John Ewing Calhoun, Ord. in
the sum of Ŀ14,000.   Dated at Long Cane the 12 March 1783.   Inventory
made 23 May 1783 by Andrew Cunningham, John McClinton, John Hall.

GRAY, WILLIAM "MINORS" Box 41 Pack 905.   Probate Judge Office.
Abbeville, S. C.   Guardianship bond, We John Pressly, James Conner
are bound unto Moses Taggart Ord. in the sum of $1,000.   Dated 22 Jan.
1801.   Whereas John Pressly gdn. of the person and personal est. of
William Gray a minor over 14 yrs. of age and John H., Lucinda, Eliza,
Amanda, Mary and Hannah Gray minors under 14 yrs. of age.   Shall
carefully and handsomely bring up said minors, etc. etc.

GREER, JOSEPH   Box 40 Pack 886.   Probate Judge Office.   Abbeville,
S. C.   Admr. bond, We Thomas Murphey, Robert Neel and Isaac Mathews
and Benjamin Kilgore free holders of Abbeville Dist. are bound unto
John Ewing Calhoun Esq. Ord. in the sum of $14,000.   Dated ___ 1783.
An inventory was made 23 May 1783, by Andrew Cunningham, John
McClinton, John Hall, Notes due est. on Wm. Thomaison for Ŀ606, another
on Elisha Brooks for Ŀ49.

GREGG, THOMAS Deed Book A, Page not given.   Clerk of Court Office.
Elberton, Ga.   This indenture made 10 May 1789 between Thomas Gregg
and Richard Colbert both of Wilkes Co., Ga.   In consideration of Ŀ20
sterling paid by Richard Colbert, have granted, sold and confirmed
a tract of land containing 150 acres, lying on both sides of dry fork
of Vanns Creek, and on the East side of Herds land, all other sides
vacant.   Wit: John Colbert, Thomas Colbert.   Signed: Thomas Gregg.
Proved before Jno. Cunningham, J.P. on 6 March 1791.

GREGORY, ISAAC Box 10 #16.   Probate Judge Office.   Greenville,
S. C.   Greenville Dist.   To Jno. Watson Ord.   The petition of Andrew
J. Ponder sheweth that whereas Isaac Gregory late of this Dist. died
intestate, leaving a small personal est. and your petitioner being a
creditor of said est. craves that a letter of admr. be granted to him
in order to secure the same, and other debts as far as the property
will go.   Dated 9 Dec. 1844.   Signed A. J. Ponder.   The admor. petition
for a sale of the personal est. on the 23 Dec. 1844.   The same was
granted the same date by Jno. Watson, Ord.   An inventory was held by
W. H. Moon and Joab Briant, no dated given.   The sale was held 4 Jan.
1845, buyers: Deborah Quinton, Mary Quinton, B. F. Dill, William

Gregory, Isaac - Continued. Peace, John Howard, A. J. Sudeth,
M. Ponder, Joab Briant, Hiram Williams, Jacob Ponder, T. Campbell,
James Henson, Isaac Below, John McClure, Saml. Craine, M. Ponder, John
Barnett, R. B. Jackson, John Walling, Esias Dill, Robt. Moon, Jefferson
Barton, Thos. Read, William Barton, Milton Ponder, J. P. Moon, J. L.
Belew, M. Lister. Final settlement was made 16 March 1846. Total
estate in cash with balance of pension was $143.52. Amount of debts
and money paid out $84.44. A sub total for distribution among three
children $59.08. Each child $19.69. A letter in file from Athens,
Tenn. Dated 6 Dec. 1859. To Clerk of Probate. Dear Sir: I am
requesting a few lines in regard to the estate of Isaac Gregory, who
died in Greenville Dist. a few years since. To it, with it is worth,
and how it has been disposed of, Gregory was a Revolutionary soldier.
Some of his grand children are in this country. I understand a man
named Ponder or some such name admr. on the est. If there is anything
there? etc. Your Obedient servant, John F. Stover. (The three chn.
not named.)

GREENLEE, PETER Pack 235. Probate Judge Office. Anderson, S.C.
I Peter Greenlee of Pendleton Co., S. C. being at this time in perfect
mind and memory. I give to my dtr. Nancy Johnson one negro named
Hannah. I give to my dtr. Elizabeth Oldhams a negro girl named
Sharlotte. I give to my son Willie Greenlee a negro woman named Grace
her child and one cow and calf. I give to my dtr. Marget Greenlee
one negro girl named Suck. I give to my son William Greenlee one
negro boy named James. I give to my dtr. Mary Oldham one negro girl
named Violet and three cows and calves. I give to my beloved wife
Deborah Greenlee 300 acres of land, being the plantation whereon I
now live, and the following negroes: Jane, Dick, Clary, Sippio,
Stephen and Daniel, with all my stock of every kind, my household
furniture, tools, it being for her support (while she is my widow) and
the support of my chn. whose names are: James Greenlee, Shadrach
Greenlee, John Greenlee, Dully Greenlee, Milley Greenlee. If my wife
get married or when she die the property I gave her to be equally
divided between my five youngest chn. at marriage or becoming of age,
till then their support. I appoint my son William Greenlee and
Reuben Johnson sole executors. Dated 28 June 1798. Stephen Willis
(name not plain), Wm. Brown. Signed: Peter Greenlee. Proven on oath
of Stephen Willis before John Harris, O.P.D. on the 3 Sept. 1802.
Appraisement warrant to Eleb More, Robert Stephenson, Robert Dowdle,
Patrick Norris, Esq., Stephen Willis or any three of you. Inventory
made 17 Sept. 1802.

GREENWOOD, JOHN Book C. Clerk of Court Office. Elberton, Ga.
This indenture made this 25 July 1795. Between John Greenwood of
Elbert Co., Ga. and Peter Brown of Abbeville Dist., S. C. Witnesseth
tha t John Greenwood Senr. and Anne Greenwood his wife, in consideration of Ł200 sterling of the State of Ga. Paid by said Brown have
granted, Bargained and sold all that tract of land containing 100
acres lying in Elbert Co., State of Ga. on waters of Savannah River,
adj. lands of John Greenwood, Jr., Fleming Greenwood and John Bowleses
land. Wit: Thomas Oliver, Fleming Greenwood, John Greenwood, B. Pace,
J.P. Signed: John Greenwood and Anne Greenwood. Recorded 28 July
1795.

GRIGSBY, JAMES Box 40 Pack 885. Probate Judge Office. Abbeville,
S. C. Abbeville, S. C. Admr. bond, We Richard Corley, Bartlet
Bledsoe and David Nicholson are bound in the sum of Ł14 current money.
Dated 13 March 1783 96 Dist. Whereas Richard Corley of Little Saluda
applied for letter of admr. of James Grigsbey decd. as highest creditor
and married to the widow. Inventory made 17 April 1783 by Bartlet
Bledsoe, Wm. Lisson, John Davis.

SKETCH OF THE GRIFFIN FAMILY No ref. Only in the margin "Please
return to H. P. Griffin, McAllen, Texas." The Griffin and Clarke
families originally came from Wales. The Griffin first settled in
Hanover, Orange Co., Va. and afterwards moved to S. C. and settled in
Laurens Dist. The Clarkes settled in Ga. The descendents of Mr.
Clarke, brother of Nancy Clarke still live in Georgia. Richard Griffin,

Sketch of the Griffin Family - Continued. B. 1734 Wales D. 25
Oct. 1805 Laurens Dist, S.C. M. Nancy Clarke in 1754, Where? They were
the parents of seventeen children namely:
    1. Nancy Griffin, b. 8 Jan. 1856 (Anne Griffin)
    2. Mary Griffin, b. 13 Sept. 1757.
    3. Elizabeth Griffin, b. 9 Dec. 1759, M. Mr. Pickens of Pendleton,
S. C.
    4. Margaret Griffin, B. 25 Apr. 1761, M. Ruben Golding.
    5. William Griffin, b. 20 Nov. 1762.
    6. Lucy Griffin b. 8 Jan. 1765, M. William Watson, 1 Jan. 1784.
    7. Major John Griffin, b. 16 Mar. 1767, M. Sallie Williams,
sister of Washington Williams.
    8. Jac. C. Griffin, b. 25 July 1769, M. Miss Goldman, #2. Miss
Case.
    9. Ruben Griffin, b. 16 Apr. 1771, M. Jane Smith Griffin.
    10. Adine Griffin, b. 15 June 1773, died in Mississippi.
    11. Ira Griffin, b. 20 June 1775, M. Susan Steinbach Wilson, dtr.
of Thomas and Patsie White Wilson.
    12. Sarah Griffin, b. 30 Mar. 1778, M. Washington Williams son of
Col. Williams, hero of Kings Mtn. battle during the Rev.
    13. Richard Griffin, b. 4 Feb. 1780, M. 1. Mary Lipcomb, dtr. of
Nathan Lipcomb, Esq. of Abbeville, 15 Oct. 1801. 2. Rebecca Wilson,
dtr. of Thomas Wilson and Rebecca Steinbach.
    14. Joseph Griffin, b. 15 Nov. 1782, M. Parthonia Coleman.
    15. David Griffin, b. 20 Jan. 1786 M. Matilda Golding.
    16. Anthony Griffin, b. 20 Jan. 1786 (twins) M. Mary Simpson.
    17. Larkin Griffin, b. 27 Mar. 1788, M. Jemima Coleman sister of
Parthonia Coleman.
    Richard Griffin the first died 25 Oct. 1805 in Laurens Co., S.C.
Nancy (Anne) Griffin died 18 Oct. 1792. Lucy Griffin, b. 8 Jan. 1765,
M. William Watson 1 Jan. 1784, children: 1. Dr. Edward Watson, b.
3 Jan. 1785, d. 14 June 1820, never married. 2. Sarrahan Watson m. 1.
Dr. Samuel Perryman, 21 Jan. 1830, 2. Capt. Henry Hunter Creswell,
6 Oct. 1840. She had three Perryman sons and one dtr. and eight
Creswell children. Died 23 Feb. 1834. William Watson died 10 Mar.
1837, they had two sons. 3. Richard Watson, b. 28 July 1787, d. 20
Nov. 1824 M. Lavina Brooks and had six children.

    GRIFFIN Power of Atty. Box 2 #39. Probate Judge Office.
Pickens, S. C. On 7 Aug. 1856, Susannah G. Griffin widow of Robt. T.
Griffin decd. of Cherokee County, Ga., Geo. W. Bush and wife Sarah,
A. D. Bush a dtr., Alva Griffin, David Dodds and wife Martha C. a dtr.
John R. Cowan and wife Mary Cowan a dtr., Amos H. McVay and wife
Sarah W. a dtr., Geo. W. Griffin and Green Griffin gdn. of Adaline R.
Griffin heirs of Robt. T. Griffin decd. appointed John C. Griffin of
same Co. their Attorney to receive from Alva Griffin admr. of Henry
Griffin late of Pickens Co., S. C. their shares.

    GRIFFIN, ABNER T. Box 87, #916. Probate Judge Office. Pickens,
S. C. Est. admr. 11 June 1866 by Sarah Griffin, Judge G. Ferguson,
Thomas R. Brackenridge who are bound to W. E. Holcombe, Ord. in the
sum of $1,000.00. Betty J. Griffin a minor in 1877.

    GILLAM, JOHN Box 39 Pack 840. Probate Judge Office. Abbeville,
S. C. 96 Dist. Admr. bond. We Robert Gillam Esq., and Robert Richey
are bound unto John Thomas, Jr. Esq. Ord. in the sum of £2000 sterling.
Dated 6 Sept. 1783. 96 Dist. To John Saterwhite, William Calwell,
Daniel McGin you are impower to make an inventory of goods and Chattels
of John Gillam decd. this 6 Sept. 1783. Signed: John Thomas, Ord.
Sale held 4 Oct. 1783, buyers, Robert Richey, Thomas Pitts, Joshua
Gillam, Robert Dunlap, Isaac Dyson, James Caldwell, Thomas Eastland,
John Wylds, Joseph Armstrong, Marmaduke Naples, Robert Gillam.

    GRIFFIN, ALVA Box 116 #15. Probate Judge Office. Pickens, S.C.
I Alvah Griffin being of sound mind and disposing memory. First pay
my just debts and funeral expenses and collect all money due me from
all and any persons. I give to my wife Lucinda Griffin one of my
feather beds and furniture, as much kitchen furniture as she may need,
the use of the house and garden as long as she remains on the plantation.

Griffin, Alva - Continued. I will that my son George W. Griffin take my plantation whereon I now live at my death, at the sum of two thousand dollars. The same to be accounted for in the final settlement. I will that my executor to dispose of all the balance of my property, and make an equal division among all my chn. (not named). I appoint my son George W. Griffin executor. Dated 28 Aug. 1883. Wit: Edwd. H. Barton, J. Calhoun Griffin, J. E. Hagood. Signed: Alva Griffin. A codicil added: I give unto my beloved son Robert T. Griffin at my death the plantation or tract of land whereon he now lives, lying on Goldens Creek, containing 70 acres and known as the Gilstrap place. Valued at $700 in the final settlement. Wit: J. E. Hagood, Thomas N. McKinney, R. M. Stewart. Dated 5 Mar. 1889. Signed: Alva Griffin. Paid on 2 March 1891, Martha Williams, Eliza A. Williams, Adeline Roberts, E. J. Robinson, G. W. Griffin each $407.37.

GRIFFIN, BENJAMIN & R. HARRISON   Pack 279 #5. Clerk of Court Office. Pickens, S. C. We Benjamin Griffin and R. Harrison Griffin both of Calhoun Co., Ala. for and in consideration of $442.24 to us paid by Robt. A. Thompson of Pickens Dist., S. C. Have granted, bargained, sold and assigned unto Robt. A. Thompson our entire remaining interest in the real est. of our father Sargent Griffin decd. which is the 2d and 3d installments in said real est. Dated 3 Sept. 1860. Wit: W. E. Holcombe, A. H. Gibson. Signed: Benj. X Griffin and R. Harrison X Griffin.

GRIFFIN, E. H. JR.   Box 108 #1034. Probate Judge Office. Pickens, S. C. Est. admr. 23 Dec. 1875 by B. F. Morgan, S. D. Keith, B. F. Lesley, A.C. Hughes who are bound unto I. H. Philpot, Ord. in the sum of $8,000. Was a merchant in Pickens. Recd. from Mrs. Sallie Griffin $2.63, Ann Griffin $49.20. Jacob Griffin $1.29. Thomas Griffin $78.00. West Griffin $1.57.

GRIFFIN, E. H.   No. 94. Clerk of Court Office. Land Warrant Office. Pickens, S. C. By W. L. Keith, Clerk to any lawful surveyor you are authorized to lay out and admeasure unto E. H. Griffin a tract of land not exceeding ten thousand acres for the purpose of regranting the tract that he lives on now and such vacant land as may be adjoining. Dated 26 Oct. 1846. Executed for 434 acres on 7 Nov. 1846. Certified the 10 Nov. 1846.

GRIFFIN, ELENDER   Box 107 #1023. Probate Judge Office. Pickens, S. C. I Elender M. Griffin of Pickens Co. being of sound mind and disposing memory. I desire that all my just debts be paid. I will and desire the rest and residue of whatever kind or nature to be divided between my children, excepting from the above devise and bequest the children of my dtr. Jane Clayton decd. as I have heretofore done them all that I feel able to do. Dated 2 Sept. 1873. Wit: W. E. Holcombe, R. A. Child, James M. McFall. Signed: E. M. Griffin. Filed 30 April 1875. Est. admr. 21 May 1875 by Aaron Garrett, Thomas Newton, B. F. Lesley who are bound unto I. H. Philpot, Ord. in the sum of $800. Heirs, W. B. McCoy, Caroline Edge, heirs of Catharine Dillard decd. Alice Dillard, James Dillard, Nancy Dillard, Cornelia Dillard, John Dillard, Henson Vaughn son of Sarah Ann Vaughn nee Sarah Ann McCoy, Emma Newton, Ellender Garrett, Jerusha A. Case.

GRIFFIN, ELIHU   Box 111 #1066. Probate Judge Office. Pickens, S. C. I Elihu Griffin, being feeble in body but of sound mind and disposing memory and understanding. First my executors to collect all debts due me, and I direct that all my just debts and funeral expenses be paid. Heirs and legatees named in will viz: son John B. Griffin, wife Elizabeth Griffin, son Elihu S. Griffin, grand daughter Elizabeth Jane Griffin, Sister Margarett Teague, Patsey S. Hendricks, the heirs of Nely Young and Elizabeth Teague. Sarah Griffin widow of my son Abner T. Griffin decd. I appoint William Smith, Esq., Col. William E. Welborn of Pickens Dist. my executors. Dated 11 Aug. 1866. Wit: Joel Bradley, Wm. H. Ariail, Harrison X Dillard. Signed: Elihu Griffin. Filed 5 March 1877. Sarah McFall recd. 25 Mar. 1878, $100 as part of her dtr. Betty Jane Griffin share from her grandfather est. Another paper in this pack: That whereas myself Elihu Griffin

Griffin, Elihu - Continued. and Eliza Durham have agreed to
marry. Now know ye that the said Eliza Durham is to have and to hold
all the property she is possed of and is not to have any dower in said
Elihu Griffin est. either real or personal. Elihu Griffin do agree to
arrange for her the Eliza Durham support during her lifetime after she
become his wife. This the 4 day May 1876. Wit: W. E. Welborn, Joab
Mauldin. Signed: Elihu Griffin and Eliza R (X) Durham.

GRIFFIN, ELIHU H.   Box 106 #1109. Probate Judge Office. Pickens,
S. C. I Elihu H. Griffin Senr. of Pickens County being in my sound
mind and disposing memory. I desire that my just debts and funeral
expenses be paid as soon as practicable after my death. I will to my
beloved wife Anna for and during the term of her life my homestead
whereon I now live, to include all land attached thereto and lying on
the West side of Main Street, with my household and kitchen furniture,
two mules and stock of cattle, eight head of hogs. With enough corn
and bacon to support my two youngest children, John C. and Susan A.
Griffin, while they remain single and live with my wife. At the
death of my wife, I will the homestead tract of land to my son John C.
and my dtr. Susan A. Griffin to divided between them. I value the same
to twenty six hundred dollars, each to account for thirteen hundred
dollars in the final settlement, each to have a good bed and bed-
clothing at their mother's death. I will to my son John C. my bay
colt and to my dtr. $100 in lieu of a horse. I have already given my
son James A. Griffin in land $1500 to my son in law Stephen D. Keith
$1,000 in land, and to my son Elihu H. Griffin in land $1200 each to
account for as advancements on a final settlement of my est. The rest
and residue of my est. to be sold, with money collected that is due me,
after my just debts are paid, the balance to be equally divided between
my chn. to make them all equal. Except the heirs of my son Robert Y. H.
Griffin decd. they have all I intend for them. Dated 22 March 1870.
Wit: John L. Thornly, John R. Petty, James M. McFall. He died on or
about 2 Oct. 1874. Filed 19 Oct. 1874.

GRIFFIN, ELIZA Box 124 #14. Probate Judge Office. Pickens,
S. C. I Eliza Griffin of Pickens County being of sound mind and disposing memory. Pay my just debts and funeral expenses from first money
coming into est. I give unto my nephew Jeptha Allen Durham all my
property both real and personal, including my home tract, containing
about 80 acres. I give him this property to prove to him my affection
for his kindness to me in living with providing for and taking care of
me in my old age. I appoint my nephew Jeptha Allen Durham my executor.
Dated 28 Mar. 1893. Wit: J. Mcd. Bruce, W. J. Gillespie, J. B. Newberry. Signed: Eliza X Griffin. Died 12 June 1895. Filed 26 June
1895.

GRIFFIN, ELIZABETH Box 95 #1002. Probate Judge Office. Pickens,
S. C. On 1 Jan. 1888 Elizabeth Griffin recd. a share from the estate
of William Hester, Jr. who died 20 Aug. 1864 in Pickens Dist.

GRIFFIN, ELIZABETH J. Box 10 #160. Probate Judge Office.
Pickens, S. C. On 19 April Sarah McFall states that Elizabeth J.
Griffin age 16 yrs. has an interest in estate of Elihu Griffin decd.

GRIFFIN, FLORENCE Box 109, $1041. Probate Judge Office.
Pickens, S. C. Floria Griffin states that her husband E. H. Griffin,
Jr. died on or about 1 Dec. 1875. Minor chn. Anna M. Griffin, Benjamin M. Griffin, Walter Griffin. James H. Morgan the guardian, a
brother to Florence Griffin.

GRIFFIN, J. C. Box 118 #1. Probate Judge Office. Pickens, S.C.
Est. admr. 20 June 1890 by James A. Griffin, J. J. Lewis, J. A. Robin-
son who are bound to James B. Newberry, Ord. in the sum of $5,600.00.
Died 31 May 1890. James A. Griffin a brother. Heirs: Jas. A.
Griffin, E. H. Griffin, J. C. Griffin, S. D. Keith, Susan A. Griffin
Wyatt.

GRIFFIN, JOHN Box 39 Pack 850. Probate Judge Office. Abbeville,
S. C. Admr. bond, We Lyda Griffin, John Conner Esq. and Lewis Mitchel

Griffin, John - Continued. all of Abbeville Dist. are bound unto
Andrew Hamilton Esq. Ord. in the sum of $10,000. Dated 10 Feb. 1808.
Whereas Eliza Griffin and Jno. Conner Esq. made suit to me to grant
letter of admr. on the goods and chattels of John Griffin decd. as next
of kin. Grantes 1 Jan. 1808. Cit. Pub. 2 Jan. 1808 by Benjamin
Northcut. an inventory was made 17 Feb. 1808. (Negroes not named).

GRIFFIN, JOHN V. Box 54 #588. Probate Judge Office. Pickens,
S. C. Est. admr. 2 July 1860 by Elihu H. Griffin, Samuel A. McCracken,
Charles Thompson who are bound unto W. E. Holcombe, Ord. in the sum of
$320.00. John V. Griffin late of Calhoun Co., Ala. Recd. 1 Jan. 1861
of E. H. & Thomas Griffin admrs. of est. of Sargent Griffin decd.
$123.03.

GRIFFIN, HENRY Book A, Page 98. Probate Judge Office. Pickens,
S. C. Pickens County. To W. D. Steele, Ordinary. The undersigned
sheweth to this Court that he has four ninths of two thirds and one
sixth of one ninth of the real estate of Henry Griffith late of Pickens
Dist. decd. He petitioned your Court for a division or sell the same.
Filed 31 Dec. 1847. Signed: Benjamin Hagood. Other heirs are Eliza-
beth Griffin, Alvah Griffin, Joseph Leage and wife Elizabeth Leage,
Heirs of William Griffin, Heirs of Robert Griffin, Thomas J. Griffin,
Samuel B. B. Stevens.

GRIFFIN, IRA Box 38 Pack 817. Probate Judge Office. Abbeville,
S. C. I Ira Griffin of Abbeville Dist. being of sound mind and memory
etc. It is my desire that my executors sell such property as they think
proper to pay all my just debts. I desire that the whole of my estate
remain together as long as my beloved wife Susannah Griffin remain in
her widowhood for the better support of her and my children, except as
my executors think proper to dispose of as above stated. If my wife
marries then the whole to be sold and she to share with the children.
As the children come of age or marry, the executors to give them in
money or property as they think the est. can afford. I desire that my
executors to aid and assist in a special manner to my beloved wife
Susannah in the educating and raising of my chn. in a proper manner.
I appoint my three brothers Richard, Joseph, and Larkin Griffin
executors. Dated 4 Feb. 1830. Wit: Leroy Watson, Vincent Griffin,
Melissa Griffin. Signed: Ira Griffin. Proved on oath of Vincent
Griffin before Moses Taggart Ord. on the 9 Feb. 1830. An inventory
was made the 10 Feb. 1830. Negroes named, Astin, Jefferson, Lucy,
Milla and Mima (twins), Margaret, Abram, Phil, Betsy and her child
Martin, Maria, Matilda, Clayborn, Jackson, Betsy, Albert, James, Sam,
Warren, Sam Turner, Dave, Peter, Gincy and 2 children Lete and Aggy,
Dilsy and her child Ned, Sarah and her child Henry, Robert, Linsey,
Violet, Huldah and her child Mary. Notes due the estate. Matthew
Burt and L. Good $112.00, Thomas Spraggins $5.55, William Scott $16.06,
Andrew Redmond $15.25, James Henderson $3.50, William Hunt $4.00,
Robert Key, Thomas Jackson and James Harly $65.00, Mrs. Mary Ann Waller
$333.04, Mrs. Rebecca Glover, $129.75, John W. Wilson $15.19, Wm. W.
Waller Minor $8.00, W. A. Huggins $11.00. Sale held 24 and 25 Nov.
1830, buyers, Leroy Watson, Andrew Huggins, Michall Wilson, Junr.,
John Morgan, James Partlow, James Watson, Robert Crawford, Elijah
Lyon, Samuel Reddin, Albert Waller, Thomas Aiken, William Henderson,
James Dozier, Dr. Francis Williams, George Marshall, Lewis Simmons,
John Casey, Dr. Franklin Williams, Andrew Huggin, William Aiken, Robert
Henderson, Richard Griffin, John Wilson, Thomas Adkinson, Thomas
Williams, Stanmore Brooks, William Mitchell, Walter Kellar, John Casey,
Samuel Leek, Richard Henderson, John Partlow Senr., M. C. Livingston,
Joseph Griffin, Thomas Aiton, Elijah Lyon, William Aiken, John
Creswell, William Mitchell, Joseph Wardlaw, John Nichols, Samuel Redden,
Thomas Osborn, Jesse Henderson, Grigsby Appleton, John W. Turner,
William Scott, Vincent Griffin, Samuel Turner, Dewry Lipford, William
Morgan, Daniel English, Richard Henderson Senr., Lewis Simmons, Joseph
Norrell, Dewy Lipford, George Marshall, Thomas Henderson, John Partlow,
Wiley G. Bullock, Robert Hudson, John Stewart, Adam Richard, Pascal
D. Klugh, Thomas Lake, Reuben Cooper, John Waller, Larkin Griffin,
Chesley Davis, R. Yeldell, William Pinchback, Stephen Witt, John Hearst,
Stephen Ross, James Martin, E. Lyon, A. Turner, William Harris, John

Griffin, Ira - Continued. Lipcomb, William Watson, Madison Livingston, Lewis Simmons, David Anderson, William Mitchell, A. Lights, Henry Norell, Richmond Still, William Hatter, Robert Hudson, Samuel Caldwell, Joseph Norrell, Thomas Stalsworth, Robert Key, John T. Whitfield, James Patterson, Davis Morgan. Money paid out 1832, Paid David Griffin in settlement (per book a/c $1917. Paid Jas. F. Griffin for money advanced to Martha $8.00, Paid Thos. Stallworth Senr. boarding Sarah and Augustus $66.62. In another place "the property land (lent) to Madison C. Livingston and price fixed by Ira Griffin. One bed and furniture $50, one negro man Wilson $400, one negro woman Fanny $350, one negro boy Dick $350, one negro girl Telitha $200, one negro girl Marinda $200, one gray mare cora $200, one saddle, bridle $15, one cow and calf $10." What relation they are to Ira Griffin is not given.

GRIFFIN, LEWIS BROWN Box 1 #16. Probate Judge Office. Pickens, On 31 Oct. 1843 Lewis Brown, Daniel Durham are bound to James H. Dendy, Ord. in the sum of $200.00. Lewis Brown guardian for Lewis Brown Griffin minor under the age of 14 yrs. Lewis Brown grandfather states that he has raised Lewis B. Griffin from an infant who was a son of Benjamin Griffin whose wife Frances Brown before marriage is dead. On 4 Mar. 1848 Julia Brown was the widow of Lewis Brown now decd. asks that W. L. Keith be gdn. for said minor. Recd. 27 Jan. 1845 from Samuel Brown admr. of Wm. Brown decd. $52.93.

GRIFFIN, MARGARET Box 38 Pack 818. Probate Judge Office. Abbeville, S. C. Admr. bond, We John L. Griffin, Charles Pitts and George J. Heard are bound unto Moses Taggart Senr. Esq. Ord. in the sum of $2,000. Dated 3 Dec. 1821. Whereas John L. Griffin has made suit to me to grant him letter of Admr. on the est. of Margaret Griffin decd. this 28 Nov. 1821. Moses Taggart, Senr. Ord. Cit. pub. at Rockey River M. House. 29 Nov. by R. L. Edwards. An inventory was made 28 Dec. 1821 by James A. Ward, Chas. Maxwell, Nathl. Marion. No date given of sale, buyers, John Marsh, James Stalsworth, Robt. Griffin, Charles C. Mayson, Charles Maxwell, Isaac Logan, James A. Ward, James Butler, Richard Griffin, James Linton, Thomas Brighton, James Mayson, Isaac McCool, William Douglass, Vincent Griffin, Jonathan Swift, Stephen Ross, Simeon Demming, Thomas Marsh, Charles B. Foster, John L. Griffin, Martin Hacket, John Franks, Jesse Calvert, Thomas Brightman, Grigsby Appleton, John Criswell, Chas. Fooshee

GRIFFIN, MARY Pack 220 #25. Clerk of Court Office. Pickens, S. C. On 26 July 1870 an inquest was held for Mary Griffin. The jury was ordered to appear to or near Allgoods Bridge to view the body found lying dead there.

GRIFFIN, MINORS Pack 280 #1. Clerk of Court Office. Pickens, S. C. State of Ala. County of Calhoun, Clerk of Probate for Calhoun Co. Special Term the 29 Dec. 1858. This day came G. B. Douthit a citizen of said county and applied for letter of Guardianship over the est. of C. B. Griffin, Mary E. Griffin, Bailey B. Griffin, John V. Griffin, James M. S. Griffin, Margaret J. Griffin, and Martha F. D. Griffin minor chn. of William Griffin late of said county of Calhoun deceased.

GRIFFIN, MINORS Box 10 #186. Probate Judge Office. Pickens, S. C. 28 Feb. 1885, R. A. Bowen, W. T. Bowen, W. L. Young are bound to J. H. Newton, Ord. in the sum of $300.00. R. A. Bowen gdn. for Annie May Griffin, Benjamin Griffin, Walter Griffin minors under 21 years. 23 Feb. 1885 F. J. Griffin states that Susan Wyatt died March 1884. That she owned a tract of land near Pickens C. H. on Wolf Creek and was a sister to E. H. Griffin, Jr. decd. F. J. Griffin the mother states that Annie May is 14 yrs., Benjamin Griffin 13 yrs., and Walter Griffin is 10 years old. 30 Oct. 1891 Paid Anna May Griffin Sutherland share $42.85.

GRIFFIN, MINORS Box 7 #108. Probate Judge Office. Pickens, S. C. 13 Aug. 1866 Elihu H. Griffin, Lemuel Thomas, Samuel Reid are bound unto W. E. Holcombe, Ord. in the sum of $1274.86. Elihu H. Griffin gdn. for Wm. Washington Griffin, Robert Virginia Griffin minor

Griffin, Minors - Continued. under 21 years. Chn. of R. Y. H.
Griffin decd. 2 July 1874 Elihu H. Griffin the gdn. sheweth that he is
advanced in years and in bad health and desire that the minors mother
Lucy J. Griffin be their guardian.

GRIFFIN, MINORS Box 10 #163. Probate Judge Office. Pickens,
S. C. 28 Jan. 1878 E. S. Griffin, guardian for Wm. E., Eula E.,
Sarah E., Carrie J., Lula L., Warren A., Ada Griffin minors who had
an interest in the estate of Elihu Griffin decd.

GRIFFIN, OWEN Box 39 Pack 841. Probate Judge Office. Abbeville,
S. C. I Owen Griffin of Abbeville Dist. being very sick and weak but
of perfect mind and memory. I give to my dtr. Elizabeth Griffin one
negro girl Patience also the remainder of my property I give to my son
James Griffin. I appoint Peter (named torn from paper). Dated 11 Nov.
1806. Wit: Jno. Peter Knop, James Adamson. Signed: Owen Griffin.
Recorded 9 Jan. 1807. An inventory was made by Conrod Mark, Saml.
Crozier, John Pressly. on the 27 Jan. 1807. Sale held 30 Jan. 1807.
Buyers, Henry Gable, James Asamson, Margaret Gable, Coonrod Mark,
George Mark, Joseph Hearst, Robert Jones, David C. McCormick, Jonathan
Arnold, Margaret Adamson, John Airgrove, Burges Pitman, Gregory Coddle,
Peter Fritz. John Adamson Executor of est.

GRIFFIN, ROBERT C. Box 91 #971. Probate Judge Office. Pickens,
S. C. Est. admr. 16 Jan. 1884 by E. B. Richardson, Job F. Smith,
W. H. Chapman who are bound unto J. H. Newton, Ord. in the sum of
$1,000. Died 12 Oct. 1883. On 2 June 1885 collected from Dr. Moseley
at Lowndesville on note $20.00.

GRIFFIN, ROBERT Y. H. Box 63 #678. Probate Judge Office.
Pickens, S. C. Est. admr. 6 Sept. 1862 by Elihu M. Griffin, James E.
Hagood, Elijah E. Alexander who are bound unto W. E. Holcombe, Ord. in
the sum of $6,000.00. Left a widow and two chn. 13 Aug. 1866 to note
on Lucy J. Griffin being balance due by her purchases at sale after
having been paid her share $193.44.

GRIFFIN, SARGENT Box 47 #524. Probate Judge Office. Pickens,
S. C. Est. admr. 28 June 1858 by Elihu H. Griffin, Thomas Griffin,
James E. Hagood, Samuel Reid, Robert Craig are bound unto W. J. Parson,
Ord. in the sum of $50,000.00. Heirs: Elihu H. Griffin, Averilla the
wife of H. J. Anthony, Vashti the wife of Joseph Mansell, William
Griffin, Benjamin Griffin, Barton Griffin, Richard H. Griffin, Anderson
Griffin, Bailey Griffin recd. Property Dorcas Alexander, Thomas
Griffin. The widow Avarilla Griffin. 24 Nov. 1858: G. B. Douthit
guardian of G. B. Griffin, Mary E. Griffin, Bailey B. Griffin, John V.
Griffin, James M. S. Griffin, Margaret J. Griffin, Martha F. D.
Griffin, minors heirs of William Griffin late of Calhoun Co., Ala.
Minerva the wife of Henry A. Billingsly, Prior Alexander Jr., John V.
Griffin.

GRIFFIN, SARGENT, SR. Pack 417 #1. Clerk of Court Office.
Pickens, S. C. State of Alabama County of Calhoun. We Avarilla A.,
Nancy V. Griffin and Rosanah M. Kelly nee Griffin, the wife of Thomas
Kelley, all of Calhoun Co., Ala. Have nominated and appointed Gabriel
B. Douthit of the same County and State, our true and lawful attorney
for us and in our respective names to do and transact the following
business in Pickens Dist., S. C. Sargent Griffin, Sr. lately died in
Pickens Dist., S. C. Leaving considerable real and Personal property.
That William Griffin late of the County of Calhoun in the State of Ala.
was the son of said Sargent Griffin, Sr. decd. and we are chn. of said
William Griffin decd. and heirs at law of Sargent Griffin decd. That
E. H. Griffin and Thomas Griffin admr. has set up the final on the 12
June 1860. Filed this 24 May 1860.

GRIFFIN, SUSAN ALLEN #190. Clerk of Court Office. Abbeville,
S. C. Petition for guardian. In Equity. To the Honr. the Chancellors:
The petition of John Taylor of Virginia, sheweth that he was appointed
on the 20 Dec. 1858 in the county of Culpepper, State of Virginia,
guardian of the person and property of Susan Allen Griffin a minor

Griffin, Susan Allen - Continued. residing in his family in said
State and is under a bond of $12,000 with good securities. Your
petitioner sheweth that said ward lives in his family, and is likely
to remain. It is very inconvenient to manage her property in the State
of S. C. The property amounting $1734.00 in money and negroes, said
property in Beaufort Co., S. C. The sum of $2096.52 in the hands of
Commissioner in Equity for Beaufort Dist. arising from sale of the
Garey Est. also in Comm. is $875.00 from the sale of a part of the est.
of late Mrs. Lucin Allen, grandmother of said ward, also five negroes
viz: Sook and her three chn. Philby, Joe, Cumsey and Ellen. Your
petitioner wish to carry the estate to Virginia. He will ever pray.
Filed 21 March 1859. Susan Allen Griffin was 13 yrs. of age.

GRIFFIN, VINCENT Pack 297. Clerk of Court Office. Abbeville,
S. C. Abbeville Dist. In Equity, To the Honr. the Chancellors:
The petition of Vincent Griffin, sheweth that he is the son of
Vincent Griffin nee of this dist. now decd. That he is a minor of the
age of seventeen years. and is entitled to an estate under his father
will, consisting of money and negroes which owing to his minority he
cannot manage for himself, that his mother is married to Larkin Rey-
nolds. Your petitioner therefore prays that his brother John L.
Griffin may be appointed his guardian. Th ot [?] Chancellors; I give
my consent that John L. Griffin be appointed the gdn. of my son
Vincent Griffin. Signed: Agness W. Reynolds and Larkin Reynolds.
Filed 12 June 1855.

GRIFFIN, WALTER H. Box 122 #14. Probate Judge Office. Pickens
Co., S. C. On 24 July 1893, B. M. Griffin, D. F. Sutherland, J. D.
Bruce are bound unto J. C. Newberry, Ord. in the sum of $200. B. M.
Griffin gdn. of Walter H. Griffin a minor over 14 yrs. Mrs. Florence
Griffin his mother. Entitled to a share of Est. of J. C. Griffin
decd.

GRIMES (GRAHAM), HUGH. Box 40 Pack 883. Probate Judge Office.
Abbeville, S. C. Abbeville Dist. Admr. bond. We Margaret Galley
and James Galley are bound unto John Thomas Jr., Ord. in the sum of
Ŀ2000 sterling. Dated 31 July 1784. Est. appraised by Wm. Black and
John Galley as was shown to them by Margaret Graham. Due to the est.
of Hugh Graham decd. Ŀ 18 5S 3P as all the just debts due to my know-
ledge certified by me. this 21 Oct. 1784 Margaret Galley. (Note:
In the bond name is Hugh Grimes, other papers Hugh Graham.)

GRIFFIN, WILLIAM Pack 634, #169. Clerk of Court Office.
Pickens, S. C. On 4 Oct. 1844 William Griffin was appointed a constable of Pickens Dist.

GRIMSLY, ELIJAH Box 107 Pack 2844. Probate Judge Office.
Abbeville, S. C. I Elijah Grimsly of Abbeville Dist. tho weak in body,
yet of a sound and perfect understanding and memory. I will and posi-
tively order that all my debts be paid. I give to my dear and loving
wife the profits arising from the rent of 330 acres of land (being in
the State of N.C. in Dobs County and on Pettenting Creek) until my
dtr. Mary now an infant is of age, which land is in possession of my
brother John Grimsly with nine years arear in rent, likewise all my
meat stock except one cow. I will (several words worn) horses with all
my household furniture, with the monies that has arose from the sale
of sixty barrels of corn left in possession of my brother John Grimsly
in N.C. also my crop of corn and tobacco at my sister Sarah Hodges in
Larance County [sic]. I give to my dtr. Mary Grimsly all my land in
N.C. in Dobs Co. and 30 acres in Georgia State, Washington County,
waters of Broad River. If my dtr. should die without issue or under
age, the land in Georgia to desend to my sister Sarah Hodges two sons
Richard and John Hodges to be equally divided between them, the land
in N.C. to the nearest heir at law. I appoint Samuel Rosamond and
Richard Hodges executors. I have this day the 1 Feb. 1786. Signed:
Elijah X Grimsly. Wit: Ledford Payne, Robert Swain, William X
Hodges 96 Dist. S. C. this day came Ledford Payne before John Thomas,
Jr., Ord. and made oath that he saw Elijah Grimsly sign said will,
this 28 April 1786.

GRISHAM, REVD. JOSEPH #131. Clerk of Court Office. Pickens, S. C. By William L. Keith, Clk. of Court. To any lawful surveyor, you are authorized to lay out unto Revd. Jos. Grisham a tract of land not exceeding ten thousand acres. Dated 6 May 1850. Executed for 2342 acres on the 22 May 1850 certified 3 June 1850.

GRISHAM, WILLIAM S. #180. Clerk of Court Office. Pickens, S. C. By William L. Keith, Clk. of Court. To any lawful surveyor you are authorized to lay out a tract land unto Maj. William S. Grisham not exceeding one thousand acres. Dated 20 July 1853. Executed for 540 acres the 29 July 1853. Recorded 1 Aug. 1853.

GRISSOP, JOHN #157. Clerk of Court Office. Pickens, S. C. By William L. Keith Clerk, To any lawful surveyor you are authorized to lay out unto John Grissop a tract of land not exceeding one thousand acres. Signed this 1 Oct. 1852 W. L. Keith, Clk. Executed for 54 acres 2 Oct. 1852. Certified the 20 Nov. 1852.

GRUBBS, RICHARD Box 38 Pack 824. Probate Judge Office. Abbeville, S. C. Admr. bond, We Elizabeth Grubbs, Nathaniel Shirly, William Blain and Reuben Kay are bound unto Moses Taggart Esq. Ord. in the sum of $8,000. Dated 6 Sept. 1819. An appraisement made 20 Oct. 1819. by John Kay, Benjamin Shirly, William Mitchell. Negroes named, girl Fender, boy Charles, boy Peter. Sale held 28 Oct. 1819 buyers, Elizabeth Grubbs, John Kay, Benjamin Shirly, Nathaniel Shirley, Andrew Flowers, Weldon Peerman, William Grubbs, William Wray, Benjmain Griffin, William Mattison, Stephen Mitchell, Cador Gantt, James Cullins, Robert H. Kay, Lewis Anthony, James R. Evins, Charles Posey, Thomas Lord, Alexander Petty, Ephraim Mitchell, William Weldon, James W. Reeve, William Bell, James Petty.

GUERIN, JACOB Box 10 #126. Probate Judge Office. Pickens, S. C. Jacob Guerin married Abigail a dtr. of Major Thomas Henderson decd. and wife Elizabeth Henderson. Were already married when her father estate was admr. on 14 June 1841.

GUERIN, MARGARET Pack 63. In Equity. Clerk of Court Office. Pickens, S. C. Margaret Guerin wife of Nathaniel Guerin was residing in Texas on March 3, 1866. She was a sister to Jesse M. Clayton, R. Carter Clayton, S. John Clayton of Pickens Dist.

GUERIN, MARGARET & NAT Pack 232 #5. Clerk of Court Office. Pickens, S. C. The State of Texas County of Rusk. We Margaret K. Guerin and her husband Nat Guerin who joins her in this power of attorney, have this day appointed Mrs. Hannah Clayton of Pickens Dist., S. C. our lawful agent and attorney in fact for us and in our name. To demand of the admr. of Jassee M. Clayton or any other person who may have possession or control of the estate. (Margaret K. Guerin being a sister of said Jessee M. Clayton). To receive and receipt etc. This 21 Feb. 1867. Wit: J. N. Still, P. H. Still. Signed: Margaret K. Guerin and Nat Guerin. On another paper, On 19 April 1869 R. C. Clayton recd. $116.00 part of the share of his decd. brother Jessee M. Clayton est. On the 1 Aug. 1876 Nat Guerin was appointed guardian of John B. Clayton and Margaret Clayton minors, John B. being twenty years old and Margaret being eighteen years old. (In the guardianship bond or papers, says who the minors are heirs of.)

GUERIN, MARY C. Pack 278 #3. Clerk of Court Office. Pickens, S. C. Pickens Dist. I Mary C. Guerin, widow of Greenberry L. Guerin late of this Dist. now decd. In consideration of $160 to me paid by Nathaniel M. Madden, Trustee for Temperance Madden wife of Ezekiel Madden, have received and for ever release, all manner of dower and right and title of dower whatsoever which I now have to the tract of land on branches of twelve mile river, adj. land of Robert Johnson, Samuel Parson. Containing 293 acres, which my late husband was possessed with, at or during his intermarriage with me, the said Mary C. Garvin. Dated 19 March 1866. Wit: Wm. Oliver, W. T. Garvin. Signed: Mary C. Garvin. (Her name is spelled, Guerin and Garvin). Proved on oath of Wm. Oliver before J. E. Hagood. C.C.P. on the 20 March 1866.

GUESS, SOPHIA & JAMES Book A-1. Page 27. Clerk of Court Office.
Pickens, S. C. Pendleton Dist. We Sophia Gess **of** Pendleton Dist.,
S. C. and James Gess of Decalbe [sic] Co., Ga. In consideration of
$200 paid in hand by James Cary of Pendleton Dist. have granted, sold
and released a plantation or tract of land containing 80 acres, lying
on a branch of Georges Creek and Wolf Creek. Bounded by land of
Thomas Christians land, Lemuel B. Edward. Dated 18 Jan. 1825. Wit:
John Bowen, Jr., Artichible H. Burton or Barton?. Signed: Sophia X
Gess and James Gess. Proved on oath of Archable H. Burton or Barton,
before Samuel Looper, J.P. on the 15 May 1825. Recorded 5 Jan. 1829.
by W. L. Keith, Clk.

GUEST, ALLEN Pack 642 #6. Clerk of Court Office. Pickens,
S. C. On 21 June 1843 Allen Guest mentioned as a son of Capt. William
Guest decd. of Pickens Dist.

GUNNIN, BENJAMIN Box 38 Pack 827. Probate Judge Office. Abbeville, S. C. I Benjamin Gunnien, being in a low state of health but
of sound mind and memory. I will my just debts be paid. I will to
Jeal Gunnien my wife the third of all my property both real and personal during life or marriage, except the plantation, except the
plantation which is to remain to support the family. At the death or
marriage of my wife, her part to be equally divided between the
legatees, except Hannah W. Gunnien must have $150 over her share, from
her mother's part. I give to my dtr. Isabella Gunnien one bed and
furniture, over her share, also Mary Gunnien one bed and furniture over
her share. I will my son James Gunnien shall have the blacksmith
tools as part of his share. I will that the negroes shall not be sold
out of the family. I appoint James Wardlaw, Gilbert Mann executors.
Dated 6 Oct. 1811. Wit: William McGaw, John Mann, Allen W. Gillespie.
Signed: Benj. Gunnien. Proved on oath of John Mann, before Talo.
Livingston Ord. on the 4 Nov. 1811. An inventory was made 15 Nov.
1811 by Bruce Livingston, Christian Barns, John Mann, Wm. Caldwell.
Negroes named, Sary, Bob, William, Sally, Alin, Rose, Daniel.

GUSHAM, JOSEPH Deed Book D-1, Page 251. Clerk of Court Office.
Pickens, S. C. I Joseph Gusham of Pickens Dist. in consideration of
$400 paid me by James W. Harrison have sold and released unto James
W. Harrison all that town lot in the town of Pickens containing one
acre in the South West square on the South side of Broad St. known in
the plan as #29 in deed from William Hubbard to Joseph Gusham. Dated
14 Apr. 1840. Wit: P. Alexander, John O. Gusham. Signed: Joseph
Gusham. Mary L. Gusham the wife of Joseph Gusham did relinquish all
her dower on land to James W. Harrison this 13 June 1840. Recd. the
13 June 1840.

GUYTON, ABRAHAM Box 8 Pack 32. Probate Judge Office. Union,
S. C. Being of sound mind and memory, etc. Pay all just debts first.
I will to my wife Patsy all my land and negroes, horses, cattle and
all other property belonging to me, to be hers to dispose of as
she shall think best. If she marry to have an equal part with the
children. I appoint Joseph Guyton and Alexander Martin as executor.
Dated 14 Feb. 1816. Wit: Joseph Smith, Aaron Parker, Daniel Smith.
Signed: Abraham Guyton. Proved on oath of Joseph Smith before
William Rice, Esq. Ord. on the 4 March 1816.

GUYTON, ABRAHAM Will Book B, Page 18. Probate Judge Office.
Union, S. C. Being now in sound mind and memory. I will all my just
debts be paid. I will to my dear wife Patsy all my land, negroes,
horses, cattle and all other property belonging to me. To dispose of
as she shall think best among the children. If she should marry, then
to only have a child part. If she marries then all my property to be
sold and divided between all my children. I appoint my brother Joseph
Guyton and Alexander Martin executors. Dated 14 Feb. 1816. Wit:
Joseph Smith, Aaron Parker, Daniel Smith. Signed: Abraham Guyton.
Proved on oath of Joseph Smith before Wm. Rice, Ord. U.D. on the
4 March 1816. Same date qualified Joseph Guyton and Alexander Martin
Extr.

GUYTON, HANNAH Will Book B, Page 29. Probate Judge Office.
Union, S. C. I Hannah Guyton of Union Dist. being in a sick and low
condition, but of sound judgment and memory. After my lawful debts are
paid. I will to my sister Amey Crittendon my best bed and furniture,
the remainder of my est. real and personal be equally divided between
my three brothers Isaac, Nathaniel and John Guyton and my two sisters
Molley Tat, Amey Crittendin. I appoint my two brothers Isaac and
Nathaniel Guyton, executors. Dated __ Nov. 1814. Wit: James McKown,
Joseph Ashworth, Nicholas Corry. Signed: Hannah X Guyton. Hannah
Guyton will proved on oath of Nicholas Corry, before Wm. Rice, Ord.
U.D. on the 4 Nov. 1816. Same date qualified Isaac and Nathaniel
Guyton executors.

GUYTON, ISAAC Will Book B, Page 239. Probate Judge Office.
Union, S. C. I Isaac Guyton of Union Dist. a planter on Broad River.
Getting old in age but of a sound mind and perfect memory. I will and
desire my just debts be paid. The rest of my estate lands and tenements, I give and bequeath to my wife Elizabeth Guyton, during her
life or widowhood. I give to my sons Jacob and Isaac Guyton one cow
and calf, worth ten dollars, and to each household furniture to make
them as much as the rest that is married. I leave to my dtrs. Sarah
and Nancy Guyton the same amount that the rest of my dtrs. recd.
After the death of my wife shall be divided between my four sons viz:
Nathaniel, Jacob, John, and Isaac and to my five dtrs. Mary, Sarah,
Nancy, Hannah, and Elizabeth and the above heirs to pay my dtr. Martha
Mullinax one twenty five cents. If my dtrs. Sarah and Nancy does not
marry they shall have their support from the place, and a house to
live in. I appoint my wife Elizabeth Guyton Executrix and Jacob and
Isaac Jr. executors. Dated 2 Oct. 1843. Wit: Joseph Guyton, James
Patrick, Thomas N. Chohen. Signed: Isaac Guyton. Proved on oath of
Thomas N. Cohen and James Patrick before J. J. Pratt Esq. Ord. on the
__ (no date). Recorded 24 Nov. 1843.

GUYTON, JOSEPH Box 48 #8. Probate Judge Office. Union, S. C.
Union Dist., I Joseph Guyton, being of sound mind and memory. I give
unto my beloved wife Moriah Guyton the following property. One negro
boy Sam, three feather beds and furniture, three cows and calves, one
note I hold on Tersah and Marthy Leech to be hers forever. I also give
to my wife Mariah, one negro man Pompy, one boy Mager, one girl
Betsey, one woman Adeline, one boy Washington, one girl Julia Dulcena
and their increase to be hers during her natural life, at her death
to be equally divided between my heirs. I also give to my __ a tract
of land, commencing on Correys line at Dr. Davis corner West side of
the Creek, North East with Correys line to Eleazer Parker line, South
West to the road from my house to E. Parker, along said road to big
road, down big road to Rockey River, during her natural life or widowhood, wife receive other items of household and farm tools, with a
child part of all money, notes on hand. I will to my dtr. Elizabeth
Kennady one negro boy George, one girl Betty Matiah. I will unto my
son Joseph W. Guyton two negro boys Bill and Green, one feather bed
and furniture. I will unto my son John L. Guyton one negro woman
Fanney and her chn. Tom, Josephine and Mary, one feather bed and
furniture. I will unto my dtr. Vilet Mitchell one negro boy Moose.
I will unto my dtr. Mary Leeches children one negro boy Calvin. I
will that my son Isaac Guyton children have one equal share with mine
in money. I will that my son Abraham Guyton children have one equal
share in money with mine. I appoint Joseph W. Guyton, John L. Guyton,
William Mitchel and Joseph Leech executors. Dated 18 Jan. 1861. Wit:
John M. McKown, Isaac L. Parker, Eleazer Parker. Signed: Joseph
Guyton. A codicil added on the 15 July 1861, only change is in the
negroes and how distributed. Wit: John M. McKown, John Weber,
Eleazer Parker. Signed: Joseph Guyton. Recorded 2 Aug. 1865.

GUYTON, JOSEPH Will Book B Page 45. Probate Judge Office.
Union, S. C. I Joseph Guyton of Union Dist. being infirm in body
through the decay of old age, yet blessed be God of sound judgment and
memory. I will all my lawful deb-s be paid. I will to my son
Joseph Guyton all the land that I am possessed of, reserving to the chn.
of my son Abraham Guyton decd. as much of my land as will include the

Guyton, Joseph - Continued. spring and stillhouse. Also reserving to the chn. of my dtr. Betsey Parker that land they now live on. Beginning at a pine above Isaac Parker spring, along the first line of my land to a stake at the waggon road, thence a straight line to the creek near John Parker fence. Also to my son Joseph Guyton all my farming utensils and my part of our waggon and gear, also my negro man named Catto. To my son Aaron Guyton I will one feather bed and furniture. To my two sons-in-law John Smith and Jonathan Smith to each one dollar. I will my negro woman Silvy and her chn. be equally divided amongst my children as follows: The chn. of Moses Guyton decd., Hannah Jondrin, Salley Guyton and Tabitha Guyton one part to be equally divided between them. Also the chn. of my decd. dtr. Betsey Parker one share to be divided between them. Also my children Aaron, Joseph Guyton, Molly Smith, and Hann Martin, each of them a share and the chn. of my son Abraham Guyton to have a share of said negroes. The remainder of my estate to be divided amongst all my chn. to wit: Son of my son Abraham one part, the three dtrs. of my son Moses, one part, the chn. of my decd. dtr. Betsey Parker one part, my son Aaron and Joseph one share each, also my two dtrs. Molly Smith and Hannah Martin each one share. Reserving my saddle and watch which I will to my grandson Abraham Guyton by my son Joseph. I appoint my son Joseph Guyton and Alexander Martin executors. Dated 26 May 1818. Wit: Nicholas Corry, Gabriel Petty, Sally Petty. Prove on oath of Nicholas Corry Esq. before William Rice, Ord. on the 3 Aug. 1818.

GUYTON, NATHANIEL   Will Book A, Page 247. Probate Judge Office. Union, S. C. I Nathaniel Guyton of Union Dist. being of sound judgment and memory. I give to my wife Sarah Guyton all that part of my estate that I received when we were married, excepting what I paid to her children upon her and their account with the addition of my white pacing mare, the full priviledge of the house wherein we now live during her life. To my son Isaac Guyton I will the plantation where he now lives. To my son Jacob I will my land upon Cherokee Creek, Spartanburg Dist. To my son John I will the plantation whereon he now lives. To my son Nathaniel I will the plantation whereon I now live (excepting the dwelling house for his mother and sister Hannah during their lives or till their marriage) also my smith tools, reserving the priviledge for any of his brothers to work upon them when they please. To my dtr. Hannah I will a plantation or tract of land joining whereon I now live upon the river below joining Morris land, containing 120 acres, with remainder of my goods and chattles and the priviledge of my dwelling house with her mother, paying to her sisters Molley Tate and Emy Crittenden one dollar each. I appoint my sons Isaac and Jacob Guyton executors. Dated 2 Jan. 1806. Wit: Nicholas Corry, Robert Corry, James Corry. Signed: Nathaniel Guyton. Recorded: 1 Oct. 1810.

GWYNN, THOMAS   Pack 5. Clerk of Court Office. Anderson, S. C. Anderson Dist. Alien's report: Pursuant to the direction and provision of the act of Congress. The undersigned made to the Court of General Sessions of the peace and held at Anderson Court House, report of himself; viz, That the said Thomas Gwynn was born in the county Doublin in Ireland that he is about the age of twenty four years. That he was born under the allegiance of the King of Great Britain. That he arrived at Philadelphia on or about fourteen months since, that he is by profession a labourer and he intends to make his residence in Anderson Dist. I have set my hand this 3 March 1829. In the presence of J. T. Lewis. Signed: Thomas X Gwynn.

HACKET, ELIJAH C. #12. Clerk of Court Office. Abbeville, S. C. Abbeville Dist. In Equity. To their Honors the chancellors: Your oratrix America E. Hackett, that Elijah C. Hackett departed this life on the first day of Dec. 1853, intestate, leaving a widow and two chn. namely, Anna Hackett, who has since died, and Ella C. Hackett who was born after the death of the intestate. Your oratrix has taken out letter of admr. on his personal estate, and the proceeds of the personalty more than sufficient to pay the debts. The intestate was possessed with a tract of land on Cuffee Town Creek, containing 200 acres. Bounded by land of Dr. John P. Burratt, Benjamin Sales, James Partlow and others. Your oratrix informed and advised that in as such as Anna Hacket has died leaving your oratrix and the daid[?] Ella C. Hackett her infant dtr. each are entitled to receive one half of the real estate. Filed 18 May 1855. Elijah C. Hackett left surviving him also at his death, brothers and sisters. William Freeman Hackett age 38, Elizabeth wife of Lemuel Bell, Augusta C. Hackett, age 28 in Edgefield. His father and mother are both dead. Mrs. Hackett resides at Phoenix P.O. Edgefield, S. C. Ann Moore wishes her land surveyed, lives in Edgefield, 6 1/2 miles from New Market on the road.

HAIRSTON, THOMAS Box 46 Pack 1044. Probate Judge Office. Abbeville, S. C. Admr. bond, 96 Dist. We William Hairston, John McCord and Robert Maxwell are bound unto John Ewing Calhoun, Ord. in the sum of 14 thousand pounds. Dated 20 Nov. 1782. Wm. Hairston as next of kin. Inventory was made 10 Dec. 1782. by John Irwin, John Calhoun and Samuel McMurty.

HALL, FRANCES E. Pack 4. Clerk of Court Office. Abbeville, S. C. Abbeville Dist. In Equity. To the Honr. the Chancellors: Your oratrix Frances E. Stark of Anderson Dist. the wife of Samuel James H. Stark of Abbeville, Dist. by Ezekiel Hall of Anderson Dist. her father and next friend. On the 14 Feb. 1852 your oratrix intermarried with Samuel James H. Stark. This marriage was solemnized in the house of the father of your oratrix by Rev. Rice. He was invited to remain in the house of your oratrix father, until he could remove to his settlement in Abbeville Dist. this he did until about the 6 March of this year. On this day he collected his clothing and other articles at the house of your oratrix father, assigning any reason for his conduct, and left said house and has not returned. Your oratrix has information that her husband is making proprations to remove from this State. He is selling his property and collecting his debts, and declaring his intention of going to Texas or California, and leaving his wife destitute of support. Your oratrix father is of moderate circumstances, and her husband has property in value exceeding ten thousand dollars. Therefore prays for relief from this Court for an annual sum to be assigned to her for maintenance or a wife share of his property, etc. She was eighteen years of age, and he was twenty four when married. Filed 9 March 1852. Settled by arrangement of the parties the 17 May 1852.

HAMBREE, EDWARD JR. Box 48 #526. Probate Judge Office. Pickens, S. C. I Edward Hambree being in sound mind and memory. I will all my just debts and funeral expenses paid. I give to my wife Elizabeth Hambree during her life time all the land, cattle, stock and hogs plantation tools, household and kitchen furniture and the crop in the field. After her death I desire all the remains of my property sold and the money equally divided between all my chn. Dated 25 Dec. 1857 Wit: John G. Mauldin, R. H. E. Cowan, S. F. K. Cowan. Proved the 5 March 1858. Est. admr. 26 March 1858 by Wm. H. Stribling, James E. Hagood, Zacharian Hall bound unto W. J. Parson, Ord. in the sum of $1800.00. Mrs. Hambree, J. D. Lumpkin, Mary H. Johnson, Eliza Pickens bought at sale.

HAMILTON, ALEXANDER C. Pack 3374. Clerk of Court Office. Abbeville, S. C. Abbeville Dist. In Equity To the Honr. the Chancellors: Your orator John Middleton Hamilton, sheweth that he is one of the legal distributees of Alexander C. Hamilton his father decd. and is entitled to a share of the estate and is desirous of obtaining his share of the real estate. His father departed this life on the

Hamilton, Alexander C. - Continued. 27th Feb. 1835, intestate
and was possessed with considerable real estate. Surviving chn: Jane
now the wife of Genl. John Bowie, John Hamilton, your orator, Robert
B. Hamilton, Susan the wife of James S. Wilson, Richard Andrew Hamilton,
Joseph Augustus Hamilton, Alexander Hamilton, Samuel Shiels Hamilton,
Ann Augusta Hamilton, Harriet Eugenia Davis Hamilton the six latter
children are minors under 21 yrs. The land is lying on Norris Creek
a branch of Long Cane, containing 526 3/4 acres bounded by land of
Alexander Martin decd., Maj. James Alston, ___ Kary and William C.
Black. Filed 16 May 1835. At this time Robert B. Hamilton was living
out of the limits of this State.

HAMMOND, WILLIAM J. Pack 327. Clerk of Court Office. Abbeville,
S. C. Abbeville Dist. In Equity, whereas William J. Hammond the
defendant to the bill of Margaret P. Hammond complaint. He admits he
intermarried with the complainant about four years ago and they had
three children, two of whom are still living. That his wife at the
time of marriage had 14 slaves worth about $6,000 (one worth about
$300 has since died) and a tract of land worth about $2500. That the
complainant at time of marriage was largely indebted, that he collected
and applied toward the payment of her debts all the money due her,
there is still an indebtedness of sixteen or seventeen hundred dollars.
That he never abused or mistreated his wife, he denies that he ever
laid his hand upon her in anger, or committed or threatened to commit
the least violence to her person. He denies ever having charged his
wife with having any veneral disease as alleged. He admits to indulge
in intoxicating liquors and while in state of intoxication he may have
used language deregatory to her character, etc. etc. Filed 10 July
1858.

HANDLY, PETER Pack 10. Clerk of Court Office. Anderson, S. C.
This indenture made this 25 Jan. 1793 between Peter Handly of Pendleton Dist. in consideration of 60 ₺ sterling paid by John Lowry, have
granted, sold, bargained and released all that tract of land in
Pendleton Dist. on the West side of twenty three mile creek waters of
Keeowe River. Bounded by vacant land on all sides. Containing 200
acres. Originally granted to Jesse ___. 2 July 1787. Wit: Wm.
Lofton, Jas. Gaines, James Brown. Signed: Peter X Handly. Recorded
24 Jan. 1794.

HARMON, THOMAS Pack 365. Clerk of Court Office. Abbeville,
S. C. Abbeville Dist. In Equity, To the Honr. the Chancellors: Your
orator and oratrix Stephen W. Willis and wife Susan, Charles M.
Freeman and wife Cynthia, Alexander A. Laramore and wife Esther and
Anthony Harmon. That Thomas Harmon of this Dist. departed this life
intestate many years ago, possessed with about seven hundred acres
of land in this Dist. lying on Savannah and Little Rivers. Bounded
by land of William Harmon, Frederick Redmonds, James Banks, Charles M.
Freeman, Ellington Searles and others. Leaving as heirs and distributees, Mary Harmon his widow, Susan Willis, Cynthia Freeman, Esther
Laramore, Anthony Harmon, Frances the wife of Dr. Socrates N. G.
Gerguson, Dicy the wife of James Banks, John Harmon, William Harmon,
Appleton G. Harmon, Emanuel Harmon, and Luke Harmon. Admr. of the
personal est. was committed to John Harmon and Appleton Harmon, with
all debts paid and distribution amongst the next of kin. The real
estate remained in possession of the widow. She died in Nov. 1862
intestate with very few debts. The only others heirs are Mary Harmon
a minor, the only child of Emanuel Harmon decd., William and Pickens
Harmon and Cornelia Crawford children of Luke Harmon decd. Filed
21 July 1863. Dr. S. N. G. Ferguson and Frances his wife, Wm. Harmon,
Pickens and Mary Harmon were residing out of State.

HARPER, LUCINDA Box 109 #1044. Probate Judge Office. Pickens,
S. C. Lucinda Harper admr. of Elias H. Hollingsworth decd. whose
will was filed 29 April 1876 in Pickens Co.

HARRALSON, MOSES Deed Book A, Page 2 & 3. Clerk of Court
Office. Marion, S. C. This indenture made this 17 Aug. 1789.
Between Moses Harralson of Prince George Parrish and Rebeckah, Isom,

Harralson, Moses - Continued. Jesse and Paul Harralson of the
same Parrish beloved sons and dtrs. of Moses Harralson. In consideration of natural love and affections I have for my sons and dtr. and
five shilling sterling in hand paid by same children, have granted and
confirmed unto Rebeckah one negro named Phillis, to Isom one negro
girl named Peg, to Jesse one negro named Will, to Selah one negro
named Mary, to Paul the first living issue of Gillen. Wit: Abigal
Harralson, Lewis Harralson. Signed: Moses Harralson. Proved on
Oath of Benjamin Harralson, J.P. on this 17 Aug. 1789. Recorded this
25 April 1800 and examined by Sam Cooper for John Dozer Junr. Reg.

HARRIS, BENJAMIN Pack 8 Clerk of Court Office. Anderson, S. C.
I Benjamin Harris of Greenville Dist. in consideration of $57.00 paid
me by John Davis of Pendleton Dist. have granted, sold, bargained and
released two tracts of land in Pendleton Dist. one tract, bounded by
Talton Lee land, Thomas Hill and John Davis line and William Childers.
The other tract bounded by lands of Burrel Carpenters land, and the
South side of Saluda River. Dated 3 Dec. 1805. Wit: Adam Todd, John
Flowers. Signed: Benjamin X Harris. Proved on oath of John Flowers
before Abner Nash, J.P. this 23 Oct. 1809.

HARRIS, JOHN Deed Book S Page 477. Clerk of Court Office,
Anderson, S. C. I John Harris of Pendleton Dist. in consideration of
$200.00 to me paid by Lewis Stanley of same Dist. have granted, sold,
bargain and release the West end of a tract of land lying on West side
of Seneca River, it being originally granted to Field Prewet. Said
land contain 88 acres. Dated 7 May 1824. Wit: Martin McCoy, Eliza
C. Harris. Signed: John Harris.

HATCHER, WILLIAM Deed Book C. Clerk of Court Office. Elberton,
Ga. This indenture made 23 Feb. 1793 between William Hatcher of
Elbert Co., Ga. and Pricilla his wife, and William Thompson Junr. of
same county. In consideration of twenty L money of this State, have
granted, sold, bargained, and release all that tract of land containing
twenty acres. Being on the South side of Butrems Creek, bounded by
land of Nat J. Williams, William Thompson Senr. Wit: M. J. Williams,
Asa Thompson, Evan Ragland, J.P. Signed: William Hatcher and
Priscilla Hatcher. Reg. 28 July 1795.

HATTER, BENJAMIN Box 45 Pack 1002. Probate Judge Office.
Abbeville, S. C. I Benjamin Hatter of Abbeville Dist. being weak in
body but of perfect mind and memory. I will my just debts be paid,
and to enable my executors to comply with my desire, I wish them to
collect my debts due me and to dispose of my cotton crop for cash and
apply all to the debt due by me to Boyce and Johnston and Mr. Oneel
merchants of Charleston. It is my desire that my negroes be hired out
anually and the proceeds applied to the supporting of my chn. When
my son Richard shall arrive of the age of fifteen, I desire a division
be made of my negroes, among my children either by lot or sale. The
three youngest chn. to be schooled at joint expense of all, until my
executors think they are on an equallity with the older one thirdly.
My executors to comply with sale of the house and lot in village of
Cambridge, S. C. to Dr. Wm. O. A. Brown agreeable to the agreement
between us which is in hand of James Pain. I rented from Albert
Waller a plantation that shall be rented out again I have sold a small
lot to Mr. L. Miller for twenty five dollars. I appoint my sons
William and Zery Hatter with friends Thomas Hill, Sr. and Joseph Hill
and Abner Piles executors. My children are: William, Zery, Polly,
Belinda, Susannah, Elizabeth, Richard, Milly and Mahaly. Dated 21
Nov. 1820. Wit: Nancy Hill, Thomas Hill, A. Mayson. Signed: Benja-
min Hatter. Proven 14 May 1821. Inventory made by Thos. Lipscomb, Jno.
Cheatham, Martin Hackett.

HAWKINS, PINKETHAM Box 46 Pack 1042. Probate Judge Office.
Abbeville, S. C. Admr. bond 96 Dist. We Michael Harvey, James
Christopher and Allen Hinton are bound unto John Ewing Calhoun Ord.
in the sum of 14 thousand pounds. Dated 13 Sept. 1782. Michael
Harvey of Savannah River was next of kin. Sale held 12 Dec. 1782
buyers Michael Harvey, Samuel Hawkins, John Lamar, Henry Graybill,

Hawkins, Pinketham - Continued.   Clark. Inventory made 25
Sept. 1782 by Wm. Harvey, Danl. Mitchell, Henry Graybill. Expend: 10
Dec. 1779, 1 year boarding and clothing Samuel Hawkins $40.00.
Boarding and clothing Sarah Hawkins $40.00, paid Elizabeth Hawkins her
acct. against est. 44.26. Boarding and clothing Mathew and Thomas
Hawkins from 1st of Aug. 1786 to the 1st April 1785, 80.00. Paid David
Leach for teaching Stephen Hawkins 7.00. (The money paid out seem to
be in dollars, yet no dollar mark is shown, the bond is in ₺)

HAYS, JACOB Box 46 Pack 1029. Probate Judge Office. Abbeville,
S. C. Admr. bond, 96 Dist. We William Wood and John Golightly of
Fairforest are bound unto John Thomas Ord. in the sum of two thousand
pounds. Dated Oct. 1783. Inventory made 9 Oct. 1783 by John Golightly,
Wm. Prince, Rowland Courelous.

HAYS, JAMES Deed Book N. Page 101. Clerk of Court Office.
Anderson, S. C. Pendleton Dist. I James Hays of Pendleton Dist. in
consideration of $76.85 to me paid in hand by Samuel Dean of same
Dist. have granted, bargained, sold, and released that tract of land
lying on Mountain Creek, waters of Big Generstee and Savannah River.
Being part of a tract granted to James Martin. Marked by a plat now
in possession of the heirs of John Hays decd. and that said James Hays
being an heir to the will of John Hays per recorded in Pendleton Dist.
Bounded by lands of Samuel Dean, James Martain, White line, near Kennedy
house. Wit: James Kennedy, Griffin Dean, Richard Dean, Abram Dean.
Signed: James X Hays. Deed dated 20 Nov. 1813. Proven on oath of
Griffin Dean before John L. Lewis C.C. on this 28 Feb. 1817.

HAYS, COL. JOSEPH Box 45 Pack 1028. Probate Judge Office.
Abbeville, S. C. Admr. bond, 96 Dist. We Alice Hays, Henry Pearson
and James Waldrop are bound unto John Ewing Calhoun Ord. in the sum of
fourteen thousand pounds money. Dated at White Hall the 8 Nov. 1782.
Inventory made 31 Jan. 1783 by Thomas Johnson, James Smith, James
Gogens. Alice Hays was the widow. The cit. was read at a public
gathering at the house of Richard Griffin the 1 Nov. 1782. She lived
between Little River and Bush River. 96 Dist. on 29 April 1786 Henry
Pearson one of the securities to the ordinary, pr. Alice Hays (Now
Alice Stewart, admrx. of Joseph Hays decd.) On oath saith that Wm.
Stewart husband of said admrs. have done several acts lending to the
wasting of the est. by disposing of property at private sale and not
agreeable to law and applying the money arising from the same to the
discharges of his own debts and not to those of the est. He has sold
seven negroes to Samuel Aiken and Prince and Doll and three chn. to his
father in North Carolina. A wagon and some horses and a negro called
Julius that is recorded in Laurens Court House. This deponent and
others are greatly endangered and the property of the minors chn. of
the decd. Joseph Hays is wasted in a shameful manner. Sworn before me
this 29 April 1786 William Moore, J.P.

HAYS, THOMAS Pack 7, Clerk of Court Office. (Basement) Anderson,
S. C. Pendleton Dist. I Thomas Hays in said Dist. in consideration
of $10.00 to me paid by Richard Dean of same Dist. have granted, sold,
bargained and released all that tract of land lying in Pendleton Dist.
waters of Savannah River, containing 199 acres. Originally granted to
Josiah Prince the 13 Oct. 1797. Dated this 12 Nov. 1813. Wit:
Griffith Dean, James Kennedy. Signed Thomas X Hays. Proved on oath of
Griffith Dean before John T. Lewis, C.C. this 28 Feb. 1817.

HAYS, WILLIAM Box 45 Pack 1026. Probate Judge Office. Abbeville,
S. C. Abbeville Dist. Admr. bond, We Robert Hays, William McKeen
and Andrew English planters are bound unto the judge of Abbe. Co.
Court in the sum of one thousand pounds sterling. Dated 10 Nov. 1795.
Inventory made 7 Dec. 1795 by John Wilson, Robert Kirkwood, John
Simpson.."I the under named subscriber do freely allow Robert Hays
and no other person to administer on my husband deceased estate
according as the law directs in witness whereof I set my hand and seal
this 9 Nov. 1795. Test. William McKeen. Signed: Elizabeth X Hays"
[sic]

HEAD, BENJAMIN Box 46 #507. Probate Judge Office. Pickens, S. C. Est. admr. 25 Jan. 1858 by William Whitmire, A. B. Grant, Miles M. Norton who are bound unto W. J. Parson, Ord. in the sum of $500. Wm. Whitmire, A. B. Grant was of Cherokee, Pickens Dist., S. C. Widow mentioned, not named.

HEAD, GEORGE & JOHN Pack 8 Clerk of Court Office. Anderson, S. C. Pendleton Dist. We George Head of Chester Dist. and John Head of Pendleton Dist. Exctrs. of Geo. Head decd. In consideration of $690.00 in hand paid by Stephen Liddall of said Dist. and State. Have granted, bargained, sold and released all that plantation which George Head decd. lived, containing 272 acres. (Land on a creek with a mill, creek not named). Wit: Wm. Pegg, John Liddall. Signed: George Head and John Head. Deed proved on oath of John Liddall before John Fleming, J.P. this 25 March 1820.

HEAD, JAMES Book A Page 79. Probate Judge Office. Elberton, Ga. I James Head of Elbert Co., Ga. being sick and weak, but in perfect memory. I give to my loving wife Elizabeth Janett Head two negroes; one named Wigan and Sarah, with four feather beds and all my household furniture and working tools, my stock of hogs, cattle, two work horses and I lend my sorrel mare to my wife during her lifetime. I give to my dtr. Sarah Fortson one negro girl named Luscy, one feather bed and furniture, saddle and bridle now in her possession. It is my will that my land on Vans Creek after the death of my wife be divided between my two sons Benjamin Simon Head and James Head. Each of my chn. from Martha down to James have received one negro, feather bed and furniture and saddle and bridle. My tract of land of 200 acres in Wilkes Co. on Kettle Creek be sold and pay my debts. I appoint my loving wife Elizabeth Janet Head executrix and Sally Riddle, Thomas White my executors. Dated this 23 Oct. 1795. Wit: William Head, John Pollard and John Hose. Signed: James Head. Recorded the 7 Jan. 1796.

HEAD, JAPTHA Pack 650-6. Clerk of Court Office. Pickens, S. C. In Equity. Head vs Leonard Capehart. Dated 17 June 1850. Jeptha Head states that George Head went to work for Leonard Capehart. Was gone three days. His father had made a wheel for Capehart. That Capehart had come with some negroes and took the wheel away. Levi Robins sworn says, Capehart came several times to see Head about fixing the wheel. Alexander Harris sworn says, Capehart said to him that Head was working on the wheel. R. R. Boyd sworn says, that the plaintiff is a mill wright. He saw the wheel and looked to him well made, and made some like it. He thought the water was not delivered to any advantage. The wheel was 8 ft. in diameter. Leonard Rogers says Capehart spoke to Head about making a wheel for saw mill, and one for grist mill. Elijah Garrett sworn says, that he thought the buckets of the wheel was to far apart, or the water was not let in right.

HEAD, STEPHEN Pack 212 #2. Clerk of Court Office. Pickens, S. C. I Stephen Head of Edgefield Dist. am held and firmly bound unto William Hamrick of the same place, in the sum of $400. I bind myself executors Admr. and assigns to said William Hamrick to cause to be paid on a tract of land containing 100 acres, lying in Pendleton Dist. on branches of Saluda River. Dated this 6 Feb. 1810. Wit: Thomas Gibson, Silas X Sigane. Signed: Stephen Head.

HEARD, ARMSTRONG Deed Book C. Clerk of Court Office. Elberton, Ga. I Armstrong Heard of State of Ga., County of Elbert. Have bargained and sold unto James Coffee in consideration of 100 L sterling, have hereby acknowledged 300 acres on waters of Shoal Creek. Bounded by land of John Rogers, being part of a grant of 500 acres granted to John Fergus and conveyed to me. Dated 17 Feb. 1794. Wit: John Heard, John Fergus, J.P. signed Armstrong Heard, Jinny Heard the wife of Armstrong Heard, hath relinquished her dower to above land this 17 Feb. 1794. Signed: Jinny X Heard.

HEARD, ISAAC Box 45 Pack 1023. Probate Judge Office. Abbeville,
S. C. Being in perfect mind and memory, I make this my last will and
testament. I give the plantation whereon I now live to my son Eliaj[?]
John Heard, my wife is to live on it while she is my widow, there is
one half acre of said plantation that I except for a grave yard. I
leave my personal property to my wife, to do as she please. There is
a stud colt I desire him sold and my debts paid. I appoint my wife
Mary Heard executrix and Thomas Heard and William Wardlaw Long execu-
tors. Dated 20 March 1804. Wit: Thos. Brightman, Wm.Brightman.
Signed: Isaac Heard. Recorded 9 April 1804. Inventory made 16
April 1804. by Larkin Reynolds, Archibald Frith and Benj. Chiles.
Richard Heard bought 1 stud colt $93.00.

HEARON, JAMES Box 31 #1094. Probate Judge Office. Camden, S.C.
Est. admr. 20 Nov. 1846 by Catharine Hearon, B. S. Lucas, Tobias
Folsom who are bound unto R. L. Wilson, Ord. in the sum of $300. James
Hearon died 24 April 1846. Owned 375 acres on the main road leading
to Tillers Ferry or bridge bounded by J. Tillers land, E. Stokes land
and H. Hix land. Owned 300 acres lying in the fork of Lynches Creek
bounded by land of John Brannon, Alexander McCaskill. (Name written
Hearon and Heron--Catharine and Katharine.)

HEARON, SAMUEL Box 31 #1095. Probate Judge Office. Camden,
S. C. Est. admr. Feb. 1861 by Harman Arrants, J. E. Rodgers, W. W.
Stokes who are bound unto Wm. M. Bullock, Ord. in the sum of $6,166.
On 6 June 1853 Daniel Hearon states that his father Samuel Heron died
24 May 1853. Paid 27 Jan. 1864 Mariah Skinner $100. Paid 2 Feb. 1864
S. Heron for E.Heron $500. Paid W. Skinner by J. E. Rodgers $100.
Paid 1 March Nancy Loylaw by C. C. Ninon $100. J. E. Rodgers admr.
Applicant vs Manuel Heron, Elias Delk, David Delk, Robert Delk, James
Delk, Icy Moore, Nelly Segars, Mary Delk, Nancy E. Delk, Wm. Skinner,
John Skinner, James Skinner, Nancy Outlaw and Rebecca Heron, fourteen
of the defendants reside without this State. Est. admr. also by
Daniel Hearon, Daniel Bethune, and John Brannon in the sum of $4,000.

HEARST, JOHN Pack #1. Clerk of Court Office. Abbeville, S. C.
I John Hearst, Senr. in consideration of #1362.00 paid by Joseph Hearst
trustee, have granted, sold and released all that tract of land lying
in said dist. on curl tail creek, waters of long cane and Savannah
River, bounded by land of Abram Lites, James Devlin Senr., William
Wharton containing 270 acres. To have and hold said land for the use
and benefit of Jane Ansley wife of William Ansley and their children.
Dated 17 Dec. 1847. Wit: James F. Watson, Geo. Marshall, John W.
Hearst. Signed: John Hearst.

HEARST, JOHN Pack #1. Deed of Trust. Clerk of Court Office.
Abbeville, S. C. Abbeville Dist. Whereas I John Hearst having purchased at the sale of the property of William S. Ansley made by
sheriff of said Dist. the 3 Oct. 1843, certain property hereinafter
named, which property is now in the possession of said William S.
Ansley by virtue of a loan to him. Whereby my dtr. Jane the wife of
said William S. Ansley shall have the benefit of the same. I John
Hearst for in consideration of the natural love and affection which I
have towards my dtr. Jane Ansley and inconsideration of one dollar
paid by my son Joseph Lewis Hearst of said Dist. do sell and deliver
the following property to wit; one negro woman Phillis age about twenty
seven, and her chn. Sam a boy age about eight yrs., Andy a boy age
about six yrs., Jaff[?] a boy age about four yrs., Caroline a girl
age about two yrs., Oliver age six months, one sorrel horse about nine
years old, one bay mare about seven yrs. old, household and kitchen
furniture, farm tools, and feed of the stock. Said property to be
free from any debts, pledge, mortgage or engagement of her present or
future husband. Said Joseph L. Hearst shall have power to take possession of all or any to preventing a removal, sale or other separation
lost or waste, after the death of my dtr. Jane said property to be
equally divided between Jane heirs. Etc. etc. Wit: B. Jordan, Samuel
Redden. Signed: John Hearst, W. S. Ansley, Jane Ansley, Joseph L.
Hearst. Dated 2 April 1844. (Another Paper) Jane Ansley departed
this life in the month of Aug. 1848, surviving her the husband William

Hearst, John - Continued. S. and two children, viz: John Augustus, Nancy Isabells, the latter infant died in the month of April 1853. The father, William still works on the farm and manage the negroes thereby making a support for himself and his son. Filed 24 April 1855.

HEARST, JOHN & WILLIAM Box 42 Pack 944. Probate Judge Office. Abbeville, S. C. There seemed to be two wills in the same pack.) I John Hearst of 96 Dist. being very sick and weak in body but of sound and perfect mind, etc. I give to my wife Mary Hearst one third of all my moveable effects of whatsoever kind, also to enjoy the full benefit of this house and plantation where I now reside, during her widowhood. I leave unto my son Robert Hearst and dtr. Mary Hearst one shilling sterling each if demanded. Also I leave to my son John Hearst one shilling sterling if demanded, likewise unto my son Joseph Hearst, Thomas Hearst, George Hearst, and William Hearst to each 100 acres of woodland belonging to this plantation. Each to receive their land when of full age. Unto my five dtrs. Christian Hearst, Elizabeth Hearst, Mary Hearst, and Margaret Hearst and Ann Hearst the remaining two thirds of my moveable property, after my debts are paid. Also to my three youngest dtrs. 100 acres of land I purchased from Jane Humphrey's. Unto my step daughter Eloner OBryan twenty three L currency to be paid when of age. I made and appoint my wife Mary Hearst sole executrix. Dated 9 Sept. 1780. Wit: Cha Teulon, Rob X Wilson, Rob X Erwin. Signed: John Hearst. Probated: 23 Aug. 1782.

HEARST, WILLIAM Abbeville Dist., S. C. I William Hearst being weak in body but sound in mind and memory. I hereby appoint John Hearst my executor with full power to pay all debts and demands. "I will that Ebenezar Pressly receive of my estate a suffitiantey to pay for his present steadys for his colegiate course his theological steadies or other profession to the amount of $1000." [sic] The remainder of my estate to be sold and divided between the children of my full brothers and sisters. Except the tract of land lying on the Reedy Branches adj. land of Wm. Drennon, James Pennal and others, which tract I will to John Hearst. Dated 8 Jan. 1823. Wit: Samuel Pressly, Wm. B. Wardlaw, John T. Pressly, John S. Pressly. Signed: William Hearst. Settlement of the est. 8 Dec. 1834. The children living at time of the death of the testator. Brother Joseph Hearst had 8 children. Brother Thomas Hearst 8 chn. Sister Elizabeth who married Wm. Pressly 4 chn. Sister Christian who married Wilson had one child. Brother George Hearst had 5 chn.. each child received $92.07 3/4.

HEARRON, JOSIAH N. Box 27 #1. Probate Judge Office. Darlington, Co., S. C. Est. admr. 4 Sept. 1863 by Chally A. Hearron, S. Wesley Harrell, Isaiah Gallaway who are bound unto John J. Russell, Ord. in the sum of $20,000. Mrs. J. N. Hearron, Mrs. Nancy Elliott bought at sale.

HEARRON, THOMAS D. Box 27 #11. Probate Judge Office. Darlington Co., S. C. Est. admr. 24 April 1865 by Christian J. Flinn, Benjamin Clements, Christopher C. Mixon who are bound to John J. Russell, Ord. in the sum of $10,000.

HEFFENER, THOMAS Pack 214 #1. Clerk of Court Office. Pickens, S. C. On 1 March 1857 Thomas Heffener was found guilty of retailing whiskey with out a license.

HEMBREE, WILLIS Pack 11, Clerk of Court Office. Anderson, S. C. I Willis T. Hembree of Anderson Dist. in consideration of $200.00 paid me by James W. Glenn of same Dist. have granted, sold, bargained, and released all that tract of land containing 75 acres in said Dist. Bounded on East and North by land of William Long and South by land of Aaron Hall and on West by road from dark Corner to Anderson Court House. Dated 8 Dec. 1845. Wit: James X Cannon, A. O. Norris. Signed: Willis T. Hembree. Proved on oath of James Cannon before A. O. Norris this 8 Dec. 1845. I A. O. Norris, Clk. of Equity do certify that Tabitha Hembree did this day appear before me and without any compulsion dread or fear renounce and relinquish all rights and claim of dower to the above land. This 13 Dec. 1845.

HEMPHILL, MARGARET Box 45 Pack 999. Probate Judge Office.
Abbeville, S. C. Abbeville Dist. Admr. bond, We William Hemphill,
Alexander Houston and James Houston who are bound unto Moses Taggart,
Ord. in the sum of $8,000. Dated 6 Feb. 1826. Cit. Pub. at Hopewell
Church. Wm. Hemphill was next of kin. Inventory was made 17 Feb.
1826 by Joseph C. Mathews, Joseph Calhoun, Robt. H. Houston. Sale
held 18 Feb. 1826 buyers, Alexander Hemphill, Wm. Hemphill, John
Johnstone, Robert Jennings, James Conner Junr., Capt. Joseph Calhoun,
Philip Leroy Jr., Robert Foster Senr., Geo. Brough, Robt. H. Houston,
John Leroy, Henry Mouchet, Jos. C. Mathews, James R. Houston, J.
Hollinghead, John Scott, E. C. Thornton, F. Mitchell, James Hughes, N.
Fry, James Anderson, Robert Leaster. Expend. Mar. 1826, Paid John
Hemphill legatee $397.89. Paid Alexr. Hemphill $397.89.

HENCKEN, JOHN M. Box 85 #897. Probate Judge Office. Pickens,
S. C. I John Hencken being of sound mind and memory, etc. First all
my lawful debts are paid. The residue of my estate real and personal,
I give and dispose of as follows, To my beloved wife the house and lots
#18 and #33 in the town of Walhalla, Pickens Dist., also lots #54, 103,
15, 26 and 36. Also two shares in the German Settlement Society of
Charleston, S. C. The rest and remainder of my property to my children
now living. (Not named). Dated 7 Feb. 1863, Wit: John N. Tideman,
Hanke Gissel, H. C. Rochan. Signed: John M. Hencken. Proved 18 Nov.
1865.

HENCOCK, SOLOMON Box 46 Pack 1043. Probate Judge Office.
Abbeville, S. C. 96 Dist. date 2 Oct. 1782. I Solomon Hencock, being
very sick and knowing the certainty of death. I give to my son William
Hencock 300 acres whereon I now live, one negro boy named Hardy, one
feather bed and furniture. I give to my son Richard one negro fellow
named Jack, and two hogshead of tobacco. I give to my dtr. Sarah
Hancock three negroes, Tamor, Joe and Tab, also one mare, one loom and
gears and choice of beds. I give to my son William and Richard one
negro boy named Isaac. I give to my dtr. Ann Hill twenty shillings
sterling also I lend her one negro woman named Sarah during life, then
to be the property of Elisha Hill, if he has no heirs of his body, then
to the next youngest son Daniel Hill. I give to my dtr. Elizabet
Case one negro woman named Jude, also one mare now in her possession.
I give the remainder of my est. to my sons William and Richard and my
dtr. Sarah. I appoint John Gorre Senr. my executor. Wit: Daniel
Gorre, Noah X Bonds, Richard X Bonds. Signed: Solomon X Hencock.
Probated 23 Nov. 1782.

HENDERSON, DAVID Vol. 14. Probate Judge Office. Charleston,
S. C. I David Henderson of St. Michaels Parish a peruke (Man wig
maker) being sick and weak of body, but of sound and perfect memory.
First I will that all my just debts and funeral charges be fully
paid. I give unto my loving wife Sarah Henderson all my estate real
and personal of whatsoever nature or kind. I appoint my wife Sarah
Henderson sole executrix with my friend John Watson, gardener of
Charleston, S. C. Dated 11 Sept. 1771. Wit: James Thompson,
Humphrey Wady, John Kefson. Signed: David Henderson. Proved before
Lord Charles Montagu, the 27 Sept. 1771, same time qualified Sarah
Henderson and John Watson Executrix and executor.

HENDERSON, DAVID Box 45 Pack 1003. Probate Judge Office.
Abbeville, S. C. Abbeville Dist. Admr. bond, We Mary Henderson, James
Henderson, George Rievs and Thompson Hodges are bound to Talo.
Livingston, Ord. in the sum of $2,000. Dated 20 April 1811. Inventory
made 26 April 1811 by James Hodges, Gabriel Long, Richard Anderson.
Sale held 9 May 1811, widow, Robert P. Delph, Mary Henderson, Wm.
Henderson, James Henderson, Thompson Hodges, Benj. Jones, Major John
Hodges, Saml. Anderson, Wm. Williams.

HENDERSON, FRANCIS Pack 250. Clerk of Court Office. Abbeville,
S. C. Abbeville Dist. To the Honr. the Chancellors; your oratrix
Cassandra Henderson sheweth that Francis Henderson the husband of your
oratrix departed this life in Aug. 1859 possessed at time of his death
with a tract of land, on waters of Rockey Creek, containing 423 acres,

Henderson, Francis - Continued. bounded by land of Sally Wideman, Josiah Patterson, Wm. McCain. Francis Henderson died leaving his heirs, your oratrix the widow and five chn. all of whom are minors under the age of 21 years. Judson about nine years, James Lewis about seven years, Jefferson about five years, Robert about three years, and Francis Marion about one year. The admr. of the goods and chattels has been granted by William Hill, Ord. to Daniel P. Self, on the 24 Sept. 1859. The present estate is more than sufficient to discharge the debts. Your oratrix desires partition of the tract of land above described. Filed 24 Sept. 1859. Another paper stated that he died 5 Aug. 1859.

HENDERSON, THOMAS #47. Clerk of Court Office. Pickens, S. C. In Equity, Pickens Dist. To their Honr. the chancellors; Your orator John Henderson sheweth that his father the late Thomas Henderson departed this life intestate in May 1841, sized at the time with considerable real estate subject to distribution amongst his heirs at law viz; the widow, Elizabeth and four children and four grand chn. to wit, Elizabeth Henderson, Nathaniel Henderson, John Cansler and wife Ann nee Henderson, Jacob Gearin and wife Abegail nee Henderson, and your orator John Henderson, Elizabeth now decd. who intermarried with John Cansler, chn. John Cansler Jr., Thomas Cansler a minor over the age of 18 yrs., Nelson Cansler a minor over 16 yrs., Carroll Cansler a minor over 14 yrs. the grand children resides within the limits of this State. Land owned by Thomas Henderson 641 acres on Georges Creek granted to him 20 July 1792, 143 acres on Brushy Creek, granted to him 4 July 1808, 80 acres conveyed by Joab Mauldin by deed 29 May 1817, 236 and 360 acres on Mill branch Creek waters of Saluda River conveyed by deed by William Henderson the 26 March 1790, 443 acres on Brushy and Georges Creek, conveyed by Henry Terrell 10 Aug. 1823, 491 on 18 Mile and Goldens Creek granted 3 April 1815, 500 acres conveyed by Richard Terrell, 11 Dec. 1811, 50 acres conveyed by J. Maulden 19 Oct. 1815. Filed 15 March 1842. A bill of complaint in the Court of Equity was filed by Daniel Thayer on the 2 Jan. 1843, against the heirs of Thomas Henderson. The Court adjudge and decree that several tracts of land be sold at public out cry. Tract #1 and 5 was sold to Daniel Thayer for $405.00. The heirs of Elizabeth Henderson decd. petition the Court for distribution of her land as widow of Thomas Henderson, land lying on Georges Creek, adj. land of Col. Holcombe and others. Dated 4 Nov. 1847.

HENDRICKS, ABEL Box 94, #992. Probate Judge Office. Pickens, S. C. Est. admr. 18 Sept. 1884 by Joseph S. Hendricks, Jesse Crenshaw, T. A. Williams are bound unto J. H. Newton, Ord. in the sum of $2,000. Dies 10 Aug. 1884. Joseph S. Hendricks his oldest son, Frances Susan Hendricks the widow and mother of Amanda M. Hendricks, Loutie Evaline Hendricks a minor under 14 yrs., 20 Feb. 1888 Wm. Walker Hendricks, Josephine J. Alexander minors over 14 yrs., 20 Feb. 1886 heirs viz; Frances Susan Julian, Morning Jane Findley, James Mason Hendricks, Saml. D. Hendricks, Alice A. Stansell, Tyler B. Hendricks, Wm. W. Hendricks, Josephine J. Alexander, Amanda M. Hendricks, Loutie Evaline Hendricks.

HENDRICKS, CYNTHIA Book A, Page 246. Probate Judge Office. Pickens, S. C. On 6 Juen 1859, Cynthia J. Hendricks was formerly the widow of James W. Couch decd. by whom she had one minor child Matilda F. Couch of whom William Hamilton was her guardian. After the death of her husband she married a Hendricks.

HENDRICKS, DAVID Box 26 #310. Probate Judge Office. Pickens, S. C. Est. admr. 23 Jan. 1852 by George Hendricks, Moses Hendricks who are bound unto Wm. D. Steele, Ord. in the sum of $5,000. On 8 Jan. 1852 George Hendricks and Morning Hendricks states that they would administer on the est. of David Hendricks decd. Settlement: 7 Feb. 1852 paid Abel Hendricks $280.02. 21 Apr. 1852 paid David Freeman $93.33. 4 Feb. paid John B. Hendricks $280.02. 7 Aug. 1854 paid Larkin Hendricks receipt for the share of Bennett Hendricks as allowed him by the Court of Equity, $280.02, 27 Feb. 1854 paid Moses Hendricks $280.02. Sale held 26 Feb. 1852, buyers: Abel Hendricks,

Hendricks, David - Continued. Morning Hendricks, Cleveland Hendricks, Garland Jones, John B. Hendricks.

HENDRICKS, DAVID Pack 56. In Equity, Clerk of Court Office. Pickens, S. C. To the Honr. the Chancellors: Your orator George Hendricks that his father departed this life intestate in Sept. 1850. Possessed at the time of his death with 150 acres of land lying on Shoal Creek waters of Saluda River. Adj. land of A. Hendricks. The heirs were: Mourning Hendricks the widow and seven chn. Abel Hendricks, heirs at law of Elizabeth Freeman who died some years before her father, Mary Looper the wife of Henson Looper, Martha Tompkins, the wife of Thomas Tompkins and David Freeman, Moses Hendrick, Bennett Hendricks, John B. Hendricks, Susan Hill the wife of Lewis Hill, and George Hendricks. Filed 9 Feb. 1852.

HENDRICKS, GEORGE Box 113, #1091. Probate Judge Office. Pickens, S. C. Est. admr. 14 Sept. 1881 by D. E. Hendricks, H. J. Anthony, J. T. Anthony are bound to Olin L. Durant, Ord. in the sum of $4,000. Paid 13 Jan. 1883 Leuvica Hendricks, widow $427.25. W. F. Hayes $200. Mary Jane Freeman $200. E. L. Williams $200. Baylus Hendricks heirs $200. W. F. Pace share $20.64.

HENDRICKS, GEORGE H. Box 2 #115. Probate Judge Office. Pickens, S. C. On 11 Feb. 1887 Wm. Field, J. K. Latham, B. S. Freeman, E. S. Griffin, W.H. Ariail, Geo. H. Hendricks minor under 21 years, son of Moses Hendricks.

HENDRICKS, JAMES B. Pack 655 #6. Clerk of Court Office. Pickens, S. C. I James B. Hendricks of Bradford County, State of Florida. Have constituted, ordained and appointed Thomas P. Looper of Pickens County, State of S.C. to be my true and lawful attorney. To ask, demand, sue and receive and receipt all money payable or coming to me from the Estate of Harrison Mansell decd. Dated 11 Oct. 1870. Wit: Benjamin E. Tucker, John S. Ball. Signed: Jas. B. Hendricks.

HENDRICKS, COL. JOHN C. Box 22 #268. Probate Judge Office. Pickens, S. C. Est. admr. 10 April 1848 by Mathew Keith, Alexander Edens who are bound unto Wm. D. Steele, Ord. in the sum of $3,000. Mathew Keith was a brother in law to Col. John Hendricks. Was a brother to Rosey Hendricks widow of Col. John Hendricks.

HENDRICKS, JOHN O. Box 66 #712. Probate Judge Office. Pickens, S. C. Est. admr. 3 Nov. 1862 by Geo. K. Hendrick, Edmond W. Keeler, Cornelius Keith who are bound unto W. E. Holcombe, Ord. in the sum of $2,000. John Hendricks was father of Geo. K. Hendricks.

HENDRICKS, LARKIN Box 64, #690. Probate Judge Office. Pickens, S. C. I Larkins Hendricks Senr. of Pickens Dist. being of sound and disposing mind and memory and understanding. I direct that all my just debts shall be paid. I give to my beloved wife Rosa Hendricks during the term of her natural life, the tract of land containing 157 1/2 acres, on which my residence is located, which is set forth in a plat of the same made by John Bowen, D. S. on 9 June 1858. At the death of my wife Rosa Hendricks, I will and direct that said tract of land be sold by my executors and the proceeds thereof be divided equally amongst my children. The share of my decd. dtr. Temperance Looper shall be divided between her children. I give to my wife Rosa during the term of her natural life my negroes Ann, and Sy otherwise called William. At the death of my wife said negroes to be sold, and the proceeds equally divided amongst the chn. of my wife, or any future child she may have by me. In the distribution of my property, I like $250 giving to my dtr. Temperance Looper now decd. her share, I now bequeath the same sum to my three grand chn. the chn. of the said dtr. I give to my dtr. Matilda Looper the wife of Thomas Looper a negro girl Delia, to make her even with the others. I give to my step son Matthew Hendricks the sum of $100 to be paid by my executors. I give to my step dtr. Rosa Hendricks the sum of $100 to be paid by my executors. The rest and remainder of my est. to be sold, and the proceeds thereof with debts due me, to pay my just debts and money

Hendricks, Larkin - Continued. legacies herein set forth. I
direct an equal division amongst my chn. Susan Roper the wife of
Marcus Roper, Joseph C. Hendricks, Jainy Crenshaw the wife of Jesse
Crenshaw, David Hendricks, James Butler Hendricks, Matilda Looper the
wife of Thomas Looper, Milton Madison Hendricks and the three grand
children the chn. of my dtr. Temperance Looper, the said children
taking the share of their mother. I appoint my son James Butler
Hendricks, and friend Dr. A. J. Anderson and C. J. Elford executors.
Dated 2 July 1858. Wit: T. B. Roberts, A. S. Briggs, H. C. Briggs.
Signed: Larkins Hendricks. Proven on oath of H. C. Briggs before
W. E. Holcombe, Ord. on the 6 Oct. 1862.

HENDRICKS, LARKIN Pack 264. Clerk of Court Office. Pickens,
S. C. Jesse Crenshaw states that Larkin Hendricks Esq. the father of
his wife departed this life some years ago, leaving a will, Appointing
Dr. Andrew J. Anderson executor. When the sale of the property came
off, he was in the army in Virginia. That he and his wife was very
anxious to purchase the home place in partnership with her brother
J. C. Hendrick. It was agreed by Jesse and Jane Crenshaw that said
Hendricks should bid off the land containing 212 acres, and the same
would be divided between them. It was known at the sale by the
executor Anderson and the spectators that he was bidding for himself
and his sister. At one point he stopped bidding, she told him to bid
on, he did and the sale was knocked off at his bid. A note was drawn
up and sent to him in Virginia to sign and return. Another note was
sent to him for the personal property purchased by his wife. His wife
took possession of the house and a portion of the land, her brother
staked off a portion of the land for himself, he cleared and cultivated
on his side of the line. The land in said County rose 2 or 3 hundred
per cent in value. He had his wife take $600 to Dr. Anderson,
Executor, who refused to except saying the whole was paid by her brother.
When he returned home he went to see said Hendricks and tendered him
the one half of purchased price which he refused, saying your orator
had no part of the land. Filed 6 Jan. 1864.

HENDRICKS, LEMUEL Box 111 #1058. Probate Judge Office. Pickens,
S. C. I Lemuel Hendricks of Pickens Co. being of sound mind and
memory, but at present in very feeble health. I will unto my beloved
wife Elizabeth Hendricks all my estate both real and personal, consisting of land, tenements, stock of all kinds, household and kitchen
furniture, notes, cash to dispose of as she may wish. Upon the death
of my wife Elizabeth my entire estate as above stated be transfered
to my dtr. Martha D. Clayton or her heirs at law. I appoint my wife
Elizabeth Hendricks executrix. Dated 5 April 1871. Wit: S. C.
McWhorter, J. T. Hinton, F. R.McClannahan. Signed: Lemuel Hendricks.
Proven 12 Feb. 1877.

HENDRICKS, LEVI #37. (Deed) Clerk of Court Office. Pickens,
S. C. I Levi Hendricks of Pickens Dist. in consideration of $550.
Paid me by John McWhorter of same Dist. have granted, sold, bargained
and released, all that tract of land containing 203 acres, lying on
Eighteen Mile Creek, waters of Savannah River. Being part of a tract
granted to Thomas Roberts the 1 Jan. 1785. Adj. land of John Mc-
Whorters. Dated 7 Sept. 1831. Wit: James McWhorter, Robert McWhorter.
Signed: Levi Hendricks. Proved on oath of Robert McWhorter before
James Langston J.P. on the 1 Oct. 1831. This Day came Martha X
Hendricks the wife of Levi Hendricks and renounce, release and forever
relinquish all her interest and claim of dower. This 1 Oct. 1831.
Signed: James Osborn, J.Q.

HENDRICKS, LOUVCY Box 121 #8. Probate Judge Office. Pickens,
S. C. Est. admr. 8 Dec. 1892 by D. E. Hendricks, S. H. Brown, J. B. R.
Freeman are bound unto J. B. Newberry, Ord. in the sum of $1,000.
Dise 22 Oct. 1892. D. E. Hendricks a son, Heirs, M. J. Freeman, D. E.
Hendricks, L. Williams, Sarah M. Pace heirs, Rachel Hendricks heirs.

HENDRICKS, MILTON M. Box 76. #812. Probate Judge Office.
Pickens, S. C. I Larkin Hendricks of Pickens Dist. inconsideration of
the natural love and affection which I have and bare towards my son
Milton M. Hendricks of the same Dist. and divers other causes I have
given granted, bargained and sold to Milton M. Hendricks a tract of
land containing 59 acres lying on Shoal Creek of Saluda River adj. land
of Abel Hendricks and myself. Dated 1 July 1858.

HENDRICKS, MILTON M. Book B Page 70. Probate Judge Office.
Pickens, S. C. By 5 Jan. 1863 Milton M. Hendricks was decd. He owned
59 acres of land on Shoal Creek waters of Saluda River. He died
leaving neither wife or child. His est. was divided between his
brothers and sisters viz; J. C. Hendricks, Marcus Roper and wife
Susan, Jesse Crenshaw and wife Jincy, heirs of Temperance Looper decd.
viz; James Perry Looper, William Anderson Looper, Temperance Looper.

HENDRICKS, LAWRENCE A. Box 9 #147. Probate Judge Office.
Pickens, S. C. On 14 July 1873 Margaret Keasler, Basil Callahan,
W. E. Holcombe are bound unto I. H. Philpot, Ord. in the sum of
$1182.00. Margaret Keasler gdn. of Lawrence A. Hendricks minor under
21 years and son of Henry Hendricks decd. Margaret the widow of Henry
Hendricks later married Henry Keasler.

HENDRICKS, "MINORS" Box 11 #173. Probate Judge Office. Pickens,
S. C. On 25 April 1881 W. N. Hendricks, Daniel Hughes, J. R. Ross
are bound unto Olin L. Durant, Ord. in the sum of $700. W. N. Hend-
ricks gdn. of Zephaniah A., William C., John Hendricks minors under
21 years. Mary E. Hendricks decd. the mother. Paid 15 Feb. 1897 for
sickness and burial expenses of John M. Hendricks $120.17. Recd 14
April 1882 from W. A. Smith, J. T. Chamblin Admnrs. of est. of
Zephaniah Smith, decd. $114.70. On 30 March 1881 W. A. Smith states
that he is the material uncle of said minors; Zephaniah A. was 5
years old 1 Nov. past, William C., 2 years old 10 July past, John
Hendricks 6 months old 16 Feb. past. Maternal aunts Tilitha J.
Chamblin, Rebecca S. Boggs. Maternal uncle J. Clayton Smith.

HENDRICKS, MOSES Box 23 #278. Probate Judge Office. Pickens,
S. C. I Moses Hendricks of Pickens Dist. being of sound mind and disposing memory I desire that after my death that all my just debts and
funeral expenses be paid. I give to my son George W. Hendricks, one
negro boy about eight years of age named Augustus. I give to my son
Warren R. Hendricks, one negro boy about seven yrs. of age named Wain.
I give to my dtr. Mary Jane Hendricks one negro girl about five yrs.
old named Susan. I give to my son Benjamin E. Hendricks one negro boy
about eight months old named Lewis. I will unto my wife Hannah
Hendricks all the balance of my property both real and personal, of
every kind during her life or widowhood. At the death or marriage of
my wife, I desire my executor to sell the balance of my property, and
make an equal division of the same amongst my fourteen chn. I appoint
my sons Larkins and Moses Hendricks executors. Dated 5 Feb. 1844.
Wit: T. W. Harbin, E. G. Gaines, W. L. Keith, Saml. Patten. Signed:
Moses X Hendricks. Proven 7 June 1847. (On the will someone had
written that he died 15 May 1847.)

HENDRICKS, MOSES Box 38 No. 432. Probate Judge Office.
Pickens, S. C. Est. admnr. 12 Nov. 1855 by Tyre L. Roper, Rt. Stewart
Esq., St. Robert Stewart are bound to W. J. Parson, Ord. in the sum of
$2,000. Heirs John Edens, John Hood, James L. Alexander and wife,
Benjamin C. Hendricks, Jacob Hendricks, Griffin Trotter and wife,
M. D. Hendricks, Duncan Hendricks, Henry Trotter and wife, M. H. Reid
and wife recd. shares.

HENDRICKS, MOSES Box 114 #1096. Probate Judge Office. Pickens,
S. C. I Moses Hendricks being of sound mind and memory. I give to
my son Moses S. Hendricks the following tract of land, containing 153
acres known as the Barnett tract No. 2, the said Moses S. to pay his
mother 25 bushels of corn and five bushels of wheat yearly for her
lifetime. I give to my dtr. Malinda C. a part of tract no. 3 known as
the Jamison tract on which the house stands description given, she also

Hendricks, Moses - Continued. give her mother 25 bushels of corn and five bushels of wheat yearly for her life time. I give to my dtr. Susan a part of tract no. 1 or the home tract, lying North West of a branch known as the Nathaniel Duncan branch. I give to my dtr. Ann all the rest of my land being portion of tract no. 1 and 3. I give to my beloved wife tract no. 1 and that portion given to dtr. Ann unless she marry. I appoint my son Moses S. Hendricks and son in law J. M. Burdine executors. Dated 4 Feb. 1871. Wit: W. A. Hendricks, E. R. Barnett, R. Barnett. Signed: Moses Hendricks. Codicil added: By the death of my son Moses S. Hendricks, I desire that my dtr. Ann and Susan shall have the proceeds from the land will to my decd. son and they to pay for raising George H. Hendricks the son of my decd. son. When he arrives to the age of twenty one the land to be his. I further desire my executor to pay my just debts and funeral expenses. I appoint my dtr. Ann Hendricks executrix with James Burdine instead of my son M. S. Hendricks. Dated 16 Sept. 1878. Wit: Isaac Williams, Rial Barnett, William Tompkins, James Frank Tompkins. Signed: Moses X Hendricks. Proved 16 June 1882.

HENDRICKS, MOSES SENR. Box 7 #91. Probate Judge Office. Pickens, S. C. Est. admr. 30 Jan. 1837 by Moses Hendricks, Dunkin Hendricks, Wm. L. Keith are bound unto James H. Dendy, Ord. in the sum of $800. In July 1837 recd. of Larkin Hendricks $52.00, recd. of Moses Hendricks Jr. $55.00. Paid Duncan Hendricks for crying sale $1.00. Sale held 16 Feb. 1837, buyers: Larkin Hendricks, Moses Hendricks, David Hendricks, Jacob Hendricks, Susanna Hendricks, Henry Trotter, Griffin Trotter. On 8 Oct. 1838 David Hays recd. money coming to him for the land of Moses Hendricks decd. In loose papers, on 18 Feb. 1840 Elizabeth Clark and her husband Alexr. Clark asked for their part of Moses Hendricks est.

HENDRICKS, WILLIAM Pack 37. Clerk of Court Office. Pickens, S. C. I William Hendricks of Pendleton Dist. in consideration of $1,000 paid me by Levi Hendricks of same Dist. have granted, sold, bargained and released, all that tract of land containing 203 acres, lying on Eighteen Mile Creek, waters of Savannah River. Being part of a tract granter to Thomas Roberts the 1 Jan. 1785. Land bounded by Henry Hendricks land. Dated 2 Oct. 1827. Wit: F. N. Garvin, E. W. Merritt. Signed: William X Hendricks. Proved on oath of Frederick N. Garvin before John Hunter N.P. this 20 Oct. 1827.

HENDRICKS, WM. E. Pack 404, #10. Clerk of Court Office. Pickens, S. C. (Order dismissing complaint). Wm. E. Hendricks vs. James Spearman. "This was an action for the recovery and partition of a tract of land claimed by the plaintiffs to have descended to them as heirs at law of Vista Hendricks decd. who was a daughter of Caroline Prince decd. which land is now in possession of the defendant. The only contention on the part of the defendant is that Vista Hendricks the mother of the plaintiff, was born to Caroline Prince out of wedlock and was therefore an illegitimate child and could not inherit from her mother. This contention is supported by the proof in the case and is found as fact by the reference. I must conclude therefore that Caroline Prince was never married and Vista Hendricks was her illegitimate daughter and under the laws of this State an illegitimate cannot inherit and that therefore the plaintiff cannot recover in this action. No interest in the land having descended to their mother none was transmitted to the plaintiffs. It is therefore ordered, decreed and adjudged that the complaint be dismissed with cost. Dated 15 July 1896. D. A. Townsend, Presiding Judge."

HENDRIX, MOSES Book 1 Page 29. Probate Judge Office. Pickens, S. C. On 30 Jan. 1837 he owned 100 acres called the school house tract on Saluda River, bound by land of Daniel Looper, Moses Hendrix and others. Grandfather of Duncan Hendrix. Moses Hendrix applicant vizt. Susan Hendrix, the widow, David Hendrix, Alexr. Clark and wife Elizabeth, heirs of John Chapman in right of his wife, David Hays and wife Barbara, Wm. Lasley and wife Rosanna, Larkin Hendrix.

HENDRIX, MOSES S. Box 92 #976. Probate Judge Office. Pickens, S. C. He died in 1876, left one heir Geo. Hendrix a minor under 14 yrs. who now lives with his grandfather Moses Hendrix. Owned two lots in the town of Easley containing one acre each.

HENSON, HENRY Box 2 #43. Probate Judge Office. Pickens, S. C. State of Ga., County Rabun. I Henry Henson being of advanced age but of sound mind and memory. I desire that all my just debts be paid. I give to my beloved wife Rachel all my estate both real and personal during her natural life. After the death of my wife, I give to James Loveless an orphan boy that I have raised, and have tender affection for my negro boy Bob for the term of said James Loveless natural life. I do not wish him to be expose to sale, therefore in case of death of James Loveless said Bob to decend to the next eldest sons down to the youngest, so that Bob may never be sold from the family of James Loveless. I give to Henery Billingsly wife of Henry Allen Billingsly and his children my plantation lying in Pickens Dist. on Chattooga River, adj. the lower part of long bottom. Not subject to the debts or control of said Henry Allen. I give to my great favorite child, son of Henry Allen Billingsley, James R. S. Billingsley which is the eldest son of Henry Allen my plantation whereon I now live and the North part of lot #25. I give to the second son of Henry Allen Billingsley, Henry F. Billingsley the lower part of lot #25. I appoint my friend James Billingsley Jr. executor and I further appoint said James Billingsley guardian of the property of said James R. S. Billingsley son of Henry Allen Billingsley. Dated 3 Feb. 1849. Wit: Edward Coffee, James Kell, Wm. Holden, Wm. Kell. Signed: Henry X Henson. Proven 29 Aug. 1856.

HENSON, JAMES Book A, Page 22. Probate Judge Office. Pickens, S. C. A suit to sell or partition the real estate of James Henson decd. Dated this 17 May 1836. Thomas Vissage, Plaintiff, visit; Clayborn Rothel in right of his wife Delilah, Elijah Leathers in right of his wife Melinder, Walter Billingsby in right of his wife Susannah, John Grindal in right of his wife Rachel, Joseph Henson, Charles Henson, heirs of James Henson decd., Robert Taylor in right of his wife Nancy. Land on Coneross Creek, containing 100 acres.

HERING, EDWARD Will Book A, Page 30. Probate Judge Office. Spartanburg, S. C. I Edward Hering of Spartanburg Dist. This 26 July 1811 make this my last will and testament. I will my just debts be paid. I desire my loving wife Marian Hering have my real and personal property for her support during her life and after her death to dispose of as she see cause to divide amongst my children. I appoint Morgan Hering executor. Wit: Jesse Mathis, William Cantrell, Morning X Barnes. Signed: Edward Hering. Recorded 14 July 1813.

HERON, DANIEL Box 31 #1093. Probate Judge Office. Kershaw Dist., Camden, S. C. I Daniel Heron of Kershaw Dist. being of sound and disposing mind and memory. After my decease, I direct my executors to sell my negro boy Nelson and the mill tract of land lying on Big Lynchs Creek, known as the Young land and all my debts are to be paid, if not sufficient then apply the portion coming to me from my father's estate. As part of my chn. have all ready received a portion of my property, those who have received are William Heron, Zinnamon Heron, Mary Heron, Sarah Heron and Mahala Heron have received one horse, one cow and calf, one feather bed, my son James Heron has received a horse, still entitled to one feather bed, one cow and calf. My dtr. Nancy Heron, son Samuel dtr. Frances P., dtr. Margaret C., and dtr. Christian H. Heron each are to have a horse, one cow and calf, one feather bed to make them equal. I give to my wife Gilly Heron my home tract of land, remaining part of my stock, household and kitchen furniture, farm tools, and the crop now on the land. I appoint Daniel Bethune, William Heron, J. E. Rodgers. Dated 22 Aug. 1860. Wit: B. S. Lucas, John McGugan, John Leach. Signed: Daniel Herron. Filed 11 Dec. 1860.

HERREN, STEPHEN Vol. 46 Page 151. Probate Judge Office. Charleston, S. C. I Stephen Herren of St. John's, being sick in body but of sound disposing mind and memory. I will and direct that all

Herren, Stephen - Continued. my funeral expenses and other just
debts be paid. I bequeath to my loving wife Martha Elizabeth Herren
all my household and kitchen furniture, also one horse and buggy
twenty five head of cattle, also the following negroes. Moses, March,
Venus, Philis, Nelly, Amey, Nancy, Clarissa and William with their
future issue and increase for the natural term of her life. At the
death of my wife, I will the whole of the personal shall pass to my
son John Stephen Herren. I give and devise the rest and residue of
my personal and real estate of every kind to my dear son John Stephen
Herren. I appoint my son John Stephen Herren executor. Dated 27
April 1852. Wit: John Phillips, J. W. Meree, Jefferson Hurst.
Signed: Stephen Herren. Proved 30 Aug. 1852.

HERRIN, JESSE J. Box 86 #3422. Probate Judge Office. Edgefield,
S. C. Est. admr. 20 Oct. 1862 by John W. Herrin, John T. Nicholson,
William Mobley who are bound to the Ordinary in the sum of $12,000.
Paid 1 Aug. 1864 Albert May for J. C. Herrin minor $1.80. The petition
of William Herrin sheweth that Jesse Herrin died intestate in April
1862. Had a widow Martha C. Herrin and a child Jesse C. Herrin.

HERRING, ESTHER Vol. 32 Page 653. Probate Judge Office.
Charleston, S. C. I Esther Herring of St. John's Parish, Charleston
Dist. being very weak and low of body, but of sound and disposing mind
and memory, etc. To my dear dtr. Eliza Lynes my dearly beloved son
William Herring I give the plantation whereon I now reside to be
equally divided between them. All negroes I have or may have I give
to my dtr. Eliza. I give to my son Benjamin Randolph one feather bed
and furniture. The rest and residue of my estate, after paying my
just debts and legacies, I give to my dtr. Eliza and my son William.
I appoint my friend Nathl. Marion and Benjamin Howorth executors.
Dated 15 Dec. 1812. Wit: Elizabeth A. Cahusac, Elizabeth Howorth,
Susannah McKelvey. Signed: Esther X Herring. Proved the 22 Jan. 1813.

HERRING, ISAAC Box 8 #8. Probate Judge Office. Darlington Co.,
S. C. Est. admr. 18 Nov. 1812 by Obedience Herring, Daniel Hearon,
Ariss Woodham who are bound to the Ordinary in the sum of $500. Isaac
Heron son of Samuel Herron.

HERRING, JAMES M. #2106. Probate Judge Office. Anderson, S.C.
Power of attorney. I James M. Herring of Paulding County, State of
Georgia. Do hereby constitute and appoint Asa Avery of Anderson
County, S. C. my attorney for me and in my name. To receive and
receipt from Wm. W. Humphreys Probate Judge of said County, all money
due me from the estate of Mary Herring decd., Dated (no day or month
given) 1869. Signed: J. M. Herring. The above signature was true
as appears to the foregoing certificate this 11 Oct. 1869. By S. B.
McGregor, Ord.

HERRING, MARY Pack 2106. Probate Judge Office. Anderson Dist.,
S. C. I Mary Herring being of sound and disposing mind and memory.
I desire that after my death my executors sell all my personal estate
and what interest I may have in my late husband est. being one third.
From said funds executors to pay my debts and funeral expenses. I
give to my dtr. Laura N. Brooks $100 for her kindness and attention in
my sickness. I will and desire that the residue of the funds be
divided into seven equal shares. I give one share to my dtr. Laura N.
Brooks. I give one share to my son James M. Herring. I give one
share to my son Jesse M. Herring. I give to my son Francis A. Herring
one share. I give to my son Elijah Herring one share. I give to my
son James M. Herring one share in trust for the sole and separate use
of my dtr. Mrs. Sarah Ann Lilly during her natural life, at her death
to be equal divided between her children. I give to my son James M.
Herring one share in trust for the use and benefit of my grand children
viz., Francis A. Beatty and David Milton Beatty, chn. of my decd. dtr.
Ruthy Ann Beatty, to be keep on interest until said chn. are full age,
then equally divided between them. I appoint James M. Herring and
John M. Burriss my executors. Dated 11 April 1856. Wit: T. A. Evins,
Ansel Strickland, J. W. Harrison. Signed: Mary X. Herring. Codicil:
A change in the above will, etc. My will is that the said Sarah Ann

Herring, Mary - Continued. Lilly shall take her share of my
estate real and personal free from all trust conditions and limitations,
and I do hereby give it to her and her heirs for ever. Dated this 19
Nov. 1857. Wit: B. F. Crayton, T. S. Crayton, J. W. Harrison.
Will was proved on oath of B. F. Crayton and J. W. Harrison before
Herbert Hammond Ord. And. Dist. on the 5 June 1865. Same date
recorded.

HERRING, WILLIAM Will Book A, Page 139. Probate Judge Office.
Anderson, S. C. I William Herring of Pendleton Dist. being sick and
weak in body but of sound mind and memory. I bequeath unto my granddaughter Matilda Herring one side saddle, one flax wheel and cards,
one bed, two pillow and case, one home made blanket, one dutch blanket,
five counterpeane and three bed quilts. The house and land where
Elijah Herring now lives, with household furniture, horses, cattle,
etc. to be sold and after all debts and expenses are paid the remainder
to be equally divided between all my children. I appoint my son Elisha
Herring executor. This 15 June 1812. Wit: Elijah Herring, James
Drennon, Job Wood. Signed: William Herring. Proved on oath of Elijah
Herring and James Drennan before John Harris Ord., this 25 June 1812.

HERRON, ANDREW Box 50 #2114. Probate Judge Office. Edgefield,
S. C. Est. admr. 4 Oct. 1841 by Humphreys Boulware, Alexander Sharpton,
Hardy White who are bound to the Ordinary in the sum of $1,000.

HERRON, GEORGE W. Box 17 #74. Probate Judge Office. Darlington
Co., S. C. Est. admr. 10 Jan. 1862 by William H. Herron, William W.
Moore, Henry D. Campbell who are bound to John J. Russell, Ord. in the
sum of $10,000.

HERRON, MRS. FRANCES Pack 3361. Clerk of Court Office.
Abbeville, S. C. Abbeville Dist. In Equity to the Honr. the
Chancellors: Your orator William Campbell of said Dist. that on the
1 March 1846 Mrs. Frances Herron, John T. Herron and Mary T. Herron
all of Abbeville Dist. confessed a judgement to your orator in the
sum of $92.50. That in the year 1846 before any part of said judgment
was paid Mrs. Frances Herron departed this life intestate one George
A. Miller has been granted letter of admr. on her est. And the said
John T. and Mary T. Herron has departed this State. The will of
Thomas Herron decd. late of this Dist. and husband of Frances Herron,
and father of John T. and Mary T. Herron. Certain property was
bequeath to Frances during her life time and at death to be equally
divided between his chn. The estate of Frances Herron amounts to
about $1079.00. Thomas Herron left five chn. all alive except one,
who has left chn. surviving him. The admor of Frances Herron est. has
refused to pay the debt from the money in hand. Your orator will ever
pray. Filed 15 Nov. 1847.

HERRON, JAMES SENR. Apt. A, Pack 384. Probate Judge Office.
Darlington, S. C. I James Herron Senr. of Darlington Dist. being sick
and poorly in health, but of sound mind and memory. I give to my
loving wife Sarah, if she think proper to live on my plantation during
her widowhood or lifetime, also one small black mare, bridle and side
saddle, one cow and calf, one sow, one feather bed with furniture,
one spinning wheel and cards. To be her own property to dispose of
as she think proper. I give to my grandson James Herron, the son of
Daniel Herron the feather bed and furniture that I now lie on, one
small round table of mahogany. I appoint my wife Sarah Herron,
executrix. Dated 5 Aug. 1813. Wit: Wm. Bramlett, John Mattuce.
Signed: James X Herron, Senr. Recorded this 11 June 1819.

HERRON, SAMUEL Box 14 #335. Probate Judge Office. Columbia,
S. C. I Samuel Herron of the town of Columbia, S. C. being sick and
weak in body but of sound and disposing mind and memory. First I will
and direct that my debts and funeral charges are paid. I give unto
my nephew George Herron the unexpired lease of the store on Richardson Street, now in possession of George Herron and myself, with all
capital or stock which I first put in. All debts due me. (Notes as
well as book accounts) shall be collected and paid to my executors.

Herron, Samuel - Continued. The warehouse that I am building on a lot across from the Baptist Church to be sold to my nephew George Herron on three years credit. I give to my nephew George Herron my Horse and sulkey and all my beds and bedding, with household and kitchen furniture. I give to my brother David Herron $500 to be sent to him at Laubrickland County of Down Ireland, by my executors through the hands of Adger and Black merchants in Charleston, S. C. After paying all my debts and finishing the warehouse, etc. What remains I give to George Herron, Sister Mary $200 for her own use. To my nephew Samuel Herron (son of James Herron, State of Maryland) $200. The remainder to be sent by some proper agent, as Adger and Black merchants of Charleston, S. C. to my brothers William Herron, Robert Herron, David Herron, and John Herron at Laueghbrickland County of Down Ireland to be equally divided between them. I also give to my nephew George Herron my three sets of plated harness. I hereby appoint my friend John M. Creyon, Joseph Ellison and George Herron to be executors. Dated 28 Feb. 1821. Wit: E. H. Maxcy, Andrew Wallace, Henry O'Loane. Signed: Samuel Herron. Proven date not given.

HICKMAN, JOSEPH Joseph Hickman was drafted in Capt. McClure's Co., S. C. Militia on 15 Dec. 1814 and was honorable discharged on 1 May 1815. He served in the army or with the troops at Lister's ferry on Savannah River and drew two land warrants, one for 40 acres and the other for 100 acres. He migrated from Pendleton Dist., S. C. in 1817 for the Black Warrior Territory of the Territory of Ala. and settled in the western area of what became Jefferson County and is now part of Birmingham, Ala. He bought at land sale in Huntsville, Ala. in 1819. Opened a tavern for travelers which he ran until 1860 when he turned his business over to his son in law Elijah Sandifer and went to Pickens Co., Ala. on a visit to his dtr. Mary Caroline who had married James A. Burgin, he died there in 1861. He has many descendants in Jefferson and Tuscaloosa counties in the State of Alabama.

HICKMAN, JOSEPH Data on Joseph Hickman of Pendleton Dist., S. C. and Jefferson County, Ala. (no ref. as where this inf. was from). In the Bible of Joseph Hickman the following information was found "My father Jesse Hickman was born 25 Dec. 1750, my mother (but does not give name) was born 22 Sept. 1766, their chn.: Joseph, born 15 Nov. 1787 m. Martha (Patsy) Pullen. John Hillman, born 7 April 1791. William, born 16 July 1797. Jesse, born 1 Aug. 1799 m. Clarissa Pullen. James, born 25 Nov. 1801. Dave, born 5 Jan. 1807. Some descendants of Joseph Hickman do not believe that his father's name was Jesse but probably William or Joseph, most probably the William listed in 1810 census of Pendleton Dist., S. C. Joseph said his father served in the revolutionary war, we have not found a record for one Jesse, there was a William Hickman in the revolutionary war, so I have been informed, have no data personally. Joseph Hickman born 15 Nov. 1787, Pendleton Dist., S. C. died 19 June 1861, Pickens County, Ala. Married 19 March 1807 in Wilkes Co., Ga. 1st. Mar. Bk. 1806-34. (I am informed that Wilkes Co., Ga. is just across the Savannah River in Georgia from the western part of Pendleton Dist., S. C. to Martha (Patsy) Pullen, dtr. of William and Mary Haynes Pullen. She was born 8 Aug. 1790 in S.C., died 30 Nov. 1878, in Tuscaloosa County, Ala. their chn. Elizabeth Ann (Betsy Ann) b. 3 Feb. 1808 m. Paschal J. Shackelford, 2 Feb. 1825. William Pullen, b. 7 Oct. 1809, m. Liza Roebuck, 10 Feb. 1825. Nancy Croft, b. 20 May 1811, m. Zadoc Shackelford, 30 Dec. 1828, d. 8 Sept. 1893. Pleasant Argalus, b. 4 May 1813, m. Epsie Caroline Mary Burgin, 8 Oct. 1835, died 20 April 1897. Mary Caroline, b. 1 June 1816 m. Jas. A. Burgin, 18 Dec. 1834, died 7 Oct. 1870. Joseph Berry, b. 1 June 1820, m. Liza Perkins, 11 May 1843, died 28 Jan. 1895. Clarissa Mariah, b. 22 June 1822, m. Mel Logan. David Edward, b. 19 Dec. 1824, m. Liddy Timmons. Martha J., b. 19 Feb. 1826, m. Hillman McMath. Elizabeth H., B. 30 Aug. 1829 m. Elijah Sandifer.

HICKMAN, RICHARD Box 42 Pack 945. Probate Judge Office. Abbeville, S. C. Abbeville Dist. Admr. bond, we Barbara D. Hickman, William Pursell, John J. Barratt and George A. Miller are bound unto Moses Taggart, Ord. in the sum of three thousand dollars. Dated 24

Hickman, Richard - Continued. Oct. 1825. Cit. Pub. at Upper
Long Cane Church. Appraisement made 2 Nov. 1825 by John J. Barratt,
Wm. Yarbrough, James Murray and David Armstrong. Sale held 11 Nov.
1825, Buyers: James Murray, Wm. Pursell, Barbara D. Hickman, Harrison
Monday, Wm. Yarbrough, Alexr. Stewart, John C. Baker, Sterling Williams,
Moses Taggart, Joseph Black Esq., James C. Livingston, Mathew Wilson,
Hugh Kirkwood, Robert Richey, Archibald McCay, John Yarbrough, David
Armstrong, James Drennan, Hugh Prince, Henry Power, Wm. Armstrong.
Sale held at the residence of Wm. Purcell.

HIETT, MARY A. No. 11 (may be a Coroner book). Pickens, S. C.
"An inquest was taken at Fair Play, Pickens Dist. March 5, 1865 to
view the body of Mrs. Mary Ann Hiett of Talladega, Ala. The jury
brought it out that she came to her death by hanging herself by the
neck with the hem of a dress twisted into a rope, in the house of
G. T. Campbell to a joist of a back room. At Fair Play on the evening
of 4 March 1865. Mrs. E. Campbell said that the decd. appeared wrong
the morning before her death. She keep her room and when visited said
she wished she was dead. She was so distressed after a while she
heard a struggling noise and gave the alarm, when the door was open
she was found hanging by the neck." Mrs. Mary Stephen says, Mrs.
Campbell came running to me excited, saying that the decd. had a fit
and was trying to destroy herself. I called negro boy Charles to lift
her up and Rebecca Whitfield cut the rope...

HIGGINS, SAMUEL G. Box 142. #7. Probate Judge Office. Pickens,
S. C. Samuel G. Higgins est. was admr. 19 March 1903. By Augusta A.
Higgins, John A. Higgins, J. T. Lathem. He died 22 Dec. 1902, was of
Easley, S. C. On 19 April 1904 J. A. Higgins, T. B. Higgins, L. J.
Jamison, Lena F. Folger, Lola Snead recd. shares. A. J. Higgins
guardian of J. F. Higgins, H. S. Higgins, Victor B. Higgins, O. K.
Higgins, Lanny B. Higgins.

HIGHTOWER, ALFRED Book L Page 122. Mesne Conveyance Office.
Greenville, S. C. I Alfred Hightower of Greenville Dist. in consideration of $520 to me paid by John Hightower of same Dist. have
granted, bargained, sold, and released a tract of land, being part of
three surveys, lying on the North Fork of the Beaverdam Creek, waters
of North Fork of Saluda River. Two surveys granted to Martin Adams,
and the other granted to Andrew W. Walker and adj. their lines.
Dated 25 March 1820. Wit: John Hodges, Joseph Goodwin. Signed:
Alfred Hightower. Proven on oath of Joseph Goodwin before Stephen
Phillips, J.P. this 9 June 1820. The above deed was for 273 acres.

HIGHTOWER, ALFRED Book L Page 123. Mesne Conveyance. Greenville, S. C. I Alfred Hightower of Greenville Dist. in consideration
of $250 paid me by Elizabeth and Jane Hightower of same Dist. have
granted, bargained, sold and released a tract of land on North Fork
of Beaverdam Creek waters of the North Fork of Saluda River. Being
part of three grants, one granted to Robert Prince, another granted to
Martin Adams and the third granted to Andrew W. Walker. The three
tracts joins each other, containing 150 acres. Dated 25 March 1820.
Wit: John Hodges, Joseph Goodwin. Signed: Alfred Hightower. Proved
on oath of Joseph Goodwin before Stephen Phillips, J.P. this 9 June
1821.

HIGHTOWER, ELIZABETH & JANE Apt. 13 File 96. Probate Judge
Office. Greenville, S. C. We Elizabeth Hightower and Jane Hightower
both of Greenville Dist. being of sound mind and disposing memory, do
make this one last and testament. We do will and bequeath to our
nephew Alfred Cantrell a tract of land lying on both sides of the North
Fork of Beverdam Creek waters of the North Fork of Saluda River. Being
part of four surveys and adjoining each other. The first granted to
Ralph Smith, the second to Robert Prince, the third granted to Martin
Adams, the fourth granted to Andrew W. Walker. For a total of 170
acres. Will dated 29 March 1833. Wit: Alfred Hightower, George
Hightower, John H. Goodwin. Signed: Elizabeth X Hightower and Jane
X Hightower. Probated 5 April 1842.

HIGHTOWER, GEORGE Book V Page 36. Mesne Conveyance. Greenville, S. C. I George Hightower of Pickens Dist. in consideration of $50 to me paid by John Hightower of Greenville Dist. have granted, bargained, sold and released all my rights, titles and claim to a tract of land lying and being in Greenville Dist. on both forks of the North Fork of Beaverdam Creek waters of Saluda River, containing 294 acres. It being surveyed for John and George Hightower the 6 April 1816. Dated this 10 Dec. 1835. Wit: Richard Goodlett, Moses Findley. Signed: George Hightower. Proven on oath of Richard Goodlett before Richard Thruston, J.P. this 15 Jan. 1834? Recorded Jan. 1836.

HIGHTOWER, JOSEPH Box 46 Pack 1031. Probate Judge Office. Abbeville, S. C. Admr. bond, 96 Dist. We, Joseph Hightwoer, Abraham Richardson and Allen Hinton are bound unto John Thomas in the sum of one thousand pounds sterling., dated 8 Feb. 1786. Inventory made 7 Feb. 1786 by Wm. Covington, Allen Hinton, John Covinton.

HILBURN "MINORS" #21. Clerk of Court Office. Abbeville, S. C. On 23 Jan. 1860 John Link was guardian of L. J. Hilburn a minor. Was gdn. of Rebecca E. Hilburn, minor. Paid 11 Feb. 1859 Susan D. Hilburn board and etc. $20.

HILL, ABEL Deed Book A, Page 5. Probate Judge Office. Pickens, S. C. James Findley admr. of Abel Hill, ext. The petition of James Findley Jr. sheweth that in the spring term of 1830 a judgment was obtained against Abel Hill and said James Findley as Hill security. Said judgment entered against Jesse Rackley, lawful constable who hold bond on said Hill. Therefore your petitioner prays that tract of land of the decd. Hill be sold to satisfy the judgment. The widow also consenting to said sale. Keziah Hill, widow, Ashworth Hill, Huldy Hill, Lewis Hill, Elizabeth Hill, and Keturah Hill. Keziah Hill guardian ad litem of minors under 14 yrs. There was 75 acres to be sold on the 5 July 1830. Asaph Hill said land not worth $1,000.

HILL, BENJAMIN Box 48 Pack 1106. Probate Judge Office. Abbeville, S. C. Abbeville Dist. Admr. bond. We Richard Hill, James William and Johnson Ramey are bound unto Moses Taggart, Ord. in the sum of $10,000. Dated 23 June 1839. (Will) I Benjamin Hill being of sound and disposing mind and memory, but weak in body. I give to my dtr. Charity Fulton my bay mare. I give to my dtr. Elizabeth Mantz my chest of drawers and my bed and furniture. I give to my dtr. Christiana Davis $300. I give to my grand son Richard B. Fulton my bay colt. The balance of my property of four negroes, Tom, Abigail, Aggy, Letty with one sorrel mare to be sold and out of the proceeds my funeral expenses and just debts to be paid. Any over to be divided between my eight chn. Hamilton, Richard, Samuel L., Frances, Charity, Elizabeth, Lucretia and Christiana. I appoint my son Hamilton Hill executor. 18 July 1838. Wit: Frederick S. Lucius, John H. Armstrong, Saml. S. Hill. Signed: Benjamin X Hill. Inventory made 29 June 1839 by Jno. H. Armstrong, Frederick S. Lucius and Wm. Davis. Frances Mantz was wife of Wm. Mantz. Lucretia was wife of Jonathan Ramey. Christaine was wife of Joseph Davis. Elizabeth was wife of Andrew Mantz, Hamilton Hill and Charity Fulton died after execution of the will but before testator. Joseph Davis died after testator. Chn. of Hamilton Hill were Elizabeth McDill wife of Thomas McDill, Jane Amanda, Sarah Cathrine, Samuel Albert, Lewis Hamilton, James Warren the last child by a second marriage. Children of Charity Fulton, Benj. H. Fulton, Richard B. Fulton, Thomas Fulton, Augustus Fulton, Elias A. Fulton, Charity F. Fulton. Samuel Hill gdn. of Sarah Cathrine, Frances McDill is gdn. of Samuel Albert Hill, Richard Hill is gdn. of Lewis Hamilton Hill. Thos. Fulton gdn. of all his children.

HILL, BIRDWELL Book C-1 Page 521. Clerk of Court Office. Pickens, S. C. I Birdwell Hill of Pickens Dist. in consideration of $600 to me paid by Valentine M. Harrison do sell and release all that tract of land whereon Birdwell Hill now lives, containing 190 acres, lying on a branch of Choestoe Creek waters of Tugalo River, being a tract originally granted to John Lewis Davis, another part granted to Nathanial Bradwell the 3 Sept. 1784. Dated this 4 Nov. 1836. Wit:

Hill, Birdwell - Continued. Leonard Gowees, F. A. Gowers.
Signed: Birdwell Hill. On the 12 March 1838 Frances Hill did relin-
quish all her interest and dower on the above land. Recorded the 21
March 1838.

HILL, GEORGE Box 4 #49. Probate Judge Office. Pickens, S. C.
State of Georgia. Lumpkin County. This 10 May 1855, before me, a
Justice of the Peace in said County and State. Personally came Susan
Williams (before her marriage Susan Hill) age 45 yrs. a resident of
Pickens Dist., S. C. who being duly sworn. That she is the legitimate
dtr. and heir at law of George Hill decd. who was the identical George
Hill who was a private soldier in the Company Commanded by Capt.
Buttler. In the regiment commanded by Col. John Earl, in the Rev.
War. That her father volunteered and was mustered into service at
Col. John Earls in the State of N.C., about the year 1780, and con-
tinued in actual service for the term of two years, and was honorably
discharged at Charleston, S. C. That her father died in Pendleton Dist.
S. C. about the year 1841, and no widow survived him. That his wife
the mother of the applicant had died previous to that time, to wit,
at Pendleton Dist. on the 11 April 1823. That her mother name was
Ashworth. That she inform and believes that her father George Hill
never applied for or drew a pension during his life. That she makes
the foregoing declaration for the purpose of obtaining the pension to
which she may be entitled as heir at law and dtr. of said George Hill.
Signed: Susan X Williams. The foregoing was sworn to and subscribed
before me the day and year aforesaid, I certify that I am personally
acquainted with Susan Williams. Signed: John H. Covington, J.P.
State of Georgia. Lumpkin County. On this 3 Sept. 1855 before me a
Justice of the Peace. Personally appeared Reuben Hill to me a person
well known to be a pensioner of the U.S. of whom I certify to be a
respectable resident of Lumpkin Co., Ga. aged 91 yrs. Who being duly
sworn according to law declares that he is personally acquainted with
Susan Williams and knows her to be the legitimate dtr. of George Hill
decd. He further declares that the said George Hill decd. was a private in Company commanded by Capt. Butler in the regiment commanded
by Col. John Earl in the Rev. War of 1776. That the said George Hill
and the affidavit were brothers and were together, part of the time.
That he was discharged at Charleston, S. C. in Feb. 1780. That he
Reuben Hill Senr. declares that he is himself a Rev. pensioner, and
receives at the agency at Savannah, Ga. the sum of $80 per annum.
Wit: Augustine Williams. Signed: Reuben X Hill Senr. Sworn before
me this day Lewis Johnston Ledbetter, J.P.

HILL, HAMILTON Box 48 Pack 1104. Probate Judge Office.
Abbeville, S. C. Abbeville Dist. I Hamilton Hill being of sound
mind disposing memory, but weak in body. I desire that after my
decease by brother shall sell my whole estate both real and personal
of whatever kind or nature, except two negroes named Fany and Tener
and their issue, as being originally disposed of to the issue of my
first wife by their grandfather Pawl (Paul). After my just debts are
paid and equal distribution between my wife Peggy and all my chn. I
appoint Samuel S. Hill executor. 4 May 1839. Wit: G. J. Cannon,
John H. Armstrong, R. Hill. Hamilton Hill. Proven 19 May 1839.
Inventory made 3 June 1839 by G. J. Cannon, A. H. Spence, J. J. Devin.
Sale held 4 June 1839. Buyers: Joseph Davis, Thos. McDill, Robert
Devin, Saml. L. Hill, G. J. Cannon, Jno. H. Armstrong, Richard Hill,
Margaret Hill widow, Joseph P. Jones, J. Horton, James Lessly, Wm.
Sanders, James Wharton, Jeremiah Hinton.

HILL, JAMES Box 45, 1024. Probate Judge Office. Abbeville,
S. C. Admr. bond. Abbeville Dist. We Adam Hill, Samuel Foster Esq.,
and James Foster Senr. are bound unto Judges of Abbe. Court in the sum
of $1,000. Dated 12 Sept. 1797. Cit. pub. at Cedar Springs Church.

HILL, JAMES Box 46 Pack 1054. Probate Judge Office. Abbeville,
S. C. I James Hill being weak in body, but of sound and disposing
mind and memory. I give to my beloved wife Katharine Hill the tract
of land whereon I now live during her life or widowhood. To my
children hereafter named viz: Jacob Hill, John Hill, Samuel Hill,

Hill, James - Continued. Thomas Hill, James Hill, Caroline Hill, Daniel Hill, Henry H. Hill and Margaret Hill, I give an equal part of my est. both real and personal to be divided at the proper time conforming to the former part of this will. Whereas I lived with a woman Margaret Dorrah for several years and by her five illegitimate issue viz: Jesse, Eleanor, Larsey, Manes, and Malinda after which she eloped from me without any known cause and too up with another man and lived with him in the same capacity. If she should come for a share of my est. I will her one dollar. Likewise any of her chn. I will each one dollar. I appoint my wife Katharine Hill and my son Jacob Hill my executrix and executor. Dated 1829. Wit: James A. Black, A. W. Lynch, Richard Ashley. Signed: James Hill. Proved 7 Dec. 1829. Inventory made 14 Dec. 1829 by James A. Black, John B. Black, David Russell.

HILL, JAMES Pack 51 #1. Clerk of Court Office. Pickens, S. C. Pendleton Dist. I James Hill of Jackson County, State of Georgia, in consideration $200 paid me in hand by John Couch, have granted, sold, bargained and released all that plantation containing 100 acres, lying and being on waters of Saluda River, being part of a tract granted to Robert Samuel Parshens on the 5 Jan. 1789 and a part of a tract laid out for Alexander Mahan, dated 5 Jan. 1789. Dated this 6 Jan. 1807. Wit: John Hamilton, Mary Hamilton. Signed: James Hill. Proved on oath of John Hamilton before Wm. Edmondson, J.P. this 20 Feb. 1807.

HILL, JOHN SR. Pack 3375. Clerk of Court Office. Abbeville, S. C. Abbeville Dist. In Equity to the Honr. the Chancellors: Your orator Robert C. Richey and oratrix Nancy his wife and orator William C. Hill. Your orator sheweth that John Hill Senr. departed this life many years ago, having made his last will and testament. By said will he gave to his wife Susannah the plantation whereon he lived with all moveable property, also negroes, Sylla, Cessa with five boys, Lewis, Silas, John, Willis and Wiley during her widowhood if she should marry again, then she to have Cessa, one horse and saddle, one bed and furniture, with household and kitchen furniture during her life. At her death to be equally divided between his children. Son Samuel to get Lewis, William negro Silas, John to get Job, son Joseph to get Willis, son Bluford to get negro Wiley. The said negroes to be keep by the executor until sons marry or become of full age. At the death of John Hill, Senr. he left a widow Susannah and twelve chn. to wit: Betsy the wife of David Hill, by his she had several chn. only two are now living Jane or Jincy now the wife of James Dodson and Joycey now the wife of ___ Cogburn, she afterwards married Patrick Germain had one son Thomas and then died. Nancy the now wife of William Mays. Polly the now wife of Jesse Rainey. Sally the now wife of David Vines. Susannah who intermarried with Benjamin Rosamond now decd. leaving as her only heir and distributees her husband and seven chn. James, Benjamin, Samuel, John, Thomas, William and Joseph. Fanny the wife of Samuel Rosamond. Samuel Hill now dead, who left as his only heirs and dist. a widow Elizabeth who has since married with William Hodges and two chn. Nancy your orator who married Robert C. Richey and Elvira who has died unmarried and quite young, Admr. on est. of Samuel Hill was granted to William Barmore. William Hill who married and then died leaving as heir William C. Hill. Joseph Hill who died intestate, leaving as heir and dist. a widow, Eliza now the wife of John Graham and three chn. Susan, Jane and Frances. Bluford Hill who died in his minority and unmarried. John Hill Junr. died about 1824, leaving to his mother a negro named Gabriel during her life at death said negro to be sold and money divided between brothers Samuel, Bluford, and Joseph and sister Rebecca. The negro Gabriel was hired out to David Vines and his wife Nelia for the year 1838, at the end of said year, the slave was not returned. Susannah the widow brought suit against her dtr. and son in law and recovered full value of $983.00 for Gabriel. Susannah Hill died about 1842. Filed 21 June 1845.

HILL, JOSEPH Box 47 Pack 1088. Probate Judge Office. Abbeville, S. C. Charles Cullins was appointed guardian of Susan Jane and Frances E. Hill minor children of Joseph Hill decd. under 14 yrs. of age, 24 Nov. 1830. Then in 14 Feb. 1847 John Graham was made guardian. Expend 2 Jan. 1832 paid Eliza Graham formerly Eliza Hill widow, for

Hill, Joseph - Continued. maintenance and support of Susan J.
and Frances E. Hill 2 years 1829, 1830 $80. Paid John and Eliza Graham
for the same years 1831 $40. On 23 Jan. 1837, recd. of Moses Taggart
$26.50 being the full distributive share of Susan J. and Frances Hill
from the Est. of John Hill Senr. decd. Charles Cullins was made
guardian of Josey Hill a minor 1 Aug. 1825. Whereas Richard Gaines
by the appt. of Moses Taggart the former Ord. has acted as guardian for
us for a number of years but now expect to move to the State of Georgia,
desires therefore to be released from the guardianship. This is to
certify that it is our wish and desire that John Graham our step-
father be appointed gdn. for us in his stead. Given under our hands
this 15 Jan. 1847. Susan J. Hill 19 yrs. and Frances E. Hill 18 yrs.
Return of Albert M. Graham admr. of John Graham decd. who was the gdn.
of Susannah and Frances E. Hill minors. The said A. M. Graham intermarried with Frances E. who had one child and died.

HILL, JOSEPH Box 45 Pack __. Probate Judge Office. Abbeville,
S. C. I Joseph Hill of Abbeville Dist. being of sound mind and
memory, etc. I give to my son William Hill, two negroes Edmund and
Venus, two cows and calves, two sows and pigs, a bed and horse. Also
the tract of land whereon he now lives. He having property value of
$1500 when final settlement takes place. I give to my son Wiley Hill
two negroes Randal and Silvy, two cows and calves, two sows and pigs,
a bed and furniture and a horse. Also a tract of land whereon he now
lives, which I purchased of John Mitchell for thirty one hundred
dollars. He having property value of $3150 all in his possession now.
I give to my dtr. Helen Bunting two negroes, Man and Milly, two cows
and calves, two pigs and sows, a bed and furniture and a horse, all of
which are in her possession now. I give to my dtr. Helen so many
negroes from common stock, as will make her share as much as my sons,
which I will land to them. I give to my son Joseph Hill a tract of
land, amount not given, description is shown with bounded by land of
Simion Chaneys, his tract to be known as the spring tract, the other
tract known as home tract. I give to my son Josch[?] two negroes,
Bartow and Judy, two cows and calves, two sows and pigs, a bed and
furniture, a horse worth $100. I give to my son Isaac Mitchell Hill,
the mill or creek tract, two negroes Will and Nancy, two cows and calves,
two sows and pigs, a bed and furniture, a horse worth $100. I give to
my son Milton Hill the home tract, after the death of his mother, also
I give him two negroes Ann and Peggy, two cows and calves, two sows and
pigs, a bed and furniture, and a horse worth $100. I will and desire
that the residue and remainder of my property to remain in common
stock, for the support of my wife and children and their education.
Also the paying of my just debts. I appoint my sons William and Wiley
Hill and my son in law Isaac Bunting executors. Dated 13 June 1825.
Wit: Peter Cheatham, William Fooshe, Wiley Caly. Signed: Jos. Hill.
Inventory made 1 Dec. 1825 by Peter Cheatham, Wm. Fooshe, Nathan
Calhoun, Jno. Fooshe, James Gillam... "April 4, 1851 received from
Wiley Hill Exor. of the will Jos. Hill decd. $1610.46 in full of my
brothers portion of said est. whom I represent as agent. Test. Chas.
Smith. Signed: Eliza Smith." She was agent of Isaac Bunting.

HILL, RICHARD Box 48 Pack 1121. Probate Judge Office. Abbeville,
S. C. I Richard Hill of Abbeville Dist. being at this time in possession of a sound mind and having perfect reasoning faculties, but very
low in health. First I desire my just debts paid. My boy Henry to be
sold and as much of my other property as my wife may see fit, except
my boy James and girl Frances and her child Joseph. If it ever be
necessary to sell any of the above three negroes, they are to have
the privilege of choosing their master without being sold at public
sale. The above three negroes and all other property to belong to my
wife Sarah J. Hill during her natural life. My son Andw. M. Hill shall
be sent to school until he shall obtain an english education, to be
deducted from his equal part of my property. I appoint Sarah J. Hill,
Thomas Thompson, executors. Dated 19 Jan. 1841. Wit: H. H. Penny,
Andrew Monroe, Blassongim X Hodges. Signed: R. Hill. Proved 28
March 1842. Expend. Paid 2 Jan. 1844 A. Ramey legacy $84.75. Paid
Thos. McDill legacy $84.75. Paid T. McDill for S. A. Hill $84.75.
Paid Saml. Hill for L. H. Hill $84.75.

HILLBURN, JAMES Box 35 #404. Probate Judge Office. Pickens, S. C. Est. admr. 25 May 1855 by James Hagood, James T. Ferguson who are bound unto W. J. Parsons, Ord. in the sum of $500. Left a widow and seven chn. no names given. Sundry notes on various persons give in Augusta, Ga. and considered as bad in 1842 and 1843. An out of date acknowledgement of Hugh Woods at Columbus, Ga. to refund the money for a check sent him by James Hillburn for $500.

HINKLE, ELIAS Box 78 #827. Probate Judge Office. Pickens, S.C. Est. admr. 23 Aug. 1864 by Ailcey Adaline Hinkle, James Lewis, James E. Hagood are bound into W. E. Holcombe, Ord. in the sum of $1,000. James Farrow Hinckle states that James Lewis his grandfather died in 1883.

HILL, UEL Box 42 Pack 946. Probate Judge Office. Abbeville, S. C. Abbeville Dist. I Uel Hill being afflicted in body, but of sound and disposing mind and memory. I give to my niece Sarah Ann Hatfield a negro called Penny, and her two chn. Betty and Aley, a boy named Adam (child of Kitty), also a sorrel horse called Dick, one womand[?] saddle, one feather bed and furniture, one set of silver table spoons, my riding gig and harness. In consideration of her kind treatment to me in all my affliction, and also for money used of hers, during my guardianship, I give to Miriam Hartsfield, a molatto girl named Zilpha and a boy called Martin, one bed and furniture, one silver teaspoon set and my deceased wife riding saddle. Also each to have a chest made by their father, and provision for their support for one year after my decd. I give to my nephew William P. Hill a negro boy named Jerey, the youngest child of Nelly, one horse to be valued at $70.00. One cow and calf. I give to my dtr. Elizabeth Hughes wife of James Hughes a negro man Gilbert his wife Kitty and their three chn. Jo, Liddy and Caroline, and all my sheep but given to W. P.Hill. I give to granddaughter Ann Palmer, wife of Willis Palmer, an equal division, Tildy now in her possession to be included. I give to my granddaughter Catherine Hughes wife of Singleton Hughes, an equal division, the girl Penny now in her possession included. I give to my granddaughter July the wife of W. G. Williams one equal division, the girl now in her possession included. The above negroes must be valued so that an equal divide may take place with my other legatees viz: W. G. William, Catherine Hughes, Ann Palmer, Thomas Hughes, Frances Hughes, James Hughes Junr., Pamealy Hughes. I will that my negro Jack the privilege of choosing his master so he may near his wife. The moveable property as stock, cattle, horses, etc. be sold and pay my debts, and the surplus be divided amongst the seven legatees last named. I appoint my friends brother Joshua Hill, Abner Perren and William P. Hill executors. Dated 22 Aug. 1832. Wit: Jacob B. Britt, R. W. Corley, A. M. McCraven. Signed: Uel Hill. Executed 3 Nov. 1832. Appraisement made 27 Nov. 1832 by Alexander Houston, Robert McCaslan, Samuel Wideman. Sale held 28-29 Nov. 1832. Buyers, James Hughes, Thomas Brock, Alexander Houston, Washington Belcher, A. Perrin, Jno. T. Carr, P. F. Moragin, J. A. M. Duvall, W. G. Williams, Mathis Crawford, James Britt, A. Wideman, G. Crawford, Daniel Ramsey, A. T. Taylor, John Hays, J. B. Tullis, Saml. Cowan, Thos. Linsey, Singleton Hughes, Esau Brooks, Ben. Gibert, P. Gilbo, Jos. Davis, Col. John Hearst, Jos. Jacobs, R. Douglass, Dr. Saml. Pressley, Wm. King, Joshua Hill, Willia Palmer, John Hase, Richard Chasteen, Lazerus Covin, Isaac Bushel, Enoch Taylor, Wm. Hanvy, John Scott, Charles Carr, John Jones, E. Carter.

HINKLE, ELIAS H. Box 78 #827. Probate Judge Office. Pickens, S. C. Est. admr. 23 Aug. 1864 by Ailcey Adaline Hinkle, James Lewis, James E. Hagood, James Farrow Hinkle states that James Lewis his grandfather died in 1883.

HILL FAMILY BIBLE Anny Hill Book, January 4, 1824. Marriages. Robert Hill m. Nancy Patton, 26 Nov. 1812. Peggy Hill m. Pinkney White, 1 May 1823. Nancy Hill m. Amenadab Marler, 25 Sept. 1828. John Hill m. Mrs. Sarah Coleman, formerly Sarah Traylor, 25 Oct. 1836. Births: John Hill b. 1 Jan. 1807, James Hill, b. 5 Feb. 1799. Molly Hill b. 25 Sept. 1794. Pinkney White b. 24 May 1801.

Hill Family Bible - Continued. Robert Hill, b. 29 Dec. 1790.
Margaret Hill b. 5 March 1804. William Hill b. 18 Sept. 1792. Nancy
Hill b. 13 Jan. 1802. Deaths: Mollie Hill d. 29 Sept. age 8 yrs. and
4 days. William Hill Senr. d. 5 Sept. 1821, age 65 yrs. William Hill
Junr. son of Wm. Hill Sr. d. 14 Nov. 1828, age 36 yrs. 26 days.
James Hill son of Wm. Hill Sr. d. 12 Aug. 1833. Age 34 yrs. Nancy
Marlar dtr. of Wm. Hill Sr. d. 27 Aug. 1833. Age 31 yrs. Ann Hill
wife of Wm. Hill Sr. d. 23 Nov. 1835 age 73. Mother of Robert Hill,
William Hill Junr., Molly Hill, Adam Hill, James Hill, Nancy Hill,
Margaret Hill and John Hill. Adam Hill d. 7 May 1865, age 68 yrs. 5
mo. 26 days. Robert Hill d. 21 April 1867, age 76 yrs. 5 mo. 22 days.
Margaret Hill dtr. of Wm. Hill Sr. d. 15 Jan. 1870. Age 65 yrs. 9 mo.
10 days. John Hill d. 5 June 1879. Age 72 yrs. 5 mo. 5 days.

HILLEN, NATHANIEL Box 45 Pack 1021. Probate Judge Office.
Abbeville, S. C. Abbeville Dist. I Nathaniel Hillen of Enoree, 96
Dist. S. C. being weak of body but of perfect mind and memory. First
after paying my just debts and funeral charges, I give to my son Lewis
all the land and plantation I now live on containing 300 acres, also
one negro boy named Jacob and one negro girl named Darus. I give to
my friend Lazarus Bentlon 125 acres of land on the South side of Enoree.
I give to my wife Mary Hillen, one third part of the rest of my real
and personal estate, and remain in her possession until my son John
arrives at the age of twenty one yrs. I appoint my wife ___ (no more
of the will in notes. A date of 1783 is shown by the will, not part
of it.)

HILLBURN, JAMES Box 35 $404. Probate Judge Office. Pickens,
S. C. Est. admr. 25 May 1855 by James E. Hagood, James T. Ferguson
in Pickens Dist. Left a widow and seven children, no names given.
Sundry notes on various persons given in Augusta, Ga. and considered
as bad in 1842 and 1843 and out of date acknowledgement of Hugh Woods
of Columbia, Ga. to refund the money for a check sent him by James
Hillburn for $500.00.

HINTON, ELIZABETH Deed Book B, page 76. Probate Judge Office.
Pickens, S. C. On 27 Nov. 1865 Elizabeth Hinton the wife of Thomas
Hinton was a sister to William M. Fennell decd. of Pickens Dist.
Her father was Hardy J. Fennell.

HINTON, R. O. Box 138 #6. Probate Judge Office. Pickens, S.C.
Est. admr. 19 Sept. 1901. by J. A. Hinton, J. T. Hinton and W. M.
Hagood. He died 27 Aug. 1901. Paid 3 Jan. 1903 Ada Hinton, widow
$211.43. Paid W. T. Dorr guardian of Ruth Hinton minor $422.86.

HINTON, R. O. Box 138 #6. Probate Judge Office. Pickens, S.C.
Est. admr. 19 Sept. 1901 by J. A. Hinton, J. T. Hinton, W. H. Hagood
are bound unto J. B. Newberry, Ord. in the sum of $1600. Died 27
Aug. 1901. Paid 3 Jan. 1903 Ada Hinton widow $211.43. Paid W. T. Dorr
gdn. of Ruth Hinton minor $422.86.

HITT, JAMES Deed Book A. Page 234. Probate Judge Office.
Pickens, S. C. On 4 Oct. 1858 James Hitt and his wife Elendor were
the heirs of Nathaniel Duncan decd. of Pickens Dist.

HITT, PETER Apt. 4 File 223. Probate Judge Office. Greenville,
S. C. I, Peter Hitt of Greenville Dist. do make this my last will and
testament. First I will and desire that all my debts be paid. The
children by my first wife namely, Elizabeth, William, James, Nancy,
John, Henry, Robert, Susannah and Thomas having received from me
three full portion of my est. I therefore give no more of my property
I give to my beloved wife Mary Hitt my plantation with all appur-
tainances. My negro man Daniel, all stock, household and kitchen
furniture during her natural life and at her death to be equally
divided between my three youngest children, Joseph, Elisha P. and Jane
Hitt, I appoint my wife Mary Hitt my executrix. Dated 29 Feb. 1832.
Wit: R. S. C. Foster, Phebe X Young, Richard Young. Signed: Peter
Hitt. Probated 25 April 1836.

HITT, THOMAS In Equity, #654-1. Clerk of Court Office. Pickens, S. C. On 7 April 1855 Martha Robertson dtr. of Allen Robertson decd. who died in 1854 and Catharine his wife of Pickens Dist., S. C. was the wife of Thomas Hitt was living in Cherokee County, Ga.

HIX, JOHN Inquest #4. Pickens Dist., S. C. An inquest was taken at Aaron Thomases in Pickens Dist. on 25 Oct. 1866 to view the dead body of John Hix. The jury brought out that John Hix came to his death from gunshot wounds on or about the 16 Oct. 1866 that he was killed or murdered by some person unknown to the jury. Miss Sarah L. Boggs sayeth, I was coming from the spring seeing some buzzards down in the corn field. I said to my aunt Bet, lets go down there and see what is dead. When she looked in the ditch or gully and said, Ah Oh Lord there is John. She last saw John standing near the smoke house. While at the spring I heard two shots from a gun, the second was louder than the first. Mrs. D. Ann Thomas sayeth, on the morning of the 16th John was in good health and ate his breakfast at her house. I went to my father as he went out of the yard. I heard two shots but heard no hollowing nor did I see anyone. I breakfasted by sun up. I heard the guns shot about one hour and half hours after sun up. I heard Mr. Linderman say, he intended to kill him the first time on sight. I heard Mr. Balis Hendrix say Yes we will. This was the day on which John Hix whipped Mr. Linderman. Mrs. Elizabeth Hix sayeth, I was twisting thread and my niece came in the house and said that a lots of buzzards are after something, we went and found John. I told her to go tell her mother and Aunt Adeline, I came back to the house and asked my sister Dilly Ann to go down and put something over him. Mrs. M. M. Durham, sayeth the last time she saw Hix was the day he whipped Mr. Linderman. Mrs. W. A. McWhorter saith she saw Hix near the place that he lived at, near Mrs. D. A. Thomas, and she heard Mr. Linderman and Balis Hendrix say that they would kill him.

HIX, JOHN Box 91 #959. Probate Judge Office. Pickens, S. C. Est. admr. 10 Nov. 1866 by Robert A. Thompson who is bound unto W. E. Holcombe, Ord. in the sum of $300.

HERRON, THOMAS D. Box 17 #73. Probate Judge Office. Darlington Co., S. C. Est. admr. 10 Jan. 1862 by William H. Herron, William W. Moore, Henry D. Campbell who are bound unto John J. Russell, Ord. in the sum of $10,000. Wm. H. Herron father of said decd.

HERRON, WILLIAM H. Box 26 #14. Probate Judge Office. Darlington Co., S. C. On 19 Nov. 1869 Penelope M. Herron states that her husband William H. Herron died 3 March 1865 and left two minors under age (a plat of 1870 of the homestead was in package.)

HESTER, ABRAHAM Box 65 #705. Probate Judge Office. Pickens, S. C. Est. admr. 14 Nov. 1862 by Emily C. Hester, widow, James E. Hagood, Carville Hester who are bound unto W. E. Holcombe, Ord. in the sum of $20,000. Heirs, Richard A. Hester, William H. Hester, Samuel J. Jester, Elizabeth Hester, Lula and Lucy Hester, the latter four are minors above the age of 14 yrs. Owned 379 acres on both sides of Rice Creek, near Central Station bounded by land of Stephen Clayton, E. Griffin and others.

HESTER, ABRAHAM Box 15 #197. Probate Judge Office. Pickens, S. C. Est. admr. by Miles M. Norton and John O. Grisham who are bound unto William D. Steele, Ord. in the sum of $100. Dated 9 Dec. 1844. Miles M. Norton petition the Court to grant him letter of admr. on the goods and chattles of Abraham Hester decd. this 22 Nov. 1844. Cit. read at Bethel Church, P.D.S.C. Recd. from Treasurer of the United States being balance of pension due him $32.91. The only ones to recd. from est. Carville Hester and Alfred Hester $5.53 each.

HESTER, ALFRED Box 49 #536. Probate Judge Office. Pickens, S. C. I Alfred Hester of Pickens Dist. being weak in body but of sound mind and understanding. First I will that my just debts are paid. I give to my dtr. Sarah A. Burgess 200 acres of land, known as the Carwile house, and negro woman Priscilla and chn. James, Shadrack and

Hester, Alfred - Continued. Jane. I give to my son Baliss J. Hester one half of my upper plantation and what hogs I have there, one sorrel horse, Saddle and bridle, two cows and calves, one negro woman Mariah and chn. Early and Andy. I give to my son James B. Hester the other half of my upper plantation also negro woman Chancy and child Emerson, one brown horse, saddle and bridle, two cows and calves, two head sheep, two sows, two beds and furniture. I give to my wife Eady Hester the house where I now live and all the land I purchased from Mr. Packard except the 200 acres I willed to Sarah Burgess. Also one negro man Edmond and wife Hannah, Reuben, Rose and Rachel and all my household and kitchen furniture. At the death of my wife, I will my son Baliss one negro Reuben, and to my son James Hannah and Rose. After my death, I desire that Elizabeth and all other property not willed to be sold, to pay my debts and support my wife. I appoint my son Baliss J. Hester and David Blythe my executors. Dated 4 Sept. 1844. Wit: Joel Jones, Bannet Jones, Allen Keith. Signed: Alfred Hester. Proven 8 Nov. 1858.

HESTER, ALFRED Deed Book E-1, Page 57. Clerk of Court Office. Pickens, S. C. Sheriffs titles to 725 acres land. I F. N. Garvin, Sheriff of Pickens Dist.. Whereas by virtue of a Writ of Fieri Facias issue out of the Court of Common Pleas. Held the 3 April 1843 at the suit of C. Packard to me directed, that the goods and chattels land and tenements of Joseph B. Reid to levy the sum of $392.90 and $16.00 damage and costs. I have taken the land and tenements of said Reid land containing 725 acres lying in Pickens Dist. on the North Fork of Carpenter Creek adj. lands of William Kirksey, John Keith and others. By virtue of the Writ of Fieri Facias, have exposed to sale at public vendue and purchased by C. Packard and by him titles ordered to be made to Afred[?] Hester of Pickens Dist. the sum of $220 being the highest that was bidden. Wherefore I, F. N. Garvin, Sheriff for and in consideration of $220 paid me by Alfred Hester, have granted sold, bargained all that estate, right title and interest which the said Joseph B. Reid of right had, etc. etc. Dated 8 Dec. 1843. Wit: J. L. Kennedy, S. Kirksey. F.N. Garvin, S.P.D. Seal. Proven on oath of S. Kirksey before W. L. Keith, Clk. of Court this 12 Dec. 1843.

HESTER, ALFRED Deed Book F-1, page 92. Clerk of Court Office. Pickens, S. C. This indenture made 3 Jan. 1848, between M. M. Norton, Esq. Commissioner of the Court of Equity, and Alfred Hester of the Dist. of Pickens, whereas James M. Reid on the 15 Sept. 1847 exhibited his bill of complaint in the Court of Equity, against Sarah Reid and others for the partition of the est. of Stephen C. Reid decd. The said Court adjudge and decree that the real estate should be sold at public outcry. Whereas Miles M. Norton as commissioner of the said Court, did sell to Alfred Hester for $61.00 being the highest bidder. Now therefore, this indenture witnesseth that Miles M. Norton, Esq. Comm. of the Court of Equity, in consideration of $61 paid by Alfred Hester have granted, sold, bargained all the tract of land known as the Peter Weaver tract containing 200 acres. Deeded from Peter Weaver to S. C. Reid. Wit: Joseph R. Ramsey, William J. Nevell. Signed: Miles M. Norton, Esq. C.E.P.D. Proven on oath of Wm. J. Nevell before W. L. Keith, Clk. of Court the 27 April 1848. Recorded the 29 April 1848.

HESTER, BAYLIS M. Pack 230 #17. Clerk of Court Office. Pickens, S. C. (Assault on James A. Mull). Luther James sworn says, "I know the deft. James A. Mull, I saw a difficulty between them. It occured in this County on a Sunday a month ago or more at or about a school house called Midway. There was preaching there. James A. Mull went to church with my sister. We went to church and as we were gearing up our horses to return home. Mull says there is Mr. Hester now and Hester says yest sir here I am. Mull said I want to see Mr. Hester about some tales you have been telling on me. Deft. said all right. Mull said didn't you tell that I was drunk here at the time there was church here before. Hester says, Yes, I did and you are drunk now, Mull said you are a lier. Hester said that was a thing that he didn't take and put his hand on him. Mull said to him to wait there until he got back or

Hester, Baylis M. - Continued. meet him on the road that he would
meet him any where. Hester said he would meet him any where and proposed to meet him at Chapmans. We went on home. We were ungearing
our horses at my shelter in my lot. Mull went along peaceably and
quiet. Some one then said there comes your man Hester now. Hester
came up to where Mull was loosing the mule and they commenced a row
in about the same way as they commenced it at the school house. Mull
said you did tell a damned lie. Hester said he would take it and would
whip him and drew to strike Mull. I tried to get them to stop. I looked
and saw that Mull had his knife out and I told Hester to look out that
he had his knife drawn. Hester then turned and went away around a
buggy that was standing near and went out to a barn about 10 or 15
steps and picked up a stick and started back. Mull moved around towards
where he was and they meet about 6 or 8 steps from where Hester picked
up the stick. As soon as they met Hester struck him with the stick.
Hester hit him 3 times on the head. Mull staggered at every lick and
fell at the third lick, he dropped the stick on him the fourth time,
it fell on his arm after he was down. Mull got up soon after he was
down and got on his mule and went away. I know tha t Mull was drinking
at the school house, I took one drink with him. I don't think that
Hester was drinking." (The named James maybe Jones.)

HESTER, CARVILLE Deed Book D-1, Page 551. Clerk of Court Office.
Pickens, S. C. I Eli Fitzgerald of Pickens Dist. have granted, bargained, sold unto Carville Hester of the same place, all that tract of
land whereon I now live for and in consideration of $1200. Containing
200 acres lying on Cane Creek and Little River, it being the same
which was by John Adair, Esq. devised to James Adair and from James
Adair to Eli Fitzgerald. Adj. land of Ira G. Gambrell, Mrs. Sloan,
Adam Lands so called and Thomas Margan[?]. Dated 10 Nov. 1842.
Wit: James Cannon, John G. Roland. Signed: Eli Fitzgerald. Proved
on oath of James Cannon before Silas Kirksey, N.P. this 9 Dec. 1842.
This day came Margaret the wife of Eli Fitzgerald and freely and
voluntarily renounce, release and forever relinquished, all interest
and claim of dower on the above land. Dated 15 Dec. 1842. Signed:
Silas Kirksey, N.P. and J.Q.

HOLDEN, JOSHUA Deed Book A, Page 222. Probate Judge Office.
Pickens, S. C. On 21 June 1858 Joshua Holden and wife Keziah were
heirs of Thomas Alexander decd. of Pickens Dist.

HOLLWEYS, HENRICH Box 84 #888. Probate Judge Office. Pickens,
S. C. I Henrich Hollweys of Pickens Dist. being of sound mind and
memory. First after my lawful debts are paid and discharged. I give
to my beloved wife Helene Catharine Hollweys during the term of her
natural life all my real and personal estate. After her death to be
divided between my children (not named) in case she marry again, my
wife Helene to have one third and the chn. two thirds. I appoint my
wife Helene Catharine Hollweys and John ___ executors. Dated 31 Aug.
1863. Wit: James G. Watt, A. E. Norman, C. H. Issertel. Signed:
Henrick Hollweys. Proven 9 Nov. 1865.

HOOD, ANDREW Servie #S 7030. Anderson Dist. Andrew Hood applied
personally in Anderson Dist. on 17 May 1834 before James A. Black, J.P.
to obtain the benefit of the act of Congress 7 June 1832. States he
entered service under Capt. McClare in Capt. Polk's regiment of
infantry N.C. militia at Charlotte court house, as stated in his
original declaration he believes in Aug. 1779, served the latter part
of 1779 and in spring of 1780. He was born in county Entrim Ireland
1744. I have no regular record of my age, I have seen an entry of it
in my father's Bible in Ireland, but I have not seen it for the last
sixty years. He was living in Mecklinburg Co.,N.C. when I entered
service. I have lived in Pendleton Dist. now Anderson Dist. since the
Revolution and still live there. He is acquainted with Revd. Wm.
Carlile, Archibald Simpson, Esq., Genl. Joseph N. Whitner, Wm. Sherad,
Joel H. Berry and Revd. Ebenezer Pressley. His age is 89 years. I
served at Fort Johnston in Brunswick under Col. Polk and Gen. Winn in
S. C. I joined a scouting party commanded by Capt. Walker, we took
one route after the British and one after the tories. I was discharged

Hood, Andrew - Continued. verbally by Capt. McClure.

HEAD, WILLIAM & PEGGY Deed Book A, Page 48. Clerk of Court
Office. Elberton, Ga. State of Georgia, County of Wilkes. This
indenture made 14 Aug. 1790 between William Head and Peggy his wife
of County and State aforesaid and Noah Harbour of Halifax County,
State of Virginia. In consideration of 50Ł sterling, hath bargained,
sold and confirm all that tract of land containing 400 acres on Cold
Water Creek, being part of a tract granted to Nick Long. Wit: Reuben
Allen, J.P. Signed: William Head and Peggy X Head. Reg. 6 Feb. 1792.

HOOD, JOHN Box 38 #432. Probate Judge Office. Pickens, S. C.
John Hood an heir of Moses Hendricks decd. whose estate was admr.
Nov. 12, 1855 in Pickens Dist.

HORTON, GRIEF Pack 6. Clerk of Court Office. Anderson, S. C.
Pendleton Dist. I Grief Horton in consideration of $520.00. Paid
me by Nimrod Nash of same Dist. Have granted, sold, bargained and
released unto said Nimrod Nash 170 acres it being part of a tract of
land where Thomas Garner formerly dwelt lying on Big Creek, waters of
Saluda River and Cason line. Dated 15 Dec. 1810. Wit: Cain Broyles,
Joshua Halbert. Signed: Grief Horton. Proved on oath of Joshua
Halbert before Abner Nash, J.P. on this 28 Dec. 1814. I Abner Nash
J.Q. to all whom it may concern that Mimey Horton the wife of Grief
Horton did this day relinquished her dower on the above land. this
28 Dec. 1814.

HOSE, JOHN Box 48 Pack 1095. Probate Judge Office. Abbeville,
S. C. I John Hose of Abbeville Dist. being in perfect mind and memory.
I desire after my death my wife Elizabeth to have the mare, saddle
and bridle. I desire that my oldest son Wm. Hose to have the eldest
horse, saddle and bridle. I desire that my son Henry to have the
youngest horse, saddle and bridle. I desire my youngest son Samuel
to have the colt that will be born this spring and to get him saddle
and bridle. I desire that my plantation be kept together till my son
William become the age of twenty one years, then to be divided equally
I appoint my wife Elizabeth Executrix and sons William and Henry Hose
executors, dated 10 March 1806. Wit: John P. Knop, G. Henry Casper,
Frederick X Knop. Signed: John X Hose. Recorded 25 Aug. 1806.

HOSKINS, NINIAN Box 46 Pack 1046. Probate Judge Office.
Abbeville, S. C. Admr. bond, Abbeville Dist. We Margaret Hoskison,
Charles Johnson, William Caldwell and Saml. Harris are bound to Andrew
Hamilton, Ord. in the sum of $10,000. Dated 1 Feb. 1805. Inventory
made 3 June 1805 by Thos. Shanklin, Wm. Davis, Wm. H. Caldwell.
Buyers at sale, Peggy Hoskinson, Alexr. Harris, B. Houston, Nathaniel
Norwood, Donald Fraser, Martin Shoemaker, John Ellington, Charles
Johnson, Wm. Davis, Wm. Caldwell, James Vernon, John Cameron.

HOUSTON, ALICE Box 45 Pack 1004. Probate Judge Office. Abbe-
ville, S. C. Admr. bond, We James R. Houston, James Hughes and John
Ferguson are bound unto Moses Taggart, Ord. in the sum of $3,000.
Dated 5 Dec. 1825. Inventory was made 20 Dec. 1825 by Jos. C. Mathews,
Philip Leroy, and John Dickson. James R. Houston was next of kin.
Sale held 20 Dec. 1825. Buyers, Jos. C. Mathews, Randolph Cain,
Martha Harris, Jno. Ferguson, James R. Houston, Nancy Houston, Alexr.
Houston.

HOUSTON, BENJAMIN Box 45 Pack 1018. Probate Judge Office.
Abbeville, S. C. I Benjamin Houston of Abbeville Dist. being weak in
body but of sound mind and memory. First my burial expenses and debts
to be paid. I give to Alice the negro girl Melinda over and above
an equal share with the rest of my heirs, I allow her to have her
mare and saddle at their value. I wish no public sale be made of my
estate, let each one take their part by valuation. I give to my wife
Betsey what the law allow and negro Rendor at her value. I wish my
executors to exchange Prince (Negro) for one that mite suite the family
better or sell him, and let his price buy one in his place. I give to
James and Benjamin and Alice equal in horses and saddles, I wish that

Houston, Benjamin - Continued. negro Rendor nor her children be
sold, I wish them to stay amongest my children. I give Alexr. Pleasent
the negro boy Tom at his value and that he gets his learning equal to
his brothers out of the estate. I allow Rendors second son for Amsey
at his value or my executors change him with a brother for a girl that
mite suit her better. I appoint my brother Alexander Houston and John
Gray and my son James executors. N.B. I allow Alexr. Pleasent to have
my wife interest in the land at her death. (Dated, not given in will)
Recorded 5 Aug. 1816. The inventory made 25 Sept. 1816 by A. Houston,
James Hutcheson, Joseph Calhoun.

HOWARD, BENJAMIN Box 45 Pack 1020. Probate Judge Office.
Abbeville, S. C. I Benjamin Howard of Abbeville Dist. being in a sick
and weak condition of body but of sound mind and memory. I desire my
just and lawful debts and funeral expenses be paid. I give to my son
Martin Howard one dollar. To dtr. Sally Nelson one dollar, to my
dtr. Catty Norris one dollar. I give to my dtr. Nancy Carson the
residue of my estate, negroes, Cealey, Ibb, Toney, and Joe, my horse
and riding carriage, saddle and bridle, all household furniture, I
appoint my son in law William Carson executor. Dated 10 Aug. 1813.
Wit: Robert Carson, Thos. Lindsay. Signed: Benjamin Howard. Recorded
18 Sept. 1813. Inventory made 2 Oct. 1813 by Thos. Lindsay, Robert
Carson, Wm. Martin.

HESTER, ELIZABETH E. Box 7 #112. Probate Judge Office.
Pickens, S. C. On 19 Nov. 1866, Bird Caradine, Joseph M. Adams,
Samuel Reid are bound unto W. E. Holcombe, Ord. in the sum of $25.60.
Bird Caradine gdn. of Elizabeth E. Hester, minor about 19 yrs. Dtr.
of Leonard Capehart decd., Bird Caradine her uncle.

HESTER, HENRY Deed Book D-1, Page 141. Clerk of Court Office.
Pickens, S. C. I Henry Hester of Pendleton Dist. for the love and good
will that I have for my beloved dtr. Sare Hester. I will and bequeath
to my dtr. the tract of land whereon I now live, containing 150 acres,
lying on a branch of Dodes Creek waters of Saluda River, also three
head horses, six head of cows, ten head of sheep, sixteen head hogs,
three feather beds and furniture, all kitchen and table furniture.
The land I gave to my dtr. is bounded to James Lathem, James Saturfield,
Enoch Hood, Robert H. Briges, and John Freeman's decd. Dated 28 Sept.
1826. Wit: John Bowen, Elizabeth Bowen. Signed: Henry X Hester.
Proved on oath John Brown before David McCollum, J.P. on this 2 March
1827. Recorded the 14 Oct. 1839 and examined by me, W. L. Keith, Clk.
of Court.

HESTER, HENRY Pack 263. Clerk of Court Office. Abbeville,
S. C. In Equity, To the Honr. the Chancellors: Your orator Thomas
Hester sheweth that Henry Hester late of this Dist. departed this life
1844, leaving as next of kin and distributees your orator, Thomas
Hester, Louisa Hester the widow, Robert Hester, Samuel Hester, Sarah
Ann Norwood the wife of James Norwood, who are of age. Rebecca
Hester, John Henry Hester, Elijah Hester who are minors under age.
At time of his death the said intestate was possessed with a tract
of land containing 450 acres, lying on Bear Garden Creek, bounded by
land of Williamson Norwood, George Gray, Richard Harris. That Louisa
Hester is administratrix and he believes that the personal property
will pay the debts and he desires a partition of the land. Filed
8 May 1845.

HESTER, JANIE Box 10 #157. Probate Judge Office. Pickens,
S. C. 26 April 1876, Mary Jane Hester states that she 21 yrs. 26 Dec.
1875. Samuel J. Hester her husband. Dtr. of T. A. Rogers, decd.

HESTER, JEPTHA Box 26 #314. Probate Judge Office. Pickens,
S. C. Est. admr. 16 Apirl 1850 by Henry Hester, W. L. Keith who are
bound unto Wm. D. Steele, Ord. in the sum of $500. Henry Hester a
brother of said decd.

HESTER, WILLIAM SENR. Box 57 #619. Probate Judge Office.
Pickens, S. C. Est. admr. 4 Feb. 1861 by A. J. Anderson, James E.

Hester, William Senr. - Continued. Hagood, Reese Bowen are bound
unto W. E. Holcombe, Ord. in the sum of $800. Sale held 25 Feb.
1861. Buyers Susan Hester the widow, J. B. Hester, Margaret Hester,
A. B. Hill, Mary Hester, James Hester. Had note on Susan Hester, James
Hester, Henry Hester, Margaret Hester, William Hester and Mary Hester.

HESTER, JOHN B. Box 83 #882. Probate Judge Office. Pickens,
S. C. Est. admr. 9 Oct. 1865 by James B. Hester, James E. Hagood,
Robert A. Thompson are bound to W. E. Holcombe, Ord. in the sum of
$1,000. Paid 27 Jan. 1876. Margaret E. Burgess heir $5.00. Paid 6
Sept. 1872 J. B. Burgess receipt $37.25. John B. Burgess $40.00.
W. F. Burgess $37.00.

HESTER, JOHN B. #36. In Equity. Clerk of Court Office. Pickens,
S. C. (Basement). To the Honr. the Chancellors: Your orator James
B. Hester of Pickens Dist. sheweth that his brother John B. Hester
and himself owned two tracts of land jointly and equally. First the
home tract containing 725 acres adj. land of Esther Keith, William
Holder and others, the other tract, the Ooleney place on Oolenoy
Creek containing 283 acres, adj. land of Marcus D. and Stephen D.
Keith, Philip Martin and others. His brother John B. died in April
1865, intestate, unmarried and leaving as his only heirs at law your
orator and six children of his pre-deceased sister Sallie Burgess.
Viz: James, William, Balus, Ruggles, Ruggles Wardlaw, Margaret and
Susan Burgess all are minors except James. A letter of Admr. was
granted to your orator by this Court, and the personal estate will be
sufficient to pay his debts. Therefore your orator prays for a partition of the said land and that a guardian ad litem be appointed for
the minors. Filed 17 May 1866.

HESTER, L. C. Box 94, #987. Probate Judge Office. Pickens,
S. C. Est. admr. 10 Sept. 1866, by James E. Hagood, Robert A. Thompson
who are bound unto W. E. Holcombe, Ord. in the sum of $500. Heirs
Elizabeth widow, Elizabeth E. Hester Jr., heirs of Mrs. Robinson,
heirs of Mrs. Fisher, heirs of Henry Hester decd., Heirs of Abraham
Hester decd.

HESTER, "MINORS" Box 9 #146. On 12 Dec. 1872 W. H. Hester, Wm.
B. Allgood are bound unto I. H. Philpot, Ord. in the sum of $76.00.
W. H. Hester gdn. of Samuel J. Hester, Elizabeth Hester, Lula Hester,
Lucy Hester. Chn. of Abraham Hester decd. Entitled to a share of
est. of Carwell Hester decd. Bettie and Lula J. Hester over 14 yrs.
Lucy M. Hester near 14 yrs. W. H. Hester, Richard A. Hester their
brothers. 7 June 1875 Emily Hester recd. one third of est. Carwell
Hester their uncle.

HESTER, WILLIAM JR. Box 95 #1002. Probate Judge Office.
Pickens, S. C. On 4 Jan. 1869 He owned 160 acres on waters of Saluda
River, adj. lands of Esli Hunt, A. J. Anderson and others. Died 20
Aug. 1864. Louisa Hester the widow. Children: Michael Hester,
Mary Jane Hester, Louisa J. Hester, Wm. Anderson Hester, John Butler
Hester all minors. On 1 Jan. 1888 Mary Jane Riddle recd. share.
Elizabeth Griffin recd. share.

HESTER, WILLIAM JR. Box 89 #941. Probate Judge Office.
Pickens, S. C. Est. admr. 27 Sept. 1866 by Louisa Hester, Michael
Whitmire, Redin Rackley who are bound to W. E. Holcombe, Ord. in the
sum of $1,000. Widow recd. $107.55 Elizabeth Griffin, Mary J. Riddle,
John B. Hester, W. A. Hester, M. W. Hester each recd. $43.02. (In
same Pack) 22 Sept. 1866 Robert A. Thompson made suit for letter of
admr. on est. of Henry Hester late of the State of Texas.

HESTER, WILLIAM SENR. Box 92 #980. Probate Judge Office.
Pickens, S. C. On 1 Jan. 1877, owned 162 acres on the East, bounded
by Saluda River, on North by land of R. G. Hunt, on South by land
belonging to the est. of Wesley Hunt decd. Whereon Margaret and Mary
Hester now resides. Susan Hester his widow died after he did. Chn.
Margaret Hester, Ann Williams, Henry Hester, Nancy wife of Abraham
Williams, Elizabeth Hunt widow of Wesley Hunt decd., Abraham Hester,

Hester, William Senr. - Continued. Jobbery Hester, Mary Hester.
The chn. of Thomas Hester decd., all of age, Rebecca Hester, John
Hester, Joseph Hester, Taylor Hester, Harriet Hester. The chn. of
William Hester decd. Michael Hester age 23, Mary Hester age 21,
Elizabeth Hester age 20, John Hester a minor, William Hester over 14
yrs. The chn. of Robert Hester decd. Louisa Hester, William Hester,
Susan Hester all over 21 yrs., Martin Hester, Catharine Hester,
Elizabeth Hester over 14 yrs. Robert Hester under 14 yrs. The chn.
of James Hester, Julia the wife of Wm. Hawkins, Amanda Hester over 21
yrs., Mary Hester over 14 yrs., and James Hester. Rebecca Hester,
John Hester, Joseph Hester, Taylor Hester, Harriet Hester, Nancy wife
of Abraham Williams resides out of State. Susan Hester married a
Green. Nancy Williams resides in Georgia. Henry Hester living in
Greenville, S. C. Thomas Hester who died and his chn. moved to Ga.
Chn. of Robert Hester living in Greenville, S. C. Abraham and James
Hester both resides in Greenville.

HUGER, BRIGR. GENL. ISAAC Land grant to Brigr. Genl. Isaac Huger
for 400 acres lying on the West side of Keowee River and adj. the same.
Bounded on all sides by vacant land when surveyed by William Tate on
the 30 of last May. Recorded 14 June 1784.

HUGGINS, ENSGN. BENJAMIN Land grant for Ensgn. Benjamin Huggins
for 150 acres situate on the West side of Sennekaw River adj. the
same about three miles below Conneross Creek, bounded on all sides by
vacant land when surveyed by William Tate, D.S. the 20 May last.
Recorded 14 June 1784.

HESTER, MARGARET Pack 653-2. Clerk of Court Office. Pickens,
S. C. Margaret Hester of Pickens Dist. charges John H. Williams as
being the father of a male bastard child that was born to her on 11
June 1858.

HESTER, SAMUEL R. Box 70 #753. Probate Judge Office. Pickens,
S. C. Est. admr. 29 June 1863 by James E. Hagood, W. N. Craig, are
bound unto W. E. Holcombe, Ord. in the sum of $1200.

HESTER, SUSAN Box 110 #1055. Probate Judge Office. Pickens,
S. C. Est. admr. 15 Nov. 1876 by Henry Hester, W. R. Phillips, J.
Whitmire who are bound unto I. H. Philpot, Ord. in the sum of $60.00.

HUGHES, FRANCES Box 45 Pack 1019. Probate Judge Office.
Abbeville, S. C. Abbeville Dist. Admr. bond, We Williamson Norwood,
Samuel Young and Joshua Dubose are bound unto Talo. Livingston, Ord.
in the sum of $5,000. Dated 24 Aug. 1812. Inventory made 29 Aug.
1812 by Charles Britt, Leonard Wideman, Moses Tullis.

HUGHEY, JEFFERSON Box 48 Pack 1094. Probate Judge Office.
Abbeville, S. C. Expend of Jefferson E. Hughey a minor with Joseph
Hughey the gdn. 1832, paid William Rusel for tuition $7.53. 1831 paid
Owen Selby for boarding $30.00.

HUNT, RICHARDSON Deed Book C. Clerk of Court Office. Elberton,
Ga. This indenture made this 11 Aug. 1794 between Richardson Hunt and
Nancy Martin his wife of state of Ga. County of Elbert and Josias
P. Adams (late of Virginia but of Augusta) in consideration of five
negroes, healthy and sound, not over the age of twenty five or under
the age of sixteen yrs. to be paid on or before 1 Jan. 1788. Said
Richardson Hunt and his wife Nancy Martin hath, granted, sold,
released until Josias P. Adams a tract of land lying in Elbert Co., Ga.
on Beaverdam Creek, containing 100 acres, that land was granted to
Richardson Hunt 1787 by George Mathews Governor, bounded on East by
land of Walker Richardson, vacant on other sides. Wit: Francis S.
Carter, M. Woods, J.P. Signed R. Hunt and Nancy M. Hunt. Nancy M.
Hunt the wife of R. Hunt, appeared before M. Woods, J.P. and relinquish-
ed her rights to dower to the above land this 11 Aug. 1794. Signed:
Nancy M. Hunt.

HUTTON, REBECCA   Box 47 Pack 1079. Probate Judge Office. Abbeville, S. C. I Rebecca Hutton of Abbeville Dist. (widow) being weak
in body but of sound mind and memory. I give to my dtr. Martha Gaston
the sum of $600. I give to my dtr. Rebecca Dichson[?] the sum of $400
and one feather bed and furniture. I give one feather bed and furniture
to Polly Hutton. I give to my granddaughter Rebecca Gray $300 to be
kept on interest by John Gray one of my executor, until marriage or
age of eighteen, also one feather bed and furniture, one walnut chest,
and all my pewter. I give to my grand dtr. Acquilla Hutton one negro
man named March, for the purpose of defraying the expenses of a
classical education. I appoint my son Joseph Hutton guardian to care
for said negro, in case Acquilla not live to finish her education, the
negro to belong to grandson John Newton Hutton. My wearing apparel
to be divided between my three dtrs. My negro Cloe is to have her
freedom and I appoint my son Joseph her guardian, and take care of
her while she lives, for doing so I give him my negro man Tombo and
quit him of $100 due me from rent on land. The money one hand to be
divided between Joseph Hutton and Mary Gray. I appoint John Gray and
Joseph Hutton executors. Dated 16 May 1814. Test. Anna C. Gray (only
one). Signed: Rebecca Hutton. Recorded 1 Sept. 1814. Expend. Paid
29 Aug. 1815, Saml. H. Dickson as part of his legacy $155.00. Paid
8 Oct. Joseph Gaston as per order to Pressly as part of his legacy
$100.00. Paid 6 June 1816 Revd. Daniel Gray by hand of John Gray as
per order $74.00. Paid 26 July 1816 Rebecca Gray by John Gray her
gdn. $26.25. Paid 1 Sept. 1814. Revd. Daniel Gray as part of legacy
$30.00.

HUTTON, WILLIAM   Box 46 Pack 1047. Probate Judge Office. Abbeville, S. C. I William Hutton of Abbeville Dist. being of disposing
mind and memory. After my funeral expenses and just debts are paid,
my wife Rebecah shall have the full use of the plantation I now live
on and all lands belonging to me adj. the same containing upward to
800 acres, during her natural life. At her decease it is my will that
my son Joseph Hutton shall have said land, on his paying to my
three dtrs. as follows, to my dtr. Martha Gaston (if alive) in three
yearly payments the sum of $200, if decease to her heirs, to my dtr.
Rebecah if alive $200 in three equal annual payments, if decease to her
heirs. To my dtr. Mary, if alive the sum of $200 in three equal annual
payments, if decease to her heirs. If my son Joseph does not take said
plantation as aforesaid. It to be sold at public outcry the purchaser
shall give four equal notes for the land, one for each of my said
children. I give my son Joseph my wearing apparal. I give to Martha,
one negro named Ran during her life time, I give to my dtr. Rebeccah,
one negro named Phillis during her life time. To my son Joseph one
negro named Sall, during his life time. To my dtr. Mary one negro
named Amber, during her life time. Each negro to become the property
of the heirs of their body. That all my be equal, Martha Gaston has
recd. $536. (Several words worn from page, maybe Joseph amount.)
Rebeccah Dickson $404, Mary Gray $404. (No more of this will found in
notes the date of 1806 is on side of will, not part of it.)

IRWIN, ALEXANDER   "Old Records B.B." No County given. All land
grants. For Alexander Irwin as a citizen, 610 acres on both sides of
Great Rockey Creek, bounded on N.W. by River, on S.E. on the old
Indian line, all other sides vacant land, when surveyed by Bennett
Crafton D.S. as appears by his certificate bearing date 31 May 1784
with the form and marks as per platt. Recorded 2 June 1784. Robert
Anderson, C.L. 16 ___

IRWIN, JAMES   #189. Clerk of Court Office. Abbeville, S. C.
Abbeville Dist. To the Honr. the Chancellors: The petition of Samuel
Perrin of this Dist. sheweth that James Parr Irwin a son of John Irwin
decd. is a minor under the age of choice (14) to wit. 12 yrs. old. He
is entitled to an estate from his father and by reason of his minority
he cannot manage for himself. Your petitioner therefore prays he may
be appointed guardian. Filed 8 June 1857. On 4 June 1857. I consent
to Mr. Samuel Perrin should act as the guardian of the estate of my

Irwin, James - Continued. infant child James Irwin, twelve years and nine months. Test: John Pardue. Signed: Mary A. Pardue.

IRONS, JOHN Box 50 Pack 1173. Probate Judge Office. Abbeville, S. C. Admr. bond, dated 2 May 1814. We John Wright, John Stuart, Joshua Davis are bound unto Telo. Livingston, Ord. in the sum of $1,000.

ISBELL, ELIZA A. M. Box 88 #5. Probate Judge Office. Pickens, S. C. I Eliza A. M. Isbell of Pickens Dist. After my just debts are paid, I will and bequeath unto my sisters Nancy M. Isbell and S. Emily Isbell all my worldly effects, to be divided between them equally. My negro girl Harriet 28 yrs. old and Josephine 2 yrs. old, all cattle, household furniture. I desire that none of my effects to be sold, only as my two named sisters think best. Dated 15 June 1864. Wit: David S. Stribling, Samuel Isbell, Balus Hix. Signed: E. A. Isbell. Proved 19 March 1866.

ISBELL, PENDLETON Box 15 #196. Probate Judge Office. Pickens, S. C. I Pendleton Isbell of Pickens Dist. First I give unto my beloved wife Clarkey Isbell all my land, a negro girl named Harriet about thirteen years of age. All my household furniture of every kind, during her natural life. I give to my dtr. Lucinda one dollar if called for within twelve months, which I consider to make her equal portion of my property. I give to my dtr. Arminda in addition to what she has, one dollar to make her equal. I give to my dtr. Nancy Mariah a bay mare named Jim, bed and furniture, cow and calf. I give to my dtr. Sarah Emiline a sorrell horse named Lacksley, a bed and furniture a cow and calf, and the cupboard at her mother death. I give to my two sons James Sidney Isbell and William Lawhorn Isbell at the death of their mother all my land. Division given with the East and South part for the oldest son Sidney, and the opposite side to Wm. Lawhorn. Each to have a bed and furniture, William to have the smithtools. I give to my youngest dtr. Eliza Almarinda a bed and furniture and at her mother death the negro Harriet. The increase of negro Harriet with remaining stock to be sold and proceeds be divided between all my chn. I appoint Joberry Maret executor. Dated 21 June 1846. Wit: David S. Stribling, Benjamin X Maret, Frederick B. Hodges. Signed: Pendleton X Isbell, Will proved 2 Nov. 1846.

ISSOM, EDWARD Box 50 Pack 1161. Probate Judge Office. Abbeville, S. C. 96 Dist. Whereas Robert Bond and Abidier Issom of said Dist. have applied to me for letter of Admr. on the goods and chattels of Edward Issom late of this Dist. The said Abidier Issom being the next of kin, who request the said Robert Bond as assistant. Dated this 17 June 1782. Admr. bond, We Robert bond, Abidier Issom, Aaron Steel and Thomas Harris of 96 Dist. are bound unto John Ewing Calhoun Esq. Ord. in the sum of fourteen thousand pounds current money or two thousand pounds sterling. Dated at Long Cane, this 20 July 1782. The above citation was publicly read at a funeral near my plantation the 30 June 1782. Appraiser were Aaron Steel, Thomas Harris, Robert Bell to view all goods and chattels as directed by Abidier Issom administratrix and Robt. Bond administrator. To make a true inventory and appraisement. Dated 12 day July 1782.

IVESTER, HUGH Box 39 #442. Probate Judge Office. Pickens, S.C. I Hugh Ivester of Pickens Dist. being of sound mind but feeble in body do make this my last will and testament. I give to my wife Eve all my stock of hogs, cattle, sheep, horses also all household and kitchen furniture, and the crop in the field, giving her full charge and control, for her use and benefit I give to my dtr. Rebecca ten dollars. I give to my dtr. Levina ten dollars. I give to my son Anderson ten dollars. I give to my son Solomon Young all that plantation or tract of land lying on Cane Creek, adj. land of John Fredricks and the tract I now live on containing 150 acres. I appoint my friend William S. Grisham executor. Dated 2 Oct. 1855. Wit: J. McNevill, Andrew Dickson, James Kistler. Signed: Hugh X Ivester. No probate date given.

JACK, JOHN   Box 51 #1193.   Probate Judge Office.   Abbeville, S.C. Admr. bond, We Mary Jack, Cahrles Caldwell, Samuel Feemster are bound unto Andrew Hamilton in the sum of $10,000.   Dated 2 June 1806. Inventory made 6 June 1806 by Wm. Lesly, James Wardlaw, Saml. Feemster. Sale made 30 Jan. 1807.   Buyers, Mary Jack, G. Bowie, A. Hamilton.

JACKSON, AARON   Deed Book 35 Page 350.   Probate Judge Office. Abbeville, S. C.   I John Pressly of Edgefield Dist. in consideration of $400 paid me in hand by Aaron Jackson of the same Dist. have granted, sold, bargained, and released all that plantation or tract of land containing 256 acres lying on the waters of Turkey Creek and Savannah River.   Bounded by land of Joseph Minter, John Blocker Junr., William Strom.   Dated 3 March 1818.   Wit: Lee Blackburn, Surles McCreless.   Signed: John X Presley.   Proved on oath of Surles McCreless before Jesse Blocker, J.Q. this 27 Sept. 1818.   Recorded 1 Feb. 1819.

JACKSON, ABEL   Box 51 Pack 1194.   Probate Judge Office.   Abbeville, S. C.   I Abel Jackson being very sick, but of sound judgment, mind and memory.   My negro boy Julius I bequeath to my son Matthew. My boy Booker to Hezekiah.   My girl Daphne to Robert.   My girl Hannah to my dtr. Patsey.   I desire all my property be expose to sale and the money keep until my children come of age, on interest, then an equal distribution be made between my children, with the exception that my youngest child Patsy receive $100 more than my sons.   I appoint Josiah Patterson and Robert Foster executor.   Dated 3 March 1806.   Wit: Robert Clark, John Moore, William Clark.   Signed: Abel X Jackson. Recorded 29 March 1806.   Inventory made 9 April 1806 by Saml. Patterson, Thos. Morrow, James McCarter.   Sale held 11-12 April 1806.   Buyers, James Boyd, Thomas Morrow, Phillip Leroy, Jno. Barksdale, Alexr. Houston, Jno. Logan, James Collier, Saml. Patterson, Thos. Crawford, Peter Gibert, Margaret Hemphill, Robert McComb, Wm. Gray, Artur Bowie, Rhoda Craig, Jno. Moore, Thos. Atwood, James Craig, David Boyse, Jas. Conner, Robt. Clark, Geo. Palmer, Margaret Bates.

JACKSON, ELIJAH   Deed Book 36, Page 280-281.   Probate Judge Office.   Abbeville, S. C.   I Elijah Jackson of Edgefield Dist. in consideration of $50 to me paid by James Jackson of the same Dist. have gra nted, bargained, sold and released a tract of land containing 50 acres.   Being part of a tract originally granted to George Gabriel Powel.   A corner in Log Creek another corner on M. Mims line, to J. Grices line.   Dated 19 March 1814.   Wit: Samuel Walker, Samuel Jackson, Signed: Elijah X Jackson.   Proven on oath of Samuel Jackson before Isaac Kirkland, J.Q. on the 9 April 1814.   Recorded 23 Nov. 1819.

JACKSON, JOHN   Box 40 Pack 1599.   Probate Judge Office.   Edgefield, S. C.   I John Jackson of 96 Dist. being of sound mind and memory.   I give to my son Henry Jackson five pounds sterling.   I give to my son Drewry Jackson five pounds sterling.   I lend to my dtr. Abigall Duncomb one negro girl named Dicey during her natural life, and after her death I give the said girl Dicey to Abigall Duncomb children viz: Elizabeth, James, Jennett, John, Wiley, ___ Duncomb.   I give to my son James Jackson one negro woman named Diner and one negro boy named Will.   I give to my dtr. Betsey Cimbrell one pound sterling. I lend to my dtr. Ann Miller one negro girl named Silva during her natural life and after her death, I give the said negro to Ann Miller children, viz: Rdmond Langford, Elizabeth Langford, and Nancy Miller. I give to my son John Jackson one negro man named Ted and one negro girl named Lile.   I give to my son Green Jackson one negro lad named Criffee and one girl named Sall, also the plantation whereon I now live, containing 100 acres, with all stock, cattle, hogs and household and kitchen furniture.   I will that my sons James, John and Green Jackson pay in equal proportion of the eleven pounds given to my three chn. in cash.   I appoint my sons James and Green Jackson my executor. Dated 26 Feb. 1787.   Wit: John Bostick, Thomas Furguson, Thomas Anderson.   Signed: John X Jackson.

JACKSON, MARTIN & ADALINE Box 73 Pack 2941. Probate Judge
Office. Edgefield, S. C. Guardianship bond, We James Tompkins, Saml.
S. Tompkins and W. H. Tompkins are bound unto the Ordinary of said Dist.
in the sum of $4,000. Dated this 6 Oct. 1856. The said James Tompkins
guardian of the persons of Martin V. and Adaline C. Jackson. To
provide them with meat, drink, washing, lodging and learning according
to their degree etc. To the Ordinary of Edgefield Dist. The petition
of Martin V. and Adeline C. Jackson sheweth that they are minors under
the age of twenty one, and are entitled to a small estate of their
late Mother Henriett Jackson decd. That they pray your Honor to
appoint Col. James Tompkins as their gdn. Signed: M. V. Jackson,
Adaline C. Jackson. I consent to accept the above appointment.
Signed: James Tompkins.

JACKSON, RALPH Box 50 Pack 1158. Probate Judge Office. Abbeville, S. C. 96 Dist. admnr. bond. We Ralph Jackson Junr., Thomas
Scales or Seales and Fredrick Jackson are bound unto John Thomas in
the sum of two thousand pounds sterling dated 20 Sept. 1783.

JACKSON, TABITHA   Deed Book 32, Page 420. Probate Judge Office.
Edgefield, S. C. I Ephraim Franklin of Edgefield Dist. in consideration of $100 to me paid by Tabitha Jackson of the same Dist. have
granted, bargained, sold and release a tract of land containing 400
acres, lying on Bridge Creek waters of South Edisto River, being part
of a tract of 575 acres granted Ephriam Franklin by patent dated 23
July 1793. On the old road from Monks to the head of Bridge Creek.
Dated 3 Jan. 1811. Wit: Lewis Holmes, Amos Holmes. Signed: Ephraim
X Franklin. Proved on oath of Lewis Holmes before Matthew Bettis, J.P.
this 31 Dec. 1811. Recorded 18 Jan. 1816.

JAMES, DAVID No ref. Clerk of Court Office. Pickens, S. C.
I W. L. Keith of Pickens Dist. in consideration of $15 to me paid by
David James of the same Dist. have granted, bargained, sold and
release all the tract of land whereon said David James now lives. The
same that was sold as property of Benj. Neighbors by W. D. Sloan then
Sheriff, adj. land of Isaac Durham, W. G. Newton. Lying on Mile Creek
containing 100 acres. Dated 28 Aug. 1840. Wit: P. Alexander,
Alexander Harris. Signed: W. L. Keith.

JAMES, GEORGE W. Box 117 #1. Probate Judge Office. Pickens,
S. C. On 23 Aug. 1889. J. E. Boggs the admnr. Dise[?] 2 March 1889.
Dianna James the widow. John W. James a brother is the plaintiff
against Dianna James, Amanda Kennemore and Julius E. Boggs (loose
papers).

JAMES, T. E.   Box 136 #4. Probate Judge Office. Pickens, S.C.
Est. admnr. 18 Jan. 1900 by L. P. James, G. W. Durham, D. C. Tomphiks[?]
who are bound unto J. B. Newberry, Ord. in the sum of $150. Dise
17 Nov. 1899 L. P. James a son.

JAMESON, CARROLL Box 75 #801. Probate Judge Office. Pickens,
S. C. I Carrol Jameson of Pickens Dist. being in good bodily health
and of sound mind and memory. I will that all my just debts and funeral
expenses shall be paid. I gi-e and bequeath to my beloved wife Amanda
Jameson the tract of land on which I live, containing 260 acres, also
two negro girls named Antinett about 12 yrs. of age and Adeline about
8 yrs. of age, to have the said property so long as she remain unmarried and my widow. Should she marry, I devise my property to be
sold and divided between my wife and my chn. as the law directs.
Should she not marry, she is to remain in full possession of all
property until death, then to be sold and proceeds to be divided
equally between my children (not named). The balance of my property
to be sold and proceeds applied to the payment of my just debts and
funeral charges. I appoint John Jameson, Benjamin F. Williams executors. Dated this 28 March 1862. Wit: Mary E. Bowen, Moses Hendricks,
R. E. Holcombe. Signed: Carrol Jameson. Proven 3 March 1864. Owned
260 acres on Georges Creek adj. land of James McAdams, Marthey Burdine
and others.

JAMESON, DORCAS In Equity, Box 2 #37. Clerk of Court Office.
Pickens, S. C. On 6 Jan. 1868 Dorcas P. Jameson, Mary A. Couch, William
Couch are bound unto Robt. A. Thompson Clk in Equity in the sum of
$4,200. On 13 Aug. 1866 Dorcas P. Jameson gdn. of Mary J. Jameson,
Wm. C. Jameson, Margaret A. Jameson minors over 14 yrs. Wm. M.
Jameson decd. their father. Dorcas P. Jameson their mother.

JAMESON, "MINORS" Box 8 #126. Probate Judge Office. Pickens,
S. C. On 15 Nov. 1869 Amanda M. McAdams, James Orr, John O. Davis
are bound unto I. H. Philpot, Ord. in the sum of $4,000. Amanda M.
McAdams gdn. of Thomas O. Jameson, Sarah A. R. Jameson, John C.
Jameson minors under 21 yrs. Amanda M. McAdams their mother. Entitled
to shares of est. of Carrol Jameson decd. In Oct. 1877 Sarah A. R. had
married a Orr.

JAMESON, REBECCA Box 25 #293. Probate Judge Office. Pickens,
S. C. Est. admnr. 3 Nov. 1851 by Wm. M. Jameson, Joshua Jameson, John
Jameson, Thomas H. Bowen who are bound unto Wm. D. Steele, Ord. in the
sum of $5,000. Piad 10 Feb. 1854 Wm. H. Perry and wife Frances $42.03.
Paid 13 Jan. Madison Jameson $42.03. Wilkerson Jameson $42.03.
Carrol Jameson $42.03. John Jameson $42.03. McElroy Jameson $42.03.
Louisa J. Jameson $42.03. Wesley Jameson $42.03.

JAMESON, WILLIAM Box 22 #269. Probate Judge Office. Pickens,
S. C. Est. admnr. 6 May 1850 by Wm. M. Jameson, Joshua Jameson, W. L.
Keith, P. Alexander are bound unto Wm. D. Steele, Ord. in the sum of
$10,000. Settment. Louisa, Carrol, William, Wilkenson, Madison,
Joshua, John, Wesley Jameson, Wm. Perry each recd. $285. Paid
McElroy Jameson $258.03. Paid 18 Jan. 1853 Wm. H. Perry and wife
Frances $267.76.

JAMESON, WILLIAM In Equity #39. Clerk of Court Office. Pickens,
S. C. In Equity, To the Honr. the Chancellors: Your orator William
M. Jameson and Joshua Jameson that William Jameson of Pickens Dist.
departed this life intestate on the 4 April 1850. Possessed of considerable real estate consisting of five tracts, viz. The home tract
on Georges Creek waters of Saluda River containing 768 acres. The
Singleton tract on Georges Creek, containing 146 acres. The Bowen
tract on Georges Creek, containing 15 acres, the cedar Rock tract
on head waters of George Creek, containing 662 acres. The medlock tract
lying on 12 Mile River, containing 221 1/2 acres. The Barnett tract
on Georges Creek containing 50 acres. Said lands are subject to
division amongst Rebecca Jameson the widow of the decd. and ten chn.
to wit, Frances the wife of William H. Perry, Madison Jamison,
Wilkinson Jameson, John Jameson, your orator William Jameson, Wesley
Jameson, Your orator Joshua Jameson, McElroy Jameson, Louisa J. Jamison
and Carrol Jameson a minor the age of 14 yrs. to wit twenty yrs. old.
Your orator sheweth that P. B. Jameson one of the heirs of William
Jameson decd. departed this life in 1846 four years before his father,
leaving no heirs, save his mother and brothers and sisters, having
never intermarried. The lands cannot be divided without manifest
injury to some of the parties. Filed 13 Nov. 1850.

JAMESON, WILLIAM Pack 124. Clerk of Court Office. Pickens,
S. C. I William Jameson of Pickens Dist. in consideration of $28 to
me paid by Josiah Trotter of the same Dist. have granted, sold, bargained and released a tract of land containing 9 1/2 acres, adj.
Trotters land on the East, and Wm. Jameson on the East. Dated 23 June
1849. Wit: B. J. Williams, Carrel Jameson. Signed: William
Jameson. Proved on oath of B. J. Williams before L. Hendricks M.P.D.
on the 8 Aug. 1850.

JAMESON, WILLIAM M. Box 78 #834. Probate Judge Office. Pickens,
S. C. Est. admnr. 30 Sept. 1864 by Dorcas P. Jameson, Wm. Couch,
Richard Lendhart who are bound unto W. E. Holcombe, Ord. in the sum
of $25,000. Inventory made by Moses Hendricks, John Jemson, Benjamin
F. Williams, Joshua Jameson.

JARVIS, DRUSCILLA Box 14 #185. Probate Judge Office. Pickens,
S. C. Est. admnr. 2 March 1846 by Miles M. Norton, J. B. E. Carodine
who are bound unto Wm. D. Steele, Ord. in the sum of $150 on 17 March
1846 cash on hand at her death being bal. of pension collected for her
$43.62. Paid 1 Sept. 1846 Ben. Jarvis acct. $4.62 1/2. Paid 29 Mar.
1847 Levi Brewers share $1.77 1/2. Paid Isaac Baldwin his share
$1.77 1/2. Paid 24 Feb. 1848 Mary Jarvis her share $1.77 1/2. On 26
Nov. 1846 Isaac Baldwin and Drusillah Baldwin recd. share.

JARVIS, ELISHA Deed Book A, Page 65. Probate Judge Office.
Pickens, S. C. Pickens Dist. To the Honr. Wm. D. Steele, Ord. The
petition of William H. Coxe sheweth that he is entitled to one third
of the real estate of Elisha Jarvis decd. as assignee of Drucilla
Jarvis widow, and two sixth of the balance as assignee of Benjamin
Jarvis and Mary S. Jarvis. Therefore your petitioner request that the
land be sold for a division amongest the heirs. Filed 17 June 1845.
Signed: Wm. H. Cox. Wm. H. Cox assignes of Drucilla Jarvis widow,
Benjamin Jarvis and Mary S. Jarvis. Applicants, vs Isaac Baldwin in
right of wife Drucilla, heirs of Levi Brewer, John Jarvis and William
Jarvis. The two last named heirs are without the limits of this State.
They are to appear within three months on their consent. Dated 30
June 1845.

JAY, WILLIAM Box 51 Pack 1200. Probate Judge Office. Abbeville,
S. C. Admnr. bond dated 27 Oct. 1829. We Wade S. Cotgran, Lewis S.
Simmons and John Hearst Junr. are bound unto Moses Taggart Ord. in the
sum of $1400. Cit. published at Damascus Meeting House. Inventory made
11 Nov. 1829 by Saml. Caldwell, Lewis S. Simmons and Thomas Harris.

JEANES, ELSEA Pack 439 #18. Clerk of Court Office. Pickens,
S. C. Pickens Dist. Be it remembered that on 31 Oct. 1843 Moses
Terrell, Thomas Fitzgerald and Jesse Jenkins appeared before me Clk.
of Court, acknowledge themselves to owe jointly $600 to be levied on
the if [?] Moses Terrell fail in the condition hereafter written.
Whereas Elsea Jeanes a single woman of Pickens Dist. in the month of
Jan. 1842 was delivered of a male child and hath on her oath charged
Moses Terrell with being the father. Whereof the said Moses Terrell
has this day come forward and entered into recognizance as the law
directs. Now the said Moses Terrell shall pay the sum of $25 annually
for the maintainance of said child from the day of birth until it shall
attain the age of twelve years old. Signed: Moses Terrell, Thos.
Fitzgerald, Jesse Jenkins.

JENKINS, ALVIN Box 85 #904. Probate Judge Office. Pickens, S.C.
Est. admnr. 12 Jan. 1866 by Robert A. Thompson C.E.P.D. bound unto
W. E. Holcombe, Ord. in the sum of $200. Jesse Jenkins, A. A. Hunni-
cutt, W. P. McCall bought at sale.

JENKINS, ANDREW Box 67 #720. Probate Judge Office. Pickens,
S. C. I Andrew Jenkins of Pickens Dist. At this time being under some
bodily afflictions but of perfect sound mind and memory. I give to
my beloved wife Elizabeth Ann Jenkins my entire estate, consisting of
my lands, negroes, stock of all kind, household furniture, notes at
interest and any property I may die with. I desire my wife to have
the right at any time she may think proper to trade away any of the
property she may think fit. I appoint E. P. Varner with my wife
Elizabeth Ann Jenkins as executor and executrix. Dated 5 Sept. 1862.
Wit: John S. Dickson, Wm. B. Land, E. P. Varner. Signed: Andrew
Jenkins. Proven 15 Dec. 1862.

JENKINS, ANN Box 35 Pack 1245. Probate Judge Office. Camden,
S. C. Est. admnr. 25 Nov. 1835 by Benjamin Williams, Elizabeth Farly,
Wiley Jenkins, James T. Jenkins, John Fraser who are bound unto the
Ordinary in the sum of six thousand dollars. Expend, 25 Nov. 1833
amount due by John Jenkins estate to Anne Jenkins $2,448.50.

JENKINS, CLAYTON Box 85 #905. Probate Judge Office. Pickens,
S. C. On 11 Dec. 1857 owned 100 acres on Toxaway Creek joining lands
of R. A. Gilmer, Isaac Standridge and others. Owned 75 acres on waters

Jenkins, Clayton - Continued. of Colonal Fork on the road leading
from Jarretts Bridge to Pickens C.H. joining lands of Dr. Earle,
Thomas Jones and others. Heirs, widow, Elizabeth Jenkins, John M.
Jenkins, Mary Jane Jenkins, Geo. M. Jenkins, James G. Jenkins, Asa A.
Jenkins, Uriah Jenkins all minors. On 20 Oct. 1857 Thos. Smith of
Walton Co., Ga. appointed Grafton Jenkins of Pickens Dist., S. C. his
atty. to receive his share of est. of Rebecca Simpson decd. late of
Pickens Dist. which is now in the hands of the admnr. as part of said
est. coming to Wm. Edwards as next of kin to said Rebecca Simpson decd.

JENKINS, DORATHEA Box 35 #403. Probate Judge Office, Pickens,
S. C. Est. admnr. 1 June 1855 by Jesse Jenkins, Alexr. Bryce, B. F.
Reeder who are bound unto W. J. Parson, Ord. in the sum of $600.
To W. J. Parson, Ordinary. The undersigned one of the heirs at law of
Frances Jenkins late of this Dist. Petition your Court to sell or
divide the real estate lying on Choestoe Creek waters of Tugaloo
River. Adj. land of Richard Dean, Samuel Varner, containing 240 acres,
heirs, Synthe wife of Richard Dean, Thomas Jenkins, William Jenkins,
Jesse Jenkins, Eliza the wife of James N. Dean, Heirs of John N.
Jenkins, Lowizy C. Jenkins, Alvin Jenkins, Archibald E. Jenkins, Nancy
Jenkins. Filed 3 Aug. 1855. Signed: Jesse Jenkins (on this paper
her name is written Frances instead of Doreathea or Dorothy.)

JENKINS, FRANCES Book 2, Page 42 (rel. est.) Clerk of Court
Office. Pickens, S. C. On 28 Nov. 1859. Owned 122 acres on waters
of Cane Creek waters of Little River adj. land of W.H. Stribling, T. J.
Hall and others. Heirs of decd. viz. heirs of Abner Jenkins decd.
number and names unknown, one of the heirs of Anderson Jenkins decd.
Thos. Jenkins, ___ Stewart and wife Eliza out of the State,
Zachariah Hall and wife Ruth, Wm. Hall and wife Sarah, Rufus Ward and
wife Belinda, Henry Myer and wife Nancy, heirs of Anderson Jenkins viz,
David or Daniel Hall and wife Caroline, Mary Jenkins out of State.
Signed: James Jenkins a heir.

JENKINS, JOHN T. Box 35 #1251. Probate Judge Office. Camden,
S. C. Est. admnr. 15 March 1847 by Elias L. Fraser, Ch. L. Dye and
Daniel D. Perry who are bound unto the Ordinary in the sum of two
thousand dollars. John T. Jenkins died in 1843 but his estate wasn't
admnr. until 1847. He was late of the Isle of Wright Co., Va. On
26 March 1849 Thomas R. Jenkins of the Isle of Wright Co., Va. men-
tioned as admnr. of his brother estate John T. Jenkins, decd. (Note,
In this package there was only one administration bond.) John T.
Jenkins left 3 distributees viz. Mary Ann Parkinson, Willie Jenkins,
Exum Jenkins.

JENKINS, JOHN Box 35 Pack 1248. Probate Judge Office. Camden,
S. C. Est. admnr. 24 March 1830 by Benjamin Williams, John Williams,
Elias L. Fraser who are bound unto the Ordinary in the sum of ten
thousand dollars. This estate was first admnr. 17 May 1825 by Ann
Jenkins, Elizabeth Farley, John Fraser who are bound unto the Ordinary
in the sum of 30 thousand dollars. Citation was read at Flat Rock
Church. Legatees, William M. Brett and wife Mary Ann, Wiley Jenkins,
James T. Jenkins, Margaret Jenkins, John Jenkins, Exum Jenkins, Thomas
R. Jenkins, Joseph Jenkins. On 9 Dec. 1840 Exum Jenkins, James T.
Jenkins, William Brett and wife Mary Ann were mentioned as being of
Tallubusha Co., Miss. Mary Ann Jenkins was a sister to Joseph and a
heir at law of John Jenkins.

JENKINS, JOSEPH Box 35 Pack 1250. Probate Judge Office.
Camden, S. C. Est. admnr. 10 Jan. 1850 by J.B. F. Boone, E. L. Fraser
who are bound unto the Ordinary in the sum of two thousand dollars.
Joseph Jenkins was a minor and was late of Yellowbusha Co., Miss. He
died in Miss. He had an interest in an Estate here, but the name of
estate not given.

JENKINS, JOSEPH A citizen Grant. Book A, Page 11. 96 Dist.
Joseph Jenkins as a citizen 340 acres situate and lying on both sides
of the South fork of Saluda River bounding NW on land of William
Reighley and all others sides vacant when surveyed by Bennett Crafton

Jenkins, Joseph - Continued. D.S. as appears by his certificate,
dated 22 May 1784.. with the form and marks as pr. platt. Recorded
27 May 1784. Pr. Robert Anderson C.L. 11...

JENKINS, JOSEPH B. Box 35 Pack 1249. Probate Judge Office.
Camden, S. C. Est. admnr. 22 Feb. 1845 by Thomas R. Jenkins, John B.
Tillman and G. W. Pope who are bound unto the Ordinary in the sum of
$600. Joseph B. Jenkins died in 1839. Was late of Yalobusha County,
Miss. and formerly of Kershaw Dist.

JENKINS, RICHARD Box 35 Pack 1252. Probate Judge Office.
Camden, S. C. Est. admnr. 10 Sept. 1782 by John Mobberly, William
Mobberly and Henry Rogers who are bound unto the Ordinary of Kershaw
Dist. in the sum of 14 thousand pounds. Richard Jenkins was a planter
of Camden Dist. Admnr. was first granted to his widow Catharine Jenkins
who later intermarried with James Matthew. She died without completing
said admnr. of her husband estate. This was dated 14 Aug. 1782.

JENKINS, REBECCA Box 2 #51. Probate Judge Office. Pickens, S.C.
Est. admnr. 23 March 1855 by Grafton Jenkins, Geo. W. Phillips who
are bound unto W. J. Parson, Ord. in the sum of $500. Grafton Jenkins
gdn. of Rebecca S. Jenkins minor under 21 yrs. dtr. of Grafton Jenkins.

JENKINS, THOMAS WILLIAM Box 35 Pack 1253. Probate Judge Office.
Camden, S. C. Saint Marks Parish the 1 Aug. 1786, I Thomas William
Jenkins, the son of William Jenkins, maltster and store keeper of the
town of Usk in the County of Monmouth South Wales and nephew to Walter
Jenkins Esq. High sheriff for the city of Bristol in England, being
of perfect mind and memory. I give to my dtr. Susannah the wife of
James Corbet, one negro named Sue, now in their possession. I give to
my good friend Richard Richardson, 40 pounds, whom I appoint with my
dtr. Elizabeth Jenkins executors and executrix of this my last will.
The remainder of my est. to be divided amongst my other chn. Viz;
Mary Jenkins (now in London), Ann Jenkins, Elizabeth Jenkins, Sarah
Jenkins, Caroline Jenkins. I desire my executors to pay to each of my
dtrs. their share anytime they shall call or desire it, after one year
of my decease. Wit: Richard Newman, Benny Corbett, Thomas Richard
Davis. Signed Thos. Wm. Jenkins. Recorded date not given.

JENNINGS, CALEB Box 51 Pack 1198. Probate Judge Office. Abbeville, S. C. I Caleb Jennings of Abbeville Dist. Being in a moderate
state of health and my mental powers and mind in moderate exercise and
with my own hand have indited what is here wrote. I leave the plantation with house furniture and stock, tools whereon I now live except
one feather bed, one cow and calf, one sow and pigs which I leave to my
son Robert T. Jennings to my beloved wife Mary Jennings during her
life if she survives me. I give to my dtr. Catharine Medlin a part of
a tract of land that I bought of Peter Moragne that he sold of the
estate of John Eymore he acting as executor for his father for said
estate. (description given) also fifteen dollars to be paid out of
my est. after her mother decd. I give to my son John Jennings apart
of the land he now lives on adj. the land I have given to my dtr.
Catharine Medlin on the same side of the road from Martin Mill to the
cross roads, formerly known as the Delanah Carrell lane. The balance
of my land of both tracts I give to my son Robert after his mother
decease. I appoint my wife and two sons executors. Dated 13 Aug. 1816.
No witness given. Signed: Caleb Jennings. Proven 2 Oct. 1816.
Inventory made 30 Oct. 1816 by Jno. L. Gibert, Joseph Richardson,
Michael Medlin.

JENNINGS, THOMAS Box 15 Pack 545. Probate Judge Office.
Edgefield, S. C. I Thomas Jennings of Edgefield Dist. being very weak
in body, but of sound mind and memory. I give to my wife Lucy Jennings
to get all my distributee share of the real and personal estate of
Landon Hicks, which I have not received. I give to my chn. or any
my wife may have by me, namely Henry Jennings, Atlicus Jennings, and
Huldah Jennings, one negro boy named John now in my possession which
has been given to my chn. by father Joseph Jennings, each to share and
share alike. The residue of my estate be keep for the use, benefit,

Jennings, Thomas - Continued. support and education of my chn. and wife during widowhood or life. At her death or marriage the said portion to be divided amongst all my lawful chn. My negro John not subject to any other division. I desire my estate be divided when my eldest son Henry arrives at full age, if he should die, then when my son Atlicus arrives at full age, or when my dtr. Huldah marry or become 21 yrs. of age. I appoint my brother Robert Jennings executor. Dated 19 March 1835. Wit: James Tomkins, Drury Morgan, Elizabeth Searles. Signed: Thoms. Jennings. Proved on oath of James Tomkins before J. Richardson, Ord. Dated 8 April 1835.

JETER, WILLIAM Pack 349 A & B. Clerk of Court Office. Abbeville, S. C. I William Jeter of Edgefield Dist. do make this my last will and testament. I give to my dtr. Becky Glover a negro woman, Esther and her chn. who has long been in her possession, I also give her five shillings, which is all she to have of my est. To my executors herein after named, I give a negro girl named Sylva and her issue in trust for the sole and separate use of my grand daughter Charlotte Elvira Glover (in exclusion of any right or control on the part of any husband she may have) to be equally divided between any chn. she may have, if she has none. I give said Sylva and her issue to the chn. or grand children of my late dtr. Charlotte Phillips that may be alive. To my dtr. Mary P. Jeter so long as she remains unmarried, I give the use of my two tracts of land adj. Henry Waldmin, Edmond Martin and the estate of George Martin, and negroes Abram, Harper, Liberty, Phebe, and her child Melinda and any other child that Phebe may have. Also household furniture and stocks. In case of the marriage, the said negroes shall be retained by my executors for the sole use of my dtr. during her natural life, at her death to be equally divided amongst such children or grand children as she may have. I give to my dtr. Sally Martin negroes Vina and her chn. Jefferson, Jacob, Tom and Esther also any other child she may have, with Balock or Peter which she may choose. I give to my son John L. Jeter, negro Ben now in his possession and Dave. Also one fifth part of my est. both real and personal property. To my executors I give negroes Rachel and her chn. Sylva, Ben and Hannah as well as other child she may have, also Jacob and Joe commonly called Joe Dart to be held in trust for the sole use of my dtr. Patsey A. Williams during her life and at death to be divided among her chn. and grand chn. I direct my executor to raise $1500 within one year and put same on interest, and pay two thirds of the principal and interest to my grand son Charles Elbert Jeter when he arrives at the age of twenty one, and the other third to my grand dtr. Lucy L. Peter when she is twenty one or marry. The rest and residue of my estate be put in five shares, one share for my decd. dtr. Charlotte Phillips children, one share to my son John L. Jeter. The other three shares be keep for the use of my three dtrs. I appoint Edmond Martin, William W. Williams my executors. Dated 31 July 1818. Wit: Henry Lake, John Doby, David Doby. Signed: W. Jeter. On 29 Jan. 1856. Mary P. Mantz signed a contract with Samuel Maxwell as she overseer and manager of her farm for the sum of $180 per year.

JOHNS, EMMA Box 50 #547. Probate Judge Office. Pickens, S.C. Est. admnr. 4 July 1859 by James Johns, Leonard Towers, F. N. Garvin who are bound unto W. J. Parson, Ord. in the sum of $200. Paid 26 Feb. 1861 Martha Johns, Eunica Addis, Aaron Eubanks and wife, W. P. Cole and wife, James O. Sanders guardian, John Johns, L. B. Stone and wife, James F. Sanders and wife, James Johns each recd. in full $6.26.

JOHNS, HENRY Box 41 #461. Probate Judge Office. Pickens, S. C. Est. admnr. 13 Oct. 1856 by James Johns, Alexander Bryce, John Hardin are bound unto W. J. Parson, Ord. in the sum of $2,000. Left a widow and nine heirs. Paid 6 June 1859 the widow her share $439.70. Paid Emma Johns $97.62. Paid Aaron Eubands and wife Harriet $97.62. Paid Samuel Addis and wife Eunice $97.62. Paid L. B. Stone and wife Mary by power of Atty. $97.62. Paid James F. Sanders and wife Dicy $97.62. Paid John Johns $97.62. Paid James Sanders gdn. for his wife's chn. $97.62.

JOHNS, HENRY In Equity #14. Clerk of Court Office. Pickens,
S. C. Petition for division, To the Honr. the Chancellors; Your
oratrix Martha Johns of Pickens Dist. that her husband Henry Johns late
of this Dist. departed this life intestate in Nov. 1855. Possessed at
time of his death with considerable real estate, one tract on Little
Beaverdam Creek waters of Tugaloo River, containing 184 acres, adj.
land of Robert A. Maxwell, A. F. Hutchins and others. That the said
real estate is subject to distribution amongst your oratrix and eight
chn. and the heirs of another deceased child to wit, James Johns;
Eunice the wife of Samuel Addis, Emily Johns, Harriet the wife of
Aaron Eubanks, Anna wife of Wiley Cole, heirs of Jemima Sanders decd.
Viz, Henry, Anna, Elias, Reese and John Sanders all minors. All
resides in Pickens Dist. except John Johns resides in Texas, James
Anders and wife Dicey resides in Alabama, Berry or Benjamin Stone and
wife Mary resides in Georgia. Your oratrix prays that a writ of partition may be issued out of this Honr. Court. Filed 15 Nov. 1856. John
Johns of ___ County, Texas appointed James Johns his attorney to
receive and receipt all money from his father estate, dated 21 Dec.
1857. Wit: James E. Morriss, W. L. Wade. Signed: John Johns. The
power of attorney was made from Kaufman County, Texas as sworn to by
J. T. Rayel, J.P. Mary Stone and L. B. Stone made their power of attorney from Cherokee County, Georgia, also appointed James Johns their
attorney to receive and receipt any money from her father estate.
Dated 11 April 1859. Wit: John B. Brock, Willia H. Foster. Signed:
L. B. Stone and Mary Stone. Sworn to by John B. Brock before Henry
Tedder, J.P. dated 11 April 1859. James Sanders and wife Dicey made
a power of attorney from Angeline County, Texas. They appointed James
Johns as their attorney to receive and receipt any money from her
father estate. Dated 11 April 1859. Wit: James R. Arnold, W. W.
Banet. Signed: James F. Sanders and Dicy Sanders.

JOHNSON, BENJAMIN Box 51 Pack 1182. Probate Judge Office.
Abbeville, S. C. Admnr. bond, We George Lomax, James S. Wilson, Thomas
J. Douglass are bound unto Moses Taggart, Ord. in the sum of $15,000.
Dated 19 Dec. 1836. Cit. Pub. at Bulow Church. Inventory made 4 Jan.
1837. Sale held 5-6 Jan. 1837. Buyers, Elizabeth Johnson, Jno. D.
Adams, Larkin Butler, Harrison Monday, Charles Stewart, Archd. Holt,
Thos. Fortiscue, Jno. Roberson, Thos. Strawhorn, Wm. Talbert, Thos. J.
Douglass, Wm. J. Paul, Oliver Grealey, Wm. Smith, Talliver Johnson,
Jno. White, Robert McWilliams, H. B. Campbell, David Keller, Thos. Burt,
Wm. Adams, Nathl. Cobb, Nathl. Rowland, Henry Norrell, P. D. Klugh,
Jno. Campbell, Archd. Arnold, Wm. Calvert, Tidence Johnson, Francis
Devlin, Jas. Martin, Jackson Paul, Jno. Burnet, Robt. C. Wilson, Malen
Morgan, Nicholas Miller, Silas Pace, G. Lomax. Elizabeth Johnson was
the widow. Expend. paid 1838 Amy Johnson $10.00. Paid Rachel Johnson
$10.00. Paid Tidence Johnson $400.00. Paid W. Smith for Benjamin
Johnson $23.31.

JOHNSON, BENJAMIN Box 50 Pack 1175. Probate Judge Office.
Abbeville, S. C. Admnr. bond, We Elizabeth Johnson, Abbeville Dist.
Henry G. Johnson, Clement T. Latimer and Richard Gaines are bound unto
Talo. Livingston, Ord. in the sum of five thousand dollars. Dated 19
Oct. 1814. Inventory made 23 Nov. 1814 by Edward McCrawn, C. T.
Latimer, Rich. Gaines. Sale held 23 Nov. 1814. Buyers, Elizabeth
Johnson, Daniel Cook, Arch Camron, Moses Myres, Thos. Norwood, Daniel
Gent, Edward Ware, Stephen Mitchel, Lankfork Hughes, Micahjah Jones,
Geo. Freeman, Reuben Nash, Henry Delh, Robt. V. Posey, Joseph Cooper,
Wm. Long, Wm. Gaines, Micajah Jones, Jordon Mosely, Henry Johnson,
Clement T. Latimer, John Gray, Robt. Bagwell, Thos. Sprewell, Abner
Nash.

JOHNSON, FRANCES ANN ELIZABETH Box 52 Pack 1214. Probate Judge
Office. Abbeville, S. C. Guardianship bond. We William C. Cozby,
Francis B. Clinkscales, and Newton Davis are bound to Moses Taggart,
Ord. in the sum of two thousand dollars. Dated 13 Nov. 1839. She a
minor under 21 yrs. Recd. 13 Nov. 1839 $1,009.91. from Francis B.
Clinkscales admnr. of the est. of John Johnson decd.

JOHNSON, GABRIEL WALKER #200. In Equity. Clerk of Court Office. Abbeville, S. C. In Equity, Abbeville Dist. To the Honr. the Chancellors; the petition of Gabriel Walker Johnson sheweth that he is a son of James Johnson decd. and entitled under his will to a legacy of about $3500, which is in the hands of G. M. Mattison and A. H. Magee exors. That your petitioner is over the age of 14 yrs. But is unable on account of his age to manage or receive his legacy. He therefore prays that his uncle Gabriel M. Mattison be appointed the gdn. of his person and estate. I Julia Johnson do consent and it is my desire that my brother G. M. Mattison be appointed guardian for my son Gabriel Walter Johnson. Dated 15 June 1859. Signed: Julia X Johnson.

JOHNSON, ISAIAH Box 52 Pack 1215. Probate Judge Office. Abbeville, S. C. I Isaiah Johnson of Abbeville Dist. planter tho feeble in body yet of sound discriminating mind and judgment. I will that my just debts be paid, for this I set aside my crop as can be spared, also my negro boy Joe which I value at $400, I allow my son Leroi T. Johnson to take said boy at this price with all notes to pay my debts, should any remain, it to be divided between my son Leroi T., and dtrs. Jane, Caroline, Amanda and Martha Johnson. I give to my son Isreal P. Johnson my negro boy George and girl Silvey. I give to my son Robert D. Johnson my negro woman Pat and boy Antony. I give to my dtr. Frances Bowie my negro girls Rachel and Lucy. I give to my son Henry O. Johnson my negro Richard. I give to my son Leroi T. Johnson my negro girl Mary and boy Henry. I give to my dtrs. Jane, Caroline, Amanda, and Martha Johnson my negro man Jim, boy Lous, boy Franklin, woman Lucinda also my plantation and tools waggon, all stock, etc. I appoint my son Leroi T. Johnson executor. Dated 17 Aug. 1841. Wit: Nathaniel Moore, George A. Ruff, John Link. Signed: Isiah Johnson. Proved 24 Sept. 1844. Inventory made 11 Dec. 1844 by Christian Barnes, J. Pressly, John Link. Sale held 12 Dec. 1844, Buyers Leroy Johnson, Davis Johnson, Chas. Bowie, Walter Barnes, Wm. Henderson, Andw. Gilespy, G. C. Bowers, C. V. Barnes, Henry Simpson, Jno. Campbell, S. Reid, W. M. Calaham, James H. Cobb.

JOHNSON, ISAAC SENR. Box 51 Pack 1192. Probate Judge Office. Abbeville, S. C. Admr. bond, Abbeville Dist. We Jacob M. Johnson, Ebenezer Hammond and Moses Jacobs are bound unto Moses Taggart, Ord. in the sum of five hundred dollars. Dated 11 Jan. 1830. Citation published at Willington Church. Also read at a public congregation at Plum Branch.

JOHNSON, JAMES Box 52 Pack 1213. Probate Judge Office. Abbeville, S. C. Abbeville Dist. Guardianship bond. We Grigsby Appleton, Joel Smith, William Buchanan are bound to Moses Taggart, Ord. in the sum of two thousand dollars. Dated 2 Nov. 1840. Whereas Grigsby Appleton made gdn. of James Johnson a minor under 21 yrs.

JOHNSON, JAMES Pack 281. Clerk of Court Office. Abbeville, S.C. Abbeville Dist. To the Honr. the Chancellors: The petition of Samuel V. Johnson sheweth that James Johnson the father of your petitioner died last year (1858) leaving a will, after some specific bequeaths he directed his executors to sell the residue of his est. and divide the proceeds among six of his chn. Your petitioner is one. The will make the following provisions. The portion falling to my son Samuel V. Johnson is under the control of Abner H. Magee, who I appoint trustee for that purpose to manage the same for the family during his natural life, and after his death be divided between his children. Filed 11 June 1859.

JOHNSON, JOHN Box 51 Pack 1191. Probate Judge Office. Abbeville, S. C. Admnr. bond 96 Dist. We Thomas Johnson, Joseph Kelso, James McElwayne are bound to John Thomas in the sum of % hundred pounds. Dated 28 June 1786. Inventory made 16 Aug. 1786 by Wm. Hamilton, Edward Finch, Joseph Hamton.

JOHNSON, JOHN Box 51 Pack 1190. Probate Judge Office. Abbeville, S. C. Admnr. bond, 96 Dist. We Sarah Johnson, Samuel Otterson, Daniel Duff and Chandler Aubry are bound to John Ewing Calhoun in the sum of

Johnson, John - Continued. 14 thousand pounds. Dated 2 Dec. 1782.
Sarah Johnson and Samuel Otterson applied for letter of admnr. as next
of kin. John Johnson was to Tyger River in 96 Dist. Inventory made
3 Jan. 1783 by Wm. Murray, Thos. Gordon, Thos. Brandon.

JOHNSON, MARGARET M. Box 139 #6. Probate Judge Office. Pickens,
S. C. I Margaret Matilda Johnson of Pickens Dist. being of sound mind
and memory. First I will my just debts and funeral expenses be paid.
I give the rest and residue of my estate to my sister Sarah A. Johnson
to have and hold during her natural life. After her decease I give to
my brother Benjamin J. Johnson and sister Mary J. Barr each one
dollar, to be paid within three months after her death. I give to my
brothers William F. and Thomas G. Johnson each the sum of $125.00
to be paid three months after my sister death. The rest and remainder
of my est. both real and personal to my three nephews and two nieces
(heirs of my brother Thomas G. Johnson) viz; William R., Joseph D.,
and Benjamin H. Johnson, Hattie M. and Margaret F. Johnson. I appoint
my brothers William F. and Thomas G. Johnson executors. Dated 24 Feb.
(torn). Wit: M. E. Garvin, Mattie Sheriff, B. D. Garvin. Signed:
Margaret Matilda Johnson. Filed 1 May 1902.

JOHNSON, ROBERT Pack 100. In Equity. Clerk of Court Office.
Pickens, S. C. Robert Johnson states that in the year 1818 he was
residing in Ireland when he received a letter from his brother Thomas
Johnson, informing him that he had purchased a tract of land in upper
S.C. and requesting him to come and take possession. He decided to
accept the same and landed with his family in Charleston on 3 Dec.
1818. Robert was to pay for the land by allowing his son Robert Jr. to
work for his brother Thomas at a sum of $8 per month. The land was in
Pendleton Dist. When he arrived on said land was worn out and inade-
quate to support his family. A tract joining his land belonging to
Cunningham, if he could get both tracts he could make a go of it. He
built a log house and cleared about 20 acres, by the year 1821 had
paid his brother $1,100. Having never received a deed from his brother.
He assumed the land was his. In the year 1833 the said land was sold
by the sheriff as the proerty of Thomas Johnson and was purchased by
Col. Robert Anderson. Your petitioner will ever pray. Filed 15 March
1833.

JOHNSON, SAMUEL W. Box 52 Pack 1212. Probate Judge Office.
Abbeville, S. C. Abbeville Dist. To David Lesly Ord. The petition
of David F. Cleckly sheweth that Samuel W. Johnson late, departed this
life intestate as it is said leaving an estate in personality. That
your petitioner is a brother in law of the decase and that the said
decease has but one brother who is under age and that the father and
widow of the decease has declined administration and requested your
Petitioner to take the same. Signed: D. F. Cleckley. Settl. made
13 Jan. 1844. Present D. F. Cleckley admnr. and J. L. Lesly who
intermarried with the widow. No other names given. (No date shown on
the petition, after the ref. the date 1841 is shown.)

JOHNSON, URLSEY Pack 491. Clerk of Court Office. Abbeville,
S. C. Abbeville Dist. I Ursley Johnson inconsideration of $100 to
me paid by Isaav Busby of Abbeville Dist. have granted, sold, bargained
and released one tract of land containing 69 acres, lying on Johnsons
Creek and Savannah River. Adj. land of John Langered formerly belonging to John Oakley. Dated 6 Oct. 1809. Wit: Joseph Pratt, David
Patrick, Signed: Ursley X. Johnson. Proved on oath of Joseph Pratt
before Jos. Black, J.P. this 17 Oct. 1809.

JOHNSON, WILLIAM Book E-1, Page 1. Clerk of Court Office.
Pickens, S. C. I William Johnson of Pickens Dist. inconsideration of
$104, to me paid by James Hughes of the same state and Dist. Have
granted, bargained, sold and release all that plantation of land lying
and being on Boroughs Creek, waters of Keowee River. Originally
granted to Robert Grant, containing 208 acres. Adj. land of Thomas
Garvin, Daniel C. Monk and others. Dated 6 June 1843. Wit: John X
Howard before W. L. Keith, Clk. of Court this 21 June 1843. Recorded
the same date.

JOHNSON, WILLIAM #26. In Equity. Clerk of Court Office.
Pickens, S. C. I William Johnson, Temperance P. Pool and John Howard
all of Pickens Dist. in consideration of a dispute of the rights of
land situated in said Dist. on waters of Six Mile Creek it being the
same land whereon the above Wm. Johnson and Temperance P. Pool now
lives. That for the sake of peace and expense of going to law, we have
entered into an artical of agreement on a conditional line it beginning
on a stake corner near the foot of Six Mile Mountain running on a
strait line to the fork on the main Creek to Temperance P. Pool line.
Dated this 15 March 1844. Wit: R. Stewart Esq., Wm. J. Parson.
Signed: William X Johnson, Temperance P. X Pool, John X Howard and
Seth S. Pool. Proved on oath of Wm. J. Parson before Rt. Stewart,
M.P.D. this 15 March 1844.

JOHNSON, WILLIAM In Equity. Clerk of Court Office. Pickens,
S. C. I William Johnson of Pickens Dist. in consideration of fifty
dollars to me paid by John Howard, Miles Yancy, James Hughes, and John
Clayton of Pickens Dist. have granted, sold, bargain and released all
that tract of land lying on six mile creek and its branches, waters
of Keowee River. Adj. land of said, Johnson, Garvins, Garner Evans
and others. Originally granted to ___ Swift containing 500 acres.
Dated 20 June 1843. Wit: W. L. Keith, Watson Stewart. Signed:
William X Johnson. Proved on oath of Watson Stewart before W. L. Keith,
Clk. of Court. This 20 June 1843.

JOHNSTON, LUCINDA ELIZABETH Box 135 #6. Probate Judge Office.
Pickens, S. C. I Lucinda Elizabeth Johnston of Pickens Co. being of
sound mind and memory. All my just debts and funeral expenses shall be
fully paid. I give to my brother Benj. Jackson Johnson and my sister
Mary Jane Barr the sum of one dollar each to be paid one month after
my decease. I give to the rest and remainder of my est. both real
and personal to my two sisters, Sarah Ann and Margaret Matilda Johnston.
To have and hold during their natural life, then to be equally divided
between my two brothers William Frederick and Thomas Garvin Johnston.
I appoint my two brothers William Frederick and Thomas Garvin Johnston
my executors. Dated 30 Oct. 1899. Wit: D. B. Owens, M. E. Garvin,
B. D. Garvin. Signed: Lucinda Elizabeth Johnston. Filed 10 May 1900.

JOHNSTON, "MINORS" In Equity. Box 2 #50. Clerk of Court Office.
Pickens, S. C. On 2 Sept. 1856 Mary H. Johnston, Wm. H. Stribling,
Wm. H. Johnston, James T. Johnston are bound unto Robert A. Thompson
Clk. of Equity in the sum of $1200. 30 June 1856 Mary H. Johnston gdn.
of Elijah M. Johnston, Edward F. Johnston minors under 21 yrs. Also
gdn. of Saml. R. Johnston, Eliza J. Johnston minors under 21 yrs.
Mary H. Johnston gdn. of Joseph W. Johnston a minor under 14 yrs.
Son of Mary H. Johnston.

JOHNSTON, ROBERT Box 94 #978. Probate Judge Office. Pickens,
S. C. I Robert Johnston of Pickens Dist. I bequeath my estate both
real and personal unto my wife Mariah F. Johnston and my four dtrs.
viz, Lucinda E. Johnston, Mary J. Johnston, Sarah A. Johnston and
Margaret M. Johnston. My real estate being 360 acres, bounded by land
of Dr. S. W. Clayton, J. J. Garvin, Thos. G. Johnston, Air line R.R.,
B. J. Johnston. At the death of my wife then to be divided between
the four named dtrs. I give to my son Wm. F. Johnston one bed and
beding, one cow. I bequeath unto my sons B. J. and T. G. Johnston one
dollar each. I appoint B. F. Johnston and Wm. F. Johnston executors.
Dated 3 Feb. 1882. Wit: J. J. Garvin, B. D. Garvin (Benj.), Wm. H.
Perry. Signed: Robert Johnston. Filed 16 Aug. 1884.

JOHNSTON, SAMUEL Box 21 #260. Probate Judge Office. Pickens,
S. C. Est. admnr. 29 April 1850 by Wm. H. Stribling, J. A. Doyle,
David S. Stribling who are bound unto Wm. D. Steele, Ord. in the sum of
$6,000. Paid Mrs. Mary H. Johnson, gdn. for minors $58.12 1/2.

JOHNSTON, T. M. Box 128 #1. Probate Judge Office. Pickens,
S. C. I, T. M. Johnston of Pickens Dist. make this my last will. I
give and bequeath my estate and property both real and personal to my
wife Charlotte Louisa Johnston to have and hold all property during

Johnston, T. M. - Continued. her natural life then to my children. I appoint my wife Charlotte Louisa Johnston my executor. Dated 11 Nov. 1896. Wit: J. J. Heard, J. W. Johnston, John W. Thomas. Signed: T. M. Johnston. Filed 20 March 1897.

JOHNSTON, WILLIAM Box 22 #270. Probate Judge Office. Pickens, S. C. Est. admnr. 19 Aug. 1850 by Robert Stewart Esq. Isaac Durham are bound unto Wm. D. Steele, Ord. in the sum of $200. Widow mentioned, not named.

JOLLY, WILLIAM Box 11 #148. Probate Judge Office. Pickens, S. C. Est. admnr. 18 Mar. 1843 by Martin Harrison, Leonard Towers, E. P. Verner are bound unto James H. Dendy, Ord. in the sum of $500. Cit. Pub. at Bethel Church.

JOLLY, WILLIAM SENR. Box 3 #27. Probate Judge Office. Pickens, S. C. I William Jolly of Pickens Dist. being weak of body but of sound mind and memory. It is my will that after my death that all my property of every kind be sold at public sale. That credit of twelve months be given. That after all my just debts are paid the residue of the money be divided in the following manner. To my son James Jolly, his son, and son in law one seventh part to be equally divided between them. To my son Joseph Jolly widow one seventh part. To my dtr. Patsey Hunnicut to her son and dtr. one seventh part equally divided between them. To my son William Jolly one seventh part, deducting twenty five dollars which he owes me. To my son Jesse Jolly's child one seventh part, deducting from the said child part $100 which I gave to Elenor Land. To my son Mansey Jolly one seventh part. To my son John Jolly one seventh part. Having given my land to my son William Jolly and to my son John Jolly's son the above property consists of negroes and other goods and chattels. I appoint my son William Jolly executor. Dated 6 July 1829. Wit: John Verner, Richard Dean, Andrew Jenkins. Signed: W. Jolly. N.B. also I desire that Charles I. or J. Verner be an executor with my son William. Dated 6 May 1831. Proven in open Court by Richard Dean in Franklin County, Georgia. this 7 May 1832. Proved in Pickens Dist., S. C. on the 1 Aug. 1831, on oath of Andrew Jenkins, before J. H. Dendy, Ord. P.D. Paid 6 Jan. 1834 Birdwell Hill on power of Atty. from Willis Hunnicut $32.00. Paid 15 Jan. James Jolly on power of Atty. from Jane Jolly legatee $175.00. Paid 7 May 1832 cash for proving and recording the will at Carnsville, Ga. $5.75. Paid 26 Feb. 1833 to John Calhoun for Elijah Land legatee $21.00. Paid 16 Mar. to George Kennedy legatee $60.00.

JOLLY, WILLIAM SENR. Book 1 Page 47. Real Estate. Clerk of Court Office. Pickens, S. C. On 3 April 1843 owned 200 acres on Choestoe Creek waters of Tugaloo River. Adj. land of Richard Dean, Nancy Perry, Josiah F. Perry, Martin Harrison, Margaret Jolly had an interest in estate. In an order to sell the above land, the petitioners Martin Harrison and Margaret X Jolly are the only heirs of the deceased William Jolly Senr. Dated 29 June 1843.

JONES "In Equity" Box 2 #52. Clerk of Court Office. Pickens, S. C. Dec. 1842 F. M. Jones and wife Mary P. Jones nee Mary P. Richards sheweth that James Richards is indebted to them. That he has left this State." As the son of Adams Richards decd. of Pickens Dist. (Loose Papers) 10 Nov. 1852 John Jones of Rutherford Co., N.C. appointed Abel Robins of Pickens Dist. his atty. to sell a certain piece of land lying in said Dist. containing 123 acres on Long Creek waters of Chattooga River, belonged to his father John Jones decd. 21 March 1859 Wilson C. Jones, Geo. W. Hendricks, Wm. M. Jones bound to Robert Thompson C. in E. in the sum $600. Wilson C. Jones gdn. of Lucy Catharine Jones, Joel J. Jones, minors under 21 yrs. Allen Robinson decd. their grandfather.

JONES, ANDREW Box 50 Pack 1155. Probate Judge Office. Abbeville, S. C. Abbeville Dist. Admnr. bond, we Catharine Jones, Moses Jones, Jonathan Essery all of this Dist. are bound unto Andrew Hamilton, Ord. in the sum of $5,000. Dated 4 May 1802. Wit: Jos. Sanders. Warrant

Jones, Andrew - Continued. of appraisement to John Hairston, John
Sanders, Charles Cladwell, Joseph Caldwell and Robert Thompson, all or
any three of you to appraise the goods and chattels of Andrew Jones
decd. Signed A. Hamilton O.A.D. Appraisers were Major Charles Caldwell,
Robert Thompson, John Sanders.. (this may be a second admnr. bond and
appraisement). In expend paid Jos. Jones for schooling Samuel and
Cathrin in 1800, paid Wm. McClanahan for schooling Sarah Jones in 1802.
In 1800 paid part of Legacy to Agnew Massey and wife legacy, also paid
Betsey Jones part of her legacy, also paid Andrew Jones part of his
legacy. Sale held 27 Nov. 1798. Buyers, Wm. Camron, Wm. Dale, Joseph
Jones, Andrew English, Andrew Weed, Alx. Porter, Jno. Gray, Thomas
Morrow, Adam Stuart, James Williams, Reuben Weed, Robert McComb, Wm.
Atwood, Arthur Morrow, James Boyd. Cash paid est. by Patrick Bradly,
Enos Crawford, Wm. Clavick, John Young. Debts owed by est. Thomas
Morrow, John Pettigrew, Jane Patton, James McCarter, Samuel Leard,
John Jones, Thomas McMillan, Adam Stewart, David Pressly, Robert
Crawford, Hugh McBride, Joseph Calhoun, John McKinley, Wm. McDonnald,
Mary Morrow, Andrew Weed, Jean Patton.

JONES, BENJAMIN SENR. Box 50 Pack 1153. Probate Judge Office.
Abbeville, S. C. Admnr. bond, We Benjamin F. Jones, Wm. H. Kirtpatrick
and F. C. P. Jones are bound unto Moses Taggart, Ord. in the sum of
$2500. Dated 19 Nov. 1839. Inventory made 14 Dec. 1839 by Abner H.
Maga, Enoch Barmore, Thos. A. Rosamond. Sale held 18 Dec. 1839.
Buyers: Wm. Kirtpatrick, A. C. Jones, H. A. Jones, Benjamin F. Jones,
C. Cullins, Isaac Agnew, S. Williamson, Wm. Wilson, Rebun Robertson,
W. T. Jones, A. J. Anderson, J. Moore.

JONES, DUDLEY #87. Land warrants. Clerk of Court Office.
Pickens, S. C. By W. L. Keith, Clk. To any lawful surveyor you are
authorized to lay a tract of land unto Edley Jones not exceeding ten
thousand acres. Dated 5 Nov. 1845. Executed for 68 acres the __ Dec.
1845. Certified 27 Dec. 1845.

JONES, GARLAND F. Box 121 #13. Probate Judge Office. Pickens,
S. C. 13 April 1893 G. W. Singleton, S. F. Robinson, Miles Singleton
are bound unto J. B. Newberry, Ord. in the sum of $26.26. G. W.
Singleton gdn. of Garland F. Jones a minor under 21 yrs. Born 24 Sept.
1879. Son of J. H. Jones decd. and his widow Mrs. S. E. Dulin.

JONES, GARLAND F. Box 70 #750. Probate Judge Office. Pickens,
S. C. I Garland F. Jones of Pickens Dist. being of sound mind and in
good health. I give to my beloved wife Gracia Caroline during her
widowhood all my real and personal estate. She paying my just debts
and funeral expenses. If my wife marry again before her death, my
will is that my executors sell at public outcry all my estate from the
proceeds one third and my children two thirds, viz; James Henry, Emry
Lawrence and Zeley Ann Jones. I desire when my chn. come of age,
each to get some household furniture if it can be spared. I appoint
my wife Gracea Caroline, Jorl Jones and Alva Griffin executors.
Dated 4 July 1862. James Burdine, Joel Jones, Joseph B. Reid. Signed:
G. F. Jones, proved on oath of Joseph B. Reid before W. E. Holcombe,
Ord. P.D. this 25 May 1863. Alva Griffin Execr. In final settlement
W. N. Hughes and wife recd. one third and a share of Zelia Ann decd.
est. Hughes and wife were gdn. for the two boys who were minors. This
settlement was made 25 Feb. 1867. (The papers does not state that the
widow married W. N. Hughes, but seem so).

JONES, ISSAH (No ref. First part of will not found in notes.)
Abbeville, S. C. And Darke and all my real estate, except a tract
lying on the other side of the branch it being apart I bought from
Stephen Jones also four head of horses, all my stock of hogs, cattle,
sheep and household and kitchen furniture during her life or widowhood,
if she marries I will her a child part, and after her decease to be
equally divided amongst my children or their heirs. I give to my son
William Jones on negro boy Donnel by him paying my executor $50.
I give to my son Wiley Jones the balance of my real est. the other
side of the branch, one horse called Dick, one cow. I give to my dtr.
Nancy Greyham one cow and fifty dollars paid by Wm. Jones. I give to

Jones, Issah - Continued. Milly or Nelly Watson one negro boy
Edmon. I give to my dtr. Polly Glover one negro girl lanner. I give
to my dtr. Jeuly F. Morgin one negro girl Sindy. I give to my dtr.
Sarah Waters one negro boy Joel. I give to my dtr. Derotha F. Jones
one negro boy Mose when come of age or marry. I give to my dtr.
Emley G. Jones one negro girl Huldy when she come of age or marry. I
give to my wife Elizabeth Jones one wagon and farm tools, also the
property I willed to my four minor children until they come of age
marry. I appoint my wife executrix and my son William Jones executor.
Dated 12 July 1831. Wit: Stephen Jones Junr., Benjamin Jones, Riel
Jones. Signed: Isaah X Jones. Proven 3 Aug. 1831. Inv. made 2
Sept. 1831 by Wm. A. Moore, Robert Y. Jones, Thomas Redden.

JONES, JABEZ Pack 653. #9. Clerk of Court Office. Pickens,
S. C. I James R. Wyley of Habersham Co., Sta te of Georgia in
consideration of $1200 to me paid by Jabez Jones of Pickens Dist.,
State of S.C. have bargained, sold and released a certain tract of
land lying in Pickens Dist. on the North side of Tugaloo River on both
sides of Cleveland Mill Creek. Being the same tract whereon Col.
Benjamin Cleveland last resided containing 250 acres. Adj. land of
Henry Shell, Moses Shannan, Micahaj Bryan. Land originally granted to
William Lott and Robert Grooms. Being the same that Moses Shannan
bid off at sale of property of the estate of Absalom Cleveland decd.
Dated 10 Aug. 1829. Wit: James Blackstock, James Eddins. Signed:
James R. Wyley.

JONES, JACOB Pension Schedule. Probate Judge Office. Pickens,
S. C. Pickens Dist. This 5 Oct. 1829 personally appeared in open
Court of General Sessions being the Court of Record. Jacob Jones aged
seventy six years, resident in Pickens Dist., S. C. who being duly
sworn declare that he served in the Revolutionary War as follows.
He enlisted in the month of May, one year and a few months over before
the battle at Brandywine under Captain William Brinkley of the third
Regiment, Commanded by Col. Jethro Sumner of the North Carolina line
for the term of two years and six months. Was in the battle of Brandywine and Monmoth at camp about seventy miles from New York. Lost
his discharge. Received only thirty dollars and one suit of clothes
for his service. Original declaration was made on the 15 May 1818.
number 8924. That he has no income other than what is contained in
the schedule annexed viz. one cow, two yearling, two sheep, two sows,
four pigs. He had a sickness about three years ago and expected to
die, and spent nearly all his property except his land, he then gave
it to his son in law and daughter, as he was unable to work it, and
could get nothing for the rent. His mill the only resource for many
years got washed away by a freshet, and unable to rebuild it. His
son lost his mental power and unable to help. He now depend on the
charity of the community. His wife Martha is aged sixty nine years
and also sickly. He lives with his son in law. Who is also poor.
Sworn to this 5 Oct. 1829. Si-ned: Jacob X Jones. William L. Keith
Clk. of Court I certify that I am of opinion that the property in the
annexed schedule does not exceed the sum of thirty dollars. Dated 5
Oct. 1829. Signed: Jno. B. O'Neall, Presiding Judge. Statement of
Joseph Grisham states that he has been acquainted with Jacob Jones
about twenty years. He to be an honest man, I have the most implicit
confidence. He is very poor and helpless etc. William Simpson Esq.
and Asa Smithson both respectable men of Pickens Dist. has been
acquainted with Jacob Jones many years. That he is poor and afflicted
with pain. They doubt his property is worth thirty dollars. Signed:
before Joseph Grisham not. Pub.

JORDON, JAMES A Citizen Grant. Book A, page 10. 96 Dist.
James Jordon as a citizen, 400 on both sides of Deep Creek and in
the fork of said Creek, waters of Savannah River. bounded on all sides
by vacant land, when surveyed by Bennet Crafton D.S. as appears by his
certificate, dated 24 May 1784. with the form and marks as per platt.
Recorded 27 May 1784, pr. Robert Anderson C.L. 10 ___

JONES, JAMES H. Box 130 #5. Probate Judge Office. Pickens, S. C. On 11 Feb. 1898 Genie Jones, Mrs. M. A. Smith, Allen Mauldin are bound unto J. B. Newberry, Ord. in the sum of $822.90. Genie Jones gdn. of her chn. James H. Jones age 7 yrs., Happie A. Jones age 5 yrs., Rebecca G. Jones age 6 months.

JONES, JAMES H. Box 119 #5. Probate Judge Office. Pickens, S. C. Est. admnr. 10 Oct. 1891 by W. N. Hughes, Miles Singleton, G. W. Singleton are bound unto J. B. Newberry, Ord. in the sum of $1,000. Died about 10 Feb. 1891. Paid 3 April 1893 Mrs. Sarah E. Dulin, gdn. of Mary L., Gracy A., Maggy D., Thomas H. and Charles W. Jones minors $78.81. Paid G. W. Singleton gdn. of Garland Singleton $13.13.

JONES, JAMES Y. Pack 380. Clerk of Court Office. Abbeville, S. C. Will in package. I James Y. Jones farmer of Abbeville Dist. do make this my Last W & T. etc. After my death I direct my just debts and funeral expenses be paid. I direct that the tract of land which I now live on be divided into three parts, first the home place and spring, containing 200 acres. The remainder divided into two parts as equal as possible. I intend said three parts as settlement for my three sons Dewitt, Thomas and Robert. The home place I bequeath to my wife Elizabeth during her life or widowhood, at her death or marriage then it to fall to my son Dewitt, Robert is to have choice of the two, with Thomas is to take the third part. I give to my wife Elizabeth the service of negroes Sam, Delf, George, Allen, Jourdan and Fanny, wife to have household and kitchen furniture, stock, cattle, hogs and sheep. I direct that my youngest son receive a solid education independent of his equal share. To my dtr. Mary I give my negro girl Lydia and her children for ever. I give to my dtr. Willey upon like terms my negro girl Eliza also to my dtr. Jane my negro girl Sylvia, and to my oldest dtr. and her children Nancy the wife of B. F. Roberts, I bequeath my tract of land called the Boyd Tract, now in their possession, containing 173 acres. I appoint my son Robert Jones and my wife executor and executrix. In Equity, To the Honr. the Chancellors: Your oratrix Mary Miller the wife of Andrew J. Miller by Thomas Jones her next friend, sheweth that in the year 18__ your oratrix married Andrew J. Miller then of Newberry Dist. of S. C. Since that time have removed to the State of Georgia and that your oratrix now resides with her husband in Richland County, that your oratrix by her marriage has one child Adelia now about ten years of age. That your oratrix father, bequeath to his wife negroes (named in will) with other effects and at her death or when she thinks proper, she may have my executor sell or divide her property, this was done on the 27 Dec. 1858. The proceeds in the hands of Robert Jones executor. Your oratrix has about $900 to her share. That her husband Andrew J. Miller is an intemperate man, thriftless and imprudent and your oratrix is unwilling that her share fall in his hands. That she willing and desire that when a settlement of the account be made, that this Court shall order and direct the executor to secure to her sole and separate use in strict orders of this Honorable Court. Filed 20 Feb. 1860.

JONES, JOEL #52. Land Warrant. Clerk of Court Office. Pickens, S. C. By W. L. Keith, Clk. of Court. To any lawful surveyor you are authorized to lay out a tract of land unto Joel Jones whereon he now lives and other land adj. the same and vacant land not exceeding ten thousand acres. Dated 24 Feb. 1843. Executed for 527 acres the 27 Feb. 1843. Certified 4 April 1843.

JONES, JOEL Box 91 #967. Probate Judge Office. Pickens, S. C. I Joel Jones of Pickens Dist. being of sound mind and disposing memory. First I desire my executors to collect all money due me, and to pay my just debts and funeral expenses. I give to my loving wife Jane during her life, all my property, both real and personal, notes and monies. I direct that my executors lay out my land into four lots and put a value on each, any of my children may take any at the value so put on said lot. My personal property to be sold and the money equally divided between my children. I appoint my sons William M. Jones and Van S. Jones executors. Dated 21 March 1871. Wit: J. E.

Jones, Joel - Continued. Hagood, Wm. Kirksey, J. Brown Kirksey.
Signed: Joel Jones. Proven 2 Sept. 1886.

JONES, JOHN Pack 4-A. Clerk of Court Office. Pickens, S. C.
Pendleton Dist. I John Jones of Dickson Co., Tenn. have this day
bargained, sold unto John Gambrell of Pendleton Dist., S. C. in consideration of $25 to me paid by sd. John Gambrell all my claim, right,
title to or in that part of my father in law estate that is by will
left to my mother in law now the wife of William Harper during her .
naturah life. All my part of the estate both real and personal at
the death of my mother in law Nancy Crenshew and when the said property
is sold agreeable to the will of my deceased father in law then said
John Gambrell to receipt my part of the property thereof with the other
legatees. Dated 5 Jan. 1813. Test John Booth. Signed: John X
Jones. Pendleton Dist. I do hereby certify unto all who it may concern that I John Gambrell of the same place do hereby for ever relinquish unto James Adams all my rights and title of in or to all and
singular the premises above mentioned etc. Dated 18 Jan. 1821. Test:
James Gambrell. Signed: John Gambrell.

JONES, JOHN Box 50 Pack 1171. Probate Judge Office. Abbeville,
S. C. Abbeville Dist. I John Jones, Layman of State and Dist. being
weak of body but of sound mind and memory. I wish my just debts to be
paid. I give to my wife Elizabeth Jones one third part of my land
during her widowhood also a bay mare, two cows, with all the moveable
property that is in being that she had when we were married. I give
to my son that piece of land that he sold to John Harris, I give unto
my son John Jones all the remainder of my land with my wifes third
after her death or marriage. I give to my son Joseph Jones one bay
mare named gin and a walnut chest. I give to my son Harris Jones one
hundred acres of land for which I gave him a penned bond, I give to
my dtr. Agnes Jones all my household and kitchen furniture. I give to
my grandson John Jones one feather bed and clothes which my dtr. Agnes
is to make. I appoint my son John Jones and my trusty friend James
S. Baskin executors. Dated 24 May 1803. Wit: Elizabeth Jones, Robert
F. Jones, John Jones. Signed: John Jones. Recorded 17 Oct. 1809.
Inventory made 6 Nov. 1809 by A. E. Scudday, John Baskin Senr., John
Harris, Thomas Ansley. Buyers at sale: John Cole, Lewis Howland,
Elizabeth Jones, A. E. Scudday, John Jones, John McKinley, Nancy Jones,
John McLendon, Geo. Wilson, John Harris, Benjamin Terry. Dated 8 Nov.
1809.

JONES, JOHN Box 50 Pack 1168. Probate Judge Office. Abbeville,
S. C. I John Jones of Abbeville Dist. being of sound mind and memory
understanding. It is my request that my wife Mary Jones hold in
possession all the land I now own. The plantation whereon my son
Edward F. Jones now lives, containing 181 acres, my son to pay rent to
his mother, as much as my executor think necessary, for her comfort
and support, after paying my just debts. I give to my son Edward F.
Jones after his mother death a tract of land whereon he now lives
containing 125 acres, and at his death to be divided between his
children. I give to my son Wm. P. Jones 131 acres to be taken off the
North side of the tract whereof I now live, he paying his mother
reasonable rent for land he may cultivate during her life, also one
sorrel horse named Jerry at his mother death.   The balance of my land
say 50 acres to be divided between my two dtrs. Damarish and Mariah to
be equally divided between them after their mother death. Also I give
them one bed and furniture. I also give one bed and furniture each.
I also give to my grand dtr., one bed and furniture and I allow her to
receive a common English education at the expense of my two sons
E. F. Jones and Wm. P. Jones. I allow Robert Cpwen[?] and Saml. Cowen
$15 each and Robert S. Edwards and Garret Morris or Norris to receive
one dollar each as their full portion and estate. I also allow my
grand son John J. Cowan son of Robert Cowan one bed and furniture at
his grand mothers death. I appoint Robert Cowan and Samuel Cowan my
executor. Dated 2 Aug. 1829. Wit: Abraham Bell, John Harris. Signed:
John X Jones. Proven 4 Dec. 1829.

JONES, JOHN Box 26 #301. Probate Judge Office. Pickens Dist.
S. C. Admnr. bond missing. Cit. pub. 9 Feb. 1852 mention that Abel
Robins applied for letter of Admnr. John Jones owned 120 acres lying
on Long Creek in Pickens Dist. adj. land of Jacob Butt and others.
Heirs Elias Jones lived in this State. James Young and wife Cassa,
Willis Dillback and wife Sarah, Nancy Hasty, Rachel Jones lived out of
State. On 7 Feb. 1852 D. P. Robins of Whetstone, Pickens Dist. stated
that his father when he left for Georgia wished to admnr. on the est.
of John Jones decd. as soon as possible as the property may be moved.
Abel Robins recd. share of est. 12 June 1854.

JONES, LEWIS Box 10 #335. Probate Judge Office. Anderson, S.C.
I Lewis Jones of Pendleton Dist. being sick and in a low condition
but in my proper senses and knowing that I must die. I give to my
wife Cherry Jones the plantation I now live on while she lives and at
her death the land to be my son Joabs, also I give to my wife all my
household furniture but one bed. All my stock of cattle, cows, hogs and
horses. I give to my dtr. Rebekah Jones one cow and calf. To my son
Lewis Jones my upper plantation lying on the same creek I now live on
containing 100 acres. To my dtrs. Mary Morehead, Sarah Jones and Nancy
Jolly one shilling each of them. I give to my son Lewis one eagle
horse which is in his possession now if he pays $70 to his mother by
next Christmas, if not the horse to be returned and be sold to pay my
debts, if Lewis returns the horse in good order then I allow him $30
on a note on his cousin Lewis Jones, given under my hand this 20 Sept.
1803. Wit: George Forbes, John Hunnicut. Signed: Lewis X Jones.
Sale held (no date). Buyers, Robert Dickerson, William McGuffin,
Absalom Tims, Lewis Jones, Wm. Tims, Ephraim Robbosson, William King,
John Watson.

JONES, "MINOR" Box 121, #14. Probate Judge Office. Pickens,
S. C. 3 April 1893 Sarah E. Dulin, Miles Singleton, S. F. Robinson
are bound unto J. B. Newberry, Ord. in the sum of $157.62. Sarah E.
Dulin gdn. of Mary L., Gracy A., Maggy D., Pinkney N., Thomas H. and
Chas. W. Jones minors under 21 yrs. 27 May 1899 paid Mary Lois Bridges
share $13.10.

JONES, "MINORS" Box 7 #115. Probate Judge Office. Pickens,
S. C. On 25 Feb. 1867 Wm. N. Hughes, Henry Williams, Andrew J. Anderson are bound unto W. E. Holcombe, Ord. in the sum of $1150. Wm. N.
Hughes gdn. of Jas. H. and Emery L. Jones minors under 21 yrs. Garland F. Jones decd. their grandfather Grace C. Hughes wanted her husband Wm. N. Hughes to be gdn. of her chn.

JONES, M. M. Box 91 #967. Probate Judge Office. Pickens,
S. C. Est. admnr. 9 Nov. 1883, by J. R. Gossett, A. G. Wyatt, H. J.
Grignillat who are bound unto J. H. Newton, Ord. in the sum of $600.
17 Oct. 1883 Margaret Jones, Wm. Jones asked for letter of admnr.

JONES, "MINORS" Box 122 #3. Probate Judge Office. Pickens, S.C.
7 Feb. 1893 J. F. Williams, Elliott Williams, W. D. Jones are bound
unto J. B. Newberry, Ord. in the sum of $381.20. J. F. Williams gdn.
of John Jones, James F. Jones, Paul Jones minors under 21 yrs.
Children of R. R. Jones decd. 3 Feb. 1896 Malinda Williams, T. A.
Williams Jr., T. A. Williams, Allen Mauldin, S. M. Looper are bound
unto J. B. Newberry, Ord. in the sum of $381.20. Malinda Williams
gdn. of said minors. Paid James Freeman Jones share $61.95. John C.
Jones born 2 Nov. 1882. James F. Jones born 1 Nov. 1885. Paul Jones
born 27 July 1889. Children of R. Jones decd. and Mrs. Lucy Cox. In
one place her name written Lucy Owens.

JONES, REBECCA Box 128 #11. Probate Judge Office. Pickens,
S. C. Est. admnr. 5 Nov. 1896 by Genie Jones, John A. Smith, Harrison
Jones are bound unto J. B. Newberry, Ord. Died 24 Sept. 1895. Genie
Jones is a daughter in law. Late of Easley. Paid 4 Feb. 1898
Harrison Jones $55.43. Mrs. Gene Jones $36.95. Paid Jimmie H. and
Happie A. Jones $73.91. Minor chn. of Tolbert Jones.

JONES, SAMUEL   Box 143 #6.   Probate Judge Office.   Pickens, S. C.
Est. admnr. 25 Nov. 1903 by H. L. Clayton, B. H. Callaham, W. H.
Chapman who are bound unto J. B. Newberry, Ord. in the sum of $300.
Died Sept. 1897.   Paid 16 Aug. 1905 Flemming T. Jones share $13.75.
Paid J. B. Newberry for Hattie Julia Jones minor $13.75.   Paid J. B.
Newberry for Judge T. or L. Jones not known where he is his share
$13.73.

JONES, S.T.C.P.   Pack 251.   Clerk of Court Office.   Abbeville,
S. C.   (Will found in package. I S.T.C.P. Jones of Mount Pleasant,
Abbeville Dist. do make this my last W & T. etc. I will and direct
that all my just debts and funeral expenses be paid. I will and direct
my executors to sell all my estate both real and personal, and from the
proceeds pay to my wife Hellena the sum of $300 annually for her support
and maintenance. I will after the death of my wife $1500 to my niece
Mary Elizabeth Jones dtr. of H. A. Jones Esq. That it shall be in
trust for her sole and separate use and not subject to the control
management of any husband she may have. I will $1500 to my niece Sarah
Fickling Jones the second dtr. of my brother H. A. Jones, subject to
like trusts and restrictions, after the death of my wife. If my wife
marry again she to have $200 annually instead of $300 as in clause #2
for her sole and separate use, not under the control of any husband she
may have. I will to my two nieces Eugenia Barmore and Frances Barmore
dtrs. of Enoch Barmore Esq. $350 each for their sole and separate use
after the death of my wife, not subject to any control of any husband
they may have. I will that my executor pay to my niece Mary Townes
Jones, and Calhoun Jones, chn. of Dr. N. S. Jones of Wetumpka, Ala.
each five hundred dollars, to be paid after the death of my wife.
Should any of my nieces die without leaving chn. at their death, their
share shall be vested in the surviving sister of such deceased. My
nephew D. F. Jones is now indebted to me for about $740 by notes
should this not be paid in my life time. I will that this indebtedness
be cancelled. Except the old clock, family Bible, chest and folding
table, I give to my niece Sallie F. Jones. Library of books which I
give to my nephew D. F. Jones. I give the rest of my household furniture, except one set of china I now will to Eugenia Barmore. I will
after the death of my wife $450 to my niece Sarah Williamson $350 in
like trust as above stated. Also $350 in like trust to Mary Traynham
and her heirs forever. I appoint my brother H. A. Jones executor.
(No more of this will found in notes.) In Equity. Abbeville Dist. in
Equity. To the Honr. the Chancellors: Your orator and your oratrix
Hugh M. Brownlee and Eugenia E. his wife sheweth that S.T.C.P. Jones
departer this life in the month of August 1854, leaving unrevoked and
in full force his will. In the sixth clause of said will he bequeath
to your oratrix Eugenia E. and her sister Frances Barmore the sum of
$350 each after the death of his wife, etc. In the eight clause he
directed that should either of his said nieces die without leaving
children, that the portion given to her should be vested in the surviving sister. The wife of the testator departed this life a few weeks
prior to the death of her husband. That in the month of March 1856
the sister of your oratrix the said Frances Barmore departed this life
without leaving chn. she having never married. Thus entitling your
oratrix to the legacy given by her uncle. That Henry A. Jones, Esq.
was appointed executor and qualified as such on the 29 Aug. 1854.
That no accounting has ever been made. That since the intermarriage
of your Orator and oratrix which occured in Sept. 1858 and before the
said marriage, Henry A. Jones, Esq. was respectively applied to in a
friendly manner to have an accounting and to secure the legacy. He
has refused and still refused to do holding said legacies in his hand
without security. Your oratrix will ever pray. Filed 18 June 1859.

JONES, "MINORS"   Box 1 #17.   Probate Judge Office.   Pickens, S.C.
On 14 Nov. 1851 Wm. H.Stribling, Saml. Reid are bound to W. D. Steele,
Ord. in the sum of $500.   W. H. Stribling gdn. of David Jones, Susan S.
Jones, Nancy C. Jones, Rebecca Jones, Matilda Jones minors under
21 yrs. Chn. of Hartwell Jones. Entitled to share of Est. of Eliza-
beth Stribling in right of their mother who is dead. M. S. Stribling
their uncle. 1 Jan. 1856 recd. of B. F. Sloan Exor. of Est. of Susan
Sloan Jones decd. for the above minor $34.00. 1 Jan. 1867 paid

166

Jones, Minors - Continued. H. R. DeSay and wife Matilda S.
DeSay formerly Jones $75.74.

JONES, THOMAS Box 50 Pack 1164. Probate Judge Office. Abbeville,
S. C. 96 Dist. Admnr. bond, We Elizabeth Jones, James Jones, Solomon
Langston and Ralph Smith are bound unto John Thomas Junr., Ord. in the
sum of two thousand pounds sterling. Sealed at Spartan Plain, this
30 July 1783. Appraisers are Moses Casey, Sampson Bobo, William
Wilder. (in same Pack) 96 Dist. By James Yancey, Esq. Surrogate to
John Harris, Ord. Whereas Henry Parkman hath applied to me for letter
of admnr. on goods and chattels of Thomas Jones decd. of this Dist.
Dated 30 Oct. 1786. The appraisers are Jesse Scrugs, John Thurman,
Nathan Tally. Dated 10 Nov. 1786. Col. Purvis is authorized and
requested to swear the appraisers. Signed: J. Yancey. Edgefield
Dist., S. C. the appraisers were sworn the 2 Jan. 1786 by John Purvis,
J.P.

JONES, TOLBERT H. Box 129 #1. Probate Judge Office. Pickens,
S. C. On 15 Dec. 1896 admnr. granted to Genie Jones of Easley on est.
of her husband who died 12 Oct. 1896.

JONES, WILLIAM & A. J. Box 14 #180. Probate Judge Office.
Pickens, S. C. Cobb Co. State of Georgia. We William Jones and A. J.
Jones of Cobb Co., Ga. for divers good causes and consideration have
this day made ordained and appointed Robert Stribling our true and law-
ful attorney to receive and receipt for our portion of the estate of
Jesse Stribling late of Pickens Dist. Dated 7 Nov. 1854. Wit: R. M.
Moore, Willis Roberts, J.P. signed William Jones and A. J. Jones.
(Also in same pack). Recd. of the Comm. in Equity of Pickens Dist.
Miles M. Norton, Ord. the sum of $10.16 1/2 cents in part of my dis-
tributive share of the real estate of Elizabeth Stribling decd. this
7 Jan. 1853. Test Thomas M. Stribling. Signed: Adam S. Jones and
Zelia E. M. Jones. Recd. of J. W. Ross Comm. in Equity for Pickens
Dist., S. C. $10.15 in part of my dist. share of the real estate of
Jesse Stribling decd. Dated 21 April 1853. Signed: William Jones
and Abigail Jones.

JONES, WILLIS (Same as above). Box 10 #335. Probate Judge
Office. Anderson, S. C. The estate of Willis Jones was admnr. 14 May
1803 by Rebecca Jones, James Morehead who are bound unto John Harris,
Ord. in the sum of $1,000. Recd. of Rebecca Jones one dollar fees for
attending to swear appraisers of est. of Willis Jones decd. Dated 8
March 1805. Signed: Rt. McCann.

JONES, WILSON C. Box 94 #997. Probate Judge Office. Pickens,
S. C. Est. admnr. 24 Mar. 1884. by Jas. P. Jones, Perry D. Dacus,
W. K. Masingill are bound unto J. H. Newton, Ord. in the sum of $500.
Died 14 Feb. 1884. J. P. Jones, Caroline Jones, Jasper Jones, Wm.
Jones bought at sale.

JONES, W. T. & LOUISA Pack 3370. Clerk of Court Office. Abbeville, S. C. Bill of Alimony, Abbeville Dist. To the Honr. the
Chancellors: Your oratrix Louisa Jones who sues by her next friend
Beaufort T. Watt. That in Dec. 1840 your oratrix married Dr. W. T.
Jones and continued to live with him until Nov. 1841. At all times
she was a kind and affectionate and obedient wife in every respect.
That he W. T. Jones was cruel by coarse and offensive language and
remarks catoulated[sic] to motify your oratrix. He encouraged his
children by a former wife to treat your oratrix with great rudness. He
locked her in the house with only her slaves. When she married she
owned eight slaves which said W. T. Jones still have, they are, a girl
named Emily and Fanney with her six chn. viz: Tom, Hannah, Deal, Mary,
Betsey and Jenny and others chattels that is in her possession. That
she finding that living with him was not in her safety that he struck
her with a hickory and his hands. He has refused to support her or
return her property. Your oratrix will ever pray. Filed 26 April
1843.

JORDON In Equity. Box 2 #53. Clerk of Court Office. Pickens,
S. C. Feb. 1853 Paul L. Jordon of Monroe Co., Miss. gdn. of Isaac
P. Jordon infant child over 14 yrs. of Saml. B. Jordon and Ruth Jordon
and one of the heirs of Wm. McDow decd. late of Pickens Dist., S. C.
Ruth a dtr. of Wm. McDow who died in Pickens Dist. in 1851. Her mother
died in Miss. in 1838 before her father death.

JUNK, JAMES Box 51 Pack 1181[?]. Probate Judge Office. Abbeville,
S. C. Abbeville Dist. admnr. bond. We John Lipscomb, Ira Griffin, and
Wm. Hamilton are bound unto Moses Taggart, Ord. in the sum of $2,000.
Dated 3 Nov. 1828. Cit. Pub. at Rehoboth Church. Inventory made 10
Nov. 1828 by James Patterson, John Hearst Sr., Stephen Witt. Sale held
10 Nov. 1828 buyers are: Jno. Lipscomb, James Patterson, Jno. P.
Barratt, Wm. Hamilton, James Chiles, Wm. Pritchard, Jno. Hearst,
Stephen Witt, Jacob Slappy, Lewis S. Simmons, Vincient Griffin, Henry
Pritchard, John Timmerman, Peter Cook.

JUNKINS, WILLIAM Box 67 #717. Probate Judge Office. Pickens,
S. C. Est. admnr. 13 Dec. 1862 by Wesley Junkin, James King, John C.
Snipes are bound unto W. E. Holcombe, Ord. in the sum of $400. Mary
Jane Junkin, Wesley Junkin, Elizabeth Snipes recd. share $33.22. On
5 Apr. 1863 J. C. Snipes recd. $13.50.

KALMBACK, JOHN C. Box 48 #530. Probate Judge Office. Pickens,
S. C. Est. admnr. 28 June 1858 by G. H. Kerber, John W. F. Thompson,
N or M. F. Mitchell who are bound unto W. J. Parson, Ord. in the sum of
$100. Sale made at Wallhalla 15 June 1858. Owned lot in town of
Walhalla on Main Street No. 77 adj. lots of Menke Bullwinkle and others
containing one half acre, with a confortable dwelling house and work
shop.

KAREY, "MINORS" Pack 430. Guardianship. Clerk of Court Office.
Abbeville, S. C. Abbeville, S. C. In Equity, To the Honr. the
Chancellors: The petition of William Adams sheweth that on the 10 June
1851 he signed as surety along with J. W. Ramey and Luke Mathis the
guardianship bond of Jane A. Karey at the preceding June term of Court.
That said Jane Karey had been appointed gdn. of her minor chn. viz;
James, Laura Ann, John, Mary Jane, Lewis, and Samuel Karey. Your
petitioner is about to remove from the State and desires to be
released from further liability as surety on said bonds. (No more of
the petition in notes.)

KAY, ALBERT B. Box 144 #1. Probate Judge Office. Pickens, S.C.
I Albert Kay of Pickens Dist. being of sound mind, etc. First I will
that as soon as practicable my executors to pay all just debts and
funeral expenses out of the money I may leave. I will unto my wife
Telular E. Kay during her natural life the house and lot in Greenville
City on Pendleton Street adj. Mrs. T. F. Gossett, Mrs. Cureton and
others, being the lot I bought from S. M. Cox and after her death to
be equally divided amongst my children. All the rest and remainder
of my estate, life insurance, rents and income from any sources be
keep by my wife for her support and maintainance and education of my
children (not named). I appoint my wife Telular E. Kay executrix.
Dated 17 Jan. 1902. Wit: Elliott Williams, John H. Davis, W. D.
Garrison. Signed: Albert B. Kay. Filed 6 May 1904. Mrs. Telular
died 10 Jan. 1927.

KAY, ELIZABETH & POLLY Pack 140. Probate Judge Office. Anderson, S. C. In the will of Francis Clinkscales dated 18 Nov. 1831.
He bequeath to his dtr. Elizabeth Kay $130. To his dtr. Polly Kay
decd. $75. To be paid to her heirs when they become of age (not named).
He appoints his son Francis B. as guardian of said minors.

KAY, JAMES H. Pack 295. Clerk of Court Office. Abbeville, S.C.
Abbeville Dist. In Equity, to the Honr. the Chancellors: Your orators
Charles W. Kay and George W. Richey. That on the 2 Dec. 1862 James
H. Kay departed this life intestate, leaving considerable real estate,

Kay, James H. - Continued. to wit, 284 acres in this dist. on the Greenville and Columbia Rail Road and waters of Covin Creek adj. lands of Isabella Kay, James A. Bigby, Melissa Kay, J. L. Davis and T. M. Branyon. The deceased left no wife, children or father living at his death. But as next of kin, a mother, brothers and sisters and the children of a decd. brother and sister, to wit, Isabella Kay the mother, George H. Kay and Charles W. Kay (one of your orators) brother of decd., Caroline a sister who married James F. Maddison and the chn. of John B. Kay, to wit., Savannah Kay, Caroline Kay and John B. Kay all minors, and your orator George W. Richey the only child of Emilly Richey decd. sister. Filed 18 March 1863.

KAY, JINNETE Box 32 #379. Probate Judge Office. Pickens, S. C. Jinnete Holden a legatee of James Holden decd. of Pickens Dist. whose est. was admnr. 30 June 1854. On 22 Nov. 1855 Jinnete Holden Kay and husband Emry Kay of Gordon Co., Ga. Appointed John Holden of Blount Co., Ala. their atty. to receive their share of James Holdens decd. estate.

KAYSER, JOHN HENRY Vol. 1. Probate Judge Office. Union Co., S. C. Dated 8 Jan. 1789. I John Henry Kayser of Union County, 96 Dist. being very sick and weak in body, but of perfect mind and sound memory. I give to my well beloved son Henicus Mooitus Kayser my two horses, one desk, all my working tools, household furniture, clothing. I appoint my friend Daniel Wooden my sole executor. Wit: Wm. Wadlington, James Caldwell, Nathl. Littleton. Signed: John Henry Kayser. On back of will: Memorandum: I give unto Hermon Mederman one small bellows, one small anvil, two hand hammers, two pr. tongs. Given under my hand this 7 Jan. 1789. John Henry Kayser. Memorandum that I give unto Mary Caldwell for her services one small Cambrick, one phancey canister, one mohogoney box, one copper laddle. John Henry Kayser. Recorded 23 March 1789.

KEAS, MALCOM Box 53 Pack 1241. Probate Judge Office. Abbeville, S. C. I Malcom Keas of Abbeville Dist. being in sound mind and memory. First I will to my loving wife Elizabeth Keas my plantation with horses, cows, hogs, and all personal property after discharging what debts the est. may have. For her support during her life or state of widowhood. At the decease of my wife, my property both real and personal to be my dtr. Jean Keas. I will my dtr. Betsey one English shilling and with special host and confidence. I leave Thos. Fulton, Henry Fulton and John Fulton executors to act in the best manner for my wife and dtr. Jean interest and support. Dated 29 Nov. 1819. Wit: James Frazier, James Richey, Henry Wiley. Signed: Malcom X Keas.

KEASLER, HENRY Pack 544 #1. Clerk of Court Office. Pickens, S. C. The State vs Henry Keasler. "Bigamy" 1st living wife name Lucinda Wardlaw before marriage. 2nd living wife, Rosa Stephens. 3rd living wife Margaret Hendrix. Witnesses to prove the first marriage. Richd Owens and his wife, also J. C. Eaton who lives at Central, S. C. 2nd. Rosa Stephens pros. R. W. Folger. Keaslers acknowledgement of the second wife. Were married at Carnesville by license about the year 1868. Thomas Gary married them, and to prove the marriage. Rosa Stephens to prove her marriage with the deft. Richard Owens to prove deft. marriage with widow Wardlaw. Lucinda Keasler the widow Wardlaw to prove her marriage with deft.

KEASLER, HENRY Box 9 #147. Probate Judge Office. Pickens, S.C. Margaret Hendrix who was the widow of Henry Hendrix who later married Henry Keasler. On 14 July 1873, Margaret Keasler was also the guardian of her son Lawrence A. Hendrix.

KEENAN Union Cemetery, in the Town part. Union, S. C. Sacred to the memory of James D. Keenan, born 10 April 1823, died 20 Feb. 1865. In memory of Rachel Keenan wife of Malachi Keenan, born 18 Jan. 1797. Died on the 11 Sept. 1835.

KEITH, JOHN Book F, Page 267. Clerk of Court Office. Pickens, S. C. This indenture made 1 Feb. 1849, between John Keith Senr. and

Keith, John - Continued. Joel M. Keith son of said John Keith
Senr. In consideration of natural love and affection which he hold and
beareth into the said Joel M. Keith. Hath given, granted, aliened
and confirmed unto said Joel M. Keith all that tract of land lying on
the Oolenoy Creek waters of Saluda River. Containing 160 acres, adj.
land of A. Hester on the East, my son James Keith Jr. on the West and
land I purchased from Cornelius Keith Senr. upon which I formerly lived.
Wit: J. B. Southerland, David Blythe. Signed: John Keith Senr.
Proved on oath of J. B. Southerland before W. L. Keith Clk. of Court.
Dated 1 Nov. 1849.

KERNON, JAMES Box 52 Pack 1232. Probate Judge Office. Abbeville,
S. C. Admnr. bond. Abbeville Dist. We Nathaniel Henderson, James
Henderson and John Sandersare bound unto Talo. Livingston, Ord. in the
sum of $10,000. Dated 22 Nov. 1813. Inv. made 4 Dec. 1813 by Joseph
Stalworth, Richard Henderson, and William Henderson. Sale held 7 Jan.
1814. Buyers: Nathaniel Henderson, James Pollard, Samuel Henderson,
N. Stallworth, Wm. English, James Mathews, Ira Griffin, John Foster.

KERR, MARY Box 52 Pack 1231. Probate Judge Office. Abbeville,
S. C. I Mary Kerr of Abbeville Dist. being very sick and weak in body,
but of perfect mind and memory. I give to my dtr. Ruth Kerr one negro
boy named George and one girl named Nancy also all the tract of land
on which I now reside. With my black silk gown cardian and jewelry.
I bequeath to Ruth Kerr all my right of dower to the land I got by
Samuel Kerr until her marriage, after which I wish the value be divided
equally amongst said Ruth, and my dtr. Catherine McLain and Jane Green.
I also bequeath unto Ruth Kerr one half of the one hundred dollar note
due me by James Vernon, the other half I give to my son John Kerr. I
also give to my dtr. Ruth Kerr two of my horses, the other two I give
to my son John Kerr with a note on George Alexander for $50. I appoint
Andrew Norris Esq., John Green, and George Bowie Esq. executors.
Dated 21 Jan. 1805. Wit: Samuel Savage Junr., A. Hunter, J. Pringle.
Signed: Mary Kerr. Recorded 12 Feb. 1805. Inv. made 22 Feb. 1805.
By Samuel Savage, Agripa Cooper, Sterling Bowen. Sale held 23 Feb.
1805. Buyers: Samuel Aston, Ruth Kerr, John Kerr, John Green, Hugh
McLin Junr., James Abell, Wm. Dunlap, James Caldwell, Wm. Caruthers,
Eli Calahan, James Pringle, Wm. Campbell, David Caldwell, Samuel
Savage, Joseph Black, Garrett Vandegrift, James Dawson, John Bowen,
Robert Beard, Isaac Bowen, Andrew Milligan, Moses Parnell, John
Roberts, Agrippa Cooper, John Miller, Sterling Bowen, Archibald Campbell,
Wm. Crawford, James Harkness, Samuel Tucker, Wm. Kelly, Wm. Warren.

KERR, WILLIAM Box 52 Pack 1229. Probate Judge Office. Abbeville,
S. C. I William Kerr Senr. of Abbeville Dist. being very sick and
weak in body but of perfect mind and memory. First I give unto my
nephew Wm. Kerr Junr. the hundred acres of land on which my house
stands and my best gun, my oven pot and pan and my deer skins. Also
to Andrew Kerr 50 acres of land lying and joining himself and my buck
horse, my youngest cow and calf and saddle and german gun and little
pot. The other 50 acres I allow to be sold and divided between David
Kerr and my sister in law Mary Kerr. I allow to Rachel Caruthers the
sorrel mare running on Savannah River. I allow John Kerr five
shilling cash likewise the hogs to be sold and divided among David and
Wm. I do allow Mary Kerr, Charles Loves note what is unpaid. Dated 9
Sept. 1795. Wit: James Caldwell Senior, Alexander Foster, James
Caldwell Junr. Signed: William X Kerr Senr. Recorded 27 March 1798.
Admnr. bond, Abbeville Dist. We David Kerr, John Robinson, Archibald
Walker and Martin Loftis are bound unto Andrew Hamilton Ord. in the sum
of $5,000. Dated 13 Dec. 1805. Inventory made 3 Jan. 1806 by James
Foster, Milton Paschal and William Bole, this inv. was of Wm. and
Lettice Kerr. Sale held 6 Jan. 1806. Buyers: Nancy Kerr, Jenney
Kerr, David Kerr, John Robeson, Archiles Walker, Edward Prince, Joseph
Prince, Wm. Crawford, Freman Willis, David Richeson, Pheby Barksdel,
Isebella Kerr, James Vernon, George Beard, John Robeson.

KERSEY, "MINORS" Pack 462. Clerk of Court Office. Abbeville,
S. C. In 1851 Luke Mathis was the guardian of William Kersey a minor
who become of age in 1858. Also Thomas Kersey, Robert Kersey. Thomas

Kersey, Minors - Continued. Kersey was of age in 1853. March
1851 recd. of Jane A. Kersey admnrx. $111.53.

KERSEY, STEPHEN & NANCY Pack 10. Clerk of Court Office. Anderson,
S. C. Pendleton Dist. We Stephen Kersey and Nancy Kersey relict of
Stephen Kersey decd. of Dist. and State aforesaid in consideration of
$1100 to us paid by Francis Young Senr. of Abbeville Dist. have granted,
sold, bargained, released a tract of land containing 215 acres. Being
part of a tract granted unto Stephen Kersey decd. lying on Crooked
Creek waters of Savannah River. Adj. land of Isom Bond, Jessy Carrol,
F. Beaty, A. Simpson. Dated 14 May 1828. Wit: Dilly X Kersey, G. W.
Simpson J.P. Signed: Stephen Kersey and Nancy X Kersey. Proved on
oath of George Simpson, J.P. this 14 May 1828. Polly Kersey the
wife of the within Stephen Kersey did this day release and forever
relinquish her dower on the above land before James Turner, J.P. this
27 Dec. 1830.

KELLER, DAVID Pack 314. In Equity, Clerk of Court Office.
Abbeville, S. C. Abbeville Dist. In Equity, to the Honr. the
Chancellors: Your orator and oratrix James A. McCord and Sarah A.
McCord, sheweth that David Keller late of this Dist. departed this life
in the year 1860 possessed with considerable estate, both real and
personal, leaving as next of kin, his widow Nancy Keller, children, your
oratrix Sarah A. McCord, J. J. Keller, Elizabeth Lomax the wife of
John W. Lomax, Elvira the wife of Samuel Lomax, Angeline R. the wife of
William A. Lomax, James W. Keller, Nancy Anna the wife of William H.
Wilson, David Z. Keller, Mary Julia the wife of James F. Mabry, Isaac
Alphus Keller, a minor about 18 yrs. of age, William Wauew Keller
about 16 yrs. of age, Sarah Emma Keller about 14 yrs. of age. The
admnr. was granted unto Nancy Keller and the personalty has been sold.
At time of death the intestate was possessed with real estate of about
one thousand acres, in Abbeville Dist. on Long Cane Creek adj. lands of
J. Foster Marshall, John Cowan, J. J. Gilmer and William Smith. Your
orator and oratrix prays for a partition of said land, Filed 11 March
1863. In 1863 John J. and James W. Keller were living in Claiborne,
Miss.

KELLY, A. JACKSON Box 100 #1049. Probate Judge Office. Pickens,
S. C. On 15 March 1871 Mary Hunt nee Kelly and wife of J. J. Hunt
shows tha t A. Jackson Kelly owned 52 acres on branches of Town Creek
adj. lands of J. G. Ferguson, J. E. Hagood and others. Heirs, Mary
Kelly the widow, chn. Sarah, Anna and John Kelly. 20 Nov. 1884 M. A.
Taylor, Sallie E. Gantt recd. share of their father est.

KELLY, ANDREW Box 43 #478. Probate Judge Office. Pickens, S.C.
Est. admnr. 1 March 1858 by Joseph W. Kelly, Elizabeth Kelly, M.
Mitchell, A. B. Grant are bound unto W. J. Parson, Ord. in the sum of
$300. J. W. Kelly, Ezekiel Kelly, the widow etc. bought at sale.
Owned 228 acres of land on Keowee River adj. land of M. M. Norton,
Mrs. Anderson and others. Owned 75 acres on waters of Little River
adj. land of Levi N. Robin and others. Heirs, Elizabeth Kelly the
widow, Lucy the wife of Thomas Jackson, Samuel C. Kelly, Feeby the
wife of John Chastain, Adaline Kelly, James J. Kelly, Joseph M. Kelly,
James J. Kelly resided out of State. (Loose Papers) Ailsey wife of
Joseph Kelly decd. chn. Wm. A., Adaline, Mary, Naomi, Lucy Kelly.
Joseph Kelly died July 1862.

KELLY, ELISHA Box 93 #986. Probate Judge Office. Pickens, S.C.
On 21 Oct. 1876, he owned 146 acres on branches of Town Creek adj.
land of James E. Hagood, Mary Hayne and others. Died in 1865. Heirs
Lucinda A. Kelly the widow, G. W. Kelly, Jas. A. Kelly, Nancy C. Smith,
Frances M. Norris, E. J. Kelly, Elisha Kelly, Lucinda E. Kelly, Jr.,
John W. Kelly, Survella Kelly. 24 March 1879 Terry Kelly recd. share
(Loose Papers) 7 Oct. 1846 Hiram Kelly recd. share of James Kelly
decd. 6 Oct. 1846 Lucinda Kelly recd. share of James Kelly decd.
(Loose Papers) 17 Feb. 1866 Daniel Broom was trustee for Barbara Kelly
who is without the limits of this State.

KELLY, HENRY   Pack 125 #10.   An Inquest.   Pickens Dist., S. C.
An inquest held at Tunnel Hill in Pickens Dist. the 18 Dec. 1857 upon
view of the body of Henry Kelly of Tunnel Hill.   The jury brought it
out that he came to his death on 17 Dec. 1857 by falling into No. 2
shaft at the Stump Hill Tunnel.   By misfortune or accident.   Frederick
Shershal says, That I am an engine driver at No. 2 shaft Tunnel Hill,
Henry Kelly hollowed out, are you alright Fred, I told him I was,
Kelly looked into the shaft as if to listen to hear them below hollow
out "hoist away" which is the rule in coming out of the shaft from a
blast.   Kelley immediately said hoist away.   I then hoisted the bucket
15 or 16 feet slowly to steady the bucket.   I then hooked on the engine
and gave her steam.

KELLY, HIRAM   Pack 646 #6.   Clerk of Court Office.   Pickens, S.C.
In 1860 Hiram Kelly of Pickens Dist. age about 50 yrs. was sent to the
asylum.

KELLY, JAMES   Apt. 1 File 63.   Probate Judge Office.   Greenville,
S. C.   To James and Susannah Kelly, you are required to appear at the
Court of Ord. holden at Greenville Court House on the first Monday in
Dec. next to show cause if any why the real est. of Jacob Black decd.
should not be divided.   James and Susannah Kelly resided in Elbert Co.,
Ga.   Dated 23 Sept. 1839.

KELLY, JAMES   Book 1 Page 50.   Clerk of Court Office.   Pickens,
S. C.   1 May 1843 owned 120 acres on Little River adj. lands of Joseph
Burnet, M. M. Norton, John J. Howard.   John O. Grisham applicant vist.
in hehalf of Sarry Kelly, Rebecca Kelly, Ezekiel Kelly, Talton Kelly,
Hiram Kelly.

KELLY, JAMES   Deed Book A, Page 50.   Probate Judge Office.
Pickens, S. C.   John O. Grisham, applicant viz Surry Kelly, Ezekiel
Kelly, Rebecca Kelly, Talton Kelly, Hiram Kelly, Ann Calhoun (widow),
Andrew Jackson and wife, Richard Jackson in right of his wife, Lucinda
Kelly minor over 14 yrs.   F. N. Garvin guardian of said minor.   Your
petitioner prays for sale of the real estate of James Kelly decd. con-
taining 120 acres, lying on Little River.   Whereon Mrs. Ann Calhoun
now lives.   Filed 1 May 1843.

KELLY, "MINORS"   Box 6 #99.   Probate Judge Office.   Pickens, S. C.
On 15 March 1864 Joseph J. Norton, Robert A. Thompson are bound unto
W. E. Holcombe, Ord. in the sum of $1802.18.   Joseph J. Norton gdn. for
Wm. A., Sarah A., Mary M., Naomi C., and Lucy E. Kelly minors under 21
yrs.   Chn. of Ailcy Kelly and chn. of Joseph W. Kelly decd.

KELLY, WILLIAM   Pack 187.   #28.   Clerk of Court Office.   Pickens,
S. C.   Levena Kelly was the wife of a William Kelly in 1858 in Pickens
Dist. as mention in peace warrant.

KEMP, LEONARD D.   Box 63 #682.   Probate Judge Office.   Pickens,
S. C.   Est. admnr. 16 Sept. 1862 by Sarah A. Kemp, Morris Miller,
Edward Rankin are bound unto W. E. Holcombe, Ord. in the sum of $1600.
Paid 1 Dec. 1863 note to Wiley Kemp $4.05.   The widow at sale, no
names given.

KENNEDY, EDMUND   Box 52 Pack 1230.   Probate Judge Office.   Abbe-
ville, S. C.   Inventory made 24 July 1805 by Samuel Foster Senr., James
Foster Senr. and James Foster Junr.   Sale held 5 Dec. 1805.   Buyers:
James Foster Senr., James Foster Junr., Jean Kenedy, John Foster,
James McClinton, George Kidd, David Cochran.   Expend.   Paid 9 June 1809
Nancy Kenedy $12.76.   23 Sept. 1807 to Jean Kenedy admnr. her third of
est. $122.07.   To her four children each 22 dollars. $91.04.   Paid
Elizabeth Camp $5.75.   Paid William Kenedy on proven account $10.
Paid Edmond Kenedy his part of estate $22.76.   Paid William Kenedy his
part of est. $22.76.   Paid Elijah Ragsdale in right of his wife her
part of est. $8.   Paid Wilson Kenedy his part $22.76.   Paid Robert
Kenedy his part $22.76.

KENNEMORE, JOHN & MARTHA   Box 1 #1.   Probate Judge Office.
Pickens, S. C. On 14 Dec. 1847 Wm. L. Smith, D. Harvey Kennemore,
Lewis H. Kennemore are bound unto W. D. Steele, Ord. in the sum of
$235. Wm. L. Smith gdn. of John S. and Martha Kennemore minors under
21 yrs. Elizabeth Jonas their Mother. They entitled to share of Elias
Kennemore Estate.

KENNEMORE, NOAH   Box 30 #360.   Probate Judge Office. Pickens,
S. C. Pickens Dist., S. C. "Noah Cannemur his will by word of mouth
made and declared by him on the twenty fourth day of August in the
year 1838 in the presents of us who have hereunto subscribed our names
as witnesses hereto, my will is that Elias shall have fifty four acres
of land off of the lower part of the plantation and the balance of
the plantation with the personal property be left at the disposal of
his widow her lifetime and at her death to be divided amongst his
daughters, signed, sealed and delivered in presents of us this 10 Sept.
1838. "Test. Joshua Burts, Geo. Dilworth, Harvey Kennemur, Lewis
Kennemur, Jane Kennemur..." This is to certify that Joab John Harvey
and Lewis here by acnollede[?] that they have had certain pieces of
land and other property given to them by their father previous to his
death which we take our part of the estate in full. Signed: Sealed,
and delivered in presents of us." Dated 10 Sept. 1838. Wit: Joshua
Burts, Geo. Dilworth. Signed: Joab Kennemur, Harvey, Lewis Kennemur.

KENNEMORE, RIAL   #38.   Clerk of Court Office. Pickens, S. C.
I Rial Kennemore of Pickens Dist. in consideration of the $450 to me
paid by Israel Mayfield of the same Dist. have granted, bargained, sold
and released all that tract of land, containing 177 acres. Lying on
branches of Goldens Creek, waters of 12 Mile River, being part of a
tract originally granted unto Henry Norton, 3 Dec. 1792. Dated this 29
Nov. 1838. Wit: Micajah Hughes, Benson Kennemore. Signed: Rial X
Kennemore. Proved on oath of Micajah Hughes before James Henderson,
J.P. this 5 Jan. 1839.

KENNEMORE, RILEY   Box 114 #1098.   Probate Judge Office. Pickens,
S. C. I Riley Kennemore of Pickens County. Do make this my last W. &
T. I will and direct all my real and personal property or mixed to my
beloved wife Judy Kennemore to hold and posses during her natural life,
after which I will that it shall be equally divided between my two
adopted daughters fiz: Julia A. or M. Cantrell and Judy C. Cantrell.
My wife may sell, barter or dispose of as much of my estate or personal
estate as may be necessary to pay all just claims against my est. I
appoint William Kennemore and my wife Juda Kennemore executor and
executrix. Dated 11 July 1882. Wit: M. F. Williams, E. H. Phillips.
Signed: Riley Kennemore. Filed 2 Sept. 1882.

KENNEMMORE, ELIAS   Box 20 #242.   Probate Judge Office. Pickens,
S. C. Est. admnr. 15 Sept. 1845 by Lewis H., D. H. Kennemuer, Alexr.
McMahan are bound unto Wm. D. Steele, Ord. in the sum of $800. Wm. L.
Smith, gdn. of John and Martha Kennemore minors heirs of said decd.
Paid the widow one third $78.34 1/2 (no name given). Elizabeth, J.
Harvey Kennemore bought at sale.

KENNEMUR, "FAMILY"   Pack 623 #1.   Clerk of Court Office. Pickens,
S. C. Noah Kennemur died intestate on 31 Aug. 1838. Left a widow
Rebecca Kennemur who died 28 July 1860. Children, Mary Kennemur who
died 8 Feb. 1872. Joab Kennemur who died 21 Jan. 1867. Margaret
Dacus who died 25 June 1890. Cynthia Kennemur died 15 Sept. 1888.
John Kennemur died 26 March or April 1872. Elizabeth Kennemur died 15
July 1869. Jane McMahan died four or five years ago. (Probably
meant from the date this paper was written which was dated 10 Sept.
1891.) Elias Kennemur died 24 Aug. 1845. Eady Smith died 14 June 1877.
D. H. Kennemur is still alive. Mary, Cynthia, Elizabeth and Joab
Kennemur all died without children. Joab left a wife who is now dead.
The children and grandchildren of William Dacus who was a son of
Margaret Dacus, gets a share. John R. Kennmur and Martha Looper,
children of Elias Kennemur take the same as heirs at law, but under the
will John S. Kennemur takes all. Mary Kennemur and children, widow and
children of Lewis H. Kennemur. Sarah Kennmur and chn. and grand chn.

Kennemur, "Family" - Continued. (heirs of John Kennemur). The husband and children of Eady Smith and the children of Jane McMahan. At the death of Margaret Dacus she had $57.97 which she gave to N. K. Smith to keep for her and which he turned over to the admnr. (Noah Smith).

KENNEMUR, AMANDA Pack 637 #7. Clerk of Court Office. Pickens, S. C. Amanda Kennemur in 1889 was mentioned as a sister to George W. James decd.

KENNEMUR, ELIAS Pack 225 #9. Clerk of Court Office. Pickens, S. C. I William Odell of Pickens Dist. in consideration of $65 to me paid by Elias Kennemur of the same Dist. I have granted, sold, bargained, and released a certain tract of land lying on both sides of Goldens Creek of 12 Mile River. Containing 13 acres. Dated 17 Jan. 1848. Wit: J. A. Smith, John Bowen, Signed: Wm. Odell. Proved on oath of J. A. Smith before John Bowen, N.P. this 17 Jan. 1848.

KENNEMUR, JOAB Box 91 #964. Probate Judge Office. Pickens, S.C. I Joab Kennemur of Pickens Dist. being sound in mind but weak in body, etc. First I will and desire my just debts are paid. I will and bequeath to my beloved wife Sarah Kennemur all my effects that may belong to me, my household and kitchen furniture, stock of all kinds. As for my land, my wife is to have the income thereof during her life time of widowhood. She may dispose of it in any way she may choose, if she fail to make distribution of my land, I impower my executor to sell my effects and land as they may think best. I appoint my wife executrix and my brother D. H. Kennemur executor. Dated 24 Sept. 1866. Wit, J. H. Clement, Wm. L. Smith, J. L. Clement. Signed: Joab X Kennemur. Filed 11 Feb. 1867.

KENNEMUR, MARY, SYNTHA & MARGARET DACUS Box 118 #10. Probate Judge Office. Pickens County, S. C. Do jointly and seperately make this our last will and testament. First that all our just debts be paid. Secondly we Mary Kennemur and Syntha Kennemur do will all of our property at our death to be sold and divided as follows, equally between our brothers and sisters that may be alive, any being dead, their portion to be equally divided amongst their children, except brother Elias Kennemur our will is that John S. Kennemur his son to have the portion going to his father if he was alive. We have it from good authority that our brother Lewis H. Kennemur died justly owing D. H. Kennemur $25 and he promises not to exact it off of his estate widow or heirs and if he does not, that the $25 be taken from his heirs and given unto the children of D. H. Kennemur. As for me Margaret Dacus, I will all of my estate to be equally divided between the chn. of William Dacus my son. We Mary Kennemur, Synthe Kennemur and Margaret Dacus do hereby appoint D. H. Kennemur our executor. And if any or all of us becomes so incapacitated that none is able to manage our affairs that he do so for us. Dated this 20 Feb. 1871. Wit: W. L. Smith, J. F. Smith, J. H. Hammond. Signed: Margaret Dacus, Synthe X Kennemur, Mary X Kennemur. I D. H. Kennemur authorize Perry D. Dacus and N. B. Smythe to take charge of the personal property and the place whereon Margaret Dacus late decd. and dispose of the same. Dated 27 June 1890. Filed 19 July 1890.

KENNEMUR, NOAH Book E-1, Page 103. Clerk of Court Office. Pickens, S. C. I Noah Kennemur of Pickens Dist. In consideration of $15 to me paid by Benjamin Saterfield of the same Dist. I have granted bargained, sold and released a certain tract of land containing 7 1/2 acres on waters of Saluda River. Adj. lands of James Satterfield, Joshua Barton. Dated 4 Jan. 1837. Wit: John Bowen, Harvey Kennemur, Signed: Noah Kennemur. Proved on oath of Harvey Kenamor[sic] before George Dilworth M.P.D. this 29 March 1844.

KENSLER, MICHAEL Pack 5 (basement). Clerk of Court Office. Anderson, S. C. Court of Common Pleas and General Sessions. Anderson Dist. Before me Elijah Webb, Clerk, Personal appeared Michael Kensler a native of Baden in Germany about the age of 30 yrs. Who being duly sworn according to law, his intention to become a citizen of the U.S.

Kensler, Michael - Continued. and to renounce forever all allegiance, etc. This 25 Oct. 1852. Elijah Webb, Clk.

KEOWN, JAMES A. No Ref. Clerk of Court Office. Anderson, S. C. Deed, Anderson, S. C. I James A. Keown of Anderson Dist. in consideration of $942 to me paid by Barnett S. Tucker of Abbeville Dist. have granted, sold, bargained and released all that tract of land containing 88 acres in said Dist. adj. land of Elizabeth Robinson, E. H. Speer, G. W. Kelly and Robert Keown. 21 Sept. 1857. Wit: Wm. G. Speer, E. H. Speer. Signed: James A. Keown.

KILPATRICK, ALEXANDER Box 14 #179. Probate Judge Office. Pickens, S. C. On 25 April 1845 G. A. L. Bolles of South Mount, Pickens Dist. applied for letter of admnr. on the estate of Alexander Kilpatrick late of Alabama. (Formerly of Pendleton Dist., S. C.)

KILPATRICK, BENJAMIN F. Box 14 #180. Probate Judge Office. Pickens, S. C. Nesheba County, State of Miss. We Benjamin F. and Rebecca Cammella Kilpatrick his wife, citizens of said County, being one of the heirs and distributees of the estate of Elizabeth Stribling decd. and consent to an order for the sale of the estate. Dated 19 July 1850. Signed: Benjamin F. Kilpatrick and R. C. Kilpatrick. On 6 Feb. 1860 B. F. and wife Rebecca C. Kilpatrick were heirs of Jesse Stribling decd. of Pickens Dist.

KILPATRICK, CLARA Pack 643. Clerk of Court Office. Pickens, S. C. Whereas by a deed of Marriage settlement made and executed this 29 April 1858 between Clara Kilpatrick now Clara Livingston, of first part, J. W. Livingston of the second part and John S. Lorton as trustee of the third part. It is stipulated and agreed between the parties that in case the said John S. Lorton trustee should depart this life or resign, the said Clara Kilpatrick shall have the right and power to nominate, substitute and appoint a new trustee to this deed. With the same power, rights and authority as the original trustee. Whereas the said John S. Lorton trustee departed this life on the 16 Oct. 1862. Now I Clara Livingston have nominated, substitued and appointed my husband J. W. Livingston as trustee, etc. dated 6 Feb. 1866.

KILPATRICK, F. WHITNER Box 2 #55. In Equity, Clerk of Court Office. Pickens, S. C. On 21 Dec. 1857 John S. Lorton, Clara Kilpatrick, and S. F. Warren Miller of Anderson Dist. are bound unto Robert A. Thompson, Clk. of Equity in the sum of $2,700.34. 29 June 1857 John S. Lorton gdn. of F. W. Kilpatrick minor over 14 yrs. 30 June 1857. recd. $508 a division of est. of J. C. Kilpatrick, Jr. and J. C. Kilpatrick, Senr.

KILPATRICK, COL. F. W. Box 72 #772. Probate Judge Office. Pickens, S. C. Est. admnr. 21 Dec. 1863 by James W. Livingston, John F. Livingston, Eliza A. Lorton are bound to W. E. Holcombe, Ord. in the sum of $150,000. J. W. Livingston was of Pendleton. Paid Wm. Geiger for bringing body home $100. Heirs: Mother Mrs. E. A. Lorton, Clara Livingston and husband J. W. Livingston.

KILPATRICK, JOHN C., JR. Box 15 #191. Probate Judge Office. Pickens, S. C. I John C. Kilpatrick Jr. of Pickens Dist. being of sound and disposing mind and memory, but weak in body, etc. I desire my executors shall make provision for payment of my just debts. I desire that all my property remain in common stock and undivided until my oldest dtr. Clarissa or Clara arrives at age, or marries. At that time a division be made into four equal shares. One share to Clara, one share to Franklin Whitner, one share to Amanda and one share to my beloved wife Amanda. I give to my wife Amanda the legacy given her by her father and any she may receive from his est. without any control from this will. I desire that my family should remain in this Country, and my executors not to permit my property to be removed from this State. I appoint my father John C. Kilpatrick, Joseph N. Whitner, John Maxwell, and Aaron Shannon of Alabama executors. Dated 30 May 1840. Wit: Robert A. Maxwell, F. W. Symmes, Tilmon C. McGee. Signed: J. C. Kilpatrick, Jr. Proved 5 Oct. 1840.

KILPATRICK, COL. JOHN C. Box 12 #157. I John C. Kilpatrick of Pickens Dist. being of sound mind and memory, but advanced in years and feeble in health. I desire that sufficient property be sold to pay all just debts. I desire my executors to dispose of the mill and the adj. land first, reserving the home tract for the chn. of my decd. son John C. Kilpatrick Junr. to be equally divided between them when they come of age. Negro girl Fanny I desire be given to Clara and Delilah given to Whitner. The management of my property after paying the debts, I leave to my executors will so manage the most beneficial to my grand children. I appoint my friends John S. Lorton, John Maxwell, and F. W. Symmes. Dated 21 Nov. 1843. Wit: Tilmon C. MeGee, John Coates, Elizabeth Maxwell, John Arnold. Signed: J. C. Kilpatrick. Proved on 18 Dec. 1843.

KILLINGSWORTH, MARK Box 53 #1244. Probate Judge Office. Abbeville, S. C. Est. admnr. 14 Oct. 1840 by Nancy and James Killingsworth, Wm. Ware, Thos. S. Wilks who are bound unto Moses Taggart, Ord. in the sum of $40,000. Died about 19 July 1840. Nancy the widow, chn. James Killingsworth, Wm. Killingsworth, Sarah the wife of Saml. H. Lockhart, Susan the wife of James W. Black, and Martha.

KILLINGSWORTH, MARK In Equity. Pack 3219. Clerk of Court Office. Abbeville, S. C. In Equity, To the Honr. the Chancellors: Your orator and oratrix Jeremiah D. Gibson and Martha his wife late Martha Killingsworth. That on or about 2 Sept. 1843 James W. Black was appointed by this Court guardian of the person and estate of said Martha your oratrix and gave bond for same. That he took possession of the estate. That in 1846 your oratrix intermarried with Jeremiah D. Gibson and has requested an account with your orator, with the money due his wife, etc. Filed 19 April 1847. Answer of the deft. That he married a sister of the complainant Martha. That upon the death of the mother in Jan. 1842 applied for and was received into his house and took possession of ehr est. that came to his knowledge. That she resided with him at all times, except about three months when in school in Laurens. About four or five weeks before her marriage to J. D. Gibson she went to Richland Co., S. C. to visit an uncle. Where she married to the co-complainant, who was a stranger to this deft. and without his knowledge or consent.

KILLINGSWORTH, NANCY Box 53 Pack 1246. The petition of James W. Black to David Lesly, Ord. The petition sheweth that Mark Killingsworth departed this life in 1840 intestate, leaving a widow and five chn. The widow Nancy and her son James received a letter of admnr. and has admnr. on the estate, and is partially admnr. That the said Nancy Killingsworth the widow also died intestate. That your petitioner has intermarried with Susan E. Killingsworth a dtr. and is desirous to obtain letter of admnr. on the est. of Nancy Killingsworth decd. on the usual terms. Filed 12 Jan. 1842. Sale was held 4 Feb. 1842. Buyers: James W. Black, Wm. Killingsworth, James Killingsworth, Saml. Lockhart, E. Moeun, Robert C. Harkness, F. P. Robertson, Jno. Swilling, Jno. Campbell, Thos. Low, Joseph F. Black, Peter S. Burton, Caleb Burton, Hudson Prince, J. R. Black, Clayton Jones, A. N. Lynch, Daniel Boyd, Thos. J. Hill, Woody Bowen, E. P. Holomon. Settlement was made 10 Aug. 1843.

KING, GEORGE W. Box 2 #43. Probate Judge Office. Pickens, S. C. On 4 April 1856 John W. L. Cary, E. E. Alexander, Geo. M. Reid, are bound unto W. J. Parson, Ord. in the sum of $557. J. W. L. Cary gdn. of George W. King a minor under 21 yrs. About 19 yrs. of age. Deed of Conveyance. I Thomas Yow of Pickens Dist. in consideration of $125 to me paid by George W. King of the same Dist. have granted, sold, bargained and released all that tract of land situated on branches of Martins Creek waters of Keowee River, containing 100 acres. Bounded by land of T. M. Sloan, being part of a tract surveyed for Daniel Mason decd. 22 Oct. 1823. Dated 16 Dec. 1874. Wit: Samuel Dean, Thomas Baldwin, Signed: Thomas A. Yow.

KING, GEORGE W. Box 23 #279. Probate Judge Office. Pickens, S. C. Est. Admnr. 21 Jan. 1850 by Lucinda King, Elizabeth Massy are bound unto Wm. D. Steele, Ord. in the sum of $400. Had only one child Geo. W. King. "Owned land lying on Martins Creek waters of Seneca River bounded by land of Baylas Earle, Dempsey Yow and others." Lucinda King the widow later married Warren Phillips. 6 Oct. 1835 Benjamin King of Buncombe Co., N. C. shows that (he) is a nephew of Joseph Underwood decd.

KING, JACOB M. Box 123 #2. Probate Judge Office. Pickens, S. C. Est. admnr. 13 April 1894 by Margaret C. King, J. Monroe King, J. N. Howard, Mary King who are bound unto J. B. Newberry, Ord. in the sum of $300. Died 20 March 1894. Margaret C. King his wife. J. Monroe King a brother.

KING, JAMES Pack 222. In Equity. Clerk of Court Office. Pickens, S. C. James King of Pickens Dist. died 5 Sept. 1851 admnr. on the est. was granted to William Cope. He had at time of death a tract of land containing 530 acres purchased from Charles McClure. His est. in equity because his personal property has fallen short of paying his debts. King left neither wife nor child surviving him, his heirs being brothers and sisters to wit. Heirs at law of Elijah King decd. who are scattered westward, name and numbers unknown, Isaac King who resides in N.C., Sally Robinson wife of Zachariah Robinson of Ala., Nancy King an unmarried sister, residing in this State, Elizabeth Cope wife of William Cope, Narcissa Thrift the wife of Allen Thrift.

KING, JAMES Grant #95. Clerk of Court Office. Pickens, S. C. By W. L. Keith, Clk. To any lawful surveyor, you are authorized to lay out unto James King a tract of land not exceeding ten thousand acres and make a true plat thereof. Dated 21 June 1847. Executed for 117 acres the 23 June 1847. Certified 10 July 1847. Tyre B. Mauldin, D.S.

KING, JOHN JR. Pack 364. Probate Judge Office. Anderson, S. C. Will dated 1 March 1841. Recorded 3 April 1841. Heirs J. E. King, Robert King Junr., Sarah King, William King, Elisha King, John King, Nancy King, Lurena King, Polly King, the widow Mary King.

KING, JOHN SENR. Pack 361. Probate Judge Office. Anderson, S. C. Est. admnr. 4 July by Jesse King, William Ingraham. Citation published at Linn Meeting House.

KING, JONATHAN Box 91 #968. Probate Judge Office. Pickens, S. C. This 10 Aug. 1882, I Jonathan King being frail in body but of sound mind. My just and lawful debts to be paid, and the remainder of my property, be divided between my lawful heirs as the law directs, to the property I own in this State. Having full confidence in my old tried friend David Harvey Kennemur after my death to take charge of all my property both real and personal to sell to the best interest of their heirs. That my land be laid off in convenient tracts and sold seperately. Wit: Noah R. Kennemur, Elias C. Hollingsworth, Henry B. Brookshire. Signed: Jonathan King. Filed 8 Oct. 1883. Samuel King of N.C. a son requested the est. to be admnr. dated 17 Dec. 1885. Heirs: Nancy King the widow, Samuel King, Jacob King, James King, Jeremiah King, Mary A. Hamlin, Hariet Barton, Rebecca E. Clark and the heirs at law of Eliza Holbert decd. to wit, B. F. Holbert, Rebecca Love, M. L. Patilo, Littleton Patilo and heirs of David King decd. to wit, Mary England, Matilda Wheeler, William Stone husband of Lizzie Stone decd. and the heirs of Hanah Clark decd. to wit. Perry C. Clark, George H. Clark, Matilda Brascomb, Rebecca Saterfield, Missouri Ware. 6 Dec. 1883 Nath. McMin Sheriff of Brevard, N.C. recd. $9.88 from Saml. King for Jonathan King for taxes.

KING, MARY Deed Book B, Page 76. Clerk of Court Office. Pickens, S. C. On 27 Nov. 1865. Mary King was a sister of William M. Fennell decd. of PIckens Dist. Her father was Hardy J. Fennell.

KING, "MINORS" Box 3 #123. Probate Judge Office. Pickens, S.C. On 18 Jan. 1894 John B. King, Warren Hamilton, Elias Day are bound

King, Minors - Continued. unto J. B. Newberry, Ord. in the sum of
$594.62. 31 Jan. 1894 J. B. King gdn. of James B. King, Clarence King,
Arthur G. King, Chas. S. King, Ruth King minor under 14 yrs. J. B.
King of Easley gdn. of Warren M., John Milton King minors over 14 yrs.
chn. of Mrs. Lou M. King of Easley.

KING, "MINORS" Box 6 #126. Probate Judge Office. Pickens, S.C.
On 3 Feb. 1896 Margaret C. King, J. Monroe King, Mary King are bound
to J. B. Newberry, Ord. in the sum of $100. Margaret C. King gdn. of
Vester E. and Flora Margaret King minors under 21 yrs. Chn. of
Margaret C. and Jacob M. King decd. Vester E. was born 24 Oct. 1880,
Flora M. was born 12 Sept. 1882. On 8 Dec. 1905 Vester E. Holcombe
and Flora M. Smith recd. shares.

KING, ROBERT SENR. Pack 363. Probate Judge Office. Anderson,
S. C. Est. admnr. 25 Jan. 1797 by Elizabeth King, James Anderson,
William Owen. Elizabeth was an Anderson in 1799. Note. She either
married an Anderson after she become a widow or she was an Anderson
before her marriage.

KING, THOMAS J. Box 115 #5. Probate Judge Office. Pickens, S.C.
Est. admnr. 28 Dec. 1887 by R. F. Smith, J. P. Smith, F. C. Boggs who
are bound to J. B. Newberry, Ord. in the sum of $200. Died 28 Aug.
1887. W. J. King a son.

KING, WILLIAM Grant #134. Clerk of Court Office. Pickens, S.C.
By W. L. Keith, Clk. To any lawful surveyor you are authorized to lay
out unto William King a tract of land not exceeding ten thousand
acres and make a true platt thereof. Dated 15 Aug. 1850. Executed
for 1455 acres. Certified the 3 Oct. 1850.

KINGSLEY, CHESTER. Deed Book Y, Page 12. Clerk of Court Office.
Anderson, S. C. I Edward M. Hall of Anderson Dist. in consideration
of $300 to me paid by Chester Kingsley of the same Dist. Have granted,
sold, bargained and released a tract of land containing 60 3/4 acres.
Lying on Cherokee Creek waters of Rockey River, bounded by land of
Burwell Magee and E. Mitchel. Dated 1845. Wm. B. Hall, Armstead M.
Hall. Signed: Ed. M. Hall. Proved on oath of Wm. B. Hall before
W. Magee Ord. this 21 Nov. 1845.

KINGSLEY, CHESTER Deed Book V, Page 8. Clerk of Court Office.
Anderson, S. C. I John Maxwell of Anderson Dist. in considera tion of
$2,600 paid me by Chester Kingsley of Abbeville Dist. Have granted,
sold, bargained and released all that tract of land whereon I now live
containing 300 acres, lying on Hencoop Creek, it being a tract granted
to myself. Dated 10 Sept. 1835. Wit: Wm. Kay or Hay Jr., Geo.
Mattison. Signed: John Maxwell. Proved on oath of William Kay
before Wm. F. Clinkscales, J.P. this 2 Nov. 1835. Jane Maxwell the
wife of John Maxwell released and relinquished her interest and claim
of dower in the above land. Dated 2 Nov. 1835. Wm. F. Clinkscales,
J.P.

KINGSLEY, CHESTER Deed Book Y, Page 103. Clerk of Court Office.
Anderson, S. C. I David Alexander of Anderson Dist. in consideration
of $343 paid me by Chester Kingsley of the same Dist. Have granted,
sold, bargained and released a certain tract of land containing 76 1/4
acres, lying in Anderson Dist. on Cherokee Creek waters of Rockey
River. Bound by land of David Alexander, Jonathan Duease and Chester
Kingsley. Tract granted to John Buchanan. Dated this 13 Nov. 1843.
Wit: Hugh C. Alexander, Stewart Strickland. Signed: David Alexander.
Jane Alexander the wife of David Alexander, renounce and relinquish her
interest and right of dower in the above land before R. N. Wright,
M.A.D. this 13 Nov. 1843.

KINGSLEY, CHESTER Deed Book W, Page 436. Clerk of Court Office.
Anderson, S. C. I James F. Wyatt of Anderson Dist. In consideration
of $138 to me paid by Chester Kingsley of the same Dist. have granted,
sold, bargained and released a tract of land containing 19 and eight
tenths, lying on a branch of Cherokee Creek waters of Rickey River.

Kingsley, Chester - Continued. Dated 28 Jan. 1840. Wit: Asa
Clinkscales, M. Magee. Signed: James F. Wyatt. Proved on oath of
Asa Clinkscales before Elijah Webb Clk. of Court. This 3 Jan. 1840.

KINGSLEY, CHESTER Pack 127. In Equity, Clerk of Court Office.
Anderson, S. C. Anderson Dist. In Equity. Writ of Partition. To
George R. Brown, Mastin Williams, Enoch Breazeals, Joseph Cox, and
James Wyatt, Esquires. You and each of you are authorized and required,
on the receipt hereof, that you do partition and fairly divide between
Erasmus R. Kingsley, Eugene T. Kingsley, and Francis E. Kingsley
minors children and heirs at law of Chester Kingsley decd. the real
estate of which he died possessed with. If land could not be divided
with out harm to one or all then a public sale to be held. Signed by
and the witness A. O. Norris, Esq. Comm. in Equity. Dated 22 Aug. 1846.

KIRKLAND, RICHARD Bundle 21 Pack 8. Probate Judge Office.
Barnwell, S. C. I Richard Kirkland of Barnwell Dist. Planter, being
of good and perfect health and of sound mind and memory. First I
desire my just and lawful debts and funeral expenses be first paid.
The tract of land on which I now reside and two adj. tracts, also three
tracts in the swamp, I leave to my beloved wife Mary Kirkland during
her natural life, at her death, the land to belong to my son Richard
Kirkland. He to have equal control over all land except the plantation
and buildings whereon I now live. The tract of land I purchased from
Benjamin Blount, containing 363 acres, I leave to my son Richard
Kirkland. The one tract I purchased from Charles Blount, and one tract
I purchased from James McKay, I leave to my dtr. Lydia Kirkland. I
leave to my wife negro named Charles during her life time at her death
said negro to belong to my son Richard Kirkland, I also leave to my
wife negroes, Tamar and her two chn. Sophia and Moria, also molattoo
girl Cassey, also Sill and her chn. Jenney and Primas, also Jonny and
George. I leave to my wife my stock of horses, Cattle, hogs with all
household and kitchen furniture and at her death to be divided between
my two youngest chn. Richard and Lydia. I leave to my son Richard a
negro named Moses a boy named Joe. I leave to my dtr. Eliza Carvin
(this may be Garvin), a negro named Isaac. I leave to my dtr. Ann
Beal my negro named Stepney during her natural life, at her death to be
her son Richard Beal. I give to my son William T. Kirkland a negro boy
named Frank, also a girl named Lucy, which negro was deeded to my dtr.
Tempey Kirkland decd., whose dying request was that her brother William
should have what belonged to her. I give to my dtr. Lydia a negro
named Pattey. I give to my grand daughter Eliza Garvin and Sarah
Smith Garvin, four head of cattle to be equally divided between them.
I appoint my wife executrix and my son William T. Kirkland executor.
Dated 15 Aug. 1812. Wit: Sarah Buxton, John Mixon, Jonas Elkin.
Signed: Ricd. Kirkland. Recorded 9 Nov. 1813.

KIRKPATRICK, JAMES Box 52 Pack 1233. Probate Judge Office.
Abbeville, S. C. Abbeville Dist. Admnr. bond. We William Mayn,
Robert C. Gordon, William Crawford and Ezekiel Evans are bound unto
Andrew Hamilton, Ord. in the sum of $5,000. Dated 23 Oct. 1809.
Inventory made 23 Oct. 1809 by Ezekiel Evans Senr., Wm. Hadden, and
James Stevenson. Sale held 14 Nov. 1809. Buyers: Robert Allis,
James Hawthorn, Thos. Hawthorn, Robert C. Gordon, Wm. McAlwain, David
Cummins, Andrew Kirkpatrick, Thos. Beaty, Oliver Martin, Dr. John
Miller, Thomas Cunningham.

KIRKPATRICK, JANE Pack 494. Clerk of Court Office. Abbeville,
S. C. Petition for guardianship. Abbeville Dist. The petition of
Jane Kirkpatrick the widow of Thomas Kirkpatrick decd. and the follow-
ing chn. Barbary about eleven yrs. old, Richard about eight yrs. old,
Jane about seven yrs. old, Elizabeth about five yrs. old, and Hannah
Kirkpatrick about two yrs. old. Who are entitled to an interest in the
estate of their father. Your petitioner prays that she the mother of
said minors may be appointed guardian. Filed 9 June 1851.

KIRKPATRICK, THOMAS Pack 356. Clerk of Court Office. Abbeville,
S. C. Abbeville Dist. In Equity, To the Honr. the Chancellors: Your
oratrix Jane Kirkpatrick of said Dist. That her husband Thomas Kirkpatrick late of this Dist. departed this life intestate 22 Nov. 1848.
Possessed with two tracts of land situated in Laurens Dist. One tract
lying on Reedy River containing 365 acres bounded by land of John
McKnight, Joseph Sullivan and others, the other tract on waters of
Rabuns Creek, containing 175 acres, bounded by land of John Garrett,
Jesse Garrett, William Mahaffy and others. That the said husband left
as distributees your oratrix and his chn. Mary, Margaret, Barbery,
and Richard Kirkpatrick and ___ a child has since his death been born
of your oratrix, a postumores child of said deceased. The admnr.
was committed to your oratrix and Gabriel M. Mattison and William
Maddox. The personal est. more than sufficient to pay all debts. Your
oratrix prays for a partition of said land. Filed 4 June 1849.
Barbary Kirkpatrick was about 10 yrs. old when filed. Thomas Kirkpatrick purchased said land the 2 Feb. 1837 from John Kennedy of
Laurens Dist. Land originally granted to James Abercrombie. Witness:
John Kennedy Jr. and Alfred Perritt. John Kennedy wife was Barbary
Kennedy, who released her dower on the land before Alfred Perritt, J.Q.
the 4 Feb. 1837. Deed proved on oath of John Kennedy Jr. before
Alfred Perritt, J.Q. on the 4 Feb. 1837. Recorded 29 Jan. 1838.

KIRKSEY, EADY CATHERINE Box 112 #1069. Probate Judge Office.
Pickens, S. C. I Edy Catherine Kirksey now being of a sound mind and
memory. I give to my dtr. Rebecca Kirksey all my real estate consisting of two tracts, one known as the home tract on which I now live,
the other known as the Wm. Holden tract, with all personal property,
etc. I appoint my son Joseph Brown Kirksey my sole and lawful executor. I desire my executor to pay all debts and funeral expenses.. and
shall dispose of any or all the said legacy for the support and comfort
of my dtr. Rebecca. It is well known that my dtr. is not of mind
sufficient to manage her affairs, therefore, I request my son and
executor is hereby directed to do so for her. Dated 26 Sept. 1874.
Wit: A. J. Anderson, J. B. Hester, J. B. Reid. Signed: Eady Catherine
Kirksey. Filed this 26 May 1877.

KIRKSEY, E. W. Box 31 #365. Probate Judge Office. Pickens,
S. C. Est. admnr. 11 Sept. 1854 by Robert Kirksey, Thomas J. Keith
who are bound unto W. J. Parson, Ord. in the sum of $3,000. Expend
Paid D. Garvin. $580. Jared Kerksey $765. Robert Kirksey $765. Wm.
Kirksey $1056.33. Christopher Kirksey $643. Catharine Hallum $700.
B. F. Halland $1140.

KIRKSEY, FAIR Pack 210. In Equity. Clerk of Court Office.
Pickens, S. C. Fair Kirksey of Anderson Dist. died intestate 24 April
1845. His brother Silas Kirksey applied for letter of admnr. upon
his est. Among the papers he found that he (Fair Kirksey) had two
deeds of trust making him trustee for his two sisters Mrs. Catherine
Hallum and Penelope Holland. Fair Kirksey died without wife or
children having never been married, his heirs were his father William
Kirksey and brothers and sisters viz. Nancy Garvin wife of David
Garvin, the heirs of at law of Jared Kirksey decd. who died since Fair
Kirksey, to wit. Jerod Kirksey, Isaiah Kirksey, Mary Kirksey, Robert
Kirksey, William Kirksey, Catharine Hallum wife of T. J. Hallum,
Christopher Kirksey, Penelope Holland who married B. F. Holland and
the said Silas Kirksey. Silas Kirksey states that E. W. Kirksey one
of the brothers died shortly after his brother Fair Kirksey never
having married and leaving no chn. Filed 16 Mar. 1852. Deed of Trust
William Kirksey Senr. to Fair Kirksey, Anderson Dist. I Jefferson
Hallum of Anderson Dist. in consideration of natural love and affection
which I have toward my wife Catharine Hallum, and the sum of five
dollars to me paid by Fair Kirksey of the same dist. have granted
bargained, sold and released all that tract of land lying on 23 Mile
Creek water of Seneca River. Containing 345 acres, conveyed to me by
Franklin Holland called the Polly Symmes place, adj. lands of Reuben
Cason, Michael Miller, Jesse Martin, William Dasmore decd. The said
premises in trust for the only and seperate use benefit and behoof of
said Catharine Hallum, during her natural life and at her death to the

Kirksey, Fair - Continued. only use and benefit of the heirs of her body forever. I give Fair Kirksey as trustee full power and authority to sell and dispose of part or all of said premises if he shall deem it to the interest of the parties, etc. Dated, 25 March 1843. Wit: John B. Benson, B. F. Holland. Signed: T. F. Hallum. We George Seaborn and Benjamin or (Berry) Sloan executors of J. B. Earle late of Anderson Dist. in consideration of $1,035 to us paid by Fair Kirksey of Pendleton Dist. have bargained, sold and delivered the following slaves, viz, Loyuda, Clarissa, Grant and Jane to the said Fair Kirksey in trust for the sole use and benefit of Catharine Hallum during her natural life, and free from debts or control of her husband, and after her death in trust for such child or chn. she may have. Dated this 12 Nov. 1844. Wit: J. B. E. Sloan. Signed: B. F. Sloan, Executor and Geo. Seaborn, Extor. Wm. Kirksey to Fair Kirksey, Pickens, Dist. I William Kirksey of Pickens Dist. in consideration of love and affection which I have toward my dtr. Penelope Holland and the sum of $5 to me paid by Fair Kirksey of Anderson Dist. have sold bargained and delivered the following slaves, Malinda about 14 yrs. old. Rose about 14 yrs. old in trust for the only, separate use and benefit of Penelope Holland during her natural life, and at her death to the heirs of her body only. Dated 5 Feb. 1842. Wit: Christopher Kirksey, E. W. Kirksey. Signed: Wm. Kirksey.

KIRKSEY, JAMES K. & SILAS Pack 212 #7. Clerk of Court Office. Pickens, S. C. We James K. and W. Silas Kirksey and Elizabeth Clayton of Pickens Dist. in consideration of $70.50 to us paid by Jno. B. Clayton, have granted, sold, bargained and released all that tract of land being in the County of Oconee on waters of Boon's Creek and branches of McKinneys Creek. Adj. lands of B. F. Robinson, James McKinney, containing 375 acres. Dated 26 July 1875. Wit: D. F. Bradley, W. E. Nimmons. Signed: J. K. Kirksey and W. S. Kirksey. Note: Elizabeth Clayton did not sign this deed.

KIRKSEY, MARK Deed Book A-1, Page 10. Clerk of Court Office. Pickens, S. C. Pendleton Dist. I Mark Kirksey of Pendleton Dist. in consideration of the sum of $300 to me paid by Daniel Rector of the same Dist. have granted, sold, bargained and released a part of a tract of land originally granted to John Robertson of Charleston, S. C. containing 300 acres, except one half an acre including the family buring ground, situated on the East side of 12 Mile River and on the West side of Rice's Creek. Dated 21 March 1828. Wit: Thomas X Lively, Allen Powel. Signed: Mark Kirksey. Proved on oath of Allen Powel before James Langston, Justice. This 26 June 1828. Recorded the 6 Nov. 1828 and examined by W. L. Keith, C.C.R.M.C.

KIRKSEY, ROBERT Box 101 #1058. Probate Judge Office. Pickens, S. C. I Robert Kirksey of Pickens Dist. being of sound mind and memory, etc. First I direct all my debts and funeral expenses be paid. I will my land in the State of Mississippi that I purchased from Samuel Reid lying in Gauderdale County, containing 1,080 unto to my three chn. viz; W. S. Kirksey, M. E. Clayton, and J. K. Kirksey to be equally divided amongst them after my death. I will unto W. S. Kirksey my tract of land I purchased from Jeremiah Looper on Wolf Creek, containing 160 acres. I will unto my dtr. M. E. Clayton $500, if there is that much left after carrying out my will. I will unto J. K. Kirksey my home tract viz, the Barton tract of 247 acres, the Christopher Kirksey tract of 504 acres, the Giton tract of 160 acres. With all household and kitchen furniture, my blacksmith tools, stock, cattle, etc. I appoint J. K. Kirksey executor. Dated 30 March 1870. Wit: Joseph J. Norton, Wm. C. Keith, W. C. Hillhouse. Signed: Robert Kirksey. Proven 3 July 1871. He owned 600 acres on Eastatoe adj. lands of Elijah Henkle, John McKinney. 200 acres on Crow Creek, adj. lands of C. C. Parson, est. of Saml. Maverick, a tract in Oconee Co. on Boons Creek, adj. lands of Mrs. Robinson, Jas. J. Kirksey, Mary E. Clayton a dtr.

KIRKSEY, SILAS Box 32 #366. Probate Judge Office. Pickens, S. C. I Silas Kirksey of Pickens Dist. Do make this my last will and testament. I desire my executors first pay my just debts and funeral

Kirksey, Silas - Continued. expenses. I will to my nephew
William Silas Kirksey son of Robert Kirksey the following negroes viz;
Vina and her chn. Wesley, Mahala, Brazeale, Harriet, Julia Ann, Eli and
Sarah Elizabeth and their increase. I will to my nephew Silas K.
Kirksey son of B. F. Holland and my sister Penelope the following
negroes. Dulla and her chn. Harrison, Mary Ann, George. I will to my
father William Kirksey Senr. my negro Sam during his natural life, at
his death to my brother Robert Kirksey forever. I will to my nephew
Silas Garvin son of David Garvin Senr. and my sister Nancy the following negroes, Jincy and Tom with all their increase. I will to my
brother Robert Kirksey the following negro Isam forever. I will to my
sister Penelope Holland wife of B. F. Holland my negro man Frank forever. I will that after my debts and funeral charges are paid the
remainder of my property be sold and equally divided amongst my brother
and sisters viz; Christopher Kirksey, Heirs of Jared Kirksey, William
Kirksey Jr., Catharine Hallum. I desire my executors have the marble
slab now at my house placed over the grace of my brother Fair Kirksey
and procure a similar one, and have placed over my brother E. Winchester
Kirksey grave and pay for same out of my est. I appoint William L.
Keith and John S. Lorton my executors. Also to take charge of the
property willed to my nephews William Silas Kirksey and Silas K.
Holland until they arrive at age. Dated 5 Oct. 1853. Wit: James
George, Jos. or Jas. W. Ross, L. C. Craig, W. N. Craig. Signed:
Silas Kirksey. Proved 23 Jan. 1854.

KIRKSEY, WILLIAM SENR. Box 31 #364. Probate Judge Office.
Pickens, S. C. Est. admnr. 25 Aug. 1854 by Robert Kirksey, Fountain
Alexander, Joseph W. Ross are bound unto W. J. Parson, Ord. in the sum
of $30,000. 30 Jan. 1861 Robert Kirksey petition the Court for a final
settlement of Wm. Kirksey's est. as to his share of the est. of Silas
Kirksey decd. the same having come into my hands since the settlement
of Wm. Kirksey's individual est. Heirs: Nancy the wife of David
Garvin, Heirs of Jared Kirksey decd. viz; Isaiah A., Jared E. F., Mary
L. P., Christopher Kirksey, Catharine Hallum, Penelope the wife of
B. F. Holland resides out of State, Wm. Kirksey the admnr. 1 Sept. 1855
Catharine the wife of T. J. Hallum recd. $1634. In this same pack, a
letter from Jared E. F. Kirksey, Isaiah W. Kirksey and Mary P. L.
Kirksey of Tuscaloosa Co., Ala. Romulus Post Office. Dated 3 Nov.
1855. To Messers B. F. Perry and E. W. Keith attorney at law;
requesting them to represent them on the 14 Dec. 1855 at the final
settlement of the estate of Wm. Kirksey Senr. est. and the est. of
E. W. Kirksey decd. est. Jared Kirksey was their father. Notes on the
family, William Kirksey was the husband of Edy C. Kirksey who was a
niece to William L. Keith. Their chn. Joseph and Rebecca Kirksey.
Silas Kirksey died 10 Oct. 1853.

KIRKWOOD, HUGH Land warrant, Book A, Page 6. 96 Dist. For the
est. of Hugh Kirkwood decd. On the bounty, two hundred acres of land
situate on both sides of Conneross Creek, waters of Keowee River.
Bounded by land of Capt. John Bowie, all others sides vacant when
surveyed by Bannett Crafton, D.S. per platt recorded this 26 May 1784.
Robert Anderson C.L.

KIRKWOOD, HUGH Box 108 Pack 2922. Probate Judge Office.
Abbeville, S. C. I Hugh Kirkwood serjeant of the Second Company of
Independants in the service of the State of S. C. being at all appearance at this point of death occasioned by a wound I received the 9th
inst. in an attack made on the town of Savannah, Thanks be to God,
sound in mind, memory and judgement do make this my last W. & T. etc.
I order and impower my hereafter named executor to make titles unto
Genl. Andrew Williamson Esq. to a tract of 250 acres of land lying on
the waters of Little River of Savannah River in 96 Dist. Which land
was originally granted to me and in my name, he the Genl. Williamson
having fully paid me the purchase money thereof. I give unto my three
children all my ready money, outstanding debts, and all other property
that I shall die possessed of. I give unto my three children any land
I may be entitled to as serving and dying in my countrys service, to
be equally divided between them. I appoint Major John Bowie, my
executor of this my last W. & T. also guardian of my three children,

Kirkwood, Hugh - Continued. leaving their education and bringing up entirely at his discretion. Dated 10 Oct. 1779. Wit: Jno. Caldwell, John Moore, Benet Crafton. Signed: Hugh X Kirkwood. Proved on oath of Bennett Crafton before John Thomas Jr. of 96 Dist. on the 27 April 1785.

KLEINBECK, JULIANA Box 2 #57. Clerk of Court Office. Pickens, S. C. In Equity, on 5 July 1858 Juliana Kleinbeck a minor over 14 yrs. Parents are both dead. John Henry Kleinbeck her uncle her gdn.

KLEINBECK, JOHN D. Deed Book 1 page 179. Clk. of Court Office. Pickens, S. C. On 17 March 1857 he owned a mill tract of land on Cane Creek of 118 acres. Also 50 acres, a small farm near Walhalla. Also 2 town lots in Walhalla of one and one half acres. Mrs. Gesina Kleinbeck was admnr. John H. Kleinbeck was admnr. of Mrs. Gesina Kleinbeck est. Chn. Juliana, Eliza, John H. Kleinbeck.

KNIGHT, EUGENIA M. Box 118 #7. Clerk of Court Office. Pickens, S. C. On 10 Nov. 1885 Geo. R. Knight, W. W. Knight, John Knight are bound unto J. H. Newton, Ord. in the sum of $125.30. George R. Knight gdn. of Eugenia M. Knight a minor of 17 yrs. old. Dtr. of Geo. W. McWhorter decd.

KNIGHT, JAMES H. Box 103 #1080. Clerk of Court Office. Pickens, S. C. On 4 March 1872 had a nervous breakdown since his return from Alabama. Miss Louisa Knight his sister.

KNIGHT, MARTHA A. Deed Book D-2, Page 157. Clerk of Court Office. Pickens, S. C. I Martha A. Knight of Pickens Dist. in consideration of $350 paid me by Samuel S. Knight of Pickens Dist. have granted, sold, bargained and released all that tract of land lying in Pickens Dist. on waters of Praters Creek, waters of 12 Mile River. Adj. land of H. Hagood, Mary Chapman, Larkin Hughes. Containing 74 acres, conveyed to me by James W. Hughes the 8 Jan. 1874 and known as the Jimmy Hughes place in Pew Ridge. Dated this 8 Oct. 1878. Wit: J. K. Kirksey, C. L. Hollingsworth before Julius E. Boggs, N.P. this 8 Oct. 1878. Recorded the 10 Oct. 1878.

KNOX, MRS. FRANCES Pack 227 #13. Clerkof Court Office. Pickens, S. C. On 15 March 1860 George Whisemant was arrested on oath of Warren R. David that he did some time in Feb. last unlawfully trade with George a slave of Mrs. Frances Knox by trading and buying corn.

KNOX, JOHN A. P. Box #360. Probate Judge Office. Pickens, S.C. Est. admnr. 15 Sept. 1834 by Samuel Knox of the State of Georgia and William D. Sloan are bound unto James H. Dendy, Ord. in the sum of #20. Cot. Pub. at Poplar Springs Church.

KNOX, JOH[sic] C. Box 81 #858. Probate Judge Office. Pickens, S. C. Est. admnr. 28 Nov. 1864 by Elizabeth Knox, Elisha M. Alexander, Robert Knox are bound unto W. E. Holcombe, Ord. in the sum of $6,000.

KNOX, JOHN ESQ. Box 47 #518. Probate Judge Office. Pickens, S. C. Est. admnr. 19 Oct. 1857 by B. F. Okelly, Miles Knox, Jesse Jenkins, Robert Knox are bound unto W. J. Parson, Ord. in the sum of $5,000. Paid 16 Feb. 1860 Nancy Knox widow in full $611.53. Paid Jeremiah Moody in full $203.84. Paid Narcissa Knox $203.86. Paid Sarah M. Knox $203.86. Paid Mamnda[sic] Crain $201.00. Paid B. F. Okelly $203.84. Paid Miles Knox $203.84.

KNOX, JOHN Pack 365. Probate Judge Office. Anderson, S. C. Pickens Dist. I John Knox of said Dist. being of sound and disposing mind and memory, but weak in body. I give to my wife Fanny Knox one negro woman named Phillis, also the plantation whereon I now live containing 950 acres, one still, waggons, tools, household and kitchen furniture and five negores viz; Girl Jinny, girl Celia, girl Mattey, Girl Hannah, boy named Bob to be her property during her natural life or widowhood. At the death or marriage of my wife the willed property to her, I give to my two sons Washington Knox and Andrew Knox. I give

Knox, John - Continued. to my son Isaac Knox one negro girl named Jenny. I give to my son Matthew Knox one negro girl named Celia. I give to my son James Knox one negro girl named Mattey. To my dtr. Sarah McClure I now at this time give her one negro girl named Lame now in her possession. I give to my dtr. Elizabeth Dandy one negro girl named Lucinda, now in her possession. I give to my son William Knox one negro named Bob. I give to my dtr. Mary Ann one negro girl named Mariah at the day of her marriage or at my wife death or marriage. I give to my dtr. Susanah one negro girl named Frances at her marriage or at my wife death or marriage. I give to my son Samuel Knox one negro named Hannah. The first issue of Jenny or Celia shall be the property of my son Washington Knox. The second issue shall be the property of my son Andrew Knox. The plantation in the State of Georgia to be sold by my executors for the use of the family or put on interest as they think best for the family. I give to my son John Knox $150 to my son James Knox I give $50. The balance to be divided amongst sons Washington and Andrew and dtr. Susannah. I appoint my wife executrix and my son Samuel Knox executor. Dated 20 Jan. 1828. Wit: Alexr. Ramsay, William Knox, Thomas Lamar, Jacob (O) Frederick. Signed: John Knox. Proven on oath of Alexander Ramsay, and same time qualified Frances Knox and Samuel Knox executors. Dated 21 July 1828 by John Harris Ord. Pen. Dist. Est. appraisers were Alexander Ramsay, Geo. W. Liddell, J. Stribling was made 11 Aug. 1828.

KNOX, SAMUEL Pack 5 (Basement) Clerk of Court Office. Pickens, S. C. Samuel Knox married Mary Swift an heir of Nancy Swift decd. They were residing in Franklin Co., Ga. Filed 24 March 1855. (Taken from the Equity records of Thos. W. Harbin.)

KNOX, SARAH ANN Pack 439. #19. Clerk of Court Office. Pickens, S. C. Pickens Dist. Bastardy bond: Whereas Col. Jesse McKenney, William McKinney and Pleasant Alexander, on the 18 June 1836 before W. L. Keith Esq. Clk. of Court acknowledge themselves jointly and severally to owe the State the sum of ₤60 sterling or $257.16. On condition that the said Jesse McKinney shall pay five pounds sterling or $21.43 annually for the maintainance of a female bastard child of which Sarah Ann Knox a single woman was delivered in the month of June 1836, until said child is twelve years old. Whereas the said Jesse McKinney hath not at any time since the birth of said bastard child was born, paid the sum due for the maintainance, and has refused to do so. It is therefore ordered that William McKinney and Pleasant Alexander do appear at the next Court of General session to show cause if any why their recognizance bond should not be forfeited, and further proceeding had thereon. Dated this third Monday in March 1838. Signed: W. L. Keith, Clk. C.

KUHTMANN, H. W. Land Warrant. Pack 630 #6. Clerk of Court Office. Pickens, S. C. I James E. Hagood, Clk. fo Court. To William Cook or any other lawful deputy surveyor, you are authorized and required to lay out unto H. W. Khutmann a tract of vacant land in this Dist. and make a true platt thereof. Dated 19 Nov. 1860. Executed for 158 acres for Col. H. W. Kuhtmann this 23 Nov. 1860 on Mill Creek waters of Little River. Filed 13 Dec. 1860.

KUHTMANN, H. W. Land Warrant. Pack 603 #83. Clerk of Court Office. Pickens, S. C. By James E. Hagood, Clerk of Court, to any lawful surveyor you are authorized to lay out unto H. W. Kuhtmann a tract of land not exceeding one thousand acres, and make a true platt thereof. Dated 14 Dec. 1857. Executed for 900 acres the 15 Dec. 1857. Filed 8 Feb. 1858.

KYLE, JAMES Box 52 Pack 1226. Probate Judge Office. Abbeville, S. C. Abbeville Dist. Admnr. bond, We Mary Kyle, Samuel L. Watt, Patrick Noble, William Lesly and Robert H. Lesly are bound unto Talo. Livingston, Ord. in the sum of $20,000. Dated 1 Feb. 1815. Expend Paid 4 May 1816 cash to Louisa Kyle by Mary Kyle when going to Mrs. Gregories school $7.37 1/2. Paid 31 Jan. 1817 Hunter Kyle for an arithmetic book $1.00. Paid 3 Mar. 1817 James Curry tuitition for James Kyle $5.00. Paid 30 June 1817 which I charged myself being the

Kyle, James - Continued. valuation assessed by three men for
3 1/2 acres of Jews land near Abbeville Village in which Mr. Kyle had
a claim. Saml. L. Watt admnr. 2 Dec. 1817 paid Uriah Barron for shoes
for Jane Kyle $1.75. Paid 3 Jan. 1818 Samuel Houston tutition for
Margaret Kyle $4.00. Paid 27 Feb. for 2 1/2 yds. apron checks for
Eliza Kyle .93 3/4. Tuitition for William Hunter Kyle $2.57 3/4.

LAFFOON, WILLIAM Deed Book G, Page 323. Mesne Conveyance.
Greenville, S. C. I William Laffoon of Pendleton Dist. in consideration of $500 to me paid by Elias Earle, have bargained, sold and
released all that tract of land lying in Greenville Dist. between the
North and South forks of Saluda River, granted to Daniel Kelly and by
him conveyed to William Laffoon the 18 May 1790 and including the
plantation where William Blitcher formerly lived, also one tract
purchased of William Right adj. land of Elias Earles, near the bridge
below the iron works. Containing 100 acres. Dated 16 Nov. 1805.
Wit: Wm. Anderson, Jo. Crawford, Geo. W. Earle. Signed: Wm. Laffoon.
Proved on oath of Geo. W. Earle before J. Thomas, J.Q. this 3 Dec. 1805.
Recorded 3 Dec. 1805.

LANE, SAMUEL Box 53 Pack 1260. Probate Judge Office. Abbeville,
S. C. I Samuel Lane of Abbeville Dist. First pay my just debts and
funeral expenses. I give to my wife Charity Lane, three negroes, Nanny,
Florer and Isaac a chesnut sorrel mare, a tract of land containing
100 acres, property of the late Benjamin Hill. An instrument of writing
left in the hands of Mr. James W. Cotten of Charleston giving from
Miss Millecent Colcock to Samuel Lane for the sum of $936. All the
household and kitchen furniture and my wearing apparel. Thirdly I
give devise and... No more of will found in notes. Dated June 6,
1805. Recorded 2 Nov. 1805.

LANGERDS, JOHN Deed Book __, Pack 502. Clerk of Court Office.
Abbeville, S. C. This indenture made this 2 Aug. 1791 between John
Langerds of Abbeville Dist. and William Burton of the same Dist. In
consideration of Ŀ12 sterling to me paid by William Burton, have
granted, bargained, sold and released all that tract of land containing 109 acres, lying on Johnsons Creek of Savannah River. Being part
of a 733 acres granted to Henry Watkins on the 6 April 1783. Wit:
Adam Crain Jones, Jr., Nathaniel Barnes, Henry Tallow. Signed: John
Langerds. Recorded 28 March 1792.

LANGARD, JOHN Pack 482. Clerk of Court Office. Abbeville, S.C.
This indenture made this 17 Aug. 1797. Between John Langard and his
wife Catron, of Abbeville Dist. and Zedekiah Wood of Dist. aforesaid.
In consideration of Ŀ12 sterling in hand paid by Zadekiah Wood. Have
sold, bargained, and released a certain tract of land containing 100
acres. Being on the Rushe Branch, bounded by land of Ruthledge and
Gottanis, Wm. Bertens and John Langard. Wit: James Langham, Robert
Green. Signed: John Langards and Catron X Langard. I A. C. Jones,
J.P. do certify that Catherine Langard the wife of John Langard did
this day voluntarily renounce, release and relinquish all her interest
and right and claim of dower on the above land. Signed: Catherine
X Langham. Dated 26 Aug. 1797. Adm. C. Jones J.A.C. Proved on oath
of James Langham, before Adm. C. Jones, J.A.C. this 28 Aug. 1797.

LATIMER, MICAJAH Pack 427. In Equity. Clerk of Court Office.
Abbeville, S. C. Abbeville Dist. In Equity. The petition of Micajah
B. Latimer sheweth that he was appointed by this Court guardian of the
est. and person of his nephews Charles C. A. Latimer and James S.
Latimer and niece Mary K. Latimer. (Same info. as in the 1851 Court
suit). except Mary K. Latimer departed this life __ day in Oct. 1854,
leaving her brothers as only heirs. Filed 22 May 1855.

LATIMER, SARAH ANN Pack 496. In Equity. Clerk of Court Office.
Abbeville, S. C. In Equity, to the Honr. the Chancellors: The
petition of Ezekiel Trible of Abbeville Dist. Sheweth that on 13 April
1851 Edmund Peyton Holleman and Sarah Ann Latimer entered into a

Latimer, Sarah Ann - Continued. marriage settlement. Whereas
Sarah Ann with the consent of Edmund Peyton Holleman, sold and released
and conveyed a tract of land, seven slaves, hogs, mules and cattle in
trust for uses and purpose to wit, dishcarge all debts and for her
sole use until her marriage to Holleman, and after their marriage for
the joint use of them. After her death for and to her heirs of her
body. That on the 8 Dec. the present month Sarah Ann died. At the
time of her marriage she was indebted greatly and the indebtness has
not diminished, but increased. Sarah Ann at her death left three chn.
to wit: Charles A. C. Latimer age about 11 yrs., James S. Latimer
aged about 9 yrs., and Mary K. Latimer aged about 7 yrs., being her
only chn. The land is described in the deed, the slaves to wit,
Edmond aged about 45 yrs., Charles aged about 28 yrs., Bob aged about
22 yrs., Satire aged 12 yrs., Martha aged about 9 yrs., Middleton aged
about 7 yrs., the last named five chn. of Edmond and Letty his wife.
Your petitioner is advised that no power is given by the deed to sell
any of the property. Therefore without power to proceed in the matter
and need the direction of this Court. Filed this 24 Dec. 1851.

LAWRENCE, BENJAMIN Land grant. Book A, Page 8. Clerk of Court
Office. Abbeville, S. C. Grant for Benjamin Lawrence as a citizen for
395 acres, on E. side of Keowee River. Bounded by said river and vacant
land when surveyed by Bennett Crafton D.S. Dated 21 May 1784. Platt
recorded 27 May 1784. Signed: Robert Anderson C.L.

LAWSON, WILLIAM Box 53 Pack 1259. Probate Judge Office.
Abbeville, S. C. I William Lawson of Abbeville Dist. now being weak
of body but of sound mind and memory and understanding. First my lawful
debts be paid. My dtr. Ann shall have a feather bed and furniture.
The balance of my property I give to my beloved wife Mathew Lawson
as long as she lives, also the plantation whereon I now reside, and at
her death to my dtr. Ann Lawson and her heirs. I appoint my wife
Mathew Lawson and James Lawson executors. Dated 3 Dec. 1807. Wit:
George Foreman, Archd. Douglass, J. or W. Mackney. Signed William
X Lawson. Inventory made 24 Dec. 1807 by John Conner, Esq., John
Arnold, James Arnold. Sale held 11 Jan. 1808. Buyers, Nancy Lawson,
Jno. B. Burn, John Lawson, Dabney Megehe, David Lawson, Silas Pace.

LEATHERS, ASA Pack 634. #177. Clerk of Court Office. Pickens,
S. C. On 3 Feb. 1845 Asa Leathers was appointed a constable of Pickens,
Dist.

LESLEY, ELIZA LULA #25. Clerk of Court Office. Abbeville, S. C.
In 1842 James L. Lesley was the guardian of Eliza Lula Lesley a minor.
On 5 Jan. 1857 she was mentioned as the wife of James M. White.
James L. Lasley the father of said minor.

LEATHERS, BENGAMAN Deed Book A, Page 78. Probate Judge Office.
Pickens, S. C. To W. D. Steele, Ord. The petition of Nimrod Leathers
sheweth that he is entitled to a share of the real est. of Bengaman
Leathers late of Pickens Dist. consisting of three tracts. On tract
of 173 acres on Shoal Creek adj. land of Thomas R. Shealor, Asa
Leathers. Another tract of 119 acres adj. land of Cleveland Merratt.
Another tract of 115 acres on Toxaway adj. land of Elijah Deaton.
Dated 2 Nov. 1846. Tohers[sic] heirs Nancy the wife of Jabel Carver,
William W. Leathers, Asa Leathers, Clarissa Leathers, Anson Leathers,
Elizabeth the wife of William McMurphrey, Mariam the wife of Samuel
Fuller. The last three resides out of State.

LEATHERS, WILLIAM Pack 630 #197. Clerk of Court Office. Pickens,
S. C. Pickens Dist. Land Warrant: By W. L. Keith, Clk. of Court.
To any lawful surveyor you are authorized to lay out unto William
Leathers a tract of land not exceeding ten thousand acres, and make a
true plat thereof. Dated 19 Nov. 1853. Executed for 96 acres by
E. R. Doyle Dep. Sur. Certified 5 Dec. 1853.

LEE, ANDREW Only ref. State of S. C. Souther Circuit. In
Equity. (Only last part of will found) I will to my dtr. Nancy Lee
two negroes named Jeff and Dinah and the land that was granted to

Lee, Andrew - Continued. Mathias Perfender, one horse, six cows and calves. To my dtr. Sara Lee, one negro named Marget, one tract of land on the North side of Saluda River and Lick Creek, and one other slave bought by my executors from the mill and bridge money, when she arrives at eighteen. I leave to my wife Nancy Lee the house I now live in and all negroes, stock that she want to keep for support of the children. She to use the money due from Andrew Robertson in North Carolina, and other debts due. "I desire that John Lee and Wilson Lee shall give a free passage over their bridge to all passangers that come to their brother mill that bring two bushels of grain at one time to be free toalage as long as them or their heirs keep aforesaid bridge." I appoint my wife Nancy and dtr. Susannah Lee and Mr. Jacob Smith executor. Dated 31 Dec. 1795. Wit: M. W. Moon, Hannah Patrick, Beverly Borrum. Signed: And. X Lee. In Equity. Southern Circuit. To the Honr. the Chancellors: Cullen Lark as well on behalf of himself and Andrew Lee Lark his son a minor about seven years old. sheweth that Andrew Lee departed this life in the month of Jan. 1795 (note will was dated 31 Dec. 1795, must be 1796) at time of death seized and possessed of divers ests. both real and personal. Leaving a widow and six chn. then living to wit: Dtr. Hannah who married before his death with George Lewis Patrick, dtr. Susanna who married since his death with Stephen Hearndon, dtr. Nancy who married since his death with Cullen Lark, your orator, and had two sons, one whom is since dead, and the named Andrew Lee Lark, a son Gershom Lee who also has departed this life intestate under the age of twenty one and unmarried. A son John Lee, a son Wilson Lee, and a dtr. Sally Lee who are still under the age of twenty one. Nancy Lee the relict and executrix, some time after the death of Andrew Lee married one Nicholas Vaughn by whom she had two chn. now living. But both herself and the said Nicholas are dead. Filed 11 Feb. 1805.

LEE, ANDREW Land grant. Book A, Page 17. Clerk of Court Office. Abbeville, S. C. Grant for Andrew Lee as a citizen for 100 acres lying in the fork of Great Rockey Creek and Hencoop Creek. Bounded on all sides by vacant land when surveyed by Bennett Crafton D.S. on 31 May 1784. Recorded this 5 June 1784. Robert Anderson, C.L.

LEE, THOMAS Land grant. Book A, page 17. Clerk of Court Office. Abbeville, S. C. Grant for Thomas Lee for 200 lying on E. side of Rockey River, bounded by the river and vacant on all sides when surveyed by Bennett Crafton, D.S. dated 29 May 1784. Recorded 5 June 1784. Robert Anderson, C.L.

LENDERMAN, PETER Apt. 8 File 595. Probate Judge Office. Greenville, S. C. On 7 Jan. 1841 John Lenderman was mentioned as the administrator of the est. of Peter Lenderman decd. of Greenville Dist. Heirs: Barbary Lenderman the widow. Henry Lenderman in Alabama. Nancy the wife of Hiram Hyde, out of State. Polly the wife of Thomas Hyde, Georgia. Caroline the wife of ___ Davis, Tennessee. Eliza the wife of John Kelly, Texas. John Stagner and child, Missouri. John Lenderman, Your petitoner. Catherine Lenderman, Alabama. Priscilla the wife of William Smith, Alabama.

LIDDELL, GEORGE Box 108 Pack 2958. Probate Judge Office. Abbeville, S. C. "The last will and testament of George Liddell, dictated and delcared by himself on Monday the twenty eight day of Dec. A.D. 1789 and committed to writing on Friday the first day of January A.D. 1790." [sic] First that all his just debts be paid. Next, that his wife Rachel may live on which ever of his plantation she pleases and have the negro wench Tab during fifteen years. Next, that his son James shall have the plantation on which the family now lives. Next, That his son George Washington shall have the plantation by Seneca River. Next, That the child of which his wife is now pregnant, if a daughter, shall have his negro wench Tab and that his negro fellow Jame shall be sold in such manner as the executors may judge to the best advantage and his price divided equally among the three children, but if a son, he shall have the wench Tab and the whole price of Jame. Next, that Capt. John Norwood shall see to a certain suit of him the said George Liddell now pending in Abbeville Court. Lastly.

Liddell, George - Continued. That Capt. John Norwood and Moses Liddell shall be executors of this his last will and testament. Wit: Robert Hall, H. Reid, Andrew Liddell. (No name signed to the will. No more papers in pack.)

LIDDELL, JAMES A. Pack 316. Clerk of Court Office. Abbeville, S. C. Abbeville Dist. In Equity, to the Honr. the Chancellors; Your orator William Wilson sheweth that James A. Liddell and himself on the 1 Jan. 1853 formed a partnership in the trade of Carriage making. That the partnership was dissolved in the month of Dec. 1855. That the said James A. Liddell left the State in the month of June 1855 and by letter has given information he never intends to return. Also that he purchased a tract of land in the town of Lowndesville, containing three acres, which contain a brick shop and a blacksmith shop, to which said Liddell has not a title to the land, or can he make one. Your orator prays that funds in the partnership be applied to his debts. Filed 6 July 1857.

LIDDLE, ANDREW Land Grant. Book A, Page 18. Clerk of Court Office. Abbeville, S. C. Grant for Andrew Liddle as a citizen for 400 acres lying on Six and twenty Mile Creek, a branch of Savannah River. Vacant land on all sides when surveyed by David Hopkins, D.S. certified 28 May 1784. Recorded 11 June 1784. By Robert Anderson, C.L.

LIDDLE, CAPT. GEORGE Land grant. Book A, Page 9. Clerk of Court Office, Abbeville, S. C. Grant for Capt. George Liddle as a citizen 400 acres on both sides of great Rockey Creek, a branch of Savannah River, known as the Great Sholes. Bounded on all sides by vacant land when surveyed by David Hopkins, D.S. on 22 May 1784. Platt recorded 27 May 1784, Robert. Anderson, C.L.

LIDDLE, CAPT. GEORGE Land Warrant. Book A, Page 2. Clerk of Court Office. Abbeville, S. C. For Capt. George Liddle on the Bounty, 300 West side of Keowee River bounding E. and E.S. on the River, the others sides vacant land. per plat. Recorded 26 May 1784. Robert Anderson, C.L.

LIDDLE, JAMES Box 54 Pack 1278. Probate Judge Office. Abbeville, S. C. I James Liddle of Abbeville Dist. being weak in body, but of sound mind and memory. I will my just debts are paid. I give to my wife Sarah the plantation on which I live, as much of my stock as she thinks best. Also as much as the household and kitchen furniture as she think proper to keep. I also leave her negroes Jemima and her family, also Dave and Tab his wife during her natural life. I give to James T. Liddell negro Florow and her increase. I give to my dtr. Eliza Ann Davis one negro named Mariah and Rinda and Robert. I give to my son George Washington Liddell at the age of twenty one, all my plantation West side of Parks Creek up to Reid Creek to my line, also negroes Sambo, Lewis and Rose. I give to my son James Thomas Liddell all my plantation East side of Parks Creek and negro George and Ransom, and Florow when he arrives at age of twenty one. I give to my dtr. Rachel Lucinda Liddell negroes Hannah, Mary, Vashti, a horse, saddle, bed and furniture. I give to my step son Joseph J. Jerkins[sic] a negro boy named Simon at his mother's death. I give to my brother W. Liddell all my wearing apparel. I appoint my wife executrix and my brothers Washington and Alexander Bowie executors. Dated 12 March 1823. Wit: Jas. Thomson, John Martin, John Liddell. Signed: J. Liddell. Proven 6 Feb. 1824.

LIDDLE, CAPT. MOSES Land Grant, Book A Page 10. Clerk of Court Office. Abbeville, S. C. Grant for Capt. Moses Liddle as a citizen 640 acres lying in the fork of Big Generostee Creek. Bounded by vacant land on all sides when surveyed. Certified by Bennett Crafton D.S. dated 24 May 1784. Recorded the 27 May 1784. Robert Anderson, C.L.

LIGHT, JACOB JUNR. Pack 7 (Basement) Clerk of Court Office. Anderson, S. C. Pendleton Dist. I Jacob Light Junr. of Pendleton Dist. in consideration of $300 to me paid by John Smith of the same Dist. Have granted, sold, bargained, and released all that tract of

Light, Jacob, Junr. - Continued. land on the North side of 12 Mile
River, containing 100 acres. Dated 31 March 1818. Wit: James Hunter,
Matthew Moore. Signed: Jacob Light Junr. Proved on oath of James
Hunter before Bailey Barton J.Q. this 26 March 1821.

LILES, JAMES Box 54 Pack 1283. Probate Judge Office. Abbeville,
S. C. 96 Dist. Admnr. bond, We John Goarey, Armanious Liles, John
Liles and William Liles are bound unto John Thomas Jr., Ord. in the
sum of two thousand pounds sterling. Dated 5 Sept. 1783. Sale held
15 Oct. 1783 buyers, John Gory, Williamson Liles, Wm. Liles, Joseph
Dawkins, Thos. Hill, Wm. Taylor, Clodis Gorey, John Green, Henry Liles,
Ephraim Liles, Alexr. Danel, John Roberson, Arramanos Liles, Little-
foot Jones, Menoah Bonds, David Fargason.

LILES, SALINA Book B Page 86. Probate Judge Office. Pickens,
S. C. 20 Nov. 1865 Salina Liles a dtr. of Letty A. Liles decd.
another dtr. was also entitled to a share of estate. Salina Liles out
of State. The heirs of Letty A. Liles decd. were Joseph Liles, Arena
Liles, Fanny Liles, Derby Ann Liles, Rachel Liles, Nancy J. Liles,
John Bell Lyles.

LILLY, EDMOND B. Box 54 Pack 1282. Probate Judge Office.
Abbeville, S. C. Abbeville Dist. Admnr. bond, We William Chiles,
Samuel Perrin, and Thomas W. Chiles are bound unto Moses Taggart, Ord.
in the sum of $5,000. Dated 11 Oct. 1820. Cit. Pub. at Cambridge
29 Sept. 1820. Sale held 9 Nov. 1820. Buyers: Wm. Collier, Uriah
Grigsby, Coln. Richard Griffin, Wesly Brooks, Joseph Talbert, Leonard
Walker, Littleton Myrick, Charles C. Mayson, Elihu Creswell Senr.,
John Talbert Jr., Robert Pollard, Simeon Demming, Wm. Chiles, John
Spikes.

LINDSAY, JOHN No. Ref. Probate Judge Office. Abbeville, S. C.
I John Lindsay of Abbeville Dist. First all my just debts are to be
paid. A plain tomb stone be bought and put up at my grave. I give
to my two sons James and John Lindsay all my real estate, to be
equally divided between them. I give to my dtr. Mary the wife of James
Martin the sum of $5.00 as her portion of my est. I give to my dtr.
Elizabeth the wife of Joseph Fields five dollars as her part of my est.
I give to my grand son Abner Nash the sum of $150.00. The residue
of my personal est. be divided amongst my other chn. To Nancy the
wife of John Murphy one part. To Jane the wife of Alanson Nash one
part. James Lindsay my oldest son one part. To my dtr. Margaret the
wife of Larkin Latimer one part. To John Lindsay my youngest son one
part. To Alley my youngest dtr. the wife of Daniel Pruett one part.
I appoint my sons James and John Lindsay executors. Dated 9 Feb. 1841.
Wit: Abram Haddon, Lydall Williams, Robert Elles. Signed: John
Lindsay. Proved on oath of Abram Haddon and Lydall Williams, before
Moses Taggart, Ord. on the 5 March 1841.

LINDSAY, HUMPHREY Deed Book A, Page 39. Probate Judge Office.
Pickens, S. C. To the Ordinary of Pickens Dist. The undersigned
Jemima Wright a first cousin to the said Lindsay formerly of this
Dist. who died about 10 yrs. ago having neither wife nor children.
Was possessed with a tract of land containing about 100 acres lying
on Chauga Creek, adj. land of Joseph Liles. The petitioner therefore
prays that the Ord. advertize for the legatees, and sell the land and
distribution if their be any other heirs. Filed 11 Oct. 1841.

LINDSAY, ISABELLA Box 57 Pack 1355. Probate Judge Office.
Abbeville, S. C. Abbeville Dist. Guardianship. To the ordinary of
Abbeville Dist. The petition of Isabella Lindsay a minor over the age
of 14 yrs. sheweth that she is entitled to a small est. from her aunt,
Isabella Bradly decd. of about $50. That she is desirous that Adam
Wideman, Jr. be appointed her gdn. on the usual terms and as in duty
boudn will ever pray. Filed 15 Jan. 1842. Isby Lindsay. Witness:
Joseph Lindsay, Jr.

LINDSAY, SAMUEL #11. Clerk of Court Office. Abbeville, S. C. Abbeville Dist. In Equity, to the Honr. the Chancellors; your orator Samuel Lindsay formerly of Lowndesville in the Dist. aforesaid, now of Elberton, Ga. That on the 11 Dec. 1854 your orator made with Jesse W. Norris a contract for the sale of a house and lot in the village of Lowndesville, bounded by lot owned by James M. Latimer Esq. Formerly owned by Dr. A. B. Arnold, for the sum of $600. Two bills or notes was made in the sum of $300 each. One note on W. A. Giles for $232.86 was paid to your orator and placed as credit on said notes. The said Jesse W. Norris has neglected and failed to pay your orator the full purchased price etc. Filed 28 April 1856.

LINDSAY, THOMAS No Ref. Probate Judge Office. Abbeville, S. C. I Thomas Lindsay of Abbeville Dist. being in full possession of mind and memory. I desire that my funeral expenses and just debts are paid. I give to my wife Grizel Lindsay the plantation whereon I now live, at her decease to descend to my son Joseph C. Lindsay and my two dtrs. Grizel and Polly. As long as they remain single, if they remove or marry then Joseph to pay each the sum of fifty dollars and the whole of the land belong to him. Wife to have use of all household and kitchen furniture, stock, tools, other personal property, at her death to decend to my five children viz; Names six: Thomas, James, John and Joseph Lindsay and Grizel and Polly Lindsay. I appoint my wife executrix and John and James Lindsay executors [sic]. Dated 25 May 1820. Wit: Patrick Gibson, William Bond, Hugh Coughran. Signed: Thomas Lindsay. Proved on oath of William Bond, before Moses Taggart, Ord. this 27 Dec. 1821.

LINN, JAMES H. Pack 501. Clerk of Court Office. Abbeville, S. C. Cass County. State of Georgia. Power of Attorney. I James H. Linn of Cass County, Ga. Have constituted and appointed John W. Weems of the same County and State, my true and lawful attorney. To ask, demand, receive and receipt. All money due me from the Commissioner of Equity of Abbeville Dist., S. C. from the estate of J. H. Hill and Eliza M. Hill formerly Linn. Dated at Cassville this 31 Aug. 1859. Wit: Thomas M. Compton, John A. Crawford. Signed: James H. Linn.

LIVELY, THOMAS Box 8 #110. Probate Judge Office. Pickens, S.C. I Thomas Lively, Senr. of Pickens Dist. being of sound mind and memory, but weak in body. I give to my beloved wife Rachel Lively a lifetime estate in all I possess and after her death, I desire that my dtr. Jane Lively and my grand son Mark Lively have all stock, household and kitchen furniture, farm tools, etc. If either die without issue the whole shall fall to the other. I give to my son John Lively the West side of Stewarts Creek. Adj. land of Robert McCanns. The East side I do give to my dtr. Jane Lively and Mark Lively and their heirs. To each and every other legal heir of mine I give ten shillings sterling. (None named.) I appoint my son John Lively executor. Dated 8 May 1836. Wit: Bailey Barton, Tho. Garvin, Vincent X James. Signed: Thomas X Lively.

LIVINGSTON, EUGENIA Pack 298. Clerk of Court Office. Abbeville, S. C. On 22 June 1829 Thomas Livingston mentioned as gdn. of Eugenia Livingston a minor child of Taliaferro Livingston decd. Territory of Florida, Madison County. Personally appeared before one of the Justices of said County. Taliaferro Livingston gdn. of Eugenia Livingston a minor and made oath to the account as just and true. Paid 28 April 1830 one third of $113 for bringing her and felex[?] from Alabama.

LIVINGSTON, THOMAS Box 54 Pack 1268. Probate Judge Office. Abbeville, S. C. I Thomas Livingston of Abbeville Dist. being in a weak state of body, but of disposing mind and memory, etc. Executors to sell his horses and negroes, Edom, Abram and Big Sam, if this not enough, sell the tract of land at Hard labor. The plantation whereon I now live for the support of the family, if wife remaines his widow she to have her support from the land. One son named Madison is named, some children are married, and have minor chn. when will was made in 1809. (Only part of said will in notes.)

LIPSCOMB, WILLIAM Box 54 Pack 1267. Probate Judge Office.
Abbeville, S. C. Abbeville Dist. Admnr. bond, we Nathan Lipscomb,
Smith Lipscomb, Nathaniel Burdine are bound unto Andrew Hamilton, Ord.
in the sum of $10,000. Dated 1 Dec. 1802. Inv. made 10 Dec. 1802 by
John Scogin, Richard Henderson, and Benjamin Chiles. Sale held 7 Jan.
1805. Buyers: Michael Taylor, Lewis Youngblood, Joseph Wardlaw,
Richard Griffin, Nathan Lipscomb, Wm. Taylor, Andrew Calhoun, Richard
Bullock, Alexr. Turner, Robt. Todd, Wm. Waller, Benj. Chiles, Wm.
Ramsy, Bird Martin, Larkin Reynolds, John Scogin, Benj. Morgan, Thos.
Stallsworth, John Moore, John Webb, David Thomas, Robert Wilson, Hugh
Toling, Maryan Heard, Wm. McCool, Abraham Thornton, Shadrack Henderson,
Thomas Heard, James Watson, Benj. Chiles, John Meriwether, ARchd.
Frith, Thos. Brighton, Jas. Campbell, Wm. Moore, Jno. Glover, Richard
Eskridge, Smith Lipscomb, Jno. Stevens, Leonard Waller, Andrew
McCallister, Robt. Gray.

LITES, ABRAHAM #475. Clerk of Court Office. Abbeville, S. C.
Abbeville Dist. In Equity, to the Honors the Chancellors; Your
orators Robert W. Lites and John Lites, sheweth that Abram Lites the
father of your orators formerly of this Dist. departed this life the
17 July 1859, intestate surviving him as heirs at law and distributees
are six chn. Joel W. Lites, James C. Lites, Eliza J. the wife of Dr.
Adam P. Boozer, Frances M. J. Lites and your orators, all over the age
of twenty one, except Frances who is now about 17 yrs. old. Abram
Lites had a large est. worth about $30,000 with debts of about $4,000.
With sons Joel and James Lites as admnr. He had a tract of land containing about 1227 acres, on waters Long Cane Creek and Curtail Creeks
bounded by land of Bartholomew Jordon, John D. Adams, Augustus H.
Morton and Dr. Joseph W. W. Marshall. Your orators prays for a partition of the said land. Filed 23 Sept. 1859.

LOGAN, ANDREW Pack 429. Clerk of Court Office. Abbeville, S. C.
I Andrew Logan of Abbeville Dist. being of sound and disposing mind
and memory. I direct all my debts and funeral expenses be paid. I
have heretofore advanced my children in property and money as follows.
Son Zachary Logan, negro girl Linda. Son John L. Logan, negro Tom and
Sam. Son Francis Logan, negro woman Ciler and child boy Jerry. Son
Tyler Logan, negro woman Tabitha and child boy Alexander. Son Leroy
Logan, negro woman Franky and Esa. Son Willis Logan negro woman Lilly
and child. Son Andrew J. Logan, negro woman Rosa and child Waller.
Dtr. Huldah Crawford, negro woman Silvey and Morris. Son Frederick
Logan, negro woman Phillis and child. Son Isaac Logan, negro woman
Betsy and two children. (The value not listed.) All personal and real
property to be sold, after debts are paid, to be equally divided
amongst my children. The children of a deceased parent shall take the
share. The share of Huldah Crawford shall not be vested in her, but
I give the same to my executors in trust for her sole use and support,
not subject to the debts or contracts of her husband. I appoint my
sons Zachary and Isaac Logan and my nephew Dr. John Logan executors.
Dated 7 Jan. 1851. Wit: Wm. T. Blake, Cabel A. Blake, A. M. Blake.
Signed: Andrew Logan. To the Honor the Chancellor: Your oratrix Jane
Arnold and her husband Wm. G. Arnold, sheweth that your oratrix grandfather Andrew Logan, departed this life testate[sic] and under said will
she and her brothers and sisters are entitled to the share of their decd.
father Francis Logan then deceased. The negroes not already given to
his chn. Are to be equally divided into ten lots, the lot of Francis
Logan to be divided between your oratrix, Lewis Logan age twenty one
years, Francis Logan, Nancy Logan and James Logan who are minors. Filed
19 April 1858. John Lewis Logan deeded to Isaac Logan and James W.
Buchanan, for $600 all his interest of what so ever nature in the
personal property, in his grandfather est. Dated 27 May 1856. Wit:
John A. Wier, B. J. Cocran. Signed: John Lewis Logan. Proved on oath
of John A. Wier before Matthew McDonald, C. C. on the 29 May 1856.

LOGAN, COL. JOHN SENR. Box 53 Pack 1256. Probate Judge Office.
Abbeville, S. C. Abbeville Dist. Admnr. bond, We Dr. John Logan,
James A. Black, Richard Griffin, and Joseph Black are bound unto Moses
Taggart, Ord. in the sum of $50,000. Dated 20 Sept. 1820. Another
bond. Abbe. Dist. Admnr. bond, We John Logan, Richard Griffin, James

Logan, Col. John Senr. - Continued. Pulliam are bound unto Moses
Taggart, Ord. in the sum of $50,000. Dated 6 March 1822. Sale held
3 Jan. 1821. Buyers, Joseph Foster, Chasley Davis, John Coleman,
Robt. Young, Edmund Beasley, Jno. Logan, James Black, John McFall,
Donald Douglass, Canady H. Blake, Thos. Gains, Jno. Buchanan, Thos.
Cobb, Richard Griffin, Dudley Richardson, Saml. Davis, Richd. Plunkett,
Elias Teague, Barbara Logan, Wm. Berry, Abram Pool, David Gillam,
Andrew Logan. Expend: 1833 paid cash to Sarah Black and John Logan,
Andrew Logan est. due them from est. of Col. John Logan as per the
decree of the Court of Equity for Abbeville, $995.44. In same pack a
petition whereas James C. Logan made suit to grant him letter of admnr.
as next of kin. Dated 23 July 1807.

LOGAN, LOUISA In Equity, Pack 10. Clerk of Court Office.
Abbeville, S. C. On 9 June 1856 William Raiford Logan and Alice Logan
chn. of Louisa Logan decd. of Abbeville Dist. Were grand children of
Henry F. Power who died in 1856. For more info. on H. F. Power see his
est. papers and Equity records.

LOGAN, MARY No Ref. Mary Logan wife of C. M. Logan and Dr.
George Logan recd. a legacy from the will of Hugh George Campbell of
Charleston in 1820.

LOGAN, "MINORS" Pack 302. Clerk of Court Office. Abbeville,
S. C. Recd. of Dr. John Logan former gdn. of my wife Jane. The
titles to a tract of land belonging to my wife, known as the plantation
whereon Barbara Logan resided at time of death, called the home tract
containing 475 or 480 acres. Dated 2 Oct. 1839. Signed: Wm. C. Black.
Paid 1 Jan. 1837 amt. for tuition of Jane Logan at Greenwood Academy
$20.00. Expenses in getting to Yorkville School $17.87 1/2.

LOGAN, "MINORS" #24. Clerk of Court Office. Abbeville, S. C.
1862 Dr. John Logan was the gdn. of Mary Susan Alice and William R.
Logan, Minors. The return of Mary Susan Alice Logan for 1862. paid
funeral expenses 7 Jan. 1863. By cash recd. from est. of Louisa Logan
$9.82. Recd. Feb. 1855 from admnr. of est. of W. W. Logan $56.00.
W. R. Logan was of age in 1870.

LOGAN, SARAH Pack 385. Clerk of Court Office. Abbeville, S. C.
Abbeville Dist. In Equity, Your oratrix Sarah Logan the wife of
Isaac Logan by her next friend, James W. Fooshe. That your oratrix
and said Isaac Logan were married 9 March 1843. That within four years
after their marriage, without provication or cause inflicted violence
upon her person until the month of June 1860, merciless beating from
his hands drove her from his house for several weeks to seek shelter
in the house of relatives. On his pretended penitence, and fair
promises, induced her to return to his house. Then on 28 Sept. 1861
in his own house inflicted many blows and threatened her life in a
manner she sought safety in the house of her brother John B. Sample.
To avoid the legal siding to which your oratrix was entitled. Isaac
Logan executed a deed for a tract of land for 150 acres and two slaves,
She rented the two slaves for the present year. Said Isaac Logan has
taken one of the said slaves, and is endeavoring to get the other.
Her counsel has informed her the deed is articfical, incomplete and
defective. Your oratrix will ever pray. Filed 20 June 1862.

LOMAX, JAMES N. Box 57 Pack 1354. Probate Judge Office.
Abbeville, S. C. Abbeville Dist. Admnr. bond. We William A. Lomax,
George W. Lomax and William H. Ritchey are bound unto David Lesly, Ord.
in the sum of $2,000. Dated 7 Oct. 1844. Petition to David Lesly, Ord.
The petition of Wm. A. Lomax sheweth that his brother James N. Lomax
departed this life intestate having no wife or child and your petitioner
is desirous to sell all personal property of said est. on the 31 Oct.
1844 on credit of 12 months. Dated 9 Oct. 1844. Inv. made 31 Oct.
1844 by Aaron Lomax, B. W. Stewart, Thos. Strawhorn, W. H. Ritchey,
Settlement of est. of James N. Lomax decd. before the Ordy 25 Aug.
1846. Present Wm. A. Lomax, Jefferson Douglass who married Matilda
a sister of decd. and John W. Lomax. Absent Geo. W. Lomax, James Lomax
left a mother and brothers as his heirs.

LONG, WILLIAM Pack 65. In Equity, Clerk of Court Office.
Abbeville, S. C. To the Honr. the Chancellors: Your oratrix Mary A.
Long sheweth that William Long her late husband departed this life in
June 1861, intestate, possessed with real est. the Home place on Turkey
Creek, adj. land of Stephen Latimer, William Mosely, containing 260
acres, and the Mattison tract of 190 acres. He left as his heirs at
law and distributees, your oratrix the widow, chn. William W. Long,
Henry S. Long, Sarah the wife of William M. Callaham, Minerva the wife
of James R. Latimer, Permelia Caroline Long, Emma Eliza Long, Mary Jane
Long, Margaret R. Long, Alpha A. Long, Alice L. Long, the last six are
under the age of twenty one. Admnr. of the personal est. was committed
to William P. Matin[?] and James R. Latimer. Filed 1 Oct. 1863.
William W. Long was killed in the war, his wife died before him. They
left some chn. name and number unknown, and reside out of State.

LOW, JESSE SENR. Box 6 #77. Probate Judge Office. Pickens,
S. C. Est. admnr. 16 May 1836 by Henry Whitmire, Wm. L. Keith,
Pleasent[sic] Alexander who are bound unto James H. Dendy, Ord. in the
sum of $1,000. Left a widow and ten chn. Paid 5 days traveling to
Buncombe (Buncome Co., N. C.) $5.00. Share were paid to Jesse, Abram,
Phillip Low, Viney Cross, Conrad Low, Eliza Millsap, Nancy Dodgen,
Nathaniel Low.

LUMPKIN, GEORGE Deed Book C. Clerk of Court Office. Elberton,
Ga. State of Georgia. This indenture made this 24 May 1792. Between
George Lumkin of Wilkes Co. and William Skelton of Elbert Co. In
consideration of ₤100 sterling paid by said William Skelton, have
granted, bargained, and sold all that tract of land lying in Elbert Co.
on Sider Creek, bounded by land of James Hannah, John Scales, Julien
Nail. Being the land George Lumkin purchased from John Smith also
where said William Skelton now lives, containing 100 acres. Wit:
Thomas Woodard, Archer Smith. Signed: George Lumkin. Proved on oath
of Archer Smith before Moses Haynes, J.P. this 28 Aug. 1794. Registered
14 May 1795.

LYLES, SAMUEL ___ Book B, Page 34. Probate Judge Office.
Pickens, S. C. 19 Oct. 1859 Samuel Lyles and wife Mary, W. D. L.
Lyles and wife Martha Ann were heirs of Joel Mason decd. of Pickens
Dist. and his widow Frances Mason.

LYNCH, HENRY Pack 15 In Equity (Basement). Clerk of Court
Office. Pickens, S. C. Henry Lynch died 1862 in Pickens Dist. Owned
239 acres lying on Oolenoy River adj. lands of Nathaniel Lynch,
Banister S. Lynch, James Burdine. Owned 180 acres on Oolenoy River,
adj. lands of James Burdine and others. Left no wife or chn.
Brothers and sisters viz; Gideon M. Lynch, Nathaniel Lynch, Banister
S. Lynch, Harriet wife of Cornelius Keith, Charles F. or T. Lynch,
Jackson Lynch, Calvin Lynch, Eliza the wife of John Robinson, Nancy
the wife of Richard Robinson, Mary the wife of John Lewis, Sarah the
wife of William Baker, Elizabeth the wife of Jason Gillespie, the last
eight resides out of State. On 17 Feb. 1864 John and Louisa Robinson,
Richard and Nancy Robertson, B. S. Lynch and W. J. Lynch brothers to
Henry Lynch, G. M. Lynch recd. shares from the est. of Henry Lynch decd.

LYNCH, ISAAC Deed Book A Page 1. Clerk of Court Office.
Anderson, S. C. This indenture (lease) made the 8 April 1790 between
Isaac Lynch of Pendleton Co. Ninety Six Dist. of the one part and
Andrew Pickens, John Miller, John Wilson, Benjamin Cleveland, William
Holbert, Henry Clarke, John Moffet and Robert Anderson Esquires of
said County of the other part. In consideration of five shillings in
hand paid by (above named Esqs.) hath granted, sold, bargained the
above Justices of the Peace for Pendleton County in trust for the said
County. All that tract of land containing 885 acres, being in the Dist.
of 96 on branches of Eighteen Mile Creek and Three and twenty Mile
Creek, bounded on N.E. and S.E. and S.W. by land laid out to Isaac
Lynch, others sides vacant, granted to said Isaac Lynch 2 July 1787.
Wit: Henry Burch and Joseph Box. Signed: Isaac X Lynch. (Release
to same land.) This indenture made 9 April 1790. To the same Esq.

Lynch, Isaac - Continued. in consideration of 25 pounds current money of the State. Same Wit: Proved on oath of Joseph Box, before Andw. Pickens, J.P. on the 14 April 1790. Filed 10 May 1790.

LYNCH, NATHANIEL SR. Pack 15. In Equity. Basement. Pickens, S. C. Nathaniel Lynch, Sr. died 20 Feb. 1861 owned 161 acres lying on Oolenoy Creek adj. land of S. E. Southerland, Alexander Edens and others. Heirs. Widow Jane Lynch in Pickens Dist. chn: G. M. Lynch, B. S. Lynch, Nathl. Lynch, Henry Lynch, Harriet wife of Cornelius Keith all of Pickens Dist. Eliza wife of John Robinson in Georgia. Nancy wife of Richard Robinson in Georgia. Sarah wife of Wm. Baker in Texas, Mary the wife of John Lewis of Georgia, Elizabeth wife of Jason Gillespie in North Carolina, Calvin Lynch in Texas, C. F. Lynch in Georgia, Wm. J. Lynch in Georgia.

LYON, JOSEPH Box 125 pack 3690. Probate Judge Office. Abbeville, S. C. I Joseph Lyon of Abbeville Dist. being of sound mind and memory etc. Each of my sons to have $1,000 at the age of twenty one yrs. Some have been advanced at various times, the sum so advanced shall accounted for, if any should not receive the amount at age, then the principal and lawful interest shall be paid. I have given my son James A. Lyon one thousand dollars. I give to my son John T. Lyon $1,000 and a good horse when of age. I give my son William Lyon $1,000 and a good horse. I give to my son Harvey L. Lyon $1,000 and a good horse, when of age. I will that of my daughter in law Mary Ann Lyon shall have a child by her marriage with my son Samuel Lyon, such child to have all the money and effects which he was possessed of at time of his death, to be put on interest by the lawful gdn. of said child till it come of age. I give to my wife Elizabeth Lyon all land, horses, cattle, hogs and eight negroes, household and kitchen furniture. To sell if she and my executors think best. I appoint James A. Lyon, John T. Lyon and Benjamin P. Hughs executros. Dated 26 Feb. 1850. Wit: Wm. Barr, Thomas B. Dendy, A. L. Gillespie. Signed: Joseph Lyon. Filed 27 March 1850. Proved on oath of Thomas B. Dendy, before F. W. Sellick O.A.D. this 27 March 1850. Inventory made 29 March 1850 by Wm. Lesy, A. L. Gillespie, Joseph Aiken, J. A. Donald, R. C. Richey. Negroes named, viz; Aggy, Molly, Joe, Ella, Wesley, Linda, Sarah and Hannah. The estate settled 21 Feb. 1852. The legacy having been paid to Harvey T. Lyon the youngest son who is the age of twenty one.

LYON, "MINORS" #22. Clerk of Court Office. Abbeville, S. C. In 1864 Margaret C. Lyon was gdn. of Martha Lyon. 9 Dec. 1860 Margaret C. Lyon in account with James Lyon, same date amount recd. from J. H. Wideman $874.14. Was gdn. of Thomas J. Lyon. We the undersigned called on by Margaret C. Lyon gdn., and Martha F. Lyon and James W. Lyon to examine and appraise the tract of land now owned by Margaret C. Lyon, containing 342 acres. Valued at $7.50 per acre or $2565.00 and we recommend that they receive the tract jointly. Dated 16 Sept. 1875.

LYTHGOE, COL. A. J. Pack 342. Clerk of Court Office. Abbeville, S. C. Abbeville Dist. In Equity. To the Honr. the Chancellors: Your Oratrix Margaret J. Lythgoe sheweth that on the 31 Dec. 1862 her late husband Col. A. J. Lythgoe of this dist. in the battle of Murfeesboro fell at the head of his regiment, mortally wounded, and in a few hours there after died. At time of his death, said Augustus J. Lythgoe was seized in fee simple a parcel of land in the town of Abbeville. Bounded by land of W. Joel Smith, Col. A. M. Smith, B. P. Hughes. Containing 19 acres well improved. The admnr. on the est. has been committed to John A. Weir, the brother of your oratrix. Your oratrix the widow and Meta A. Lythgoe, George B. Lythgoe and Hattie H. Lythgoe her children, all minors the oldest about seven yrs. old. Your oratrix prays for partition amongst herself and children. Filed 25 May 1863.

McADAM, CAPT. JOHN #3341. Clerk of Court Office. Abbeville, S. C. Abbeville Dist. In Equity. To the Honr. the Chancellors: Your orators Ezekiel Tribble and John Tribble sheweth that John McAdams Esq. late of Abbeville Dist. died in Nov. 1834 intestate leaving as his only heirs and distributees, a widow Sarah McAdam and ten chn. to wit., Polly now the wife of James Fisher, Grizella now the wife of John Wright, Sarah Elizabeth McAdams, John McAdam, Jane now the wife of Thomas Davis, Robert McAdam, James J. McAdam, Rachel McAdam, the last named a minor over the age of 14 yrs., and the chn. of a decease dtr. named Margaret, who was the wife of Lemuel W. Tribble and who died before her father leaving a husband, Lemuel W. and seven ch. to wit, your orators and Polly Ann since married to George Grubbs, Nancy Emily Tribble, James R. Tribble the last three named now minors over the age of 14 yrs. and Stephen M. Tribble and Lemuel W. Tribble minors under the age of 14 yrs. The admnr. was granted to Lemuel Tribble and John McAdam. The said John McAdam was possessed with a tract of land on Little Hogskin Creek a branch of Little River. Originally granted to John McAdam in 1804. Containing 365 acres, bounded by land of Robert Right, ___ McKinney, Patt Bell, Elijah Tribble, Joseph Burton and John Fish. Filed 13 June 1836.

McADAMS, JAMES Pack 632. #1. Clerk of Court Office. Pickens, S. C. James McAdams husband of Amanda M. McAdams died in Pickens County, 5 March 1881. Father of George A. McAdams and Mason B. McAdams.

McADAMS, RACHEL Box 13 #8. Probate Judge Office. Orangeburg, S. C. Rachel McAdams formerly Jeffcoat, was written on back of Mrs. Ann P. Staley will who died in 1864 in Orangeburg Co. Mentions a child.

McADAMS, Tombstone inscriptions taken from Lindsay Cemetery. 2 Miles South of Due West, Abbeville County, S. C. Enoch H. McAdams, born 25 Dec. 1840. Died 2 Dec. 1864.

McAFEE, JAMES Pack 495. Probate Judge Office. Anderson, S. C. Whereas Patsey or Martha McAfee and Joseph McAfee made suit to me to grant them letter of admnr. on the estate of James McAfee late of Pendleton Dist. Dated this 21 July 1806. John Harris O.P.D. Pub. at Keowee Meeting house, the 26 July 1806. Admnr. bond, Pendleton Dist. We Patsay McAfee, Joseph McAfee, William Humphries and William McFarling are bound unto John Harris, Ors. in the sum of $3,000. Dated 4 Aug. 1806. The final decree before the Ordinary filed 13 June 1825. On application of Joseph McAfee admnr. The heirs of James McAfee decd. Patsey the widow with her husband Isaac Thomas with whom she married, Jordan McAfee, Hugh McAfee, in their own persons, and Joseph and Patsey McAfee minors chn. over 14 yrs. of age with Hugh McAfee as guardian of minors. The admnr. collected $1,018.34. He has expended the sum of $516.17. It appeared to the Court that Patsey McAfee now Patsey Thomas has received $341.22 which it appears to be $60.09 over her share. The administratrix and administrator is liable to pay Jordan, Hugh, Joseph and Patsey the chn. of said James McAfee their share with interest. On 13 June 1825 Jordan McAfee recd. $272.84. as his share. Same date Hugh McAfee recd. $818.52 his share with the share of Joseph and Patsey minors.

McBEE, VARDRY Pack 31 #1. Clerk of Court Office. (Basement). Pickens, S. C. I Vardry McBee of Lincoln County in N.C. in considera- tion of the sum of $40.00 to me paid by John Couch of Pendleton Dist. have granted, sold, and released a certain lot in the village of Green- ville described in McBee plan of said village by the no. of 18. Dated 7 March 1824. Wit: Thomas Allen, Davis Whitman. Signed: Vardry McBee.

McBETH, GEORGE Land Platt. Book A, Page 1. Probate Judge Office. Abbeville, S. C. To George McBeth on the bounty 200 acres on the W. side of Keowee River, bounded on the river and vacant land as per platt. Recorded 25 May 1784.

McBRIDE, JOHN Pack 421. Clerk of Court Office. Abbeville, S.C.
Abbeville, S. C. In Equity, To the Honr. the Chancellors; your orator
Samuel McBride of Texas, sheweth, that many years ago John McBride
departed this life leaving in full force his last will and testament.
By which he gave to his dtr. Jane the wife of Joseph Criswell a tract
of land on Long Cane Creek, bounded by Wm. K. Bradley, James Drennan
and others. Containing 120 acres. The said Jane and her husband
Joseph Creswell, occupied the said land until Jane departed this life
without chn. or lineal descendants. The interest of Joseph Criswell
in the said tract of land has been sold by the sheriff of this Dist.
under execution brought by one Andrew Weed. Who bought Creswell
interest in said land. The same Andrew Weed was the executor of the
last will of John McBride. Filed 28 Feb. 1860. Will of John McBride.
I John McBride of Abbeville Dist. being weak and feeble in health, but
of sound mind and memory. I will my just debts be paid. I will and
bequeath to my loving dtr. Jane who has nursed and cared for me day and
night through my declining health, all my tract of land on the North
side of the spring Branch, two beds and furniture, one cow and calf,
one trunk, etc. I will to my son Josiah one bed and furniture, one
cow and calf, my saddle. I will to my grand son John McBride all my
land on the South side of spring Branch. I will to my grand son John
Andrew McBride $20. I will my remaining property be sold and proceeds
equally divided among all my ch. viz, Thomas, Joseph, James, Samuel,
Josiah and Jane. I appoint my trusty friend Andrew Weed. Wit: Geo.
W. Pressly, George McYoung, Simpson Evan. Will proved on oath of
George McYoung before Wm. Hill Ord. this 6 Jan. 1854. Another paper,
States that John McBride died Dec. 1853. His chn. Joseph, Joshua,
Thomas resides in Abbeville Dist. Samuel McBride resides in Texas,
James McBride resides in Miss. John McBride resides in Alabama.
Power of Attorney. Samuel McBride of Cherokee County, State of Texas
has appointed William Bradly who resides at Indian Hill in Abbeville
Dist. to receive and receipt in my name etc. from the est. of my father
John McBride who at his death resided at Indian Hill in Abbeville Dist.,
S. C. Dated 13 Oct. 1854. Wit: A. J. Coupland, R. H. Guinn.
Signed: Samuel McBride.

McCAW, MARGARET FRANCES Pack 284. Clerk of Court Office.
Abbeville, S. C. Abbeville Dist. In Equity, to the Honr. Chancellors;
The petition of Margaret Frances McCaw sheweth that she is a minor
over the age 14 yrs. That her father William H. McCaw of this Dist.
departed this life in 1852, intestate, leaving a considerable est.
she is entitled to share of about six or eight thousand dollars, owing
to her minority she is unable to manage. Therefore she prays that
Dr. Joseph J. Wardlaw be appointed her guardian. Filed 13 June 1854.

McCAW, WILLIAM H. Pack 407. Clerk of Court Office. Abbeville,
S. C. Abbeville Dist. In Equity, To the Honr. the Chancellors; your
oratrix Elizabeth McCaw sheweth that her husband William H. McCaw
departed this life intestate in 1852. Leaving as heirs and distributees
your oratrix his widow and six chn. all of whom are minor. Julia
Carolina agreed about 14 yrs. Margaret Frances about twelve yrs. old,
John Todd about ten yrs. old, Mary McGehee about eight yrs. old,
William Henry about six yrs. old, Alexander Barr about two yrs. old.
Your oratrix sheweth that the admnr. was granted to Thomas C. Perrin
Esq. and that the personal est. will be more than sufficient to pay
all debts. Your oratrix further sheweth that her late husband was
possessed with a large tract of land, containing about three thousand
acres on waters of Little River, bounded by land of D. L. Wardlaw,
John Baskin, Dr. Yarbrough, Charles T. Haskell, Mrs. Witherspoon, Col.
Huger, Thomas Cunningham and Ed. Tilman. Your oratrix prays for a
sale of said land, she is unable to manage and the chn. are minors.
Filed 13 Nov. 1852.

McCELVEY, JAMES L. Box 152 Pack 4289. Probate Judge Office.
Abbeville, S. C. Est. admnr. 23 March 1861 by William McCelvey,
James McCaslan and M. O. McCaslan who are bound unto William Hill, Ord.
in the sum of $10,000. James L. McCelvey died in Texas. Power of
Attorney. State of Texas, County of Houston. We Mary J. McCelvey
widow of the late J. L. McCelvey decd. and Martha J. McHenry wife of

McCelvey, James L. - Continued. Wm. P. McHenry and dtr. of J. L. McCelvey decd. and Wm. P. McHenry husband of Martha J. McHenry, all of Houston County, State of Texas. Have appointed John A. Ansley of Houston County, Texas, our true and lawful attorney. To use our name to represent us in anything necessary to be done in relation to the estate of J. L. McCelvey decd. in S. C. or Georgia. To receive and receipt anyone, etc. Dated at Crockett Texas this 11 July 1866. Signed: H. M. McCelvey, J. H. McCelvey, Wm. P. McHenry, Mary J. McCelvey, Martha J. McHenry. Proved on oath of O. C. Arbsick, C.C. this 11 July 1866. His name is proven by J. M. Odell, Chief Justice, Houston County, Texas. This 12 July 1866.

McCELVEY, "MINORS" #45. Clerk of Court Office. Abbeville, S.C. On 17 Feb. 1848 James L. McCelvey was the guardian of Hezekiah C. McCelvey a minor. 22 Jan. 1849 Paid George W. McCelvey account $45. The settlement was made 4 Oct. 1852 between James L. McCelvey gdn. and Hezekiah C. McCelvey who has come of age. 17 Feb. 1848 James L. McCelvey mentioned as the gdn. of George W. McCelvey a minor. The settlement was made 22 Sept. 1851 between James L. McCelvey gdn. and George W. McCelvey who has come of age. 1848 also gdn. of Hugh M. McCelvey a minor.

McCELVEY, "MINORS" #45. Clerk of Court Office. Abbeville, S.C. 17 Feb. James L. McCelvey was guardian of Hezekiah C. McCelvey a minor Paid 22 Jan. 1849 George W. McCelvey for a horse forward to farm with $80. Paid 1852 William McCelvey account $45. The settlement was made 4 Oct. 1852 between James L. McCelvey gdn. and Hezekiah C. McCelvey who has come of age. 17 Feb. 1848 James L. McCelvey gdn. of George W. McCelvey a minor. Their settlement was made 22 Sept. 1851 when George W. came of age. 1848 James L. McCelvey was gdn. of Hugh M. McCelvey.

McCLELLAN, ROBERT Pack 425. Clerk of Court Office. Abbeville, S. C. Abbeville Dist. In Equity. To the Honr. the Chancellors; your orator Elijah McClellan and your oratrix Jane McCellan sheweth That their father Robert McCellan late of this Dist. died intestate. Leaving as his only heir and distributees his widow Charity McCellan, your orator and oratrix, Mary and Margaret sisters. At the death of Robert McCellan, he was possessed with a tract of land on waters of Curtail Creek, bounded by land of Bartholomew Jordan, Francis Atkins, Samuel Marshall, containing 116 acres. No admnr. was sent out upon the estate of the intestate, which was unnecessary as he owed no debts. The tract of land and personal est. was taken possession by Charity McCellan the widow, for her support and that of her chn. Your orator and oratrix sheweth that Charity McCellan departed this life intestate, leaving the four chn. as heirs and distributees. No admnr. on her est. has been sent out from any Court. Your orator and oratrix further states that their sisters Mary and Margaret hath from their birth and still are wholly deficient in reason and understanding, and to all intents and purposes are idiots and unfit and unable to govern themselves or manage their est. Barthow. Jordan states that he has known the said Mary and Margaret for 40 yrs. and lived within half mile of his resident. Dr. John Davis states that he has been their doctor for 9 yrs. Filed 28 April 1851.

McCLELLAND, JOHN Pack 326. Clerk of Court Office. Abbeville, S. C. Abbeville Dist. In the Court of Common Pleas. To the Honr. the Judge of the Judicial Circuit of the State. Your orator and oratrix Patrick H. Bradley and Mrs. Mary Jane Dendy, executor and executrix of the last will of John McClelland decd. and all unsatisfied creditors of the est. of Allen Vance, decd. Allen Vance late of the said County was indebted to John McClellan in the sum of $3,500 by a note under seal with James Cresswell as surety. The said note was in part the purchase money for a tract of land, conveyed in the fall 1862, in the full sum of $7,700. Tract of land contained 500 acres on waters of Coronaco Creek, adj. lands of Dr. John Logan decd. Mrs. Magee and others. After the execution of said bill, the said John McClellan departed this life, leaving his will in full force. Your orator and oratrix are qualified as such. After the death of John McClellan, the said Allen Vance departed this life, leaving his will in full force. His son

McClelland, John - Continued. John C. Vance and James W. Vance
a brother were appointed executors. Of these John C. Vance alone
qualified, the brother James W. Vance resides in the State of Louisiana
where if still living he still reside. Allen Vance left a widow and
three chn. to wit, Mary E. the wife of C. A. C. Waller, John C. Vance,
Laura C. Vance, the last named a minor under the age of twenty one.
The real estate of Allen Vance decd. in this State are, a house and
lot in the village of Greenwood, a tract of 23 acres adj. land of
Simon P. Boozer, William A. Bailey, Bennett Reynolds, Jr., J. T.
McKeller. Also a tract near Greenwood called the Wier tract of about
485 acres, bounded by land of Dr. W. B. Millwee. The widow of said
Vance sold the house and lot and part of the Wier tract to Dr. John
C. Maxwell, and has removed to the State of Louisana to reside. The
son John C. Vance, the executor of said will also removed to the State
of Louisana and the son in law C. A. C. Waller, has been paid for some
of the property described. Filed 14 Feb. 1870. In the will of John
McClellan of Abbeville Dist. being sorely afflicted in body and having
lived out the days usually alloted to man. I wish the plantation to
constitute a comfortable home for my wife during her natural life.
Also for my dtr. Mary Jane Dendy during her natural life, and at her
death I give the said plantation to the grand chn. E. E. Dendy, James
N. Dendy, Thomas M. Dendy to share and share alike. I give to my wife
my servants Barbary, Mary, John, Bufort, Ben, Lewis and wife Fanny,
also Charity and her dtr. Betsy, with her dtr. Jane. I give to my
grand chn. a good horse, and saddle and bridle and cow and calf. I
appoint my dtr. Mary Jane Dendy and my friend Capt. P. H. Bradley and
my grand son James Nevin Dendy my executrix and executors. Dated 14
May 1863. Wit: S. A. Wilson, Larkin Reynolds, John McDowell. Signed:
John McClellan.

McCLINTOCK, HENRY K. Deed Book S, Page 617. Clerk of Court
Office. Anderson, S. C. I Henry King McClintock of Anderson Dist. in
consideration of $1800 to me paid by Henry G. Dreffen of the same Dist.
have granted, sold and released all that tract of land situate in the
village of Pendleton in Anderson Dist. which is a house and other
buildings on said lot designated as lot No. 47 and 47 containing one
acre each. Adj. land of Major Elam Sharp, Martin Palmer. Dated 12
July 1830. Wit: George E. W. Foster, Joseph N. Whiter, Moody Burt.
Signed: Henry K. McClintock. Proved on oath of G. E. W. Foster before
James E. Reese, N.P. this 12 July 1830. Recorded 14 July 1830.

McCLINTON, ALEXANDER Deed Book X, Page 398. Clerk of Court
Office. Anderson, S. C. Anderson Dist. I Robert Henderson of said
Dist. in consideration of $500 to me paid by Alexander McClinton of the
same place. Have granted, sold, and released all my interest claim of
right or title as legatee to a share in the Northern part of half of
a tract of land containing 290 acres in Anderson Dist. on waters of
Great Generostee Creek waters of Savannah River. Originally surveyed
by David Hopkins the 24 June 1784 for John Perrman, resurveyed by
James Gilmer the 8 Dec. 1827 making 320 acres, which was conveyed from
Peerman down to John Henderson from whom I derived my right as a
legatee. Dated 24 Sept. 1842. Wit: J. J. Norris, P. K. Norris.
Signed: Robert Henderson. This day came Mary Ann Henderson the wife
of Robert Henderson, did renounce, release and relinquish all her
interest and claim of dower. Before E. L. Norris, M.A. This 30 Sept.
1842. Proved on oath of P. K. Norris before Elijah Webb, Clk. of
Court, this 30 Sept. 1842.

McCLINTON, ALEXANDER S. Deed Book P-2, Page 138. Clerk of Court
Office. Anderson, S. C. I Alexander S. McClinton of Anderson County
in consideration of $700. to me paid by John H. McClinton of the same
place, have granted, sold, released all that tract of land containing
99 acres. It being the North end of a tract containing 323 granted
to Alexander S. McClinton the 29 Dec. 1859. Lying on Big Generostee
Creek. Bounded by land of Mrs. L. A. M. Vanwyck, James Montgomery,
Charles K. Willerford, M. Lesser. Dated 17 Sept. 1870. Wit: James
Adams, Wm. S. Shaw. Signed: A. S. McClinton. Proved on oath of
Wm. S. Shaw before John B. Moore N.P. this 4 Dec. 1871. Recorded the
17 Dec. 1871.

McCLINTON, ALEXANDER S. Deed Book P-2, Page 140. Clerk of Court Office. Anderson, S. C. I Alexander S. McClinton of Anderson Dist. in consideration of five dollars to me paid by W. McDuffie Cochran of the same place. Have granted, sold, and released one third interest in a certain tract of land containing five and one tenth acres, on Big Generostee Creek, water of Savannah River. It being part of a tract granted to Alexander S. McClinton the 13 Jan. 1800. Dated 22 Dec. 1874. Wit: George M. McLee, J. J. Gilmer. Signed A. S. McClinton. Proved on oath of George M. McClinton before J. J. Gilmer, J.P. this 22 Dec. 1874. This day came Hannah McClinton the wife of Alexander S. McClinton and released and renounced and forever relinquished all interest of dower in the above land. Dated (No date). Signed: J. J. Gilmer, Trial Justice. Recorded the 13 July 1875.

McCLINTON, ALEXANDER S. Deed Book V, Page 114. Clerk of Court Office. Anderson, S. C. I Alexander S. McClinton of Anderson Dist. in consideration of $150. To me paid by Peyton R. Shaw of same place, have granted, sold, bargained, released all that tract of land containing 80 acres lying on Sadlers Creek waters of Savannah River. It being the Eastwardly part of a tract originally surveyed for Shederick Irgram by Thomas Fiendly, D.S. the 20 April 1786. Near the Shockley Ferry Road. It being the same land sold at sheriff sale property of Jacob Dillishaw. Dated 9 Sept. 1836. Wit: George X Bushby, James Gilmer. Signed: Alexander S. McClenton. Proved on oath of George Bushby before James Gilmer, J.Q. this 9 Sept. 1836.

McCLINTON, ALEXANDER S. Deed Book U, Page 191. Clerk of Court Office. Anderson, S. C. I Andrew N. McFall, sheriff of Anderson Dist. Whereas by virtue of a writ of Feri Facias issued from Court of Common Pleas. The 8 Oct. 1833 at the suit of Samuel Maverick and Major Lewis to James McKinney then sheriff commanding him that the goods and chattels of Jacob Dillishaw be levy the sum of $57.08 and cost. The said property was exposed to sale and purchased by Alexander S. McClinton (bid off by Major Lewis) in the sum of $75. Whereas said sheriff has sold, granted, released unto Alexander S. McClinton that tract of land of Jacob Dillishaw. This 20 March 1834. Wit: Joseph P. Lawhorn. Signed: A. N. McFall, Sheriff. Proved on oath of Joseph P. Lawhon, before George E. W. Foster, N.P. this 20 March 1834.

McCLINTON, JAMES Box 58 Pack 1383. Probate Judge Office. Abbeville, S. C. Abbeville Dist. Know that we Samuel B. McClinton, John McClinton and Alexr. Spence are bound unto Moses Taggart, Ord. in the sum of $1200. Dated 13 April 1835. Citation pub. at Hopewell Church. Inventory made 27 April 1835. by Dr. Robert Devlin, James W. Frazer, John McClinton, and Samuel McClinton. Rosannah McClinton bought at sale.

McCLINTON, JAMES R. Box 58 Pack 1838. Probate Judge Office. Abbeville, S. C. I James R. McClinton being of sound mind and disposing memory. First I will to my brother William McClinton and to my sisters Jane and Caroline McClinton and to my neice Elizabeth Richey, making in all four shares. To them all my personal and real estate. Having two tracts of land, the home tract and the other adj. to it. With negroes Jack, Caroline, Jane, Cornelia and Harry, also all household and kitchen furniture, stock, tools, wagons and gears, buggy and harness. Each to have an equal share. I appoint R. C. Sharp executor. Dated 10 May 1856. Wit: James Y. Sitton, Robert Drennon, Robert A. Archer. Signed: J. R. McClinton. Proved on oath of Robert Drennen before me, Wm. Hill, Ordinary of Abbeville Dist. this 2 June 1856. Recorded the 27 Nov. 1856.

McCOLLUM, DAVID Pack 124. Clerk of Court Office. Pickens, S.C. I David McCollum of Pendleton Dist. in consideration of the sum of $18 to me paid by John Stanley of the same Dist. have granted, bargained, sold and conveyed all my interest or claim in or to a part of a tract of land lying in Pendleton Dist. on Town Creek being a branch of Twelve Mile River. Containing ten acres. Adj. land of James Ferguson and others. Dated 17 Feb. 1816. Wit: James Ferguson, Hundley Evatt. Signed: David McCollum.

McCOOL, GABRIEL   In Equity, Book B-1, Page 75.   Clerk of Court Office. Pickens, S. C. A marriage artical between Gabriel McCool and Nancy Turner. Agreement before marriage that the property of the intended wife should be conveyed to trustee, the profits to be at the disposal of the husband during their joint lives. But the wife to have power to dispose of it by will not withstanding her coverture or if she survives the husband by decd. or otherwise and to claim no part of her husband estate. Dated 1 July 1831. Signed: Gabriel McCool, Miss Nancy Turner and Francis F. Burt Commissioner. Nancy Turner has in her possession a tract of land of 100 acres, now in possession of her brother Jackson Turner, adj. lands of John Hunt decd. est. Joseph Williams, Samuel Looper, John S. Edwards, six head of cattle, three head of hogs and shotes[?], three beds and bed steads and furniture, one pine cupboard and furniture, three tables and some household furniture. Dated 1 July 1831. Wit: John S. Edwards, G. W. Hawkins. Signed: Gabl. McCoole and Nancy X Turner. Recorded this 14 Sept. 1831.

McCLURE, EDWARD J.   Pack 630 #38. Clerk of Court Office. Pickens, S. C. By James E. Hagood, Clk. by virtue of my office. To any lawful surveyor you are hereby authorized to lay out unto Edward J. McClure a tract of land not exceeding ten thousand acres, and made a true platt thereof. Dated 26 Jan. 1858. Executed the 27 Jan. 1858 by Robert Fullerton D.S. Amount not given.

McCRARY, ALFRED   Pack 632. #6. Clerk of Court Office. Pickens, S. C. Alfred McCrary died in 1877 in Pickens Dist. Owned 126 acres of land on waters of Little Eastatoe Waters of Keowee River, adj. land of John Gilstrap, Waddy B. Graveley and others. Left a widow Elizabeth McRary, and chn; Hester Ann Stansell, Alfred M. McCrary, Charity C. Malone, Sarah E. McCrary, Lettie J. Reid, Mary M. McCrary, William J. McCrary, J. B. McCrary. After his death Sarah E. and Mary M. McCrary died intestate and unmarried being minors. W. J. and J. B. McCrary under 14 yrs. and Lettie J. Reid, Sarah E. McCrary and Mary M. McCrary over that age.

McCRADY, JAMES W.   Pack 95. Clerk of Court Office. Abbeville, S. C. Abbeville Dist. In Equity To the Honr. the Chancellors; your orator John T. Wait of Laurens Dist. sheweth. On the 12 June 1854 James W. McCrady living at that time in Belton, S. C. Anderson Dist. In consideration of love and affection to his wife Parthena and her children by their marriage, made a deed by which he "bargained, sold, and released" unto your orator, one negro woman named Lydia about 26 yrs. old and her two chn. to wit, Henry about two yrs. old, Daniel about one year of age. Said James W. McCrady to have negroes their life time, then to their chn. so on. Your orator having married the sister of Parthenia McCrady felt duty bound to accept the property in trust and subscribing his name to the deed and had same recorded in the Court House in Anderson Dist. Soon after the deed was recorded James W. McCrady contracted a number of debts which he has been unable to pay. One John Smith knowing of the said deed, has ordered the sheriff of Abbeville Dist. to levy his execution upon the whole family. Filed 30 April 1860.

McCREARY, JOSEPH   Box 59 Pack 1412. Probate Judge Office. Abbeville, S. C. Petition of David McReary to grant him a letter of admnr. on the est. of Joseph McReary decd. Dated 30 Oct. 1827. Granted Moses Taggart, Ord. Admnr. bond granted to David H. McReary, John McComb and Robert McBride all of Abbeville Dist. are bound unto Moses Taggart, Ord. in the sum of $10,000. Dated 5 Nov. 1827. Inventory made 20 Nov. 1827. Sale held 20 Nov. 1827. Buyers: Mary McCreary, Peggy McCreary, John Stover, John C. McCreary, Frances Wilson, John C. Covy, William Giles, Samuel B. Robertson, James Spence, William Cowan, John Yarbrough, George Presly, Andrew Redmond, John F. Busby, Young Ragon, John Gray, Samuel Jordan, Thomas P. Dowden, William Chiles, William Dale. Notes due the est. James Richey $11.83. John Cochran $10. Samuel B. Robertson $6. William S. Pritchard $8.50. John Chiles $5.75. Frances Wilson $10. John McCombs $10. John Ruff $3. Expenses paid 3 Nov. 1834. Joseph McReary $280. Paid 29 Nov. 1834.

McCreary, Joseph - Continued. Margret McReary $23.06. Paid schoolan[sic] for James Richey years 1834-37. Paid James Richey 12 Oct. 1830 $22.25. (The others seem to take their share at the sale.)

McCORMICK, "MINORS" Pack 392. Clerk of Court Office. Abbeville, S. C. In 1839 William J. Thompson was the guardian of the minor children of Hugh McCormick decd. Viz; Mary McCormick, John C. McCormick, Elvira J. McCormick.

McCURRY, MATILDA In Equity. #649. Clerk of Court Office. Pickens, S. C. On 13 May 1867 Matilda McCurry wife of W. McCurry who resides in Anderson Dist. was a dtr. of Hundley E. Campbell decd. of Pickens Dist. who died in 1859.

McDANIEL, ANGUS Will Book A, Page 77. Probate Judge Office. Edgefield, S. C. I Angus McDaniel of Edgefield County, being in a low state of health, but of sound reason, mind, and memory. I give to my wife Ann my two negroes Simon and Milley, with the plantation whereon I now live, three head of horses, four cows and calves, household and kitchen furniture, except two feather beds which I reserve for my son John McDaniel and my dtr. Ann McDaniel. I give to my son the tract of land whereon I now live at the decease of my wife, with one mare, three cows and calves, one sow. I give to my dtr. Ann McDaniel three cows and calves, one sow and pigs. At the death of my wife my property not already mentioned to be equally divided amongst all my chn. viz; Thomas McDaniel, Patty White, Ann McDaniel, Elizabeth Thompson, and John McDaniel. I appoint my wife Ann McDaniel and Elias Blackbourn executrix and executor. Dated 24 Feb. 1795. Wit: Richard Tutt, Lewis Youngblood, Stephen Norris. Signed: Angus McDaniel. Codicil. It is my will and desire, I hereby give to John Blackbourn an equal dividend in the last remaining part of my personal est. Said John is the son of Elias Blackbourn. Wife to collect all debts due and pay all debts owed and to purchase another negro for the place. No date on Codicil. Proved on of Lewis Youngblood in open Court before Richard Tutt, C.E. this March term 1795.

McDANIEL, ARCHIBALD No Ref. Probate Judge Office. Laurens, S. C. I Archibald McDaniel of Laurens Dist. being of sound mind and dis- psing memory, but weak in body. I desire all my just debts be paid. I give to my beloved wife Margaret Wade McDaniel, all my estate both real and personal during her widowhood or natural life. I give to my son Thomas McDaniel two negroes Isaac about twenty five yrs. and girl Enzee. I give unto my son Mathew McDaniel one negro boy Stephen about twelve yrs. I give to my son Joel McDaniel a negro boy Samuel about five yrs. I have heretofore given my dtr. Elizabeth Moore a negro girl Grace. I have given to my dtr. a horse valued about $80. I have given to my son Thomas a horse valued about $80 both to be accounted for in the final settlement. I give to my son Joel a black filly about two yrs. old worth about $40, to be accounted for. I give to my son Mathew my rifle gun not to be accounted for. I give to my sons Mathew and Joel a negro girl Anne about nine yrs. of age not to be accounted for. At the death of my wife, the residue of my est. to be sold and divided amongst my children. I appoint Elias Brock, John Burton, James Boyd executor. Dated 5 Oct. 1815. Richardson __, Joel X Withers, Polly Strain, James Boyd. Signed: Archibald X McDaniel. Proved on oath of Turner Richardson before D. Anderson, Ord. this 2 Jan. 1826.

McDANIEL, CAROLINE Will Book F, Page 315. Probate Judge Office. Edgefield, S. C. I Caroline McDaniel of Edgefield Dist. being of sound and disposing mind and memory and understanding. My will and desire is that my dtr. Elizabeth Thomas have 100 acres of land adj. the land of William Glanton. That my two dtrs. Millie Glanton and Frances receive $5.00 each. I wish the rest and residue of my property both real and personal go to my dtr. Martha, to be possessed by her as long as she is single. At her death or marriage to be divided between her two dtr. Mary Ann McKenny and Frances America Holmes. I appoint Mr. William McDaniel. Dated 26 Oct. 1875. Wit: G. W. Bussey, D. C. Bussey, Wm. L. McDaniel. Proved on oath of D. C. Bussey before L. Charlton, J.P.C. this 31 Oct. 1878.

McDANIEL, CAROLINE Will Book F, Page 315. Probate Judge Office.
Edgefield, S. C. I Caroline McDaniel of Edgefield Dist. being of
sound mind and memory and understanding. I will and desire that my
dtr. Elizabeth Thomas have 100 acres of land adj. the land of William
Glanton, and that my two dtrs. Millie Glanton and Frances Holson receive
$5.00 each. I wish the residue of my property both real and personal
go to my dtr. Matha[?] to be possessed by her as long as she lives a
single or unmarried life. But if she marry or dies, said property to
be divided between her two chn. Mary Ann McKenny and Frances America
Holmes. I appoint Mr. William McDaniel executor. Dated 26 Oct. 1875.
Wit: G. W. Bussey, D. C. Bussey, Wm. L. McDaniel. Signed: Caroline
X McDaniel. Proved on oath of D. C. Bussey before L. Charlton J.P.C.
this 31 Oct. 1878.

McDANIEL, JOHN Will Book A, Page 395. Probate Judge Office.
Edgefield, S. C. I John McDaniel of Edgefield Dist. being weak in
body, but of sound mind and memory. First I lend to my beloved wife,
Mary McDaniel all my estate both real and personal during her widowhood,
unless as is herein after mentioned it is my desire that the whole of
my est. with the debts due me, be divided equally amongst my wife Mary
and my children, Edmund McDaniel, John Harden McDaniel, Sherlett McDaniel,
Martin R. McDaniel and Eliza Ann McDaniel. It is my desire that as
soon as the children come of age they shall have their part. I appoint
my wife Mary McDaniel and William Robertson executrix, and executor.
Dated 3 Jan. 1818. Wit: Benjamin Harrison, Burgess White, James H.
Mosley. Signed: John McDaniel. Proved on oath of Burgess White
before John Simpkins O.E.D. this 24 Jan. 1818.

McDANIEL, JOHN Will Book A, Page 395. Probate Judge Office.
Edgefield, S. C. I John McDaniel of Edgefield Dist. being weak in
body but of sound mind and memory. I lend unto beloved wife Mary
McDaniel all my estate both real and personal during her widowhood.
My will and desire that the whole of my est. both real and personal,
with all debts owing to my est. be equally divided between my wife
Mary McDaniel and my chn. Edmund McDaniel, John Harden McDaniel,
Sherlett McDaniel, Martin R. McDaniel, Eliza Ann McDaniel. I appoint
my wife Mary McDaniel and William Robertson executrix and executor.
Dated 3 Jan. 1818. Wit: Benjamin Harrison, Burgess White, James H.
Mosely. Signed: John McDaniel. Proved on oath of Burgess White
before John Simkins, Ord. this 24 Jan. 1818.

McDANIEL, LEVI SENR. Will Book E, Page 253. Probate Judge
Office. Edgefield, S. C. I Levi McDaniel of Edgefield Dist. being
weak in body but of sound mind and memory. I will my just debts be
paid. I give to my wife Ann McDaniel all my estate both real and
personal, at her death, it to be sold. The money arising to be divided
as, To my dtr. Caroline Calahan five dollars. I give to my son Fed.
one sixth, to my son Erasmus one sixth, to my son Oliver one sixth, to
my son Levi Jr. one sixth, to my dtr. Patie Holmes one sixth, to my two
grandchildren William and Anna Cartledge jointly one sixth. I appoint
my two sons Fed and Oliver McDaniel executors. Dated 13 Oct. 1847.
Wit: J. B. Harris, James Tompkins, Martin Holmes. Signed: Levi
McDaniel. Proved on oath of James Tompkins before W. F. Durisee,
O.E.D. this 13 May 1858.

McDANIEL, ROBERT S. Box 45 Pack 24. Probate Judge Office. Union,
S. C. I Robert S. McDaniel, desiring to dispose of what earthly
effects. I desire my debts, both personal and copartnership due by me
be paid by Sims McDaniel. I will all my brother Sims McDaniel all my
interest being one half, in the tract of land purchased by us from
Dr. W. K. Sims lying on Broad River. The remainder of my estate of
what ever nature or kind soever, I desire to be equally divided among
my sisters Mary A. L. Gist, wife of N. Gist Jr., Deusilla Beard, wife
of W. B. S. Beard and said Sims McDaniel. Dated 10 June 1861. Wit:
Julius Kaiser, Wm. W. Perry, George Fant. Signed: R. S. McDaniel.
Proved on oath of Julius Kaiser before Columbus Gage, Esq. Ord. this
15 April 1862.

McDANIEL, THOMAS SR. Pack 650 #5. Clerk of Court Office.
Pickens, S. C. I Thomas McDaniel Senr. of Pickens Dist. in consideration of $80 to me paid by David Sloan of the same Dist. have sold,
bargained, and released all that tract of land whereon I now live,
containing 150 acres. Being part of the tract I purchased from John
Gregory. Bounded by land of Thomas McDaniel Jr., James H. Dendy,
Nathaniel Hull, lying on Coneross Creek. Dated 28 Feb. 1828. Wit:
Amon Rowland, James Peterson. Signed: Thomas McDaniel. Proved on
oath of Amon Rowland before Wm. L. Keith C.C. this 8 May 1829.

McDILL, THOMAS Box 68 Pack 1669. Probate Judge Office. Abbeville,
S. C. I Thomas McDill of Abbeville Dist. being of sound and disposing
mind and memory, but weak in body. I desire that my wagon, blacksmith
tools and all such effects as my executors think best be sold after
my decease, and the money arising to pay my just debts and funeral
expenses, after paying such debts. I give to my beloved wife Jane
McDill all my est. both real and personal. After the decease of my
wife, I give to my son Wm. McDill one fourth after all debts are paid.
To my grand son Thos. R. McDill my shot gun. I give to my son Thos.
McDill one fourth of my est. I give to my dtr. Jane one fourth part
of my est. also one cow and calf. I give to my two grand dtrs. heirs
of my dtr. Molly Lagron decd. viz; Rebeca Lagron and Mary Lagron, also
one spinning wheel, one pot, one chest. I appoint Thomas McDill
executor. Dated 8 April 1843. Wit: David M. McDill, G. J. Cannon,
Vena X Anderson. Signed: Thomas McDill. Proven on oath of David
M. Wardlaw before David Lesly Ord. this 14 July 1843. Inventory was
made 18 Nov. 1843 by David Wardlaw, Tompson Shoemaker, J. A. Donald,
Larkin Harris. Sale held 23 Nov. 1843. Buyers: William McDill,
Thomas McDill, Jr., William Harris, David M. Wardlaw, Harris Alexander,
Alexander Ghastin, Isaac Kenneday. Settlement of the est. was made
5 Jan. 1847. Present Thos. McDill, exor. Wm. McDill, John H.
Hutchison only son of Jane. The decd. dtr. two chn. gdn. not present.

McDONALD, THOMAS Box 3 Pack 7. Probate Judge Office. Union,
S. C. I Thomas McDonald of Union Dist. do make this my last will and
testament. I appoint my friends Charles McDonald, Richd. Farr. Robt.
Crenshaw Junr. my executors. The plantation whereon I now live, my
desire my beloved wife Frances may remain in possession of the same
and that my dtrs. are permitted to live with her until my son Robert
doth arrive to the age of twenty one. At the death of my wife the
named tract of land to become my son Robert McDonald property in fee
simple. To my sons Charles and Thomas McDonald one tract of land in
Chester County, I purchased from John McCool, also one tract in Union
County, I purchased from W. Parson to be equally divided between them.
I give to my wife Frances one ball faced mare, exclusive of a child
part which I give her forever. I give to my dtr. Sarah S. McDonald one
celar colt, named Harpoon. I give to my dtr. Sebellow B. McDonald,
one celar colt named Snip. When my dtr. Lucy Farr was married I gave
her three negroes, Jude, Mill and Lewis, these are to be appraised,
and be partof her legacy of my est. Likewise after my decease I desire
my executors to have three for each of my children, as near the same
value as convenant, each child to draw a lot for their negroes.
Children to draw lots are: Charles McDonald, Sarah S. McDonald,
Thomas McDonald, Sebello B. McDonald, Elizabeth L. McDonald, Jensey
McDonald, Robert McDonald and Matilda McDonald. I desire my just debts
be paid. The remainder of my estate be equally divided amongst all
my chn. Dated 11 Aug. 1800. Wit: Thos. Shelton, Elesebeth[sic] X
Grenshaw, Charlott X Davis. Signed by Frances X McDonald. Signed:
Joseph McJunkin, J.P. Proved before Joseph McJunkin, J.P. on oath of
Thomas Shelton, Elesebeth Grenshaw and Charlott Davis on the 11 Aug.
1800. The named witnesses saith that Thomas McDonald was perfectly in
his senses when he dicted[sic] the within, as his last will and
testament.

McDOW, GEORGE W. Pack 225 #7. Clerk of Court Office. Pickens,
S. C. Whereas Elisha Lawrence of Pickens Dist. did on the 12 Nov.
1842 execute and deliver to W. L. Keith and G. W. Liddell trustees a
deed of trust by which Elisha Lawrence conveyed to said trustees certain property to be held for the separate use, benefit of his wife

McDow, George W. - Continued. Martha Lawrence during her natural
life and after her death to the heirs of her body. Said trustees shall
have power to sell any part of said property to pay existing debts.
Now know all, that we George W. McDow and Mary Margaret McDow of
Pickens Dist. in consideration that the said trustees have consented
that the remainder of the property so deeded, not already sold to pay
debts of Martha Lawrence, who has removed to the State of Texas. Dated
9 Oct. 1852. Wit: Wm. G. Mullinnex, Wm. C. Mullennex. Signed:
Mary Margaret McDow.

McDOW, MARGARET J.   , Box 97 #1020. Probate Judge Office.
Pickens, S. C. Est. admnr. 11 Dec. 1869 by John McDow, Joseph Warner,
J. C. Watkins, and J. D. Gassaway are bound unto I. H. Philpot, Ord.
in the sum of $1,000. Died about 18 Sept. 1869. Paid 3 Dec. 1877
E. M. Bruce heir $162. Paid Susan J. McDow $45.35. Paid Sarah E.
McDow a minor $37.60.

McDOW, "MINORS" Box 3 #70. In Equity, Clerk of Court Office.
Pickens, S. C. On 18 Oct. 1861 Margaret J. McDow, Robert Craig, Jr.,
David S. Craig are bound unto Robert A. Thompson Clk. of Equity in the
sum of $12,600. Margaret J. McDow gdn. of John W., Mary C., Martha L.,
Sydney McDow their father. Ellender, Sarah and Susan are minors under
12 yrs.

McDOW, SIDNEY Box 52 #570. Probate Judge Office. Pickens, S. C.
Est. admnr. 7 Nov. 1859 by Margaret J. McDow, Robert Craig, John H.
Arial, R. E. Holcombe are bound unto James E. Hagood, Ord. in the sum
of $20,000. Heirs Mary J. McDow the widow (in bond written Margaret J.)
William A. McDow, John W. McDow, Mary C. McDow, Martha L. McDow,
Elender M. McDow, Sarah E. McDow, Susan McDow all of this Dist. except
Wm. A. McDow who resides out of State. On 23 Oct. 1872 Sallie is
16 yrs. of age, Sue McDow is 14 yrs. of age. They are the minors of
Sidney McDow and reside with their brother John McDow. Sidney McDow
owned 450 acres on 18 Mile Creek adj. land of W. C. Miller, Ed. Martin,
and others. The widow Margaret McDow has also died. The chn. Mary
Werner, Martha Brock residing in Georgia, Ellen Bruce, Sallie McDow,
Sue McDow are minors. Dated 23 Oct. 1872.

McDOW, CAPT. WILLIAM Box 27 #322. Probate Judge Office. Pickens,
S. C. Est. admnr. 20 Dec. 1850 by G. W. McDow, Thomas Gassaway, Miles
M. Norton, Samuel Reid, E. G. Gaines who are bound unto W. D. Steele,
Ord. in the sum of $8,000. Expend: Paid 3 March 1854 Sidney McDow
$120.00. Paid 7 Feb. 1853 Nancy Hopkins $2.50. Paid 20 Sept. 1855
James Gassaway guardian for Matilda A. Gassaway and Thomas Gassaway
minors $177.95. Paid 1 March 1852 Jonathan McDow $471.35. Paid
Samuel McDow $471.35. Paid G. W. Mitchell $471.32. Amount due the
heirs of Reuben Mitchell decd. $97.06. Amount due the heirs of Westley
Gassaway decd. $60.26.

McDOW, WILLIAM P. Box 7 #92. Probate Judge Office. Pickens,
S. C. Est. admnr. 4 Dec. 1837 by William McDow, Robert Gaines, who
are bound unto James M. Dendy, Ord. in the sum of $900. William McDow
was the father of said decd. Expend, paid 2 Dec. 1850 George Mitchell
guardian for William H. McDow, Elizabeth A. McDow $893.38 1/4. On
6 Dec. 1850 George W. Mitchell in right of his wife Margaret A.
Mitchell sheweth that William P. McDow died some 10 or 15 years ago,
intestate, leaving a widow and two chn. William P. McDow died possessed
with 60 acres of land lying on waters of 18 mile creek. Adj. land of
G. W. McDow, William D. Arnold, W. G. Mullinix. Your petitioner prays
for a partition, one third in right of his wife Margaret, one third to
William H. McDow, and one third to Elizabeth McDow chn. of said William
P. McDow. State of Mississippi County of Monroe, on filing the return
of William H. McDow and Elizabeth McDow minors heirs of Pinchney McDow
late of Pickens Dist. Praying that George W. Mitchell be appointed
their legal gdn. It appeared that the minors residing in this County
and are over the age of 14 yrs. Dated 4 Nov. 1850.

McDOWELL, MALINDA Book B, Page 97. Probate Judge Office.
Pickens, S. C. Malinda McDowell mentioned on 27 Aug. 1866 as sister
of E. G. Hudson decd. of Pickens Dist.

McELMOYLE, ELIZABETH Box 90 #950. Probate Judge Office. Anderson, S. C. I Eliza McElmoyle being of sound mind and memory. All my
property, including the dwelling house, lots, stock, cattle and my
gold watch, which was given to me by my father and mother, all notes,
money to my dear sister Eleanor J. Walker. The property in Charleston
to be for my sister maintenance. I appoint my sister Eleanor Janes
Walker executrix. Dated 21 Sept. 1883. Wit: J. P. Glenn, W. W.
Martin, N. T. Martin. Elizabeth McElmoyle. Filed this 12 Jan. 1884.

McELVANY, ANDREW K. Box 2 #16. Probate Judge Office. Pickens,
S. C. Est. admnr. 1 Feb. 1830 by William Oliver, Robert Gaines, James
Gaines, Esq. are bound unto James H. Dendy, Ord. in the sum of $200.
Citation pub. at Mount Zion Meeting House. Expend 31 Jan. 1812.
Andrew K. McElvany minor in acct. with William Oliver his guardian
for boarding 4 yrs. $80. 10 Jan. 1830 Andrew K. McElvany decd. debtor
to William Oliver for 15 months boarding and nursing in sickness $150.

McFALL, JAMES M. Box 107 #1026. Probate Judge Office. Pickens,
S. C. Est. admnr. 24 July 1875 by W. T. McFall, D. F. Bradley, J.
Riley Ferguson are bound unto I. H. Philpot, Ord. in the sum of $3,000.
16 June 1896 C. W. McFall of Winston, N.C. recd. share from his father
est. Was merchant in the town of Pickens. Left a widow Mildred
McFall and five chn. minors, Kate, Minnie, James and Eloise McFall.
(One name not given.)

McFALL, "MINORS" Box 95 #6. Probate Judge Office. Pickens,
S. C. On 25 June 1875 W. T. McFall, D. Frank Bradley, J. Riley
Ferguson are bound unto I. H. Philpot, Ord. in the sum of $1667.00
W. T. McFall gdn. of Kate McFall, Minnie Lee McFall, James Henry
McFall, Eloise McFall, Clarence McFall all minors under the age of
21 yrs. Chn. of James McFall decd. and wife Mildred McFall. James
McFall decd. had a policy of insurance upon the Piedmont and Arlington
Insurance Co. of Richmond, Va. On 7 June 1894 Mrs. W. C. Langley recd.
a share her her father estate.

McGEE, ANNA Box 58 Pack 1381. Probate Judge Office. Abbeville,
S. C. I Anny Magee [sic] widow of Michael Magee decd. of Abbeville
Dist. being of sound mind and memory. First I give my grandson Michael
Magee Senr. forty dollars, then the balance, I desire to be equally
divided between my children viz; John Magee, Jane Dodson, Elizabeth S.
Sims, Polly Dun, Burrel Magee, Michael Magee, Abner H. Magee, William
Magee, Nancy Barmore decd. her part to be equally divided between
Malinda Brownly and Margaret Marmore and my grand son Michael Magee
Senr. I desire to receive an equal part of all my est. that is to be
divided after my death. I appoint my son John Magee my executor.
Dated 25 Sept. 1837. Wit: Wm. Barmore, Washington Youngblood,
Isaac Agnew. Signed: Anna X Magee. Inventory made 26 Nov. 1838 by
Benjamin Smith, Ezekiel Rasor, John Rasor.

McGEE, MICHAEL Box 66 Pack 1589. Probate Judge Office. Abbe-
ville, S. C. Est. admnr. by Burrell McGee, Abner H. McGee, William
Barmore and Ezekiel Rasor who are bound unto Moses Taggart, Esq. Ord.
in the sum of $20,000. Dated 10 Nov. 1834. Inventory made 24 Nov.
1834. Slaves named Dick and Siller, Tim Florah and Mahaly, George,
Harry, Jack, Joe, Fillis, Lewis, Amy, Rachel, Reuben, Black Man, Shake,
Tom, Snipe, Ball. Appraisers, Ezekiel Rasor, Albert N. Ware, W. T.
Jones. Citation published 9 Nov. 1834 at Turkey Meeting House.
Signed: Arthur Williams. Sale held 25-26 Nov. 1834. Widow (Anna
McGee), Wm. Ware, A. H. McGee, D. Prowitt, A. H. McGee, W. F. Jones,
Isaac Agnew, James Agnew, William Richey, Wm. Kay, D. Roney, G. Wallace,
A. N. Ware, J. Dodson, S. Kinman, Wm. Mattox, William Long, Charles
B. Foshee, James Dodson, D. Maybury, M. Henderson, A. Norris, M. McGee
Senr., Wm. Barmore, D. O. Hawthorn, J. Burnes, Harrison Hodges, S.
Kinman, H. Dixon, J. Robertson, J. W. Norris, R. V. Posey, Joseph
Richey, M. Killingsworth, J. Raysor, widow Kinman, W. Drummond,

McGee, Michael - Continued. S. Agnew Jr., widow Mattox, J. McCullough, S. Jones, Jr., S. Dodson, J. S. McGee, A. H. McGee, Asa Franklin, Abner Nobbs, B. McGee, R. Robertson, S. Williamson, Price Posey. Paid to Polly Dunn for Samuel Dunn on power of Attorney, resided in Indiana $600. Michael McGee $545. William McGee $335. G. H. Brownlee $360. John McGee $250. James Dodson $598.84. Wm. Barmore for his dtr. Margaret $395. Elizabeth Sims as legatee $496.

McGRAW, JOHN No. 9 An Inquest. Pack 125. Probate Judge Office. Pickens, S. C. An inquest was held at Tunnel Hill in Pickens Dist. 21 Jan. 1858 upon the body of John McGraw of Tunnel Hill. The jury brought it out that he came to his death by falling into the shaft of #4 of Stump House Tunnel on the morning of 21 Jan. 1858 by misfortune or accident. John Knight said that he was working between 3 or 4 o'clock, I heard something strick[sic] the bottom, John T. Williams asked if it was a rock fell in the shaft. James Cunningham looked around and saw no one, he took up the lamp and looked and said there is a man lying here and I found him to be dead. We took him up in the barrel and went with him. William Gassaway says that he was down in the bottom, and thought it was a rock falling.

McGRIFF, JOHN Book Q, Page 162. Clerk of Court Office. Chester, S. C. I John McGriff of the State of Georgia and Laurence Co. in consideration of $100 to me paid by Alexander Donald of the State of S. C. Chester Dist. have bargained, sold and released all that tract of land on Sandy River, containing 174 acres. Granted to said John McGriff the 3 Dec. 1767. Dated this 9 Sept. 1813. Wit: Wm. McGriff, Hezh. Donald. Signed: John McGriff. Proved on oath of Hezh. Donald who said he saw John McGriff of the State of Georgia sign the within deed before Henry Head, J.P. this 20 Nov. 1813.

McGUFFIN, JOSEPH B. Pack 115 #3. Clerk of Court Office. Pickens, S. C. An inquest was held at the house of Joseph B. McGuffin in Pickens Dist. on the 14 Dec. 1864 to view the dead body of Joseph B. McGuffin. The jury brought it out that the decd. came to his death by a wound inflicted by a knife in the hands of a man supposed by evidence to be Peter L. Barton of the town of Walhalla on the 6 Dec. 1864. Capt. C. H. Taylor sworn sayth, I was present in the town of Walhalla on 6 Dec. and saw a man called Peter Barton and J. B. McGuffin have a fist fight. McGuffin wanted to borrow 50 dollars from Barton. Barton told him he did not have it. McGuffin swore he did have it. Then he chased Barton. Barton drew his knife and made at McGuffin with it open. McGuffin broke and run. Barton stabbed him in the back and then in the side and shoulder. They were then parted by the former sheriff of the Dist. (W. N. Craig). On cross examination he stated that McGuffin pulled Barton off his horse, pushed him up against a shady tree with violence. McGuffin called him a G.D. liar and scoundel and that he was not worth a dogs notice, and swore he would whip him before he left the place. Barton did not abuse him with his tongue. Both were drinking to some extent. Signed: C. H. Taylor.

McHUGH, CORNELIUS #1. Clerk of Court Office. Abbeville, S. C. Abbeville Dist. Court of General Sessions and Common Pleas: To the Honr. J. D. Witherspoon, Judge. The petition of Cornelius McHugh, aged 32 yrs. following the profession of merchant. Your petitioner was born in Glenties County, Donugal Ireland. That he arrived in U.S. at New York City on the 5 Sept. 1874. Has resided in S.C. for 9 yrs. That he did declare his intention of renouncing all allegiance to any foreign power, etc. He therefore prays that the oath which in such cases is provided, may be administered to him, and that he may be admitted as a citizen of the U.S. Thomas McGelligen and James H. Simmons states that they have known said Cornelius McHugh for five years and that he has been a good citizen. Signed: Thomas McGelligan and James H. Simmons. He was sworn in the 12 Feb. 1886.

McKEE, KEZIAH Box 53 #580. Probate Judge Office. Pickens Dist., S. C. Est. admnr. 27 Feb. 1860 by William G. Newton, Watson Collins, Joshua Holden who are bound unto W. E. Holcombe, Ord. in the sum of $500.

McKELLAR, "MINORS" Pack 436. Clerk of Court Office. Abbeville, S. C. In 1825 C. C. Mayson was the guardian of the minor children of John McKellar, Jr. decd. viz; John W. McKellar, William N. McKellar, James D. McKellar. 1 Jan. 1820 recd. from Donald McKellar for sale of land $1490.00. In 1828 John W. McKellar was the guardian. 1838 paid taxes for land in James D. McKellar in acct. in Edgefield $2.50. Aug. 1838, Expenses to Mississippi $17.00. 27 Sept. 1834 paid Mrs. Nancy McKellar $200. Paid 1822 for repairs done on the house in Cambridge $34.

McKOWN, JOSEPH Box 66 Pack 1594. Probate Judge Office. Abbeville, S. C. Abbeville Dist. Admnr. bond, we Robert McKown, Joseph McKown, 7 Robert Sharp are bound unto Moses Taggart, Ord. in the sum of $4,000. Dated 3 Nov. 1834. The appraisment was taken the 15 Nov. 1834 by Robert C. Sharp, William Sharp, A. C. Hawthorn. Sale held the 18 Nov. 1834, Buyers, the widow is listed as "the widow" Robert McKown, Johnston Sims, John McKellar, Katherine McKown, Robert Ellis, William Sharp, Joseph McKown, Samuel Pruit, James P. Bowie, James Wilson, Joseph J. McKeller, Joseph J. Hawthorn, Donnald Douglass, Poly McKown, D. O. Hawthorn, Edward Haggan, John Webb, Hesekiah Bowie, Thomas Hawthorn, Richard P. Doyl, William McGree, Michael Wilson, John Waer, John A. Burton, Robert Caldwell, James Burnes, Wm. Barmore, James Cowan, Henson Posey, John Givens, William McCree, David Anderson, William Simpson, Sarah McKown, John Richardson, Andrew Richey, Jos. Aiken, William McKay, John Collins, William D. Reeves, James Moore, Notes due the est. John Allgier, George Wallace, Joseph J. McKown, George W. Sims, Robert McKown, Joseph Sharp. Two slaves were bought by Widow McKown named Bob and Flora. One negro girl, named Susan was bought by John Givens. The widow may have been named Catherine as she paid the est. $899.22 as she bought two negroes and many other items. The legatee listed as Mary McKown. Margaret A. McKown, John Wear (legatee by note). Not listed as legatees, but paid Sarah McKown.

McKEE, JAMES A. Book B, Page 27. Probate Judge Office. Pickens, S. C. On 14 Dec. 1859 James A. McKee and wife Elvira E. McKee were mentioned as heirs of Jacob B. Perry decd. and his widow Mary A. Perry of Pickens Dist. Tombstone inscriptions taken from "Eakin Cemetery" Central Community. Abbeville County, S. C.
James J. McKee, 9 March 1877, 20 Jan. 1941
Thomas J. McKee, 3 Dec. 1873, 24 Sept. 1931
Janie Bryson Nickles wife of William J. McKee, 4 Aug. 1852, 22 Nov. 1929.

McKINNEY, DANIEL Box 48 #534. Probate Judge Office. Pickens, S. C. Est. admnr. 27 Sept. 1858 by Robert A. Thompson who is bound unto W. J. Parson, Ord. in the sum of $100. Sale held 20 Nov. 1858. Buyers: Rachel McKinney and W. R. Durham.

McKINNEY, JAMES Deed Book A, Page 43. Probate Judge Office. Pickens, S. C. The undersigned sheweth that he has an interest in the surplus land of James McKinney Senr. decd. Therefore petition this Court to sell said land as soon as possible. Dated 17 Jan. 1842. Signed: John McKinney. To Charles McKinney, James Lay, David McKinney, Jesse Preston and Wilson McKinney, James Robertson legal heirs of James McKinney. You are required to appear at Pickens Court House and show why 133 acres lying on water of Devils Fork should not be divided. Filed this 17 Jan. 1842.

McKINNEY, JAMES Pack 58 #8. Clerk of Court Office. Pickens, S. C. On 18 May 1834 James McKinney appeared before David McKinney, J.P. and made oath that on Sunday evening last that John Corbin Junr. and James Corbin and John Corbin Senr. did felonously and wholly lay way him at the foot of Capeharts Mountain in the intention of murdering and robbing him, they shot at him three times. He met John Corbin Jr. and James Corbin in the road, after they passed, they turned and shot at time, his horse throwed him, when he looked up he saw the Corbins boys running up the road, he heard another one which he belives to be John Corbin Senr. which he gave him a fatal and mortal wound near the back bone. Witnesses were Nancy Readman, John Knox, Jesse McKinney, Alfred Moss, Jeptha Moss gave evidence against the Corbins.

McKINNEY, JAMES SENR. Pack 296. Clerk of Court Office. Pickens, S. C. I James McKinney Sr. of Pickens Dist. in consideration of $1500 to me paid by Ephraim Perry of the same place. Have granted, sold, bargained and released all that tract of land on the North fork of Little River waters of Seneca River. Being the tract granted originally to Jane Peteat the 2 April 1821. Adj. lands of Martins Reserve. Dated this 5 Oct. 1840. Wit: Thos. D. Garvin, David McKinney. Signed: James McKinney Senr. This day came Mrs. Mary McKinney the wife of James McKinney (now decd.) and freely renounce, release, and forever relinquished all interest of dower in the above land. Dated this 18 Jan. 1842. Signed: Mary X McKinney. Proved on oath of Thomas D. Garvin before W. L. Keith C.C. this 25 Jan. 1842.

McKINNEY, JAMES SENR. Pack 296. In Equity. Clerk of Court Office. Pickens, S. C. Ephraim Perry states that he purchased of James McKinney, now decd. in his life time lying and being in Pickens Dist. on the North fork of Little River, and paid James McKinney Senr. $1500 in cash. That the said land had been granted unto Jane Bruce by the State of S. C., while she was a feme sole (a woman unmarried) by the name of Jane Peteat, brought her action of tresspass to try titles in Court. Said James McKinney departed this life before the action of trespass. Jane Bruce joined her husband in the deed to said James McKinney had relinquished her estate of inheritance in the land. Jane Bruce husband John Bruce is now dead. The heirs of James McKinney are John McKinney residing in Pickens Dist., Elizabeth the wife of James Lay resides in Pickens Dist., James McKinney Jr. resides in Cherokee Co., Ga. Sarah the wife of James McKinney resides in Jackson Co., N.C. Hester the wife of James Robinson resides in Pickens Dist., Preston McKinney resides in California. The following grandchildren, sons and dtrs. of Charles McKinney decd. Eliza the wife of Robert Knox resides in Pickens Dist., John McKinney resides in Pickens Dist., Sarah the wife of Wiley McConnell resides in Pickens Dist., Rosey L. Martin the wife of Stephen Martin resides in Anderson Dist., George W. McKinney resides in N.C., Caroline McKinney resides in Pickens Dist. The following grandchildren, sons and dtr. of David McKinney decd. Nancy the widow, living in Georgia, James McKinney, Mary the wife of Mr. Murphy, Francis McKinney, Preston McKinney and Nancy McKinney all resides in Georgia. Nancy Earnest a widow and dtr. of James McKinney Senr. resides in Ga. William McKinney resides in Texas, Jesse McKinney decd. died without wife or chn. Wilson McKinney decd. died without wife or chn. The wife of James McKinney survived her husband but has since departed this life. Filed 29 Oct. 1858.

McKINNEY, JESSE In Equity, #69. Clerk of Court Office. Pickens, S. C. I Jesse McKinney of Pickens Dist. in consideration of $45 to me paid by Joseph Grisham of the same place, have bargained, sold, granted and released all that town lot in the village of Pickens known as Robertson barn lot and numbered as 47 containing one acre and 11 3/4 rods. Dated 22 March 1837. Wit: Miles M. Norton, Naaman Curtis. Signed: Jesse McKinney. Proved on oath of Naaman Curtis before Miles M. Norton J.P. this 22 March 1837. Here Jesse McKinney is Col. Jesse McKinney.

McKINNEY, MAJOR JAMES ESQ. Box 11 #150. Probate Judge Office. Pickens, S. C. Est. admnr. 2 Nov. 1843 by James Robertson Esq., Benjamin Hagood who are bound unto James H. Dendy Ord. in the sum of $2000. State of Georgia, Cherokee County. James McKinney states that he paid his father James McKinney Sr. $1185.00 for a tract of land. His father keep the title and let Preston McKinney have same, therefore, his father estate is indebted to him. James McKinney Sr. owned on 17 Jan. 1842 a tract of land on Boon Creek containing 800 acres, also a tract on White Water River, another tract on the Devils Fork. Heirs: Charles, David, Jesse, Preston, Wilson, James Jr. McKinney, James Lay and James Robertson, Sarah McKinney.

McKINNEY, JOHN Box 104 #1090. Probate Judge Office. Pickens, S. C. Est. admnr. 6 Sept. 1873 by Elizabeth McKinney, Thos. W. Alexander, Thos. N. McKinney are bound I. H. Philpot, Ord. in the sum of $800.

McKINNEY, JOHN W. Box 93 Pack 976. Probate Judge Office.
Pickens, S. C. On 10 Aug. 1866. John W. McKinney decd. owned 120
acres the home place on Indian Branch, waters of Three and twenty mile
Creek, adj. land of Lem Hendricks, Jane McWhorter and others. Owned
39 1/4 acres on waters of 18 mile Creek adj. land of Lem Hendricks
and John Hinton. Heirs Sarah G. McKinney, Alice T., Vesta K., John
C. McKinney. On 17 Dec. 1870 Margaret A. E. Durham recd. her third of
said est.

McKINNEY, JOHN W. Box 77 #822. Probate Judge Office. Pickens,
S. C. Est. admnr. 12 Aug. 1864 by Margaret A. E. McKinney, Robert
Knox, Daniel Hughes are bound unto W. E. Holcombe, Ord. in the sum of
$1,000. Left widow and 4 chn. Margaret A. E. Durham, admnrx. Paid
29 July 1880. Sarah G. Kelly $39.77. Alice T. Taylor, paid $39.77.
Paid Vester K. and John McKinney $79.50.

McKINNEY, MRS. MARY Box 43 #477. Probate Judge Office. Pickens,
S. C. Est. admnr. 16 July 1858 by John Robertson, W. F. Mitchell,
L. C. Craig are bound unto W. J. Parson, Ord. in the sum of $600. Her
est. was derelict and consists of her share in the estates of her sons,
Jesse and Wilson McKinney. Recd. 8 Aug. 1860 of John McKinney Admnr.
of Jesse McKinney Est. $232.89. Recd. of John McKinney admnr. of
Wilson McKinney decd. est. $51.20.

McKINNEY, "MINORS" Box 11 #166. Probate Judge Office. Pickens,
S. C. On 1 Dec. 1879 Margaret A. E. Durham, A. G. Wyatt, H. A. Richey
are bound to Olin L. Durant, Ord. in the sum of $150. Margaret A. E.
Durham gdn. of Vesta K. McKinney, John C. McKinney minors under 21
yrs. Chn. of John McKinney decd. Margaret A. E. McKinney their mother.

McKINNEY, "MINORS" Box 5 #84. Probate Judge Office. Pickens,
S. C. On 9 Feb. 1861 C. C. McKinney, John McKinney, Samuel Reid are
bound to W. E. Holcombe, Ord. in the sum of $208. Claiborne C. McKinney
gdn. of Preston McKinney, Nancy McKinney minors under 21 yrs. Nancy
McKinney their mother. David McKinney decd. their father. Wilson
McKinney and Jesse McKinney both dead were their uncles.

McKINNEY, PRESTON Box 2 #61. In Equity, Clerk of Court Office.
Pickens, S. C. On 22 March 1858. Elijah E. Alexander states that
Preston McKinney removed from this State to Texas many yrs. ago. Son
of James McKinney decd. Mother Mary McKinney, brothers, Jesse, Wilson
McKinney decd. 15 Feb. 1859 Dyer McKinney son of David McKinney saith
that Preston McKinney boarded at fathers 8 or 9 yrs. and left our
house 2 Feb. 1852. Took off with fathers mare, work horse and sold it
at Spring Place, Ga. Nancy McKinney widow of David McKinney.

McKINNEY, THOMAS N. Box 100 #1059. Probate Judge Office.
Pickens, S. C. I Thomas McKinney of Pickens County, being of sound and
disposing mind and memory. First I desire my executrix as soon after
my decease as possible to collect all monies due me and pay my just
debts and funeral expenses. I give unto my loving wife Mary E.
McKinney during her natural life or widowhood, all my property both
real and personal, for the family support and education of my chn.
Should my wife remarry, I desire my estate be divided according to law
in such cases. I appoint my wife executrix. Dated 25 Sept. 1883.
Wit: J. E. Hagood, R. M. Stewart, Morris Miller. Signed: Thomas N.
McKinney. Filed 20 July 1885.

McKINNEY, ZACHARIAH Pack 297 #143. Clerk of Court Office.
Pickens, S. C. Whereas I Zachariah McKinney is confined in the common
jail of Pickens Dist. on a Capeas at the suit of Benjamin Hagood. To
the Commissioner of special bail, your petitioner is desirous to file
his schedule in the Clerk Office of all his effects and be discharged
agreeable to the prison board. Filed the 8 Feb. 1854. Monies owed
to Zach. McKinney, James D. Wright for $34 with interest for 13 yrs.
Another on Wright for $12 with interest.. one on David White for $3.50.
He a runaway. A true account of all property is listed, with a sow
given to his son by his grandfather. Zachariah wife was named Nancy L.
McKinney. See Pack 289 #5. Pro. Jed. Office. Pickens, S. C.

McMASTER, WILLIAM Box 67 #1647. Probate Judge Office. Abbeville,
S. C. I William McMaster being sick and low in condition. I will my
executors to pay all my just debts, and the rest of my property to be
divided amongst my legatees, viz, my wife Rebecker McMaster, my dtr.
Martha B. Thornton and Susannah T. Thornton and this to be upon record
until all parties are fully satisfied if my wife should have a desire
that Rachel and her children should more be with her than any of the
rest it is my it should be so. Dated 24 Nov. 1823. N.B. I wish
Hammer be set free, to be compelled to live with his mistress or either
of my dtr. Proved on oath of James Allen made oath that he belives the
signature to the within instrument to be the proper hand writing of
William McMaster decd. This 18 March 1824. Signed: James Allen.
Admnr. bond to Rebecca McMaster, John Cameron, James Allen. in the sum
of $10,000. Dated 18 March (written out, one thousand eight hundred
and eighty four) must be 1824. Recd. 27 April 1824, $2,087.60 my
distributive share. Signed: Jonathan Thornton. Recd. 27 April 1824,
$2,087.60. Signed Jonathan Thornton, Attorney in fact for Sandford
Thornton.

McLENNAN, JOHN Pack 321. Clerk of Court Office. Abbeville,
S. C. Abbeville Dist. To the Honr. the Chancellors: Your oratrix
Catharine Ann Watson of Abbeville Dist. an infant of the age of nine
yrs. by John P. Barratt of the same dist. as her next friend, sheweth,
that John McLennan late of Marion Co., State of Florida decd. was
possessed with personal and real estate of considerable amount and value.
Also considerable estate in this Dist. A paper purporting to be his
last will and testament, dated 3 Jan. 1852. The legal execution of
which said will your oratrix and her next friend declares to be null
and void, and an appeal has been taken by your orator in the Court of
Ordinary of this Dist. In said will, #3 "I bequeath to my granddaughter Catharine Ann Watson five hundred dollars." #4. I bequeath
to my father Alexr. McLennan five hundred dollars, in case of his
death, two thirds I bequeath to my brothers to be equally divided
among them, the other third to bequeath to my sisters. My father and
mother, brothers and sisters may be found in Locholsh Scotland. I
appoint James Wesley child and Thomas Thomson Esq. Attorney at law at
Abbeville C.H. my executors. Your oratrix sheweth that John McLennan
departed this life in the year 1853, that she is his only lineal
descendant, and next of kin. That John McLennan was a native of Scotland, and when quite young came to America about the year 1820, and
settled at Cambridge in Abbeville Dist. and the said John McLennan
married Catherine McKellar, and the issue of which marriage was Ann
McLennan alone, who was the mother of your oratrix, Ann McLennan who
had intermarried with Edward Watson, the father of your oratrix who
died in the city of Mexico in the service of his Country in the year
1847, and the mother of your oratrix died in the year 1845. Your
oratrix is informed and believes that the father and mother of her
grand father has long since been dead, and the suppose brothers and
sisters of her grandfather has never been known to anyone in this
Country, etc. etc. Filed 11 Jan. 1854. (Anyone that is a descedant of
the Catherine Ann Watson, will find valuable information in this
depositions were taken from people who knew the family in Scotland.)

McMAHAN, CLEO F. J. Box 115 #1. Probate Judge Office. Pickens,
S. C. On 4 Feb. 1887 Wm. T. Field, Wm. B. Allgood, J. N. Wyatt are
bound to J. B. Newberry, Ord. in the sum of $709. W. T. Filed gdn. of
Cleo Agnes and Franklin J. McMahan minors under 14 yrs. Cleo Agnes
aged 8 yrs. Franklin J. aged 6 yrs. chn. of F. J. McMahan who died
26 Nov. 1879. 11 March 1897 paid E. B. Latham gdn. for Cleo Latham
nee McMahan $189.53.

McMAHAN, "MINORS" Box 136 #1. Probate Judge Office. Pickens,
S. C. On 9 April 1900 Mamie Barton McMahan, J. E. Barton of Anderson
Co. Mary J. Barton are bound to J. B. Newberry Ord. in the sum of
$317.52. Mary B. McMahan gdn. for James Barton McMahan age 15 yrs.,
Bessie Virginia McMahan age 13 yrs. Eula May McMahan age 9 yrs., Thos.
Thornwell McMahan age 7 yrs., Alexr. Calvin McMahan, age 1 yrs.
Children of T. A. McMahan decd.

McMAHAN, "MINORS" Box 10 #185. Probate Judge Office. Pickens, S. C. On 27 March 1885. Wm. McMahan, T. H. McMahan, Elbert E. Perry are bound unto J. H. Newton, Ord. in the sum of $434.76. Wm. McMahan gdn. of E. A. McMahan, J. W. E. McMahan, Ida E. McMahan minors under 21 yrs. Chn. of G. W. McMahan who died in 1879.

McMAHAN, NANCY E. Book H-1. Page 214. Clerk of Court Office. Pickens, S. C. A deed of assignment, Pickens Dist. Whereas Lemuel A. Perry of the same place did on the 15 Aug. 1848 sign a deed of gift bequeathing to Nancy E. McMahan and Jesse R. Perry a certain portion of his real estate. To be equally divided between them at his death, which deed is recorded. Now be it known in conveyance of other arrangements that Nancy E. McMahan does freely relinquish all claims to her portion of said deed and all claim of any portion of the personal and real est. of Lemuel A. Perry forever. Dated 26 Dec. 1865. Wit: D. Grice, John G. Bowen. Signed: Nancy E. McMahan. Proved on oath of John G. Bowen before John R. Gosett Mag. P.D. this 17 March 1866.

McMAHAN, T. A. Box 132 #5. Probate Judge Office. Pickens, S. C. Est. admnr. 9 March 1899 by Wm. McMahan, E. A. McMahan, M. M. McMahan are bound unto J. B. Newberry, Ord. in the sum of $1,000. Died 1 Feb. 1899. Heirs, Mamie Barton McMahan the widow, James McMahan, Bessie McMahan, Eila McMahan, Thomas McMahan, Archibald McMahan. Owned 309 acres in Pickens Co. on George Creek. One tract on Cedar Rock road on waters of Georges Creek and Saluda River, containing 123 acres. Also 130 acres which formerly belonged to est. of Alexander McMahan decd. Owned 100 acres on Georges Creek, adj. land of R. F. Benhardt, J. B. Mauldin, and Furman University being on both sides of Cedar Rock road to Greenville, Dated 16 Oct. 1899.

McWHORTER the father of your oratrix died in June 1858 leaving the following children his only heirs ti wit, David C. McWhorter who resides in Pickens Dist., Sarah C. McWhorter who resides in N.C., Louisa C. Brown who resides in Georgia, John McWhorter who resides in State of Texas, James McWhorter who resides in Abbeville Dist., the chn. of Jeremiah McWhorter decd. to wit. Margaret E. wife of John, McKinney who resides in Pickens Dist., Martha M. McWhorter who resides in Pickens Dist., Charlotte L. McWhorter a minor under the age of 21 yrs. old resides in Pickens Dist. Filed 30 March 1861.

McWHORTER, DAVID Pack 2-A. (Basement) Clerk of Court Office. Pickens, S. C. I David McWhorter of Pickens Dist. in consideration of $250 to me paid by J. V. Coffee of same Dist. have sold, bargained and convey a tract of land containing 150 acres, lying on East fork of Little River. It being all the land I own on that side of the River. Dated 29 Dec. 1857. Wit: L. N. Robins, Samuel Capehart. Signed: David X McWhorter. Proved on oath of Samuel Capehart before L. N. Robins, J.P. this 29 Dec. 1857. Recorded 4 Jan. 1858.

McWHORTER, DAVID Box 30 #359. Probate Judge Office. Pickens, S. C. On 15 July 1853 John McWhorter, Mary McWhorter, Jane McWhorter, S. C. McWhorter, Daniel or David Gassaway, Coleman and Elizabeth A. Gassaway recd. shares from est. S. C. McWhorter was a brother to David McWhorter.

McWHORTER, GEORGE W. Box 90 #949. Probate Judge Office. Pickens, S. C. Est. admnr. 14 Dec. 1881 by Wm. W. McWhorter, H. B. Hendricks, E. F. Looper are bound unto Olin L. Durant, Ord. in the sum of $400. Died on or about 7 Dec. 1881. Wm. W. McWhorter his eldest brother. 14 March 1883 paid Mrs. H. E. McWhorter, gdn. of her chn. $50.68.

McWHORTER, GIDEON E. Box 104 #1088. Probate Judge Office. Pickens, S. C. I March 1873. Owned 113 acres on waters of Wolf Creek bounded by land of Reese Bowen, W. T. Field and others. W. A. G. McWhorter a son. L. H. McWhorter the widow.

McWHORTER, GIDEON E.   Box 39 #441.   Probate Judge Office.
Pickens, S. C.   Est. admnr. 16 May 1856 by Reese Bowen, R. A. Thompson
are bound unto W. J. Parson, Ord. in the sum of $600.   On 12 Oct. 1854
Moses E. McWhorter, Miles M. Norton of Athens, Clark Co., Ga. are
bound to Wm. J. Parsons, Ord. in the sum of $60.00.   Wm. J. Parson, Ord.
has paid to Moses E. McWhorter $26.26 as the share of Andw. P. McWhorter
in the est. of his decd. sister Melinda McWhorter.   Paid 1 Jan. 1859
L. H. McWhorter widow of Gideon McWhorter $147.81.

McWHORTER, JAMES BAILUS   Box 83 #883.   Probate Judge Office.
Pickens, S. C.   I James Bailus McWhorter, planter of Pickens Dist.
being of sound mind and body.   The dangers which are unseperable from
the life of a solider in the war.   I will my just debts be paid.   I
give to my three chn. John Thomas McWhorter, Margaret Jane McWhorter,
Robert Earle McWhorter the whole of my est. both real and personal.
I will that as soon after my death as practicable my est. be sold and
the proceed invested to the advantageous of my chn..   I appoint my
father Robert McWhorter Executor.   Dated 23 March 1863.   Wit: W. J.
Gantt, W. N. Craig, S. H. Johns.   Signed: J. B. McWhorter.   Proven
25 Oct. 1865.   Owned 170 acres lying on Goldens Creek adj. land of
Elihu Griffin, Est. of J. H. Boggs, decd., J. B. Clayton, paid 4 Dec.
1867 Winney A. McWhorter dower $75.

McWHORTER, JAMES   Box 65 #697.   Probate Judge Office.   Pickens,
S. C.   Est. admnr. 17 Oct. 1862 by Judah McWhorter, widow, Gideon
Ellis, John Ariail are bound unto W. E. Holcombe, Ord. in the sum of
$3,000.   Expend Paid M. A. Oneal $70.10.   Paid W. B. McWhorter $23.25.
Paid Lucinda McWhorter $97.90.   Paid E. A. White $35.18.   Paid R. A.
McWhorter $218.   Paid J. B. McWhorter $149.50.

McWHORTER, JEREMIAH   Box 112 #1078.   Probate Judge Office.
Pickens, S. C.   Abbeville Dist.   I Jeremiah B. McWhorter being of sound
and disposing mind but weak in body.   I desire that one bay mare be
sold and pay my just debts and funeral expenses be paid.   I will to my
wife Jane all my estate, both real and personal during her natural life
or widowhood.   If she marry then the property be sold and proceeds
divided amongst my children, Margaret Ann Elizabeth Sarah Jane Rebecker
Martha Mariah Charlotte Lettesha.   [Written this way]   I appoint my
wife Jane executrix.   Dated 13 Feb. 1844.   Wit: James ___ ?, William
L. Briant, William X McAdams.   Signed: Jeremiah B. X McWhorter.
Proven in Pickens Dist. 26 Feb. 1844.

McWHORTER, JOHN   Box 15 #201.   Probate Judge Office.   Pickens,
S. C.   State of Arkansas County of Washington.   I Hugh Rogers of said
State and County do hereby appoint John McWhotter of Walker County,
Georgia as my true and lawful attorney.   To ask, demand, sue, receive
and receipt for any money or other property due or owing me from the
estate of James Rogers decd. late of Pickens Dist.   Dated 25 April
1859.   Wit: Thomas M. Gunter, James W. Carny.   Signed: Hugh Rogers.
Proven on oath of James W. Carny before Cyrus G. Gilbreath, J.P. this
25 April 1859.   P. R. Smith certified that Cyrus G. Gilbreath, J.P.
signature was genuine, this 25 April 1859.   Signed: P. R. Smith,
Clerk of Court.

McWHORTER, JOHN   Pack 15 #201.   Probate Judge Office.   Pickens,
S. C.   Power of Attorney, State of Georgia, County of Walker.   I John
McWhorter attorney in fact for Hugh Rogers, Prudence Drenon, Temperance
McWhorter and Sarah McWhorter and for myself John McWhorter do hereby
appoint William McWhorter of Pickens Dist. my true and lawful attorney
in my name, for the use and benefit, to act, carry out and execute a
power of attorney made to me by Hugh Rogers of the State of Arkansas
and County of Washington and also a power of Attorney made to me by
Prudence Drennen, Temperance McWhorter and Sarah McWhorter of the
County of Walker and State of Georgia, etc. etc. to sue, receive and
receipt all sums of money, property either personal or real due me from
the est. of James Rogers decd. late of Pickens Dist., S. C.   Dated
31 Oct. 1859.   Wit: T. E. Patton, J. T. Deck.   Signed: John
McWhorter.

McWHORTER, JOHN Box 63 #676. Probate Judge Office. Pickens,
S. C. Est. admrn. 25 Aug. 1862 by Harriett E. McWhorter, John W.
Walker, Saml. C. McWhorter who are bound unto W. E. Holcombe, Ord. in
the sum of $1200. Expend: Paid 24 Sept. 1862 S. C. McWhorter, $66.04.
Mrs. H. E. McWhorter, John W. McWhorter, R. Rufus Oats, Frank Cobb,
etc. brought at sale. On 11 Oct. 1869 Jacob Mauldin, S.P.C. recd. of
H. E. McWhorter $148.75 in the case of Elihu Griffin Vs. H. E. McWhorter.

McWHORTER, JOHN Box 94 #989. Probate Judge Office. Pickens,
S. C. On 15 Feb. 1867. Owned 116 acres 1 mile below Pickensville adj.
land of Fields Mullinax, W. A. Lesley and others. Heirs Marcus L.,
Francis C., Mary T., Allen D. and Andrew F. McWhorter.

McWHORTER, JOHN In Equity, Pack 37. Clerk of Court Office.
(Basement) Pickens, S. C. To the Honr. the Chancellors: Your orator
Robert E. McWhorter, that the father of your orator John McWhorter,
Senr. departed this life, in the year 1858, leaving as heirs at law his
widow Dolly McWhorter and his ten chn. Harriet the wife of Gideon
Ellis, Eliza the wife of George W. B. Boggs, Matilda the wife of George
Chapman, Malinda the wife of Columbus L. Hollingsworth, your orator
Robert E. McWhorter, Mary Ann McWhorter, James A. McWhorter, Laura
J. McWhorter, and William A. McWhorter, all living in this State and
Dist. the last three are minors over the age of choice. Your orator
sheweth that his father possessed considerable real estate, one tract
on 18 mile creek, waters of Seneca River, containing 400 acres. Also
a tract of 165 acres adj. land of Thomas G. Boggs, Thomas E. Willard,
W. S. Williams. Another tract of 230 acres adj. land of Jeremiah
Prater, G. J. Chapman, W. S. Williams, in another paper Gideon Ellis
and the wife Adaline. Your orator prays for oertition [?] of said
land. That the Court appoint guardian of the minors chn. Tyre B.
Mauldin was appointed gdn. of the minors.

McWHORTER, JOHN SR. Box 45 #496. Probate Judge Office. Pickens,
S. C. Est. admnr. 28 Nov. 1857 by Robert E. McWhorter, John McWhorter,
James E. Hagood, Joseph J. Norton are bound to W. J. Parson, Ord. in
the sum of $10,000. Paid 6 Jan. 1859 the widow in full $1636.11. Paid
John McWhorter 4 Jan. #389.60. Paid Gideon Ellis & wife, G. M. Boggs
and wife, Malinda A. McWhorter, Matilda McWhorter, Mary Ann McWhorter,
R. E. McWhorter, each recd. $389.60. Paid R. E. McWhorter gdn. of
Jas. A., and Wm. A. McWhorter minors $1,168.80.

McWHORTER, JUDA Box 113 #1103. Probate Judge Office. Pickens,
S. C. Est. admnr. 21 March 1883 by R. S. McWhorter, W. W. McWhorter,
T. H. McWhorter are bound to J. H. Newton, Ord. in the sum of $300.
Died 10 Jan. 1883. 30 Jan. 1884 J. N. McWhorter, W. B. Bruce, S. R.
Robinson, their shares of est.

McWHORTER, MELINDA Box 18 #227. Probate Judge Office. Pickens,
S. C. Est. admnr. 31 Oct. 1848 by Thomas W. Harbin Esq., John L.
Gordon who are bound unto Wm. D. Steele, Ord. in the sum of $600.
Heirs brothers and sisters, heirs of John McWhorter, Mary McWhorter,
Sarah L. McWhorter, Moses McWhorter, David McWhorter, Isaac McWhorter,
Andrew McWhorter, Mary Matilda and Henry Myers, Eliza Ann wife of
Robert M. Beaty. Paid to H. L. Davis. (The name Melinda was also
written Belinda on some papers.)

McWHORTER, "MINORS" Box 10 #167. Probate Judge Office. Pickens,
S. C. 1 March 1883 Hester E. McWhorter, W. W. McWhorter, T. H.
McWhorter are bound unto J. H. Newton, Ord. in the sum of $100.
Hester E. McWhorter gdn. of her chn. Eugenia Malissa, Robert E.,
Earnest H. and Susan W. McWhorter minors under 21 yrs. Chn. of G. W.
McWhorter who died 8 Dec. 1881. 1 Mar. 1883 paid Geo. R. Knight gdn.
of his wife Eugenia M. her share $13.32.

McWHORTER, "MINORS" Box 4 #91. Clerk of Court Office.
Pickens, S. C. 20 April 1859 Robt. E. McWhorter, James E. Hagood,
W. N. Craig are bound unto R. A. Thompson in the sum $4,200. Robert
E. McWhorter gdn. of James Alvah, Laura Jane and Wm. Alfred McWhorter
minors under 21 yrs. John McWhorter their father, Robert E. McWhorter
their eldest brother.

McWHORTER, REBECCA Box 3 #35. (B. Armstrong will). Probate
Judge Office. Pickens, S. C. Rebecca McWhorter was the dtr. of
Benjamin Armstrong decd. of Pickens Dist. will proved 13 Dec. 1832.
She was probably the wife of Ezekiel McWhorter who was exor. of her
father will. The following are brothers and sisters, viz. his will,
Nancy Gaines, Gillah wife of John Wooten, Syntha Armstrong, Abner
Crosby Armstrong, Charles Armstrong, Benjamin Cornelius Wooten was
the son of Gillah and John Wooten. On 7 June 1875 B. C. Wooten's
widow, Mrs. Charlotte Wooten was living at Tunnel Hill, Ga. She wrote
a letter to the Ordinary of Pickens Dist. stating that her husband
B. C. Wooten had died in the war. Letter in Armstrong pack.

McWHORTER, ROBERT Box 110 #1049. Probate Judge Office. Pickens,
S. C. Whereas I Robert McWhorter of Pickens Dist. being of sound mind
and memory. It is my will and desire that my executors collect any
and all debts and monies that may be due me, and pay my just debts
and funeral expenses. I give to my wife Jane Matilda McWhorter, with
my two sons William Wesley, and Thomas Harlesto McWhorter, all my
property both real and personal. At her death I will the same to my
two above named sons upon the payment of certain sums of money to my
two dtrs., Louisa E. Ferguson and Martha Malissa Looper, and the
children of my decd. son Baylus McWhorter decd. I will to my two named
dtr. the sum of $450.00. This sum to be their full share of my est.
I give to the chn. of my son Baylus McWhorter decd. the sum of $450.00
to be equally divided between them, which sum is their share of my
est. I have already advanced to my son George W. McWhorter the tract
of land whereon he now lives and other property, which is all I desire
for him. If my sons and daughters and grand children can agree and
get along well, that they all shall live together on the place. I
appoint my sons William Wesley McWhorter and Thomas Harleston McWhorter
executors. Dated this 31 July 1873. Wit: J. E. Hagood, S. D. Keith,
W. A. Wesley. Signed: Robert McWhorter. Filed 9 May 1876.

McWHORTER, SAMUEL CHERRY Box 140 #9. Probate Judge Office.
Pickens, S. C. I Samuel Cherry McWhorter of Pickens Dist. being of
sound mind and memory. I give to my wife Sarah Jane all my personal
property during her natural life. If anything is left after that it
is to go to our children share and share alike. My sons G. L. Mc-
Whorter and Berry W. McWhorter are appointed executors. Dated 14 May
1901. Wit: Julius E. Boggs of Pickens, A. C. Jones of Rockford, Ill.
J. M. D. Bruce of Pickens. Codicil. The interest I have in machinery
in with my sons, I give to my son Julius Gray McWhorter and my dtr.
Martha Jane Brown and children having been fully advanced during her
life time, her chn. are to receive nothing further from my est. except
one dollar is given to the children of Mary Jane Brown who survive.
Dated this 24 May 1901. Wit: C. Gravly, J. R. Ashmore, B. F. Freeman.
Filed 3 Feb. 1903.

McWHORTER, SARAH C. Pack 2-A (Basement). Clerk of Court Office.
Pickens, S. C. Pickens Dist. I Sarah C. McWhorter for the natural
love and affection, I have for my beloved son Dr. Abner L. Clinkscales
of Macon, Georgia. In consideration of one dollar to me paid by Dr.
A. L. Clinkscales, I do sell, bargain and convey a negro girl named
Louisa and her increase if any. Dated 28 Dec. 1858. Wit: L. N.
Robins, M. J. Robins. Signed: Sarah C. X McWhorter. Proved on oath
of Mrs. Mary J. Robins, before L. N. Robins, J.P. this 28 Dec. 1858.
Signed: M. J. Robins. Recorded 23 Jan. 1859.

McWHORTER, DAVID Pack 2-A. In Equity (Basement). Clerk of
Court Office. Pickens, S. C. To the Honr. the Chancellors: Your
orator and oratrixs, Green W. and his wife Elizabeth A. Massengale
and A. D. and Mary C. Rogers that David ...

MADDING, GEORGE No Ref. Probate Judge Office. Laurens Dist.
Laurens, S. C. I George Madding of Laurens Dist. being of sound mind
and disposing memory. I desire as much of my property to be sold as
needed to pay my debts and funeral expenses. I give to my wife Nancy
Madding the balance of my est. both real and personal, during her life
or widowhood. If she marry again she to get only a child share. If

Madding, George - Continued. she should not marry, at her decease the estate shall be sold and the amount divided equally amongst my chn. Except Elizabeth Wilborn and Locklin L. Madding to have none until the other chn. gets as much as they have. Elizabeth Wilborn to receive ten dollars for her full share. The balance divided amongst Nancy Madding, Locklian L. Madding, Fanny Madding, Sarah Madding, Rebekah Madding, Molly Madding, Amy Madding, Lewcy Madding. I appoint my wife executrix and my son Locklin L. Madding executor. 3 Oct. 1842. Wit: Wm. Graves, Thomas X Dison, Obed W. Graves. Signed: Geo. Madding. Proved on oath of Wm. Graves before M. D. Watts, O. L. D. this 28 Aug. 1844.

MAGEE, JOHN No ref. Probate Judge Office. Anderson, S. C. (The first page of will not found in notes) -- the amount which he has received and is to receive is not to come into the division with the balance of my est. Benjamin Mattison an equal share. Theodosia Amanda Harkness an equal share. Caroline Richey an equal share. Gabriel an equal share. William an equal share. Hillman an equal share. James an equal share. Elizabeth Liddle an equal share. Nancy an equal share, Harriet Martha an equal share. John an equal share. Lucy Christian an equal share. My present wife Nancy to have an equal share with the chn. If any child die before maturity, its share to revert to the other chn. My just debts and funeral expenses are to be paid before the division is made. I appoint my sons Gabriel L., and William Magee executors, and to keep the shares of my minors chn. until they become of age, or to defray expenses of their education. Dated 21 June 1850. Wit: E. J. Earle, Nathan Harris, M. Magee. Signed: John Magee. Proved 7 Oct. 1850 before Herbert Hammond, O.A.D.

MALONE, CHARITY C. Pack 632 #6. Clerk of Court Office. Pickens, S. C. Charity C. Malone a dtr. of Alfred McCrary decd. who died in 1877 in Pickens Dist. and of his widow Elizabeth McCrary.

MANCIL, GREEN Box 116 #4. Probate Judge Office. Pickens, S.C. I Green Mancil of Pickens County being of sound mind and memory. I desire that all my just debts be paid. I desire that all my personal and real estate be sold and divided amongst my six chn. to wit, Harriet Gordon, Amanda Johnson, Perry Mancil, Merida Mancil, James Mancil, Caroline Miller. This will to go into effect at my decease. I appoint G. M. Lynch my executor. Dated 14 May 1888. Wit: G. M. Lynch, Ira T. Roper, M. R. X Chapman. Signed Green Mancil. Filed 29 June 1888.

MANN, JOHN G. Pack 443. In Equity, Clerk of Court Office. Abbeville, S. C. Abbeville Dist. To the Honr. the Chancellors: Your orator Isaac Branch of said Dist. sheweth that John G. Mann departed this life intestate on the 1 Oct. 1848. Leaving a widow Elizabeth Mann and chn. Franklin Mann, Amanda Mann and Sarah Mann. Admnr. on said est. was granted to your orator 20 Nov. 1848. Your orator soon found the est. involved deeply in debt, and conflicting and disputed claims presented for payment, etc. Your orator has been compelled to resort to this Honorable Court for directions and advice. John Mann the father of said intestate devised by his will a tract of land containing 250 acres on Flag Reid Creek, bounded by lands of James Pursly, Mrs. Susannah Brooks, Robert Wilson to his wife Margaret Mann during her life time, at her death to his three sons viz; John G. Mann, Michael S. Mann and William R. Mann. William R. Mann conveyed to his two brothers, his interest in said land. The widow conveyed to her two sons her interest in the said land for an annuity of $25 per year for her support. Your orator has paid the widow this amount to her, she now lives in Newton Co., Ga. The two brothers agreed to divide the land but no agreement on payment of their mother annuity, he is bound with security to pay the said amount. (No more of this suit found in notes.)

MANSELL, JAMES Deed Book E-1, Page 88. Clerk of Court Office. Pickens, S. C. James Mansell bought from James D. Saterfield both of Pickens Dist. for the sum of $50, the Widow Gorman tract of land. Saterfield was a legatee of the said land. Dated 8 Feb. 1834.

Mansell, James - Continued. Wit: Abraham Burdine, Mason Burdine.
Signed: James X Saterfield. This day came Sarah Saterfield the wife
of James D. Saterfield and released all interest and right to dower in
the land. Dated 25 Jan. 1837.

MANSELL, JAMES Pack 106. Clerk of Court Office. Pickens, S.C.
Pickens Dist. To the Honr. the Chancellors: Your orator Joseph
Mansell sheweth that James Mansell departed this life 184_? intestate
Possessed with real estate, consisting of four tracts as follows.
Tract one known as the home tract, lying on both sides of Doddy's
Creek, waters of Saluda River, adj. land of Matthew Mansell, Lewis
Hill and others, containing 800 acres. Tract two, known as the Widow
Gorman tract, containing 290 acres, adj. land of A. Burdine, R. Bowen,
William Gilstrap. Tract three, known as the Flat Rock tract, containing
240 acres, adj. land of Joseph Young, John Higgins, William Gilstrap,
Tract four, the Davis tract containing 250 acres, adj. land of E. Lee,
N. Gassaway, J. Norton, lying on waters of Little River. Your orator
shews that the land is subject to distribution amongst Sarah Mansell the
widow, and eleven chn. Joshua Mansell, Matthew Mansell, Frances the
wife of ___ Barrett, Jane Ferguson, the wife of J. G. Ferguson, William
Mansell, Lemuel Mansell who resides in Georgia, John Mansell who
resides in Alabama, Richard H. Mansell a minor, Juliet the wife of
Merida Freeman who resides in N.C. The home tract was bought by Sarah
Mansell and Joshua Mansell, the Gorman tract was bought by James Latham,
the flat rock tract was bought by Pearson Mayfield, the Davis tract
was bought by Isreal Mayfield. Power of Attorney, Lemuel Mansell of
Cherokee County, Ga. appointed Samuel Mansell his attorney to receive
and receipt any money from his father James Mansell est. and from the
est. of his brother John Mansell both decd. Dated 22 May 1849. Samuel
Mansell was also a brother to John and a son of James Mansell. Robert
was a son and brother also who lived in Georgia, Cherokee County.
William Mansell was residing in Tippah County, Miss. and appointed
Josiah Mansell his attorney to receive and receipt for any money due him.
Dated 4 June 1849.

MANSELL, JOHN Pack 214 #11. Clerk of Court Office. Pickens,
S. C. On 4 Nov. 1856 John Mansell was found guilty of retailing whiskey
without a license.

MANSELL, JOSHUA Pack 31 #3. (Basement). Pickens, S. C. On 2
Nov. 1829 Arranah Sitton dtr. of Phillip Sitton decd. was mentioned
as the wife of Joshua Mansell. Elizabeth B. Sitton her mother.

MANSELL, JOSHUA Box 32 #371. Probate Judge Office. Pickens,
S. C. I Joshua Mansell of Pickens Dist. being in a low state of health
though of a sound and full disposing mind. First after my debts and
funeral expenses are paid. I will to my wife Mahala Mansell 100 acres
of land enclosed my house, enduring her widow or natural life time.
Her land to include the spring, adj. land of Austain Day field. Also
one negro woman called Matilda and one boy named Laurense (Matilda
and increase). With all stock, tools, household and kitchen furniture,
one horse, the crop in field, rent from the land. After her natural
life or marriage I devise the same to my six youngest children to wit;
Cumilla Jane, Tinsa Emmer, Thomas Fletcher, Abi., Baily, Malinda
Allice Mansell to be divided equally. I give to my oldest son John B.
Mansell and my third son Addison Mansell the remainder of my land to
be divided at their pleasure. I give to my oldest son my double
barreled shot gun and blacksmith tools. To my son Addison my rifle
gun. To my second son Westly Mansell I will one negro named Ester
the oldest dtr. of Matilda. To my dtr. Sarah the wife of John R.
Trotter, I will one negro named Hannah second dtr. of Matilda. To my
second dtr. Anny I will one negro girl Permelia youngest or third dtr.
of Matilda. Dated 6 March 1854. Wit: Joshua Jameson, Reuben Ellis,
Gideon Ellis. Signed: Joshua Mansell. Codicil: I have neglected to
appoint an executor to the said will. I do appoint my trusty friend
and brother in law Judge G. Ferguson as my lawful executor. Dated
this 9 May 1854. Wit: Gideon Ellis, John Ferguson, Reuben Ellis.
Signed: Joshua Mansell. On 5 June 1854 Gideon Ellis Senr. states he
saw the other witnesses sign the will.

MANSELL, MATTHEW Box 100 #1056. Probate Judge Office. Pickens,
S. C. I Matthew Mansell of Pickens County make this my last will and
testament. First I will my just debts and funeral expenses be paid.
I will to my beloved wife Polly my home tract of land, except 150
acres to be laid off to my dtr. Nancy F. the wife of Harvey H. C. Hunt,
as well as my ready money and personal property, at her death I devise
my home place to my son Samuel T. Mansell. I will to my dtr. Sarah
the wife of George W. Cox 216 acres lying in Pickens and Anderson
counties on branches of Brushey Creek adj. land of Joel Ellison,
Sterling Turner and others. At the death of my wife Polly, I will to
the heirs of my dtr. Mary T. Reid decd. the sum of six hundred dollars,
to be equally divided between them (not named). I appoint my wife
Polly Mansell executrix. Dated 18 March 1876. Wit: T. M. Welborn, J.
Riley Ferguson, W. E. Holcombe. Signed: Matthew Mansell. Filed
5 Sept. 1885.

MANSELL, MATTHEW Box 76 #811. Probate Judge Office. Pickens,
S. C. Matthew Mansell was granted 158 acres on Wolf Creek in Pickens
Dist. by Martin Barrett on 11 July 1834.

MANSELL, RICHARD HARRISON Box 78 #829. Probate Judge Office.
Pickens, S. C. Est. admnr. 26 Aug. 1864 by Matthew Mansell, Judge
G. Ferguson, Madison F. Mitchell, Isaac Wickliffe are bound unto W. E.
Holcombe, Ord. in the sum of $30,000. L Aug. 1871 L. C. Mansell
widow of Wm. Mansell decd. as gdn. for John Cobb, Saml. Lewis, Wm.
Dunkin, Geo. Washington minors of Wm. Mansell and his wife L. C. Mansell
and Jas. Henry Mansell, Josiah Thompson Mansell now of age, also heirs
of Wm. and L. C. Mansell of the County of Madison, Miss. Appointed:
J. G. Ferguson of Pickens Co., S. C. their Attorney to receive their
part as heir of Wm. Mansell in and to the est. of Richard Harrison
Mansell decd. Matilda A. Mansell received a share.

MANSELL, SAMUEL T. Box 142 #5. Probate Judge Office. Pickens,
S. C. I Samuel Mansell of Pickens County. Being of sound mind and
memory, etc. I will that my just debts be fully paid, and the remainder
of my est. both real and personal go to my beloved wife Janey Mansell.
Dated 5 May 1902. Wit: W. M. Hagood, W. W. Robinson, J. N. Howard.
Signed: S. T. Mansell. Filed 19 Oct. 1903. Est. admnr. 5 Nov. 1903
by M. Jane Mansell, W. W. Robinson, J. A. Robinson who are bound unto
J. B. Newberry, Ord. in the sum of $200. He died 10 Oct. 1903.

MANSELL, WILLIAM Pack 274. #16. Clerk of Court Office. Pickens,
S. C. On 6 July 1842 William Mansell made oath that Tilman Roper on
the 4 of this inst. (month) died at the house of Robert Malears did
assault him with his fist twice and afterwards caught him by the skirt
of his coat tail and tore it off and threw it away.

MANTZ, CHRISTOPHER Pack 349. Clerk of Court Office. Abbeville,
S. C. Abbeville Dist. In Equity To the Honr. the Chancellors: Your
orator David Glover of Edgefield Dist. sheweth, Christopher W. Mantz of
Abbeville Dist. being possessed with considerable real and personal
property did make and publish his last will and testament. The testator departed this life near the end of Dec. 1851. Said will was
probated in the Ordinary Office, and John W. Hearst on the 5 Jan. 1852
qualified as executor, Mary P. Mantz the widow of the testator having
been appointed executrix declined to qualify as such. The said widow
took possession of the estate of her decd. husband until her death
in the year 1856 when she leaving an unaltered will. Your orator was
appointed executor, and qualifed as such the 8 Sept. 1856. John W.
Hearst proceeded to take possession of the plantation under the will
of C. W. Mantz. The testatrix bequeath articles to her grand neice
Harriet Glover and her grand nephew Vandall M. Glover chn. of your
orator, and other property bequeathed by her late husband. The said
John W. Hearst has made a crop of grain, corn, cotton upon said land
and your orator belive he is indebted unto the estate with interest for
said crop. John Cothran Esq. Sowrn says, Think C. W. Mantz settled
the place in the year 1821 or 1822. Thinks Mrs. Mantz said they were
married in 1823, always understood Mrs. Mantz carried the property,
does not known how much in 1829 lived at Mrs. Sproul. Mr. Mantz

Mantz, Christopher - Continued. died in 1851. Mrs. died in 1856. Filed 27 March 1857.

MARTIN, AGNES RICHARD   Pack 292.   Clerk of Court Office.   Abbeville, S. C. Abbeville Dist. To the Honr. the Chancellors: The petition of Joseph W. W. Marshall of Abbeville Dist. sheweth that at June term 1852 Margaret P. Martin the then widow and mother of Agnes Richard Martin was appointed guardian of the estate of her minor child, who is at the age of three yrs. That on __ Feb. 1854 Margaret P. Martin married one Wm. J. Hammond, and is now desirous of relinquishing the guardianship of the estate, which is worth about five thousand dollars, her share of said minor father est. Your petitioner prays to be appointed the gdn. of said est. Filed 21 March 1854.

MARTIN, ALEXANDER   Box 58 Pack 1387.   Probate Judge Office. Abbeville, S. C. I Alexander Martin of Newberry Dist. being called into the service of the United States, being of sound mind and memory. First I wish as much of my property to be sold to pay all my debts, after collection of the debts due me. The balance of my estate both real and personal, I lend to my wife Agnus Martin during her life or widowhood. At her death or marriage, my property to be divided amongst my children (not named). I appoint John Martin and James Caldwell as executors. Dated 30 Jan. 1814. Wit: John M. Morris, W. M. Rutherford, Thomas Gordon. Signed: Alexander Martin. Inv. made 10 Jan. 1832 by Samuel Watt, Wm. Lesly, Samuel A. Jack. Cit. Pub. at upper Long Cane Church Recd. from Gordon Martin $11. James P. Martin $8. Richard Martin $7.38.

MARTIN, JAMES O.   Box 31 Pack 1209.   Probate Judge Office. Anderson, S. C. To the Honr. Herbert Hammond, Ordinary of Anderson Dist. The petition of the undersigned sheweth that he is a brother of James O. Martin, late of Anderson Dist. decd. who died intestate. Your petitioner prays for and will accept letter of admnr. on the est. Filed 17 Dec. 1849. Est. admnr. on 2 Jan. 1850 by John A. Martin and Pheby Martin who are bound unto Herbert Hammond, Ord. in their sum of $500. Sale of personal property was held 24 Jan. 1850. Melissa Martin bought most of the household furniture and some stock and feed. John A. Martin bought most of the tools and stock, others buyers are Charles Bowie, Joe Obrian, Joshua Buchanan, C. D. Giles, William Cook, R. Boyd, A. J. Smith, Alexr. Gray, J. Abels. The sale brought a total of $224.75. Amt. paid out $220.72. Notes due, or accounts due, William Sherrod, John H. Reid, Jacob Whitman, Melissa Martin, Jas. T. Baskin, B. F. Crayton, L. Buchanan, E. S. Martin, R. Sullivan Esq., Saml. E. Parker, John Golden, Charles Bowie, Del. Tucker, James H. Miles, J. T. White-field, J. W. Buchanan.

MARTIN, JOHN ALLEN   #195.   Clerk of Court Office.   Abbeville, S. C. Abbeville Dist. In Equity, To the Honr. the Chancellors: The petition of William Q. Martin sheweth that John Allen Martin the father of your petitioner was appointed by this Court guardian of your petitioner in the year 1842, and gave bond for this trust on the 10 Sept. 1844, in the sum of $500. He received in 1845 the sum of $250 and about the year 1850 further sum of $107.50. Your petitioner sheweth that he has become of full age, and desires a settlement with his said guardian. He has made several appointments for a settlement in the Commissioners office, but has been disappointed, and is compelled to apply to this Court for its aid, etc. Filed 12 April 1855. On another paper, the answer of John Allen Martin states that Wm. Q. Martin recd. a legacy from the estate of his great grandmother, Mrs. Quarles. Also that he knew his son to be wild and reckless, but he had supposed the many acts of kindness which he had bestowed upon him and the many difficulties from which he had releaved him would have induced some emotion of gratitude which this defendant is pained to see is not exhibited by the petitioner.

MARTIN, GEORGE   Box 58 1376.   Probate Judge Office.   Abbeville, S. C. Admnr. bond, We Sarah Martin, William Thompson and Jacob Thornton are bound unto Moses Taggart, Ord. in the sum of $1,000. Dated 5 Dec. 1820. Citation published at Hopewell Church. Sale held

Martin, George - Continued. 22 Dec. 1820, Buyers: Mrs. Sarah
Martin, George Creswell, Nancy Martin, Sarah Martin, Sr., Sarah Martin
Jr., Saml. Wideman, Jacob Thornton, George Martin, Jr., Wm. Patton,
Robt. Margy Jr., Patrick Bradly Sr.

MARTIN, RICHARD A. Pack 376. Clerk of Court Office. Abbeville,
S. C. Abbeville Dist. In Equity, To the Honr. the Chancellors: Your
oratrix Margaret P. Martin the relict of Richard A. Martin decd. sheweth
that Richard A. Martin on the 3 Sept. 1852 departed this life intestate possessed with four tracts of land. Tract one, the home tract,
bounded by land of Patrick McCaslan, John Martin, Robert McDonald,
Thomas Thomson, containing 96 acres. Second tract, called the Wideman
tract on waters of Long Cane Creek, bounded by land of Mrs. Sarah
Kenedy, John Creswell, Frederick Roberson, containing 127 acres, third
tract, called the Dillse tract lying on Long Cane Creek, bounded by
land of Wm. K. Bradley, A. Littes, Mrs. Sarah Kenedy, Thomas Creswell
containing 201 acres, the fourth tract called the McDonald tract,
lying on Long Cane Creek, bounded by land of A. P. Conner, Samuel
Jordan, Patrick McCaslan, James McClain, containing 327 acres. Said
Richard A. Martin only heirs and distributees, your Oratrix and his
only dtr. Kitty Foster, who is now a minor. A sale of the personalty
of the said Martin was held the 19 Nov. 1851, and prays for a partition
of the real estate. Filed Nov. __ 1851.

MARTIN, WILLIAM Pack 451 #2. Clerk of Court Office. Abbeville,
S. C. I William Martin of Abbeville Dist. in consideration of $200
to me paid by Benjamin South of the same dist. have granted, sold
released all of two tracts of land in said dist. one tract containing
58 acres on a branch of Hogskin Creek, waters of Savannah River, having
such shape and form as platt annexed. Conveyed from William and Mary
Bell to said William Martin, dated 11 April 1801. The second tract
containing 37 acres, on Hogskin Creek, granted to William Martin the
6 July 1801, having such shape and form as platt annexed. Dated this
30 Dec. 1803. Wit: William X Grub, Nat. J. Rosamond. Signed:
William Martin. Rebeckah Martin the wife William Martin did appear
before me Adam Jones, J.Q. and renounced, released and relinquish her
dower to the above land. This 30 Dec. 1803. Proved on oath of Nathaniel
J. Rosamond before Adam C. Jones, J.Q. the 31 Dec. 1803.

MASINGILL, JOSEPH Box 84 #894. Probate Judge Office. Pickens,
S. C. I Joseph Masingill of Pickens Dist. being of sound mind and
disposing memory. I desire my executor pay my just debts and funeral
expenses, from the first money that come into their hands. I give to
my beloved wife Jane Masingill all my property both real and personal
during her natural life or widowhood. For the use and support and
education of my chn. (not named). At the marriage or death divided
equally according to law. I do appoint my friend James E. Hagood
executor. Dated 9 June 1863. Wit: John Hagood, J. O. Mosley, L. W.
Hagood. Signed: Joseph Masingill. Proven 24 Nov. 1865. 1 Oct.
1844 Dread Masingill, Deborah Masingill were legatees of Hannah
Nicholson decd.

MASON, JOEL Book B Page 34. Probate Judge Office. Pickens,
S. C. On 19 Oct. 1859 Joel Mason decd. of Pickens Dist. owned 280
acres of land lying on waters of Choestoe, adj. lands of Thomas W. H.
Harbin, Thomas Jenkins, John Mason and others. Heirs were, Frances
Mason his widow, Milly the wife of B. C. Whiseant, Mary W. the wife of
Samuel Lyles, Martha Ann the wife of D. L. Lyles, Charles W. Mason
all resident of Pickens Dist. and of full age except Charles W. Mason.

MASON, JOHN Book A, Page __. Probate Judge Office. Pickens,
S. C. On 5 July 1858 John Mason and his wife Elizabeth were heirs of
William Abbott decd. and his wife Julia Abbott of Pickens Dist.

MATHIS, ISABELLA Pack 440. Clerk of Court Office. Abbeville,
S. C. Abbeville Dist. In Equity To the Honr. the Chancellors: Your
orator Luke Mathis sheweth that Isabella Mathis the mother and surviving parent of your orator, departed this life in the month of Feb.
1854. On the 19 May 1841, the said Isabella Mathis executed as she

Mathis, Isabella - Continued. supposed her last will and testament. This paper was submitted to William Hill Esq. Ord. of this Dist.
for probate, but the executor named in said will was a witness thereto,
he refused to admit the same to probate. The said Isabella Mathis left
heirs at law, two dtrs. Jane the wife of Charles B. Griffin and Sarah
now the wife of Thomas M. Morrow, three sons, your orator, William
Mathis and Elford Mathis (the last of whom is a minor about 17 yrs. old.)
and the grand children to wit, Armistead Burt Hill, Elizabeth Hill, and
Benjamin Hill the children of her dtr. Mary who married Samuel Hill
many years ago. Admnr. was granted unto Charles B. Griffin and Thomas
M. Morrow. The personal est. has over paid any debts on the est. Your
orator sheweth that the decease was possessed with a tract of land,
about ten miles South East of Abbeville on both sides of the Augusta
Road, containing 365 acres, bounded by land of Efferd Owen, W. J. Davis,
Jane A. Karey. This tract of land is subject to partition among those
entitled to the same. Filed 1 Nov. 1854.

MAYS, MEDY No Ref. Clerk of Court Office. Abbeville, S. C.
I James Graham son of Will and in consideration of $750 to me paid by
Medy Mays of Abbeville Dist. have granted, sold and released all that
tract of land on waters of Little and Mulberry Creeks of Saluda River.
Containing 225 acres bounded by land of James Graham, James John
Huskerson, John Williams, Geo. Higans. Dated 13 Nov. 1844. Wit:
Thos. Rosamond, Elihu Campbell. Signed: James Graham Senr., Thursey
X Graham, the wife of James Graham died this day renounce, released and
relinquished all interest of dower in the above land before John C.
Waters, Mag. this 12 Dec. 1844.

MAYS, MEDY No Ref. Clerk of Court Office. Abbeville, S. C.
I William Pope of Abbeville Dist. in consideration of 214 to me paid
by Medy Mays of the same Dist. have granted, sold released all that
tract of land containing 50 acres lying on Little Mulberry Creek.
Bounded by land of Medy and Larkin Mays and George Higans, Robert
Smith, John Williams. Dated 17 Nov. 1844. Wit: John Williams, John
C. Waters. Signed: William Pope, Margaret X Pope, ronounce, released
and relinquished her interest in the above land before John C. Waters
Mag. this 27 Nov. 1844.

MAYS, MEDY No Ref. Clerk of Clerk Office. Abbeville, S. C.
I Larkin Mays of Abbeville Dist. in consideration of $100 to me paid
by Medy Mays, have granted, sold, released all my part of that tract of
land lying and being on Little and Big Mulberry Creeks waters of Saluda
River, containing 45 acres, adj. land of William Pope and John
Williams and the land whereon Needy Mays now lives. Dated this 12
July 1845. Wit: Thos. Rosamond, John Rosamand. Signed: Larkin Mays.

MAYS, MEEDY No Ref. Clerk of Court Office. Abbeville, S. C.
I John Williams of Abbeville Dist. in consideration of $220 to me
paid by Meedy Mays of the same Dist. have granted, sold, and released
all that tract of land containing 40 acres. Bounded by land of Greyham,
Hoskinson and myself. Dated 17 Nov. 1844. Wit: John C. Waters, John
C. Fowler. Signed: John Williams. Proved on oath of John C. Fowler
before John C. Waters, Mag. This day came Rebecca X Williams the wife
of John Williams before me John C. Waters, Mag. and renounce, released
and relinquished all her interest of dower in the above land. Dated
25 Nov. 1844.

MAYS, MEEDY JR. Pack 347. Clerk of Court Office. Abbeville,
S. C. Abbeville Dist. In Equity, To the Honr. the Chancellors:
Your oratrix Mary Elizabeth Mays sheweth that Meedy Mays Jr. lately
the husband of your oratrix departed this life intestate on the 11 Jan.
1849. His heirs and distributees, Your oratrix the widow and two chn.
John Mathew Mays, about four yrs. old, and Lucretia Ann Mays about two
yrs. old. At his death he was possessed with a tract of land on
Saluda River containing about 400 acres, bounded by land of Capt. J. W.
Waren, George Higgins, Robert Smith and others. The personal est.
was admnr.by Larkins and Henry Mays, granted on the 13 Jan. 1849. The
personal est. is more than sufficient to pay all debts of the intestate.
Your oratrix prays for a partition of the real estate. Filed 21 May
1850.

NASH, JOHN Box 70 Pack 1720. Probate Judge Office. Abbeville, S. C. I John Nash of Abbeville Dist. being very sick and weak in body but of perfect mind and memory. I give to my beloved wife Polly Harrison my whole estate both real and personal during her natural life or widowhood and after her death or marriage, I give to my three sons Abner, Ezekiel, Nimrod all that tract of land whereon I now live. Containing 401 acres to be equally divided amongst them. The remainder of my est. to be divided amongst my four sons, Reuben, Abner, Ezekiel and Nimrod and my five dtrs. Theodoshe Bettey Evans Melinda Lusinda and mertilday[?]. I appoint my wife Polly Harrison and my three sons executrix and executors. Dated this 20 Oct. 1794. Wit: William White, John White, James Smith. Signed: John Nash. Recorded this 25 March 1795. Inventory made 8 July 1795 by Robert Elgin, Nicholas Long, James Kay. Negroes named, Pollis age 20 yrs., Caroline age 21 yrs., Hannah age 14 yrs., Edmond age 30 yrs.

NASH, COL. REUBEN Box 70 Pack 1717. Probate Judge Office. Abbeville, S. C. Abbeville Dist. We John J. Nash, Valentine Nash, William Ware and Henry Delph are bound unto Moses Taggart, Ord. in the sum of $5,000. Dated 3 June 1822. John J. Nash and Valentine Nash made suit for letter of admnr. on the est. the 7 May 1822. Inventory made 25 July 1822. Appraisers not named, Negroes Tom, Ben, Armsted, Pierce, Sarra, Orange, Harry, Sarah, Caroline, Sally, Edy, Laura, Matiller, Levenia, Elena, Jack.

NEALE, ANDREW Vol. 17, Page 522. Probate Judge Office. Charleston, S. C. I Andrew Neale do make this my last W & T. I give all my estate and personal property after payment of my just debts are paid in manner following. I will all my land be divided equally betwixt my sons Thomas and Aaron, all other property to be divided betwixt, Thomas Neale, Aaron Neale, Elizabeth Neale, Sarah Neale and Ann Neale my children. I appoint my mother Sarah Neale executrix and Thomas Neale Esq. executor. Dated 13 Aug. 1776. Wit: John Purves, William McDowell, Nat. Abney. Signed: Andrew Neale. Recorded in Will Book 1774-1779.

NEALE, WILLIAM Vol. 25 Page 112. Probate Judge Office. Charleston, S. C. I William Neale of the Parish of St. James Santee. Do make this my last W & T. I give to my dtr. Sarah Fraser and her heirs after my funeral expenses are paid, one shilling. I give to my dtr. Ann Beerman and her heirs one shilling. I give to my dtr. Rebecker Neale and her heirs, all the rest and residue of my estate, to be paid and delivered to her when she arrives to the age of 18 yrs. I appoint my friend Edward Jerman and Samuel Warren of the parish aforesaid executors. Dated 1 Sept. 1791. Wit: Ezekiel Farramore, John Deliefseline. Signed: William W. Neale. Proved by virtue of a Dedimus from Charles Linning, O.C.T.D. before Charles Gaillard Esq. on 28 Dec. 1793.

NEELY, CHARLES Box 52 Pack 835. Probate Judge Office. Chester, S. C. Est. admnr. 23 Dec. 1832 by William Poag who are bound unto Peter Wylie Ord. in the sum of $1,000. Paid 27 Aug. 1833 William Neely on account $2.00. Paid 6 Jan. 1834 John Neely on account $13.99 1/2. On 23 Dec. 1832 William Neely, Edward Crawford, James D. Crawford, Joseph Paog were ordered to appraise the estate. John Neely, William Neely, Widow Neely, Jane Neely, Harvy Neely, Nancy Neely bought at sale.

NEELY, JAMES Box 52 Pack 822. Probate Judge Office. Chester, S. C. Est. admnr. 18 Nov. 1804 by Dr. James Simpson, Robert Neely, William Whiteside, Samuel Whiteside who are bound unto Joseph Brown, Ord. in the sum of $4,000. Cit. was pub. in Bethesda Congregation 4 Nov. 1804. Robert Neely, Jane Neely, John Neely, Thomas Neely, Sarah Neely, Mary Mills bought at sale.

NEELY, JOHN S. Box 52 Pack 836. Probate Judge Office. Chester, S. C. Est. admnr. 3 April 1838 by William Neely, A. H. Gaston, Isaac McFadden who are bound unto the Ordinary in the sum of $10,000. Cit. was pub. at Fishing Creek Church on 1 April 1838. Paid 1 Oct. 1842

Neely, John S. - Continued. Mary S. Neely guardian $2278.81.
Paid her share 8 Oct. 1842 of $1860.50. Polly Neely, William Neely,
G. Harvy Neely, James Neely, Widow Neely bought at sale.

NEELY, SAM Will Book #, Page 17. Probate Judge Office. York,
S. C. I Samuel Neely of York Dist. being of sound and disposing mind
and memory. I desire all my just debts and funeral expenses be paid
from money on hand, if not enough executors to collect enough from
debts due me from money loaned. I give to my dtr. Nancy Warren one
dollar. I give to my dtr. Elizabeth McElwee one negro girl named
Phobe. I give to my grand son Samuel son of Nancy Warren formerly
Nancy Miller, one negro named Polly about eight yrs. old. I give to my
grand son James son of William McElwee one negro girl named Vincy. I
give to my grand daughter Jane dtr. of William McElwee a negro girl
named Eliza. I give to my son in law John Miller one dollar. I give
to my grand children, Drusilla, Jane and Joseph chn. of John Miller,
one dollar. I desire my executors continue to put out at interest,
until my wife decease all money which I have heretofore loaned. I give
to my wife Elizabeth all household and kitchen furniture, stock of
cattle, negroes, Tom Poll and the youngest child of Poll at my decease.
All money not used in paying my debts and funeral expenses. I give to
my wife during her natural life the house I now live in and as much
land as she thinks she can tend. She may choose as much horses and
farming tools as she choose. At my wife decease, I give to my grand
son Samuel, son of Benjamin two negroes Ason and Yellow girl called
Mary or ma. All remainder of in this item contained both real and
personal to go to my son Benjamin. I give to my wife and son Benjamin
the two houses and lots in Yorkville. Son Benjamin to get most of the
property after wife decd. I appoint my wife and son Benjamin executrix
and executor. Dated __ June 1838. Wit: Benjamin Chambers, G. W.
Williams, Ja. Kuykendal. Signed: Sam Neely. Probated 15 Feb. 1841.

NEELY, CAPT. THOMAS Box 52 Pack 821. Probate Judge Office.
Chester, S. C. Est. admnr. 13 Jan. 1816 by John Neely, John Boyd,
John Lattice who are bound unto E. Lyles, Ord. in the sum of $5,000.
Legatees: John McFadden advanced in the life time of said decd. $197.50.
Andrew Bradford advanced $514.75. John Neely advanced $35.00. Samuel
Neely advanced $25.00. Paid the widow $533.91. Left 7 legatees in
all. Other 2 not named. Mary Neely bought at sale.

NELSON, SAMUEL Deed Book C. Clerk of Court Office. Elberton,
Ga. This indenture made 16 Aug. 1794. Between Samuel Nelson of
Elbert Co., Ga. and James Leper of the same place. In consideration of
Ł200 lawful money, have granted, sold, bargained and confirmed a tract
of land containing 269 acres lying on the South fork of Broad River,
being part of an originally survey for Samuel Neldo by Hor. Samuel
Elbert the 10 Aug. 1785. Wit: Mathew X Nelson. Dated this 16 Aug.
1794. By Wm. Jodg, J.P.

NELSON, SAMUEL JAMES Box 73 Pack 6. Probate Judge Office.
Sumter, S. C. I Samuel James Nelson of Sumter Dist. do declare this
to be my last will and testament. I give to my wife Caroline Nelson
the following negroes, Harriet and her child Binkey, Boomer, and Sam.
Also Amelia and her dtr. Yanica. The two last named negroes is given
in lieu of her dower on any land I may have, if claims her dower, then
the named negroes to be divided between my chn. I also give to my wife
the use of my plantation during her natural life or widowhood, with my
riding chair and chair horse, one bedstead and furniture, eight head
of milking cows. I desire my sons James Harvey Nelson, John M. W.
Nelson all my real estate, after the death of their mother, to be
divided between them. I desire the rest and residue of my personal
property to be divided amongst my chn. James H. Nelson, John M. W.
Nelson, Sarah S. W. Nelson. I desire my cattle, hogs, household and
kitchen furniture be sold and the money for the payment of my debts.
I appoint John M. Witherspoon, Jared J. Nelson and Samuel E. Conyers
executors. Dated 1 1830. Wit: John Potts, John Hemphill, I. M.
Bostwich. Signed: Samuel James Nelson. Recorded 18 Oct. 1830.
Citation to account dated 7 June 1847 mention that the mother of James
Nelson died about 14 yrs ago.

NEWELL, ISAIAH J. #2361. Probate Judge Office. Anderson, S. C.
I Isaiah J. Newell of Anderson Dist. being of sound and disposing mind
and memory. First I will $100 be set aside to be expended in my funeral
and as much as may be necessary to buy tomb stones to be put to the
graves of my sister Susan M. Tucker and Thomas A. Newell. I will my
tract of land known as Thomas A. Newell tract containing 149 acres to
my sister Jincy L. Newell during her life time. If she die without
heirs, the land is to revert back to my executor to be divided among
my sister and brothers. I will my part of the home tract of land to
my brother Reuben D. Newell on the following conditions, he is to pay
my executor $420.00 which is to be equal with my personal estate
divided among my brothers and sister. I appoint my brother Newton J.
Newell executor. Dated 2 Feb. 1869. Wit: Ezekiel Hall, E. Hall, Jr.,
W. Morison. Signed: I. J. Newell. Filed 6 March 1869. Inventory
made on the 20 March 1869 by Wm. Tucker, James R. Little, A. Todd,
D. L. McKee.

NEWELL, JOHN J. #2017. Probate Judge Office. Anderson Dist.
I John J. Newell of Anderson Dist. being of sound mind and going to the
army and service of Country and knowing the uncertainty of life. I
give to my brother Samuel Newell the tract of land on which we now
live on, that we purchased at mothers sale, also a negro woman named
Fereby. I give to my brother J. J. Newell the tract of land I purchased
from Thomas J. Newell, containing 149 acres and one male saddle and
bridle. The balance of my est. to be divided between my brothers and
sisters to share equal, after paying my nephew John James Newell to
N. J. Newell as trustee for Jno. J. Newell for his education or in any
manner he may think best for him. I appoint N. J. Newell and Samuel
Newell my executors. Dated 26 Aug. 1863. Wit: J. D. M. Dobbins,
Elijah Webb, S. V. Gentry. Signed: J. J. Newell. Proved on oath of
Elijah Webb before Herbert Hammond O.A.D. this 19 Sept. 1864. Est.
appraised 3 Oct. 1864 by A. D. Gray, A. Todd, William Tucker, James
Tucker. Sale held 3 Jan. 1865. Buyers: N. J. Newell, S. S. Newell,
William B. Newell, Miss Jane L. Newell, Frank Robinson, W. J. Robinson,
Peter Burton.

NEWELL, REUBEN D. #2789. Probate Judge Office. Anderson, S. C.
I Reuben D. Newell of Anderson Co. being of sound and disposing mind
and memory. I will $100 for defraying my funeral expenses. I will my
land containing 211 acres known as the home or Stephen Leverette's
tract to my son William B. Newell for life, for the purpose here in
after named. He is to pay my sister Jincy L. Newell the sum of $50
annually during her life or while she is single, if she should marry
then the said anuity is to cease. Upon the demise of William B.
Newell the land to revert back to my executor. If Jincy L. Newell is
still living and single, the sum to be paid, if she is not living, or
is married then the land to be sold and equally divided between my
brothers and sisters. I will all my personal property of horses, hogs,
cows, household furniture be sold and the money equally divided among
my brothers and sisters. Newton J. Newell, Samuel S. Newell, Hannah
E. Price and James Tucker my nephew. I appoint my brother Newton J.
Newell executor. Dated 10 Jan. 1871. Wit: James Tucker, J. J. Tucker,
V. A. S. Moore. Signed: R. D. Newell. Proven 25 April 1871. On
24 June 1884 Jincy Newell was mentioned as Jincy Moore. One paper for
10 Dec. 1884 mentioned Dr. N. J. Newell.

NICHOLS, THOMAS A. #199. Clerk of Court Office. Abbeville,
S. C. In Equity, To the Honr. the Chancellors: The petition of
Nimrod W. Stewart sheweth that Thomas Nichols lately departed this
life intestate, leaving among other heirs a son Thomas A. Nichols
who is a minor about 19 yrs. of age. Has an estate of about $1,000
from his father's est. The mother has given her consetn, and the minor
himself has expressed before the commissioner his desire that your
petitioner be appointed gdn. of his est. the money is now due. I
consent that Nimrod W. Stewart be gdn. of my son Tho. A. Nichols, this
14 Jan. 1859. Signed: E. B. Nichols. Henry Beard states that Thomas
Nichols left a widow and five chn.

NOBLE, EDWARD ESQ. Pack 423. Clerk of Court Office. Abbeville, S. C. In Equity, to the Honr. the Chancellors: Your orator James A. Norwood of Abbeville Dist. On the 20 Feb. 1847 Edward Noble Esq. was possessed of a tract of land in Abbeville Dist. known as the Upper part of Fort Charlotte tract. Sold and conveyed to Dr. Nathaniel Harris for the sum of $2675.00. Payment was secured by a note by F. W. Pickens and a mortgage on a tract of land on Savannah River containing 700 acres, adj. land of John Cunningham, (now W. D. Partlow) D. B. Kade, Dr. A. Armstrong, lately belonging to Mary H. Noble and the estate of John A. Noble decd. Filed 4 May 1854.

NICHOLS, SAMUEL Deed Book E-1, Page 256. Clerk of Court Office. Pickens, S. C. I Samuel Nichols of Pickens Dist. in consideration of $60 to me paid by L. A. Perry of the same place. Have granted, sold, bargained and released a tract of land containing 52 acres lying on Georges Creek of Saluda River. Adj. land of L. A. Perry, H. C. Briggs and Samuel Nichols. Dated 1 Jan. 1845. William Ellison, H. C. Briggs. Signed: Samuel Nichols. Proved on oath of William Ellison before John Bowen N.R.P. this 3 Jan. 1845. Recorded 31 March 1845.

NOBLE, JAMES SENR. Box 70 Pack 1707. Probate Judge Office. Abbeville, S. C. I James Noble of Abbeville Dist. being of sound mind and memory. I give to my wife Anne one negro woman named Sarah, my will is that my wife have one third of my land including my dwelling house and clear land during her life or widowhood, also one third of moveable estate. The value of negro Sarah is given in fee simple. My sons James and John shall have the shole of my land after the death of my wife. The whole of my moveable estate to be divided among my four chn. James, John, Mary and Sarah when they come of age. I appoint my brother Alexander Noble and Joseph Calhoun executors. Dated 5 Nov. 1796. Wit: Flm. Bates, William Noble, Nancy McFarland. Signed: James Noble. Recorded 8 Nov. 1796. Inventory made by Benjamin Howard, Capt. John McCarter, William Gray on 19 May 1797.

NORWOOD, JOHN CAPT. Book A, Page 9. Clerk of Court Office. Abbeville, S. C. For Capt. John Norwood as a citizen, grant of 352 acres on both sides of the South fork of Saludy River, bounded by land of Robert Anderson Esq. Vancant land on all sides. Surveyed by Bennett Crafton D.S. this 27 May 1784.

NORWOOD, THEOPHILUS Box 70 Pack 1721. Probate Judge Office. Abbeville, S. C. I Theophilus Norwood being sick and weak of health, but of perfect mind and memory. I appoint John Middleton and Samuel Porter my lawful executor. I will unto my wife Elener all my moveable affects. I will all my land and tenements unto my three sons, Samuel Norwood, John Middleton Norwood, Richard Norwood. All debts own to me and all that I may owe to be paid from the boys est. Dated 13 April 1787. Wit: Samuel Norwood, John Middleton. Signed: Theophilus Norwood.

NORWOOD, WILLIAMSON Pack 372. Clerk of Court Office. Abbeville, S. C. In Equity, to the Honr. the Chancellors: Your orator Alexander Scott sheweth that in Nov. 1842 and for some time before that period your orator was pressed by executions in the hands of the sheriff, to meet these claims upon him. James H. Cobb then the sheriff was unwilling to delay the sale of your orator property. Mr. W. Norwood said he was willing to cash notes in the sum of said debt. On day of sale Norwood refused to do, instead he offered to lend him the money, in the amount of $400 and another $150 for interest.

NORRIS, ELIZA Real est. Book B, Page 86. Probate Judge Office. Pickens, S. C. 20 Nov. 1865, Eliza Norris decd. was a dtr. of Christopher Whisenant decd. of Pickens Dist. her heirs were Nancy wife of J. J. Hunnicut, Barbary Alverson, T. R. Norris, Rebecca Norris.

NORRIS, ESTHER A. Es. Recd. E. C. Hackett. Pack 12. Clerk of Court Office. Abbeville, S. C. On 12 June 1854 Esther A. Norris states that some years ago Thomas Chatham was appointed her gdn. in

NORRIS, ESTHER A. Abbeville Dist. Her parents were dead. She states that in the year 1846 she went with some of her relatives and friends who was residing in Montgomery, Ala. to spend some time with them, and while there she married Jasper J. Norris. That shortly afterwards differences accrued between them and caused their separation. They have been living separate for two yrs. That she arrived of full age in 1853 and no settlement had been made between her husband her her gdn.

NORRIS, JESSE W. Es. Recd. Samuel Lindsay, Pack 11. Clerk of Court Office. Abbeville Dist. On 28 April 1856 Jesse W. Norris of Lownesdville bought a house and lot from Samuel Lindsay formerly of Lownesville but now of Elbert Co., Ga.

NORRIS, MARY, ELIZABETH, ELENOR Pack 261. Clerk of Court Office. Abbeville, S. C. Abbeville Dist. This indenture made the 9 Aug. 1796. Between Elenor, Mary and Elizabeth Norris and William Speer of the same place. In consideration of ₤50 sterling in hand paid by William Speer have granted, sold, bargained and released all that tract of land containing 150 acres, lying on Frasera Creek a branch of Long Cane Creek. Wit: Robert Norris, Thomas Kyes. Signed: Mary Morris, Elizabeth Norris, Elenor Norris. Proved on oath of Thomas Kyes before Phm. Buford, J.P. this 24 March 1813. Recorded 14 Jan. 1818.

NORRIS, PATROCK Book A, Page 12. Clerk of Court Office. Abbeville, S. C. For Patrock Norris as a citizen 300 acres lying on Great Rockey Creek a branch of Savannah River. Bounded on all sides when surveyed by David Hopkins S.S. Certificate dated 26 May 1784. Recorded 29 May 1784. Robert Anderson, C.L.

OATS, RUFUS Box 112 #1076. Probate Judge Office. Pickens, S.C. Died 18 April 1876. Est. admnr. 6 Oct. 1876 by Mary A. Oats, Alonzo M. Folger, W. A. Lesley who are bound unto I. H. Philpot, Ord. in the sum of $800. Mary A. Oats the widow. Mary A. Oats, Alonzo M. Folger plaintiffs against T. W. Russell, J. E. Peoples, Wm. McMahan, F. J. McMahan, Archie McMahan defendants.

OATS, MARY A. Box 128 #7. Probate Judge Office. Pickens, S.C. Est. admnr. 29 July 1897 by N. Oats, J. Mcd. Bruce, C. L. Hollingsworth are bound unto J. B. Newberry, Ord. in the sum of $1100. Died 8 July 1897. N. Oats a son, Will Oats, Sam Oats, Joseph Oats, Newton Oats, Joe Oats bought at sale.

OBRIEN, TIMOTHY Box 84 #891. Probate Judge Office. Pickens, S. C. I Timothy Obrien of Pickens Dist. being of sound mind and disposing memory. I desire my executor pay all my debts and funeral expenses as soon as possible. I give to my loving wife Delilah OBrien all my property both real and personal during her natural life, after her death, then I will all my property to my young friend James E. Hagood, Junr. son of James E. Haggos[?] Senr.. I desire that after my death that J. E. Hagood Sr. to take my property and see that none is wasted, and that my wife has a good, comfortable support. The young Irish boy Richard Harty now living with me. does his duty to me and my wife, when he arrives at twenty one yrs. of age shall have 200 acres of land, one horse, one cow. If he should leave me or my wife before full age then he is not to have any part of my estate. I appoint James E. Hagood Senr. executor. Dated 25 Sept. 1876. Wit: T. G. Hawkins, W. N. Hagood, P. McD Alexander. Signed: Timothy X Obrien. Proved 24 June 1879. His widow died 10 Jan. 1901.

ODELL, ABNER Deed Book A, Page 150. Probate Judge Office. Pickens, S. C. Mary Smith wife of Abner Odell was probably the dtr. of Sussannah Smith of Pickens Dist. For they were ordered to appear in Court on the first Monday next to show cause if any why the real estate of Sussannah Smith decd. containing 145 acres on waters of Goldens Creek, bounded by land of Elihu Griffin, Barnett H. Allgood, Joseph Boggs should not be sold and a division made among the heirs.

Odell, Abner - Continued. Others ordered to appear were: Z.
Smith, William Smith, Fields Mullinin and wife Mary. Dated 26 Dec.
1853. W. S. Williams, Alexander Bryce were guardian of the heirs of
Thomas Smith decd. and legal representatives of Susannah Smith decd.

O'DELL, MAY A. Box 83 #874. Probate Judge Office. Pickens, S.C.
May A. O'Dell and Amanda O'Dell were heirs of Henry Hendrix decd.
whose's will was proven 27 March 1865 in Pickens Dist. Probably were
children.

O'DELL, W. T. Obituary notice of W. T. O'Dell. From Pickens,
Sentinel. No date of paper. W. T. O'dell of Pickens County passed
away at his home between Pickens and Liberty at 1:30 a.m. Friday, May
19. He was born 21 May 1847, was educated in public and private
schools of Pickens Co. and in the Citadel and served in the war between
the States during the latter part. He would have been 86 yrs. of age
Sunday following his death. He served in the State Senate from 1890-
1898 and 1915-1919. He was a member of the First Baptist Church of
Liberty, being an Honorary deacon at his death. Survived by his widow
Mrs. Ary Parson O'dell, three sons S. W. O'Dell, W. C. O'Dell, T. R.
O'Dell and three dtrs. Mrs. J. A. Allgood, Mrs. T. A. Bowen, Mrs. A. D.
Chapman with 20 grandchildren, and six great grandchildren. Services
were held at the home at 2:30 p.m. Sunday by Rev. George Pennell of
Liberty assisted by Rev. H. A. Knox. Grandsons were active pall-
bearers: Joel Allgood, W. Taylor O'Dell, Otis O'Dell, T. R. O'Dell,
Jr., Billy Bowen, Otis Bowen, Alfred T. O'Dell, D. G. O'Dell, and
Willis Chapman.

OLIVER, DIONYSIUS Deed Book C. Clerk of Court Office. Elberton,
Ga. This indenture witnesseth that I have in consideration of ₺14
sterling money of Georgia. Wherefore, I herby acknowledge I hath sold
to William Hatcher a lot in the town of Petersburg the fork of Savannah
and Broad River, marked as #29 which lies on the East side of Front
Street. Lot contains one half acre, forty yards on street, fifty five
yards outward. Dated 29 Sept. 1786. Wit: John Oliver, Elizabeth
Ragland. Signed: Dionysiua Oliver and Mary An Oliver. Proved by
John Oliver before M. Wood, J.P. 15 May 1795.

OLIVER, DORCAS ANN Box 102 #1070. Probate Judge Office.
Pickens, S. C. I Dorcus Ann Oliver, being of sound mind and calling
to mind the uncertainty of this life. I desire my just debts and
funeral expenses be paid. I give to my dtr. Lucy Ann Josephine Oliver
two bedsteads and furniture, one buro and one cloth or weaving loom
and one trunk. I will to my sons Thomas G. A. Oliver and William A.
Oliver one bed and stead and furniture. I desire all rest of my
property be turned over to my executor, to be sold or divided as my
executor thinks best for the children. I ordain my brother James D.
Gassaway my executor. (No more of will in notes.)

OLIVER, ELIZABETH Pack 645. #3. Clerk of Court Office.
Pickens, S. C. On 20 Oct. 1863 Elizabeth Oliver age 85 yrs. was
living in the poor house in Pickens County.

OLIVER, JAMES #139. Petition for Naturalization. Clerk of
Court Office. Chester, S. C. The petition of James Oliver sheweth
that he is a native of Ireland in Great Britian and a subject of the
kingdom. That he is a free man. That he has been residing within the
U.S. since Feb. 1810. That it is his bona fide intention to become
a naturalized citizen of U.S. upon the terms and pursuant to the act
of Congress in such cases. Therefore prays that he may be admitted
to take the oath required by law. Wit: Abn. Nott. Signed: James
Oliver. Chester Dist., S. C. personal appeared Dr. Charles Boyd, and
Patrick Spence and on oath said they were acquainted with the above
James Oliver and believes he has resided within the limits of this
Dist. and that he is a man of good moral character, etc. Sworn to this
4 April 1821 before Joseph Gaston, J.P. Signed: Charles Boyd,
Patrick Spence.

OLIVER, JAMES Deed Book Y, Page 131. Clerk of Court Office. Alberton, Ga. This indenture made this 14 Nov. 1833 between James Oliver, Charles S. Merriwether and Milly T. Merriwether wife of Charles S. and Simeon Oliver. In consideration of $2,000 in hand paid, hath bargained, sold, conveyed unto said Simeon Oliver all that tract of land lying in Elbert Co., Ga. Lying on Broad River containing 400. It being part of the land granted to John Eades Senr. Adj. land of Shelton White's on the road from Webbs Ferry to Petersburg, known as the River road. Also part of land belonging to Elizabeth Glenn. Also a small island known as the Clarks fishery. With all rights herediti- ments and appurtenances there to except the grave yard. Wit: Willis Banks, Shelton Oliver. Signed: James Oliver, C. S. Merriwether, Milly T. Merriwether. Proved on oath of Shelton Oliver before Z. Smith, J.P. this 23 Dec. 1839. Recorded the 23 Dec. 1839.

OLIVER, JOHN #16. Lunatic. Clerk of Court Office. Abbeville, S. C. Settlement of the transactions of James M. Latimre[sic] who was the committee of John Oliver and is now the executor of his last will and testament, being a statement of the amounts between himself as such committee until he assumed the duties of an executor of said John Oliver will in 1854.

OLIVER, WILLIAM Pack 13. Clerk of Court Office. Pickens, S. C. William Oliver deeded 167 acres to John Hollingsworth in 1824 on Six Mile Creek. Later became the Gaines estate. Ruth Oliver his wife.

OLIVER, WILLIAM Box 100 #1053. Probate Judge Office. Pickens, S. C. I William Oliver of Pickens Dist. being of sound mind and memory First after my lawful debts are paid, the residue of my estate, I give to my beloved wife Dorcas Ann during her natural life or widowhood. After her death to be divided between my children. I appoint my wife Darcus Ann to be executrix and her brother James D. Gassaway executor. Dated 23 Feb. 1864. Wit: A. C. Campbell, J. L. Simpson, John T. Sloan. Signed: Wm. Oliver. Filed 19 May 1871.

ORGAN, SOLOMON Vol. 17 Page 792. Probate Judge Office. Charles- ton, S. C. I Solomon Organ of St. Bartholomews in S.C. being weak of body but of perfect mind and memory. I desire my lawful debts and funeral charges be paid with all convenient speed after my decease from money on interest. All other money to be called in and my executors to purchase negroes for the benefit of my est. I give to my loving wife Elizabeth Organ and to any child she may have by me, an equal division to be made when the oldest child attain the age of fifteen yrs. or is married. In the mean time till such division is made, I require that my wife and child or children have decent maintenance and brought up and educated out of the profits and income of my est. I appoint my friend William Clay Snipes, Edmond Cousins, and John Sanders to be executors. Dated this 7 Feb. 1777. Wit: Sarah Culliaw, Sarah Findley, And. Cunningham. Signed: Solomon Organ.

OSBORN, JAMES No ref. Clerk of Court Office. Pickens, S. C. (First page of deed not found in notes.) Dated 19 Nov. 1828. Wit: Sidney Smith, Benjamin Mcord[sic]. Signed: James Osborn. Proved on oath of Sidney Smith before J. Douthit, J.Q. Dated 19 Dec. 1828. Came this day Patsey Osborn the wife of James Osborn and freely renounce, release and forever relinquish unto the within William Sitton his heirs and assigns all her interest, and claim of dower. Dated this 19 Dec. 1828. James Douthit, J.Q. Signed: Patsy Osborn. Recorded 5 Jan. 1829.

OSBORN, THOMAS Pack 358. Clerk of Court Office. Abbeville, S. C. I Thomas Osborn of Abbeville Dist. in consideration of $200 to me paid by John Adams, have granted, bargained, sold and release a tract of land containing 65 acres. Being part of a tract of 350 originally granted to Samuel Foster Senr. decd. on branches of Norises Creek. Adj. land of Adams and Thomas Osborn. Dated 12 Oct. 1827. Wit: Simeon S. Bonhom, Edward Vann. Signed: Thomas Osborn. Proved on oath of Edward Vann before James Foster, J.Q. this 9 Oct. 1838. State of Alabama, Chambers County. I Benjamin B. Patrick a Justice of

Osborn, Thomas - Continued. the peace for said County, do certify
that Sarah Osborn the wife of Thomas Osborn. Did appear before me and
voluntarily, renounce, release and forever relinquish unto John Adams
all her interest and all right of dower of the above land. Dated this
14 May 1842. Wit: Henry Norell, Jefferson E. Hughey.

OSHEALS, R. Y. H. Pack 278 #5. Clerk of Court Office. Pickens,
S. C. This is an account of a school R.Y.H. Osheal taught in the year
1864. Osheal states that he lived with Mr. Brock. The school was
commenced 2d Monday in Jan. 1864 taught for 10 months. School open at
9 O'clock, a recess at 10 O'clock at 12 I gave 2 hours and at 3 O'clock
a short recess. In the summer time dismissed between 5 and 6 O'clock.
I was away from the school one day attending medical board in Pickens
C.H. and was hurt four days at a molasses mill. There was some dissatisfied employers, they are Mrs. Chesly, Mr. Masingill, Mr. Johnston,
Mr. Parson, Mrs. Elizabeth Smith, Mr. Stephens. Oseal[sic] was paid
ten dollars per schooler for the teaching Spelling, Reading, Writing,
Arithmetic and sixteen dollars for teaching English, Grammer, Geography
and analysis per session (5 months).

OWEN, JOHN Deed Book F, Page 197. Clerk of Court Office.
Chester, S. C. I John Owens of Chester County. In consideration $100
to me paid by Hezekiah Donald of the same place, do grant, bargain,
sell and release all that tract of land granted to George Miller the
20 Aug. 1767. Conveyed from George Miller to William Saunders by
lease and release. From Saunders to Francis Jenkins by deed. From
Francis Jenkins to John Reice the 16 Dec. 1774. Then by mortgage unto
Hezekiah Arnold. Wit: This 16 Oct. 1797. Wit: John Clark, Joseph
McElhenney. Signed: John Owens. Proved in open Court 1798. Recorded:
10 May 1798.

OWENS, ADAMS Pack 213 #3. Clerk of Court Office. Pickens, S.C.
On 17 May Adam Owens was charged with stealing a turkey from John
Brian. On 14 June H. A. Richey made oath that on or about the 17th
May 1880 one Adam Owens did assault and resist him in discharge of his
duties as special constable. Richey saith that he was bringing Adam
Owens from Easley to the Pickens C.H. on 17 May 1880. On the way to
the C.H. they had a fight. He had to use his gun on him to subdue him.

OWENS, JOHN Book A, Page 17. Clerk of Court Office. Abbeville,
S. C. A citizen grant of 620 acres, lying on both sides of Twenty Six
Mile Creek waters of Savannah River. Bounding on North and N.E. on
land fresh marks not known. On South by land for Benjamin Waller,
other sides vacant when surveyed by Bennett Crafton D.S. Dated 27
May 1784. Recorded 5 June 1784. Robt. Anderson, C.L.

PACE, SARAH Pack 353. Clerk of Court Office. Abbeville, S. C.
Abbeville, S. C. In Equity, to the Honr. the Chancellors: Your oratrix Lucinda Jane Cannon, granddaughter of Sarah Pace, decd. An infant
under the age of twenty one yrs. of said Dist. by Philip Cromer of the
same Dist. That Sarah Pace departed this life in 185__. Leaving in
full force her last will and test. which Thomas Eakin was appointed
executor. Said will was lost or destroyed and not admitted to probate.
That in 1855 John Davis was duly appointed admnr. of said estate. An
appeal was made from the ordinary and the jury verdict gave your oratrix
"negroes Hester, Adline and Frankie a gray pony, two mules, kit and
sal, and all property to remain in possession of Mr. Breazeal until
she came of age or married. All other stock and cattle to be divided
between Lucinda Jane and Mrs. Brazeal. Some items were sold by the
appointed admnr. sale. After the will was made valid, neither the
admnr. or the executor will account to your oratrix guardian. Filed
22 April 1859. In Jan. 1850 Louisa Pace was appointed gdn. of Lucinda
J. Cannon a minor. Lucinda Pace intermarried with Eakin Breazeal, and
the plaintiff resided with them. She now resides with her father, and
James Irwin her gdn. On one paper that was rejected it mentioned the
chn. of Richard Pace decd. On another paper mention Thomas Eakin
claiming to be executor vs. John Davis and wife and others. Filed 22
April 1859.

PACE, W. F. Box 113 #1091. Probate Judge Office. Pickens, S.C. W. F. Pace was an heir of George Hendricks decd. whose est. was admnr. 14 Sept. 1881 in Pickens Dist.

PALMER, BENJAMIN Box 34 #3. Probate Judge Office. Pickens, S.C. Est. admnr. 2 April 1832 by Lewis Barker, Francis Burt who are bound unto James H. Dendy, Ord. in the sum of $70.00. Banj. Palmer was late of Tuscaloosa, Ala. The name written Palmer and Palmour.

PALMER, HELLEN Pack 388. Clerk of Court Office. Abbeville, S. C. Abbeville Dist. In Equity, to the Honr. the Chancellors: Your orator sheweth that Robert M. Palmer his father of this State and Dist. on the 10 of April 1848 by deed duly executed, conveyed to William A. Wardlaw twenty negroes and their increase, viz, Basil and his family Hannah Caty, Sucky, Grace, Harriet, Marcus and Rena and Anthony and his wife Lines and her chn. Sam, Cy, and Simeon and his family Molly, John, Mack, Billy, Dave, Harry and Jinney in trust for the sole use of his wife Hellen St. Julien Palmer during her life. At her death to be divided among her children share and share alike. His mother Hellen St. Julien Palmer died in June 1857, leaving the following chn. Your orator John Marion Palmer who attained legal age in Nov. 1860. Sarah R. Palmer, Harriet R. Palmer, Frances M. Palmer and Robert Germain Palmer who are all minors. Some negroes has died and some born, since the date of said deed, viz, Katy, Sucky, and a child about one year old, Marcus, Rinda, Anthony, Sam, Simeon, Molly, Mack, Billy, Dave, Harry, Jenny, Amelia, Present, Basil, Bick, London, Style and Libby. After the death of his mother, his father was appointed guardian of the estate of the above named chn. and now has possession of said property. Your orator having attained full age desires a partition of said negroes. Filed 2 Dec. 1861.

PALMER, WILLIAM R. Pack 269 #10. Clerk of Court Office. Pickens, S. C. On 9 Aug. 1858 appeared William W. Hays who made oath that William R. Palmer did threaten to kill his wife Mary Palmer repeatedly and on the 8 Aug. did fall upon her and beat and bruised her in a shamefully manner.

PARK, ROBERT Bundle 100, Pack 6. Probate Judge Office. Barn- well, S. C. Est. admnr. 6 May 1850 by Wm. H. Thomson, Ord. who is bound in the sum (none given). The petition of James Moorhead states that Robert Park (blacksmith) late of Blackville Village in Barnwell Dist. died intestate on or about the beginning of Sept. leaving a widow his only legal representative. Filed 1 Oct. 1849. Mark Park the widow. Owned one and a half lot of land in the town of Clinton formerly known as the village of Blackville.

PARKSON, ELIZABETH P. Will #17. Probate Judge Office. York, S. C. Elizabeth P. Parkson mentioned in will of a Jane Campbell of York Dist. in 1860.

PARSONS, F. V. G. Box 72 #775. Probate Judge Office. Pickens, S. C. Paid 4 May 1865 F. V. G. Parson his share, H. R. Parson her share, Samuel Parson his share each $9.30 from the est. of John F. Herd decd. of Pickens Dist. whose est. admnr. 1 Jan. 1864.

PATTERSON, CARY P. #192. Clerk of Court Office. Abbeville, S.C. Abbeville Dist. In Equity. To the Honr. the Chancellors: The petition of Cary P. Patterson formerly of this Dist. and State. But now of Jasper County State of Miss. Sheweth that before his removal from this Dist. The children of your petitioner to wit, Ann O. E. Patterson, W. T. Patterson, Sarah J. Patterson and Eliza P. Patterson became entitled to an estate under a deed of their grandfather Moses Taggart decd. in value of about $1500. These chn. are all under age and unable to manage their est. Your petitioner was about to remove from the State, given written consent that the relative of his chn. and his personal friend Moses T. Owen might be appointed their gdn. In the term of 185 court Moses T. Owen was appointed gdn. of said minors. In order to handle the minors estate better, he prays that the estate may be removed to Jasper Co., Miss. Filed 1 June 1857.

PATTERSON, JOSIAH   Pack 438.   Clerk of Court Office.   Abbeville,
S. C. Abbeville Dist.   In Equity, to the Honr. the Chancellors: Your
orator Josiah Patterson and your oratrix his wife Nancy Patterson sheweth.
Your orator being now near seventy years of age is very old and feeble.
Has not only brought up on his physical weakness, but also greatly
impaired his intellect, which was never strong. He is childless and
his wife is almost as old as himself. A few years ago he possessed
with about 200 acres of land and about ten slaves, sufficient to have
supplied himself and wife in their years. They have been deprived
of the possession and use of their property. In the year 1852, John
Patterson one of the nephews of your orator, under the pretext of paying
off their debts out of their property. Procured Josiah to sign a
paper conveying his whole estate to said John Patterson. Who has taken
the whole of the property, leaving them unprotected and almost unpro-
vided for. The fatal paper purported to be a trust deed, and provides
first for the use and benefit of Josiah and wife Nancy during their
natural lives. And in case Mrs. Jane Bradley the then wife of Archibald Bradley should die without heirs which has since has happened.
The whole was to be the property of John Patterson. Josiah and wife
states they had full confidence in the said nephew, as their trustee
or agent. Therefore your orator prays that the said paper be set
aside, as unjust in these terms. Filed 29 April 1858. Archibald
Bradley states that the old folks lived in the same house he was born
in, near Patterson Bridge. Joseph Britt states that Mrs. Josiah
Patterson was an aunt. That she lived some maiden sisters before
marriage. James H. Britt states he lived all his life with his aunts.
Dr. John Sanders has been their physician.

PATTERSON, JOSIAH   Pack 384.   Clerk of Court Office.   Abbeville,
S. C. Abbeville Dist.   In Equity. To the Honr. the Chancellors: Your
orator Alexander Patterson of Dallas County, State of Arkansas, and
your oratrix Nancy Patterson of Abbeville Dist., S. C. Sheweth that
Josiah Patterson the husband of your oratrix and brother of full blood
of your orator departed this life intestate about the 6 Aug. 1860.
Possessed with a tract of land in said Dist. lying on Long Cane Creek
at the Patterson Bridge, containing 193 acres. Bounded by land of
Archibald Bradley, John Wideman. Admnr. on the est. was granted to
Nancy Patterson and Archibald Bradley. The intestate departed this
life without children, his only heirs and distributee, your oratrix
his widow, your orator a brother of full blood, the chn. of James
Patterson decd. another brother of whole blood, namely John Patterson,
Jane Patterson, Mary Patterson, Alexander Patterson a son of James
Patterson decd. died leaving a dtr. Mary Ann now the wife of William
Clay. The family of James Patterson lives in Abbeville Dist. and all
of full age. Also a brother Malcolm Patterson decd. of whole blood
who died in Morgan County, Ala. in Feb. 1859. Heirs: Andrew M.
Patterson, Jane Patterson the wife of Daniel Patterson, John Patterson,
Josiah Patterson and Catherine M. Patterson a minor who lives in Morgan
Co. and ___ Patterson and Malcolm Patterson Jr. now living in State
of Texas. Alexander Patterson a son of Malcolm Patterson decd. died
in Texas leaving chn. name and number unknown. Malcolm Patterson Senr.
died leaving a widow Mary Patterson who has no interest. Samuel
Patterson another brother decd. of whole blood, who last known living
in Ala. Filed 24 Jan. 1861.

PATTERSON, "MINORS"   Pack 52.   Clerk of Court Office.   Abbeville,
S. C. On 12 Dec. 1851 Moses T. Owen was the guardian of Eliza Perrin
Patterson. Carey Patterson has presented an account for board for
1853 and 1854 $100. Est. of Eliza Patterson, ward of M. T. Owen, made
by M. T. Owen and Dr. J. W. Heartagent for C. P. Patterson gdn. in
the State of Miss. M. T. Owen made gdn. of Ann E. Patterson a minor.

PATTERSON, ROBERT S.   Pack 3360.   Clerk of Court Office.   Abbeville, S. C. To the Honr. the Chancellors: Your Oratrix Mary D.
Patterson, sheweth that Robert S. Patterson late of this Dist. died
intestate leaving as his heirs and distributees your oratrix the widow
and two infant children, to wit. James Napoleon Patterson and Robert
Lewis Patterson. Soon after the death of Robert S. Patterson his son
Robert, died, then being an infant of tender years. Wade S. Cothran

Patterson, Robert S. - Continued. has been appointed guardian
of the estate of James Napoleon Patterson by this Court. Robert S.
Patterson was possessed with a tract of land lying on Beaver Dam
Creek, waters of Hard Labor Creek, containing 950 acres, being the
same land alloted to Robert S. Patterson by a division of the est. of
Robert Smyth Senr. to the chn. of Nancy Patterson of whom Robert S.
was one. The admnr. was granted to Josiah C. Patterson who has sold
all the personal est. and paid all debts. Only the real est. remains
to be divided between your oratrix and her infant son. Filed this
14 June 1836.

PATTERSON, WILLIAM Pack 3349. Clerk of Court Office. Abbeville,
S. C. Abbeville Dist. In Equity, to the Honr. the Chancellors:
Your orator James Patterson sheweth that William Patterson a son of
your orator departed this life about May 1837, intestate and under
age, leaving no wife or child. Leaving as heirs and distributees your
orator the father, his brothers Josiah C. Patterson, Napoleon Patterson, and James N. Patterson the only child of a decease brother Robert
Patterson. Napolean Patterson has since died, and by his last will
made Josiah C. Patterson his sole devise and executor. Larkin
Reynolds has been appointed guardian of James N. Patterson, yet a minor
of tender age. William Patterson decd. at his death was seized of a
tract of land containings 520 acres, known as the Robert Smith lands,
the Parks tract, and the Andrew Gray place. Lying on branches of
Reedy branch, Lesly branch, and Hardlabor. Bounded by land of Wm.
Lipford, George Red, Charles Sproulls, Robert D. Gray and Robert
Patterson decd. Filed 12 June 1839.

PEARSON, HENRY Pack 290 #28. Clerk of Court Office. Pickens,
S. C. Henry and Arminda were the children of Polly Pearson of Pickens
Dist. No date.

PEDAN, JOHN SENR. Apt. 6 File 374. Probate Judge Office.
Greenville, S. C. I John Pedan Senr. of Greenville Dist. being of
perfect mind and memory. After all my lawful debts are paid. I give
to my beloved wife the use of my dwelling house and fourth part of
what shall be raised on the place for her support. I give to my son
Samuel, 200 acres of land where he now lives. I give all the rest of
my land to be equally divided between my three sons John, James and
William. I give to my wife, my sons, John, James and William likewise
my dtrs. Peggy, Polly, Jenny and Lizy an equal share of the rest of my
property. I give to Polly Gregory one suit of house spun and one suit
of store cloathing and a bed and furniture. I appoint my sons Samuel
and James Pedan my executors. Dated 13 May 1810. Wit: Thomas Pedan,
Anthony Savage. Signed: John Pedan. Proved on oath of Anthony
Savage before David Goodlett, Ord. this 3 Dec. 1810. Recd. 26 Dec.
1810.

PEDAN, JOHN SENR. Apt. 6 File 374. Probate Judge Office.
Greenville, S. C. I John Pedan Senr. of Greenville Dist. being of
perfect mind and memory. First I desire all my lawful debts be paid.
I give to my wife the use of the dwelling house and a fourth part of
what is raised on my plantation for her use during her life. I give
to my son Samuel 200 acres of land where he now lives. I give the
rest of my land to be equally divided among my three sons John, James
and William. I also give to my dtrs. Peggy, Polly, Jenny and Lucy an
equal share of the rest of my property. I give to Polly Gregory one
suit of home spun and one suit of store cloathing, a bed and furniture.
I appoint my sons Samuel and James executors. Dated 13 May 1810.
Wit: Thomas Pedan, Anthony Savage. Signed: John Pedan. Proven on
oath of Anthony Savage before D. Goodlett Ord. this 3 Dec. 1810.
Recorded 26 Dec. 1810.

PEDIGREW, EBENEZER Old records, Book A, page 14. Clerk of Court
Office. 96 Dist. A citizen grant for Ebenezer Pedigrew for 340 on
both side of Generostee Creek a branch of Savannah River. Bounded on
all sides by vacant land when surveyed. Dated 22 May 1784. Recd. 29
May 1784.

PEDIGREW, WILLIAM Old Records Book A, Page 14. Clerk of Court Office. 96 Dist. A citizen grant for William Pedigrew for 400 on Generostee Creek a branch of Savannah River, bounded by land of Ebenezer Pedigrew and all other sides vacant when surveyed. Dated 22 May 1784. Recd. 29 May 1784.

PELFREY, JAMES ESQ. Box 49 #542. Probate Judge Office. Pickens, S. C. "Personally appeared brfore me Huldah Hinton and made oath that she was present and saw James Pelfree and Martha Hinton married by Henry Griffin, Esq. in Pickens District in Martha Hinton's own house near Robert Boyd's about eighteen years ago and that John Masingill and wife Sindarilla and Harrison Boyd and Warren Boyd was present at the time they was married." Dated this 7 May 1860. Before J. W. Singleton, N.P.D. Signed: Huldah X Hinton.

PENNEL, "MINORS" Pack 61. Clerk of Court Office. Abbeville, S. C. In 1858, M. O. McCaslan was guardian of William H. Pennal, James A. Pennal minors. Expend: 1 Jan. 1859 paid Esther Pennal $84.

PERKINS, JOSHUA Deed Book E-1, page 30. Clerk of Court Office. Pickens, S. C. I Joshua Perkins of Pickens Dist. in consideration of $1,000 to me paid by E. B. Verner, have granted, bargained, sold unto E. P. Verner a tract of land lying on Choastoe Creek waters of Tugalo River. Bounded on North and West by land of Shannons, on East by Smithsons, on South by Andersons, containing 165 acres. Dated this 20 Oct. 1843. Wit: Joseph Dickson, William Roper. Signed: Joshua Perkins. This day came Hannah Perkins the wife of Joshua Perkins and relinquished all her rights and claim of dower. This 28 Oct. 1843. Signed T. W. Harbin, Mag. P.D. Hannah X Perkins. Recorded 10 Nov. 1843.

PERKINS, JOSIAH Deed Book H-1, Page 501. Clerk of Court Office. Pickens, S. C. I Josiah Perkins of Pickens Dist. in consideration of $2,000. To me paid by Lofayette [sic] M. Allen, have granted, sold, bargained and released all that plantation of land lying on Coneros and Colonels Fork Creek waters of Seneca River. The same where I formerly lived, adj. land of F. S. Mavericks, N.J.F. Perry, G. W. Phillips. Containing 332 acres. Dated 4 Oct. 1855. Wit: J. W. Earle, Saml. X Perkins. Signed: Josiah Perkins. Hannah Perkins the wife of Josiah Perkins released and relinquished all interest in the above land before E. Haynes a Mag. This 23 Feb. 1858.

PERMENTER, ELIZABETH Pack 417. Clerk of Court Office. Abbeville, S. C. On 30 Dec. 1851 a statement of the account of John T. Carter who was gdn. of Elizabeth S. Permenter with a view to a settlement with John H. Cook admnr. of the ward who has died. Paid 15 Jan. 1839 Alsela Permenter for boarding $35.00. Paid 30 Dec. 1845 Judy Ross for boarding $60. On one paper name was written Saran Ann E. Permenter.

PERRIN, ROBERT #228. Bill for account. Clerk of Court Office. Abbeville, S. C. Abbeville Dist. In Equity, to the Honr. the Chancellors: Your orator Francis L. Pelot, an infant who sues in behalf by his uncle and next friend Abner Perrin, Robert Perrin late of Edgefield Dist. departed this life in 1826. Leaving his will and testament in full force and executed on the 31 Jan. 1826. He gave to his wife the land South of Mantz's branch, during her natural life and at her death to his lawful heirs, to share equal, he also gave to his wife ten negroes (not named) during her natural life, and at her death to his heirs, equally. To his daughters Catharine and Eliza or the lawful heirs of their body, other legacies, some to be enjoyed after the death of his wife, who died in the year 1829, leaving a considerable estate, most subject to her husband will. The dtr. and heir Catherine intermarried in the year 182_ with John F. Pelot and on the _ Nov. 1828 departed this life, leaving your orator the only issue of her body. That after the death of your orator mother Catharine, certain proceeding were presented in this Court for Edgefield Dist. by Llewellyn Oliver and wife, she being Eliza dtr. of said Robert Perrin against your orator and his father John F. Pelot. In the June Court 1829 said John F. Pelot was appointed guardian of the estate of your orator.

Perrin, Robert - Continued. That said John F. Pelot did sell to
Wade S. Cothran a tract of land on the South side of Hard Labor Creek
in Edgefield Dist. containing 390 acres. He now seeks confirmation of
said sale. Filed 6 Feb. 1843. In another paper John F. Pelot states
he removed to Washington in Wilks County, Ga. in the year 1836. Also
his son is now between 10 and 11 yrs. of age, dated 6 Feb. 1843.

PERRY, LEMUEL A. Apt. 86, Pack 915. Probate Judge Office.
Pickens, S. C. I Lemuel A. Perry of Pickens Dist. being of sound mind
and disposing memory. First I will and direct that all my just debts
and funeral expenses be paid. I will that my three children Emma Etny
Parry, Ebvin Early Perry, Ella Cornelia Perry shall have my land, Lot
No. 1 whereon the dwelling houses stands containing 32 1/2 acres.
Bounded by land of McMahan and John Perry Martin. The wood shop that
stands on said land to be the property of my sons, Ebin Earley Parry,
Elbert Earle Perry, Ellis Ray Perry, with the right to work the shop
where it stands or to move it if they desire. Mrs. Lucinda Perry to
have a home for her natural life or widowhood. I will that John Perry
Martin shall have Lot No. 2, containing 4 1/4 acres. I will that Nancy
Emily McMahan shall have Lot No. 3 containing 30 1/4 acres, bounded on
West by Holcombe land. I will that Mary Ann Nally shall have Lot No.
4, containing 17 acres bounded by land of Holcombe and heirs of Jesse
Perry decd. I will that Elbert Earle Perry shall have Lot No. 5
containing 10 acres, and that Ellie Ray Perry shall have Lot No. 6,
containing 10 acres. I will that my son Irby Leland Perry shall have
my rifle gun and my black mule (Jack), Ella Camelia Perry to have my
bay mare (Bob), Ebin Early Parry to have the bay mare (Molly Elbert
E. Perry to take possession of the plantation and to pay unto Adetlee
Perry Martin ten dollars on the first of Jan. each year for ten years.
I appoint my son Elbert Earle Perry my executor. Dated 14 June 1878.
Wit: J. F. Barnes, E. T. Holcombe, R. E. Holcombe. Signed: Lemuel
X Perry. Recorded the 27 May 1879.

PETTIGREW, GEORGE Pack 315. Clerk of Court Office. Abbeville,
S. C. I George Pettigrew of Abbeville Dist. being weak in body but of
perfect mind and memory. First I desire all my just debts be paid
with funeral expenses out of my estate. I give to my dtr. Sarah
Oliver $600 which she already received and negro girl Olly appraised
at $800. I give to my dtr. Margaret Robinson $300, she already received,
also negro woman Easther and child Della Ann, appraised at $850. I
give to my son John Even Pettigrew $300, he already received, also negro
Isaac appraised at $1,000. I give to my son Robert H. Pettigrew the
tract of land whereon he now lives, at $736, also negro boy Elijah
appraised at $400. I give to my dtr. Rosa Anna Brownlee a negro girl
Milla, appraised at $350, also two boys named Edman and Joe Appraised
at $750. I give to my grandchildren Mary T. and Sarah J. Paskel a
negro woman Sharlet, with the increase from said Sharlet to go to the
chn. share and share alike. If either should die, the other to be sole
heir. At the death of their grandmother they are to have their mother
share, all to be keep in the hand of John Brownlee, till they become
of age or marry. I give to my son George P. Pettigrew two negroe
boys, Dave and Alexander appraised at $800, also the tract of land
whereon I now reside. After the death of my wife I desire all my
personal estate be sold, and the money equally divided between all my
chn. except Perry, he is to have no part as I think the land is a good
portion. I appoint my son Robert Pettigrew and son-in-law John Brownlee executors. Dated 1 March 1839. Wit: Joel Lockhart, John
Robinson, S. T. Baskin. Signed: George Pettigrew. Codicil. I give
to my (grand)daughter Jane Paskel on negro woman appraised at $800.
I give to my son Robin Pettigrew on negro boy Lewis in place of one
that died. I give to my son Perry Pettigrew one negro named Frank, also
250 acres of land, taken off to upper end of this tract. I will that
Jeff, Allen and Siller be sold, with the cotton crop to settle the
debts. I will to my wife the following negroes, Ben, Fanny, Cole,
Sarah, Lillan, Harriet and Black Harriett, Redler, Wiley, Augustus
and Pegga and Alfred. Dated this 27 June 1843. Wit: Joel Lockhart,
F. Y. Baskin, John N. Brown. Signed: George Pettigrew. Filed 26
Feb. 1850. In Equity. Your orator and your oratrix John Brownlee and
his wife Rosann. Sheweth that George Pettigrew decd. made his last

Pettigrew, George - Continued. will and testament 1 March 1839, with a codicil dated 27 June 1843. In his will he devise to his wife Mary for life a tract of land, in the codicil he gave to his son George F. Pettigrew 250 acres from the upper end of this said tract, after the death of his wife, with the other part of the land and personal estate sold and equally divided between all his children and grand children, viz; Robert H. Pettigrew, George P. Pettigrew, Margaret Robinson a widow, Rosannah Brownlee your oratrix, John Pettigrew residing in Georgia, Sarah the wife of Robert Oliver residing in Miss. his grand children Mary and Jane Pashell the children of a decd. dtr. Jane, who married William M. Pashell residing in Miss. Your oratrix sheweth that Mary Pettigrew the widow is living and has consented to surrender her life estate in the tract of land for the purpose of division. The land lying on Rockey River, adj. land of Margaret Robinson, John Mauldin and George F. Pettigrew containing 430 acres. Your orator will ever pray.

PETTIS, ANNA No ref. or County given. Settlement of the est. of Anna Pettis, widow of James Pettis decd. as sold by Geo. Lomax Exor. After the death of the widow. The matter in the will of James Pettis all being settled in full between the exor and legatee. Present at this settlement Geo. Lomax Exor. James A. Jay who married Clotilda Pettis, Edward Lipford who married Ellnor. James A. Jay holding power of Attorney for H. Owens, who married Louisa, who resides in Miss., Jno. Stone

PETTY, ABSOLOM Box 3 Pack 49. Probate Judge Office. Union, S. C. I Absolom Petty of Union Dist. farmer, being sick and weak in body but of perfect mind and memory. First I will, all my estate to my beloved wife Molly Petty during her natural life or widowhood (and to my children Charles and Sarah, I give a moity of five shillings). To my son John, William and James to dtrs. Isabel and Nancy shall have an equal division of my estate at the death of my wife. I appoint my wife executrix and sons John and William Petty executors. Dated this 20 June 1801. Wit: Gabreil Petty, John Durborow, Martha X Petty. Proved on oath of Gabriel Petty before Benjamin Haile Esq. Ord. This 4 June 1802.

PETTIT, JANE E. Pack 633. Record of Richard Burdine. Clerk of Court Office. Pickens, S. C. On 23 March 1861 Jane E. Pettit wife of James E. Pettit was a dtr. of Polly Latham decd. and husband John Latham of Georgia. Polly Latham a dtr. of Richard Burdine of Pickens Dist.

PETTY, JAMES Box 5 Pack 3. Probate Judge Office. Union, S. C. I James Petty of Union Dist. farmer being of sound mind and memory. First I will all my just debts and funeral expenses be paid, then it is my will that my wife Martha enjoy as her right all my estate during her natural life or widowhood (excepting a moity of five shilling to each of my children viz; Ambrose, James Absalom, Joshua, Thomas and George also a moity of five shilling to each dtr. Rachel, Sarah, Martha, Catherine, and Polly to be paid after the death of my wife. At death or marriage of my wife I give my plantation containing 327 acres to my son Gabriel Petty in fee simple, also two thirds of my personal estate, the other third I give to my wife to dispose as she pleases. I appoint my wife executrix and my son Gabriel with my trusty friend Nicholas Corry executors. Dated this 14 March 1806. Wit: Charles Petty, Jepthah Harrington, John Petty. Signed: James Petty. Proved on oath of Jepthah Harrington before Wm. Rice, Ord. this 3 Nov. 1809.

PHEIFER, FRED Petition for citizenship #6. Clerk of Common Pleas and Common Sessions. To the Honr. James S. Cothran one of the Judges of the State. The petition of Frederick Pfeifer age 47 yrs. Occupation of farming, your petitioner sheweth that he was born in Naussaw[sic] Germany. That he arrived in this country in June 1867 and in this State for eleven yrs. and is sincerely attached to the constitution of the U.S. He prays the oath which in such cases is provided may be administered to him, and that he be admitted as a citizen. Be it so. Signed: James Cochran, Circuit Judge. Dated this 24 Oct. 1882.

PICKENS, ANDREW #37. Clerk of Court Office. Pickens, S. C.
I Andrew Pickens of Pendleton Dist. are held and firmly bound unto
Henry Hendricks of the same place in the sum of $240. The condition
of the above obligation is such that if the said Andrew Pickens shall
well and truly make unto Henry Hendricks a good and sufficient title
to a tract of land lying in said Dist. against Oct. 1823 when the said
heir come of age. Land adj. Joshua Smith and Clabourn Pools. Dated
22 Dec. 1820. Wit: William Dowis, James Hendrick. Signed: Andrew X
Pickens. Proved on oath of William Dowis before Rt. MCann[?], J.Q.
this 29 Nov. 1821.

PICKENS, ANDREW #37. Clerk of Court Office. Pickens, S. C.
Pendleton Dist., S. C. I Andrew Pickens are held and firmly bound
unto Henry Hendricks of this same Dist. in the sum of $240. Condition
of the above obligation that Andrew Pickens shall make unto the said
Henry Hendricks a good and sufficient right and title to a tract of
land, against Oct. 1823 when the said heir come of age. Adj. lands
of Joshua Smiths, Clabourn Pools. It being one third part of 136
acres, or 45 and one third acres. Dated 22 Dec. 1820. Wit: William
Dowis, James Hendricks. Signed: Andrew X Pickens. Proved on oath of
William Dowis before R. T. McAnn, J.Q. this 29 Nov. 1821.

PICKENS, ANDREW SENR. Deed Book H, Page 420-21-22. Clerk of
Court Office. Anderson, S. C. I Andrew Pickens Senr. of Pendleton
Dist. in consideration of ten shillings sterling to me paid by Ezekiel
Pickens of St. Thomases Parish have granted, sold, bargained and
conveyed all that tract of land lying in Pendleton Dist. containing
394 acres one quarter and twenty one poles. On the East bank of Keowee
River (the same being the lower of the Hopewell tract.) Dated 7 Feb.
1805. Wit: B. R. Montgomery, Andrew Pickens, Junr., Signed: Andrew
Pickens. Proved on oath of Andrew Pickens, Junr. before M. Hammond
D.C. this 15 Dec. 1806.

PICKENS, ELIZA Pack 47. Clerk of Court Office. Abbeville,
S. C. Marriage settlement: This indenture made the 10 July 1832
between Eliza Pickens and Floride Calhoun, guardians appointed by the
will of the father of Mary Barksdale Pickens, dtr. of Ezekiel Pickens
late of St. Thomas Parish, in Charleston Dist. decd. Mary Barksdale
Pickens of the first patr. Robert Anderson of Pickens Dist. of the
second part, and Patrick Noble of Abbeville Dist. as trustee names and
chosen by the parties of this settlement of the third part. Whereas
by permission of God a marriage is to be had between Robert Anderson
and Mary Barksdale Pickens. Whereas Mary Pickens is possessed in her
own rights the following negroes, to wit: Romeo and Aggy and child
Isham, Rose and child July and child Milly, **Jerry, Judy, Nelson**, Frank,
Fanny and Rebecca. Also a share of her grandfather George Barksale
decd. est. after the decease of her mother Eliza Pickens. In consideration of one dollar paid by Patrick Noble, have bargained, sold the
above named slaves and their increase, with the share of George Barksdale est. to have and hold the said property in trust, for the use and
benefit of Mary Barksdale Pickens before and after her marriage, for
her lifetime, then to the lineal descendants of Robert Anderson and
Mary Barkesdale Pickens. Wit: T. J. Pickens, Kezia A. Pickens,
Eliza Pickens. Signed: E. Pickens Noble, Robert Anderson, Mary B.
Pickens. Patrick Noble. Proved on oath of Thomas J. Pickens before
Wm. L. Keith clk. this 13 July 1832.

PITMAN, BURGESS Box 71 Pack 1758. Probate Judge Office.
Abbeville, S. C. Est. admnr. the 19 Nov. 1819 by John Glasgow, James
Glasgow, William McDonald Senr. and James McAllister who are bound
unto Moses Taggart, Ord. in the sum of $7,000. Citation was published
at Hopewell Church. Paid 7 April 1821 Mary Pitman $17.00, Paid 7 Jan.
1817 Burgis Pitman Jr. $10.00. By a note of hand on Peter Pitman and
H. M. Pitman for $8.06 not good.

PRICE, REBECCA Box 11 #138. Probate Judge Office. Pickens,
S. C. Rebecca Price was a dtr. of Jesse Nevill of Pickens Dist. her
father will was proven in 1842.

POLIAKOOFF, DAVID No. 4. Petition for Citizenship. Clerk of Court Office. Abbeville, S. C. In the Court of Common Pleas. To the Honr. J. C. Klugh, Judge presiding at the June term 1901. The petition of David Polakooff, aged 27 yrs. Occupation of a merchant sheweth. Your petitioner was born in Mensk in Russia on the 11 Oct. 1875, and arriver in New York on the 15 Aug. 1893. He has resided in N.Y. State about 6 months, and has resided in Aiken, Spartanburg and Abbeville counties in this State since. Your petitioner was 18 yrs. on the 11 Oct. 1893 and is desirous of becoming a citizen of the U.S. That he is willing to renounce all allegiance and fidelity to every foreign prince, potentate, state and particularly the Czar of Russia of whom he was born a subject. The above petition was sworn before J. L. Perrin Clerk of Court. This 4 June 1901. There are sworn statement of M. Poliakoff of Gaffney, S. C. States he has known David Polia- kooff for six years, etc. dated 28 May 1901. Another sworn statement from J. S. Poliakooff who resides at Langley, S. C. saith he known David Poliakooff for eight years, and he has good moral character, etc. Dated 28 May 1901.

POOLE, MICAJAH Pack 3215. Clerk of Court Office. Abbeville, S. C. I Macajah Poole, being of sound and disposing mind and memory, but weak in body, etc. I desire my just debts and funeral expenses be paid. I desire my son Robert Poole shall have the tract of land whereon I now live, supposed to be 360 acres, by paying my son in law Robert Young $650. My son Robert shall have negro woman Lucinda, also my desk and Silver watch. I have advanced my son in law Robert Young about $750 and the use of it for about four or five years, with the $650 to be paid in one year, I consider him equal with my son Robert. Also I give to my dtr. Nancy Young a negro woman named Pat. All other negroes not disposed of to be equally divided between dtr. Nancy Young and son Robert Poole by valuation during their natural life and then to their heirs, if either dies without heirs, their share shall return to my estate and decend to the heirs of my body. I appoint Alexr. W. Adams and Francis White executors. Dated 3 Sept. 1819. Wit: Joel Lipscomb, Alexr. Stuart, W. Wier. Signed: Micajah Poole. Recorded 16 May 1825. In Equity. To the Honr. the Chcanellors: Your oratrices Caroline, Matilda and Tabitha Poole, drtrs. of Robert Poole late of this dist. deceased, infants under the age of twenty one, by their guardian William Eddins. Sheweth that Micajah Poole gave to their father Robert Poole negro Lucinda and her increase, with other negroes to be divided between their father and his sister Nancy Young, during their natural life, then to their heirs. Their father died intestate and James Sample was granted admnor. of the est. with the widow. The said widow (not named) has intermarried with James Anderson. The admnor. James Sample bought negro Lucinda and her issue for $706.00. Their guardian has applied to the admnor. for the money of Lucinda and child. The admnor. pretending that your oratrices are entitled to only two thirds of the price of negroes and the widow the other third. Filed 23 May 1825.

PORTER, HUGH L. In same file with John Proter. Box 119 Pack 3532. Probate Judge Office. Abbeville, S. C. Power of Attorney from Hugh L. Porter of Tishamingo County, Miss. the surviving brother of Jane E. Porter decd. of Itawamba County, Miss. Who died without issue and without any sister or other brother surviving her, children of Andrew R. Porter decd. of Abbeville Dist., S. C. and Nancy H. Porter alias Nancy H. Davis being now the wife of Isreal N. Davis. Do hereby nomi- nate and appoint David Lesly of Abbeville Dist., S. C. my true and law- ful attorney for me and in my name and for my use and benefit, to receive and receipt of and from Robert late the guardian of Jane E. Porter decd. Dated this 13 Nov. 1852. Wit: J. T. Brown, John S. Harrison. Signed: Hugh L. Porter.

PORTER, EDWARD SANDERS Will Book A, Page 6. Probate Judge Office. Union, S. C. I Edward Sanders Porter of Union County, S. C. Tho weak in body, yet of sound mind and perfect understanding, etc. First I desire my lawful debts be paid. I give to my loving wife during the term of her widowhood this house where I now dwell, with all tenna- ments about it, with all cattle, hogs, sheep and one bay mare named John.

Porter, Edward Sanders - Continued. At her marring or death, to
be equally divided among all my children. I will to my son Calvin one
bay mare named Doe. Likewise I will to my son Epaphroditus a "Statling"
colt named Selah. I appoint my two eldest sons Lancelst Porter and
Handcock Porter executors and Trustees for my wife and children.
Dated this 1 Dec. 1791. Wit: William Campbell, Jesse X Holcom,
Nicholas X Lazarus. Signed: Edward Sanders X Porter. Recorded the
4 Sept. 1792.

PORTER, JOHN Box 119 Pack 3532. Probate Judge Office. Abbeville,
S. C. The last will and testament of John Porter of Abbeville Dist,
S. C. being of sound mind. I give to my wife E. D. Porter one sixth
part of my estate both real and personal, "after my debts are paid, and
my three youngest chn. viz, Martha M., Hugh F. and Mary E. have
received an equal portion for education with my three eldest dtrs. or
arrangement made for that purpose." At the death of wife, one half
of est. to be divided among my chn., the other half wife may dispose
as she may think proper. His chn. Hester Ann Mary Glover, Catharine
Jones, Martha Matilda, Hugh Francis and Mary Elizth Porter. I appoint
my wife E. D. Porter, exorx., Dr. T. R. Gary, T. W. Williams, and
Henry Hester my executors. Dated __ July 1838. Wit: Nathl. Marion,
Jas. Shackelford, James B. Clanahan. Signed: John Porter. Proved by
oath of James B. Canahan before David Lesly, Ord. this 25 Jan. 1847.
Codicil added the 17 Jan. 1847. He states that his estate has accumu-
lated to some extent, and one of his daughter has died. "That my only
son Hugh Francis Porter do receive of my estate over and above any of
my chn. One negro named Tom a brick layer by trade, and his wife
Sharlott." Wit: John A. Stewart, John Williams, Gabriel Hodges.
Signed: John Porter. Both will and codicil was proved by Gabriel
Hodges this 25 Jan. 1847. The Rev. John Porter died the 19 Jan. 1847.
Est. was appraised on 28 Jan. 1847 by John Vance, Larkin Mays, John
Willson, John C. Waters. Negroes named viz: Phillis, Isaac, Silvey,
Sherrod, Abby, Old Peter, July, Charles, Huldy, Abram, Jane, Tom,
Sharlott, Solomon, Alleck, Jennett and child, Anney, Moriah, Luisa,
Lucinda, Olley, Liza, Mahala, Lucius, Squir, Aaron, Little Peter, Wait.
Hugh F. Porter states that he was unwilling to take the negroes given
him by the codicil attached to his father's will. He desired all the
legatees to share equal in the estate. Dated 30 Jan. 1847. The
legatees in said will asked the Court to set aside the will, as he left
no direction as in what manner the division should be made. The
executors named in said will, who now survive, have relinquished all
right to qualify as executor or executrix. Therefore, the Ordinary
in said dist. has appointed Robert M. Davis administrator thereof.
The heirs are: Hester Ann Davis, Mary G. Porter, James T. Allen and
wife Catharine J., Hugh F. Porter, Mary E. the wife of Meady Mays,
Elizabeth D. Porter the widow. On Dec. 8, 1847 the est. was divided.
One Leroy J. Johnson recd. a share (he may be the husband of Mary G.
Porter, as she is not listed as received her share).

PORTER, MACKLIN Box 120 Pack 3533. Probate Judge Office.
Abbeville, S. C. Abbeville Dist. Admnr. Bond. We James W. Porter,
Phares Martin and A. H. McAllister are bound unto David Lesly Esq. Ord.
in the sum of $300. Dated 22 Jan. 1847. The petition of James W.
Porter sheweth that his brother Maclin Porter departed this life
intestate having no wife or children, but a mother, brothers and sisters
having a small est. Dated 8 Jan. 1847. An appraisment of the property
of the est. of Maclin Porter decd. this 28 Jan. 1847 viz: One horse,
$75.00, one saddle, one Blanket, one bridle, one neatingale[?] $6.00.
The above is a true statement of the effects of the est. of Maclin
Porter decd.

PORTER, MARY ANN Box 109 Pack 3067. Probate Judge Office.
Abbeville, S. C. Gdn. bond. We John Porter (no other person named)
of Abbeville Dist. are bound unto Taliaferro Livingston, Ord. in the
just sum of $10,000. Dated 11 June 1814. Whereas the Court of
Ordinary did appoint John Porter gdn. of the person and personal est.
of Mary Ann Porter a minor under 14 yrs. of age. Wit: John Bickly.
Letter proved by Rev. Jno. Porter. To T. Livingston, Ord. Dear Sir:
Should the Court be disposed to appoint Rev. Jno. Porter gdn. for Ann

Porter, Mary Ann - Continued. Porter the daughter of Hugh Porter decd. I will at any time become security for his guardinship, etc. This letter shall stand binding on me for that end and purpose, I am with esteem. Your Obd. Servent, Benj. Glover.

PORTER, SAMUEL Box 74 Pack 1795. Probate Judge Office. Abbeville, S. C. I Samuel Porter of Abbeville Dist., S. C. being of sound mind and disposing memory, but weak in body. I desire enough of my personal estate be sold to pay my just debts and funeral expenses. I give to my wife Susannah Porter all the remainder of my personal estate as long as she lives, at her decease I wish what property she has left be sold and the money divided into six equal shares and given to the following: 1 share to Jane L. Brownlee, two shares to Susanah Beaty, two shares to Susanah M. Dobins, the remaining share to be equally divided betwix Sinthy M. Dobins, Samuel P. Dobins, Eliza A. Dobins. I give all that tract of land where on the widow Nancy Porter now lives containing 170 acres to the heirs of Andrew R. Porter decd. I give to my son Samuel Porter all the tract of land whereon I now live, containing 250 acres. My sons Hugh Porter, John Porter and Richard E. Porter have received their full of my estate. I appoint Sugar Bonds and Samuel W. Beaty executors. Dated 4 May 1833. Wit: James Cosper, F. Y. Baskin, Thos. X Crawford. Signed: Samuel X. Porter. Proving date not given, first return to Ordinary on 15 Nov. 1837. Buyers at sale (no date). Flurnoy Davis, Watson Bonds, Archibald Maulden Jr., William Hutcheson, William Crawford, John Bonds, James K. Windfield, John McAlister, Isam Bonds, Howard B. Shackleford, Francis Y. Baskin, George Pettigrew, Wm. Crawford Jr., John Robbeson, Hugh Porter, Pickens Macklin, William Simpson, John Simpson, William Pascal, Moses W. Bonds, John W. Conner, Speer Partain, William Kelly, George Burdett, Jane L. Brownlee, Joel Galbreath, William Harper, John Stuart, Thomas Harris, Emmaline Dobbins, Stephen Cash, Uriah Barren. In an account, paid for moving Susanah Porter from S. C. to Jackson Co., Ga. $10. Dated 1841. Paid $8.00 Oct. 15, 1841 the funeral expenses of Susanah Porter. (Letter) "Mr. Sugar Bonds: Jefferson Court House. Jackson County, Ga. Abb. C. House. July 29, 1847. Dr. Sir: I am called on by the legatees of Saml. Porter decd. and will ask you to be so good as to account to my office for the balance of the estate in your hands. Your sale bill was the rise of $500.00 and you have paid out sum $290.00 which leaves $310.00 in your hands. Will you come over and attend to this matter? other wise you may be put to some trouble. Please ander[sic] me immediately or come and attend to the settlmt of your estate. Yours respectfully, David Lesly, Ordinary of Abbeville Dist." Came this day Sugar Bonds, exor. of Saml. Porter est. 18 Sept. 1847 one share to Jane L. Brownlee of Tishimingo City, Miss., two shares to Susanah Beaty who lives at Moffetsville, Andn. Dist., S. C., two shares to Susanah M. Dobins don't know where she lives. The remaining share to Sinthy M., Saml. P., and Eliza A. Dobins where living not known.

PORTER, WILLIAM B. Box 109 Pack 3058. Probate Judge Office. Abbeville, S. C. Gdn. bond. Abbeville Dist. We William C. Cozby, John Brownlee and Patrick Noble of said Dist. are bound unto Moses Taggart, Ord. in the sum of $1,000. Dated 22 Oct. 1836. Wit: John Kennedy. The petition of Wm. C. Cozby sheweth that William B. Porter a minor over the age of 14 yrs. is entitled to considerable personal estate, which by reason of his minority he is incapable of managing. Therefore your petitioner prays he may be appointed gdn. of said estate.

POSTELL, RACHEL Box 75 Pack 1841. Probate Judge Office. Abbeville, S. C. I Rachel Postell the wife of Col. James Postell of Coosawhatchie in Beaufort Dist., S. C. Having the power notwithstanding my covertur, (by virtue of a marriage settlement) of making my will and bequeathing my property do hereby declare this to be my last will and testament. First I to my dear husband Col. James Postell the use of my estate during his natural life, at his death I give to my friend Charles J. Jenkins, my faithful old man servant, Jacob, with a request that he will manumit[sic] him according to law. I leave in trust for the maintenance and support of said servant, twenty

Postell, Rachel - Continued. dollars every year as long as he
lives. The rest and residue of my estate I leave to my friend
Charles J. Jenkins in trust, after the death of my husband, for the
use and benefit of my adopted children, William Henry, E. Eliza, Mary
Hay (children of my friend Samuel Hay Esq. decd.) to them and their
heirs forever. If the above named children should not live to full
age or marry, then the trust shall be for the use and benefit of the
children of my two neices. Mrs. Eliza Postell (wife of Capt. James
Postell) and Mrs. Rachel Sweet (wife of Rev. James D. Sweet) one half
to each neices chn. I appoint Col. James Postell and my friend
Charles J. Jenkins as executors. Dated 8 March 1816. Wit: Edwd.
W. North and J. S. Petigru. Signed: Rachel Postell. Proved on oath
of Dr. Edward W. North before Robert G. Norton, Ord. of Beauford Dist.
Dated this 11 April 1818. An inventory was made of the est. the 29
June 1818 by Thos. Finley, Jos C. Mathews, J. Calhoun. Slaves only
Jacob, T. Johny, Y. Johny, Hannah, Tom, William, Betty, Rachel, Patty,
Amelia, Nancy and child Betsy, Lucy, Liddya.

POWELL, ALMON Box 47 #519. Probate Judge Office. Pickens, S.C.
Est. admnr. 21 Dec. 1857 by Robert Powell, B. E. Poole, G. W. Vanzant,
W. Leathers are bound unto W. J. Parsons, Ord. in the sum of $4,000.
Elizabeth Powell the widow. Asel Powell, Robert Powell, Thos. Powell,
etc. bought at sale. Robert Powell of Horse Shoe, Pickens Dist. was
a son.

POWELL, ALMON Pack 111 #5. Clerk of Court Office. Pickens,
S. C. An inquest was held at the house of Almon Powell in Pickens
Dist. the 2nd. Nov. 1857 that the decd. was found lying in bed at about
5 O'Clock on the first of Nov. died thru a dispensation of Providence
the cause being unknown. Mistress Powell says that the decd. ate his
supper as usual, went to bed at usual bedtime, heard no complaint.
She thought about 5 O'Clock he got up and went out of doors, came in
a few minutes. She was laying awake when he got back in bed, he said
something but did not understand, thought he was making a remark about
the weather, as he usually done when getting up at night. Their
daughter Mrs. McIntire was in the room with her children, she heard her
father say something to her mother, but didn't hear what it was. She
heard her father gron or moan after he lay down, nothing more till
mother gave the alarm which was about sun up.

POWELL, HARRISON Pack 647 #11. Clerk of Court Office. Pickens,
S. C. I Harrison Powell of Pickens County in consideration of the
sum of $300.00 to me paid by Jeremiah Powell of same County. Have
bargained, sold and released a tract of land lying on Rocky Bottom
Creek waters of Big Eastatoe Creek. Adj. land of Thomas Powell and
the Western part of my original home place containing 230 acres.
Dated 11 Oct. 1880. Wit: J. M. Stewart, Hiram X Reaves. Signed:
Harrison X Powell. I James M. Stewart do certify that Mrs Angeline
Powell the wife of Harrison Powell did this day before me, renounce,
release, and relinquish all her interest and all right of dower on the
above land. Signed: James M. Stewart, Trial Justice. Recorded 17
Nov. 1880.

POWELL, HARRISON Box 133 #6. Probate Judge Office. Pickens,
S. C. Est. admnr. 14 Oct. 1899 by Angeline Powell, B. N. Powell,
J. McD. Bruce, W. T. McFall are bound unto J. B. Newberry, Ord. in the
sum of $200.00. Died 12 Sept. 1899. Angeline Powell the widow.
B. N. Powell a son.

POWER, HENRY F. #10. In Equity. Clerk of Court Office. Abbeville, S. C. Whereas Henry F. Power lately delivered his bill of
complaint, before this Court. Against John B. Black the admnor and
Susan Black the widow of the late Robert F. Black of this Dist.
Whereas Robert F. Black agreed to convey a tract of land unto Henry
F. Power in his life time. The contract for the land was to be in
cash, Powers to pay $2650.00 in cash for 505 acres. Susan Black the
widow, and William C. Black as commissioner in equity for the chn. of
Robert F. Black decd. to wit. John W. Black, Lucy C. Black, Joseph A.
Black, William Black, and Robert F. Black. The said land on Pennys

Power, Henry F. - Continued. Creek water of Little River. Adj.
land of Craven Fraser, Hudson Prince, Hugh M. Prince, George Miller
and John Russell. Dated this 7 Jan. 1839. Wit: Susan Black.
David Lesly. John Hunter, John B. Black, Jno. W. Black. Signed:
Susan Black and William C. Black (seal) C.E.A.D. Proved on oath of
Jno. W. Black as to the signature of Susan Black. This 25 June 1839.
Proved David Lesly before J. H. Wilson J.Q. as to the signature Wm. C.
Black. Dated this 1 July 1839.

POWER, MARY LIEUEZER Box 77 #816. Probate Judge Office.
Pickens, S. C. Mary Lieuezer Power was the dtr. of Robert Gaines of
Pickens Dist. His will proven in 1864.

POWER, HENRY F. Pack 10. Equity Records. Clerk of Court
Office. Abbeville, S. C. Henry F. Power died 9 June 1856 at the time
of his death he left one child J. William Power and two grand children,
William Raiford Logan and Alice Logan chn. of a decd. dtr. Louisa
Logan. When Henry died he had a large est. with three tracts of land,
one, the home tract contained 452 acres, bounded by land of Alexander
Hunter, Joel Cunningham, second tract. The Black tract contained 700
acres, bounded by land of Hugh M. Prince, W. J. Cheatham. The
third tract, the Smith tract contained 150 acres bounded by land of
George B. Clinkscales, Benjamin W. Williams.

POWERS names in Mt. Zion Cemetery. Central, Pickens County, S.C.
Zachariah Power, born 20 June 1811, died 22 July 1878. Age 66 yrs.
11 mo. 2 days.
Victoria I. wife of J. G. Powers, 29 Sept. 1857 - 8 Oct. 1907.
James G. Powers - Co. D. 1 Bn. S. C. Vols. 1847-1925.
(2 unmarked graves with old field rocks by J. G. Powers.)
Robert K. Powers - 1887-1940
Gula P. Mauldin 1883-1918.
M. L. Powers 1835-1906 (2 old unmarked graves.)
Mariah - wife of Drury Power, aged 79 (no other dates)
Nathaniel - son of J. G. and V. I. Power, 26 Feb. 1892-28 Feb. 1892

POWERS, DREWRY Box 23 #272. Probate Judge Office. Pickens,
S. C. Est. admnr. 21 Oct. 1850 by Mariah Powers the widow, B. S.
Gaines and H. L. Gaines are bound unto Wm. D. Steele, Ord. in the sum
of $500. Left 7 heirs: Mary L., Harriet O., M. L., James G. Powers
all under age Emily C. the wife of R. P. Landrith, Della E. the wife
of Willis G. Grant, Pinckney Powers a minor. On 12 Sept. 1856 Mariah
and Mary L. Powers recd. a share.

POWERS, WM. K. AND JAMES G. Box 3 #63. Probate Judge Office.
Pickens, S. C. On 9 Feb. 1857 Robert A. Thompson, James E. Hagood and
L. C. Craig are bound unto W. J. Parson, Ord. in the sum of $591.00.
Robert A. Thompson guardian for William K. Power and James G. Power
minors under 21 yrs. Mariah Powers their mother.

POWERS, HARRIET E. Box 3 #55. Probate Judge Office. Pickens,
S. C. On 9 Feb. 1857 Robert A. Thompson, James E. Hagood and L. C.
Craig were bound unto W. J. Pardon, Ord. in the sum of $68.81. R. A.
Thompson the guardian of Harriet E. Powers minor under 21 yrs.

POWERS, PINCKEY Box 42 #474. Probate Judge Office. Pickens,
S. C. Est. admnr. 3 Nov. 1856 by R. A. Thompson, James E. Hagood and
L. C. Craig who are bound unto W. J. Parson, Ord. in the sum of $200.
Was a minor. Recd. 12 Jan. 1857 from admnrx. of Drury Powers decd.
$21.81.

PULLEN, WILLIAM From a genealogy paper written by descendant in
Bham, Ala. William Pullen was born in 1758 near Petersburg, Va. He
enlisted in the Revolutionary War, 1 Jan. 1777 in Geo. Lambert's
Company of Con. Regulars of the 14th Va. Reg. of foot. Commanded by
Col. Charles Lewis. He served in other Companys, from Va. William
first married "Patsy" no other named known by whom he had two sons
Peyton and Pleasent Pullen. About 1786 he and his second wife Mary
Haynes were married in Wilkes Co., Ga. They were of the Baptist faith.

Pullen, William - Continued. Their chn. William Jr. born 1789,
M. Mary Brooks died 1883 in Ala. Martha (Patsy) B. 8 Aug. 1790 M.
Joseph Hickman died 30 Nov. 1878. Sarah b. 1797 m. James Rowan in 1813,
died 1863. Mary (Polly Ann) m. Samuel Rowan 2 Dec. 1823. Clarissa
m. Jesse Hickman 29 Jan. 1822. Elizabeth b. 1808 in Ga. m. Richard
Tankersley. Mary Pullen applied for a widow pension in 1851 and gave
her age as 86 yrs. William Pulliam moved his family to Ala. in 1817.
He bought land in 1819 in "Jones Valley." He died the 4 April 1845
and is said to be the first Rev. soldier buried in Jefferson County,
Ala. He was in his 87 yr. when he died.

PULLIAM, JOHN Box 74 Pack 1799. Probate Judge Office. Abbeville,
S. C. I John Pulliam Senr. of Abbeville Dist. being of sound mind yet
very sick. After my just debts are paid, I lend unto my beloved wife
Sarah during her natural life the tract of land whereon I now live also
the land I bought from Robert Pollard, except the land I have given to
my son Thomas. I also lend to my wife during her natural life negroes
Bob, Barnett, Rose, Lucy, Violet, Amy and her three children Moses,
Pegg and Jim. I give to my son John one negro man Peter, also a horse
and saddle, one cow and calf and one feather bed, all which he has now.
Also part of the land I bought from Robert Pollard at the death of my
wife, his part described. I give to my dtr. Martha Fooshe Ł40
Virginia money also one cow and calf, one feather bed, one mare, saddle
and bridle, all of which is now in her possession. As my dtr. Betsey
Gholson is dead and left three chn. Nancy, Zachariah and Benjamin. My
will is at my wife death, two Ł for each to be put on interest by my
executor and paid them as they come of age or marry. I give to my
dtr. Nancy Ball Ł40 Virginia money, a feather bed and furniture, a
horse, seven hundred weight of prok and eighteen bushels of corn, all
now in her possession. I give to my dtr. Mary, one negro named Jenney
also one feather bed, a large chest, a mare called pleasure fly, a
cow and calf. I desire my dtr. Mary should have a comfortable room in
my house and use of 50 acres of the land I have given to my son
Zachary, during the time she remains unmarried and no longer. I give
to my son Thomas one negro boy named Amos also a mare and colt and
saddle he now calls his, one feather bed and furniture, some land adj.
Henry Johnson, Robert Pollard, Standfield, and the Calhoon line. I
give to my dtr. Rhoda, three hogheads of tobacco, one feather bed and
furniture, one negro boy named Will. I give to my dtr. Judy Lewis
Chiles, one negro girl named Phillis, also a horse and saddle, one cow
and calf. I give to my dtr. Fanny, one negro girl named Brenah and
Ł40 in cash, also one horse and saddle, one feather bed, one cow and
calf. I give to my dtr. Anna one negro girl named Nell, also a horse
and saddle, one feather bed, a cow and calf. I give to my son Zachary
one negro boy called Ned, also a horse and saddle, one feather bed.
At the death of my wife, he to get the rest of my land whereon the
house now stands with the mills. I appoint my wife executrix and my
son Zachary and son in law Charles Fooshe and my friend John Waller
executors. Dated 2 May 1798. Wit: John Weatherford, D. Mitchel,
Fielder Wells. Signed: John Pulliam. Recorded 11 June 1798. An
inventory was made 12 July 1798 by Nathan Sims, Robert Pollard, George
Heard, Negroes named: Bob, Barnet, Rose, Amy and 3 chn. Moses, Peggy
and Juno. Vilet, Lucy, Ano, Ned, Jany, Phillis, Nelly, Bruno. In the
account of 19 Nov. 1812, Mary Pulliam was decd. and John Pulliam was
admnr. Also Nancy Gholson was the wife of Nick Sisson.

PULLIAM, SARAH Box 109 Pack 3089. Probate Judge Office. Abbeville, S. C. I Sarah Pulliam of Abbeville Dist. being of sound mind,
yet being sick and sencable[sic]. I give to my son John $100 (which
he has) and one feather bed. I give to my dtr. Martha Fooshe $100
(which she has) and four bales of cotton. I give to my dtr. Betsey
Gholston decd. and left three chn. viz, Nancy, Zachary, and Benjamin
I give to each $50 to be paid by my executor. I give to my dtr. Nancy
Ball $100 (which she has) and a negro woman Genney. I give to my dtr.
Rhoda Pulliam $100 (which she has) and one bale of cotton, and a negro
girl Nicy during her life, at her death I give said negro Nicy to John
Coalman (son of Fanney Coalman). I give to my son Zachary $100 (which
he has) and one negro Nitt, and my cupboard and two pair of fire dogs
and tongs. I give to my dtr. Juda L. Chiles $100 (which she has) and

Pulliam, Sarah - Continued. one feather bed and furniture and
two bales of cotton. I give to my dtr. Fanney Coalman $100 (which she
has) and one black mare named Peg, one feather bed and furniture and
one bale of cotton. I give to my dtr. Anney Cooper $100 (which she has)
and one chest of drawers and four bales of cotton. After my just are
paid I desire the balance be equally divided among my children. I
appoint my son James Pulliam and son in law Peter H. Coalman executors.
Dated 4 Aug. 1812. Wit: Robert A. Cunningham, Dudley Richardson,
Champness X Turner. Signed: Sarah X Pulliam. Proved on oath of
Dudley Richardson before Talo. Livingston Ord. Abb. Dist. this 5 Sept.
1812.

PULLIAM, ZACHARY Box 75 #800. Probate Judge Office. Pickens,
S. C. I Zachary C. Pulliam of Pickens Dist. do ordain and publish
this as my last will and testament. I desire that after the payment
of all my just debts the balance of my estate be distributed among the
widows and orphans of the members of the Keowee Rifles" as to my
executor he shall think fit and proper. I appoint James E. Hagood
executor. Dated this 16 July 1861. Wit: W. N. Craig, Js. Wickliffe,
J. W. L. Cary. Signed: Z. C. Pulliam. Proven this 16 Feb. 1863.

PULLIAM, ZACHARY Box 72 Pack 1762. Probate Judge Office. Abbeville, S. C. Abbeville Dist. I Zachary Pulliam being in a low state
of health, but of sound mind and memory, etc. My will and desire is
that my estate be kept together until my youngest son Robert comes of
age. As my sons come of age or marry, each shall have two servicable
young negroes, a horse saddle, bridle and a feather bed and furniture.
When my son Robert come of age, I desire my negroes be put into equal
lots as there may be legatees. I desire that Robert A. Cunningham
shall act in the place of myself for my sister Anna Cooper. I appoint
my friend Robert A. Cunningham and Robert Turner and my son John Pulliam
when he come to the age of eighteen yrs. executors. Dated 4 Dec. 1820.
Wit: John Brown, Margret X Cunningham, John Pulliam. Signed Zachary
Pulliam. Proved on oath of John Brown before Moses Taggart, Ord. this
2 Jan. 1826. Same date, Qualified Robt. A. Cunningham, John Pulliam
Exors. The inventory was made 31 Jan. 1826 by William Calhoun, William
Fooshe, Elihu Creswell, John N. Sample. In the expenses paid for 1830
paid Thos. B. Pollard and W. B. Cooper for tuition of Z & R $33.60.

PULLUM, JOHN Deed Book C-1, Page 216. Clerk of Court Office.
Pickens, S. C. Pickens Dist. This indenture made this 26 Dec. 1833
between Grief Williams of Forsyth County, Ga. and John Pullum of
Habersham County, Ga. in consideration of $1600. to me paid by said
John Pullum, have bargained, sold and released three tracts of land
lying on Tugaloo River, viz, one tract known as the county survey
containing 200 acres, another tract granted to James Drummonda containing 150 acres, another tract that I purchased from John Barton
containing 40 acres. The land is where I formerly lived. Wit:
William C. Wyly, Young Davis. Signed: Grief Williams. Proved on oath
of Young Davis before Wm. Barton, J.Q. this 3 Oct. 1836.

PURSLEY, DAVID E. Pack 355. Clerk of Court Office. Abbeville,
S. C. Abbeville Dist. In Equity to the Honr. the Chancellors: Your
oratrix Emeline Pursley of this Dist. sheweth that on the 26 Nov.
1861 her husband David E. Pursley departed this life intestate. At
the time of his death he was possessed with a tract of land, lying on
Calhoun Creek, containing 235 acres. Bounded by land of Andrew
Gillespie, J. L. Johnson, James Pursley, Samuel Lockridge and others.
Leaving as heirs and distributees your oratrix and chn. Mary E.
Pursley and Narcissa L. Pursley who are under the age of twenty one.
Your oratrix sheweth that on the 14 Dec. 1861 admnr. of the goods and
chattels was granted to James Pursley. Your oratrix is informed and
believes that the personal est. will be more than sufficient to pay all
the debts. Filed 10 Nov. 1862.

PRATER'S Pack 51 #2. Clerk of Court Office. Pickens, S. C.
Pendleton Dist. We John, Joseph, Aaron, Josiah and Jeremiah Prater
(sons of Philip Prater decd.) of the Dist. aforesaid. In consideration
of $184.00 paid by Henry Hendrick of the same Dist. Have granted

Prater's - Continued. bargained, sold, and released a tract of
land containing 83 acres on waters of 18 mile Creek. It being part of
101 acres granted to Robert M. Cann and conveyed to Philip Prater.
Adj. land of James Chapman and Thomas Garven. Dated this 21 Dec.
1820. Wit: John Chapman, James Hendricks. Signed: John Prater,
Joseph Prater, Aaron Prater, Josiah Prater, Jeremiah Prater. Proved
on oath of James Howard? before John Clayton, J.P. this 5 Nov. 1821.
Recorded the same day.

PRATER, ELIZA A. Box 25 #297. Probate Judge Office. Pickens,
S. C. Eliza A. Prater a dtr. of Richard Hallum decd. whose will was
proven 8 Jan. 1849 in Pickens Dist. Probably the wife of J. B. Prater
who recd. a legacy of $100.00 from said est.

PRATER, JOHN Box 3 #24. Probate Judge Office. Pickens, S. C.
Est. admnr. 7 Nov. 1831 by John Couch, Reuben Baker, Wm. Nimons who
are bound unto James H. Dendy, Ord. in the sum of $1800.00. Cit. pub.
at Shiloh Meeting house. Mentions that John Prater was late of Ala.
Expend: Couch for going to Columbia 28 days, self and horse $28.00.
Paid Thos. Montgomery for traveling to Columbia and back $5.00.

PRATER, JOHN Box 26 #313. Probate Judge Office. Pickens, S.C.
Est. admnr. 1 Sept. 1851 by John A. Gunter, F. N. Garvin, Robt. F.
Morgan are bound unto Wm. D. Steele, Ord. in the sum of $150.00. John
Prater was of State of Ala. died in Benton Co., Ala. John A. Gunter
a son-in-law.

PRATER, HENRY Box 81 #859. Probate Judge Office. Pickens, S.C.
Est. admnr. 26 Jan. 1865 by Mary Prater, Robert F. Morgan, are bound
unto W. E. Holcombe, Ord. in the sum of $2,000. Est. admnr. again 15
Nov. 1864 by Robert A. Thompson, C.E.P.D. in the sum of $1,000. Exp.
1 Jan. 1866 paid Jeremiah Prater $84.50. Paid Eliza Prater $42.87
(loose papers) 16 Jan. 1854 Philip Prater of Rutherford Co., Tenn.
Appointed Austin Prater his Atty. to receive from Jeremiah Prater or
any other person his share from est. of Philip or Susan Prater decd. of
Pendleton Dist., S. C.

PRATER, MARGARET Box 27 #325. Probate Judge Office. Pickens,
S. C. Margaret Prater decd. of Pickens Dist. est. was admnr. 27 Aug.
1852 by Miles M. Norton who was bound unto the Ordinary, in the sum of
$250.00. Margaret Prater was late of Ala. On 4 Jan. 1851 Samuel
Fraser and Bethshaba Fraser of Hall Co., Ga. appointed Garner Evans
of Pickens Dist. their atty. to receive their distributive share of
the est. of Margaret Prater decd.

PRATT FAMILY Tombstone inscriptions taken from Lindsay Cemetery.
2 miles South of Due West, Abbeville County, S. C.
Elizabeth Jones, wife of Joseph Pratt, died 10 Nov. 1860. 91st year
of age.
Joseph Pratt, died 7 April 1826, 58th year of age.
Thomas Pratt, died 13 April 1826, 26 year of age.
Joseph Pratt, died 22 April 1826, 23 year of age.
John Pratt Jr., born 20 Aug. 1812, died 25 June 1849.
Cornelia Pratt, age 15 yrs.
Langden Pratt, age 21 yrs.
Nancy N. Pratt died 7 Oct. 1872, age 57 years.
Sarah Pratt, born 26 Nov. 1790, died 25 April 1840
James Pratt, born 13 March 1788, died 14 Sept. 1828.
John Lawrence, son of James and S. C. Pratt born 27 Oct. 1854, died
8 Jan. 1858.
Infant son of James and S. C. Pratt born 28 Nov. 1858.
James Alex, age 14 months son of Capt. James and Susan Pratt
Sue A. Pratt, born 18 Jan. 1848, died 15 May 1875.

PRATT, "MINORS" Pack 238. Clerk of Court Office. Abbeville, S.C.
Abbeville Dist. To the Honr. the Chancellors: The petition of Mary
Pratt sheweth that her late husband James L. Pratt has died leaving
his children James W. L. Pratt about three years old, Louisa Jane Pratt
about one year old. These have in common five negroes to wit, Wesby,

Pratt, "Minors" - Continued. Jane and her children, Thom, Milton
and William with about four thousand dollars. Your petitioner prays
to be made guardian of his said children. Filed 2 Nov. 1859.

PRATT, WILLIAM A. Bill for Injunction. #198. Clerk of Court
Office. Abbeville, S. C. In Equity, To the Chancellors: Your orator
Marshall Sharp sheweth, that William A. Pratt departed this life in
Sept. 1863 being killed at the battle of Chickawauga?. He died leaving
in full force and unrevoked his last will and testament. He left a
widow Mary Z. Pratt now married to Lucian K. Robertson, but no children.
The widow was named executrix, did not qualify, your orator was named
executor, and did qualify, and took upon himself the execution of said
will. The widow who married Lucian K. Robertson has moved to the State
of Texas. Your orator sold the personal and real estate in the month
of November 1863 on credit of twelve months, at what is known as
Confederate prices. Some is still uncollected, what is collected was
in Confederate money. Over three thousand dollars is the sale of
negroes and cannot be collected in consequence of military orders. The
return of said sale is on file in Your office. Under the circumstances
the debts of the estate are not paid. Your orator has offered to pay
some debts in Confederate money, and his offer has been refused. Your
orator will ever pray. Filed 8 April 1868.

PRATT, JOHN N. Family records and a diary as recorded by Mr.
Pratt from 1894 to 1916. (Only genealogical records given here, all
very interesting.)
Joseph Pratt was born 1 Jan. 1768, died 7 April 1826.
Joseph Pratt and Elizabeth Jones were married 15 April 1793.
Samuel Young and Emma Pratt were married 31 March 1812.
William Young and Sarah Pratt were married 29 Jan. 1815.
John Pratt (my grandfather) and Nancy N. Harkness were married 16 Feb.
1832.
Thomas Crawford and Caroline Wood were married 5 Feb. 1829.
Caroline Wood was an adopted daughter of Joseph Pratt.
Joseph Pratt was born 1 Jan. 1768 and died 7 April 1826.
Elizabeth Pratt was born 16 March 1770 and died 10 Nov. 1860.
Emma Pratt was born 1 Feb. 1794 and died 30 April 1869.
Sarah Pratt was born 18 Feb. 1796 and died 22 Jan. 1866.
William Pratt was born 27 Sept. 1798 and died 26 Jan. 1863.
Thomas Pratt was born 13 Dec. 1800 and died 13 April 1826.
Joseph Pratt was born 24 Feb. 1823 and died 22 April 1826.
Mary Pratt was born 3 July 1809 and died 13 June 1816
John Pratt was born 20 Aug. 1812 and died 24 June 1849.
Nancy Pratt was born 24 July 1820 and died 1 April 1826
Joseph Pratt mother was Emma Hage before her marriage.
Elizabeth Jones' mother was Sarah Britian.
My grandfather John Pratt died 3 Oct. 1872.
John Pratt and Nancy N. Harkness were married 16 Feb. 1832.
T. Rufus Pratt was born 10 May 1835 and died 25 Feb. 1879.
P. Hassie Pratt was born 23 July 1838 and died 23 Oct. 1898.
S. Langdon Pratt was born 26 Oct. 1840 and died 5 June 1862 (in army)
E. __ Pratt was born 25 Feb. 1843 and died 15 June 1857.
Joseph J. H. Pratt was born 1 Feb. 1845 and died 20 Dec. 1913.
Robert M. Pratt (my father) was born 10 March 1847 and died 20 Dec.
1913.
William L. Pratt was born 1 March 1849 and died 29 April 1910.
P. Minerva Pratt was born 16 May 1833 and died 3 Feb. 1887.
Robert M. Pratt (my father) and Jane A. Bowen was married 3 Oct. 1867
(first)
John N. Pratt (me) was born 9 May 1870.
W. Walter Pratt was born 13 May 1872.
Jesse P. Pratt was born 29 March 1874.
James A. Pratt died 9 Jan. 1876.
W. Walter Pratt died 24 July 1901.
Jesse P. Pratt died 10 July 1948.
Robert M. Pratt and Maggie P. McAlister were married 16 Nov. 1876
(second)
R. Lewis Pratt was born 18 Dec. 1877 and died __ Feb. 1926.
Rosa E. Pratt was born 6 March 1880 and died 13 June 1914.

Pratt, John N. - Continued.
Charles M. Pratt was born 10 Sept. 1882 and died __ Oct. 1916.
Livy E. Pratt, Pratt was born 2 March 1890 and died 14 Sept. 1933.
Lilly Pratt was born 9 March 1894 and died ___.
Robert M. Pratt was born 10 March 1847 and died 20 Dec. 1913.
Maggie R. Pratt was born ___ and died 29 Feb. 1915.
John N. Pratt and L__ Downing were married 12 Oct. 1892.
Claude A. Pratt was born 29 Oct. 1892, married Mary Anderson 28 June
1919.
J. Marion Pratt was born 28 June 1894, married Flora Kelly 29 Dec. 1921.
Burts B. Pratt was born 18 April 1896, married Frances Boggs 9 June
1923.
W. Cecil Pratt was born 18 April 1898 married Daist[?] Sawford 4 Dec.
1921.
Robert Pratt was born 25 Jan. 1901 and died 28 Jan. 1901.
second marriage
John N. Pratt and Jessie L. Parker were married 27 March 1906.
Annie Pratt was born 8 Sept. 1904 and died 17 __ 1906.
M. Elizabeth Pratt was born 5 July 1906.
Rosa Lee Pratt was born 5 Feb. 1908.
Jane B. Pratt was born 3 March 1911.
Jessie L. Pratt died 13 March 1942,
L. Annie Pratt died 13 March 1942.
In his recollections, dated 9 Jan. 1945, age almost 70 yrs. olf age
(45 page) John N. Pratt mother died 9 Jan. 1856 and was buried in
Shiloh Cemetery. In the spring Aunt Ophelia Mann (a sister) was
buried. Later Uncle Enoch Bowen, a brother took typhoid fever and
fell asleep. Three in six months from one family. (his mothers and
her brother and sister.) In Nov. Pa married Miss Maggie A. McAlister
from beyond Iva, S. C. A double wedding. W. D. Mann married Miss
Mattie making him an uncle by both marriage.

Diary of John N. Pratt
13 Sept. 1894, B. L. Young buried. Had typhoid fever. Funeral by Rev.
J. J. Farmer.
4 Jan. 1895, J. W. Brooks buried about 80 yrs. old. Funeral by Rev.
Willson.
12 March 1895, J. P. Pratt and Gussie Armstrong married.
3 Oct. 1895, Ira Carwile buried, had typhoid fever, funeral by Rev.
J. J. Farmer.
24 Nov. 1895, Rev. J. J. Farmer preached farewell sermon at Little
River Church.
6 Jan. 1896, Clarence Haddon buried, Relapes from measles. Funeral
by Rev. Arial.
5 April 1896, H. Robinson buried, funeral by M. Mgee.
26 Aug. (no year) wife of L. P. Harkness buried. By Rev. Arial.
23 Nov. 1897, Mrs. W. P. McCarter my aunt buried, funeral by Rev. Synder.
5 July (no year) Rev. P. G. Hooper, pastor of Little River and wife
died from fever within a few hours of each other.
16 June 1900, R. Lewis Pratt, brother ordained deacon of Little River
Church.
11 March 1901, P. Noble Bell buried, funeral by Rev. W. D. Moore.
24 July 1901, W. W. Pratt brother buried, funeral by Rev. Moore.
5 Aug. 1901, Mrs. John Pratt buried, funeral by Rev. Moore.
13 Aug. 1901, Mrs. T. J. Bowen buried, funeral by Rev. Moore.
27 May 1902, John N. Pratt and Jessie L. Parker married.
24 Oct. 1906, Rosa E. Pratt and Dr. D. J. Barton married.
23 July 1907, Moses L. Ashley buried about 90 yrs. of age.
11 April 1908, J. A. Busbys baby burned to death.
17 Sept. 1908, T. J. Bowen and Widow Cochran married.
1 Jan. 1908, S. S. Callaham accidentally killed his wife.
31 Oct. 1908, Thad Gambrell killed by R. R. train near Honea Path.
24 Nov. 1908, Miss Ashley died.
16 Dec. 1908, Wickliffe McCarter and Emma Stokes were married.
25 Dec. 1908, Jim P. Carwile and Josie Martin were married.
30 Dec. 1908, Calvin Crawford and Miss Price were married.
8 Jan. 1909, Jeff Winn buried, pneumonia.
16 Feb. 1909, Lee Winn brother of Jeff buried, pneumonia.
14 Feb. 1909, Mrs. Sarah G. Callaham buried, acute indigestion.

Pratt, John N. - Continued

6 Oct. 1909, Norris Wakefield and Laura Bowen were married.
13 Oct. 1909, S. F. Ellis and Eula Kay were married.
8 Dec. 1909, Furman Bowen and Lillian McCarter were married.
22 Dec. 1909, Will Crawford and Jeanette Pruitt were married.
19 Jan. 1910, Rev. O. Y. Bonner of Due West died from pneumonia.
5 Jan. 1910, Frank Arnold and Nellie Parker.
27 Mar. 1910, Mrs. Reuben Clinkscales buried.
27 Mar. 1910, Henry Davis and Essie Clinkscales were married.
17 Apr. 1910, Marion, dtr. of J. P. Pratt died, pneumonia.
17 Apr. 1910, Will Young died, pneumonia.
29 Apr. 1910, Wm. L. Pratt an uncle died, living at Fountain Inn.
5 May 1910, Edgar Hawthorne and Carrie McWhorter were married.
25 May 1910, Jim Erwin and Julia Branyon were married.
25 July 1910, J. P. Parker buried, age 73.
15 Jan. 1911, A. F. Carwile Sr. died age 82 yrs.
22 Jan. 1911, Arthur Alewine and Ethel Williams were married.
16 Feb. 1911, Jim McAdams and Vira Bowen were married.
17 July 1911, E. H. Pennel died, perforation of bowels.
29 June 1911, Manly L. McWhorter and Lindsay Grumbles were married.
8 July 1911, Mr. John Seawright died.
24 Sept. 1911, Blanche Pruitt and Bob Crawford were married.
29 Sept. 1911, Mrs. A. H. Patterson, buried.
23 Dec. 1911, J. A. Brownlee died, totally blind for good while.
21 Nov. 1912, W. P. McCarter died, pneumonia and abscess.
9 Feb. 1913. J. N. Ashley wife died confinement. No delivery.
17 April 1913, Mr. J. O. Pruitt dropped dead.
27 Apr. 1913, Charley Haddon, colored, died rather suddenly.
13 June 1913, P. T. Alewine wife died.
14 Feb. 1914, J. O. MClain died, buried the 15th, age about 70 yrs.
17 Feb. 1914, J. G. Loner died in Columbia, Thyroid buried the 18th
1 Mar. 1914, P. C. Ellis and Belle Clinkscales were married.
1 Mar. 1914, W. N. Ellis and Lula Young were married.
25 Mar. 1914, Mrs. Bernice McWhorter died.
2 Mar. 1914, Grady Young and Dora Temple were married.
15 Mar. 1914, Henry Ashley died in Columbia hospital, buried the 17th
at Little River.
12 Apr. 1914, Eli Starks, colored died.
19 Apr. 1914, Dr. John H. Bell died about 80 yrs.
6 May 1914, J. C. Clinkscales and Reba Caldwell were married.
12 June 1914, Mrs. Dr. Barton sister buried at Hartwell, Ga.
2 Aug. 1914, B. Loner died in Calif, with fever.
20 Sept. 1914, Dale Ferguson and Denifie Pruitt were married.
24 Dec. 1914, Laurense Clinkscales and Mary Gunter were married.
27 Jan. 1915, Tom Eakin died from pneumonia.
3 Feb. 1915, Mr. Zeke Norris died from pneumonia, about 80 yrs.
21 Feb. 1915, J. C. Pruitt buried.
28 Feb. 1915, Ma. died at 11:42 a.m.
1 Mar. 1915, All went to burial except little ones. Rev. Jamie
Pressley, preacher
15 Mar. 1915, Emma Crawford baby born (not named).
24 May 1915, Mr. Jim Busby died.
23 June 1915, T. C. Brownlee died, he from Due West.
20 Jan. 1916, Josh Ashley and Mannie M Whorter were married.
22 Mar. 1916, Cousin Vessie Harkness buried at Shiloh.
26 April 1916, Bessie Ashley and Mr. Wheeler were married.
30 Apr. 1916, Mr. Joshua Ashley buried in eveing about 3000 present
2 May 1916, John C. Clinkscales buried.
18 May 1916, Spent night in Asheville, N.C. at Sou. Bapt. Conv. spent
night with cousin Rev. Jno. L. Ray of Gaysville, Ala.
7 June 1916, L. O. Robinson buried at Little River.
9 June 1916, Mrs. Downing, boys grandmother buried. Good Water, Ala.
22 June 1916, Went to Due West to meet Rev. J. L. Ray of Gaylesville,
Ala. His first visit here, his grandfather John Carwile married my
great Aunt, Eater Bowen sister of G. W. Bowen. Moved to Ala. in 1860.
31 July 1916, Harvey Clinkscales, colored, died last night.
10 Sept. 1916, Jas. B. Carwole died from fever, buried about 4:00 p.m.
11 Sept. 1916, Mrs. J. C. Alewine died at 7:30 and buried in eveing
at 4:00 p.m.

Pratt, John N. - Continued.
3 Oct. 1916, 24 years ago went to Ashland, Ala. to marry Annie Dowing at noon.
12 Oct. 1916, 24 years since I first married.
15 Oct. 1916, brother Charley died at a.m. of hemorrhage from lungs, died in a few minutes. Brother Charley buried at 4:00 p.m.
11 Nov. 1916, MGregg Loner and Irene Moore were married.

PRESSLY, ANN Pack 1186. Probate Judge Office. Anderson, S. C. Est. admnr. 28 Aug. 1849 by William O'Briant, James H. Wiles and Ibzan Walters are bound unto the ordinary in the sum of $1200. She the widow of David Pressly. Ann Pressly drew a Revolutionary pension. Wm. O'Briant wife Jane M. was the sister of Ann Pressly.

PRESSLY, DAVID Pack 451 #3. Clerk of Court Office. Abbeville, S. C. I David Pressly of Abbeville Dist. in consideration of $102.00 to me paid by John Foster of the same Dist. have granted, sold and released, all that tract of land containing 102 acres lying on Fraser Creek a branch of Norrises Creek adj. land of John Stuart and John Foster. Dated this 30 Sept. 1818. Wit: Jno. Devlin, Sarah X Cochram[?]. Signed: David Presley.

PRESTON, ISAAC Deed Book E, Page 188-189. Mesne Conveyance Office. Greenville, S. C. This indenture made the 12 Aug. 1798 between Isaac Preston of Greenville Dist. and William Taylor of the same Dist. in consideration of Twerd? [word not plain] hundred dollars paid by said Taylor, hath bargained, sold a tract of land, lying and being in Greenville County on branches of Enoree River, containing 500 acres. Being the same granted unto Uriah Conner, originally, beginning at poplar on a branch whereon the old meeting house stands and running to Preston and Henry Chambles line. Wit: Isaac X Low, Ezekrel X Preston, Abuham McAfee. Signed: Isaac Preston. Proved on oath of Isaac Low before Robert McAfee, Esq. this 26 April 1799.

PREWITT, DUDLEY Deed Book W, Page 252. Clerk of Court Office. Anderson, S. C. Bond from Dudley Prewitt of Pickens Co., Ala. in the sum of $300 to be paid by me unto Alfred M. Carpenter. If ever Josiah Prewitt or the heirs of Solomon Prewitt make any claim whatever upon the tract of land owned by Dudly Prewitt decd. now conveyed to said Carpenter by the rest of the heirs of Dudley Prewitt decd. Then the above obligation to be null and void. This 27 Dec. 1838. Wit: E. Mitchell, W. Magee. Signed: Dudley Prewitt. Proved on oath of Wm. Magee before Wm. Acker, J.Q. this 25 March 1839. Recd. this 26 March 1839.

PREWITT, DUDLY Deed Book W, Page 250. Clerk of Court Office. Anderson, S. C. State of Alabama, Pickens County. This indenture made the 27 Dec. 1838 between Austin Prewitt Admnr. of the est. of Dudley Prewitt decd. and Dudley Prewitt Junr., Stephen Prewitt, Bennett Prewitt, Micajah Prewitt, Elizabeth Pearson and John Prewitt all lawful heirs of Dudly Prewitt. In consideration of $700 to them paid by Alfred M. Carpenter, have granted, bargained, sold and released all that tract of land, lying and being in Pendleton Dist. on waters of Hebcoopy Creek. Adj. land of Philmon Waters, Richard Lancaster and John Long. Containing 311 acres. Wit: E. Mitchell, Harrison Latimer. Signed: Auset Prewit, Dudly Prewit, Stephen Prewit, Micajah X Prewit, John Prewit, and Elizabeth Pierson. Proved on oath of all the above signed, before me William Sullivant, J.P. this 13 Nov. 1838.

PRICE A letter from W. W. Price of Crystal Springs, Miss. Dated 10 Oct. 1958.
Joseph Price born 1775 in S.C., died 1856 in Miss.
Sarah Wilson Price born 1779 in N.C., died 1858 in Miss.
Children:
Wilson Price born 1799 in S.C.; Eleanor Price born 1802 in S. C., wife of Cader Price; Charner Price born 1803 in S.C., W. W. Price grandfather; John Price born 1812 in S.C.; William Price born 1815 in S.C.; Joseph Price born 1822 in S.C.; Other daughters, Hannah, Sarah, Charlotte, and Mary. Family moved to Miss. between 1815-1820. Lived

Price - Continued. in Chester, Lancaster and Edgefield Counties, S. C.

PRICE, JOSEPH Deed Book 27, Page 456. Probate Judge Office. Edgefield, S. C. I Joseph Price of Edgefield Dist. in consideration of $400 to me paid by William Robinson of the same Dist. have granted, sold, bargain and release unto said Williams, all that of land containing 260 acres in Edgefield Dist. on waters of Catfish and Middle Creeks, waters of Savannah River, in four different surveys, one of 104 acres granted to Thomas Robinson, the 3 April 1785 whereon Robinson now lives, another tract of 25 acres part of a tract granted to Charles Ashley, then conveyed to Charles Fenley from Fenley to Jacob Clacker from Clacker to Joseph Price. Another tract of 31 acres, being part of a 300 acre survey granted to David Calleyham the 17 May 1774. From him conveyed to William Rennolds, and from Rennolds to Milly Peeket now Milly Seals and from Seals to Joseph Price. Another tract of 100 acres franted to John Holsonbade, being part of survey of 200 acres, being the East part adj. William Robinson, West Cooks line. Dated this 12 March 1805. Wit: Thomas Barrett, Travis Hill. Signed: Joseph X Price and Judith X Price. I John Lyon, J.Q. did this day examine Judy Price the wife of Joseph Price, who renounce and forever relinquished all interest and rights of dower on the above land. Dated this 3 June 1806. Proved on oath of Thomas Barrett before John Longmere, J.P. this 9 Aug. 1805. Recd. 23 March 1807.

PRICE, JOSEPH T. Pack 3221. Clerk of Court Office. Abbeville, S. C. In Equity, to the Honr. the Chancellors: Your orator Berry Deason, sheweth, that Joseph T. Price of Abbeville Dist. in Dec. 1845 departed this life intestate, leaving as his only heirs and distributees a widow Matilda Price and four chn. to wit. Elizabeth the wife of your orator, Martha the wife of John Holloway, Thomas S. Price and William N. Price, all of this Dist. except your orator who resides in Edgefield Dist. All are of full age except Thomas S. Price and William N. Price who are minors. A few days after the death of Joseph T. Price, in the month of Dec. 1845. his dtr. Elizabeth the wife of your orator, departed this life, leaving your orator and two chn. to wit. Matilda about two yrs. old, and Jane about two months old. Also in the month of Dec. 1845 a few days after the death of Elizabeth Deason, wife of your orator, Martha the widow of Joseph T. Price, also departed this life intestate. At the time of the death of Joseph T. Price, he was possessed with a tract of land, lying on Little Buffalow Creek waters of Little River, containing 585 acres, adj. land of Daniel New, Edward Collier, William Beasly and Levi Fulmer. The admnr. on the est. of Joseph T. Price was granted to Little Berry Freeman Esq. The sale of the personal effects are over the debts of the est. Therefore your orator prays for a partition of the real estate. Filed: 30 May 1846.

PRICE, JOSEPH W. Box 143 #11. Probate Judge Office. Pickens, S. C. I Joseph Price of Hurricane Township, County of Pickens, S. C. being of sound mind and memory. First I desire all my debts and funeral expenses be paid. Second, I give all the rest, residue and remainder of my personal property, also one piece of land, lying on Keowee River adj. land of Robt. E. Steele, W. E. Nimmons, D. H. Alexander containing 350 acres to my beloved wife Elizar J. Price, to have the above property during her natural life. At her death I give unto my dtr. Rachel F. E. J. Cox the South portion of the above mentioned real estate, I also give to my dtr. Mattie S. M. E. Price the Northern part of the above land. I give to my son Joseph S. H. Price $5.00. I appoint A. John Boggs my executor. Dated 8 Dec. 1903. Wit: John W. Stewart, B. D. Mauldin, Robert Stewart. Signed: Joseph W. X Price. Filed 12 Feb. 1904.

PRICE, RICE Vol 8 Page 135. Probate Judge Office. Charleston, S. C. I Rice Price of Charles Town, S. C. Merchant, being very sick and weak in body, but of sound disposing mind, memory and understanding. First I desire my just debts and funeral expenses be paid and satisfied. I give to my wife Jane Price two slaves of her choice, for her own use forever. After my debts are paid, I desire a sufficient sum be

Price, Rice - Continued. raised out of my est. that the interest
will amount to £400 annually, this amount to be paid my wife quarterly,
half yearly or annually as she shall choose for the term of her
natural life. I desire my executors to sell and dispose of all my
messuage[?], land tenements and hereditaments in Charles Town and else-
where, and put monies, notes and securities out at interest for the
benefit of my only son Samuel Price. If my wife think proper to return
to England, her passage shall be paid from the estate, fi she choose
to remain in the province she may choose such beds and furniture with
kitchen utensils as she desires. My son to be bound to some merchant
in Charles Town until he shall be of full age. At the death of my wife
my son Samuel shall have the whole of the estate remaining over. I
appoint my wife Jane Price, Executrix and John Remington and Hopkin
Price executors and guardian over my son Samuel estate during his
minority. Dated 10 Nov. 1757. Wit: David Dott, John Cart, Richd.
Muncreef. Signed: Rice Price. Proved the 25 Nov. 1757. Same time
qualified Hopkin Price and John Remington exors and Jane Price Exorx.

PRICE, SAMUEL Deed Book 39, Page 332. Probate Judge Office.
Edgefield, S. C. I Samuel Price of Edgefield Dist. in consideration
of $200 to me paid by Pen[?] Price of the same Dist. have granted,
sold, bargained and released all that tract of land lying and being in
Edgefield Dist. on Rocky Branch and Stephen Creek, waters of Savannah
River. Containing 103 acres, as shown by plat annexed with the excep-
tion of 3 acres sold to Allen Baily from the North West corner. Dated
11 Jan. 1823. Wit: Perry Holloway, Harmon P. Casper. Signed: Samuel
X Price. Proved on oath of Perry Holloway before William Thurmond,
J.Q. this 11 Jan. 1823. Recorded: 11 Jan. 1823.

PRICE, THOMAS Box 22 Pack 800. Probate Judge Office. Edgefield,
S. C. On the 31 Dec. 1821 William Robertson and Sandford Robertson
applied for letter of admnr. on the est. of Thomas Price decd. Admnr.
bond given to Wm. Robertson and Sandford Robertson with Bartholomew
Still and Nathan Fortner as security. Dated 14 Jan. 1822. An inventory
was made 16 Jan. 1822. by Joseph Cunningham, Joseph Jennings, Abiah
X Morgan. Sale held 28 Jan. 1822, buyers: Joseph Price Senr., Stephen
Tomkins, Senr., Christopher Cox, Richard Hardy, John Holsombeke,
Joseph Cunningham, William H. Nixon, Drury Morgan, Thomas H. Nixon,
Wily Price, John Tomkins, Elizabeth Searls, Evan Morgan, John Clagg,
Sarah Robertson, Hugh A. Nixon, Joseph Robertson, Michel Cox, Daniel
McKie, Hardy Robertson, Reuben Carpenter, Daniel Self, David Mims
Junr., James Still, Joseph Cook, Coleman Squire, Thomas Jennings,
Joseph Price Junr., Jeramiah Hardy, Richard Parks, John Holms, E. L.
Cartlege, Abraham Kilcrease, Catlet Corley, William Gray, John Chadwick,
Gilbert Fortner, Saml. Cartlege, Charles Nix, John Crawford, Learoy
Taylor, James Pickett, David George, Abner Clark, James George, Martin
Puckett, Charles Fendly, James Lockhart, J. Cartlege, Garret Freeman,
William Shannon, Charles Nix, Wily Freeman.

PRICE, WILLIAM SENR. Deed Book 29, Page 256. Probate Judge
Office. Edgefield, S. C. I William Price, Senr. of Edgefield Dist.
in consideration of $400 to me paid by Thomas Martin, Junr. of the same
Dist. have granted, sold and release unto said Thomas Martin, all that
tract of land containing 155 acres in two surveys, one tract of 80
acres, being part of a tract of 500 acres granted to Abram Biggs, one
other survey 75 acres, granted to James Simpson. Lying on Stevens
Creek and Savannah River. Adj. lands of William R. Morton, John Price,
Isiah Catledge. Dated this 5 Nov. 1808. Wit: Stephen White, Jr.,
Samuel Thomas. Signed: William Price (seal). I John Lyon, J.Q. did
this day examine Judith Price the wife of William Price Senr. and
renounce, release and forever relinquished all interest and right of
dower on the above land. Dated this 5 Nov. 1808. Proved on oath of
Stephen White before John Lyon, J.Q. this 5 Nov. 1808. Recorded the
7 Nov. 1808.

PRICE, WILLIAM Deed Book 41, Page 441. Probate Judge Office.
Edgefield, S. C. I William Price of Edgefield Dist. in consideration
of $600 paid to me by James Freeman of the same dist. hath granted,
bargained, sold and released all that tract of land containing 106

Price, William - Continued. acres, originally granted to James
Hagood (no date) lying on the dranes (drains) of Bedingfield and West-
coats Creek waters of Savannah River. Adj. land of Robert White,
McKinneys and on McCoys Road. Dated this 9 Feb. 1820. Wit: James
Tomkins, Saml. Freeman, Signed: William Price. Proved on oath of
Saml. Freeman, before William Thurmond, J.Q. this 29 Feb. 1820. I
William Thurmond one of the Justices of the Quorum did privately and
separately examine Nancy Price the wife of William Price who renounced,
released, and forever relinquished all interest and right of dower to
the above land. This 29 Feb. 1820. Recd. 13 March 1826.

PRICE, WILLIAM Deed Book 30, Page 495. Probate Judge Office.
Edgefield, S. C. I William Price of Edgefield Dist. in consideration
of $100 to me paid by Anthony Lowe of the same Dist. have granted,
sold, bargained and released all that tract of land containing 80 acres,
on Stephen Creek waters of Savannah River. Dated this 14 Sept. 1816.
Wit: Robt. Harrison, William Evans. Signed: William Price. I John
Lyon, J.Q. did this day examine Nancy Price the wife of William Price
and she renounced, and released and forever relinquished her interest
and right of dower on the above land. Dated this 14 Sept. 1816.
Proved on oath of William Evans before John Lyon, J.Q. this 14 Sept.
1816. Recorded 6 March 1819.

PRICE, WILLIAM JUNR. Deed Book 29, Page 266. Probate Judge
Office. Edgefield, S. C. I William Price, Junr. of Edgefield Dist.
in consideration of $250 to me paid by William Price Senr. of the same
Dist. have granted, bargained, sold and released unto said William
Price Senr. all that tract of land laid for and granted to Abram
Riggs, containing 75 acres (exclusion of a small part taken off the
South side by an old survey). Adj. land of Samuel Patterson, John
Price, and Richard McCary and the land whereon William Price, Senr.
now resides. Dated this 5 Nov. 1779. Wit: Stephen White Jr., Samuel
Thomas. Signed: William Price, Junr. I John Lyon, J.Q. this day did
Nancy Price the wife of William Price Junr. and renounce, release and
forever relinquished all interest and rights of dower on the above
land. Dated this 5 Nov. 1808. Proved on oath of Stephen White Junr.
before John Lyon, J.Q. this 5 Nov. 1808.

PRICE, WILLIAM Vol 6 Page 329. Probate Judge Office. Charleston,
S. C. I William Price of the Parish of Prince George in Craven County,
S. C. being of sound mind and memory. I give unto my wife Anny Ł25
currency. I give to my son Henry Ł25. I give to my son Samuel Ł25
to be paid twelve months after my death by my exor. I give to my
other two sons William and James all remaining part of my estate both
real and personal, to be equally divided between them. I appoint Thos.
Waitis my executor. Dated 11 March 1749. Wit: Saml. Jenkin, Thos.
(X) T. Brazzer, John (X) N. Neal. Signed: Wm. C. Price. Proved by
virtue of a dedimus the 9 April 1750. Same day qualified Thos. Watis
executor.

PRINCE, CAROLINE Pack 632 #5. Clerk of Court Office. Pickens,
S. C. Caroline Prince died in 1879 in Pickens County. Her heirs
were: W. M. Prince, Narcissa Prince, Elizabeth Prince.

PRINCE, CHARLES Box 121 #11. Probate Judge Office. Pickens,
S. C. Est. admnr. 19 Jan. 1893 by J. M. Stewart, M. F. Hester, W. B.
Singleton, E. M. McKissick who are bound unto J. B. Newberry, Ord. in
the sum of $300. Died Dec. 1892. Elizabeth Prince, F. M. Prince,
bought at sale.

PRINCE, EDWARD Box 83 #884. Probate Judge Office. Pickens,
S. C. Dated 4 Sept. 1865. This indenture is to show that I Edward
Prince do will unto Jencia Caroline Prince my home place where I now
live, containing 150 acres. But this place to remain mine as long as
I live binding lands of Micajah Alexander and Elisha Alexander and
W. R. Roberts and others, also one cow and calf and heifer. I do will
unto Jencia Caroline Prince nine head of hogs and one mare, the crop
that is growing with the household and kitchen furn iture. I will to
my brother John Prince one gun if he ever calls for it. I do will the

Prince, Edward - Continued. above named property, but to remain mine as long as I live and to do as I please with it. Wit: S. J. Adams, James X Sperman, S. C. Sperman. Signed: Edward X Prince. Rec. 2 Oct. 1865. Est. admnr. 30 April 1866 by Jencia C. Prince, Samuel J. Adams, Thomas M. Johnson, James C. Roberts who are bound unto W. E. Holcombe, Ord. in the sum of $1,000.

PRINCE, EDWARD SR. Pack 3357. Clerk of Court Office. Abbeville, S. C. To the Honr. the Judges of the Court of Equity: Your orators and oratrices Robert F. Black and his wife Hudson Prince and his wife and Edward Prince, Jr. all of Abbeville Dist. sheweth that Edward Prince Senr. late, made and duly executed his last will, by which after specific legacies to sundry persons he devised to his wife Lucy Prince all the remainder of his property for her support during her life time. After her death he directed it to be divided between Robert F. Black and his wife, Hudson Prince and his wife, Edward Prince Junr. and Joseph Prince and his four grand children ___ Clark. Your Orators sheweth that Lucy Prince is old and infirm and in her weakness has been induced by her son Joseph Prince to let him have the estate. He has disposed of considerable amount of the stock, negroes in the value of two thousand dollars. Your orators has applied to the widow, she will not believe the great waste which her son is making of the property. Filed this 18 Feb. 1820.

PRINCE, ELIZA Pack 220 #26. Clerk of Court Office. Pickens, S. C. On 26 March 1842 Eliza Prince took out a warrant for Ivory Howard charging him as being the father of her bastard child Hester Ann Prince.

PRINCE, JOHN Box 68 #731. Probate Judge Office. Pickens, S. C. Est. admnr. 11 Feb. 1863 by Rutha Prince widow, James E. Hagood, James Porter are bound unto W. E. Holcombe, Ord. in the sum of $1,000. Rutha Prince, Rebecca Prince, J. H. Amber, bought at sale.

PRINCE, JOHN Box 98 #1035. Probate Judge Office. Pickens, S.C. Died in 1862. Heirs Rutha Prince. chn: Williamson Prince of Pickens, Co., S. C., Margery Prince, Sarah Prince, Narcissa Prince, Rena Prince of Jackson County, N.C. Rutha Prince the widow died in June 186__ in Jackson Co., N.C. John Prince owned 174 acres in Pickens Co., S. C. on 12 Mile River adj. lands of Charles Prince, John P. Perritt and est. of R. Y. H. Griffin decd. In 1871 Margie was the wife of Chasteen Shelton of Jackson Co., N.C. Rena Prince was written Arrenia on one paper.

PRINCE, J. M. Box 18 #230. Probate Judge Office. Pickens, S.C. On 22 Jan. 1849 J. E. Hagood applied for letter of admnr. (no other papers.)

PRINCE, MARY Deed Book B, Page 10-11. Mesne Conveyance Office. Greenville, S. C. This indenture made the 13 Aug. 1788, between Mary Prince of Greenville Dist. and John McVay of the same Dist. inconsideration of £150 sterling. Paid by said John McVay, have granted, bargained, sold and released a tract of land lying on both forks of Enoree River, containing 530. Originally granted the 5 Dec. 1785 (to whom not named). Wit: John Tubb, Robert Prince. Signed: Mary X Prince. Proved in open Court on oath of Robert Prince the 16 Feb. 1789.

PRINCE, "MINORS" Box 7 #119. Probate Judge Office. Pickens, S. C. On 30 Jan. 1892 R. M. Prince, J. C. Watkins, Thos. L. Watkins are bound unto J. B. Newberry, Ord. in the sum of $187.66. R. M. Prince guardian for Norah F. Prince, Elmo M. Prince, Nina C. Prince minors under 21 yrs. R. M. Prince their father. Sarah Isabel Prince decd. their mother.

PRICHARD, W. L. Box 142 #8. Probate Judge Office. Pickens, S.C. Est. admnr. 6 March 1903 by Mary A. Prichard, J. M. Stewart, G. W. Dorr are bound unto J. B. Newberry, Ord. in the sum of $300.00. Died 29 Jan. 1903.

PRITCHETT, WILLIAM Pack 634 #184. Clerk of Court Office.
Pickens, S. C. On 2 June 1845 William Pritchett was appointed a
constable of Pickens Dist.

PRUITT, DANIEL Pack 399. Clerk of Court Office. Abbeville, S.C.
Abbeville Dist. To the Honr. the Chancellors: Your Orators Floride
Pruitt, Louvina Morrow and her husband George B. Morrow and Lany
Hawthorn and her husband A. G. Hawthorne sheweth. That in the year
18__ Daniel Pruitt died intestate, leaving his widow Alley Pruitt and
chn. G. M. Pruitt, F. V. Pruitt, and Jane Pruitt now a minor also your
orators, Floride Pruitt, Louvena Morrow, Lany Hawthorne some time after
the death of Daniel Pruitt, Alley Pruitt his widow also died intestate.
Daniel owned a tract of land in Abbeville Dist. adj. land of A. C.
Hawthorn, Samuel Pruitt and Cowan land. Containing 500 acres. Your
orators are advise that the said land is entitled to be distributed
among his heirs. A letter of admnr. was granted many years ago to
James Lindsay and Samuel E. Pruitt and the personal est. has been fully
distributed. Filed 5 Nov. 1863.

PRUITT, DAVID Book E, Page 20. Clerk of Court Office. Anderson,
S. C. We James Martin and Francis Bremar of Anderson Dist. in consideration of £60 to us paid by David Pruitt of the same Dist. have
granted, bargained, sold and released, all that tract of land in 96
Dist. on Great Generostee a branch of Savannah River surveyed for
Joseph Walker the 26 June 1784. Bounded by vacant land on all sides
when surveyed. Dated 13 April 1799. Wit: Matthew Dickson, Eliza B.
Thompson. Signed: F. Bremar. Proved on oath of Matthew Dickson
before John Wilson, J.P. this 25 June 1799.

PRUITT, DUDLY #529. Probate Judge Office. Anderson, S. C.
I Dudly Pruitt of Anderson County, Pendleton Dist. being very sick and
weak in body, but of perfect mind and memory. I will and desire that
all my lawful debts be paid out of such property as can be sold for
that purpose. I desire the remainder of my estate remain in possession
of my wife during her life for the use of my children, at her death to
be divided among them equally. I desire and will that my mother may
live with my family if she choose it. I appoint my wife Ann Pruit and
my son Solomon Pruit my executrix and executor of this my last will.
Dated 30 Oct. 1794. Wit: Thomas Scott, William Green, John Sentell.
Signed: Dudly X Pruit. Proved on oath of Thomas Scott of Edgefield
Dist. beofre Wm. Robinson J.P. this 26 April 1803. Est. appraised the
2 July 1803, by Stephen Willis, John Lauglin, Joseph Warnock.

PRUITT, FIELD Deed Book F, Page 239. Clerk of Court Office.
Anderson, S. C. This indenture made 10 July 1799. Between Robert
McCann, Deputy Surveyor and Field Prewit Sr. in consideration of £
five sterling paid by said Field Prewit Senr. have granted, bargained,
sold and release a tract of land containing 1,000 acres. Originally
granted the 29 Nov. 179o, land on Cane Creek, waters of Keowee River.
Wit: Thomas Wafer, Joseph McAphee. Proved on oath of Thomas Wafer
before Henry Burch, J.P. this 9 March 1801.

PRUITT, FIELD Deed Book G, Page 199. Clerk of Court Office.
Anderson, S. C. This indenture made the 13 Feb. 1795. Between William
Sloan and Field Prewit both of Anderson Dist. In consideration of five
shillings sterling to me paid by Field Prewit Sr. have granted, bargained, sold and released a tract of land containing 310 acres, lying
on the South Fork of Cane Creek waters of Keowee River. Originally
granted to Sloan 10 Dec. 1791. Wit: George Tarwater, Field Prewit
Junr., Signed: William Sloan. Proved on oath of George Tarwater
before John Taylor, J.Q. this 29 Jan. 1803.

PRUITT, JACOB #1324. Probate Judge Office. Anderson, S. C.
I Jacob Pruitt of Anderson Dist. in making a final disposition of such
wordly estate, etc. I order and direct son after my death the whole
of my est. be sold at publick out cry, on such credit as executor think
proper. My only real estate is a declaration by probate sent to Washington for a patent land warrant, when returned, I order it to be
sold. From the proceeds of such sale to pay my just debts, and the

Pruitt, Jacob - Continued. balance go to support my wife and the raising of my ch. I appoint A. Todd Esq. my executor. Dated 3 March 1851. Wit: A. D. Gray, Joshua Buchanan, Thos. Simpson. Signed: Jacob Pruitt. Proved on oath of Alexander D. Gray before Herbert Hammond, O.A.D. this 29 March 1853.

PRUIT, JOHN at al. Deed Book R, Page 401. Clerk of Court Office. Anderson, Pendleton Dist. We Agness Neel, Robert Neel, William Neel, John Pruit and Rosannah his wife all of this Dist. Thomas Jones and his wife Elizabeth, of the State of Georgia, Archibald Pruit and Mary his wife of the Territory of Alabama in consideration of $1400 to us paid by James Thomson of this dist. have granted, bargained, sold and released a tract of land containing 175 acres, which was granted to Adam File and two small tracts granted to Agness Neel, one containing 27 and 1/2 the other 7 and 1/2 bounded by land of Andrew McAllister, John Callaham and Alexander Caven, on East by Fanton Hall decd. Dated this 25 Nov. 1817. Wit: Matt. Thomson, William McDowall, John B. Pickens. Proved on oath of Isreal? B. Pickens before James Thomson, J.Q. this 5 Jan. 1820. I Hezekiah Rice J.Q. do certify that Agness Neil and Rosannah Pruit the wives of Robert Neil and John Pruit did this day renounce, release and forever relinquish all interest, claim and right of dower on the above land. Signed: Agness X Neill, Robert Neill, William Neill, John X Pruit, Rosannah X Pruit, Thomas Jones, Archibald Pruit.

PRUITT, WILLIAM #1502. Probate Judge Office. Anderson, S. C. I William Pruitt Sr. of Anderson Dist. being of sound and disposing mind and memory, but weak in body etc. I desire my just debts be paid. I give to my wife Frances Pruitt all my estate both real and personal for and during her natural life, at her decease I give the same to my children, to be sold and divide among them. I appoint my sons Elias D. and Tolliver Pruitt executors. Dated 4 Dec. 1855. Wit: Jas. Robinson, Hugh Robinson, John W. Shirley. Signed: William X Pruitt. Proved on oath of James Robinson before Herbert Hammond, Ord. And. Dist. this 10 March 1857. Est. appraised 10 Aug. 1858. By Robert Parker, A. M. Hall, J. N. Harkness, James A. Drake.

QUILLIAN, J. W., M.D. Pack 359 #16. Affidavit. Clerk of Court Office. Pickens, S. C. "Before me personally appears Dr. J. W. Quillian who being duly sworn says he is a practicing physician, residing at Easley Station, State and County of S. C., Pickens Co. That he was born in Union County, State of Georgia and is practicing by authority of a diploma granted by the Atlanta Medical College of Atlanta, State of Georgia bearing date March 3, 1873. Sworn to and subscribed before me the 31 May 1882. J. T. Gossett. T. J. P.D. Signed: J. W. Quillian.

QUARLES, NANCY B. Pack 220 #6. Clerk of Court Office. Pickens, S. C. On 20 Aug. 1859 Nancy B. Quarles took out a peace warrant against W. J. Quarles.

RAIFORD, WILLIAM P. #201. Clerk of Court Office. Abbeville, S. C. Abbeville Dist. In Equity, To the Honr. the Chancellors: Your orator John Montague Raiford of the State of Ala. Sheweth that about the year 1843 William P. Raiford of Abbeville Dist. the father of your orator, died intestate, leaving a handsome estate, and leaving as his only heirs at law a widow Susan C. Raiford, two chn. a dtr. Susan and your orator John M. Raiford, and two grandchildren, John William Power and Louis R. Power, the chn. of a decd. dtr. The said William P. Raiford decd. left a will which Susan C. was executrix. Widow to get all property for life. She died in 1852. On 11 June 1853 William Power one of the grandchildren filed his bill in this Court for a partition of the land, Chancellors Doogan ordered the land put on sale in Nov. 1853. Robert H. W. Hodges who had married with Susan C. (the dtr.) with George W. Hodges and Samuel A. Hodges his sureties (here

Raiford, William P. - Continued. three lines of the Court order is torn out.) The Commerission[?] let the land fall into the hands of Robert H. W. Hodges. In Dec. 1866 Robt. Hodges confessed judgment in the sum of $6284.44. Filed 28 April 1868. On 11 Nov. 1861 Robert H. W. Hodges made a deed of gift to his dtr. Susan L. Jones to William A. Giles in trust for said dtr. and her children. The granddaughter Louisa R. Power had intermarried with William W. Logan.

RAINWATER, D. T. Pack 8. Clerk of Court Office. Anderson, S.C. I, D. T. Rainwater, executor of the last will of Louisa Rochester decd. In consideration of $6125.00 to me paid by John W. Guyton of the same Dist. have granted, sold, and released all that tract or lot #4, on both sides of Beaverdam Creek and waters of Rockey River, bound by land of William Duskworth, Guyton Gyton and others. Containing 288 acres. Dated 24 Dec. 1864. Wit: John B. Watson, Thos. King. Signed: D. T. Rainwater, Exor. Proved on oath of John B. Watson before John W. Daniels, O.C.P. this 31 May 1871.

RANKIN, EDWARD Pack 71. Clerk of Court Office. Pickens, S.C. I Edward Rankin of Pickens Dist. in consideration of $250.00 to me paid by Sarah Morgan of the same Dist. have granted, sold and released a part of the tract of land, which I purchased at sale of the Richards lands. Deed made to me by the Commissioners in Equity. Dated 5 Sept. 1842 containing about 300 acres. Dated 7 Nov. 1848. Wit: Silas Kirksey, John Rankin. Signed: Edward X Rankin. I Edward Rankin agree to give Sarah Morgan and her heirs the privilege of a road to run across my field where it crosses the creek. Dated 27 Nov. 1848. Wit: Silas Kirksey, John Rankin. Signed: Edward X Rankin. Proved on oath of Silas Kirksey before L. N. Robins, N.P. this 3 Feb. 1857. This day came Mary Rankin the wife of Edward Rankin and released and relinquished all interest and right of dower. This 31 Jan. 1857 Levi N. Robin, N.P.

RATCLIFFE, SAMUEL SENR. Vol. 17, Page 744. Probate Judge Office. Charleston, S. C. I Samuel Ratcliffe of Craven County, St. Marks Parish being in perfect health of body and memory. I give to Samuel Butler my loving grandson 100 acres of land with my dwelling house wherein I now dwell. I also give to my grandson Samuel Butler and John Butler all my moveable estate, with all my household goods, to be equally divided between them after my death likewise I give to my well beloved wife her life time in my plantation house. Whom I appoint my wife executrix and my grandson Samuel Butler executor. Dated this 29 July 1772. Wit: John Hardee, Sarah Hardee, Stephen Motte. Signed: Samuel R. Ratcliffe Senr. Recorded in Will Book 1774-1779. Page 582.

RAWLINS, THOMAS W. Pack 10. Clerk of Court Office. Anderson, S. C. I Thomas Rawlins of Pendleton Dist. in consideration of $600 to me paid by Jeremiah W. Rogers, of the same place. Hath granted, sold, bargain and release all that tract of land containing 415 acres, lying in Pendleton Dist. on waters of Big Creek and Hurricane Creek, whereon Rawlins now lives. Adj. land of James Simson, Pickens Adams. Dated this 20 May 1823. Wit: Roger Murphey, Moses Murphee. Signed: Thos. W. Rawlins. Proved on oath of Moses Murphee before Henry Cobb, J.Q. this 15 July 1823. Came this day Polly Rawlins the wife of Thos. W. Rawlins and did renounce, release and forever relinquish all right and interest of dower in the above land. Signed: Henry Cobb, J.Q. this 15 July 1823.

RAZOR, CHRISTOPHER Pack 495. Clerk of Court Office. Abbeville, S. C. Abbeville Dist. In Equity To the Honr. the Chancellors: The petition of John Donnald and Polly Ann his wife. Sheweth, that Christopher Razor departed this life _ Dec. last (1848) having executed his last will, by which he disposed of his estate. John Razor one of the sons and a legatee under the will, but died after the making of the said will and before the death of the testator Christopher Razor. He left six chn. living at his death. viz; Elizabeth Jane the wife of Isaac C. Richey, Nancy O. wife of Redman F. Wyatt, Polly Ann wife of John Donnald your petitioners, George W. Razor, Sarah L. Razor, and

Razor, Christopher - Continued. Pamelia C. Razor, the last three being minors, under the age of twenty one, having a gdn. appointed by this Court. The executor having delivered to your orator, the legacy of John Razor decd. under the will of the decd. father to wit, two negroes, one boy Reuben about the age of fourteen, and a girl Lindy about fifteen years old. Your petitioner prays for an order to sell the named slaves, so an equal division can be made among the distributees. Filed: 25 Jan. 1849. Signed: John Donnald Junr.

REESE, ELIZABETH Pack 654 #1. Es. Rec. Allen Robertson. Clerk of Court Office. Pickens, S. C. On 7 April 1855 the heirs at law of Elizabeth Reese names and number unknown residing in Mississippi, when last heard from dtr. of Allen Robertson decd. and his widow Catharine Robertson of Pickens Dist.

REIGHLEY, WILLIAM Old Records B.B., Page 11, 96 Dist. Abbeville, S. C. William Reighley as a citizen 340 acres lying in the fork of Saludy River and Wollenie Creek and on both sides of the said South fork. Bounded on all sides by vacant land when surveyed by Bennett Crafton D.S. dated 22 May 1784. Recorded this 27 May 1784.

REMBERT, SAMUEL Pack 3218. Clerk of Court Office. Abbeville, S. C. Abbeville Dist. In Equity, To the Honr. the Chancellors: Your orator William P. Rembert and George L. Holmes and Elizabeth his wife sheweth, That Samuel Rembert late of Shelby County, Tenn. died about 10 Nov. 1846, intestate, leaving as his heirs and distributees a widow Rebecca Rembert and four chn. your orator, William P. Rembert, your oratrix Elizabeth Holmes, Mary H. M. Rembert, Louisa Rembert, the last two are minors under the age of 12 yrs. and nine grandchildren being chn. of his sons and dtrs. who died before the said intestate to wit. Samuel S. Rembert and Harriet M. now the wife of ___ Moon, chn. of Andrew Rembert who died about the __ April 1845 and Lewellen Rembert, Louisa R. now the wife of ___ Tresvant, and James A. Rembert, the last of whom is now a minor child of James Rembert a son of the intestate who died about 1841, and John W. Pope, Louisa M. now the wife of ___ Miller, Judith Pope and Moriah or Monah Perry Pope, the last two named are minors chn. of Louisa a dtr. of the intestate who married John Pope and died about 1837. At the time of his death, Samuel Rembert possessed two tracts of land in Abbeville Dist., S. C. on the Savannah River, one called the McMaster tract, containing 240 acres. The other tract called the Beall tract containing 410 acres, lying below the first tract, adj. land of William P. Rembert, The Roberts land, Dr. Armistead. The above property is subject to division, to wit. the widow one third, the remaining two thirds divided into seven parts for each child, or their heirs. Filed 6 Oct. 1847.

RICE, LEONARD & SARAH Deed Book A, Page 9. Clerk of Court Office. Elberton, Ga. This indenture made this 6 Jan. 1791 between Leonard and Sarah his wife of Elbert Co., Ga. and John Staples of the same County. In consideration of ₤65 paid by said Staples, have granted, sold, and released all that tract of land containing fifty acres. Originally granted to William Strong, dated 10 July 1786. Lying on David Creek. Wit: Andrew Johnson, Robert Burke. Signed: Leonard X Rice and Sary X Rice. Recorded 7 March 1791.

RICHARDS, ADAM Pack 4 (Basement). Clerk of Court Office. Anderson, S. C. Pendleton Dist. To the Honr. the Associate Judges: The petition of Adam Richards a native of the County of Antrim, Ireland. He arrived in Charleston, S. C. about the 31 May 1803. That he is attached to the principles of the constitution of the U.S. He prays that he be admitted to become a citizen of this Country. Dated this 27 Oct. 1814. We the undersigned have known the said Adam Richards since the year 1806 and he is of good moral character. Signed: Thomas Richards, John Harris, James C. Griffin, George Reese. He takes the oath on the 27 Oct. 1814.

RICHEY, "MINORS" Pack 278. Clerk of Court Office. Abbeville, S. C. The return of W. C. Moseley guardian of Benjamin A. Richey and Virginia C. Richey, minor for clothing and board. Paid 8 Feb. 1858, $83.42. For the year 1857.

RISOR, GEORGE Will Book A, Page 371. Probate Judge Office.
Edgefield, S. C. I George Risor of Edgefield Dist. being very weak
in body but in perfect mind and memory. I give to my brothers Jacob
Risor, Jacob Commick, Jacob Collins, John Lightse, John Lagrone and
Adam Koon the lad that I have raised the sum of $1887.00 to be equally
divided amongst them to be raised out those debts that are due me.
I further give to Adam Koon one negro boy named London and one negro
girl named Hannah and 200 acres of land lying on Clouds Creek, called
the Bates tract, one horse saddle and bridle, horse to be worth $60.00.
With two sows and pigs, one cow and calf, to be paid said Adam Koon
when he is 21 yrs. of age or is married. The other legacies to be
paid after my death. I give to my son George Risor the rest and residue
of my estate to be vest in him immediately after my decease. I appoint
Nathan Norris, John Bates, William Norris my executors. Dated this
16 May 1816. Wit: Jacob Long, Junr., Jno. A. Kinard, Elizabeth X
Long. Signed: George X Risor. Proved on oath of Jacob Long Junr.
this 13 Sept. 1816. Same day qualified John Bates and William Norris
executors.

RISER, H. H. Will Book, Page 185. Probate Judge Office. Edgefield, S. C. (Only part of will in notes.) I, H. H. Riser of Edgefield Dist. being weak in body and of sound mind and memory and understanding. I direct that all my debts be paid as soon as possible. I
direct that all my personal property (there being one note against my
son Jas. H. Riser) shall be sold at public outcry. One third of the
net proceeds of said sale be given to my wife Keerrenhappuck Riser,
the remaining two thirds be equally divided amongst my five chn. viz,
Marill E. Wyse, Jas. H. Riser, Sallie A. Etheredge, J. Elbert Riser
and A. Picken Riser or their heirs in case of death.

ROACH, WILLIAM Pack 630 #15. Clerk of Court Office. Pickens,
S. C. Land Warrant, By James E. Hagood, Clerk of Court. To any lawful
surveyor, you are authorized to lay out unto William Roach a tract of
land not exceeding ten thousand acres, and make a true plat thereof
and return to my office within two months from date. This 10 Dec. 1859.
Executed for 900 acres on 23 Dec. 1859. Filed 27 Jan. 1860.

ROBESON, JAMES Case 35, File 1488. Probate Judge Office. York,
S. C. Est. admnr. 18 Feb. 1857 by John H. Adams, S. C. Youngblood,
John G. Enloe, who are bound unto John M. Ross, Ord. in the sum of $600.

ROBESON, JAMES Will Book A-12, Page 104. Probate Judge Office.
York, S. C. I James Robeson being weak in body but of sound mind and
perfect memory. I give to Jephus Arnold a black heffer, I give to
Charles Robeson a black steer, I give to John Cook a spotted heffer,
I give to Thomas Thorn a spotted heifer, I give to Sarah Robeson a
sorral mare, I will that Catharine have the colt that the roan mare
is with, I give to William Robeson my son a bay mare colt, I give to
Washington Robeson my roan mare colt, I will the remaining part of
my estate to my wife and the five unmarried children to wit, John,
Sarah, Catherine, William, and Washington, during my wife widowhood.
I will that the tract of land that I now live on be equally divided
between my three sons, after the decease of my wife. I desire that
my debts be paid from the estate. I appoint my wife Lusey Robeson and
my son John Robeson my executrix and executor. Dated this 4 June 1794.
Wit: Duncan Sinclair, John Robeson, Charles Robertson. Signed:
James X Robeson. Recorded 11 March 1795.

ROBESON, JOHN W. Box 26 #643. Probate Judge Office. Columbia,
S. C. I John W. Robeson, M.D. of Columbia, S. C. I give to my
brother Jonas Robeson all and singular, my real and personal estate and
effects. Subject to the payment of my just debts and the following
legacies. I give to my sister Marie Robeson one elegant gold watch
and trinkets, to be present in my name. I give to my brother Abel B.
Robeson, one watch of value of $100 to be presented in like manner,
when he shall arrive at the age of twenty one yrs. I give to my
Nephew John Robeson Wells one watch of value of $100 to be presented
in like manner, when he arrives at age of twenty one. I appoint my
brother Jonas Robeson my executor. Dated 8 Oct. 1827. Wit: Joseph

Robeson, John W. - Continued. McClintock, W. K. D. Lindsey,
Joel R. Adams. Proved on oath of Joseph McClintock before James S.
Gurgnard, Ord. of Richland County. Dated this 26 May 1828.

ROBERSON, JOHN Box 19 #9. Probate Judge Office. Manning, S.C.
I John Roberson of Clarendon County, S. C. being of sound mind and
memory. After my just debts are paid, I give to my wife Elizabeth, all
my effects, both real and personal, household and kitchen furniture,
tools, stock during her natural life or widowhood, after her death or
remarriage then to my niece Elizabeth L. Roberson now in my house who
I have brought up from her infancy. Should she die without lawful
issue then it is my will that her brother John Ervin, my nephew shall
have all my effects. I appoint my nephew Joseph Roberson and Levi B.
Gibbons my executors. Dated 28 March 1877. Wit: J. F. Gamble,
J. W. Holladay, R. B. Gamble. Signed: John X Roberson. Proved 2 Oct.
1880.

ROBERSON, WILLIS Bundle 84, Pack 11. Probate Judge Office.
Sumter, S. C. I Willis Roberson of Sumter Dist. being sick and weak
of body, but of sound and disposing mind and memory. I lend to my
loving wife Martha Roberson during her natural life all my estate, both
real and personal. It is my desire the whole of my estate both real
and personal be equally divided after the death of my loving wife,
between all my chn. that hath not been advanced or had their portion
given them during my life time (viz) Samuel Robertson, John Robertson,
Benjamin E. Robertson, Willie Robertson, Willis Robertson, Jane Robertson and William Robertson. My dtr. Mary Singleton has been advanced
in my life time equal to what I suppose as her share, and shall have no
more. Samuel and John and Benjamin have each had a horse beast out of
my estate. I appoint Samuel and John Robertson executors. Dated this
26 Aug. 1811. Wit: Underhill Ellis, Edwd. Barrett, Felix Ellis.
Signed: Willis X Robertson. Recorded 7 Aug. 1828.

ROBERTSON, DORCAS Pack 329. Clerk of Court Office. Abbeville,
S. C. Abbeville Dist. In Equity. To the Honr. the Chancellors:
Your orators William Robertson of Tuscallosa Co., Ala. and Syth Robertson of Cherokee Co. Texas sheweth. That on the 16 Sept. 1815 the mother
of your orators, Dorcas Robertson then a feme sole (unmarried, widow)
executed in favor of her three sons, a deed of gift of land and negroes,
reserving unto herself the use and benefit until her death. The said
deed was probated on the 2nd and recorded on the 18th of Oct. 1815. In
the deed this language occurs, "To my loving son Hugh, I give and grant
one negro girl by the name of Dianh[sic] to have the immediate possession on this condition, that if he the said should die without
heirs then the said Dinah to revert to my loving sons William and
Syth. "That soon after the execution of this deed of gift, the said
Dorcas Robertson departed this life. Some time, in the latter part of
the last year or the beginning of this, Hugh Robertson departed this
life leaving a wife but no children. Hugh Robertson left a last will,
which was admitted to probate in due form of law. James W. Lipscomb is
the executor. That the said Dinah if alive and Mary at least several
of her descendants are now in possession of James W. Lipscomb and Luana
Robertson. That your orator are entitled to the said negro or negroes
by virtue of said deed. Filed 28 April 1859. Will of Hugh Robertson.
Abbeville Dist. I Hugh Robertson of Abbeville Dist. desire that my
debts are fully paid. I give to my wife Louanna Robertson the tract
of land on which I now reside, bound by land of William Sproull, John
Webber, Henry Rush, and Henry Quattlebum containing 309 acres. I give
to my wife Louanna the following negroes, Sam, Milly, Joe, Harry,
Dianah, Eliza and Philip and their increase. I will (to the dtr. of
my wife by a former marriage) Jemima Eugenia Cook one negro boy
Matthew. In case she die without heir, the said negro to be the
property of my wife Louanna. I appoint my friend James W. Lipscomb
as executor. Dated 14 Nov. 1857. Wit: Abraham P. Pool, Nathaniel
McCants, John Sadler. Signed: Hugh Robertson. Recd. 16 May 1859. In
another paper, William and Syth Robertson were brothers of the whole
blood of Hugh Robertson.

ROBERTSON, GEORGE Will 1, Probate Judge Office, Charleston, S.C. George Robertson son of John Robertson of Charleston recd. a legacy from the will of Hugh George Campbell in 1820.

ROBERTSON, JAMES Pack 244. Clerk of Court Office. Abbeville, S. C. Abbeville Dist. In Equity. To the Honr. The Chancellors: John Waddell admnor of the est. of James M. Robertson decd. sheweth that on the 4 Feb. 1831 the said James M. Robertson and Robert G. Quarles and Mary E. his wife, John Waddell and Martha Ann his wife filed their bill of complaint in the Court against Edward Collier and Mary his wife, John H. Gray and Jane his wife. Whereas about the 15 Oct. 1817 George Robertson made his last will and testament, and shortly afterwards died leaving a widow Mary and four chn. viz, James M., Mary E., Martha Ann and Jane. In said will the widow to have the household and kitchen furniture in fee simple and also during her widowhood the interest and profits from his estate, except as might be necessary for the education and maintenance of his chn. He appointed John McCalla as executor and the widow executrix. John McCalla was qualified as executor and he bore the whole burden of executing the said will, until the 2 Dec. 1824 when Mary qualified as executrix. The household furniture was appraised at $1611.75. The plantation, stock, tools, debts due, cotton was appraised at $4456.25. Other property sold for $137.96. The widow Mary intermarried with Edward Collier about 25 Dec. 1821. Filed 9 May 1834. In a deposition taken in Greene County, Ala. from Arthur Slaughter, taken Thomas Ridell, Esq. in Springfield, Greene Co., Ala. Qust. 1. Did you at any time and how long reside near Mr. Edward Collier? Answ. I resided near E. Collier, Esq. from the time of his marriage to his present wife until the Spring of 1829. Qust. 2. Are you acquainted with the value of Berry Hill Plantation the est. of the late George Robertson, decd. Answ. I have been to the said plantation many times, as to the value, it should be worth $650.00 per annum. Qust. 3. Had you an opportunity of forming an opinion of Mr. Collier's treatment of his step children, was his conduct towards them characterized by kindness and generosity? Answ. I do not think his general conduct toward them was characterized by kindness and generosity. Dated this 25 May 1833.

ROBERTSON, JOHN Case 37 File 1564. Probate Judge Office. York, S. C. I John Robertson being weak in body but of a strong dispsing mind. I give to my beloved wife Charity Robertson one bed and furniture and one cow. I give to my dtr. Sally Men Irvy Robertson one bed and furniture, and one cow. I give to my dtr. Rachael Dulathy Robertson one bed and furniture and one cow. I give to my son John H. Robertson one young mare. I desire that my sorrel mare called Match be reserved for the use of the family that may choose to stay on the land. I give unto my beloved wife Charrity Robertson the land whereon I now live and keep my two dtrs. Sally Men Ervy and Rachael Dulathy during their single life free of charge. My son Benjamin shall have a decent support from the land, during the natural life of his mother. I desire that after my decease, all my property not heretofore mentioned be put to sale, and from the money pay my just debts. Any money left shall be equal divided with, Charrity on ninth, son Thomas one ninth, son Joseph O. one ninth, son James one ninth, son Elihue one ninth, son William one ninth, son John H. one ninth, dtr. Sally Menervy one ninth, dtr. Rachael Dulathy one ninth, son Benjamin to have one half of the home place after the decease of my wife. I appoint my wife Charrity Robertson Executrix and son Thomas Robertson Executor. Dated this 11 July 1835. Wit: Wm. Anderson, William Hill Senr., Rezin Talbert. Signed: John X Robertson. Probate 22 Aug. 1836.

ROBERTSON, LEWIS Bundle 82 #13. Probate Judge Office. Sumter, S. C. On 19 July 1878 Margaret Robertson sheweth that Lewis Robertson of Sumter County died 27 May 1878. That she is the only surviving child. On 2 July 1878 Charlotte Withers of Sumter County states that Lewis Robertson died the 30 May 1878 at his residence in Sumter leaving Charlotte Withers as a sister by whole blood.

ROBERTSON, REBECCA Case 35, File 1486. Probate Judge Office.
York, S. C. I Rebecca Robertson of York Dist. being old and infirm
but of sound mind disposing memory. I give to my three sons who went
West, viz, James Robertson, Thomas Robertson, Samuel Robertson each
$300 in cash, to be paid from any fund that I may possess at death.
The rest and residue, I allow and desire to be equally divided between
all my children, as well as those named out West. I appoint my son
Allan Robertson my executor. Dated this 16 July 1851. Wit: S. Sadler,
J. S. Sadler, M. A. Sadler. Signed: Renekeh Robertson. Probated:
16 Feb. 1837? (mistake in will date or probate date.)

ROBERTSON, ROBERT Pack 3200. Clerk of Court Office. Abbeville,
S. C. I Robert Robertson of Abbeville Dist. being of sound mind and
disposing memory. I desire my debts and funeral expenses be paid. I
will to Rebben Robertson my son a man of color, the following negroes,
James and his wife Rachel, Ned, Prince, Anna, Jesse, Moses, Silvey,
Matilda, Rachel, Bethany, Albert, James, Monday, Alexander, Peggy,
Moses, Joseph, Lawson, Lewis, George, Judah, Amy, Edward, Lucy, Sally.
With two waggons and all needful tools, 11 horses, household furniture
not given to his mother Delph. A tract of land lying on the North
Prong of Mulberry, containing 200 acres, adj. land of Charles and
William Hodges and Miss Hill. I will and devise to Susannah Greer my
daughter a woman of color, the following negroes, Nancy, Hudson, Agga,
William, Dick, Westly and Bashey, James, Carlease, Mary, Catherine and
Johnson a rone mare saddle and bridle. One half of a tract of land
I bought of John and James Watt, being 200 acres, adj. the tract I
now live on. I give to my daughter Jean Greer a woman of color, the
following negroes Sharlot, Rachel, Levina, Lutisse, Emmeline, Florah,
Hagar, Almira, Little Sam, Catharine, Peter, John, Vincent, a bay mare
and a gray mare and the other half of the tract of land I bought of
John and James Watts being 200 acres adj. the land whereon I now live.
I give and devise to Elizabeth Greer my daughter a woman of color
the following negroes, Polley, Nancy, Patsey, Clary, Gabriel, Kizey,
Armstead, Old Sam, Charles, Pickney, one mare and one colt, and 100
acres of land I bought of Adam Crain Jones Junr. I will to Delph a
black woman of color whom I did imancipate on the 9 July 1812, agreeable to act of assembly of this State the following negroes, Frank,
Amy, Abraham, Old Henry, Ben, Dealph, also 100 acres of land to be
laid off where I now live so as to include the house and all buildings
with two cows, a horse, farm tools and $100 in cash. At her death the
property to return to my estate and divided among my children. The
land on South prong of Turkey Creek formerly belong to Robert Gibson
be sold and the money divided between my children or their heirs. I
will and devise that the land on the North prong of Turkey Creek to
my son Reuben Robertson, and the household furniture to be divided
between my dtrs. I give to my brother John Robertson the sum of $20.00.
I appoint H. Morrah, James Wardlaw Esq., Bazle Jay executors. Dated
5 Nov. 1819. Wit: Aug. Arnold, William McIlwain, Jr., Henson Norris.
Signed: Robert Robertson. Proven 24 March 1825. John Robertson died
in 1826, after he had filed a bill against the executors of Robert
Robertson Est. as the only full blood heir and that people of color
cannot own land. He states that Jean Greer had married Hinson
Norris. John Robertson admnr. was Andrew Robertson he and James
Richey and wife Jane, Jane Robertson, widow, Richard Mattox and Peggy
his wife, John Robertson, Augustin Mattox and Letty his wife. In the
bill, it states that Susannah Green died before the testator. The
last bill was filed on 26 April 1828.

ROBERTSON, THOMAS Box 6 #68. Probate Judge Office. Pickens,
S. C. Est. admnr. 17 Aug. 1835 by James Robertson, John McKinney,
Jesse McKinney are bound unto James H. Dendy, Ord. in the sum of
$1,000. Cit. pub. at Antioch Meeting House.

TOMBSTONE INSCRIPTIONS, taken from Eakin Cemetery, Central Community
Abbeville, S. C. Matilda C. Robinson, born 19 Oct. 1865.
Marion Archa-son of B. S. and A. V. Robertson, born 2 Dec. 1889,
24 Feb. 1890.
Bluford Walls-son of W. S. and M. A. Robertson, born 20 Dec. 1860,
22 July 1861.

Tombstone inscriptions - continued.
Mary Ann Robinson, Consort of Thomas Robinson, 3rd dtr. of Thomas and
Matilda Eakin, born 14 Dec. 1827, 2 May 1857.
Williae Robinson, infant son of Thomas and Mary A. Robinson, 27 Aug.
1856, 16 Sept. 1857.
Margaret A. wife of W. S. Robertson, born 26 Jan. 1827, 27 Jan. 1887.
W. S. Robertson, born 28 June 1816, 20 Jan. 1892.
Nancy Jane dtr. of W. S. and M. A. Robinson, 22 Sept. 1855, 18 Apr. 1856.

ROBINSON, ALEXANDER Bundle 81, Pack 10. Probate Judge Office.
Sumter, S. C. I Alexander Robinson of Clarendon Co. being weak in
body, but of sound mind and memory. This first day of Jan. 1798 do
make this my last will and testament. I give to my dtr. Ann Courtney
two negroes. A boy named Bobb and a girl named Cloe. I give to my
dtr. Mary Adkins two negroes girls, named Peggy and Sarah, to be
delivered to her when ever she demands them, after the decease of
Marmaduke Adkins her present husband, if she dies without issue, the
said negroes to be sold and the money equally divided amongst my
children, then living or their lawful issue. I give to my dtr. Elizabeth Robinson and her heirs three negroes, named Tianer, a girl named
Dolly and a boy named James with one feather bed to be delivered on
the day of her marriage or of full age. I give to my wife Elizabeth
Robinson the plantation where I now live on, containing 300 acres,
with all my household and kitchen furniture, one negro named Flander,
all stock of cattle, horses, hogs, sheep during her natural life, at
her decease the whole to go to Elizabeth Robinson my dtr. and her issue.
I appoint my wife Elizabeth Robinson, executrix and my friend William
Taylor Esq. and Mayr. Thomas McFadin of Salem County, my executors.
Wit: Saml. P. Taylor, Mary Taylor, Frances A. Taylor. Signed:
Alexander Robinson. Recorded 2 May 1800.

ROBINSON, ALLEN Apt. 1 File 26. Probate Judge Office. Greenville, S. C. Allen Robinson died on 28 March 1854 in Pickens Dist.
Owned 784 acres on both sides of the South Fork of Saluda River. Heirs
were: His widow Catha rine Robinson who resides in Pickens Dist. and
13 children, James Robinson who resides in Greenville Dist., Randall
Robinson who resides in Texas, Joseph Robinson who resides in Mississippi, Anna Whitmire the wife of Jeremiah Whitmire who resides in Pickens
Dist., Martha the wife of Thomas Hitt who resides in Cherokee Co., Ga.
Lydia the wife of Osborne Hagood who resides in Gilmer Co., Ga., Lucy
the wife of Bailey Barton who resides in Pickens Dist., Malinda the
wife of Wilson Jones who resides in Pickens Dist., John A. Robinson of
Pickens Dist., The heirs at law of Elizabeth Reese, name and number
unknown and residing in Miss., the heirs at law of Hardy Robinson name
and number unknown, the heirs at law of George Robinson viz. George
Robinson who resides in Ala. The heirs at law of William Robinson a
son of George, name and number unknown but residing in Georgia and
Jeremiah Robinson. Filed 7 April 1855.

ROBINSON, AMOS No ref. Pickens, S. C. In 1853 Amos Robinson
was mentioned as the husband of Nelly Rogers and were living in Ga.
She was the dtr. of James Rogers Sr. decd. and his wife, Ann Rogers of
Pickens Dist., S. C.

ROBINSON, ARCHIBALD Box 38 #1592. Probate Judge Office. York,
S. C. Est. admnr. 4 June 1827 by Mary Robinson, William Jamison, John
Hemphill Esq. and John King Sr. who are bound unto Benjamin Chambers
Ord. in the sum of $1500. Cit. pub. at Bullock Creek Church. (No
other papers).

ROBINSON, ARCHIBALD Case 38 File 1592. Probate Judge Office.
York, S. C. Est. admnr. 4 June 1827 by Mary Robinson, William Jamison,
John Hemphill Esq., and John King Sr. who are bound unto Benjamin
Chambers in the sum of $1500. Cit. Pub. at Bulluck Creek Church.

ROBINSON, ARCHIBALD Box 2 #54. Probate Judge Office, York,
S. C. He owned 118 acres of land on Turkey Creek, on 8 Jan. 1840
John C. Cairnes, Robert Gilfillan, Eliza Cairnes are bound unto the
Ord. in the sum of $200.16. James C. Shearer in right of wife

Robinson, Archibald - Continued. Sarah C. Decd., James C. Robinson gdn. of Charles L. Robinson, a minor over 14 yrs. Minor heir of
Archibald Robinson, decd. and James C. Shearer gdn. of his own two
ch. Wm. L., James A. Shearer ordered to appear in Court. J. C. Shearer
applicant vs. the widow Mary Robinson the gdn. of Charles I. Robinson,
Wm. Robinson minors. Nancy W. Robinson decd. 22 Oct. 1839.

ROBINSON, ARTHUR Case 38 File 1594. Probate Judge Office. York,
S. C. Est. admnr. 12 Jan. 1830 by Jonathan Roberson, John King and
Joseph Dawle, who are bound unto Benjamin Chambers in the sum of $2,000.
Cit. Pub. at Bullucks Creek Church.

ROBINSON, ARTHUR Box 38 File 1594. Probate Judge Office. York,
S. C. Est. admnr. 12 Jan. 1830 by Jonathan Roberson, John King and
Joseph Dowdle are bound unto Benjamin Chambers, Ord. in the sum of
$2,000. Cit. pub. at Bullocks Creek Church. (no other papers).

ROBINSON, BENJAMIN Bundle 86 #10. Probate Judge Office. Sumter,
S. C. On 20 Jan. 1881 Jane Robinson the widow of John H. Robinson
sheweth that her husband died leaving also children. He died in 1880.
No names given.

ROBINSON, BENJAMIN Bundle 86 #10. Probate Judge Office. Sumter,
S. C. Est. admnr. 27 Sept. 1830 by Lemuel Robinson, John Robinson and
Wiley Robinson are bound unto Wm. Potts, Esq. Ord. in the sum of
$155.00.

ROBINSON, CATHERINE Box 98 #1032. Probate Judge Office. Pickens,
S. C. I Catherine Robinson of Pickens Dist. being of sound and dispos-
ing mind and memory. I own one half of a tract of land containing 230
acres, lying on Carpenter Creek waters of Saluda River in Pickens Dist.
Said land was assigned to me in the partitioning of my late husband
Allen Robinson decd. One half of the tract I have conveyed to my
son Jeremiah Robinson who made payment for same, in the sum of $1,000.
Pay my just debts from the money owed by Jeremiah. The remainder to
be divided into three parts, one for my son Jeremiah, one part for
Lucy Barton the wife of Bailey Barton, the other part to Lucy Catherine
Jones and Joel Jasper Jones the chn. of my decd. dtr. Melinda Jones, to
be equal divided between them, when becoming of full age. I appoint
my son Jeremiah Robinson my executor. Dated this 10 March 1859.
Wit: John H. Williams, C. J. Elford, T. I. Donaldson. Signed:
Catherine X Robinson. Proven 1 July 1870. On 15 Oct. 1870 Lucy
Hindman of Cass County, P. O. Cartersville, Ga. appointed James E.
Hagood of Pickens Dist. her attorney to receive her part from est. of
Martha M. Robinson. Heirs, Julia Ann Keith and her husband John D. M.
Keith, Pinckney Robinson, Silas Robinson, Lucy C. Jones and Joel J.
Jones. Catherine Robinson died in 1869. Jeremiah Robinson died 1860.
Martha M. Robinson widow of said Jeremiah Robinson.

ROBINSON, CLARK Case 82 File 4028. Probate Judge Office. York,
S. C. Est. admnr. 30 March 1872 by Simpson W. Robison, Wm. Thomasson,
and W. B. Allison are bound to S. B. Hall in the sum of $200. Died
12 March 1872.

ROBINSON, DORCAS P. Pack 632 #2. Clerk of Court Office. Pickens,
S. C. Dorcas P. Robinson was formerly the widow of William M. Jamison
of Pickens Dist. He died in 1864. Chn. by first husband: Jane Stegall,
W. C. Jamison, A. P. Jamison, John J. Jamison, Margaret A. Chastain
wife of William Chastain.

ROBINSON, JOHN family bible in possession of Mrs. Oliva Pearman
of Anderson, S. C. She is dtr. of Weldon Pearman who married Sallie
Rickets, Weldon was the father of Ollie, Mollie, Oliva, Lizzie, James,
Nathaniel Pearman (Weldon was once the Clerk of Court in Anderson Co.,
S. C. James Pearman married Susannah Ashley dtr. of Joshua Ashley
and Mahala Moore. Buried at Bethel Church James and Susannah had Allie,
Eunice, Grase, Annie, James J. John Thomas Ashley born 20 Jan. 1837
died 5 Feb. 1922. Married Adeline B. Robinson born 26 Oct. 1844 died
7 Feb. 1879. Age 34 yrs. 3 mo. 11 days. John Thomas Ashley is a

John Robinson family - Continued. brother to Joshua Ashley who
married Mahala Moore. (The following are copies of the family records
from the John B. Robinson Bible, no information on the Bible is given,
all seems to have been written by the same person.)
Sally B. Robinson, born 22 Sept. 1799.
John B. Robinson, born on Thursday, Feb. 1800, no date.
Mary B. Robinson, was born 22 of December on Friday 1820.
Jane B. Robinson was born 9 of May, Friday 1823.
Richard B. Robinson, was born 8 April Friday 1825.
Anna Robinson, was born 22 January Tuesday 1827.
Sally B. Robinson was born 8 Dec. Monday 1829.
Rachel Robinson, was born 8 October Monday 1831.
Elizabeth B. Robinson, was born 22 January 1833.
Hannah B. Robinson, was born 20 October Monday 1834.
John B. Robinson, was born 7 August Sunday 1836.
Isaac H. Robinson, was born 3 August Friday 1838.
James H. Robinson was born 9 August Sunday 1840.
Jesse T. Robinson, was born 11 June Sunday 1843.
Addline B. Robinson, was born 26 October Sunday 1844.
Jesse T. Robinson (died) the last day of September 1843.
John B. Robinson Junr. died the 21 day of August 1858.
John B. Robinson died the 11 May 1864.
Sally Robinson died the 31 day of July 1868.
Polly B. Robinson died the 7 day of April 1877.
Anna Nelson died the 18 March 1878.
Sally Robinson died the 11 September 1878.
Jane Hogg, sister died the 19 of September 1878.
Addline B. Ashley, sister, died the 7 February 1879/
J. H. Robinson, brother, died the 18 June 1880. (The J. H. and I. H.
looks just alike, maybe wrong)
I. H. Robinson, brother died the 6 September 1880.
Hannah Kay, sister, died the 15 September 1880.
R. B. Robinson, brother died the 23 of October 1880.
E. E. Robinson died the 2 July 1886.
M. L. E. Robinson, died the 18 May 1887.
B. F. Robinson and M. L. E. Hays was married the 15 Feb. 1881.
S. A. Pearman, mother, was born 4 May 1848 and was married 28 Dec.
1871.
James N. Pearman was born 9 Dec. 1872.
A. T. was born January 28, 1875.
M. S. Pearman was born 28 August 1877.
O. C. Pearman was born 9 Aug. 1882.
S. E. Pearman was born 22 Aug. 1885.
W. C. Pearman died Dec. 7, 1888 and buried the 8th at Mount Bethel
Church.
A. T. died the 10 Sept. 1897 and was buried at Broad ?

ROBINSON, GEORGE Pack 231 #3. Clerk of Court Office. Pickens,
S. C. State of Ala. St. Clair Co. I George Robinson of said county,
son of George Robinson Sr. decd. who was a son of Allen Robinson decd.
and one of heirs and distributees of the est. of Allen Robinson decd.
Have appointed James E. Hagood of Pickens Dist., S. C. my true and lawful attorney for me and in my name. To receive and receipt any money,
goods, chattles etc. in the hands of Alvah Griffin admnr. of the est.
and R. A. Thompson Esq. Comm. in Equity. Dated this 30 July 1859.
Wit: T. S. Logan, Jasper Sibert. Signed: George Robinson. Attested
before John D. Byrne J.P. that George Robinson did sign the within
power of attorney this 30 July 1859.

ROBINSON, GEORGE Box 50 #2092. Probate Judge Office. Camden,
S. C. Est. admnr. 14 May 1808 by Elizabeth Robinson and Jesse Howard
are bound unto Isaac Alexander Ord. Kershaw Dist. in the sum of $300.00.
The property was sold at the dwelling house of Frederick Robinson in
Camden.

ROBINSON, GEORGE SR. Bundle 8 Pack 7. Probate Judge Office.
Barnwell, S. C. I George Robinson of Barnwell Dist. being of perfect,
sound and disposing mind and memory. First I direct all my just and
funeral expenses be paid out of the profits of my estate. I give to

Robinson, George Sr. - Continued. George Stewart, son of Elizabeth
Ann Stewart, all the cattle which I purchased of Thomas Nightingale,
also negroes which he has of mine to wit, Humphrey, Okerah, Jo, Tom,
Pollow, Cato, Junah, Grace, Monday, Moses, Will, Ned, Harriett, Brance,
Antoney, Seal, Popey, Young Melinda, Isaac, Glaster. I have given to
Mary Hatcher of the State of Georgia the wife of Archibald Hatcher
negroes now in her possession, to wit, Jerry, Philles, Claritta,
Carter, Mary, Mood, John, and Fanney, with all their increase.
(George Robinson, had six dtr. each to receive property in trust, some
legatees must be grand children.) Other legatees, Ann Squires, Louisa
Chevelette, Sarah Mills, Lucy Dunbar, George Robinson Dunbar, Lucy
Stewart, Lucy Dunbar, Elizabeth Ann Govan and Andrew Govan, Betsey
Dunbar, Betsey Robinson Squires. (Some of these legatees are minors.)
Dated this 31 Oct. 1803. Wit: Joseph Duncan, John Bates Junr., Tom
Castellaw. Signed: George Robinson.

ROBINSON, HARDY Box 52 #573. Probate Judge Office. Pickens,
S. C. Est. admnr. 27 Jan. 1860 by James E. Hagood, Robert A. Thompson,
Elijah E. Alexander are bound unto W. E.Holcombe Ord. in the sum of
$600. Left 9 heirs viz: James Robinson, George Robinson Jr., Joseph
Robinson, Randall Robinson, Lydia Hagood, Thomas Hill and wife Martha,
heirs of Wm. Robinson decd. number and names unknown, heirs of Elizabeth
Reese decd. number unknown, Jeremiah Whitmire and wife Anna. Was
late of Ala.

ROBINSON, HENRIETTA J. Pack 633. Clerk of Court Office.
Pickens, S. C. I Henrietta Robinson of Shelby County, Ala. in consideration of $185.00 to me paid by John T. Gossett of Pickens Dist.,
S. C. Have granted, sold, bargain, and release, all my right, title,
interest and claim in law or equity to a tract of land containing 129
acres, lying in Pickens Dist., S. C. adj. land of J. T. Gossett and
others, being the same tract of which my father Hamilton Burdine died
possessed with, in which I have an interest of one sixth of two thirds.
Also all my interest, right and title, in law and in Equity to a tract
of land of which my grandfather Richard Burdine died possessed, containing 400 acres, lying on waters of Georges Creek. In which I have
one sixth of one sixth interest in said land. Dated 3 Oct. 1863.
Wit: D. Hoke, T. Q. Donelson. Signed: Henrietta J. Robinson.
Proved in Greenville Dist., S. C. on oath of D. Hoke, before T. Q.
Donelson, M.G.D. this 3 Oct. 1863. Recd. 18 March 1867.

ROBINSON, HENRIETTA Deed Book B, Page 72. Probate Judge Office.
Pickens, S. C. On 19 Oct. 1863 Henrietta Robinson the dtr. of
Hamilton Burdine decd. of Pickens Dist. and his widow who later
married B. A. Stephens.

ROBINSON, HENRIETTA J. Equity papers, Pack 633. Clerk of Court
Office. Pickens, S. C. Henrietta J. Robinson was wife of Elijah
Robinson and lived in Shelby Co., Ala. After the death of her husband
she later married a Hand (or Hann). She was dtr. of Hamilton Burdine
decd. who died before his father Richard Burdine in Pickens Dist.

ROBINSON, MRS. J. S. #71. Judge of Probate Office. Florence,
S. C. Est. admnr. 21 Jan. 1891 by B. M. Grayson, J. R. McCay,
R. W. Fulton are bound unto J. P. McNeill, Ord. in the sum of $1400.
Was of the County of Williamsburg. Died on or about 12 Dec. 1890.

ROBINSON, MRS. JANE Bundle 176 Pack 11. Probate Judge Office.
Barnwell, S. C. Est. admnr. 14 Nov. 1868 by Stephen B. Robinson,
C. G. Tutt, J. P. McElhenny who are bound unto J. N. Teague Ord. in
the sum of $1100. On 7 Dec. 1868 cash deposited in hands of Judge of
Probate for the children of Caroline McElhany being one sixth of the
est. $86.58 on 30 Dec. 1869 paid A. E. Lark dist. share $86.58. Paid
Jane A. Robinson share $86.58. Paid M. E. Robinson $86.58. Died
in March 1867.

ROBINSON, MRS. JANE Bundle 116 Pack 1. Probate Judge Office.
Barnwell, S. C. On 28 April 1853, Ezekiel J. Williams, James J.
Wilson, Andrew Dunbar are bound unto Johnson Hagood Ord. in the sum

Robinson, Mrs. Jane - Continued. of $2000. Whereas Ezekiel J.
Williams made trustee of the estate of Jane Robinson wife of A. G.
Robinson.

ROBINSON, JEREMIAH Land Warrant. Pack 630 #4. Clerk of Court
Office. Pickens, S. C. Pickens Dist. I, J. E. Hagood Clerk of
Court, to W. D. Therlkeld D.S. for said Dist. You are authorized to
lay out a tract of land unto Jeremiah Robinson, and make a true plat
thereof dated this 19 Dec. 1860. Filed 5 Jan. 1861.

ROBINSON, JEREMIAH Box 68 #729. Probate Judge Office. Pickens,
S. C. I Jeremiah Robinson being a man of sound mind and memory. First
it is my will that all my property both real and personal remain in
the hands of my wife and mother for the benefit of my wife and mother
and children, during the natural life of my mother or my wife Martha.
Mother name is Catharine Robinson. Property to remain as it was when
I was alive unto my wife remarry or my children come of age. I appoint
my wife Marthy Robinson Executrix and A. J. Anderson executor. Dated
this 18 Jan. 1862. Wit: John A. Robinson, S. P. Henderson, Mary
Anderson. Signed: Jeremiah Robinson. Proven 25 May 1863. Owned
230 acres on both sides of Carpenter Creek. Heirs on 25 Feb. 1885 viz,
J. P. Robinson, S. T. Robinson, Julia Ann Keith. Recd. 14 Dec. 1863
of L. Latham for horse sold in Virginia $174.00.

ROBINSON, JOHN Box 59 #2095. Probate Judge Office. Camden,
S. C. Est. admnr. 4 June 1816 by Littleberry Robinson of Little
Lynches Creek, William Robinson, James Robinson and Zacharias Robinson
of Buffelow Creek, planters, the first of Kershaw Dist. and the three
others of Lancaster Dist. are bound unto Samuel Mathis Ord. in the sum
of $600.00 John Robinson was of Buffelow Creek in Kershaw Dist.
Elizabeth Robinson widow of decd. Citation pub. at Robinson Meeting
House.

ROBINSON, JOHN Pack 383. Probate Judge Office. Abbeville, S.C.
Abbeville Dist. To the Chancellors of this State, Your oratrix
Elizabeth Robinson of this Dist. sheweth, in the latter part of the
year 1857 John Robinson the husband of your oratrix departed this life
intestate, leaving your oratrix his widow and chn. James E. Robinson
over the age of twenty one yrs. and is living as your oratrix believes
in the State of Texas. Rachel the wife of Benjamin B. Hornby and died
one week after the death of her father, leaving a son John William
Hornby a lad about ten yrs. of age and her husband Benjamin B. both
residing in Abbeville Dist. Robert J. Robinson who lives with your
oratrix and will be twenty one yrs. of age in the month of May of this
year. Jabez P. Robinson a minor about eighteen years of age and
living with your oratrix. At the request of your oratrix Dr. John W.
Hearst of this Dist. has admnr. of the est. and has taken charge of
the personalty which your oratrix believes will amount in value to
about $2,000. John Robinson died possessed with a tract of land in
said Dist. containing about 490 acres, bounded by land of John G.
Thornton, William B. Dorn and others. Your oratrix is informed that
the land is subject to partition between your oratrix and the heirs at
law. Filed 1 March 1858. In a letter James E. Robinson resided at
Mill Way, Blue Hill, P.O. Texas.

ROBINSON, JOHN Box 2 #53. Probate Judge Office. York, S. C.
Minor heirs were: Thos. F. Robinson, James L. Robinson, Saml. W.
Robinson, D. G. Robinson. Dated 22 March 1841. Was late of Chester
Dist., S. C. Elizabeth Robinson widow, John Douglass in right of his
wife Eleanor, John Robinson, Thomas F. Robinson, Daniel G. Robinson,
James Robinson, Saml. W. Robinson, Catharine Robinson all of whom
live in Georgia, the last six being minors, heirs of John Robinson late
of Merriweather Co., Ga. Thos. F. Mathews in right of wife Catherine,
Wm. Robinson. Widow one third. Eight shares.

ROBINSON, JOHN Box 38 File 1598. Probate Judge Office. York,
S.C. Est. admnr. 14 April 1834 by David Robertson, John P. Glass
Esq. and David Robertson are bound unto Benjamin Chambers Ord. in the
sum of $1,000.

ROBINSON, JOHN Pack 15. In Equity (Basement). Clerk of Court Office. Pickens, S. C. John Robinson married Eliza Lynch dtr. of Nathaniel Lynch Sr. who died 20 Feb. 1861 and his wife Jane Lynch of Pickens Dist. They were living in Georgia around 1863. Richard Robinson married Nancy Lynch another dtr. and they to were living in Georgia around 1863.

ROBINSON, JOHN A. Box 102 #1068. Probate Judge Office. Pickens, S. C. I John Robinson of Pickens County. Being sick and weak in body but of sound mind. I desire my just debts be paid. I wish that none of my property be sold, and each of my children have an equal share in value. I give to each of my four children $100 each to wit. George F. Robinson, Alexander P. Robinson, Josephine D. the wife of P. Holbert Williams and Mary Robinson, the amount to be paid in money or property. The property to be valued by Stephen D. Keith and Richard H. Alexander. I give to my wife Mary Robinson all the remainder of my property during her natural life, and after her death to be equally divided between my said children. He gives to his wife Mary a tract of land, lines given, adj. land of Martin Whitmire, Peters Creek Church, Alva Griffins fence, after the death of my wife, said property to belong to my dtr. Mary Robinson. Alexander P. Robinson to have a tract of land, adj. the tract given to his wife, known as the "Lizzie Old Field" adj. land of Alva Griffins, Solomon Loopers. I give to Josephine D. Williams a tract of land lying on the West side of the tract given to my wife. I appoint my son George F. Robinson and Absolom Blythe Esq. executors. Dated 2 April 1870. Wit: G. G. Wells, G. E. Elrod, E. E. E. Clythe. Signed: John A. Robinson. Proven 1 Aug. 1871.

ROBINSON, JOHN T. Case 35 File 1489. Probate Judge Office. York, S. C. Est. admnr. 13 Feb. 1857 by J. M. Wallace, F. A. Ervin, S. G. Hemphill who are bound unto John M. Ross, Ord. in the sum of $1,000.

ROBINSON, JOHN DR. Apt. 1 File 27. Probate Judge Office. Greenville, S. C. On 16 Feb. 1824 Gen. John Blassingame of Greenville Dist. advanced property to his children during his life time. Among them Dr. John Robinson was ment.

ROBINSON, JOHN DOCTR. Pack 75 (Basement). Clerk of Court Office. Pickens, S. C. I John Robinson of Pickens Dist. in consideration of the sum of $175.00 to me paid by Lewis Mauldin of the same Dist. have bargain, sold, and release a tract of land containing 50 acres, lying on West side of Bresha Creek, waters of Saluda River adj. land of Rucker Mauldins, John Robinson. Dated this 30 March 1835. Wit: Wm. Hunter, R. Mauldin. Signed: John Robinson. This day came Eliza Robinson the wife of John Robinson and renounced, release and relinquished all rights and interest in the above land. 24 Dec. 1836.

ROBINSON, LEMUEL Will 19. (Book) Probate Judge Office. Barnwell, S. C. Lemuel Robinson of Barnwell Co. will dated 1861. Bro. Ezekiel Robinson. Gives to Mrs. Ann Allmon. Bequeath to Mary Ann Attaway wife of H. B. Attaway of Burke Co., Ga. Brother in La. W. John McChany. Land bounded by J. W. Freeman, James Kemp, Dr. Jas. E. O'Bannon and Wm. R. Halford decd. Exor. James Patterson and J. C. Buckingham.

ROBINSON, LEMUEL No Ref. Probate Judge Office. Barnwell, S.C. I Lemuel Robinson planter of Barnwell Dist. residing in the village of Barnwell do make this my last will and testament. I appoint my friends James Patterson and J. C. Buckingham both of Barnwell Court House my Executors. I give to my brother Ezekiel Robinson the sum of $500, the sum of $250 to be paid on the 1 Jan. 1863 and the other $250 to be paid 1 Jan. 1864. I give to Mrs. Ann Allmon all that tract of land whereon she now lives, lying on the West side of Turkey Creek containing 13 1/2 acres, adj. land of James Kemp, Dr. James E. O'Bannon and land belonging to the est. of William R. Halford decd. also she is to have the first years provision off my place and also pay unto her annually the sum of $70 out of my est. for her natural life. I give to my brother in law John McChany my gold watch and chain. I give the

Robinson, Lemuel - Continued. remainder of my est. both real and personal to Mrs. Mary Ann Attaway the wife of H. B. Attaway who resides now in Burke Co., Ga. I desire the property to remain as it is, and that the negroes not taken from the Dist. or State. Property not subject to her husband debts, contracts, or any future husband she may have, at her death property to be equally divided among any heirs she may have, share and share alike. I desire my executors to bind my boy Frank, who I have raised in the house, to Mr. J. C. Buckingham until Frank attains the age of twenty one, and be instructed in the art of and trade of a taylor. I do not wish that Frank be sold or put to any other trade than that of his trade. Dated this 7 Dec. 1861. Wit: J. W. Freeman, J. O. Hagood, N. G. W. Walker. Signed: Lemuel Robinson.

ROBINSON, MARTHA Box 49 File 2055. Probate Judge Office. York, S. C. On 20 July 1821 Samuel Givins Esq. Philander Moore and William Burnes are bound unto Thomas Bennett Ord. of York Co. in the sum of $10,000. Samuel Givins Esq. was appointed guardian of Martha a minor child of William Robinson decd. (no other papers).

ROBINSON, MARTHA Case 49, File 2055. Probate Judge Office. York, S. C. On 20 July 1821 Samuel Givins Esq., Philander Moore, and William Burnes are bound unto Thomas Bennett in the sum of $10,000. Samuel Givins Esq. gdn. of Martha Robinson minor. Child of William Robinson decd.

ROBINSON, MRS. MARTHA M. Bundle 83, Pack 11. Probate Judge Office. Barnwell, S. C. Est. admnr. 22 Feb. 1843 by Jacob R. Harley, William H. Peyton and James Patterson Esq. are bound unto O. D. Allen, Ord. in the sum of $10,000. On 6 July cash recd. of A. O. Norris Commissioner in Equity of Anderson Dist. $901.27. Paid 8 Feb. 1847 Robert S. Smith and wife in full for their interest in the est. of Richard Moncuiff, for which James E. Robinson had credit on settlement with Est. $500. Paid Wm. R. Erwin Guardian of Mary E. and Wm. D. Robinson $2983.27.

ROBINSON, MARY Will Book G, Page 85. Probate Judge Office. York, S. C. I Mary Robinson being very sick and weak in body but of health sound and disposing mind and memory. It is my will that my son John I. Abernethie who has been most attentive tender and affectionate child. I do give him all my real and personal estate, consisting of John S. Jones note, indorsed by Norman and Jones, dated 15 March 1819 with a mortgage on said note, also my half of the bond and mortgage given by Jacob Davis dated 1 June 1819, for purchase of a house and lot at 40 Queen Street. Amounting to $1340.00. Also bed and bedding, household and kitchen furniture. I give to my disobedient of my dtr. Mary Davis, I only will her $25.00 to purchase her a mourning suit. I desire my just debts and doctor bills and funeral expenses. I appoint my son John I. Abernethie and friend James Sweeny executors. Dated 25 June 1819. Wit: Eliza Sweeny, Frances Sweeny, Mary Kilkelly. Signed: Mary Robinson. Probated 23 April 1822.

ROBINSON, MARY C. Box 2 #79. Probate Judge Office. York, S.C. Est. Admnr. 21 Dec. 1844 by James C. Shearer, Wm. Shearer, Thomas Shearer who are bound unto John M. Ross, Esq. Ord. in the sum of $500. Charles L. Robinson, William T. Robinson etc. bought at sale.

ROBINSON, MARK Bundle 15 Pack 2. Probate Judge Office. Barnwell, S. C. Est. admnr. 17 Feb. 1809 by Capt. Robert Bradly, William B. Willard and Joseph Duncan who are bound unto O. D. Allen Ord. in the sum of $1500.

ROBINSON, NANCY W. Case 38 File 1604. Probate Judge Office. York, S. C. Est. admnr. 14 Jan. 1840 by James C. Shearer, Wm. Shearer, Richard Shearer who are bound unto Benj. Chambers Ord. in the sum of $500. Cit. Pub. at Bullucks Creek. Divided into four parts viz, Mrs. Mary Robinson widow of Robinson, Charles L. Robinson, William T. Robinson and two minor children of James C. Shearer.

ROBINSON, MARY Box 59 $2098. Probate Judge Office. Camden, S. C. On 20 Jan. 1810 James Smith and John Smith were bound unto Isaac Alexander Ord. in the sum of $1,000.00 James Smith guardian of Mary Robinson minor.

ROBINSON, NATHANIEL Pack 10, Clerk of Court Office. Anderson, S. C. Pendleton Dist. This indenture made this 2 Jan. 1806 Between Nathaniel Robinson and John Duncan both of Pendleton Dist. In consideration of $200 in hand paid, doth, bargain, sell and release a tract of land containing 200 acres, originally granted to James Scot the 6 Jan. 1785. Lying on South Broadaway, waters of Savannah River. Wit: Anderson Duncan, Wm. Johnston. Signed: Nathaniel Robinson. Proved on oath of William Johnson before E. Brown, J.Q. this 3 Jan. 1806. This day came Elizabeth Robinson the wife of and renounce, release and forever relinquish all right and interest in the above land. Dated this 3 Jan. 1806. Signed: E. Brown, J.Q.

ROBINSON, NICHOLAS Box 59 #2097. Probate Judge Office. Camden, S. C. Est. admnr. 8 Nov. 1798 by Charles Robinson, Frances Robinson, John Kirkpatrick and John Naudin are bound unto Burwell Boykin, Isaac Dubose, and James Kershaw Judges of Kershaw Dist. in the sum of $4,000.00. Robert Ford, Isham Powell, Frederick Robinson, Thomas Lankford bought at sale.

ROBINSON, MRS. Box 94 #987. Probate Judge Office. Pickens, S. C. L. C. Hester decd. whose est. was admnr. 10 Sept. 1866 in Pickens Dist. mention as heirs, the heirs of a Mrs. Robinson. No other name given.

ROBINSON, NANCY No Ref. Abbeville, S. C. Abbeville Dist. In the Court of Ordinary. The petition of John Gray, John Faulkner, Lewis Covin, Philip Leroy, and Thomas McBride as some of the heirs that would have an interest in the estate if she died intestate. States that any paper pruposing to be a will of Nancy Robinson is no will and that should any paper be presented for probate, that the same may be required to be fines? witness in solemen form of law. Dated 9 June 1851. Recd. from John Gray and Lewis admnr. of the est. of Nancy Robinson decd. the sum of $276.91 being my own share of the est. and my children viz; Elizabeth Baugh, George House, Thomas House, John House, do hereby guarantee that not one of my chn. will shall ever claim the same again from the admnr. Date ___ 1855. Signed: Thomas X House. Recd. this day from John Gray and Lewis Covin admnr. of the est. of Nancy Robinson decd. the sum of $553.82 in full of the est. of said decease. Dated April 26, ___. Signed: T. C. X McBride and Jane X McBride.

ROBINSON, PATRICK Will Book A-12, Page 86. Probate Judge Office. York, S. C. I Patrick Robinson of York Co. and Pinckney Dist. being very sick in body but of perfect mind and memory. I give to my beloved wife Sarow (Sarah) the house and land that I live on, during her life or widowhood, with all household furniture, stock. I also give to my dtr. Elizabeth Gillom the land lying between the Broad River and Gilkeys Creek and Ebets Creek. I also give to my dtrs. Cetura and Sarah my land lying on the lowest side of Bullockes Creek adj. the land I now live on. I also give to my dtrs. Agnes and Jean the land I now live on after the decease of my wife. I appoint my beloved wife and Samuel Robertson my executors. Dated 12 March 1793. Wit: Joseph Robinson, Samuel Neisbett, Isaac Leaney. Signed: Patrick Robinson.

ROBINSON, POLLY Apt. 1 File 26. Probate Judge Office. Greenville, S. C. On 16 July 1827 Nancy Benson the admnr. of the estate of Robert Benson decd. of Greenville Dist. who in his life time advanced property to his following children of which Polly Robinson was mentioned.

ROBISON, JOSEPH Case 35 File 1491. Probate Judge Office. York, S. C. I Joseph Robison of York Dist. will all my just debts and funeral expenses be paid. I will all my estate to my wife for and during her natural life. I will at the death of my wife all my estate be equally divided amongst my children share and share alike, the

Robison, Joseph - Continued. legal title of the share of my dtr. Elizabeth Jenkins is to remain in my executor hands and any interest or rent to be paid over to her annually, at her death I direct that her share to be equally divided amongst her chn. living at that time. I appoint my sons Andrew E. Robison and William Robison executors. Dated this 7 April 1856. Wit: J. L. McElwei, Wm. S. Plaxico, J. L. Crawford. Signed: Joseph Robison.

ROBINSON, SAMUEL Box 31 #160. Probate Judge Office. Pickens, S. C. I Samuel Robinson of Anderson Dist. being weak in body but of sound mind and memory. I will and desire that my just debts be paid. I devise and give to my beloved wife Louiza M. Robinson all of my estate both real and personal for her use and benefit during her natural life or widowhood, at her death or marriage, I desire all my property to be sold and distributed according I devise to my wife Louisa M. Robinson should she remain a widow until the children come of age, or marry and leave her, the power to help the child so long as she can do it without injury to the rest of my chn. Anything they take, she is to get receipt for the amount, except my son James M. Robinson is to have nothing until the final distribution. I devise to Meredith H. Brock in trust for my son James M. Robinson an equal share at the final distribution. The said share is to be for his sole use and benefit, should he die without heirs, then any property to return to my estate. I appoint my brother in law Merideth H. Brock executor. Dated this 4 Nov. 1853. Wit: C. C. Armstrong, H. N. Brock, W. H. Brock. Signed: Samuel Robinson. Proved 3 Dec. 1853.

ROBINSON, SARAH Box 62 #2848. Probate Judge Office. York, S.C. Est. admnr. 3 Oct. 1791 by Thomas Davis, Wm. Davis, Robert Adams, John Spence who are bound unto Wm. Hill Ord. in the sum of ₺100. Paid Mrs. Ann McKenzie account 31.4.0.₺.

ROBINSON, WILLIAM Case 38 File 1632. Probate Judge Office. York, S. C. Est. admnr. 17 Oct. 1879 by James L. Moss and Joseph R. Moss are bound to J. A. McLean in the sum of $300. Died 28 May 1879 leaving a brother and sister viz, Ira Robison and Mr. J. R. Ross.

ROBINSON, WILLIAM Bundle 80 Pack 9. Probate Judge Office. Sumter, S. C. Est. admnr. 1 June 1803 by Mary Robinson, Willie Robinson Senr., and Underhill Ellis of Salem County are bound unto Wm. Taylor Esq. Ord. in the sum of $1,000. Paid cash 11 Dec. 1802 in support of Martha Robinson 3 yrs. $30.00. For the support Benny R. Robinson 3 yrs. $30.00. For support of Jonathan, Sovereign and John Robinson each for 3 yrs. $50.00 total $150.00. (name written Robinson, R. Robertson).

ROBINSON, WILLIAM Box 49 #541. Probate Judge Office. Pickens, S. C. I William Robinson a farmer of Pickens Dist. being feeble in body but of sound and disposing mind and memory. It is my will that my just debts be paid. I give to the children by my first wife (not named) the sum of one dollar, not in a spirit of unkindness but in great affection and sense of duty, as the chn. by the first wife are mature in age and able to support themselves. The chn. by the second wife are young and comparitively helpless, requiring all my limited means for their nuture and education and support of their mother and themselves. I give to my beloved wife Elizabeth Robinson and my dear children to wit; dtr. Elizabeth Robinson, son, Robert Robinson, son, James Boyd Robinson, dtr. Josephine G. Robinson, dtr. Margaret Robinson, dtr. Victoria Robinson and any other child my wife may have by me before my death, all the land on which I now live to my wife and my children in fee simple, adj. lands of Robert Maxwell Jr., James L. Boyd, All my stock, tools, household and kitchen furniture. It is my will that my wife have the management of all my property of every kind, until her youngest child by me come of age, or until she marries again, if this happens, I desire that the property be sold and equally divided amongst my wife and her chn. by me, share and share alike. Dated this 18 Nov. 1858. Wit: John W. L. Cary, H. W. M. Boggs, John C. Fringe. Signed: William Robinson. Proven 6 Dec. 1858.

ROBINSON, WILLIAM D. Bundle 172 Pack 2. Probate Judge Office. Barnwell, S. C. Est. admnr. 4 March 1867 by Richard Johnson, Thos. H. Johnson, James J. Ingram who are bound unto John W. Freeman, Ord. in the sum of $8,000. Died in the fall of 1864. Left a father James E. Robinson and his sister Mary E. the wife of Richard Johnson.

ROBINSON, WILLIAM SENR. Box 36 #1534. Probate Judge Office. York, S. C. I William Robinson Senr. being sick and in a low state of body but of sound judgment and understanding. First I will that all my lawful debts be paid. I will to my beloved dtr. Martha Robinson, a negro woman named Jude and her eight chn. with all my land and grist mill and saw mill and also that a negro man named Harry and a negro man named Yogue be sold or hired and the money arising, I will to my dtr. Martha. Should my dtr. die without any lawful heirs, my property should be equally divided amongst brother Robert Robinson family. I appoint Samuel Given executor. Dated this 24 Feb. 1821. Wit: Geo. Wright, Robert Robinson, Jane Robinson. Signed: William X Robinson. Probated 7 March 1821.

ROBISON, WILLIAM Case 37, File 1565. Probate Judge Office, York, S. C. I William Robison of York Dist. being weak of body in a low state of health, but of a sound and disposing mind and memory. I give to my wife Isabell the whole of my plantation whereon I now live during her life time, at her death, I desire that the land be sold and the money equally divided among all my chn. to my wife. I also give her two horses and two plows and harness, I also give to my wife two cows and calves. I give to the deacons of New Bethel Church $100 for the benefit of said church, if the church disorganize then the money to return to my executors. To the deacons I give the sum of $75 to be disposed of in the Baptist or Burmah Mission. I give to my dtr. Melissa one cow and calf. I desire the balance of my est. of every description shall be sold and the money equally divided among my sons James Robison, Clark Robison and James Biggers my son in law, Quinn Robert Robison also my grandson James, Wilson, William, and Samuel Wilson. I desire my wife Isabell and son James Robison be executors Dated this 11 March 1838. Wit: Wm. Meek, Geo. Wright, John Minter. Signed: Wm. Robison. Probated 19 March 1838.

ROCHESTER, SARAH E. Box 2 #49. Probate Judge Office. Pickens, S. C. On 6 Nov. 1854 John Sharp Esq., John C. Nevill, John Rankins are bound to W. L. Parson Ord. in the sum of $500. John Sharp guardian of Sarah E. Rochester minor under 21 yrs. Recd. from the Ordinary of Union Dist. $157.14. Recd. of admnr. of the est. of Asberry Rochester decd. $27.00. Paid 31 Jan. 1856 C. M. Sharp and wife Sarah $144.80.

RODGERS, THOMAS Box 62 Pack 5. Probate Judge Office. Laurens, S. C. Thomas Rodgers admnr. of Letty Rodgers decd. denies that William A. Rodgers has nay right or just claim whatsoever for anything more of the estate of Andrew Rodgers decd. or of the estate of Letty Rodgers decd. than what he already has. Because he has already received more than twice as much as all the rest of the children of the deceased which is manifest by the papers herewith exhibited. And because after the death of their father Andrew Rodgers it was expressly agreed between William A. Rodgers and his mother who was the administratrix of her deceased husband Andrew Rodgers and all the others heirs that, that William A. Rodgers should have 340 acres of land which belonged to his father, in his lifetime, as his whole share of the estate, and he was never to make any claim for any thing more which said land is worth as much as all the rest of the estate of which his father died seized and possessed, and of which said land the said William Rodgers now holds uninterrupted possession. The foresaid contract can be proven by many living witnesses." Said Thomas has frequently cited William Rodgers to attend at his house, and make his claim against the estate if any or to come for an equal share with the rest of the heirs, but being fully conscious of his having no claim whatever he never attended. Therefore the said Thomas refuses to pay him any more of the estate of his deceased mother. No date given. Signed: Thos. Rodgers admnr. of Letty Rodgers decd.

ROGERS, FELEX Deed Book G-1, Page 612. Clerk of Court Office.
Pickens, S. C. I Felix Rogers of Pickens Dist. in consideration of
$263 to me paid by Calvin Odell of the same Dist. have granted, sold,
conveyed and released a tract of land containing 40 1/2 acres lying
in said Dist. on waters of 18 Mile Creek of 12 Mile River. Adj. land
of Calvin Odell and myself. Dated this 8 Jan. 1855. Wit: John Bowen,
Wm. Odell. Signed: Felix Rogers. Proved on oath of Wm. Odell before
John Bowen, J.P. this 18 Jan. 1855. This day came Cassandra Rogers the
wife of Felex Rogers and did renounce, release and forever relinquish
unto Calvin Odell all her right and claim of dower in the above land.
John Bowen, J.P. Signed: Cassandra Rogers. Recd. 2 Apr. 1855.

ROGERS, MARY Pack 332 #5. Clerk of Court Office. Pickens, S.C.
On 19 June 1851 Mary Rogers a single woman made oath that on the 13
of May last past she was delivered of a bastard female child and that
Elias Mason is the father of said child.

ROGERS, MAJOR JAMES Grant Book L, #8. Secretarys Office.
Columbia, S. C. Pursuance of an act of the Legislature, entitled.
An act for granting the land now vacant, etc. Passed 19 Feb. 1791.
We have granted unto Major James Rogers a tract of land containing 127
acres, surveyed for him the 4 March 1818 on waters of Little River and
Ocenny Creek in Pendleton Dist. adj. land of Major Rogers, McDows,
Boyd, and Wm. Hammonds. Signed: John Geddes Esq. Governor. Dated
this 4 Jan. 1819.

ROLAND, JEFFERSON Pack 31 #6. (in basement). Clerk of Court
Office. No County. In Oct. 1830 Jefferson Roland was mentioned as
the husband of Lucy Trimmier dtr. of Col. Obadiah Trimmier decd. and
his wife Lucy Trimmier.

ROGERS, MAJOR JAMES SENR. In Equity, File 35. Clerk of Court
Office. Pickens Dist. Major James Rogers Senr. of Pickens Dist. died
6 Sept. 1847. Wife Ann Rogers, Children, James Rogers, A. D. Rogers,
Edward Rogers, John McWhorter and wife Sarah, Temperance McWhorter
widow of James McWhorter, Prudence Drennan widow of Wilson Drennan,
Amos Robinson and wife Nelly all of the State of Georgia. Hugh Rogers
resides in Arkansas. The heirs at law of John Rogers who died since
his father, to wit. his widow ___ Rogers, and his chn. and their
husbands. Viz, Emerson Black and Elizabeth Rogers. Moore and Sarah
Rogers his wife, James Rogers, Zachariah Rogers who are over 21 yrs.
and William Rogers, John Rogers, David Rogers, who are minors all, of
said heirs of John Rogers reside in the State of Texas, Margaret
Rogers. James Rogers had 10 children. Filed in Equity 1858.

ROPER FAMILY of Pickens County, S. C. Who gave the irformation
is not given.
1. Benjamin Roper Sr. died 8 Aug. 1831 in Pickens County. Wife
Susannah Roper, left 12 children only 10 are mentioned. Children:
Meredith Roper, John H. Roper, Jacob Roper, Aaron Roper, Keziah Roper,
Cazzy Roper wife of John Birus, Rachel Ward, ___ Roper M. J. M. Keith,
Benjamin Roper, Nancy Roper. After his death Moses Hendricks bought the
tract of land.
2. Aaron Roper Sr. died 17 Sept. 1855, left 10 children. Wife died
and buried about the same time Aaron Roper Sr. was buried. Children:
Lemuel Roper, John Roper, Matilda Roper married Joab Lankford, Jane
Roper married a ___ Hagood (died some years before her parents).
Tilmon Roper died before his parents. Left children, viz, Catharine
Roper over 12yrs., John Roper under 14 yrs., James Roper under 14 yrs.
David Roper under 14 yrs., Tilmon Roper under 14 yrs. Charles Roper
died in 1855 left 2 chn. Ira Thomas and Starling Roper. Tyre L.
Roper, Aaron Roper Jr., Marcus Roper married Susan Hendricks dtr. of
Larkin Henricks, Marena Roper married Simeon E. Burgess. Hamilton
Roper married Clarinda Turner. Dtr. of Benjamin of Greenville Dist.
Lemuel Roper married Jane left four chn. viz, William Noble Roper,
Bailey Roper under 14 yrs., Martha Roper, Elmina Roper under 12 yrs.
all resides in Georgia in 1855. Hamilton Roper's widow Clarinda
states that she was married to him in Greenville Dist. in Jan. 1853
and lived with him until June 1854. During which time she had a male

Roper Family - Continued. child by him which died when but a
few weeks old.
3. Rev. Tyre L. Roper, son of Aaron Roper Sr. died 27 March 1876.
Wife, Darcas Jane ___. Children: Margaret A. Roper a minor. Leander
Roper a minor, Thomas Walters Roper a minor, Rachel Roper married a
___ Gillespie, Rebecca C. Roper married David Lewis of Eastland Co.,
Texas, Jesse E. Roper, Samuel Roper, Elijah Roper, Ann Madison Roper,
married ___ Satterfield, Amos Roper, Mary O. Roper married ___ Suther-
land, Vashti Roper, married Joel R. Jones.
4. Charles Roper, son of Aaron Roper Sr. died 13 Oct. 1855. Widow
___? Children: Ira Thomas Roper a minor, Starling Roper a minor.
5. Joshua Roper, died 3 March 1856. Wife Mary ___. Children:
Absalom Roper. "Land on East side of Town Creek", Charles Roper,
Samuel Roper, Joshua Roper, Alfred Roper, William Roper, Singleton
Roper, Rutha Roper married ___ Crow, Eleanor Roper married James
Spearman, Synthia Roper married Jesse Crain, Mary Roper married William
Byers. Others heirs were: Henry and Adaline Lawson, Tyre Roper,
Rebecca Roper, Malinda Roper Newman, Elizabeth Duncan, Redin Byers.
On 6 Jan. 1868 paid 3 minors heirs of William Byers $13.45.
6. Ira T. Roper died 24 April 1895.
7. Absalom Roper died 7 Sept. 1901. Wife Nancy Roper. Children:
Mrs. Mattie A. Roper married ___ Spann. Anna married ___ McDavid,
Nannaie A. Roper married ___ Norris, John Roper, W. H. Roper, William
Roper, Ellen Roper married ___ Moor, Gideon Roper died 21 Oct. 1861.
Wife Elizabeth Roper. Other children names not given.
8. Charles Roper son of Absalom Roper died 19 Oct. 1883. Wife
Margaret ___? Children: Martha Roper married ___ Tripp, Elizabeth
Roper married ___ Kay, Adeline Roper married ___ Davis, Mary Roper
married ___ Davis, Margaret Roper married ___ Smith, A. Alonzo Roper
married ___? Sarah E. Roper married ___ Satterfield, Frances L.
Roper married ___ Kelly, Laura A. Roper married ___ Kelly, Daily Roper,
Susan Roper married ___ Lawson, dead, Martha Roper married ___ Jarratt.

ROPER, MARCUS Box 64 #690. Probate Judge Office. Pickens, S.C.
Susan Hendricks dtr. of Larkin Hendricks decd. who died in Pickens
Dist. whose will was proven 6 Oct. 1862. Wife of Marcus Roper. On
18 May 1861 Absalom Roper wife Malinda and Harrison Roper wife Susan
were the dtrs. of David Gilliland decd. of Pickens Dist.

ROPER, SAMUEL E. Deed Book B, Page 60. Probate Judge Office.
Pickens, S. C. On 23 Nov. 1861 Samuel E. Roper and his wife Louisa
Roper were all heirs of John Cassell decd. of Pickens Dist. and his
widow Fanny Cass.

ROPER, MARCUS Deed Book B, Page 70. Probate Judge Office.
Pickens, S. C. On 5 Jan. 1863 Marcus Roper and wife Susan were heirs
of Milton M. Hendricks decd. of Pickens Dist. He died leaving neither
wife or child. (Note, probably a brother to her.)

ROSEMON, EMMA Pack 647 #6. Clerk of Court Office. Pickens,
S. C. I Emma Rosemon of Pickens Dist. for and in consideration of the
sum of fifty dollars to be paid to Walter Brown also the fifty dollars
to be paid to Rosa Brown when the above named children then become
twenty one years old that is to say Walter Brown now eight yrs. old
and Rosa Brown now six yrs. old, do hereby convey to David Thomas my
two children Walter Brown and Rosa Brown until they shall become
of full age to have and hold the aforesaid children in the manner
aforesaid to the David Thomas a good and lawful deed to the aforesaid
children upon the afore condition. Dated this 17 May 1910. Wit:
J. C. Boggs, W. M. Boggs. Signed: Emma X Rosemen. Proved on oath
of J. C. Boggs before M. A. Boss Mag. P.D. this 17 May 1910. Filed
this 6 June 1910.

ROSENBURG, PHILIP Petition for citizenship #3. Clerk of Court
Office. Abbeville Dist. In the Court of Common Pleas. The Honr.
T. J. Mackey, Presiding. The petition of Philip Rosenburg aged twenty
four yrs. following the profession of a merchant, sheweth that he
arrived in the U.S. in May 1872 at New York City and resided in that
State two years, and resided in this State four yrs. He arrived in

Rosenburg, Philip - Continued. this Country under the age of eighteen and it has been his bona fide intention to become a citizen. That he is attached to the constitution of the U.S. and well disposed to the good order and happiness of the same. That he prays that he may become a citizen of this Country. Signed: P. Rosenburg. I do solemnly swear that the contents of my petition are just and true, that I will support the constituion of the U.S. of America, and that I do hereby absolutely, and entirely renounce all allegiance and fidelity to every foreign Prince, Potentate, State or sovereignty whatever and particularly to his Majesty Alexander the Czar of Russia of whom I was born a subject. Dated this 27 April 1878. Signed: P. Rosenburg. Wit: M. G. Zeigler. The petition was granted.

ROSS, GEORGE F. Deed Book B, Page 91. Probate Judge Office. Pickens, S. C. On 23 Jan. 1866, George F. Ross owned 137 acres in Pickens Dist. adj. land of John Ross, Thomas R. Davis and others. John Ross the father of said decease. Heirs were: John Ross, heirs of Willey Ross decd. viz, Thomas, Morgan, Richard, Mary and Melissa Ross. Alexander White and wife Milly, Elizabeth Barker, Reuben Lee and wife Gilla, Miles Moss and wife Manerva, Harriet Ross, Jesse R. Ross, Heirs of John Ross Jr., decd. viz, Melissa, Sarah M., William L. and Jesse A. Ross. Lunsford M. Ross, heirs of Melissa Vaughn decd. viz, Harriet Vaughn all in the State except Lunsford M. Ross.

ROPER, GEORGE Pack 640 #3. Clerk of Court Office. Pickens, S. C. On 23 June 1878 George Roper states that he is the husband of Mary Roper of Pickens Dist. and that her father B. S. Porter died about 5 yrs. ago. That her father had 12 children but only 11 were living.

ROPER, SARAH Pack 645 #11. Clerk of Court Office. Pickens, S.C. Sarah Roper died 5 Oct. 1846 in the poor house in Pickens Dist.

ROSS, JOHN File 36. No other inf. Camden Dist. John Ross of Camden Dist. was the grandfather of Green Bowen age about 5 yrs. Henry Bowen about 2 yrs. whose father was Philip P. Bowen. On 8 March 1877, Burwell Abbert their guardian.

ROSS, MARY Apt. 6 File 246. Probate Judge Office. Greenville, S. C. Drury Morris decd. of Greenville Dist. in his life time advanced property to Mary Ross. His estate admnr. 1 June 1818 by Mrs. Rachel Morris and Drury Morris.

ROSS, MARY M. Box 120 #9. Probate Judge Office. Pickens, S.C. Est. admnr. 18 Aug. 1892 by J. R. Ross, N. R. Kennemore, D. R. Jones are bound unto J. B. Newberry, Ord. in the sum of $100. Died 26 March 1892. Wife of J. R. Ross. On 23 Nov. 1898 Mrs. M. E. Bolden, J. W. Ross, Miss M. D. Ross, J. D. Ross, J. R. Ross, Mrs. L. M. Kennemore each recd. a share.

ROTHEL, CLAIBORN Pack 630 #28. Clerk of Court Office. Pickens, S. C. By James E. Hagood, Clerk of Court, To any lawful surveyor you are hereby authorized to lay out unto Claiborn Rothel a tract of land not exceeding one thousand acres, and make a true plat thereof and return to my office within two months. Dated this 20 Feb. 1860. Executed for 318 acres the 22 Feb. 1860. Tyre B. Mauldin, D.S. Filed 16 April 1860.

ROUNDTREE, JESSE Old Records B.B. Page 111. 96 Dist. Abbeville, S. C. Jesse Roundtree as a citizen 2497 acres, lying in Edgefield County on the NW side of the Big Horn Creek surveyed by Robert Lang D.S. on the 20 March 1786. Recorded this 11 April 1786. R. Anderson C.L.

ROUNDTREE, JESSE Old Records, B.B. 96 Dist. Abbeville, S. C. Jesse Roundtree as a citizen 132 acres of land lying in Edgefield County on Big Horn Creek waters of Savannah River. Bounded by land of Phillip Lamars, and vacant land, on old surveyed land surveyed by David Brooks D.S. this 29 Sept. 1785. Recorded this 16 Dec. 1785. R. Anderson C.L.

ROUNDTREE, JETHRO Box 80 Pack 1967. Probate Judge Office. Abbeville, S. C. We Jesse Roundtree, Daniel Shaw, Simeon Cushman are bound unto John Ewing Calhoun Esq. Ord. in the sum of fourteen thousand pounds current money. Dated at Cuffetown in the dist. aforesaid this 26 Nov. 1782. Wit: Andw. Pickens. Whereas Jesse Roundtree as the next of kin, to be and appear before me in the Court of Ordinary, to be held at Fort Boone, Long Canes, on the Friday after the publication hereof to show cause if any they have why the said admnor should not be granted. Dated 24 April 1782. Read publicly the 24 Novr. 1782. Wit: John Murry, Jno. Ewing Calhoun [sic]. The appraisers were Daniel Shaw, Benjamin Harris, John Sturzenegger, returned the appraisement the 16 Dec. 1782. (The inventory was to dim to copy.)

ROUNDTREE, JOB Box 81 Pack 1996. Probate Judge Office. Abbeville, S. C. 96Dist. We Jesse Roundtree, John Sturzeonaire and Leonard Myres are bound unto John Thomas Junr. Ord. of this Dist. in the sum of two thousand Ł sterling. Dated 29 Nov. 1783. Estate was appraised by Daniel Shaw, James Richard, Leonard Meyers. The 4 Dec. 1783.

RUSH, DAVID #470. Clerk of Court Office. Abbeville, S. C. Edgefield Dist. I David Rush of Edgefield Dist. in consideration of $100 to me paid by Jacob Gable and Samuel Gallaher of Abbeville Dist. have granted bargained sold and released all that tract of land containing 100 acres, lying and being in Edgefield Dist. on waters of Cuffatown Creek, adj. land of David Rush, heirs of John Shibley and land granted to Elizabeth Bowers. Dated this 18 Aug. 1818. Wit: William X Doris, Joseph X Thorenton. David Rush. N.B. It is understood by the parties above named that David Rush is not to warrant and defend the land above named against nay person or persons except himself and his heirs. Proved on oath of William Dorris before Samuel Perrin, J.Q. of Abbeville Dist. this 26 Aug. 1818.

RUSK, JAMES Pack 3 (Basement). Clerk of Court Office. Anderson, S. C. Pendleton Dist. To the Honr. John F. Grimke, Presiding Judge. The petition of James Rusk a native of County of Antrin in Ireland. He arrived in Charleston, S. C. on the 13 Nov. 1805. That he is attached to the principles of the U.S. Constitution and is desirous of becoming a citizen thereof. Given to the Oct. term of Court in 1809. We do hereby certify that we have known James Rusk since the year 1805, and that he is of good moral character and attached to the principles of the Constitution. Signed: Thomas Farrar, David Sloan, Wm. Thompson, Andrew Noble, Obadiah Trimmier, James McKinney, David Sloan Junr., B. Earle. He takes the oath in the Court held in Pendleton Dist. in Oct. 1809.

RUSSELL, Family in South Carolina before 1790. Timothy Russell had 200 acres of land in Abbeville Dist. on waters of Long Cane Creek adj. land of William McCrowns, William Robjnson, Widow Boggs. Land surveyed 15 July 1785. George Russell had 897 acres above the line on Camp Creek waters of Saluda River. Surveyed by Thomas Lofton the 3 Sept. 1787. Robert Russell had 157 acres on Westcoats Creek waters of Savannah River. Land surveyed 5 Jan. 1786. William Russell had 250 acres on water of Little River on the N. West fork of Long Cane surveyed by William Lesly D.S. the 26 Aug. 1785.

RUSSELL, JOHN Box 83 Pack 2034. Probate Judge Office. Abbeville, S. C. I John Russell Senr. of Abbeville County, 96 Dist. weaver, being not well in body, but of perfect understanding. I will and order that all my just debts be paid. I give to my dtr. Ann Russell my spinning wheel, loom, tackling, etc. household and kitchen furniture, bed, and bedding. I give to my dtr. Mary wife of Samuel Armstrong one guinea. I give to my dtr. Martha wife of James Miller one guinea. I give to my grandson William Russell a colt called the ball and five pounds to be paid to him within twelve months after my decease. The rest and remainder of my estate I give to my dtr. Ann Russell, sons John Russell and James Russell to be equally divided between them, share and share alike. I appoint my son John Russell Junr. and my son in law Samuel Armstrong executors and my dtr. Ann Russell executrix. Dated 20 Feb. 1796. Wit: John Hairson, R. A. Rapley, John Richmond.

Russell, John - Continued. Signed: John Russel. Proved on oath
of Richd. A. Rapley Esq. before Andrew Hamilton Ord. this 24 April 1800.

RUSSELL, JOHN   Pack 476. Clerk of Court Office. Abbeville,
S. C. To the Honr. the Chancellors, your oratrix Sarah Russell,
sheweth that about 23 May 1855 John Russell the husband of your oratrix
died intestate, leaving as next of kin, your oratrix his widow, and
children, Franklin Russell, Lewis Russell, Mary Jane, Anna and James.
The last two are minors. Your oratrix applied for and received letter
of admnr. upon the estate. That John Russell at time of his death
was entitled to a distributive share of his father William Russell
estate. William Russell died about the year 1847, leaving as his next
of kin his children, viz, Washington Russell, Polly Russell, Eliza
Russell, Grigzilla Russell, Jane afterwards married to Reuben Goodwin
and Rachel married to William Knox. At time of his death William was
possessed of a number of slaves to wit: Mary Ann and her chn. Tom,
George, Aaron, Adalin, Hannah and her two infant. Mary the mother of
the slaves was given by her father Samuel Huston to his dtr. the wife
of William Russell. At the time of the death of William all his
children was living with him except John and your oratrix who lived in
the same neighborhood. Filed 28 April 1859.

RUSSELL, MARTHA Deed Book R, Page 498. Clerk of Court. Anderson,
S. C. Pendleton Dist. we Martha Henderson, Mary Henderson, Ann Henderson, Robert Henderson, Alexander S. McClinton and Hannah McClinton all
of Pendleton Dist. heirs of John Henderson decd. in consideration of
$1.00 to us paid by the heirs of John Russell decd. viz Martha Russell
and the legatees and heirs, have granted, sold, bargained and released
all that tract of land containing 25 acres lying in said Dist. on the
East side of the Devils Fork of Generostee Creek waters of Savannah
River. Beginning at the fork on the Devils forks, where the road
crosses leading from James Gunnins mills to Shockleys ferry, etc.
Dated this 7 Oct. 1824. Wit: Thomas A. Patrick, Rachel McCarley.
Signed: Martha X Henderson, Mary X Henderson, Anna Henderson, Robert
Henderson, Alexander S. McClinton, Hannah McClinton. Proved on oath of
Thomas Patrick before Solomon Skelton QM this 11 Oct. 1824. Recorded
23 Oct. 1826.

RUSSELL, THOMAS H. Pack 382 #5. Clerk of Court Office. Pickens,
S. C. I Thomas H. Russell of Pickens County. In consideration of
$150 to me paid by Moses S. Hendrix of the same County, have granted,
sold, bargained and released unto Moses S. Hendrix two lots nos. 30
and 36 in the town of Easley on the North side of the Air Line Railway,
bounded by lots of W. H. Colcombe, and R. E. Bowen and by Cross Street.
Containing one acre each. Dated 23 Dec. 1875. Wit: E. B. O'Neal,
T. E. Boggs. Signed: Thos. H. Russell. Proved on oath of E. B.
O'Neal before R. E. Holcombe N.P. this 23 Dec. 1875. I T. W. Russell
N.P. do hereby certify that Mrs. Mary Jane Russell the wife of Thos.
H. Russell did freely and voluntarily renounce, release and relinquish
her interest and right of dower unto the said Moses S. Hendrix. Dated
this 17 March 1875 (1876). Signed: M. J. Russell.

SANDERS, "MINORS" Pack 412. Clerk of Court Office. Abbeville,
S. C. In 1829 John Little was the guardian of John Sanders, William
Sanders and Elizabeth Sanders minors and Thomas Sanders [sic]. On 10
July 1823 paid cash Joseph Davis for commission on the estate of John
and Anna Sanders decd. $162.25.

SATTERWHITE, BARTLETT Pack 322, Clerk of Court Office. Abbeville,
S. C. Abbeville Dist. In Equity, To the Honr. the Chancellors: Your
oratrix Susan Glover and your orator Wiley Glover of Benton County,
Ala. Sheweth that Bartlett Satterwhite formerly of Newberry Dist. in
this State the great grandfather of your orator, departed this life,
the time not precisely known. Between the 15 Feb. 1803 and the 14
April 1807, this being the interval of time between the making and
probate of his will. Under the second item in said will he gave to
his dtr. Jemima Glover then the wife of Wiley Glover your orator

Satterwhite, Bartlett - Continued. grandfather, to her and lawful heirs, the following slaves, Tener and Chaney and after the demise of his wife one negro named Jude and her increase. Your orator sheweth that Wiley Glover departed this life on the 8 Feb. 1806, leaving in full force his last will. Appointing his wife Jemima Glover executrix and James Bullock and Nathan Lipscombe executors, the first two qualified and acted and all are dead now. His wife Jemima Glover, his widow and his chn. Elizabeth Glover and Willis Satterwhite Glover, your orators father were his only devises and legatees. Jemima Glover intermarried with Nathan Lipscomb in March 1808. Elizabeth Glover married William Harris 1814. Filed a bill against Jamima Lipscomb and her husband on the 27 May 1815, to require them to account for the sale of the property of their father's estate. This filed 6 Nov. 1821. Jemima Lipcomb died 29 Jan. 1850, her will executed 18 April 1849 (these dates must be reversed) she bequeathed to her granddaughter Jemima Harris now the wife of E. S. Irvine. Another granddaughter Rebecca the wife of George A. Addison, Wiley Glover lived in Edgefield Dist. Bartlett Satterwhite of Newberry Dist. died 21 Jan. 1807. Legatees of this will, Dtr. Elizabeth Bullock, wife Rebecca, Dtr. Jamima Glover, grandson Elihu Bullock and Benjamin Franklin Bullock, grandson Satterwhite Bullock, grandson James Bullock, Whiley Bullock, granddaughter Elizabeth Glover, Grandson Willis Satterwhite Glover, Niece Martha Moor dtr. of Elish Moor and Susannah his wife. Nathan Lipscomb made his will 26 April 1820. Proved 12 April 1850.

SAXON, A. G. Letter of A. G. Saxon of Connersville, Indiana. Sent to me. My great grandfather, Alexander Saxon and wife, Mary Baldwin Saxon were living in Halifax, N.C. in the 1790 census and had three children. They probably went to S.C. and then on the Franklin Co., Ga. as William Saxon was born there, 17 March 1798. My grandfather Alexander Gillespie Saxon same place in 1802. Records shows their land was sold in 1808 to Robert Saxon and Michael Ragsdale. Then they came to Warren Co., Ohio. Stayed there almost a year, took the trail again west as far as John Conners trading post on the fork of the White Water River. This was in 1811. They did not unload the wagons, took up quarters in the Black House with the soldiers for the winter. There was a land sale held in Cincinnatti, Ohio on 8 Dec. 1811 they entered 160 acres, built a house in 1812 and run a ferry on the river. Alexander Saxon and wife had 9 children viz, James Saxon, John Saxon, William Saxon, Pheones Clayton, Alexander Gillespie Saxon, Elizabeth Saxon, Mary Ann Saxon, Robert Saxon, Selina Saxon. These were the chn. by his first wife Mary Baldwin. My grandfather Alexander Gillespie Saxon married Margaret McCrory in 1827. She came from County Antrim, Ireland with her parents at the age of 2 years during the winter of 1811-1812. Was six months on the water, landed in Philadelphia, Pa. Stayed there 7 yrs. Then came here in 1819. Alexander G. Saxon and Margaret McCrory had 12 chn. viz John Saxon, McHenry Saxon, William Saxon, Robert Saxon, James N. Saxon, Samuel Saxon, Jane Saxon, Selina Saxon, Anna Saxon, Savana Saxon, Mary Saxon, Elizabeth Saxon. My father was Robert Saxon born 31 Dec. 1842 and died 26 March 1913. My grandfather died July 1876. My great grandfather was born 11 Sept. 1767 and died Dec. 1844. Records of Georgia Rooster of the Revolution, page 316 Elizabeth M. Saxon entitled to draw in lottery of 1825 as widow of Revolutionary Soldier. Page 452, Solomon Saxon drew pension in 1840 as a Revo. soldier of Jackson County. President McKinley wife was a Saxon, my uncle McHenry Saxon went to see them in Ohio. H. B. Saxon of Abbeville was born and raised in Elbert County, Ga. brothers, R. L. and J. L. Saxon and two sisters still living at the old home, which has been in the family 136 years. One sister married S. W. Dixon. Grandfather name, Lewis Saxon born in N.C. moved to Elbert Co., Ga. when young. Grandfather name was William Yancy Saxon, killed in 1798 with 12 other Revolutionary soldiers while defending a fort in old 96 by bloody Bill Cunningham and his Indians. (This date must be wrong.)

SAXON, HUGH & MARY Deed Book D, Page 109. Clerk of Court Office. Elberton, Ga. This indenture made this 6 March 1790, between Hugh Saxon and Mary his wife of Washington Co., Ga. and Christopher Harris of Elbert Co., Ga. in consideration of 150 ℔ sterling, have

Saxon, Hugh & Mary - Continued. acknowledged, bargained, sold and released unto Christopher Harris a tract of land containing 200 acres. Adj. land of Robert Thomson, William Moss. Wit: Thomas Barton Jr., William X Thompson. Signed: H. Saxon and Mary Saxon. Proved on oath of William Thompson before James Bell J.P. this 6 Nov. 1797.

SAXON, HUGH Deed Book D, Page 109. Clerk of Court Office. Elberton, Ga. This indenture made this 6·March 1795 between Hugh Saxon and Mary his wife of Washington County, Ga. and Christopher Harriss of Elbert County, Ga. In consideration of 150Ŀ sterling, hath bargained, sold and released a tract of land containing 200 acres. Bounded by land of Robert Tomson, Brazels line, William Moss land. Wit: Thomas Barton Jr., William X Thompson. Signed: Hugh Saxon and Mary Saxon. Proved on oath of William Thompson before James Bell, J.P. this 19 March 1797. Reg. 6 Nov. 1797.

SAXON, JAMES No. Ref. Clerk of Court Office. Laurens, S. C. On this 18 April 1822, personally appeared in open Court, James Saxon of Laurens Dist., S. C. age 68 yrs. Being first duly sworn, doth on his oath declare that he served in the revolutionary war as follows, in the third regiment commanded by Col. William Thompson and Company commanded by Capt. Francis Boykin. That on the 13 April 1819 in the Circuit Court holden in Laurens Dist. that he made his declaration according with the law the 18 March 1818. He is to receive eight dollars per months, commence on the 13 April 1819. Certificate registered in Book B, Vol. 9 Page 163. His property at this time is books worth $50, a small bay mare worth $20, 12 head of sheep worth $18. He has been a planter, but from infirmity been unable to work scarcely able to walk out of the house, I have a wife named Anna aged 65 yrs. and a dtr. Sally aged 22 yrs. residing with me. Wit: John Garlington Clk. Signed: James Saxon. There are letters from Major James Dillard and William Dunlap, stating they knew James Saxon for a number of years, and that he was in need. On the 18 May 1835 a letter from J. L. Elmore, Esq. stating that the pension of James Saxon was to be transfered to the Alabama Dist. James Saxon died in Feb. 1836 in Autanga County, Ala.

SCALES, JOHN Book C (No page given). Clerk of Court Office. Elberton, Ga. This indenture made and agreed on this 7 March 1792. Between John Scales of Elbert County and William Skelton of the same county. In consideration of fifty pounds lawful money of this State, hath granted, sold, bargained, and released all that tract of land lying on North side of Big Cedar Creek containing 50 acres, bounded by land of Scales and Skelton. Wit: H. M. Donald, John Skelton. Signed: John X Scales. Proved on oath of Hugh McDonald, before M. Woods, J.P. this 31 July 1795. Registered 31 July 1795.

SCOTT, JOHN O. Pack 360, Clerk of Court Office. Abbeville, S.C. Abbeville Dist. In Equity, To the Honr. the Chancellors: Your oratrix Mary Scott, sheweth that her husband John O. Scott departed this life in the latter part of the year 1856, leaving in full force his last will. That Thomas B. Scott the brother of your oratrix husband is the sole executor. The said will directs that the entire property to remain in common for the use of his family, to receive support and maintainance and education out of the estate as long as unmarried, or upon the death of your oratrix. The chn, Maria E., Joseph A. and John O. Scott the oldest of whom is now about seven yrs. old. The testator at death possessed a small plantation but well stocked, and with five negroes, one of whom is a woman, raised to field work and unfit for house work. Your oratrix prays that her executor may purchase a young negro girl to be trained in house work. This may be done with money on hand and the proceeds of the crops upon the place. This would give her more time to prudent management of the plantation and to her three small children. Filed 11 June 1859. James McCelvey and W. M. Rogers were neighbors to John O. Scott decd. Scott will was made the 6 Oct. 1856 and named his brother-in-law Samuel R. Morrah, and his brother Thomas B. Scott as executors. Wit: M. O. Talman, P. Leroy, J. Oliver Lindsay.

SCOTT, MARY JANE Pack 309. Clerk of Court Office. Abbeville, S. C. Abbeville Dist. In Equity, To the Honr. the Chancellors: The petition of Mary Jane Scott, sheweth that she is without father or mother. Her father died about a month ago, mother has long since been dead. Mary Jane and her father lived in Anderson Dist. until his death. Since she has been living with an uncle James L. McCelvey of Abbeville Dist. and is going to school there. One William C. Scott swore that Joseph D. Scott was the father of Mary Jane Scott. This was before the Ordinary in Anderson Dist. on the 2 Oct. 1854. She prays that her uncle be made guardian of her person and her estate. Signed: Mary Jane Scott. Dated 3 Oct. 1854.

SCOTT, SAMUEL Pack 3356. Clerk of Court Office. Abbeville, S. C. Abbeville Dist. To the Honr. the Chancellors: Your orator John A. S. Martin sheweth that while an infant became entitled to a large estate both real and personal under the will of his grandfather Samuel Scott late of Edgefield Dist. By deed of gift from his late father Charles Martin of Edgefield Dist. The estate by reason of his tender age of your orator, was committed originally to Charles Martin as guardian, who died in the state of Mississippi in the year 1810. Then the said Thomas P. Martin about the year 1811 opened unofficially the management of the estate, receiving large sum of money from rent of the land and negroes. The said Thomas P. Martin was appointed guardian of the estate and person by this Court in 1814. Who continued until his death in 182__ (no number given). Who appointed his son John C. Martin as executor of his last will. The late Thomas Martin never made a return to the Court or your orator during the years he was guardian. Now his son refused an account or settlement. Your orator has only relief in this Honorable Court. Filed 2 Feb. 1830.

SHOCKLEY, RACHEL Pack 8 Clerk of Court Office. Anderson, S.C. Pendleton Dist. I Rachel Shockley (widow) of the same Dist. in consideration of $600 to me paid by Wm. Dyar of the same Dist. have granted, sell, and release all that tract of land containing 100 acres lying on waters of Savannah River. Bounded by land of Richard Shockley, William Dyar, and Mary Shockley and William Glenn. Dated this 6 July 1819. Wit: Mary Shockley, Ruth Oarley. Signed: Rachel X Shockley. Proved on oath of Mary Shockley before John T. Lewis J.Q. this 6 July 1819.

SMITH, AUGUSTUS M. Pack 311. In Equity, Clerk of Court Office. Abbeville, S. C. Abbeville Dist. In Equity To the Honr. the Chancellors: Your orators D.D. Wardlaw, W. Joel Smith, sheweth, as executors of the last will and testament of Augustus M. Smith decd. that he died 30 June 1862, having his domicil in Abbeville Dist. leaving as his only heirs and distributees, his widow Sarah M. Smith and two sons Lewis Wardlaw Smith, Augustus W. Smith, both infants who are yet under ten yrs. of age. Also James M. Perrin was appointed executor with your orators, all qualified in Aug. 1862. James M. Perrin died 4 May 1863. Smith had a large estate with about 1800 acres in Abbeville Dist. with a plantation of 2000 acres and 129 slaves with Thomas McGregor as partner. The rest of this suit deals with a note of $200,000.00 for 203 slaves to be delivered to him by Joseph H. Dallis. Filed 17 Feb. 1869.

SMITH, DAVID Will Book A, Page 197. Probate Judge Office. Union, S. C. I David Smith being weak in body but of perfect mind and memory. First all my lawful debts to be paid. I ordain and constitute my beloved wife Beershaba and Young G. Harington my executor and executrix, if my wife should marry then she retain the one third of my moveable property, with the use of negro Sue with her issue. Children to be raised and schooled out of her third with the use of negro Sam. I give the other two (one) third to my two sons James and Henry Smith, when Henry come of age, also the other two (one) third to my beloved dtrs. Fanny and Deliah to be equally divided between them, as they come of age. Dated this 1 Feb. 1806. Wit: Wm. Calter, Joseph Moorehead, Thos. Lusk. Signed: David X Smith. Proved on oath of William Colter before Nicholas Corry, J.P. this 25 Feb. 1806.

SMITH, DAVID Will Book A, Page 268. Probate Judge Office.
Union, S. C. I David Smith of Union County, S.C. being in a law
state of Health at present, but perfect in judgement and memory. First
all my lawful debts to be paid. All that I possess after my death
I bequeath to my wife Elizabeth Smith her life time, the household to
dispose of as she think proper, the land after her death to go to my
nephew Burrell Homesly or his heirs. Dated this 22 June 1811. Wit:
John Lockhart, Joseph X Ashworth, Ann Ashworth. Signed: David Smith.
Recorded 4 Nov. 1811.

SMITH, ELIZABETH Pack 112 #2. Clerk of Court Office. Pickens,
S. C. An inquest held at the house of the decd. widow Smith on 11
April 1859. The jury brought out that the decease died at her own
house on the night of 9 April 1859, the cause of death unknown to us.
Jemima Smith sworn sayeth that the baby commenced crying, she went to
the bed where the child and her mother was lying, she called to her
mother, but got no answer. She then called her brother and told him
that their mother had left them. James Smith sworn sayeth that his
sister went to the bed where their mother and baby was lying and called
to their mother, got no answer, she then called to him to get up, he
went to the bed and raised her up, and he called to Timothy Fincher
to get up. He sayeth that his mother was in her usual good health
when she went to bed. Masiah Long, sworn, sayth that he was at the
house of the decd. on the night of her death, and that she was in good
health as far as he knew. Mrs. Mary Fincher, sworn sayeth that she
help make the shroud for the decd. That she saw no marks of violence
on her body, when the shroud was put on her. Thimthy[sic] Fincher
sworn, sayeth that he was staying at the decd. house on the night of
her death. That about 4 O'clock he was awoke and heard Jemima Smith
calling to her brother to get up, James Smith then called him to get
up as their mother was dead, he arose and found her lying in her bed
dead.

SMITH, FLEET Will Book B, Page 190. Probate Judge Office.
Union, S. C. I Fleet Smith of Union Dist. being in a low state of
bodily health for a considerable time and am sensible of the change
that ever long may take place. I give to my son Levi Smith a horse
and saddle value of $50, also when he marry one bed and furniture.
I give to my son Isaac Smith a black mare and my saddle at $50, a
bed when he marry. I give to my son William Smith when he become the
age of 21, my bay mare and saddle, also one bed and furniture when he
marry. I give to my dtr. Dorcas Smith my sorrel mare colt, with a
saddle, also a bed and furniture at the age of 20 yrs. The balance
of my property to remain in possession of my executors for the benefit
of my wife and the younger children, until the youngest child become
of the age of 21 yrs. Each to have two years of schooling. My negro
boy Harry and girl Edaline, I leave with the executors for the wife as
long as she may live. I appoint my sons Levi and Isaac Smith
executors. Dated this 10 Jan. 1832. Wit: Thomas Woodson, William
Hood, Nathan Harlan. Signed: Fleet Smith. Proved on oath of Thomas
Woodson before John J. Pratt, Esq. Ord. this 27 Feb. 1832. Inventory
made 13 April 1832 by Thomas Woodson, Nathan Harlan, Henry Smith.

SMITH, JOHN Deed Book A, Page 21. Clerk of Court Office.
Elberton, Ga. This indenture made this 20 July 1790 between John
Smith and Pricillah his wife of Wilkes County, Ga. and Moses Davis
of Amhurst County, Va. In consideration of fifty pounds sterling.
John Smith and Pricillah hath granted, bargained, sold, and released
all that tract of land in Wilkes Co. on Beaverdam Creek, containing
400 acres, at time of survey bounded by land of John Tollett's and
Stathams land, other sides vacant. Granted to John Smith on the 17
April 1790. Wit: William Higginbotham, Abraham Stinchcomb, Peter
Brown. Signed: John X Smith and Pricillah X Smith. Proved on oath
of Wm. Higginbotham before R. Banks J.P. this 21 July 1790. Reg. 11
July 1791.

SMITH, MOSES Box 84 Pack 2060. Probate Judge Office. Abbeville,
S. C. I Moses Smith of Abbeville Dist. finding myself being frail
through the infirmity of old age and not knowing how soon I may be

Smith, Moses - Continued. called away being of sound mind and
memory. I give to my son George one negro girl named Ellin also $250.
I give to my son William one tract of land of 200 acres lying on
Barren Branch on which he now lives. I give to my son Robert, 335
acres lying on Turkey Creek, on which he now lives. Which will make
them equal with Joseph Ebenezer and Samuel. I give to my dtr. Jane
Cullins all my interest in a tract of land that she now lives on in the
State of Indiana. I give to my grand children Jas Dun and Moses Dun
children of my dtr. Feby Dun decd. I give to James Dun $150 with what
he has already received, and I give to Moses Dun $100 with what he
has recd. I give to my son Benjamin all the plantation which I now
live on containing 523 acres with all improvements also five negroes
named, Jack, Tilman, Sucky, Child Aggy. (no more of this will in notes).
One page of the sale, Dated 8 Nov. 1837. Buyers: William Smith,
Benjamin Smith, William T. Jones, James Agnew, Robert Smith, James W.
Richey, Allen Dobson, James Dobson.

SMITH, RICHARD Deed Book A, Page 6. Probate Judge Office.
Pickens, S. C. The petition of Samuel Smith sheweth that he having
lately come to the age of twenty one yrs. prayeth that the sale of
the tract of land lying in the Dist. that belonging to the estate of
his father Richard Smith decd. be sold on a credit of three years,
pursuant to an agreement made with his brother and sister, Moses and
Elizabeth at the end of which time the youngest will arrive at the age
of twenty one yrs. Signed: Samuel Smith. Joseph W. Looper sayeth
that the tract of land lying in said Dist. on Doudies Creek waters of
Saluda River is not worth $1000 and in his opinion it is best for the
parties that the land be sold for the purposes of division. Dated this
26 Oct. 1830. Sale to be held on the first Monday, Jan. 1831.
Postponed until first Monday in Feb. 1831.

SMITH, SAMUEL Will Book B, Page 235. Probate Judge Office.
Union, S. C. I Samuel Smith of Union Dist. being weak in body but of
sound mind and memory. First I will that my just debts be paid. I
give to my beloved wife Elizabeth all my real and personal estate,
including all land, negroes, stock, household and kitchen furniture,
wagon, horses etc. during her natural life and at her decease or
marriage to be divided in the following manner. I give to my son
William Smith $50 to be paid from the est. and I release him from all
debts due me. I give to my dtr. Elizabeth Smith $50. I give to my
son Bailey Smith $50. I give to my son Miles Smith $50. I give to
my dtr. Ginsey Vaughn and her heirs $50. I give to my children, Patsey
Coleman and her heirs, Hannah Mitchell and her heirs, Giles N. Smith,
Isaac Smith and Newell Smith all my land, stock, negroes that I may
die with to be equally divided, share and share alike, after paying
off the named sums. Estate has about 350 acres of land, with negroes,
Dilce, Mime, Nance, Ede, Sam, Lott, Rendy, Mary, Jesse, Elmina,
Carolina & Siddy. I appoint my friend Elias Mitchell, Newell Smith
and B. H. Bradley my executors. Dated this 16 April 1835. Wit:
B. H. Bradley, Thos. Hancock, Aquilla Powers. Signed: Samuel Smith.
Recorded 14 Feb. 1837. Cit. Pub. at Wesleys Chapel on the 13 March
1838 by W. E. Collier.

SMITH, WILLIAM H. In Equity #168. Clerk of Court Office. Abbeville, S. C. Abbeville Dist. In Equity, To the Honr. the Chancellors:
Your orator William Trewit, sheweth that William H. Smith late of
Abbeville Dist. departed this life, about the first of Dec. 1855
leaving in full force his last will and testament, whereof your orator
was appointed executor. The testator died seized and possessed with
property both real and personal as set forth. The testator only
heirs and distributees his widow Beda Smith, his brothers Pater Smith,
Frederick Smith, the children of Charles A. Smith decd. to wit.
Frances wife of Hazel Smith, Alexander Smith, Sophronia A. Smith,
Jewette Smith, Martha Smith and Charles A. Smith. Sophronia is now
the wife of James Owens, the latter three are under age, also the chn.
of Moses B. and Mary Collins decd. to wit. Frances the wife of
William Dinkins, Peter Collins, Moses Collins, James and Mary are all
living beyond the limits of this State. Also the chn. of John
Parnell and Elizabeth his wife now decd. to wit. William Parnell

Smith, William H. - Continued. and John Parnell living beyond the limits of this State. Your orator sheweth that Beda Smith married Dr. P. H. Bradley the 3 Jan. last past (1856) and has taken possession of the estate, both real and personal, except what was sold by your orator, which is shown to your Honors. Your orator is informed that the testator had several notes calling for considerable amount of money, one note due by the said Dr. P. H. Bradley for $150 due for board for himself and a horse in 1854 and 1855. On note on John Freeman, amount unknown, one note on Sherod Barksdale amount unknown, one still in the hand of Mrs. Bradley. Your orator prays that she may be required full true and perfect answer. Filed 5 Nov. 1856.

SMITH, WILLIAM S. Pack 333, Clerk of Court Office. Abbeville, S. C. Your orator William S. Smith, sheweth that many years ago your orator married Permelia McCrady she having a son living by a former marriage to wit, James W. McCrady. That on 7 Jan. 1856 your orator executed a deed by which he conveyed to Middleton Cobb 400 acres of land and the following slaves, to wit, Haly, Hotton, Sam, Randel, John, Gabriel, Rose, Martha, Mary the child of Jane, Sarah, Sam the child of Jane and Susan in trust for the use of your orator and his wife Permilia during their joint lives, Upon the death of the survivor, the land and slaves to the children of James W. McCrady. The trustee permitted the slaves to remain in possession of your orator until the death of Permelia, which happened in Jan. 1857. Said Cobb took possession of the slaves, and hired them out, and removed to the State of Mississippi. Cobb died in the State of Miss. in or about the 23 day. (No more of this suit in notes.)

SMITHSON, MARSON Real Estate Book A, Page 7. Probate Judge Office. Pickens, S. C. Nimrod Leathers admnr. of the est. of Marson Smithson decd. vizt. William Smithson, Lelah Smithson, Sarah Smithson, Anson Smithson and James Jolly, legal heirs of Marson Smithson. You are required to appear to show cause is any why the real estate lying on waters of Choestoe, bounded by land of Eli Davis, Benjamin Perry containing 115 acres, should not be divided or sold allotting each heir an equal share. Land to be sold by the sheriff on the first Monday of Feb. next (1831), giving twelve months credit. Filed 6 Sept. 1830.

SOUTHERLAND, AMOS L. Land Warrant. Clerk of Court Office. Pickens, S. C. #79. By W. L. Keith, Clerk of Court. To any lawful surveyor, you are authorized to lay out unto Amos L. Southerland a tract of land not exceeding ten thousand acres, and make a true plat thereof and return to my office within two months. The above warrant is for the purpose of regranting a certain tract of land whereon widow Southerland now lives, lying on the Oolenoy, and such vacant land that may be adjoining the same. Dated this 19 Feb. 1845. Received 405 acres on the 19 Feb. 1845. Certified the 1 April 1845.

SPEER, JOHN Pack 358. Clerk of Court Office. Abbeville, S.C. Abbeville Dist. I John Speer of said Dist. in consideration of $400 to me paid by Basil Darby of the same dist. have granted, bargained, sold, and released all that tract of land containing 160 acres. Being the tract originally granted to Robert Norris Junr. on Frazers branch of Norris Creek, waters of Long Cane Creek. Bounded by Jehu Foster, Samuel Foster, Esq. Dated 22 July 1818. Wit: William Ezzard, William Speer Junr. Signed: John Speer. Proved on oath of William Speer Junr. before Ezkl. Calhoun, J.Q. this ___ July 1818. This day came Elizabeth A. H. Speer the wife of John Speer and voluntarily renounce, release and relinquish all interest and right and claim of dower in said land. Signed: Elizabeth Ann Harris Speer.

SPENCE, JOHN & WILLIAM #9. In Equity. Clerk of Court Office. Abbeville, S. C. Abbeville Dist. In Equity To the Honr. the Chancellors: Your oratrix Jane Young, sheweth that her brothers, John and William Spence of this Dist. some time prior to the year 1849, they departed this life possessed jointly of a tract of land on Link Branch waters of Long Cane Creek. Adj. land of Adam Wideman, Thomas J. Lyon, John Robertson, containing 204 acres. Leaving as heirs and distributees, your oratrix, Nelly Spence, Sallie Spence, George

Spence, John & William - Continued. Spence, Thomas Creswell and Mary his wife, Jacob Creswell and Peggy his wife, the brother and sisters of the decd. and also the chn. of a predeceased brother James Spence, Samuel Spence, John Creswell and Ann his wife, John Faulkner and Mary his wife, Robert Steward and Peggy ? his wife, Oliver Spence, Lindy Spence and Carolina Spence. The last two being minors, the latter about sixteen yrs., and the former eighteen yrs. of age. (No filing date.)

SPENCER, JACKSON Box 43 #1834. Probate Judge Office. York County, S. C. Est. admnr. 18 June 1860 by Jesse Spencer, Reese W. Workman, and John F. Workman are bound unto John M. Ross, Ord. in the sum of $4,000. Estate divided into 8 shares among Martha Spencer, Jesse Spencer, Thomas Spencer, sisters and brothers, Joseph Spencer legatee of Jane Spencer and Margaret Spencer child of Robert Spencer each entitled to $59.71.

SPENCER, JENNY Box 49 #2021. Probate Judge Office. York County, S. C. I Jenny Spencer of York County do make this my last will and testament etc. I give unto my beloved relative Joseph Spencer all my undivided interest in my brother Jackson Spencer est. both real and personal, also my unaired [sic] interest in sixty acres of land given by my father to myself and two sisters Martha and May Spencer, also my unclaimed interest in the est. of decd. sister Mary Spencer, also all other property both real and personal that I may die with... I appoint Joseph Spencer my executor. Dated this 14 April 1860. Wit: Thomas Neely, Wm. H. Neely, F. B. Thompson. Signed: Jenny X Spencer. Filed 7 Oct. 1863.

SPENCER, JOSEPH Vol. 5, Page 585. Probate Judge Office. Charleston, S. C. 20 June 1746, I Joseph Spencer of James Island St. Andrew Parish, being very sick and weak of body but of perfect mind and memory. I will that my debts and funeral expenses be paid, as soon as possible. I give to my beloved brother William Spencer and his heirs, all that tract of land on which I now dwell, containing 140 acres with the dwelling house and out houses. I give to Mary Dill dtr. of Elizabeth Dill, one cedar chestnoe being in the dwelling house of the said Elizabeth Dill, with all things that are therein at the time of my decease. I order that the land which I bought of Capt. Robert Rivers lately in the possession of Stephen Russell, containing about 52 acres, with my moveable and personal estate be put at sale and the money applied to paying my debts and funeral charges, any money over to be equal divided between my sister (not named) and Mary Dill. I appoint my brother William Spencer executor with my friend Mary Dill executrix. Wit: Samuel Stent, Joseph Rivers, Will Gough. Signed: Joseph Spencer. Proved on oath of Will Gough, Saml. Stent, Joseph Rivers. On 11 July 1746.

SPENCER, WILLIAM Vol. 6 Page 482. Probate Judge Office. Charleston, S. C. The 19 Feb. 1751, I William Spencer of James Island in Berkley Co. Planter being sick and weak in body but of perfect mind and memory. I give to my wife Sarah Spencer one negro man named Robin and a girl named Flower and all the cattle and of her mark, her riding horse, her bed and furniture, two cedar chest and her poultry. I leave her a room in the dwelling house during her widowhood. I leave her negro woman Hannah during her widowhood. I leave to my son William the plantation whereon I now live and the two islands fronting the sea to him forever. I give to my son John Spencer sixty acres of land belonging to the tract that he now lives on. My will is that the tract of 200 joining John Stanyarne's land be sold and pay my debts if any. My will is that the tract of land containing 200 joining Mrs. Coles land be sold. I will that all my personal estate shall be justly appraised and equally divided amongst my children, John Spencer, William Spencer, Ann Sandiford, Sarah Holmes. My will is that after my funeral expenses is paid, I give Ⱡ80 to be paid out to interest for the support of Poor Children at a Christian School. I give Ⱡ20 for the repairing of the meeting house on James Island whenever wanted for that use. I appoint my wife Sarah Spencer, executrix and John Spencer, William Spencer, John Sandiford, John Holmes,

Spencer, William - Continued. executors. Wit: Jno. Mathewes, Mary Samvays, Mary Vanderwicke. Signed: William Spencer. Proved: 12 April 1751.

SPRIGGS, THOMAS Deed Book I, page 544. Mesne Conveyance. Greenville, S. C. I Thomas Sprigs of Greenville Dist. in consideration of $300 to me paid by John Sprigs of the same Dist. have granted, sold, conveyed and released all my part of the undivided tract of land bequeath to me and my brother John Sprigs jointly by the last will of our father Thomas Sprigs late of this Dist. bearing date 22 June 1801. Tract originally granted to John Clayton bearing date of 15 Oct. 1784. This deed dated 4 April 1811. Wit: Wm. Motlow, Geo. Salmon. Signed: Thos. Sprigs. Proved on oath of George Salmon before John Massy, J.P. this 2 Nov. 1816.

SPRIGGS, THOMAS Apt. 7 File 443. Probate Judge Office. Greenville, S. C. I Thomas Sprigs of Greenville Dist. being weak of body but of sound mind and memory. I give to my beloved wife Susannah Sprigs all my household and kitchen furniture except two beds and furniture, also two cows and calves and my brown horse. I give to my sons Thomas and John Sprigs my tract of land and tools to be equally divided between them, my wife to have a maintenance out of the proceeds during her life. I give to my son Thomas my sorrel mare and my new saddle, my son John to have my oung sorrel horse and old saddle. I give to my dtr. Mary Couch sixty dollars which her husband James Couch is indebted to me, also one cow now in her possession. I give to my dtr. Sarah Sprigs one feather bed and furniture which is called hers, also one cow and fifty dollars to be paid to her. I give to my dtr. Betsey Sprigs one feather bed and furniture also one cow, and fifty dollars to be paid to her. I give to my son Jeremiah Sprigs $100 to be put on interest with the interest to pay for his schooling, also one sorrel colt now sucking my sorrel mare. I give to my son Ezekiel Sprigs $120 to be put on interest, with the same paid to his schooling, also my stock of hogs. I appoint my friend George Salmon of Greenville Dist. as executor. Dated 22 June 1801. Wit: John Goodlett, Ann X Goodlett, Elizabeth Salmon. Signed: Thomas X Sprigs. Proved on oath of John and Ann Goodlett the 31 March 1806. Estate appraised 24 May 1806 by John Adkins, Erasmus Ford, William Lynch, John Goodlett.

STONE, URIAH Book C (No page given). Clerk of Court Office. Elberton, Ga. I Uriah Stone of the County of Elbert do appoint Marbel Stone of the State of Virginia and of Franklin County as my lawful attorney in all things, necessary for the caring on the said suits against several persons either in law or equity. I impower my attorney to demand, to receive, to collect in all my outstanding negroes, pledged for money, debts, notes etc. This 14 May 1795. Signed: Uriah Stone. Registered 14 May 1795.

SHACKLEFORD, JOHN Book C (No page given). Clerk of Court Office. Elberton, Ga. This indenture made this 22 May 1795 between John Shackleford of Elbert Co., State of Ga. and Sherwood Harris of the same place. In consideration of seventeen pounds good and lawful money of this State, hath granted, sold, bargained, and released all that parcel of land being in Elbert Co., Ga. containing 110 acres bounded by land of M. Wood and Shackleford land. Wit: Thos. Cook J.P. and M. Wood J.P. Signed: John Shackleford. Reg. 22 May 1795.

SHADRACK, JOHN B. Box 179 Pack 4740. Probate Judge Office. Abbeville, S. C. On 19 March 1868 Johnson Sales petition the Ordinary for a letter of admnr. upon the estate, and that he is a creditor. On 15 April 1868 to the Ordinary Wm. Hill. "I have declined taking the admnr. of the est. of J. B. Shadrick decd. Signed: L. C. Parks. The admnr. bond was signed by Johnson Sale, Josephine R. Lake, Irvin Hutchinson and T. J. Ouzts, dated 17 April 1868. On the 31 Aug. 1869 Emma E. Shadrick made suit to the Ordinary to grant her letter of admnr. upon the effects of John B. Shadrick. Anyone who is creditor or debtor shall appear before me at Abbeville Court House on the 17 Sept. 1869 to show cause why the admnr. should not be granted.

Shadrack, John - Continued. Signed: Wm. Hill, Ord. Sale held
on 5 May 1868. Buyers: William A. Eyton, Lewis Parks, Johnson Sale
H. H. Creswell, S. B. Brooks, William S. Shadrick, S. B. Elmore,
H. M. Spikes, Lemuel Bell, J. S. Chiply, Dr. John Maxwell.

SHELAR, JACOB Pack 9, Clerk of Court Office. Anderson, S. C.
Pendleton Dist. This indenture made this 13 Sept. 1823 between
Jacob Shelar of Mecklenburgh Co., Va. and George Shelar of Montgomery
Co., Va. In consideration of $300 to him paid by George Shelar, have
granted, sold, bargained and released two tracts of land in Pendleton
Dist. one tract adj. land of Benjamin Perry and on Tugaloo River and
Choashoa Creek, containing 340 acres. Another tract known as the
Hooper Mill and McMurter tracts containing 230 acres. Wit: Wm.
Shelar, Nancy X Logan, Jacob Shelar. Signed: Jacob Shelar. Be it
known that on 1 Jan. 1824 before me George E. W. Foster, N.P. acting
by letter patent under the great seal of the said State. Came Jacob
Shelar who acknowledge the within instrument to be his act and deed.
Signed: George E. W. Foster.

SHIELDS, "MINORS" Box 110 Pack 3142. Probate Judge Office.
Abbeville, S.C. Whereas we Samuel B. Shields, Andrew Bowie, Alexander
C. Hamilton are bound unto Andrew Hamilton, Ord. in the sum of $2,000.
Dated 19 March 1806. As guardian of person and personal estate of
Theodore C. Shields and William F. Shields during their minority.

SHIELDS, MAJOR THOMAS Box 86 Pack 2097. Abbeville, S. C.
Whereas Samuel B. Shields made application to grant him letter of
admnr. on the est. of Major Thomas Shields decd. as next of kin. Dated
this 11 April 1803. Admnr. bond signed by Samuel B. Shields, George
Bowie, Dr. Jesse C. Boushell are bound unto the Ors. Andrew Hamilton,
Esq. in the sum of $5,000. Dated this 2 May 1803. The cit. pub. at
Upper Long Cane by Robert Wilson, Min. Sale held on 31 May 1803,
buyers: Nathaniel Terry, Merriday McGee, Charles Taylor, John Bowie
Jur., Allen Glover, Cornelius B. Williams, Stephen Russell, Nathaniel
Perry, John Scudday, Harrison Posey, Andrew Milligan, Lewis Howland,
Richard M. Lewallen, Thomas Stokes, John King, William T. Moon,
Samuel B. Shields, Thomas Casey, William T. Moore, Edmund Wimbush,
Thomas Brough, James Bickley, Revd. Moses Waddel, Breefy Morris, Mrs.
Goodman, Thomas Blair, John N. Newby, George Whitfield.

SHIRLEY, LEVI THOMPSON Pack 359 #1. Clerk of Court Office.
Pickens, S. C. Personally appeared before me Levi Thompson Shirley
and made oath he is a regular practicing physician and lives at Central
in Pickens County. He was born in Abbeville County, S.C. and is 28
years of age. He graduated at the College of Physicioner and Surgeons
in the city of Baltimore, Md. on the 16 March 1888. Sworn to and
subscribed before me this 2 Oct. 1888. J. J. Lewis, Clerk. Signed:
L. T. Shirley.

SHIRLEY, NATHANIEL Pack 352. Clerk of Court Office. Abbeville,
S. C. Abbeville Dist. In Equity To the Honr. the Chancellors: Your
oratrix Nancy Shirley and orators Benjamin Shirley, Richard Shirley,
William Shirley, John Shirley, Reuben Branyon and Elizabeth is wife,
James Shirley and George Shirley some of the heirs. That on 14 July
1849 Nathaniel Shirley departed this life intestate at time of death
possessed with two tracts of land in this Dist. lying on branches of
Hogskin Creek, waters of Little River. Containing 600 acres or more.
Bounded by land of John R. Willson, John Kay, John R. Shirley, Richard
Shirley, Andrew Armstrong, Arthur Williams, Mastin Shirley, John
McClain. Leaving as heirs and distributees, your oratrix Nancy his
widow and Benjamin, Richard, William, John, James and George and
Elizabeth the wife of Reuben Branyan and four minors, Polly Ann age
about 18 yrs., Letta Masena age about 16 yrs., Nancy Arena age about
14 yrs., and Amaziah Nathaniel age about 11 yrs. The admnr. was
committed to Nancy the widow and Richard and John two sons. The
personal est. will more than pay all debts. The real est. is now to
be distributed amongst the heirs. Filed 2 Nov. 1849.

SHOEMAKER, LABAN Pack 330 Clerk of Court Office. Abbeville,
S. C. Abbeville Dist. In Equity To the Honr. the Chancellors, your
oratrix Polly M. Shoemaker sheweth. That in Nov. 1848 Laban Shoemaker
of this Dist. departed this life, leaving as his only heirs and distributees, your oratrix his widow and two chn. Hannah Elizabeth and
Thomas Shoemaker which said Thomas soon after his father death also
died without wife or child. The said Laban was possessed at his death
with a tract of land, lying in this Dist. on Mountain Creek waters
of Long Cane Creek: Containing 357 acres, bounded by __ Robinson,
James Edwards, Widow Riley and Widow Butler. Admnr. on the est. was
never prayed for, the same was admnr. by David Lesly Ord. as derelict
and your oratrix has been informed and believes that the personal est.
will more than pay all the debts. Therefore she prays that the land
be partition between herself and Hannah Elizabeth as the only heirs.
Filed 12 May 1851.

SIMMONS, FRANCIS Pack 272, Clerk of Court Office. Abbeville,
S.C. Edgefield Dist. In Equity. To the Honr. the Chancellors:
Your orator and oratrix F. G. Thomas and Mary Y. Thomas sheweth, that
the late Francis Simmons of John's Island, by his last will and testament bequeathed to your oratrix then Mary Y. Simmons the sum of one
thousand pounds, to be held in trust for her benefit upon certain
conditions. That after the death of the testator, your oratrix
married Joseph R. Arthur decd. and during their marriage the said
Joseph R. Arthur was substituted trustee of your oratrix. That the
said Arthur on the 4 Dec. 1826 purchased from Waddy Thompson, Jr. a
tract of land containing 1000 acres, using her legacy of the purchase
price. Since the death of Joseph R. Arthur, William Edward Hayne has
been appointed trustee of your oratrix est. Your oratrix sheweth that
the land is in an unhealthy section, that she has lost several children
on the land. She prays that her trustee sell the present plantation
and purchase another tract as he may deem better. Filed this 16 Jan.
1858. (This paper was in with the above.) "Settlement of the est. of
W. E. H. Arthur decd. in ordinarys office 5 Jan. 1846. Present:
Dr. F. G. Thomas and Thomas S. Arthur the only heirs and distributees
of the decd. Dr. F. G. Thomas was guardian of the decd. and made his
return in Lexington Dist."

SIMPSON, HENRY Pack 6. In Equity, Clerk of Court Office.
Abbeville, S. C. Abbeville Dist. In Equity, To the Honr. the
Chancellors: Your orator Bartlett M. Cheatham sheweth that the said
Henry Simpson formerly of this Dist. now decd. On the 14 July 1852
executed a deed by which he conveyed to your orator a negro woman
Fanny and her four chn. to wit: Charlotte, William, Sarah, and an
infant. Your orator has been unable to make any disposition of them.
Your orator is advised tha t the property conveyed is liable for all
the debts contracted before the execution of the said deed. Filed
2 June 1855.

SIMS, NATHAN Pack 3231. Clerk of Court Office. Abbeville, S.C.
Abbeville Dist. In Equity To the Honr. the Chancellors: Your orators
and oratrixs Jeremiah Walker and Lucinda his wife, Stephen Stovall
and Jane his wife (which four are of Lincoln Co., Ga.) Agness Calhoun
widow of John Calhoun decd., James McMillan and Peggy his wife (which
three are of Abbeville Dist.) William Sims Cowan of Wayne Co.,
Missouri. Sheweth, your four oratrixs and Nathan Griffin now living in
Lee Co., Ga. are children of Amelia the dtr. of Nathan Sims, by her
first husband Richard Griffin, and your orator William S. Cowan is her
child by her second husband John Cowan, and with Buckner Griffin are
the only children she had at or before the making of the deed of gift
from her father. On the 5 March 1802 Nathan Sims father of Amelia,
executed to her a deed of gift. He was residing in Abbeville Dist.
and she the widow of Richard Griffin who was residing in Lincoln Co.,
Ga. of seven negroes, these being in her possession to have and hold
during her natural life, and after her death be divided between her
children share and share alike. About the year 1803 Amelia the widow,
married John Cowan then of Lincoln Co., Ga. the said negroes came into
possession of Amelia Husband John Cowan after he prevailed against some
claim set up by the Admnr. of Richard Griffin, one of the negroes

Sims, Nathan - Continued. named in the deed, then a young woman named Isbel was sold by the sheriff to Frederick Brown of Columbia Co., Ga. Isbel remained in possession of said Brown, being called Lizzie and bore many children of whom Phillis and Milly are two. By gift and other conveyance the said Fred. Brown transferred Phillis and her chn. to his granddaughter Elizabeth White the dtr. of William White of Elbert Co., Ga. now the wife of James W. Frazier of Abbeville Dist. The said Phillis now has, chn. to wit: Jeanette, Lucinda, Jane (one name not plain) John, Betty all in possession of James W. Frazier and worth about two thousand dollars. Milly by the will of Frederick Brown who died in 1836 was also acquired by Elizabeth the wife of James W. Frazier and is now in Elbert Co., Ga. Buckner Griffin, died in Georgia about 1836 in the lifetime of his mother, leaving a widow Patsey Griffin and nine chn. to wit, Richard Griffin, Amelia the wife of Anderson B. Smith, Jane the wife of Littleton Hughes, Holman Griffin, Thomas Griffin, Margaret the wife of Lemuel McCord, William Griffin, Leonard Griffin and Sarah Griffin all whom reside in Georgia. The said Buckner Griffin in his lifetime released all his interest under the deed of gift. John Cowan removed from Georgia to Missouri and died in the latter State in 1822 and in Feb. 1841 his widow Amelia the mother of your oratrixs died in Missouri. Filed 4 Nov. 1841. The deed of gift from Nathan Sims, made in 1802 was wit. by Leonard Sims, William X Bond, and George X Sims.

SKELTON, WILLIAM Deed Book M, Page 175. Clerk of Court Office. Anderson, S. C. Pendleton Dist. This 24 Aug. 1813, know that William Skelton of Pendleton Dist. in consideration of $55 to me paid by my son Solomon Skelton of the same Dist. have granted, sold, released a tract of land containing 55 acres lying on waters of Mountain Creek a branch of Savannah River, being the tract former surveyed for David Clark, certified the 15 Sept. 1786. Wit: F. A. Herring, Charles Woods, William McCarley. Signed: William Skelton. Proved on oath of Francis A. Herring before Dennis Still, J.Q. this 24 Aug. 1813. Recorded the same date.

STANLEY, PETER Vol. 4 Page 763. Probate Judge Office. Charleston, S. C. I Peter Stanley of Saint James Parrish in Craven County, planter, being sick and weak of body but of sound mind and memory. I will that my lawful and just debts be paid. I give to John June my well beloved God-son Peter June (son of John June) ₺100 to be put on interest until he attain the age of twenty one. I give to my well beloved God-son Peter June son of Solomon ₺100 to be put on interest until he attain the age of twenty one. I give my beloved God-son Peter Whitten ₺100 to be put on interest until he attain the age of twenty one. I give to my beloved God-daughter Susannah Predriau ₺100, to be put on interest until she attain the age of twenty one. I give to my nephew Monclar son of Andrew Monclar ₺100 to be put on interest until he attain the age of twenty one. I give to my beloved wife Elizabeth Stanley all the residue, both real and personally to be her own disposal. I appoint my wife Elizabeth Stanley executrix. Dated this 6 Dec. 1736. Wit: Rich. Gough, Jno. Nicholson, James Fulton. Signed: Peter Stanley. Proved on oath of Rich. Gough and John Nicholson before Daniel Welahujsen, M.J. This 14 July 1737. Recorded 23 Aug. 1738.

STAPLES, JOHN Book C (no page given). Clerk of Court Office. Elberton, Ga. This indenture made this 27 Jan. 1795. Between John Staples of Elbert Co. and Larkin Gatewood of the same county. In consideration of one thousand pounds of tobacco, hath granted, bargained, sold and released all that parcel of land containing 53 acres, lying in Elbert Co. Adj. John Upshaws land and John Staples land and Gatewood land. Wit: John Upshaw, James Gatewood. Signed: John Staples. Proved on oath of both witnesses before M. Wood, J.P. this 14 May 1795. Registered 14 May 1795.

STARK, REUBEN Pack 3210. Clerk of Court Office. Abbeville, S. C. Abbeville Dist. To the Honors the Judges of the Court of Equity. Bill for alimony, Your oratrix Elizabeth G. Stark the wife of Reuben Stark, sueing here by Elam Sharpe her next friend. That your

Stark, Reuben - Continued. oratrix married Reuben Stark on 6 Jan.
1819 and resided with him on his estate near Camden from the time of
marriage until about the last of January 1823. Within a few months
after her marriage Reuben manifested a disposition calculated to
inspire little hope of conjugal happiness. He removed from his home
to this Dist. about the last of January 1823 and refused to live with
her. (Only one page found notes.)

STARK, SAMUEL J. Pack 273. Clerk of Court Office. Abbeville,
S. C. Abbeville Dist. In Equity To the Honr. the Chancellors: The
petition of Samuel J. H. Stark and Frances E. Stark his wife sheweth
that by a deed of trust bearing date 12 July 1852. Made by your
petitioner Samuel J. H. Stark and conveying to John Davis M.D. of
said Dist. All his estate both real and personal upon the trusts
following. In trust for the support and maintenance of your petitioner,
in the first place, and after the further trust for your petitioner and
any children I may have. With express direction to apply the rent,
issue and profits. Your petitioner becoming dissatisfied with the
manner in which Dr. John Davis was managing their trust estate. Having
filed in this Honorable Court, a bill of complaining of the acting and
doing, that he be required to account for the trust, profits, effects,
rents, issues, etc. Also his application thereof be removed from being
trustee under the said deed. In the June term 1853 Chancellor Wardlaw
granted an order in which amongest other things the said Dr. John
Davis was ordered to cease to act as trustee under said deed. Filed:
27 Oct. 1859. The est. consisting of 595 acres and seven slaves with
all other plantation tools, stock, horses, hogs, and household and
kitchen furniture.

STEGALL, BENJAMIN Pack 90, Clerk of Court Office. Pickens,
S. C. Lauderdale County, Ala. I Benjamin Stegall of said county and
state have made, appointed and ordained Kelly Green Stegall of said
county my lawful attorney, to use my name, ask, demand, sue, receive
and receipt from any representative of my father estate, etc. Dated
this 29 Sept. 1838. Signed: Benjamin X Stegall. Pickens, S. C.
I Kelly Green Stegall mentioned in the within power of attorney do
hereby assign over to John Bowen all the rights, privileges and
authority confered on me by Benjn. Stegall in the power of attorney so
far as relates to the real estate of Richard Stegall decd. Dated this
7 Nov. 1838. Wit: Wm. Holcombe, Elijah Watson. Signed Kelly Green
Stegall.

STEGALL, MARGARET Pack 90. Clerk of Court Office. Pickens,
S. C. I Margaret Stegall wife of the late Richard Stegall do hereby
appoint William Holcombe of Pickensville, S. C. as my lawful attorney
to use my name, to sue, collect, receive and receipt all sums of money
from the est. of my late husband. Wit: John Bowen, R. A. Stegall.
Signed: Margaret X Stegall. (Between the above power of attorney and
the next, is written Kingston Roan County, East Tennessee.)

STEGALL, NANCY Pack 90. Clerk of Court Office. Pickens, S. C.
Lumpkin County, Ga. I Nancy Stegall of said county reposing special
confidence and trust in my son George W. Stegall of the same place,
have ordained and appointed him as my lawful agent and atrorney, to
ask, demand, receive and receipt from the legal representatives of the
estate of Richard Stegall late of Pickens Dist. Dated 6 Oct. 1837.
Wit: S. D. Crane, Signed: Nancy X Stegall. Pickensville, S.C. this
29 Sept. 1839. I George W. Stegall do hereby assign over to John
Bowen of Pickens Dist. all the rights and authority confirmed on me
by my mother Nancy Stegall in the written power of attorney giving him
full power to collect and receipt for the same. Wit: B. Dunham,
Wm. Holcombe. Signed: G. W. Stegall.

STEGALL, RICHARD A. Pack 90. Clerk of Court Office. Pickens,
S. C. State of South Carolina. We Abel Williams and Richard A.
Stegall heirs of Richard Stegall decd. have appointed John Bowen of
Pickens Dist. our lawful attorney for us and in our name, to sue,
collect, recover and receipt for all sums of money as may come to us
through the real estate of said decease. Dated 14 Nov. 1838.

Stegall, Richard A. - Continued. Wit: Wm. Holcombe. Signed: Abel William, Richard A. Stegall.

STEGALL, RICHARD In Equity, Clerk of Court Office. Pack 90. Pickens, S. C. Richard Stegall died the 28 Dec. 1835 in the 80th year of his age. Leaving his widow Margaret and nine children to wit, Benjamin Stegall, Patsy Denny, Nancy Stegall, Kelly Stegall, Birdwell Stegall, Blackwell Stegall, Linny Yancy, Richard A. Stegall, Susan Williams. Had two chn. decd. Hensly and Spencer Stegall. Hensly Stegall died leaving five illegitimate children, Spencer Stegall died leaving a widow Sarah Stegall and seven children to wit: Hensly Stegall, William Stegall, Robert Stegall, Peter Stegall, Elizabeth Stegall, and two others names unknown. Richard Stegall Senr. was helpless about 11 years before his death and could not walk. Filed 3 Oct. 1836.

STEGALL, RICHARD Pack 90. Clerk of Court Office. Pickens, S.C. I Richard Stegall of Pickens Dist. in consideration of natural love and affection which I have and bear to my children, and in considera- tion of the sum of five dollars to me paid in hand have granted, bargained, sold, and released to Bird Stegall, Spencer Stegall, Black- well Stegall, Linny Yancy, Artemus Stegall, Susan Stegall, Benjamin Stegall, Kelly Stegall, Nancy Stegall, Patsy Denny and the five child- ren of my son Hensly Stegall decd. the following property. Negroes, Squire, Selvy, Susan, America, Angeliner, and a tract of land that contains 600 acres on Georges Creek, whereon I now live. The property to remain in the hands of Richard Stegall Senr. during his natural life. At his death to be equally divided among the chn. The share for Linny Yancy to go to Bird and Blackwell Stegall and held in trust for her and her two children to wit, Elizabeth Yancy and Baylis Yancy. Said property not subject to any debt of hers or of her husband or future husband she may have. Dated 16 March 1831. Wit: John Burdine, Zachariah Conger. Signed: Richard X Stegall. Sworn to the 25 Sept. 1831.

STEPHENS, JOHN Pack 3351. Clerk of Court Office. Abbeville, S. C. Abbeville Dist. In Equity. To the Honr. the Chancellors: Your orator John Robertson sheweth about the 21 Oct. 1839, John Stephen late of Abbeville Dist. sold to your orator a tract of land containing about 400 acres lying on Willson Creek. In consideration of $3000 to be paid in three installments the first due Jan. 1, 1840 one more due 1841 another due 1842. About July 6 1841, th said John Stephens departed this life intestate, leaving as his heirs and distrubutees his widow Mary M. Stephen and one child Sarah Jane Stephens of very tender age. The admnr. on the estate was granted to Robert Davis, Esq. Your orator has paid the last payment to said Admnor. May it please your Honors to grant a writ subponea to said Mary M. and Sarah Jane Stephens on a certain day to appear in this Court and abide and perform such order and decree. Filed: 2 Nov. 1843.

STEVENSON, ALEXANDER & EMRY VAN Pack 358. Clerk of Court Office. Abbeville, S. C. I Alexander Stevenson and Emry Van of Abbeville Dist. in consideration of $1200 to me paid by Henry Atkins of the same Dist. have granted, sold, bargained and released, all that tract of land containing 120 acres, on a branch of Norrises Creek, water of Long Cane. Bounded by land of John Adams, Hugh Armstrong. Dated this 22 Jan. 1841. Wit: Thos. Hinton, John Adams. Signed: Emry Van and Alex. Stevenson. Proved on oath of Thomas Hinton before Samuel L. Hill J.Q. this 22 Jan. 1841. This day came Edney Stevenson the wife of Alexander Stevenson and Fanny Van the wife of Emry Van, and forever renounce, release, and relinquish unto Henry Atkins all their interest and right of dower on the above land. This 23 April 1841. Edny X Stevenson and Frances Vann. Recorded the 16 Aug. 1841.

STEVENSON, ANDREW #185. Clerk of Court Office. Abbeville, S.C. Abbeville Dist. To the Honorable the Chancellors, Your orator and oratrix Francis A. Carlisle and Mary Ann Carlisle his wife, that Andrew Stevenson of this Dist. departed this life intestate. Leaving

Stevenson, Andrew - Continued. as his next of kin and distributees,
his widow Elizabeth Stevenson, ch. John Stevenson, James Stevenson,
Mary Ann Carlisle your oratrix, Elizabeth Stevenson, Thomas Stevenson,
Jane Stevenson, Sarah A. Stevenson, Rebecca Stevenson, Thompson
Stevenson. The last three named are minors. At time of his death
Andrew Stevenson was possessed with a tract of land lying on waters of
Little River, containing 300 acres, bounded by land of Allen T. Miller,
John Cunningham. Your orator and oratrix prays for a partition of
said or a sale thereof. Filed 3 Oct. 1837.

STEWART, NIMROD W. Pack 332. Clerk of Court Office. Abbeville,
S. C. Abbeville Dist. To the Honorable the Chancellors: Your oratrix
Rebecca Stewart and your orator J. J. Cooper both of this Dist.
sheweth, that Nimrod W. Stewart decd. was the husband of your oratrix.
Leaving his wife your oratrix and three children to wit, Emma J.
Stewart, Lawrence Stewart, and Rush Stewart all minors, under the age
of twenty one. Recently Emma J. has married James N. King. The
business of the said Nimrod W. Stewart was that of a merchant. With
a consideration amount of bill due him uncollected, also two tracts of
land. One tract in and near the village of 96, containing 321 acres,
part of in the village, with a house, bounded by land of John Sadler,
John Goulden, Dr. John A. Stuart. One other tract of about one half
an acre in the village, which is a blacksmith shop, bounded by land
of James Richardson, J. F. Cason. Admnr. on the est. was granted to
your oratrix by the ordinary on the 14 Jan. 1865. They found large
debts against the estate pressing for payment. With the depreciating
of Confederate currancy melting away. The estate is unable to pay its
debts. Your orator and oratrix prays the an? order for the sale of the
real property. Filed 21 Feb. 1867.

STEWART, WILLIAM AND POLLY Pack 3353. Clerk of Court Office.
Abbeville, S. C. Abbeville Dist. To the Honr. the Chancellors: Your
orator Polly Stewart by Ezekiel Leopard. That she was lawful married
unto William Stewart. That he became cruel and beat, abused and some
acts too shocking to be told. etc. She has been told that he has
removed some property to the State of Alabama. She therefore prays
that she may have a small tract of land, with a cow for her humble
support, that she will be satisfied. Filed 7 Sept. 1820.

SUMTER, THOMAS JR. Deed Book CC, page 17. Clerk of Court Office.
Sumter, S. C. I Thomas Sumter Jr. of Stateburgh, in consideration of
$4500 to me paid by Peter Whitten of St. Matthews Parish. Have granted,
bargained, sold and released all that plantation containing 300 acres,
lying in Sumter Dist. near Bay swamp, bounded by land of Edmund Roach,
James and John Atkinson and Thomas Sumter Jr. as will appear by plat
annexed, certified by Hastin Jennings and dated 15 June 1809. Being
the same date of this deed. Wit: Hastin Jenning, David Thompson.
Signed: Thos. Sumter Jr. Proved on oath of Hastin Jennings, before
John Horan J.Q. this 15 June 1809. Came this date Mrs. Natalie Sumter
the wife of Thomas Sumter Jr. and did release and forever relinquished
to the within named Peter Whitten, all her interest and right or claim
of dower on the above land. Dated this 15 June 1809.

SWAIN, WILLIAM R. Pack 416. Clerk of Court Office. Abbeville,
S. C. Abbeville Dist. In Equity, To your Honr. the Chancellors. Your
orator Joel Smith on behalf of himself and other creditors. Sheweth
that William R. Swain formerly of this Dist. but now in the State of
Miss. prior to the year 1841. Being indebted to your orator in considerable amounts, an execution against him was made on the 3 April
1842. Your orator sheweth that the said William Swain, father by will
gave unto his wife Anna certain negroes and other effects, during her
lifetime, at her decease to be divided amongst his children, of whom
William R. is one. The said Anna Swain died in Aug. 1851. In
November of last year Jesse Swain the executor of said will, proceeded
to execute that part of the will. Filed 1 Nov. 1853. In the will of
John Swain, he leaves his wife Anna Swain the plantation whereon I now
live during her natural life. With negroes, Will, Cuffey, Milley and
Eliza. The chn. were: James Swain, Jane Swain, Jesse Swain, Nancy
Swain, Mary Swain, John Swain, William Swain and Peggy Swain and

Swain, William R. - Continued. and Betsey Smith. After his dec.
negroes, Strother, Fillis, Rachel, Isaac, Manull, Caroline, Malinda,
Amy, Dick to be divided amongst my chn. equally. Sons Jesse and John
Swain are executors. Dated this 7 March 1821. Signed John X Swain.
Wit: John Weatherall, Robert Swain, William X Hodges.

SWANZY (MINORS) Pack 432. Clerk of Court Office. Abbeville,
S. C. On 21 Feb. 1824 William Wier was the guardian of Louisa Swanzy,
Robert Swanzy, Eliza Caroline Swanzy, Mary Swanzy minors of Dr. Samuel
Swanzy decd. Also Sarah Ann, Rosana Swanzy. Louisa Swanzy was of
Stoney Point, S.C. On 1 July 1822 paid Sarah Ann distributive share
of expenses allowing me for trip to Ala. to look after her father
property $12.00. In account with William Wier 2 Dec. 1822 paid Sarah
Ann share of $165 discounted in settlement with exors. of John Longs
estate, for your mother's part of $1155.00 paid by Longs est. one
seventh of which she had to loose $27.50. William Turner and Wilson
Crain recd. shares in right of their wives. One paper mentioned Sarah
Ann Swanzy and William Turner.

SWIFT, THOMAS M. Pack 106. Clerk of Court Office. Abbeville,
S. C. Abbeville Dist. In Equity To the Honr. the Chancellors:
The petition of James C. Harper, sheweth that William A. Swift late
of Elberton, Ga. departed this life possessed with a considerable est.
His wife Nancy J. Swift and several children survive him. Nancy J. is
your petitioner sister in law and desire the guardianship of one orphan
child named Thomas M. Swift, who is about ten yrs. of age. Filed:
30 Nov. 1857. Signed: James C. Harper. I wish, consent, and desire
that James C. Harper my brother in law may be appointed the gdn. of the
person and est. of my infant son Thomas M. Swift. Signed: Nancy J.
Swift. I Philip Cromer who married a sister of Nancy J. Swift swears
that he has seen the petition of James C. Harper, and believes it to
be true and that said Harper is a fit and proper person to be appointed
guardian of said minor. Signed: Philip Cromer before Thomas Thomson,
J.P. this 18 Nov. 1857.

STOKES, THOMAS Deed Book Q, Page 288. Clerk of Court Office.
Chester, S. C. This indenture made this 17 Jan. 1784 between Thomas
Stokes and Alexander Donald both of Camden Dist. in consideration of
ten shilling current money. Said Thomas Stokes hath bargained, sold,
and release a tract of land containing 250 acres lying on branches of
Sandy River. Excepting 12 acres thereof which quantity being reserved
to Thomas Roden now in the possession of Elizabeth Nance. Land first
granted to Jeremiah Potts, dated 20 June 1764. Wit: John Terry,
Jeremiah Thomas, Priscilar X Terry. Signed: Thomas Terry. Proved on
oath of Jeremiah Thomas before Hezh. Donald J.P. this 16 Aug. 1814.
Thomas Stokes wife was Sarah.

STOKES, WILLIAM Will Book A, Page 90. Probate Judge Office.
Elberton, Ga. I William Stokes of Elbert Co., Ga. Being in good
health and perfect sound mind and memory. I lend to my wife Sarah
Stokes the use of all my personal estate of every kind whatsoever, I
also lend to my wife the use of the plantation whereon I now live on
South Broad River, during her natural life or widowhood. Having given
my dtr. Elizabeth Pryor three young negroes and other property, I made
no further revision except I give her twenty shilling to buy her a ring.
Having given my dtr. Sarah Grimes one likely negro woman named Lett,
I make no other provision for her, except I give her twenty shillings
to buy her a ring. Having given my dtr. Peggy Strong one negro name
named Antoney and one negro woman named Margret and other property, I
make no other provision for her, except I give her twenty shilling to
buy her a ring. Having given my dtr. Jane Stokes one negro woman
named Edy and one negro boy named Nelson, I make no other provision
for her except I give her twenty shilling to buy her a ring. I give
to my dtr. Martha Stokes my tract of land whereon I now live on South
Broad River, containing 200 acres. I also give to Martha one negro
boy named Davis and one negro girl named Lucy, one horse and saddle,
one feather bed and furniture. I give unto my son William Munfort
Stokes my tract of land on Beaver Dam Creek, in Oglethorpe County,
containing 600 acres, Also my tract of land at the big shoals of

Stokes, William - Continued. Oconia River in Franklin Co.
Containing 300 acres, I also give to my son, negro man Charles, and
at the decease of my wife negro woman Amey, Also I give to my son all
my rent books. I give to my grandson Thomas Burdell one negro boy
named Jack to be delivered to him at his coming of age, if he should
die under that age said negro to go to Robert Burdell, if he die under
that age, said negro to go to Elizabeth Grimes dtr. of Sarah Grimes.
I give to my grandson Robert Burdell one negro boy named Coleman, to
be delivered to him at twenty one years of age, if he die before that
age, negro to go to Thomas Burdell, if both die, then to go to Sarah
Grimes. (Only one page of will found in notes.)

STUART, ROBERT An Inquest. Pack 125. Clerk of Court Office.
Pickens, S. C. An inquest was held at Jumping Off Rock in Pickens
Dist. this 20 Oct. 1857. Before Lenard Rodgers, Magistrate upon view
of the body of Robert Stuart. The jury brought it out that he came to
his death by misfortune or accident. John Hencel sworn said, that the
decd. was lying on his left side his gun lying across his neck. He
did not seem any appearance of any violence being used upon the body.
He said that Elija Jinkel, Silas Henkel, Isaac Stuart Jackson Stuart,
Thomas Stuart were present when the body was found. Dr. J. N. Lawrence
said that he examined the body and found that his neck was broken.

STUBBLEFIELD, J.W. Pack 603 #202. Clerk of Court Office. Pickens,
S. C. By W. L. Keith Clk. To any lawful surveyor you are authorized
to lay out a tract of land unto J. W. Stubblefield, not exceeding ten
thousand acres, making a true plat thereof, within two months. Dated
this 12 Dec. 1853. Executed for 25 acres this 12 Dec. 1853. Certified
2 Jan. 1854.

TAGGART, MOSES Pack 270. Clerk of Court Office. Abbeville,
S.C. Abbeville Dist. To the Honr. the Chancellors: Your orator
William Patterson by Moses T. Owen his next friend. The great grandfather of your orator Moses Taggart Esq. late of this Dist. now deceased
on the 10 April 1819 made and executed to his son James Taggart a deed
of trust in favor of his dtr. then Mary Perrin for life with certain
limitation over, certain negroes to wit. Rachel with her male child
named George and her female child Anika, to have and hold said negroes
unto the said James Taggart trustee. By said trust, James Taggart
trustee was to permit Mary Parrin then the wife of Thomas Perrin to
enjoy the interest, increase, and profits from said negroes for life.
At her death negroes to be sold and all money to be divided amongst her
chn. of her body when then arrive at the age of twenty one or marry.
After the death of her first husband, Mary intermarried with Arthur
Murphy, she and her husband are still in possession of said negroes,
sixteen in number to wit, Rachel, George, Anika, Ben, Joe, Hannah,
Lewis, Jane, Martha, Alfred, Frank, Abram, Sally, Willis, Alexander
and Adaline. Mary Murphy has no children by her last marriage, by her
first husband she made two chn. Elizabeth and Sarah Ann, Elizabeth
intermarried with Dr. Thomas Mabry and had one child, but both mother
and child died many years ago. Sarah Ann married Cary P. Patterson
and at her death on 14 Feb. 1852 had four chn. to wit, Ann Patterson,
Sarah Patterson, Eliza Patterson and the complainant William Patterson.
A division of said negroes was agreeable to Mary and her husband
Arthur Murphy and dtr. Sarah Ann Patterson, his mother share was to be
conveyed to John W. Hearst trustee. The agreement was not signed by
his mother, account of her sickness, but was signed in her present by
Dr. J. W. McKeller. Your orator will ever pray. Filed 11 June 1853.

TARRANT, BENJAMIN Apt. 7 File 465. Probate Judge Office.
Greenville, S. C. I Benjamin Tarrant of Greenville Dist. being weak
in body, but of perfect mind and memory. I give to my beloved wife
Martha Tarrant all my estate both real and personal during her life
time or widowhood after all my just debts are paid. At her death or
marriage, my estate to be divided amongst my chn. Milley Hollon,
Betsey Snow and heirs of my decd. dtr. Molley Wade and son Benjamin
Tarrant Junr. each to have five pounds sterling, having formerly

Tarrant, Benjamin - Continued. given them part of my estate, that
is twenty pounds to be paid from the est. then the remaining part to
be divded between sons Leonard, Waitt, Robert, Samuel, James, John
Tarrant. I appoint my wife Martha Tarrant and sons Leonard and Samuel
executors. Dated 15 Nov. 1808. Wit: Henry Machen Jr., James
Tarrant, Solomon Dalton. Signed: Benjn. Tarrant. Proven by Solomon
Dalton before Spartan Goodlett, Ord. on the 20 Aug. 1819. Expenditure
March 1821. Paid Mark Snow $6.87 1/2 cts. on proven account.

TATE, JAMES SENR. Old Records B.B. Page 13. Clerk of Court
Office. Abbeville, S. C. As a citizen 320 acres, lying on N.E. side
of Sennekaw River, bounded on North by land of Robert Tate, on other
sides vacant when surveyed by William Tate, D.S. Dated 21 May 1784.
Recd. 29 May 1784. Robert Anderson, Clk.

TATE, ROBERT Old Records B.B. Page 12. Clerk of Court Office.
Abbeville, S. C. A citizen grant for 640 acres, lying on the N.E.
side of Senekaw old Town, bounded on all sides by vacant land, when
surveyed by William Tate, D.S. dated 21 May 1784. Recorded 29 May
1784. Signed: Robert Anderson, C.L.

TATOM, ORVILLE Pack 3348. Clerk of Court Office. Abbeville,
S. C. Will. I Orville Tatom believing that I am about to die and
feeling unable to execute a will in due form, do ordain this as my
last will and testament in presence of William Tennant and James Norwood whom I appoint my executors. I will that my negroes Clark and
Hannah and child Margaret also her child Minna, Moses and Hanna shall
be sold after making another crop, and the money put on interest for
my son William T. Tatom, and if my wife be pregnant with child, it
shall have an equal amount with my son William T. Tatom. I further
will all the balance of my property both real and personal, after paying
my debts, to my wife Caroline S. Tatom if she should not marry and if
she should marry she is only to have one third in fee simple, the
balance to go to my child or chn. If my wife should marry, my negro
George shall be placed in hands of James Norwood for the benefit of my
chn. Effy his wife and her children to be with him. Wit: A. B.
Arnold, Thomas Graves, W. Tennant, William Bratcher. Dated 4 Sept.
1837. I will to Mr. Bratcher what he owes me. Signed: Orville Tatom.
Codicil. I wish that in case my son William T. Tatom should die before
he becomes of age, the money I willed to him to be given to my wife
and that my negro George and his wife and chn. be given to James A.
Norwood my executor. Dated 4 Sept. 1837. Wit: A. B. Arnold, W.
Tennant, T. Graves. In Equity, Abbeville Dist. Your orator George
Graves and your oratrix Caroline L. Graves his wife sheweth that
Orville Tatom died about __ Sept. 1837. Leaving in full force his last
will and testament. Stating that if she married again she shall have
one third of the estate in fee simple. That she and William T. Tatom
are the only devisees and legatees of said Tatom. He leaving a tract
of land containing 700 acres adj. land of Michael Speed, A. F. Winbish,
Littleton Yarbrough and others. Your oratrix on about 30 Jan. 1844
intermarried with George Graves, some parts of said will executed
under her widowhood, now she seeks a final settlement under partition
according to his will. Filed 30 April 1844.

TATOM, WILLIAM T. Pack 404. Clerk of Court Office. Abbeville,
S. C. On 26 March 1857 a statement of the estate of William T. Tatom
in the hands of his guardian Dr. William Tennant. W. T. Tatom has now
come of age.

TAYLOR, ANDREW #3345. Clerk of Court Office. Abbeville, S. C.
Will, I Andrew Taylor of Abbeville Dist. being sick of body, but of
good disposing mind and memory. First to my beloved wife I leave 75
acres of land to wit that place I bought from Samuel McKinney and to
be laid off along Henry Wideman line including the cabin and spring
where James Sims lately lived and this during her natural life only.
I then devise said land of 75 acres to my grandson Andrew Anderson.
To my daughter Jane Moragne I leave my two negroes to wit a fellow
named Sam and a wench named Delia during her natural life only, at her
death, I will the fellow to my grandson David Taylor and the wench to

Taylor, Andrew - Continued. my granddaughter Jane Anderson and
further to my grandson David Taylor I will the house and plantation
on which we now live. To my grandson Robert Taylor I will the
remainder of the land I bought from Saml. McKinney to wit 75 acres,
having formerly settled with my son Robert (who is since dead) on a
tract of land I bought from John Carson, with mare added to it.
I will the same to his widow during her widowhood at her death or
marriage I will it to her son James Taylor. All remainder of my
property not willed to be sold and money preserved and paid to my.
granddaughter Jane Anderson as soon as she come of age or marry. I
allow to be paid to my granddaughter Susan Sims twenty dollars and to
my granddaughter Polly Anderson ten dollars. I appoint my friend
Andrew McComb and his son John as my executors. Dated this 13 Jan.
1818. Wit: Robert McCaslin, Archibald Bradley, George X McFarlin.
Signed: Andrew Taylor. In Equity. To the Honr. the Chancellors:
Your orator and oratrix Calvin Pressly and Jane his wife late Jane
Anderson. Sheweth that Andrew Taylor the grandfather or your oratrix
in the year 1818 departed this life, having previously made his will
whereby after various particular disposition of his property, he
directed that all the residue shall be sold at public sale one half
of the money used for paying debts and legacies made in his will, the
other half or remainder keep for your oratrix, paying to her on
becoming of age. Your oratrix was of full age in July 1826, and was
married to your orator in 1825. About 1819 Andrew McComb died intestate and to his son John McComb was committed the administration of
his est. Your orator and oratrix has applied to said John McComb
for an account and settlement of her account. Filed 21 April 1828.

TAYLOR, JOHN Will Book A, Page 31, 32. Probate Judge Office.
Union, S. C. I John Taylor of Union County in Pinkney Dist. being
sick in body, but of good and perfect memory. I will and order all
my just debts be paid with my funeral expenses. I give to my beloved
wife Susana Taylor, all and singular of my stock, household furniture
for her use and disposal. I appoint Susana Taylor my wife and Moses
Guyton as my executors. Dated this 17 Sept. 1794. Wit: John Mitchell,
Moses Guyton, James May Jr. Signed: John Taylor. Recorded this 17
Sept. 1794. Debts paid, Enoch Garrett, Edwin Prince, Thomas Harris.
Debts due est. John Hutton, Enoc Davis, Richard Burgess, Hilaz Garrett
Junr., Enoch Floyd, John Prince Senr. Admnr. bond dated 10 Sept. 1795.
Inventory made 28 Sept. 1795.

TAYLOR, SAMUEL Pack 255. Clerk of Court Office. Abbeville, S.C.
To all and sundry to whom these presents shall come Mary Taylor otherwise Raney spouse of William Raney preacher of the gospel in the parish
of Drumblade and County of Aberdeen and lawful daughter of deceased
Samuel Taylor of Drumdole, in the parish of Forque and County of
Aberdeen aforesaid and Elizabeth Forbes his spouse also now deceased,
with consent of my husband and the said William Raney for myself, my
own right and interest where as William Forbes of Philadelphia, brother
german of the deceased Elizabeth Forbes my mother died some time ago
intestate possessed of certain houses in the city of Philadelphia
and houses and lands in and about the village of German Town, and certain lands in the State of Kentucky to all which Nathaniel Forbes his
son also now deceased, succeeded subject to the dower of Mrs. Mary
Forbes his mother, that the said Nathaniel Forbes having also died
intestate the said Elizabeth Forbes my mother came to have right to the
lands and houses aforesaid, and she having also died intestate, I the
said Mary Taylor and Samuel Taylor of Lesendum in the parish of Drumblade and County of Aberdeen aforesaid my brother being the only
surviving children of the said Elizabeth Forbes and the only heirs
representatives of the said William Forbes, and Nathaniel Forbes his
son have now the sole right to the lands and houses and all other
subjects means and estate wheresoever situated which belongs to the
said William and Nathaniel Forbes subject always to the dower of the
said Mrs. Mary Forbes and whereas William Forbes Taylor of Cambletown,
So. Carolina by brother died sometime ago leaving a will by which he
appointed William Ross and Deencein Mathison both now deceased, and
Patrick McDowel of Savannah and Savage of ___, his executors and
bequeathing to me, and my said brother Samuel the whole of his

Taylor, Samuel - Continued. residuary estate and where as it is
requisite and necessary that I authorize some proper person or persons
to manage and recover for my behoof my share of the property aforesaid.
Therefore know ye, that I the said Mary Taylor with the consent of my
husband, and I the said William Raney for my own right and interest
and we both with one consent have made constituted and appointed and
by these present make constitute and appoint the said Patrick McDowel
and Samuel Taylor jointly and severally to be our true and lawful
attorney, to ask, sue, demand, recover, from all and every person
or persons in any State of America all debts, sums of money, goods,
wares, effects, etc. [sic]. Dated this 14 Sept. 1815. Wit: Allen
Donald, John Spence. Signed: Mary Taylor and William Raney. Seals.
8 Sept. 1760 Samuel Taylor in Loanhead had a son baptized named William.
William Forbes and Nathaniel Forbes witnessed 15 June 1721, Samuel
Taylor had a son baptized names Samuel. William Forbes and Robert
Forbes witnessed 5 Jany. 1778. Samuel Taylor in Loanhead a daughter
baptized named Mary. Nathaniel Forbes and John Allen witnessed.
Extract from the register of baptisms of the Parish of Drum Blade this
27 Aug. 1815. Signed: Alex Sims, Session Clerk P.T. That the written
is a just and faithful extract, and that Samuel and Mary Taylor therein
mentioned are lawful brother and sister to the late William F. Taylor
Esq. merchant of So. Carolina, is attested in presence of the Church
Session by Robert Gordon Minister of the parish of Drumblade. John
Jones and John Spence elders of said parish at Drumblade this 29 Aug.
1815. Signed: Robert Gordon, Min. David Jones, Elder, John Spence,
elder. I Hereby certify that the said General Alexander Hays of Raines
is one of the justices of the peace for the County of Aberdeen and that
the above affadavid was made and attested in my presence. Signed:
Alexr. Stewart, N.P. Richmond County, Georgia. Superior Court, 21
Dec. 1815. Recorded in Book N, folio 371 to 374 and examined. Signed
John H. Mann, Clerk. Edgefield Dist. So. Carolina. I do hereby
certify that the foregoing instrument of writing is a true copy from
the records remaining in my office, in Book J.J. from page 528 to 533
and examined by this 5 day Feb. 1818. Signed: M. Mims, C. & R.M.C.

TAYLOR, SAMUEL Old records B.B. Page 7. Clerk of Court Office.
Abbeville, S. C. For Samuel Taylor a citizen grant for 640 acres,
lying on the East side of Keowee River, bound on the West by the River,
all other sides by vacant land, when surveyed by Bennett Crafton D.S.
this 21 May 1784. Platt recorded 27 May 1784. Signed: Robert
Anderson C.L.

TEASLEY, SILAS & FANNY Deed Book A, Page 30. Clerk of Court
Office. Elberton, Ga. This indenture made 26 March 1791. Between
Silas Teasley and Fanny his wife and Oliver Crafford of the same place.
In consideration of twenty Ł sterling in hand, hath granted, sold, and
bargained a tract of land on a branch of Cold Water Creek, containing
200 acres. Wit: R. Banks J.P. Signed: Silas Teasley and Fanny X
Teasley. Registered 19 Aug. 1791.

TERRELLS, LEWIS Deed Pack 350 #7. Clerk of Court Office.
Pickens, S. C. I James K. Sutherland of Pickens County in consideration of $95 to me paid by Lewis Terrell of the same place, have
granted, sold, bargained and released a certain tract of land lying
in Pickens County on waters of Weaver and Latners Creek waters of
Oolenoy River. Adj. land of James W. Friddle, W. Burgess. Containing
95 acres. Dated 23 April 1883. Wit: W. U. Hunt, Merida X Mancell.
Signed: James K. Southerland. Proven on oath of W. U. Hunt before
J. J. Lewis, C.C.P. on this 23 April 1883.

THOMAS, MARY ANN Pack 408. Clerk of Court Office. Abbeville,
S. C. In 1857 Dr. F. G. Thomas was the guardian of his daughter Mary
Ann Thomas. Recd. 1 June 1847 from William Chiles Exor of Richard
White $59.15. Recd. 19 Nov. 1845 from L. White, Admnr. of Nancy
Coleman personal estate $486.80. Recd. from Wm. Waller by L. White
admnr. of George White est. $557.20. Recd. from John White admnr. of
Wm. Bullock wards share of grandfather real est. $901.81. In 1848
Mary Ann Thomas had intermarried with John W. Suber.

THOMAS, THOMAS WALTER   No ref. Probate Judge Office.   Abbeville,
S. C.   I Thomas Walter Thomas of Abbeville Dist. being in sound mind
and at this time in tolerable health.   I hereby appoint my wife Elizabeth Hamilton Thomas my executrix and my son James Walter Thomas my
executor, enjoining my son always to act in obedience to the wishes of
his mother, to treat the negroes with special consideration and be kind
and attentive to his brothers and sisters without expecting to exert
too much control over them in his capacith of my executor.   All money
of the estate shall be invested in bank stock as the safest investment.
If the land and negroes cannot be managed, they have the power to sell
and invest the money.   They will divide the property in an equitable
manner, each to have an equal share.   The bank stock shall be used to
the education of the children, until they are all educated, then a
division to be made.   I give to son Robert Walter Thomas my gold
sleeve buttons.   In consequence of the youth of my son James I direct
that he must not qualify or act as my executor until he is directed to
do so by his mother. Wit: Charles T. Haskell, James Taggart, R.M.M.
Palmer. Signed: T. W. Thomas, seal. As no date in will. Abbeville,
Dist. In Equity, I William Hill, Ord. certify that the foregoing is
a true copy of the last will and testament of Thomas W. Thomas decd.
Taken from the original which is on file in my office. This 16 April
1857. Signed: William Hill, Ord. Abby. Dist.

THOMPSON, JOHN FARLEY   Will Book 1791-1803, Page 31.   Probate
Judge Office.   Elberton, Ga.   I John Farley Thompson of Elbert Co., Ga.
being in a low state of health and weak in body, but of perfect mind
and memory.   I will and desire that my just debts and funeral expenses
be paid.   My desire that my negro wench Peg and my riding horse with
tobacco crop be sold in Peterburg to the highest bidder, and the profits to be equally divided amongst my seven children, to wit, John,
Isham, Peter, Sally, Mary, Mily and Tabby.   I give to my son William
Thompson 100 acres of land whereon he now lives, also three negroes
named Frank, Ivey, Nancy.   I give to my son Robert Thompson all that
tract where he now lives, containing 300 acres, also negro boy now in
his possession, named James.   I give to my dtr. Milly Ragland the
negro named Silas now in her possession.   I give to my son Farley
Thompson that part of my land on Butrams Creek lying on West and North
West of Harris Nunneler and William Thompson Senr.   Also one negro
named Isaac, one bay mare, half of the stock of cattle and hogs, household furniture.   I give to my son Lewis Bevel Thompson all that part
of my land on Butram Creek whereon John Harris now lives, not already
given to sons William and Farley, Also the other half of my stock of
cattle, hogs, household furniture.   I give my sons all debts due
either by bond or open account, and they are to pay all my debts, out
of what I have given them.   I appoint my two sons Farley and Lewis
Bevel Thompson executors. Dated this 3 Sept. 1792. Wit: Robert
Thompson Senr., William Thompson Senr., Stephen Ellington. Signed:
John F. X Thompson. Recorded this 5 Feb. 1793. W. Higginbotham,
Reg. Pro.

THOMPSON, RACHEL   Old records B.B., Page 10.   Clerk of Court
Office. Abbeville, S.C.   For Rachel Thompson widow a citizen grant
for 300 lying on South side of Great Rockey Creek a branch of Savannah
River.   Bounded on all sides by vacant land, when surveyed by David
Hopkins D.S. dated 24 May 1784. Recorded the 27 May 1784. Signed:
Robert Anderson C.L.

THOMPSON, ROBERT SR.   Pack 5187. Clerk of Court Office. Abbeville, S. C. Abbeville Dist. To the Honr. The Chancellors, Henry
Desaussure, William Harper. Your orators Robert Thompson, Elijah
Teague and Margaret his wife, and John Sloan and Sarah R. his wife
that they are children of the late Robert Thompson, Senr. who departed
this life intestate, possessed with considerable real and personal
estate.   That Elijah Foster in tye year 1818 was appointed guardian
of the goods and effects of your orators by this Honr. Court.   That in
the June Court of 1824 your orator filed a bill against the said
Elijah Foster, their gdn. for an account.   Also that in the June term
of this Court in 1826, the report filed a balance of $3672.62 against
the defendant as guardian was confirmed and made the decree of this

Thompson, Robert Sr. - Continued. Court. Your orators sheweth
that the said Elijah Foster now lives beyond the limits of this State.
He was sized of a tract of land containing __ acres. Which tract was
levied on and was sold at sheriff's sale. The highest bidder being
Owen Selby who received the title for said land, and who was employed
by said Elijah Foster as his agent to purchase the land for him,
having furnished the said Owen with funds. Filed 27 April 1829.

THOMPSON, WILLIAM SR. Deed Book C. Clerk of Court Office.
Elberton, Ga. This indenture made this 25 March 1793. Between William
Thompson Senr. and Mary his wife of Elbert Co., Ga. and William
Thompson Junr. of the same place. In consideration of good will, love
and affection that we bear for our son, have freely given and granted
all the tract of land whereon he now lives. Being on the East side of
Butrams Creek. Adj. land of Stephen Ellingtons, James Morrisons,
Benjamin Cook, Walker Richardsons, Eliah Brewer, William Brewers,
Matt J. Williams, William Hatchers and Stephen Ellinftons. Containing
1300 acres. Wit: Samuel Watkins, Drury Thompson Junr., Isam Watkins.
Evan Ragland J.P. Signed: William Thompson and Mary Thompson,
seals. Recorded 28 July 1795.

TILLISON, ANNANIAS Pack 405 #100. Clerk of Court Office.
Pickens, S. C. Know all men that we Annanias Tillison and George W.
Phillips of Pickens Dist. are bound unto Joseph Black and William Laval
treasurers for the time being and to their successors in office in the
sum of $500, the payment well and truly be made and done, we bind
ourselves, our executors, admnr. etc. This 19 March 1839. The above
bound Annanias Tillison hath been appointed the office of constable.
Signed: Annanias X Tillison, Seal. G. W. Phillips. To W. L. Keith
C.C. I Saml. Mosley J.Q. do certify to the Clerk that Annanias Tilliso
expresses a willingness to serve as constable and I think him to be a
fit person. Signed: Saml. Mosley.

TOLBERT, JAMES In Equity, Pack 306. Clerk of Court Office.
Abbeville, S. C. Abbeville Dist. To the Honr. the Chancellors: Your
oratrix Rebecca Talbert relict of James Tolbert decd. Sheweth that
James Tolbert on the 21 Aug. 1853 departed this life intestate seized
and possessed of a tract of land on the waters of Curtail Creek
containing 275 acres bounded by land of James Martin, Louisa Logan,
Ephraim Davis, the tract on which said James Tolbert lived the time of
his death. Leaving as heirs and distributees, your oratrix his widow
and chn. John H. Tolbert, Mary Isabella who married John F.H. Davis,
Nancy Jane who married James W. Buchanan, William K. Tolbert, Joseph
Marshall Tolbert minors under the age of twenty one and Levi Strawhorn
who married Martha Rebacca, dtr. of the said James Tolbert decd. who
died on the 2 Aug. 1853 leaving an only child named William H. Strawhorn which said child has died since the death of its grandfather James
Tolbert decd. Your oratrix sheweth that in Oct. 1853 the admnr. on the
est. was committed to your oratrix and her son John H. Tolbert, and she
is satisfied that the personalty of the est. will meet all demands
and she believes that it would be in the interest of all, that a
partition of the land be made. Filed 17 Nov. 1853 (The name is
written Talbert and Tolbert.)

TOLBERT, RACHEL Pack 293. Clerk of Court Office. Abbeville,
S.C. In Equity, Abbeville Dist. To the Honr. the Chancellors: The
petition of James P. Martin sheweth that Rachel Tolbert is an idiot
aged about forty five yrs. That in 1846 a writ was issued from the
Court of Common Pleas. That upon due examination the said Rachel
Tolbert was found to be an idiot. Therefore her brother William Tolbert
was appointed her Committee. That he soon afterwards died. That upon
his decd. James Tolbert was appointed. That he is now also deceased.
That the said idiot is entitled to an estate of about $1200.00 from
the est. of her deceased father Daniel Tolbert, which was in the hands
of the admnr. of James Tolbert. That the idiot has been living with
your petitioner since the death of her mother. That by an order of
the Court of Common Pleas about $85 was allowed for the support of
said idiot. This amount was paid to your petitioner until the year
1853 when James Tolbert died before making his return and his admnor.

Tolbert, Rachel - Continued. having neglected to pay. Your petitioner has married a sister of said idiot. That her next of kin has given their consent to the appointment. The mother, in her last will and testament requested that your petitioner take care of said idiot. Your petitioner will ever pray. Filed 1 June 1854. Signed: James P. Martin.

TOLBERT, REBECCA Pack 58. Clerk of Court Office. Abbeville, S. C. On 10 Sept. 1862 Jos. or Jas. M. Tolbert was guardian of Rebecca Tolbert minor who has now come of age. (no other date.)

TOLLETT, JOHN Deed Book A, Page 7. Clerk of Court Office. Elberton, Ga. This indenture made the 17 Jan. 1790. Between John Tollett of Wilkes Co., Ga. and John Allbriton of Union Co., S. C. In consideration of 60 ₺ sterling, hath bargained, sold one tract land lying in Wilkes Co., Ga. on Beaverdam Creek, adj. land of Thomas Carter, Richardson Hunts all others sides vacant. Containing 200 acres. Wit: Richardson Hunt, Thomas Carter, Jesse Holbrook. Signed: John Tollett, seal. Personally appeared Margret Tollet wife of John Tollet and consented to her husband selling and disposing of the within named land and relinquished all right to dower before Richardson Hunt, J.P. Dated 24 Feb. 1791. Ch. Wood Pro. and Matthew Tollet C.E.C.

TODD, ARCHIBALD #1681. Probate Judge Office. Anderson, S.C. To the Honr. Herbert Hammond Ord. The petition of A. O. Norris sheweth that Archibald Todd late of Anderson Dist. died intestate with diver goods, rights and credits. Your petitioner prays for letter of admnr. Filed this 17 Dec. 1860. Admnr. bond. We A. O. Harris, C. L. Gillard and J. W. Harrison are bound unto Herbert Hammond, Ord. in the sum of $2500. This 31 Jan. 1861.

TODD, JAMES JR. #946. Probate Judge Office. Anderson, S.C. The petition of Andrew Todd sheweth that James Todd Jr. the brother of your petitioner late of Anderson Dist. decd. It is believed that he died intestate. That he left a small ste[?] on hand unsettled. There are some debts due the est. which cannot be recovered without some person is authorized to do so. Your petitioner prays for letter of admnr. on the est. Dated this 29 Aug. 1842. Admnr. bond. We Andrew Todd, Robert Todd and A. N. McFall are bound unto John Martin Esq. Ord. of Anderson Dist. in the sum of $300. Dated this 12 Sept. 1842. The inventory was made 30 Sept. 1842 by Robert Todd, John McPhail, Nathan McAlister.

TODD, ROBERT No Ref. Probate Judge Office. Anderson, S. C. Anderson Dist. I Robert Todd Senr. being feeble health but of sound and disposing mind. First after my decease, my will is that my funeral expenses and just debts be paid. I will that the whole of my estate both real and personal be sold except two tracts of land, viz. one tract that David Gordon lives on, called the Jarrett tract. The other where James Jarrett now lives, called the old McDaniel tract that I bought from John M. McKee, a feather bed and furniture. The personal property be sold on credit of one year. The real estate and negroes be sold on one half twelve months credit and the other two years [sic]. I will the tract of land called the Jarrett tract to the heirs of the body of Jane M. Gordon, containing 230 acres, and that Jane M. Gordon live on said during her natural life. I will to my son in law James Martin the tract called the old McDaniel tract, containing 128 acres. It shall be his part of my estate. I will to my wife one feather bed and furniture and the third of my estate. I will besides the land to the heirs of my dtr. Mary Ann Martin body, that the money be put on interest until said heirs become the age of twenty one. I will that Andrew Todds son, my grandson Robert Todd $100 after my wife gets her share put on interest until he is twenty one yrs. I will to my grandson Robert C. Pressly son of David and Elizabeth Pressly $100 to be put on interest until he is twenty one yrs. I will to my grandson Robert Gordon son of David and Jane M. Gordon $100 to be put on interest until he is twenty one yrs. I will to my grandson Robert (Todd) Branyan son of Henry and Margaret Branyan

Todd, Robert - Continued. $100 to be put on interest until he
is twenty one yrs. I will to my brother John Todd that is in Ireland
or on his way from there $400 when he arrives. If he never arrives,
said money to be divided among my heirs and legatees. The balance
after the four hundred dollars to my grandsons and the third to my
wife, to be divided equally among my son Andrew Todd, John Todd and
Henry Branyan my son in law and David A. Pressly my son in law. I
appoint my son Andrew Todd my executor. Dated this 13 June 1844.
Wit: James Herron, Nathan McAlister, George W. Long, John McPhail.
Signed: Robert Todd. Proved on oath of John McPhail, before W. Magee
O.A.D. this 26 July 1844. By the year 1856 the legacy given to John
Todd of Ireland was divided among the heirs. In the inventory the
following negroes are named, Tom, Ned, Calop, Katy, Mary, Elsy, Mandy,
Gilbert. The est. sale was held 6 Nov. 1844. Buyers, Samuel Brown,
Andrew Todd, Henry Branyan, James A. Rampy, Thomas Branyan, David
Gordon, Samuel M. Webb, Robert Duncan Sr. Andrew Latham, Robert Duncan
Junr., John Herron, John Cantrel, James Stevenson, Joseph Jarrett,
Lent Hall Jr., David Hall, Fenten Hall, Olive Todd, Thomas Duncan,
David A. Pressly, John Scott, Maulding R. Manning, William B. Elrod,
Drewry Hall, John Todd, Jacob Sligh, James Cockrane, Daniel H.
Cochrane, James Martin, Lenton J. Hall, Robert D. Gray, Stephen
Haynie, William Lesly, Jackson Carter, David S. McKindy, James Burton,
John McPhail, Lewis Sherrill, Elijah Webb, John M. Hamelton, Hiram
Howard, Luke Hamelton, Andrew W. Hawkins, John McFall.

   TODD, ROBERT Pack 4 (basement). Clerk of Court Office. Anderson,
S. C. Pendleton Dist. To the Honr. the Court of Common Pleas now
sitting. The petition of Robert Todd, lately called and known by the
name of "Irish Robert." A native of the County Antrim in Kingdom of
Ireland. Your petitioner has resided within the jurisdiction of the
U.S. since 23 April 1802 and has resided for the last ten years and
upward in this State, and has behaved himself as a man of good moral
character, etc. and is desirous of becoming a citizen of the U.S.
Your petitioner is about 29 yrs. old. Dated 26 Oct. 1813. We the
subscribed citizens and freeholders do hereby certify that we have
been personally acquainted with Robert Todd from early in the year
1802 etc. Signed: Nathan McAlister, Capt. T. Thoms (rest torn from
page), Capt. T. McAlister, T. T. Beaty, Q.M., John Bryce, J.P.,
Samuel Black J.P., John McMillion. Robert took oath as a citizen
on 26 Oct. 1813. Wit: John T. Lewis, C.C.

   TORRANCE, ANDERSON Pack 3209. Clerk of Court Office. Abbeville,
S. C. Southern Circuit, In Equity. Abbeville Dist. To the Honrs.
the Judges, Hugh Rutledge, William James, Waddy Thompson. Your orator
Andrew Torrance of Union Dist. Sometime in or about the month of March
1781. Your orator being at that time in the County of Essex, Va.
Happened in the company of John Rennolds, after the usual course of
bargaining and ealing, did purchased from said Rennolds a certain
horse for the price of 2,000 weight of tobacco to be delivered in
Fredericksburgh, at the price of ten shillings per hundred weight
Virginia money. Which valued the horse at ten pounds Virginia money.
John Rennolds having or pretending to have anote or bond owing to
him from Berkett Davenport of Culpepper County, Va. for the sum of
48 ₺ five shilling and two pence, Va. money. Your orator having some
business in Culpepper Co. Said John Rennolds entreating and requesting your orator to take said note or bond to Berkett Davenport or
leave same with some other person to collect. Your orator having no
interest or fee from the note or bond. He did deliver said note to
Davenport, who said that he could not pay off the note or any part
thereof. He left the said note in the hand of Joseph Wood Esq.
deputy sheriff under his father who was high sheriff of the county and
lived within a few miles of Davenport. That when he returned to him
home, he told John Rennolds what Davenport had told him and where the
note or bond was. He shortly after, he had this conversation with
Rennolds he left Essex Co., Va. and removed himself to S.C. and has
resided to this present time in this Dist. That he has never seen or
heard from John Rennolds, Bickett Davenport or Joseph Wood. In the
month of February 1791 a person who called himself John Rennolds Junr.
came to my house in Union Dist. and produced an account in the amount

Torrance, Anderson - Continued. of 115£ 10 shillings and 10 pence for the above mentioned note or bond, for the horse with tobacco selling at thirty six shillings per hundred weight and three bushels of rye. Filed 1 Jan. 1807.

TRAVERSE, JOHN Old Records B.B., Page 20. Book A. Clerk of Court Office. Abbeville, S. C. as a citizen 640 acres lying on both sides of Broadway Creek a branch of Savannah River. Bounded on S.W. on Capt. George Liddle, other sides vacant when surveyed by David Hopkins, D.S. the 24 May 1784. Recorded the 11 June 1784. Robert Anderson, C.L.

TRIMBLE, MOSES & CATERUN Deed Book A, Page 33. Clerk of Court Office. Elberton, Ga. This indenture made this 1 April 1791 between Moses Trimble and Caterun [sic] his wife both of Elbert Co., Ga. In consideration of __ paid by John Balinger. Have granted, sold, bargained and released a tract of land containing 600 acres, lying on Beaver Dam Creek. It being the tract whereon Philip Vineyard now lives. Bounded by land of Vineland, John Statham, Richardson Hunt. Land originally granted to John Tottel on the 5 Oct. 1785. (No mare of this deed found in notes.)

TRIMMIER, COL. OBADIAH Pack 31 #6. Clerk of Court Office. Pickens, S. C. In Equity. To William Clark, Jabes Jones, John T. Humpries, John Robertson, Edward Hughs. Whereas Oliver Clarke and Elizabeth his wife, Staret Dobson and Mary his wife, James Blair or Blain? and Arrina his wife, George Blair? and Maria his wife, Jefferson Roland and Lucy his wife, Thomas Trimmier, William Trimmier and Selina Trimmier by their petition in the Court of Common Pleas. Sheweth that Col. Obadiah Trimmier was in his life time seized and possessed with several tracts of land to wit, one tract of 200 acres purchased from P. Carpenter, one tract of 25 acres purchased from James Doran. One tract of 200 acres, one tract of 115 acres, another of 116 acres all three purchased from Henry Dobson another tract of 300 purchased from John Nichols. Containing in the whole 956 acres, it being which he lived on at time of his death, lying on Toxaway Creek, waters of Tugaloo River. The said Obadiah Trimmier died intestate. Therefore the land descended to the said petitioner. The first five in right of their wives, the next three in their own rights as children and also the widow Lucy Trimmier and his other chn. David Sloan and Nancy his wife, and two minors, Obadiah and Marcus Trimmier. The petitioner are desirous of a partition of said land or a sale thereof, with the widow taking one third, and the eleven children the other two thirds. Dated this 4 Oct. 1830. Obadiah W. and M. T. Trimmier are mover 14 yrs. of age.

TURNER, FRANKEY Pack 339 #3. Clerk of Court Office. Pickens, S.C. On 12 Jan. 1850 Frankey Turner took out a bastard warrant for Archibald Anderson as being the father of her two children. That on 27 Nov. 1844 she was delivered of a female bastard child named Matildah who has red hair and blue eyes, that on 1 July 1849 she was delivered of another female bastard child named Liza Jane which had black eyes, and that Archibald Anderson is the father of said children.

TURNER, THOMAS Family as given by Mrs. Edmon L. Crow of Dallas, Texas, dated 7 Aug. 1853. The will of Thomas Turner, Sr. was probated in Marlboro Dist., S. C. 26 July 1822, he named the following chn. James, Aaron, Jane, Thomas Jr., (my great grandfather) Moses, John, Mark, and Mary. His wife Chairity was not named in the will, so presume she was dead before this date. In April 1803 is a transfer of 200 acres of land by Thomas Turner, to Alex Rascoe, the wife's dower in this deed is Chairity Turner. So we know she was living in 1803. In the History of Old Cheraw's, by Bishop Alexander Gregg, that Thomas Turner Sr. was Clerk for Cheraw Dist. in 1773. He further states on page 226 on 9 June 1775 the Lt. Governor named twelve magestrates for Cheraw Dist., S. C. Thomas Turner Sr. being in the list of names. Aaron Turner, married Sallie English, had Joe, Aaron Jr., Esater, Sallie and Anne. Thomas Turner Jr. (my great grandfather) married a sister to Sallie English, do not know her, they had Thomas,

Turner, Thomas - Continued. married a Miss Skipper, lived in
Tenn. Chairity, married Joe Parish, lived in Lee Co., Ga. Mark married
Drucella Harris, lived in Fayette County, Ga. Isham was a preacher,
married Anna Driggens, lived in Ark. and Ga. John, married Betsy
Archibald, lived in Randolph Co., Ga. and Harriett no record. Thomas
Turner Jr. wife died and he married the second time in S.C. place and
date __? to Gincy Parish (Parrish) was Gincy her name or nickname?
They had following chn. William Kennedy Turner, born 29 Jan. 1824.
Marlboro Dist., S. C. came to Texas when he was young was a M.E.
preacher have complete data on his decandants. Nancy Turner born about
1825 in S.C. married John Arnold, lived in Calhoun, Ga. Patsy Turner
born about 1827 Fayette Co., Ga. Married John Booker and moved to S.C.
they had chn. Lizzie Turner born about 1829 Fayette Co., Ga. Married
___ Williams, school teacher. Durury Turner died in infancy. George
Washington Turner (my grandfather) born 13 Nov. 1833 Henry Co., Ga.
came to Texas when he was twelve years and lived with his uncle Aaron
who had moved to Texas a short time before from Ga. another child
Malissa Turner, no record. Gincy Parish Turner, second wife of Thomas
Turner Jr. died about 1844 in Henry Co., Ga. Thomas is said to have
married twice after her death, no chn. by last two marriages. Thomas
was a soldier of the war of 1812 and is buried in or near Tunnelhill,
Ga. would like to locate his grave and place a marker. Any information
on Thomas Turner Sr. and wife Chairity, of Marlboro Dist., S. C. and
their ancestory, and any information on their son Thomas (my great
grandfather) who moved to Ga. about 1826 will be greatfully received.
If any other children of Thomas and Chairity, moved to Ga. except
Aaron and Thomas, I have no record of it. Thomas Turner Jr. had four
sons who were pioneer Methodist preachers, Isham, William Kennedy,
George Washington, and Aaron Turner. I feel sure there are many of
Thomas Turner Sr. and wife Chairity's decandants still living in South
Carolina.

TYGER, L. L. Box 920. Probate Judge Office. Pickens, S. C.
I L. L. Tyger being of sound mind and memory. First I desire to be
buried in a matalic case by my wife at Mrs. Elizas Walthalla old family
burying ground in Amelia County, Ga. I will to my beloved sister-in-
law Laiser Egelston Walthall the town lots #2, 3, 4 each containing
three fourths of an acre, in the town of Central in Pickens County.
Also lots #11, 12, 23, 24, 25, 28, 29, 42 43 and 44 being part of
Eatons lost by Bronson's survey. Also I desire that a heavy marble
head and foot board be placed at my own and wife graves and after
expenses and just debts are paid, I will the remainder of my money and
notes to my sister Louiser Egleston Walthall. I will to Albert
Walthall one open face silver watch also one ring (with stamp B on it).
I will to Kit Walthall one double case silver watch. I appoint my
friend John J. Thrasher, executor. Dated this 30 Jan. 1879. Wit:
D. O. Thrasher, J. D. Warnock, Ellen B. Terrie. Signed: L. L. Tyger.
Filed: 13 March 1879.

UNDERWOOD, GEORGE Apr. 10, File 5. Probate Judge Office.
Greenville, S. C. Summons in Partition. To Amasa Underwood, Nimrod
Underwood the legal heirs of William Underwood. The legal heirs of
Elijah Underwood. The legal heirs of Enoch Underwood, The legal heirs
of George Underwood. The legal heirs of John Underwood, Harris Puckett
and Alsabeth his wife, and John Chamness and Martha his wife. All
legal heirs of the late George Underwood of Greenville Dist. You are
hereby required to appear in the Court on the first Monday in Dec.
next to shew cause, if any, why the real estate lying on waters of
South Tyger River, bounded by land of Wm. Fuller, Joseph McKinney,
Wilson Goodlett and Thos. Barton, containing 230 acres. Allotting to
each a share thereof. Dated this 4 Aug. 1840. (in another place
states that) Amasa and Nimrod lives in S.C., William and John Lives in
Alabama, Elijah, heirs of Enoch, heirs of George lives in East
Tennessee, Harris Puckett and wife lives in Georgia, does not say
where John Chamness lives. Sale of the personal estate was sold 17
Oct. 1840. Buyers: Wm. Fuller, Amasa Underwood, Alped Turner, John
Brison, Charles Howard, Philip Ross, Jeremiah Tramel, Wilson Goodlett,

Underwood, George - Continued. Henry Kelly, John Hodges Senr.,
James Ward, Joseph McKiney, Thomas Clabourn, John Hudgeons, Toliver
Tramel.

UNDERWOOD, JOSEPH Book A, Page 20. Probate Judge Office.
Pickens, S. C. Partition of the real estate. Benjamin King viz.
John Devenport, Elizabeth Lewis (widow) of Charles Lewis decd., heirs
of John Whitesides decd., George Russell, Joseph King, Jonathan King,
Mary Kelly, Samuel King, Letty Griffin or heirs. Bill for partition
of real estate of Joseph Underwood decd. lying on waters of Cane Creek,
containing 500 acres. Originally granted to John C. Kilpatrick and
Jesse Nevill. After advertizing in the Messenger for absent legatees,
all being absent and without the limits of this State. Land to be
sold by sheriff on first Monday in January next. Dated 7 Dec. 1835.
Jas. H. Dendy, O.P.D.

VANCE, ALLEN Pack 326-B. Clerk of Court Office. Abbeville,
S. C. Abbeville Dist. I Allen Vance being frail in body, but of
sound mind and calling to mind the uncertainty of life. First I desire
that my just debts be paid. The property in Abbeville Dist. and in
Bosier Louisiana both real and personal, the Louisiana plantation
contains 1700 acres with all stock, tools, crops and interest I have
in ten to twenty negroes, hired by Mr. E. J. Wiss. I bequeath to my
three children viz, John C. Vance, Mary E. Vance and Laura C. Vance.
I desire this property to remain together under the control and
direction of my executors until my dtr. Laura C. Vance is at the age
of eighteen or marry. Chn. to educated from the Louisiana property.
I give to my wife instead of dower on the Louisiana property a house
and lot in the village of Greenwood containing 23 acres, also the
Wier tract containing about 485 acres, at death of my wife, the property
to go back to the estate. I am indebted to my brother J. H. Hairison
on note of five thousand dollars, which amount I request my executors
to pay. I appoint my brother Jas. W. Vance of Louisiana and my son
John C. Vance executors. Dated this 29 July 1865. Wit: John T. Parks,
W. C. Vance, Emanuel J. Wiss, J. Bailey. Signed: Allen Vance.
Codicil. I wish my executor to carry into effect a contract made by
me and J. K. Vance, to loan him 100 bales of cotton, also loan 100
bales of cotton to E. J. Wiss, secured to my estate by a merchantile
house in Charleston, S. C. of which J. K. Vance, M. Strauss, E. J.
Wiss and Jno. C. Vance are to be partners. I also loan my son 100
bales fo cotton all of which to come from the Louisiana property, my
son to use fifty bales in the merchantiles house. Dated: 27 Aug.
1865. Wit: Thomas H. Chappell, J. F. Davis, J. T. Parks, J. H.
Vance, J. Bailey. Signed: Allen X Vance. Codicil #2. I desire my
executors to pay my dtr. Mary on arriving at age or marry the sum of
ten thousand dollars, or what they think is one third of the Louisiana
property. I desire that my son not pay interest on the cotton loaned
to him. Dated 29 Aug. 1865. Wit: Wm. Williams, John McLees, J. F.
Davis, J. Bailey. Signed: Allen X Vance. Filed 15 Feb. 1870.

VAN WYCK, WILLIAM Pack 114. Clerk of Court Office. Pickens,
S. C. By W. L. Keith, Clk. to any lawful surveyor, you are authorized
to lay out unto William Van Wyck a tract of land not exceeding ten
thousand acres, and make a true platt thereof. Dated this 11 June
1853 executed for 672 acres on 5 July 1853. By Thomas D. Garvin, D.S.
recorded 8 July 1853.

VARNER, EBENEZER P. "Slave Papers" Pack 89. Clerk of Court
Office. Pickens, S. C. #4. On 17 July 1856 appeared. Ebenezer P.
Varner and said Sam Oglesby a free man of color, did on the night of
the 17th perpetuate the crime of feloniously breaking open the store
of Ebenezer P. Varner and stealing some money. Negro evidence,
Quince says that about 9 o'clock he saw Sam at the corner of the yard
going a different way home to what Sam had told him he was going the
same evening. Also a few days before Sam wanted to know of him how
the windows was gastened, the same window was broken open. Negro
Anderson says that Sam wanted him to go with him to see if they could

Varner, Ebenezer P. - Continued. get in the back window. Negro
Martin says that on the night of the 17th Sam came home about 11 or
12 o'clock. The jury are: Leonard Towers, James Johns, Aaron Terrell,
Richard Dean, Andrew Jenkins, Squire Hughès, John Bowman and D. E.
Smithson. Sam found guilty. Fined $15.00 and 110 lashes on his back.

VAUGHAN, FRANCES Pack 275. Clerk of Court Office. Abbeville,
S. C. Abbeville Dist., in Equity. To the Honr. the Chancellors:
The petition of James M. Perrin of the dist. aforesaid sheweth. That
Thomas B. Boyd of this Dist. departed this life in February 1857,
leaving in full force his last will and testament. By said will, the
testator divised to your petitioner one third of his estate (after
certain specific legacies) to be held in trust for the sold and separate
use of his daughter Frances, wife of Edward Vaughan, not subject to
debts, contracts or liabilities of her husband. The executors sold
the land and personal estate except the negroes who were divided into
lots, as instructed to do. The lot of negroes drawn for Frances, were
turner over to your petitioner. Your petitioner sheweth that Edward
Vaughan lives in the Dist. of Newberry, remote from the residence of
your petitioner, who cannot give the trust, attention which it may
require. Your petitioner prays that he be released from the office of
trustee and substitute Mr. James C. Vaughan the father of said Edward
Vaughan, who your petitioner is informed is a gentleman of great moral
worth, and possessed of a large estate. Filed 24 April 1857.

VAUGHN, P. Pack 11 #7. Clerk of Court Office. Pickens, S.C.
An inquest was taken at the home of Miles McCallister the second day
of July 1859 before John Adair Magistrate and acting coroner upon the
body of P. Vonn (Vaughn) Jury, Alexander Bryce Senr., foreman, J.
Leopold, Elijah Deaton, Alexander Grayham, Lewis Abbott, Mannon Phillips,
Franklin Phillips, Joseph Brewer, Michael Broom, William Lady. James
Hull witness sworn sayeth that, that he came from Walhalla on the night
of first of July and found the now dead man sitting on the road with
his back against a tree and his head leaning down. He gave him a dram
to drink. He helped him up and they went about fifty yards down the
road, he set down again and asked for another dram, and said that he
was hungry. I went to McCallister for food and told them about him and
Miles McCallister and Franklin Phillips came to where he was lying and
he told us that he thought he was dying. I sent Sarah Satterfield for
the provision. Henry Goodwin sworn sayeth that he saw the decease in
Walhalla on the 30 June and he was sick then. They started home and
came to the fork in the road. The decease set down and would not get
up, he stayed with him till after dark, and he built him a fire and
left, he thought him drunk. Dr. Norman sworn says that he examined
the body. The death was caused by suffication from an excess of strong
drink and privation of food, being exposed all night and day.

WADE, EDWARD Deed Book H, Page 198. Clerk of Court Office.
Anderson, S. C. This indenture made 3 March 1804 between Edward Wade
of Elbert Co., Ga. and Moses Holland of Pendleton Dist., S. C. In
consideration of twenty pounds paid by said Moses Holland, hath
bargained, sold, a certain tract of land containing 79 acres in
Pendleton Dist., S. C. lying on Neels Creek. Being part of a grant
of Samuel Dalrymple on the 3 July 1787. Wit: James Ridgway, Abner
Sutton, Thomas Burford. Signed: Edward Wade. Attested to by Thomas
Burford, before Jno. George, J.P. on the 6 March 1804. Mrs. Ann Wade,
being examined apart from her husband, have relinquished her interest,
rights on the above tract of land before Ro. B. Christian, J.P. this
3 March 1804. Recorded 19 April 1805.

WAITES, MAINORS #183. Clerk of Court Office. Abbeville, S.C.
Abbeville Dist. In Equity, To the Honr. the Chancellors: The petition
of William E. Sharp sheweth that he has been appointed in the County
of Marion state of Florida, guardian of W. Franklin Waites, Telitha
Ann Waites, Emeline Waites, and Elizabeth Ellen Waites, children of
Simon Wait who has died in Florida. The said minors have a share of
the est. of Sarah Wait their grandmother, who some years ago departed

Waites, Mainors - Continued. this life in this Dist. The four
minors have about $500 from the est. The same is in the hands of
the Admnor. Simons Wait. A small part of the minors share in the real
estate, their father consented to the sale, but didn't sign a written
consent for the sale. Your petitioner prays that the sale be confirmed.
Filed 22 Sept. 1859. Letter, dated 5 March 1859. Mr. J. M. McIntosh.
Sir, as it is out of my power to get to Ocala to see you, I would be
glad you would Mr. W. E. Sharp guardian of my four children and give
him power to get the money for them. Signed: Elizabeth X Waites.
Wit: W. E. Sharp, J. C. Sharp. In another paper, Marshall Sharp
states that W. E. Sharp is his son. Larkin Mays states that he knows of
the land formerly belonging to Sarah Wait decd. That she was his Aunt.
A. H. Magee states that the parties were originally from S. C.

WALKER, HENRY G. Box 96 Pack 2359. Probate Judge Office.
Abbeville, S. C. Est. admnr. 3 Dec. 1827 by Lettice Walker, James W.
Prather, Alexander Scott and Matthew Young who are bound unto Moses
Taggart Ord. in the sum of $10,000. Citation published at Vianna
the 27 Nov. 1827 by Kenneth Murchison, Est. appraised 6 Dec. 1827
by Andrew Rembert, William Gray, Matthew Young. Negroes named:
Alfred, Backus, Isaam, Betty, Ben, old woman and her child Mary,
Agness. Notes due the est. Jos. B. Gilbert, Lewis Howland, William
Pate, Lidiel Bacon, R. Posey, Benjamin Cook, W. Rucker, J. Hatcher,
A. McDaniel, John M. Whitney, Rowlin Stone, Joseph Williams, Grant
Taylor, J. R. Whitney, John Dyre, Charles Yarbrough, William Maxwell,
Robert Stewart, T. W. Whitehead, S. Higgenbottom, L. Hunt, John Morris,
John Blake, William Taylor, George Alexander, C. Harriss, Randolph
Cook, John Scuddy, Able Whitty, Zack Bowman, Jerry Walker, Thomas
Burton Senr., William J. Dennis, Saml. Goolsby, Willis Rucker, C. S.
Causby, William Blunt, Ledford Parret, Dabney and Wany, John S. Head.
Sale held 19 Dec. 1827. Buyers, Robert Howard, Alexander Scott, Capt.
William Drennan, Charles B. Herrod, William Gray, James R. Houston,
Peter Bird, John Scott, James Rembert, Samuel Cole, Thomas Hamilton,
William Reed, John H. Walker, Jeremiah G. Walker, Phares C. Walker,
James V. Oalds, Thomas Jones, John S. Trunbull. In another paper
dated 9 Aug. 1824 Andrew Rembert Exetor. of Robert Winn and Henry G.
Walker admnor. of Lettice Winn. It states that Robert Winn willed to
his mother Lettice Winn, stock, and two negroes, named Sarah and Lucas.

WALKER, RICHARD Box 94 Pack 2327. Probate Judge Office. Abbeville, S. C. Est. admnr. 27 Oct. 1832 by Thomas Ferguson, A. T.
Trailer and Pleasant Searls who are bound unto Moses Taggart, Ord. in
the sum of $1,000. Cit. Published at Republican Meeting House the 23
Oct. 1832. Expends for the year 1 June 1836 to 1 June 1837 for board
and clothing of Frances, Willard, Mary and Manda $100. Est. appraised
9 Nov. 1832 by Isaac Hawes, Peter Smith, John Martin. Sale held 12
Nov. 1832. Buyers: Elizabeth (Widow), Thomas Freeman, Cutberth Price,
Isaac Hawes, Widow Johnson, James Garret, Samuel Walker, Abner Banks,
C. Carey, Joseph Garrett, William Fendley, Sanders Walker, Ivy Taylor,
Robert Jennings, Henry King, Adkin Corley, Squire Hill, Moses Jones,
Pharis Martin. Whereas it is inconvenient and almost impracticable
for me to attend the Court at Abbeville on the 3 June 1834. I do therefore certify that the settlement made on that day by Thomas Ferguson
admnr. of the est. of Richard Walker decd. and Moses Taggart Esq. Ord.
shall be final and conclusive in relation to said est. Dated 2 June
1834. Sgn. Elizabeth Walker.

WALKER, SOLOMON Box 143 Pack 4047. Probate Judge Office.
Abbeville, S. C. I Solomon Walker of Abbeville Dist. being of sound
and disposing mind and memory. After paying my debts, I give to my
wife Nancy a negro girl 12 yrs. old named Moriah, during her natural
life and after her decease, I give the same to all my chn. to be
equally divided amongst them. I give to my dtr. Elizabeth Dillishaw
one negro girl named Martha about ten yrs. old. All the rest of my
personal est. I give to be equally divided between the whole of my six
chn. Lucy Hardy, Samuel Walker, Sanders Walker, Margaret Martin, Barton
Walker, and Elizabeth Dillishaw. I appoint my son Sanders Walker
executor. Dated 29 Jan. 1847. Wit: Thomas Ferguson, Geo. W. Mitchell,
L. Newby. Signed: Solomon Walker. Sale held on 21 Nov. 1855.

Walker, Solomon - Continued. Buyers: John Deason, William Harman, John Elkins, Redman Brown, William McKiney, Sanders Walker, Charles Freeman, Andrew Harris, Henry McKiney, Uriah Brown, Nancy Walker (widow), Chesley Walker, James Brown, Burton Walker, Isaac Caldwell, James Carrel, Richard Barret, Sampson Carrel, Peter Smith, Red Brown, Willard Smith, Allen Weeks, William McCain, Iven Robeson, William Dillishaw, Samuel Walker, Samuel Stuart. Negroes sold at sale, Bill, Hanner and child, Molly, Hester, Susan, Toba, York, May, Fany, Andrew, Edna, Lucy, Tilda, Peter. Will was probated 19 June 1855. Power of attorney from Samuel Walker of Coweta County, Ga. Appointing Burton Walker as his lawful attorney. Dated 24 Nov. 1857. Two more power of attorney from Gallant H. Hardy and Lusinday X Hardy and from James F. Martin and Margret X Martin both dated 30 Oct. 1857 and witnessed by John J. Allen, Place not given or where they resided. Final settlement was made after three months notice in the "Independant Press." This 12 Feb. 1858. Present: Sanders Walker and Thomas Thomson, Esq., Burton Walker in his own right and representing James F. Martin and wife, Gallant Hardy and wife, also William Delashaw, guardian of John Wesley Delashaw only child of Elizabeth Delashaw decd.

WALLACE, ALEXANDER Box 40 #1723. Probate Judge Office, York, S. C. Estate admnr. 25 Oct. 1858 by Sarah Wallace, James A. Barnett, Arthur A. McKenzie who are bound unto J. M. Ross Ord. in the sum of $1,000. The estate was divided into two shares.

WALLACE, ANDREW Box 62 Pack 1539. Probate Judge Office. Columbia, S. C. I Andrew Wallace of Richland Dist. being of sound and disposing memory. I devise to my beloved wife (Sarah) during her natural life, my dwelling house, out buildings and lot opposite the Lunatic Asylum and about ten acres of land. I also give to my wife during her life time only all my household and kitchen furniture, my gold watch, my plate, library of books, etc. a carriage and pair of good horses, etc. Also negroes, Bella and her son Joseph, Mima and her dtr. Beckey, Mary, Julia, Cornelia and her son Charles, Warren, Poinsett, Bob, Eliza and her dtr. Catharine, Emma, and Rosina, Old Harriet, Hester, Jack, Darkey and Polydore. I also give to my wife, the annual interest on $20,000 during her life time. I devise to my son Dr. John Wallace the Borad River plantation now in his possession, which I bought from William Thompson, also the house and lot where he now resides, which he conveyed to me by deed dated 16 July 1856, also the Welch tract and I hereby cancel any bond, mortgage or other obligation, also negroes, now in his possession, Tom, Moses, Abram, Toby, Jim, Sam, Dinah, Caroline, and her child Richard, Sylvia, Cressy, Dolly, Old Suckey, Jesse and his wife Allin, Jim, Sarah, Sam, and Old Jim and wife. The value in the general distribution of $30,000. Also my blacksmith James now in my possession. I devise to my son William Wallace the Molly Horn plantation in Newberry Dist. which I bought of Chancellor Caldwell and others, now in his possession, which was conveyed to me by deed dated 18 Aug. 1857. I also give to son William the house and lot where he now resides adj. the city of Columbia. I also give to my son William negroes, Charles, Sally, Venus, Bob, Gorgianna, Nancy, Spencer, Elsey, Rosetta, Eliza, Milton, Jeffrey, Adalina, Jane, Sancho, and William also George and Frank. Value in the general dist. at $20,000. Also my blacksmith Joshua now in my possession. I devise to my son Alfred Wallace the plantation in Richland Dist. which I purchased from Gen. Samuel Owens, which formerly belonged to Ethel Heath. Also negroes Billy and his wife Eliza and their son Edmund and dtr. Milly, Gabriel, Isom, Henry, Jacob, Nancy, Mary, Martha and her dtr. Eliza. Joe and his wife Rachel and their chn. Dinah, Major, Centy, Caesar, Isreal, Jeffry also mules and horses. The property to be valued at general dist. at $26,000. I also give to son Alfred the house and lot in Columbia between my house and son William house. I devise to my son Edward Wallace the Wyche tract, containing about fifty acres, and all the Phillips tract (except the portion which belongs to the house tract where I now live. I also give him negroes, Old Lewis, Rose, Nelson, Charley, Billy, John, Old Sam, Clarressey, George, Henry, Lieber, Young, Sam, Ephraim, Hope and Doughey. I devise to my dtr. Mrs. Jane Yates for her life time, the house and lot on Church Street in the City of Charleston where she now

Wallace, Andrew - Continued. resided, the $6,000 paid by me of
the purchased, also all the negroes now in her possession bought from
the est. of John C. Taylor and delivered to her, with the ones I
advanced to and put in her possession. The value at the General Dist.
at $15,000. I devise to my dtr. Mrs. Ellen Pearson, the house and lot
in the town of Columbia, S. C. where she now resides with her husband
John H. Pearson Esq. Also the tract of land in Richland Dist. known
as the Glover or Daniel plantation, also negroes, Henry, Emily, David,
Mary, Susan, Laura, Ben, Hardy, Maria, Lavinia, Melinda, Warley,
Susannah, Lucinda, John, Margaret, Lewis, Frank, Randall, Edmund.
Also all claims, demands, judgments, mortgages, or other liens, which
I hold against her husband John H. Pearson Esq. The above property
value in the General dist. at $20,000. I devise to my dtr. Mrs. Emma
Murdock wife of Dr. John S. Murdock the house and lot in the town of
Jacksonville, Fla. also negroes, Bill, Amanda, Cressey, Maria, Frances,
Lydia, Harriet, Margaret, Caroline, Milly, Collin, Mary Jane and Winny.
Also all demands and claims of whatever description which I hold
against her husband Dr. John S. Murdock. The property to be valued
in the general Dist. at $20,000. I devise unto my dtr. Mrs. Agnes
Barton, the house and lot in the city of New Orleans, where she and
her husband formerly resided Also the negroes heretofore advanced to
her by deed of gift. Also a house and lot in Columbia, S. C. adj. my
residence, with negroes Harriet and her chn., Alonzo, Ameratta, Henry
the carpenter son of Claresey. The property to be valued at $13,000
in the general dist. I devise to my dtr. Mrs. Alexina Evans wife of
Samuel W. Evans, negroes, Frank, Jenny, Anna, Erasmus, Osborne, Young,
Frank, Dick, Jacob, and Martha, also the following negroes purchased
from her husband by me, and now in his possession. Randolph, Dinah,
Louisa, Clara, Julia, Lisbon, Sophy, Nelly, Sam, Rodger, William,
Keziah, Massey, Solomon, Absalom, and Sylvia. The property to be
valued at $16,000 in the general dist. I devise unto my dtr. Eliza
Wallace a lot in the city of Columbia, S. C. also negroes, Fanney and
her chn., Harriet and John, Harriet the dtr. of Eliza, Bill, Simonds,
Lewis, Ben (a bricklayer) Lisbon (a carpenter), Ben (a bricklayer)
Alick, Little Billy, and Edward (a carpenter). The house and lot I
gave to my wife in the first clause, I give to my son Edward after
her death. All household and kitchen furniture, plates, carriage,
portraits, library, horses and other items, I wish at her death to be
divided amongst my chn. Alfred, Edward, and Eliza. Negroes given to
my wife, I give to Edward, Old Harriet, Eliza (wife of Bill Simonds),
Mary, Julia, Warren, Polydore, Bob, Poinsett and Bella. To my dtr.
Mrs. Jane Yates I give, after the death of my wife, negroes, Catherine,
Emma, and Rosina (dtr. of Eliza). To my dtr. Eliza Wallace, I give
after the death of my wife, negroes, Cornelia and her son Charles.
To Mrs. Agnes Barton I give after the death of her mother, negroes,
Hester, Mima, Beckey. To my son John I give after the death of his
mother, negroes, Jack and Darkey. I give to my son William after the
death of his mother, negroes, Joseph the son of Bella. I give to my
neices Jane and Isabella Wallace of Castle Douglas, Scotland the sum
of $500. Also $500 in trust for said neices to use as they think
best for the support of Nathaniel Burkeby and his family. Also $5,000
in building a new Methodist Church in lieu of the present Washington
Street Church. (city not given). I appoint John A. Crawford, Dr. J. W.
Parker, Robert Bryce, and Edward J. Arthur to make the valuation of
my estate. I hereby appoint my wife Sarah Wallace and sons William
and Edward executrix and executors. I do hereby declare the foregoing
twenty two and one fourth pages to be my last will and testament. This
23 May 1860. Wit: J. A. Crawford, S. Olin Tally, Henry E. Scott,
Signed: Andrew Wallace. Codicil: Whereas my dtr. Emma Murdock has
been left a widow and returned to me with her chn. and need a dwelling
house. I therefore declare as null and void the cause giving to dtr.
Eliza a lot in Columbia. I give the same to dtr. Emma Murdock. I
hereby give to my dtr.Eliza the lot I bought at sale of Jesse DeBruhl.
The clause to subscribe $5,000 to the Methodist Church, I now declare
the same to be null and void and stricken from my will. In the ___?
clause, I devised to my dtr. Agnes Barton now Agnes Taylor a lot of
four acres on the West side of the Asylum road, I declare to be null
and void. Dated this 22 Oct. 1861. Wit: And. Crawford, S. E. Capers,
Henry E. Scott. Signed: Andrew Wallace. Will proved before Jacob

Wallace, Andrew - Continued. Bell, Ord. on the 6 Jan. 1863.
Sarah Wallace and William Wallace qualified as executrix and executor
on the 7 Jan. 1863.

WALLACE, ANN Vol. 41, Page 624. Probate Judge Office. Charleston, S. C. I Ann Wallace of the City of Charleston, S. C. I direct
that my just debts and funeral expenses shall be paid as soon as convenient. I give unto Lydia, Serena and George MaCaulay the younger,
the children of my brother George McCaulay $1,000 to be divided among
them, share and share alike. I give to David Christie the only
surviving and now blind son of my old and intimate acquaintance Mrs.
Joanne Christie $300. I give unto the Presbyterian Church of the City
of Charleston of which I have been so long a member $300. I give to
the orphan house of Charleston $300. By the last will of my deceased
step father George McCaulay, gave unto me three of his negroes, to wit.
Betty, Mary and Richard with power to dispose of the same in my life
time. I think best for them and Fanny of whom I purchased from his
est. The said negroes shall have three months to procure themselves
owner or owners at a moderate valuation. The ones not sold after three
months after my decease shall be sold at public or private sale, and
the money go into the est. I give the rest and remainder of my est. to
my brother Daniel Macaulay, if he should die before me then the property
to be his heirs. I appoint my brother Daniel Macaulay and my friend
Mitchell King executors. Dated 1 March 1827. Wit: Wm. Broadfoot,
Thomas Ogier, Neill McNeill. Signed: Ann Wallace, seal. Codicil.
I give unto my friend Samuel MacCartney $500. I give unto Jane Douglas
Morrison the sum of $200, and I wish her to allow her brother such part
of this legacy as she think proper. I give my negro Fanny and her
child to my dear brother Daniel Macaulay. Dated this 2 April 1834.
Wit: Walter Knox, Henry D. Lesesne, Nelson Mitchell. Signed: Ann
Wallace. Proved before Thomas Lehre, O.C.T.D. this 11 July 1837. Same
time qualified Mitchell King exor.

WALLACE, BEAUFORT A. Will Book D, Page 140. Probate Judge
Office. Edgefield, S. C. I Beaufort A. Wallace of Edgefield Dist.
being somewhat feeble in body but of sound and disposing mind and memory.
First I desire that my just debts be paid from cash on hand, or notes
and accounts due me. It is my desire that my Executrix sell the tract
of land I bought from Benjamin T. Mims adj. land of J. Glover, or the
store in the village of Edgefield occupied by G. L. and E. Penn Co. or
she may sell lot in the village. I desire that no division of my
estate be made until my wife gets married again or until one of my
children comes of age or marries, the est. to be held in common, until
my children are educated. When either of my children come of age or
marries or my wife marries again, I desire a division of my est. be
made between my beloved wife Ellen T. Wallace and my chn. I appoint
my wife Ellen T. Wallace executrix. Dated this 13 May 1841. Wit:
P. Schoppert, John Lark, Mary B. Schoppert. Signed: B. A. Wallace.
Recorded and proved this 22 Sept. 1841.

WALLACE, DOUGLASS No ref. Probate Judge Office. Spartanburg,
S. C. I Douglass Wallace do make this my last will and testament.
First I will my just debts and funeral expenses be paid. I will that
my wife sell the mule and wagon, and apply the proceeds to the paying
of my debts. I will that my real and personal of every description
to my beloved wife Meoriah Wallace, during her natural life. At her
death on half of the property to go to my grandson Lewis Wallace and
his heirs. The other half of my property to go to the heirs of my said
wife forever. I appoint my wife Moriah Wallace, executrix. Dated 19
June 1900. Wit: Geo. W. Nicholes, John M. Nicholes, Andrew Peak.
Signed: Douglass X Wallace.

WALLACE, ELIZABETH Box 66 #3189. Probate Judge Office. York,
S. C. On 4 March 1816 James Wallace Sr., James Wallace Jr., Elizabeth
Wallace were bound unto Henry Middleton Gov. of the State in the sum
of $1,000. James Wallace the guardian of Elizabeth Wallace a minor.

WALLACE, HUGH B. Case #59. File 2707. Probate Judge Office.
York, S. C. I Hugh B. Wallace of York Dist. being sensible of the

Wallace, Hugh B. - Continued. uncertainty of life. To my
beloved wife Mary Ann I give all my property of every description for
her use and for the purpose of bringing up and education of my children.
When the children come of age, I leave to my wife, what and how much
they shall receive, having regard to the interest and comfort of the
remainder of my family. I appoint my wife Mary Ann as executrix and
guardian of my children. Dated this 21 Aug. 1866. Wit: I. L. Watson,
J. L. Adams, L. L. Adams. Signed: H. B. Wallace. Probated 25 Sept.
1866.

WALLACE, ISABELLA Box 51 #2263. Probate Judge Office. York,
S. C. On 14 Oct. 1837, William Wallace, Henry Carroll Esq., Thomas H.
Smith were bound unto Benjamin Chambers Ord. in the sum of $500.
William Wallace made guardian of his dtr. Isabella Wallace a minor.
A legacy from the estate of Elizabeth Brumfield decd.'

WALLACE, JAMES Box 72 Pack 1149. Probate Judge Office. Chester,
S. C. In April 1813 Jacob Smith a constable received from Charity
Wallis $5.00 in full of a execution of William Smith. Harbert Wallace
a Justice said the account was true. (No other papers in pack.)

WALLACE, JAMES Vol 24 Page 826. Probate Judge Office. Charleston, S. C. I James Wallace of Jacksonborough, S.C. a Practitioner of
Physic being sick and weak in body but of sound mind and disposing
memory. First I desire that my just debts and funeral expenses be
paid from the ready money and the balance equally divided among my five
brothers to wit, Gustavus Wallace, Michael Wallace, William Wallace,
Thomas Wallace and John Wallace, share and share alike. I also give
to my five brothers all my land in the states of Virginia and Kentucky
and slaves in S.C. to wit, Jim, Minda, Little Jim, Abraham and a female
infant dtr. of Minda, also all notes, bonds and book debts. The negro
I bought from the sheriff sale named Stephny who is now in possession
of Mr. Joseph Marquiss and by him detained contrary to my consent as
soon as he is recovered, he to be sold with my stock of medicines and
instruments and stock of horses, mares, colts and sheep. Whereas my
negro woman named Diana has served me well and with obedience. I
therefore declare that after my death she be free and liberated from
all servitude. I give unto said Diana and her heirs forever negroes
Peter and July, also all household and kitchen furniture. I appoint
my five brothers and my friend Colo. William Washington and Paul
Hamilton executors. Dated this 10 Dec. 1790. Wit: Thomas Murphy,
Gabriel Lewis, John Caskin. Signed: James Wallace. Codicil. Whereas
I James Wallace have made application for letter of Admnr. upon the
est. of Richard Warrington as greatest creditor and have obtained a
cition[?] but have not admnr. I desire the whole of my demands
against the said est. with debts due my est. be equally divided among
the heirs of Mr. John Riley of Jacksonborough. Dated this 10 Dec.
1790. Wit: Thomas Murphy, Gabriel Lewis, John Caskin. Signed:
James Wallace. Proved before Charles Lining Esq. O.C.T.D. on 4 March
1791.

WALLACE, JAMES Case 36 File 1538. Probate Judge Office. York,
S. C. I James Wallace of York Dist. do make this my last will and
testament. I will unto John James McArter all my land lying on the
East side of the creek and $100. I also give to Elias Gimelin the one
third of all the balance that I possess. I also give unto Rebacka Rhea
of Pike County Misura one third of my estate. I also give unto
Margret Wallace of York Dist. one third of my est. I appoint James
Caldwell my executor. Dated: 14 Nov. 1856. Wit: Robert Neelands,
Abram Neelands, John Whitesides. Signed: James Wallace.

WALLACE, JAMES Box 71 #2520. Probate Judge Office. Camden, S.C.
I James Wallace of Carshaw (Kershaw) being very sick and weak in body
but of perfect mind and memory. First I leave all my real and personal
estate to be equally divided amongst my four small children (not named).
Secondly, I appoint Mr. Donul McMillen my executor and request that
he dispose of my estate to the best advantage at my death for the
support of my children. Dated this 17 July 1806. Wit: Saml. Dunlap,
Robert Thompson. Signed: James X Wallace, seal. Proved 19 July 1806

Wallace, James - Continued. before Thomas Gardner, J.P. On 7 Jan.
1818 recd. of William Randolph $52.00 in payment of rent of the planta-
tion of James Wallace of Whiteoak decd. Signed: Daniel McMillen,
exor.

WALLACE, JAMES F. Box 14 #614. Probate Judge Office. York, S.C.
On 26 May 1849 John R. Wallace states that James F. Wallace owned 40
acres of land on Fishing Creek and left heirs, Rachel Wallace his
widow, who has married Thomas Milner, chn. James M., Terissa M.,
Matilda J., Elizabeth N., and John R. Wallace, all of age except
Elizabeth who is a minor.

WALLACE, JAMES F. Box 10 #444. Probate Judge Office. York,
S. C. Estate Admnr. I July 1848 by John R. Wallace, Rachel Milnor,
Alexander Fewell, who were bound unto J. M. Ross, Ord. in the sum of
$400. The widow recd. one third and five shares divided. James
M. Wallace, Matilda Wallace, Terace Wallace recd. shares.

WALLACE, JAMES JR. Box 2 #72. Probate Judge Office. York, S.C.
No date, James Wallace Jr. was heir of James Wallace Senr. decd.
Aaron Boggs in right of his wife Elizabeth, Wm. Wallace, heirs of
John Wallace seven in number, heirs of Margaret Burris decd. seven in
number, Robert Wallace, heirs of Jane Robinson decd. two in number,
heirs of James Jr. decd. are ordered to appear in court. Owned land
on Fishing Creek. Also Edward, Isabella, Isaac H., Mary, Saml. W.
Wallace.

WALLACE, JONATHAN Box 71 Pack 1113. Probate Judge Office.
Chester, S. C. Est. admnr. 30 Oct. 1821 by Elizabeth S. D. Wallace,
William L. Wallace, John Kidd, Hugh Wallace who are bound unto E.
Lyles Ord. in the sum of $6,000. Left nine heirs. Expend 1822,
Paid M. Teresa for school and board, paid Robert (minor) school and
board, paid Margaret school and board, paid Matilda school and board.
Paid Sarah school and board. Paid Jonathan David school and board,
paid 1828 John Gill and wife Margaret $130.07. Paid 1831 William D.
Wallace $34. Paid 6 Feb. 1833 William C. Walker in right of his wife
Sarah $103.97. Paid Aug. 1832 R. M. Wallace share $121.09. Paid
10 Sept. 1832 Thomas Wallace in right of his wife Matilda $72.75.

WALLACE, JOHN Box 44 #1853. Probate Judge Office. York, S.C.
Est. admnr. 11 Nov. 1816 by Thomas Wallace, Robert Watson, Nathaniel
Philips, John Bennett are bound unto the ordinary of York County in
the sum of $3,000. John Wallace and Samuel D. Wallace of Lauderdale
Co., Ala. on 29 Nov. 1826 appointed Thomas of same State and County
their attorney to receive their share from the estate of John Wallace,
decd. Thomas Wallace of Lauderdale Co., Ala. appointed guardian of
Catherine and Samuel Wallis. Thomas Farris wife was a dtr. of said
decd. (name written Wallace and Wallis.)

WALLACE, JOHN C. Box 44 #1874. Probate Judge Office. York,
S. C. Estate admnr. 20 Feb. 1860 by Robert Whitesides, John Brown,
Thaddeus Bolen who are bound unto J. M. Ross, Ord. in the sum of $500.

WALLACE, JOHN R. H. Box 81 #3989. Probate Judge Office.
York, S. C. Est. admnr. 26 Sept. 1862 by James Wallace, Joseph A.
McLean are bound unto the ordinary of York County in the sum of $400.
No other papers.

WALLACE, MARGARET Box 96 File 4709. Probate Judge Office.
York, S. C. I Margaret Wallace of York County, S. C. being impressed
with the uncertainty of life, etc. I will all my property of which
I may die with, both real and personal be equally divided between my
children Martha Ruth Eeixina? and Alice W. Wallace. They are jointly
paying my debts and funeral expenses. I appoint A. W. Wallace
executor. Dated this 10 Dec. 1888. Wit: A. P. Campbell, Zimri
Carroll, W. B. Glass. Signed: Margaret X Wallace. Probated 7 Jan.
1889.

WALLACE, MARY   Box 91 Pack 1448.   Probate Judge Office.   Chester, S. C.   Est. admnr. 15 April 1844 by Thomas Torbitt, Joseph Dickey and Samuel McCaw who are bound unto Peter Wylie Ord. in the sum of $500. Expend as of 1 March 1857.   Paid Thomas Wallace $121.   Paid Robert Wallace $68.68.   Paid Nancy Wallace $52.13.   Paid William Wallace $67.36.

WALLACE, MCCASTLAND   Case 81, File 3962.   Probate Judge Office. York, S. C.   I McCastland Wallace of York Dist. being in good health and disposing mind and memory.   First I direct that my body be decently buried and my just debts be paid.   Having given my children and grandchildren except my son Alexander S. Wallace all that I wish or intende to.   I hereby will to my son Alexander S. Wallace all my estate of every description whatever to him and heir heirs forever. I appoint my son Alexander S. Wallace executor.   Dated 28 (no month given) 1847.   Wit: Jas. Brian, J. Bolton Smith, S. W. Melton.   Signed: Mcnd. Wallace, seal.   Probated 21 Aug. 1862.

WALLACE, MINORS   Box 48 #28.   Probate Judge Office.   Darlington Co., S.C.   Martha L. Wallace aged 20 yrs., John B. Wallace aged 17 yrs., Margaret G. Wallace aged 15 yrs., James H. L. Wallace aged 13 yrs., petitions by their father James G. Wallace, sheweth that they reside with their father and mother and they have no guardian.   That they all have an interest in a tract of land in Darlington Co., S. C. and that they reside in Arkansas.

WALLACE, OLIVER   Box 66 #3203.   Probate Judge Office.   York, S.C. On 21 Jan. 1804, James Wallace, Thomas Wallace Esq., and John Wallace were bound unto James B. Richardson Gov. of the State in the sum of 2,000 pounds.   James Wallace appointed guardian of Oliver Wallace a minor.

WALLACE, OLIVER   Box 66 #3161.   Probate Judge Office.   York, S.C. On 5 March 1806, Samuel Carson, Reuben McConnel and William Hovis were bound unto Paul Hamilton Gov. of the State in the sum of $1,000.

WALLACE, OLIVER JR.   Case 64, File 459.   Probate Judge Office. York, S. C.   I Oliver Wallace Junr. of York County, being weak in body but of sound mind and disposing memory.   I desire that my just debts and funeral expenses be fully paid.   I give to my wife Judith Wallace my oldest mare with a woman saddle and bridle, an equal share with my three daughters in my household furniture, for her use forever. Wife to have her support from the plantation with the service of negro boy Snow in supporting my four chn.   I also give to my wife one cow and calf to be chosen from the stock.   I give to my three dtr. an equal share of my stock, and to my oldest dtr. my sorrel mare.   I give to my son Oliver Berry Wallace the plantation whereon I now live, containing 100 acres, with all tools, one horse colt.   I appoint my friend Thomas Wallace and Andrew Love executors and my wife Judith Wallace. Executrix dated 17 July 1789.   Wit: Jas. Mitchell, Jas. Wallace, Wm. Davison.   Signed: Oliver Wallace.   Recorded 28 Dec. 1789.

WALLACE, ROBERT   Box 102 Pack 2505.   Probate Judge Office.   Abbeville, S.C.   I Robert Wallace of Abbeville Dist.   Being weak in body. I desire that my just debts paid.   I give to my wife Nancy Wallace two negroes Mahaly and Peter one half of my land, two feather beds and furniture, other house furniture to be divided between my wife and son George Wallace.   I give to my son George, negroes Ann and Andrew and one half of my land, one feather bed and one half of the household furniture and one small wagon.   I give my old negro Hanner to son George, I conceive a charge to my son, one hundred dollars to support said negro Hanner, which is not to be sold.   The balance of my est. to be divided among my wife Nancy, son George, Allen McCullough, Ruben Richey of Anderson Dist. my wife son and my daughter Elizabeth Drennon, Elizabeth Drennon part to be left in the hands of John Donald Senr. in trust during her natural life.   I appoint Larkin Barmore and Samuel Donald executors.   Dated this 16 Aug. 1837.   Wit: Jno. Donnald, Richard P. Bowie, Wm. Barmore.   Signed: Robert X Wallace.   (No recording date)   Est. appraised on 12 Feb. 1840 by

Wallace, Robert - Continued. Robert Dunn, Benjamin Smith, Richard P. Bowie. Sale held 13 Feb. 1840, Buyers: Geo. Wallace. The Widow, Reuben Richey, Benjamin Smith, E. D. Mitchell, Robert Seawright, James Lindsey, A. C. Jones, Isaac Richey, Andrew Pruit, Ezekial Razor, Wm. Robertson, Robert Smith, Joseph Richey, James Killingsworth, Saml. Bratcher, Alax. Miller, Wm. Richey, Mastin Shirley, Saml. Kinmon. Richard Bowie, Jno. R. Richey, James W. Agnew, Wm. Ware, Aaron Drummond. Final settlement Nancy Wallace the widow, Geo. Wallace, Reuben Richey (Ellen McCalla and Elizabeth Drenan), Majr. Jno. Donald being trustee for E. Drennon and atty. for Ellen McCalla. Present Saml. Donald, L. Barmore Exors. On another paper written Elinor McCollough.

WALLACE, ROBERT Box 3 Pack 13. Probate Judge Office. Union, S. C. I Robert Wallace of Union Dist. being in perfect mind and memory. I give to my son William all my land in Union County, also seven negroes to wit, Harry, Long, Jude, Old Jude, Sam, Millbry, Winn, Lowden. I give to my stepson John Parham all my right title and interest to a tract of land lying on Cape Fear River in the County of Chathem in N.C. Land granted to me by said State in 1780. Land adj. land of John Parham in right of his father John Parham decd. I also give him a bay mare by the name of Ham. I give to my dtr. Martha six negroes known as Sambo, Phebe, Phill, Sockey, Rose and Peter. I give unto my dtr. Elizabeth seven negroes, known as Will, Tom, Suke, Jame, Ellock, Phillis and Dembo. I give unto Polly Pinnell, dtr. of Tabitha Pinnell two negroes known as Sambo and Myry, also a good feather bed and ten pounds sterling. My land in Greenville? and Moore counties N.C. to be sold as soon as my dtr. Elizabeth shall be of age of eighteen or marry, and the money divided among chn. William, Martha and Elizabeth. I appoint my friends Frances Deake and George Harlen of Union Co., S.C. and my son William Wallace and William Deake of Chatham Co., N.C. executors. No date given. Wit: Sarah Darby, Wm. Darby, And. Torrance?, James Darby. Signed: Robt. Wallace. Recorded 31 March 1800.

WALLACE, THOMAS Box 44 #1855. Probate Judge Office. York, S. C. Est. admnr. 6 May 1816 by Margaret Wallace, Daniel Seehorn or Seehone?, James Stewart, Robert McCullough are bound unto Benjamin Chambers Ord. in the sum of $1,000. Citation published at Buraheba Church. On 24 Feb. 1819 Mary Hood recd. $22.07. Left five legatees, no names given.

WALLACE, THOMAS Vol. 49, Page 930. Probate Judge Office. Charleston, S. C. I Thomas Wallace of Charleston being of sound mind and memory. I will unto Martha McKinley a free woman of color for whom Charles Edmondston Esq. is guardian, all that lot on West side of King Street in the city of Charleston, S. C. with all buildings thereon, consisting of a two and half story brick house, the title she now holds as security for $1200 loaned to me. I desire that all my other property be sold and after paying my just debts and funeral expenses, the proceeds be divided between my sister Agness Councell, my niece Agnes Martin and niece Julia Ann Francis. To my sister Agness Councell wife of Edward C. Cauncell I give one third of the proceeds after my debts are paid, to my neice Agnes Martin wife of Jacob J. Martin one third, the other third to be put in bank stock and the interest paid to my niece Julia Ann Francis during her life time. I appoint John Phillips Esq. as executor. Dated this 14 April 1854. Wit: Samuel Wiley, W. J. Wiley, Cornelius OMears. Signed: Thomas Wallace. Probated 3 Jan. 1862. At same time qualified John Phillips as executor.

WALLACE, THOMAS Vol 33 Page 1167. Probate Judge Office. Charleston, S. C. I Thomas Wallace of Charleston, S. C. cabinet maker, being sick and indisposed of body but of sound mind and dis- posing memory. First, I direct my just debts and funeral expenses be paid. I will and direct that all my property both real and personal be kept together in the hands of my executors, until my youngest child attain full age of twenty one years. The money from said property shall be applied to the maintenance of my wife and the education of

Wallace, Thomas - Continued. my three youngest children. (Wife
not named.) When my three youngest chn. come of age, the whole of my
property to be sold and my wife to have one third, and the other two
thirds divided among all my children, share and share alike. I hereby
appoint my friend Dr. Aaron W. Leland and Mr. Robert Walker, cabinet
maker, as guardian of my children and of the property. I hereby
appoint Rev. Aaron W. Leland and Mr. Robert Walker Executors. Dated
15 Nov. 1816. Wit: Geo. Kidd, John Reid, James Calder. Signed:
Thomas Wallace, seal. Proved before James D. Mitchell Esq. on the
27 Nov. 1816. At same time qualified Rev. Dr. Aaron W. Leland and
Robert Walker.

WALLACE, WILLIAM Box 51 #2253. Probate Judge Office. York, S.C.
On 6 Jan. 1840 M. Wallace, Thomas Whitesdies, John Nickles are bound
unto the Ordinary of York County in the sum of $4,000. Myles Wallace
made guardian of William Wallace a minor.

WALLACE, WILLIAM Case 86 File 4277. Probate Judge Office.
York, S. C. I William Wallace of York County do make this my last will
and testament. I desire that my executors pay my just debts and
funeral expenses as soon as possible from the money on hand and to sell
the two tracts of real estate, one known as the H. H. Simeril land.
I will to my wife Rebecca the Suthern half of the plantation on which
I now live, known as the Jancy Simeril tract. Also all my stock and
household furniture of every description during her natural life or
widowhood. If she marry or at her death, the said property to be my
sons's Janies Robert Wallace. I will to David G. Wallace the Northern
half of the said James Simeril tract. D. G. Wallace to pay James Robert
$100 to his schooling. I will to my dtr. Isabella Jackson $200. I
appoint W. B. Allison executor. Dated this 21 May 1876. Wit: J. A.
M. L. Stewart, John R. Long, Wm. W. Robinson, W. B. Allison. Signed:
William X Wallace. Probated 18 July 1876.

WALLER, ALBERT Pack 253. Clerk of Court Office. Abbeville,
S. C. In Equity, Abbeville Dist. To the Honr. the Chancellors:
Your oratrix Jane Elizabeth Waller sheweth that in the month of August
last (1859) Albert Waller whilst on a visit to his plantation in
Florida departed this life intestate, leaving as his only heirs and
distributees your oratrix his widow and eight chn. Pelius A. Waller,
Codnes D. Waller, Rody E. wife of William E. Kilcrease, Robert A.
Waller, Criswell A. Waller, James L. Waller, Cadmus G. Waller, and
Edward Henry Waller the last four are minors. Said Albert Waller was
possessed at time of his death with property in Alabama, Florida and
this dist. of S. C. The home tract containing about 300 upon which he
resided in the village of Greenwood, bounded by land of R. G. Levell,
James Bailey, Bennett Reynolds, John Hinton and others. Another tract
containing 80 acres, bounded by land of Richard M. White, Bennett
Reynold and others, on this lot stands the Male Academy formerly known
as the Hodges Institute, which was conveyed to Albert Waller the 25
Jan. 1847 agent of the board of trustees of the Greenwood Male and
Female Academies under the control of the Baptist denomination which
all interest was released and relinquished for a valuable consideration
to Albert Waller on the 4 Feb. 1859. Another lot in village of Greenwood containing about 2 1/4 acres, bounded by land of William P. Hill,
Thomas L. Coleman, Felix G. Parks, a house stands on this lot built for
the female Academy formerly known as the "the Fuller Institute," which
was conveyed to Albert Waller the 4 Jan. 1847 by William P. Hill.
Admnor of the est. was granted to Codnes L. Waller, Pelius A. Waller
and William P. Hill Esq. Filed 12 Nov. 1859.

WALLER, MINORS Pack 301. Clerk of Court Office. Abbeville,
S. C. In Jan. 1827, James Coleman Senr. was the guardian of John
Waller and William Waller minors. Recd. 4 Jan. 1823 from sheriff of
Abbeville dist. of a claim on Nathan and Thomas Lipscomb $1234.06 1/2
On 15 Feb. 1818 James Sales was guardian of John H. Waller, Guilford
Waller. On 15 Jan. 1821 James Coleman was guardian of Susan Waller.
In 1823 Leonard Waller was the guardian of Amelia Waller a minor.

WALLIS, JANE   Vol 5 Page 264.   Probate Judge Office.   Charleston,
S. C.   I Jane Wallis of St. Bartholomew's Parish, Colleton Co., S. C.
being sick and weak in body but of perfect mind and memory, etc.   First
I will that my just debts be paid.   I leave to my granddaughter Kanny
one negro named Cate, when arrived at twenty one yrs.   I give to my
daughter Mary Lawson one negro named Sambo.   I leave to my granddaughter
Ann Lawson one negro named Ealcey.   I leave to my granddaughter Mary
Lawson one negro named Phillis and one boy named Joe with my bed and
beding, horse and saddle, when she come of age of twenty one yrs. or
marry.   I leave to Joseph Mackey one negro named Stephney and one girl
called Bess, to be given at age of twenty one or marry.   I give to
Jane Mackey one negro named Clarinda when she arrives at twenty one or
marry.   I leave to John Lawson one negro named Scipio when he arrives
at twenty one yrs.   I leave to Alexander Lawson one negro boy named
Cyrus when he arrives at twenty one.   I leave all my stock, cattle to
be divided equally among Joseph Mackey, Jane Mackey, Margaret Lawson,
each to have their share at twenty one yrs. of age.   I appoint my
friend John Good my executors.   Dated 1 Nov. 1743.   Wit: Mary Good,
Mary Lawson, Elizabeth Page.   Signed: Jane X Wallis.   Proved by virtue
of a dedimus before Charles Wright Esq. this 14 Feb. 1743/4.   Recd.
19 Mar. 1743/4.

WALLIS, MARGARET   Vol. 42, Page 196.   Probate Judge Office.
Charleston, S. C.   I Margaret Wallis, widow, do make this my last will
and testament.   I desire my executor to pay my just debts and funeral
expenses and procure a tomb stone to be placed over the family graves.
I give to my three nephews John E. Dunn, William Dunn and Charles
Dunn one half of my est. the other half to Edmund Dunn and the chn. of
Mary McQuire the chn. taking one share to be divided among them.   I
also desire my executor to pay Peggy or Margaret Wallis twenty guiness.
I appoint John E. Dunn and William Dunn executors.   Dated 18 June
1838.   Wit: Geo. B. Eckard, J. O. Street, Benjamin Daneuil Hunt.
Signed: Margaret X Wallis.   Proved before Thomas Lehre Esq. O.C.T.D.
on the 6 Nov. 1840.   On 7 Nov. 1840 qualified John E. Dunn and William
Dunn executors.

WALLIS, MARTHA   #679.   Probate Judge Office.   York, S. C.   I
Martha Wallis of York Dist. being in a low state of health but of
perfect mind and memory.   My husband the Rev. James Wallis having by
a deed of trust made to David Hutcheson dated 9 May 1818, authorized
me to dispose of the property agreeable to my own will and pleasure.
I give and it is my earnest desire that my beloved husband James
Wallis except $200 to be paid to him as soon after my death as possible
for the great care and attention he has paid me since our marriage.
My brother has a gin, being in his possession, which I paid for, I
allow him to keep and gin by paying to my son William E. White, when
he come of age the price I paid for it without interest, also the hire
of a negro man called Dick which he had in the year 1818.   I give to
my sister Doreas one good bed with curtains also all my wearing
apparel.   Negro Man Ben named in the deed of trust to be sold, with
stock of cattle, household furniture, shop and tools, from the proceeds,
my executors shall endeavour to give my son William E. White an education and pay for the same from the est. bequeathed to him.   I appoint
my brother Samuel Elliot and David Hutcheson executors.   Dated 21 Oct.
1819.   Wit: John Cathey, George Cathey, James Perry.   Signed:
Martha Wallis.

WALLIS, THOMAS   Vol. 5 Page 373.   Probate Judge Office.   Charleston, S. C.   I Thomas Wallis of Stono Colleton Co., S. C.   Cooper,
being in perfect health and mind.   I give to Mary Woodbury my land and
slaves and all that I have in this world.   She the Mary Woodbury paying
my debts and give Rose her freedom if she require it.   Dated this 26
Sept. 1741.   Wit: Thomas Farr, Hum Elliott.   Signed: Thomas Wallis.
Proved 14 March 1744.

WARDLAW, ALICE R. P.   #215.   Clerk of Court Office.   Abbeville,
S. C.   In Equity, Abbeville, S. C.   To the Honr. the Chancellors:
The petition of Alice R. P. Wardlaw sheweth that she is a minor over
the age of twelve yrs.   That there is coming to her a small est. or

Wardlaw, Alice R. P. - Continued. part of an est. in St. Lukes
Parish in the Dist. and State aforesaid, amounting to about one
thousand dollars. She will be unable to manage on account her minority.
That your petitioner is desirous that her father Judge D. L. Wardlaw
who lives in Abbeville Dist. be appointed her guardian. Filed 11
Sept. 1857.

WARDLAW, JOSEPH No ref. Probate Judge Office. Abbeville, S.C.
(only the latter part of his will, in notes). It is my will that in
case of the death as above of my son Hugh W. Wardlaw that my son
Benjamin F. be joined to Thomas C. Perrin as trustee for my dtr.
Harriet Whitlock and her children. I will under trust to my dtr.
Harriet Whitlock and her chn. all my land in Florida, and all the
negroes now in their possession, with the following negroes, Abraham,
Patsy and her chn., Dick and his chn. Jane, Cynthia and Toby. Billy,
also Harriet and her chn. and Little Fanny and her family or chn. with
one half of my mules and horses not disposed of. I hereby appoint my
son Hugh Waller Wardlaw and Thomas C. Perrin Esq. trustees of all
property given to my dtr. Harriet Whitlock and her chn. I will to my
son Benjamin F. Wardlaw one half of all my land in Abbeville Dist. to
be divided by five disinterested men my son Hugh W. Wardlaw taking the
homestead into his half. I also give to my son Benjamin F. Wardlaw
all the negroes now in his possession, with Little Nancy and her chn.
also Washington and his wife Louisa and her chn. also the whole of
Lilly's family, children and grandchildren, born of Lillys dtr. also
my blacksmith Stephen, also the remainder of my mules and horses. I
appoint my son Hugh W. Wardlaw and Thomas C. Perrin executors. Dated
22 May 1852. Wit: W. L. Templeton, J. R. Ellis, James Douglass,
Henry H. Creswell. Signed: Joseph Wardlaw. Proved on oath of Henry
H. Creswell before F. W. Selleck, O.A.D. this 7 June 1852. In another
paper, In Equity, Thomas L. Whitlock and his wife Harriet states
that they lived in Madison Co., Fla. and have been a citizen of that
state for many years before her father death. That they have a large
family of chn. eleven in number, viz; William W. Whitlock, Lewis A. M.
Thomas and Frances Amanda his wife, Joseph N. Whitlock, Harriet N.
Whitlock, Ann Eliza Whitlock, Charles A. Whitlock, Edward C. Whitlock,
James R. Whitlock, David L. Whitlock, Benjamin F. Whitlock, John H.
Whitlock. The last nine named by their gdn. The last named child
John H. Whitlock having been born after the death of Joseph Wardlaw.
Filed 20 Oct. 1854.

WARLEY, MAJOR FELIX Land Platt. Book A, Page 2. Probate Judge
Office. Abbeville, S. C. For Major Felix Warley 400 acres, bounty on
the West side of Keowee River, bounded on the said river other sides
vacant land known by the name of the halfway house as per platt.
Recorded this 26 May 1784. Robert Anderson Clk.

WATKINS, DR. D. M. Pack 634. #189. Clerk of Court Office.
Pickens, S. C. On 31 Oct. 1846 Dr. D. M. Watkins was appointed a
constable of Pickens Dist.

WATKINS, ELIZABETH Pack 214 #7. Clerk of Court Office. Pickens,
S. C. On 2 Dec. 1856 Elizabeth Watkins made oath that on 14 Nov. last
Randel Lee and Henry Roach did assault her by striking and pushing her
in an angry manner.

WATKINS, HENRY Pack 471. Clerk of Court Office. Abbeville,
S. C. This indenture made 5 Nov. 1789 between Henry Watkins of
Abbeville Dist. and John Longards, carpenter of the same place. In
consideration of five shillings sterling of this State, have granted,
bargained, sold and released all that tract of land containing 733
acres lying in 96 Dist. on Johnson Creek of Savannah River. Granted to
Henry Watkins the 6 April 1789. Wit: Nelson Fields, John Jones,
Adam Crain Jones Junr. Signed: Henry Watkins.

WATKINS, JOSEPH Land Warrant. Pack 630 #17. Clerk of Court
Office. Pickens, S. C. By James E. Hagood, Clk. to any lawful
surveyor you are authorized to lay out unto Joseph Watkins a tract
of land not exceeding one thousand acres and make a true plat thereof.

Watkins, Joseph - Continued. Dated 15 Dec. 1859. Executed for 266 acres on 22 Dec. 1859. By Tyre B. Mauldin D. S. Recorded 27 Jan. 1860.

WATSON, JAMES F. #218. Clerk of Court Office. Abbeville, S.C. Abbeville Dist. In Equity, To the Honr. the Chancellors: Your orator James H. Wideman, executor of the last will of James F. Watson late of Abbeville Dist. Said James F. Watson died on the 6 Sept. 1851. Leaving as heirs and distributees, his widow Margaret Watson and five chn., William E. Watson, George McDuffie Watson a minor about the age of nineteen, James F. Watson about the age of fourteen, Dorothy Jane Watson about the age of ten yrs., Thomas A. Watson about the age of eleven yrs. The testator directed that his property should be divided without sale. He made no provision for the payment of debts. The monies, notes, bonds and accounts is not sufficient for the large sum of debts of the testator. Your orator sheweth that the said will was written on the 17 May 1850, and the time of his death he acquired two tracts of land in or near the village of Greenwood, one purchased from Capt. Thomas B. Byrd, containing ten acres, adj. land of John Logan, Bennett Reynolds, Thomas Coleman and Allen Vance. The other tract purchased from Wm. N. Blake and Dr. E. R. Calhoun, it is near the contemplated depot at Greenwood. The rail road is expected to reach Greenwood by the first of May or June next. As these tracts of land was purchased after the will was written and is not included in and conveyed by said will. Therefore your orator prays that the tracts may be sold as if the testate had died intestate, and apply the proceeds to his debts. Filed 12, 1852.

WATSON, JOHN Pack 435. Clerk of Court Office. Abbeville, S. C. Abbeville Dist. In the Common Pleas, Equity Side. To His Honor the Judge of the Seventh Judicial Circuit of the said State setting in Equity. Your orator Edmund W. Watson for himself and as next friend, his brothers, Archibald K. Watson, and John Watson. Sheweth that in 1852 their father departed this life intestate, possessed with a small estate, consisting of a tract of land on Persimmon Branch, waters of Long Cane. Containing 300 acres. Bounded by land of Patrick McCaslem and others. The intestate leaving a widow Mary Watson and three infant chn., your orator Edmund William Watson, Archibald K. Watson and John H. Watson. A brother of the decease, William Watson admnr. on the estate until his death in 1855. Then the grandfather of your orator, Isaac Kennedy, took out letter of admnr. and gave bond to the Ordinary on the 29 Jan. 1855. He received from A. B. Kennedy the admnr. of William Watson, the first admnr. the sum of $711.44 arising from the personal est. of John Watson decd. and he took possession of the est. until 1866 when also died, not having fully admnr. on the est. or at least not having paid out any of the shares of the distributees. In Oct. 1853 Mary Watson the widow petition the Court for a partition of the real estate. Land was ordered to be sold 22 Oct. 1853 at sheriff sale. The sheriff sold the land to Isaac Kennedy for the sum of $3210. He had never paid the sheriff for the land when he died in 1866. Isaac Kennedy will appointed his dtr. as executrix and on 1 Sept. 1866, Wm. Hill Esq. Ord. now Judge, stated that the est. of Kennedy was indebted to the heirs of John Watson as, the widow $966.17, each heir $644. 12. In the year 1867 your orator the oldest son of John Watson became of age and applied to the executrix of Isaac Kennedy est. for his share of his father est. Under advice of other legatees and devisees, she refused to pay your orator his share. Therefore your orator took out letter of admnr. on the estate of his father, being the third one to do so. Therefore he demanded an account and payment of the said money due himself, his brothers and his mother. Filed 12 April 1869. Edmund W. Watson was 22 yrs. of age, Archibald K. Watson was 19 yrs. of age, John H. Watson was 17 yrs. of age.

WATSON, MARY PETTUS Pack 337. Clerk of Court Office. Abbeville, S. C. The petition of Benjamin S. Pulliam, sheweth that by the will of Mary P. Watson who has lately died, a legacy is given to your petitioner in trust as trustee for his aunt Belinda Cunningham wife of Charles Cunningham, which is in the hands of the executor, which

Watson, Mary Pettus - Continued. will amount to about $1,000.
The legacy is given for the sole use of Mrs. B. Cunningham during her
life and at her death, to be equally divided between your petitioner
and Mary Ann Tharp a dtr. of John J. Tharp, and about thirteen yrs.
of age. Mrs. B. Cunningham is very poor and is over fifty yrs. of age,
and need a man servant to work around the house. She has made application for the purchase of a man servant named Albert and pay for him
from the legacy. Your petitioner in order to oblige his aunt Belinda,
has purchased said Albert, who is about 21 yrs. old and valuable boy
for the price. Your petitioner prays that this Court will confirm the
purchase and direct the legacy to be paid. Filed 6 May 1859. In the
will of Mary P. Watson she directs that negroes Susan and her five
chn. be sold and to pay her debts and the balance divided into five
parts, her son Jubal Watson to have three fifths. One fifth, to
Benjamin S. Pulliam to have and hold in trust for the use of my dtr.
Belinda Cunningham wife of Charles N. Cunningham, and at the death of
my dtr. Belinda, to be divided between my two grandchildren Benj. S.
Pulliam and Mary Ann Tharp. If Mary die without children her portion
to be divided equally between her brothers and sisters. I will that
my dtr. Nancy Tharp wife of John J. Tharp to have one fifth. At her
death to be divided among her chn. Walnut folding table and looking
glass to my granddaughter Mary Ann Tharp. (no more of will in notes.)

WATSON, MINORS Pack 303. Clerk of Court Office. Abbeville,
S. C. Abbeville Dist. In Equity, To the Honr. the Chancellors:
The petition of Archibald B. Kennedy sheweth that Sarah L. Watson,
Elizabeth J. Watson, and Margaret W. Watson chn. of your petitioner
sister, are of very tender age the oldest not over six yrs. They are
entitled to a share of the est. of their father William Watson, decd.
The mother is desirous that your petitioner be appointed gdn. of the
person and estate. To the Chancellor. I give my consent and desire
that my brother A. B. Kennedy be appointed the gdn. of my infant chn.
(named). Filed 29 May 1857. Signed: Margaret E. Watson.

WATSON, RICHARD Pack 435. Clerk of Court Office. Abbeville,
S. C. In Equity, To the Honr. the Chancellors: Deed of trust, I
Richard Watson Senr. in consideration of love and affection I have for
my wife Elizabeth and my chn., Anna Lucy about three yrs. of age,
William Edward about four months of age. My wife having brought me
considerable property at her marriage. Having granted, bargained, sell,
and released unto my friend and neighbor John Foster, the following
property, part of my plantation that lies between Beaverdam and Heron
Creeks, bounded by land of Widow Hearst land, the est. of Vincent
Griffin, Dr. Samuel Marshalls. The dwelling now stands on said tract.
Also the following negroes, Hannah age about forty yrs., Frank about
twenty one, Oliver about eighteen, Sarah Ann about sixteen, James about
twelve, Charles about twenty five, Kitty about thirty, Bob about forty,
Lix thirty and her five chn. Isabella about twelve, Charity about
eleven, Benjamin about nine, Savannah about five, Jack about two, and
Amanda a woman about twenty two and her chn. Mary about two, Kate about
six months, Patty a woman about sixty yrs. of age, Marshall about
twenty three, Martha about twelve, Ann about four, and Anaky and her
three chn. Anana about five, Aggy about three, and Frank about one,
with all household and kitchen furniture. Said property to be in
trust for the use of his wife and their chn. etc. Dated 27 March 1852.
Wit: Willie Smith, Thos. Thomson. Signed: Richard Watson. Proved
on oath of Willie Smith before Mathew McDonald C.C. on the 29 March
1852. Recorded 29 April 1852. In Equity. Your Oratrix Lucy A.
Watson by next friend Mrs. Elizabeth Harris, sheweth. Your oratrix
under the age of twenty one to wit the age of ten yrs. the oldest
of three chn. of Richard Watson, who departed this life in 1859, some
years before her father conveyed to John Foster a large portion of
his estate in trust for the use and benefit of his wife and chn.
Soon after the execution of this deed the mother of your oratrix departed this life in her last illness by virtue of a power given her
in said deed released John Foster the original trustee, and substituted
in his stead William W. Perryman. Your oratrix sheweth that since the
death of her father and mother the property named in said trust is now
vested in herself and her brothers Richard Watson and Samuel M. Watson.
Filed 30 April 1859.

WEST, JAMES P. Box 62 Pack 25. Probate Judge Office. Spartanburg, S. C. I James P. West of Campobello Post Office, in Sptg. Co.,
S. C. being of sound mind and memory. First, I desire my funeral
expenses and just debts be paid. I give to my wife Mariah West all
my personal property, money, notes and accounts, I also give to my wife
all real estate. I appoint my wife Mariah West executrix and Joseph
R. West executor. Dated 29 May 1895. Wit: M. L. Adair, J. H. Farmer,
M. E. Johnson. Signed: James P. West. No Probate date.

WEST, OSBORN Box 33 Pack 4. Probate Judge Office. Spartanburg,
S. C. I Osborn West of Spartanburg Dist. being not well in body but
of perfect mind and memory. I leave unto my well beloved wife Dorcas
West all my personal estate, that is to say, land, negroes, stock
moveable of every kind, bonds, notes and debts due during her natural
life or widowhood and after her marriage of decease the estate to be
equally divided among my nine chn., Casey, Catty, Peggy, David, Masey,
Anny, Liley, William, Genny. I appoint my wife Dorcas West executrix.
Dated this 31 Aug. 1804. Wit: George T. Sloan, Wm. Wofford, Thomas
Meaders. Signed: Osborn West. Recorded 17 Aug. 1814.

WEST, THOMAS Box 37 Pack 6. Probate Judge Office. Spartanburg,
S. C. I Thomas West of Spartanburg Dist. being of sound mind and
memory, but weak in body. I give to my wife Mary Minerva West all my
property both personal and real of every description to have and hold
during her natural life or widowhood. At her decease or marriage, I
will the property to be divided as I will to my dtr. Christina Smith,
one negro named Lucinda and her child Caleb. I will to my dtr. Jane
Fidele Grogan one negro woman by the name Harriet. I give to my dtr.
Asenath one negro woman called Mahala and her child Gina. I give to
my son Elias Franklin West three negroes, Alfred, Sam and George. It
is my will that the property willed to my wife at death or marriage,
shall be divided among my sons. Joseph Washington West, Theodore
Jefferson West and Baylies Earle West when this division takes place,
I desire that my son Theodore J. West have the Nicholas tract on
Dutchman's Creek. I desire that my two unmarried dtrs. Christina Smith
and Asenath shall live with my wife Mary and be supported from the
place. I appoint my wife Mary executrix and son Joseph W. West executor
Dated 7 May 1856. Wit: B. B. Foster, Robert West, Wm. Smith. Signed:
Thos. West. No probate date given.

WESTBROOK, SAMUEL Deed Book B-1, Page 43. Clerk of Court Office.
Pickens, S. C. Whereas James Tatum of Pickens Dist. by four notes
stands justly indebted to Samuel Westbrook in the sum of $175. I am
willing to secure unto the said Samuel Westbrook the true and faithful
payment of said notes, have granted, bargained, sold and released a
tract of land in Pickens Dist. being the same tract conveyed to me by
Samuel Westbrook. Dated this 4 Feb. 1831. Wit: John Hunter, James
Henderson. Signed: James X Tatom. Attested by James Henderson before
James Osborn, J.Q. this 25 March 1831. Recd. same date by William
L. Keith, C.C.

WHARTON, SAMUEL F 2, Page 120. Clerk of Court Office. Anderson,
S. C. This indenture made the 5 Jan. 1863 between O. Norris Esq.
Commissioner of the Court of Equity for Anderson Dist. of the one part
and Samuel Wharton and Esse M. Wharton his wife of the other part.
Whereas John B. Clinkscales on or about 30 Aug. 1862 did exhibit his
bill of complaint, against Rebecca Clinkscales, A. G. Cook and others
heirs at law of Abner Clinkscales decd. Said Court ordered that lot
#4 be sold. Whereas Samuel Wharton and wife being the highest bidder
in the sum of $597. Whereas this indenture witnesseth that for the
consideration sum A. O. Norris as Commissioner hereby grant, sold,
bargain and release lot #4 containing 99 1/2 acres on Browns road and
branches of Big and Little Generostee Creek, waters of Savannah River.
Land bounded by Jesse McGee, George Stephenson. Wit: J. Dill Dobbins,
A. Langston. Signed: A. O. Norris, CE A.D.

WHARTON, SAMUEL J 2, Page 412. Clerk of Court Office. Anderson,
S. C. I David Sherard of Anderson Dist. in consideration of $1800 to
me paid by Samuel Wharton of same Dist. have granted, sold, bargained

Wharton, Samuel - Continued. and released. All that tract of
land containing 379 acres, lying on Little Generostee Creek, waters of
Savannah River. Bounded by land of Mrs. P. H. Sherard, J. G. McCurry,
R. A. Pressley, Jas. Simpson, S. Wharton, Mrs. J. C. Wharton, David
Sadler and Dr. A. Walker. Dated 15 Feb. 1870. Wit: T. A. Stevenson,
J. A. Gray. Signed: D. J. Sherard. Came this day Margaret C.
Sherard the wife of David J. Sherard and renounce, release and forever
relinquished unto Samuel Wharton all her interest in the above land.
Dated 15 Feb. 1870.

WHARTON, SAMUEL   No Ref. Clerk of Court Office. Anderson, S.C.
Anderson Co., S. C. I Mary A. Cook wife of Dr. A. G. Cook, Esse M.
Wharton wife of Samuel Wharton, Sallie F. Hamilton wife of Wm.
Hamilton, R. P. Clinkscales, Dr. W. A. Clinkscales, M. B. Clinkscales
of Anderson Co., S. C. heirs of the estate of Rebecca Clinkscales decd.
in consideration of our distributive share to us paid by Lawrence S.
Clinkscales of Anderson Co. have granted, bargained, sold, and
released unto Lawrence S. Clinkscales all that tract of land of the
est. of Rebecca Clinkscales decd. lying on waters of Little Generstee
Creek. Containing 170 acres, bounded by land of Dr. W. A. Clinkscales,
on the West, R. P. Clinkscales on the South, M. B. Clinkscales on the
East. The same being known as the home tract. Dated 18 Jan. 1871.
Wit: E. J. McGee, A. E. Scudday. Signed: R. P. Clinkscales, M. B.
Clinkscales, W. A. Clinkscales, Esse M. Wharton, Sallie F. Hamilton,
Wm. Hamilton, Mary A. Cook. Attested by E. J. McGee, before Wm. L.
Bolt, N.P. this 3 Feb. 1879. Recd. 3 Feb. 1879.

WHITE, SARAH Box 69 #741. Probate Judge Office. Pickens, S.C.
Est. admnr. 18 March 1863 by John B. Sitton, Joseph J. Norton who are
bound unto W. E. Holcombe, Ord. in the sum of $3600. Left seven
heirs. Expend 5 Dec. 1864 paid Jane Lanier admnr. Mrs. Elizabeth
Lanier decd. Share $270.09. Paid 23 June John Addis his share
$43.50. Paid Mary Addis her share $9.75. Paid 8 Sept. Sarah E. Nimmons
share $9.75.

WHITE, SARAH S. S. #133. Clerk of Court Office. Abbeville,
S. C. Abbeville Dist. In Equity, To the Honr. the Chancellors:
The petition of Abner G. White sheweth that by the last will of
Christopher W. Mantz, late of this Dist. his dtr. Sarah S. S. White
is entitled to a small legacy. That the said Sarah is an infant about
eleven yrs. of age. Your petitioner prays that he be appointed
guardian of her est. Filed 15 June 1859.

WHITE, THOMAS A. Box 79 #844. Probate Judge Office. Pickens,
S. C. Est. admnr. 28 Nov. 1864 by Madison F. Mitchell, William N.
Craig, Zachariah Gibson who are bound unto W. E. Holcombe, Ord. in the
sum of $5,000. Owned 50 acres of land adj. land of Gideon Ellis,
Jacob Boroughs. Elizabeth White the widow, was the only heir.

WHITE, J. B. Box 77 #825. Probate Judge Office. Pickens, S.C.
Est. admnr. 22 Aug. 1864 by Archibald D. Gaillard, John W. L. Cary,
Wm. N. Craig, are bound unto W. E. Holcombe, Ord. in the sum of $1500.

WHITE, FRANCES #123. Clerk of Court Office. Abbeville, S. C.
I Frances White of sound and disposing mind and memory. First I
desire that my just debts be paid. I have placed in the hands of my
trusty friend Thos. J. Lyon my notes, land warrant which I own, on
account my son James M. White now decd. I have let said Lyon have
negroes Joe, Lark, Lewis, and Randoll. The interest and profit from
said property to be divided between my four grandchildren, Frances
Gillam Harrison, Ann Virginia Harrison, Mary Longmire Harrison and
James White Harrison. I appoint my friend Thomas J. Lyon as executor.
Dated 11 Feb. 1851. Wit: Adam Wideman, R. W. Lites, John P. Quattlebaum. Signed: Frances White. Codicil. I do by this codicil, give
one bed and furniture and a silver salt spoon to my granddaughter
Emma Pauline Evans. I give my family testament to my dtr. Kesiah
Evans and three silver tablesppons that has been in the family over a
hundred years, I give to my three granddaughters, Frances Harrison,
Ann Harrison and Mary Harrison. Dated 17 May 1852. Wit: Adam Wideman,

White, Frances - Continued. Anthony Harmon, R. W. Lites. Signed: Frances White. Filed 25 April 1856. In another paper, Mrs. Frances White was the dtr. of William Evans. In 1850 she had two chn. living, viz, Mrs. Keziah Evans and Mrs. Lucy Lyon and grandchildren of a decd. dtr. Mary Harrison. Mrs. White died in June 1853.

WHITE, ALEXANDER Pack 3222. Clerk of Court Office. Abbeville, S. C. Abbeville Dist. In Equity, to the Honr. the Chancellors: Your orator William Sherard sheweth that he contracted with William Crawford for a small tract of land, containing 100 acres, adj. land of Robert Simpson, Miles J. Hardy, Arch. Mauldin Senr. and Junr. That the said William Crawford had long resided and represented himself the true owner. That having paid him the consideration price on the 26 March 1842, and took possession, in the latter part of 1844 one Jackson McCurry intruded himself and took possession. Your orator inform that said Jackson McCurry has recently married with one Sarah White, the widow of John White, through whom they claim to have an interest on the land, rests on the following statement. That William Crawford purchased the land in the year 1820 from David Gillespie, being embarrassed circumstances, was promise aid from his brother-in-law John White, and he became surety for the price, except a portion paid by the mother in law of William Crawford and received a title in his own name, and was in possession until sold to your orator. Some time after he took possession one ___ Purcell in the Court of Common Pleas, a recovery being had, and that David Gillespie procured a second deed to be executed to John White. That William Crawford paid the consideration price to either Gillespie or White. When John White departed this life intestate leaving his widow and two chn. Alexander White and Rosanna White each minors, the former being about 11 yrs. and the other about nine yrs. Nathan McCallister was admnor. on the est. of John White. Who collected the entire sum due from the advances made in his lifetime. During the twenty years Crawford lived on the land on rent was paid to White of Gillespie. Said White held title as security. Filed 6 May 1845. Testimony. Robert Simpson states that William Crawford had a family of five sons and three dtrs. all of age except two and living in his family except two, who lived in the neighborhood. Nathan McAlister sworn that he admnor on the est. of John White being a brother of the widow, the present Mrs. McCurry. About the year 1833 Sarah and John White were married. In the year 1836 John White died intestate. (Part of Alex. White, will in notes.) No date, Wife Elizabeth White to have one third during her life time or widowhood. After all debts are paid the remainder to be divided among my five youngest chn. John, Nancy, Catorena, Martha. Sons John and James White to have the other two thirds of the land by sale or division.

WHITING, GEORGE Vol. 30 Page 769. Probate Judge Office. Charleston, S. C. I George Whiting of Charleston, S. C. watchmaker, being of sound mind, memory and understanding. I give to my brother John Whiting of Boston in Mass. state, turner, all and every my effects both real and personal that I may be possessed of at my decease. Also all sums of money that may be owing me at my decease. Also I appoint him whole and sole executor. Dated 24 June 1803. Wit: Peter O. Fitzpatrick, Joseph Jepson. Signed: George Whiting. Proved before Charles Linning, Esq. O.C.T.D. this 25 Jan. 1805.

WHITLOCK, HARRIET AND THOMAS L. Clerk of Court Office. Abbeville, S. C. Abbeville Dist. In Equity, To the Honr. the Chancellors: The petition of Harriet Whitlock the wife of Thomas L. Whitlock of Madison Co., Fla. Sheweth that Edward Collier late of this Dist. by his will bequeathed to your petitioner a certain negro man named Dave and four hundred dollars. Sheweth that the said slave is still in possession of the executor of said will namely David Lesly Esq. Your petitioner is desirous of having the legacy settled upon her, she has selected as her trustee to preserve the said legacy, her brother Hugh Waller Wardlaw. I Thomas L. Whitlock the husband of Harriet Whitlock has read and carefully considered the petition of my wife and have signed the same. This 6 May 1849.

WHITMIRE, LILY & SAMUEL   Pack 339 #3.   Clerk of Court Office.
Pickens, S. C.   On 4 March 1829 Lily and Samuel Whitmire made oath
against Robert Cobb of having gotten Delilah Whitmire a single woman
with a bastard child which was born on 8 April 1825.

WHITNEY, JOHN Deed Book 1, Page 233.   Clerk of Court Office.
Anderson, S. C.   I John Whitney of Pendleton Dist. in consideration of
$320.02 and mills to me paid by James Carson Hamilton of the same Dist.
Whereas John Whitney have granted, bargained, sold and released all
that land containing 240 acres laid out for Robert Lusk lying on the
15 Mile Creek waters of the 18 Mile Creek. Dated 22 Nov. 1802. Wit:
James Garvin, Jeremiah Whitney, John Whitney, Jr. Signed: John
Whitney. Attested to me by James Garvin on 28 April 1804. Sworn to
1 Aug. 1808.

WHITNEY, JOHN Deed Book L, Page 67.   Clerk of Court Office.
Anderson, S. C.   John Whitney of Pendleton Dist. in consideration of
$160. Paid by William Eubanks of the same Dist. have sold and
released unto William Eubanks 150 acres of land, being part of a tract
granted to George Shuler or Miller? lying on Goldens Creek waters of
12 Mile River, it being the plantation that formerly belonged to
William Rillen. Dated 19 March 1804. Wit: James Garvin, James
Gillam. Signed: John Whitney.

WHITNEY, JOHN Deed Book B, Page 311.   Clerk of Court Office.
Anderson, S. C.   This indenture made 26 Feb. 1789 between Robert Lusk
of Union Co., S. C. and John Whitney of Pendleton Dist. In consideration of fifty pounds sterling paid by John Whitney before the sealing
and delivery of this deed. Robert Lusk hath sold and released a tract
of land containing 240 acres in 96 Dist. on the North fork of 18 Mile
Creek, on waters of Savannah River. Wit: Wm. McCullough, Aaron Lockert,
Mary McCullock. Signed: Robert Lusk. Union Co., S. C. Aaron Lockert
made oath that he saw Robert Lusk sign the within deed. Recorded:
15 Sept. 1794.

WHITTEN, ELIZABETH Box 89 #936.   Probate Judge Office. Pickens,
S. C.   I Elizabeth Whitten of Pickens Dist. being of sound mind and
memory. First I desire that my just debts be paid. I will the
balance of my property placed in the hands of my two chn. Mary A. C.
Whitten and Augustus M. Whitten to be placed in the hands of my
executor for the support of the said children in raising and schooling
them. I appoint William J. Smith my executor. Dated the 26 Sept.
1866. Wit: J. C. C. Parson, Augustus M. Hamilton, Thomas R. Gary.
Signed: Elizabeth X Whitten. (In same pack) 28 Sept. 1866, F. E.
Willard petitioned the Court for letter of admnr. on the est. of
Ledford P. Whitten decd. late of this Dist. who died intestate,
leaving personal property in this dist.

WHORTON, BARTLETT Deed Book P, Page 319.   Clerk of Court Office.
Spartanburg, S. C.   I John Townsend of Greenville Dist. in consideration of $130 to me paid by Bartlett Whorton of the same Dist. have
granted, sold, release and conveyed a tract of land lying and being
on both sides of Mill Creek a branch of South Pacolet. Containing 99
acres, being part of a survey dated 5 April 1790. Conveyed to him by
John Gowen. Dated 5 Oct. 1808. Wit: John X Whorton, Wiley S. Brown.
Signed: John X Townsen. Attested by John Whorton before Benjamin
Pollard, J.P. this 14 Dec. 1808. Recd. 4 Dec. 1818.

WHORTON, BENJAMIN Deed Book C, Page 133.   Clerk of Court Office.
Anderson, S. C.   This indenture made 18 May 1793 between Robert Anderson of Pendleton Dist. and Benjamin Whorton of the same Dist. in
consideration of fifty five pounds sterling. Have bargained, sold,
released and confirmed unto Benjamin Whorton a tract of land lying in
said Dist. containing 275 acres. Wit: Jos. Sanders, James Hendrix.
Signed: Robert Anderson. Attested by James Hendrix before J. B.
Earle, J.P. this 20 Jan. 1796. Recd. the 26 Jan. 1796.

WHORTON, BENJAMIN Deed Book C, Page 134.   Clerk of Court
Office. Anderson, S. C.   This indenture made this 15 April 1790.

Whorton, Benjamin - Continued. Between Fields Prewet of Pendleton Dist. and Benjamin Whorton of the same Dist. in consideration of
thirty pounds current money of this State, have acknowledged, bargained,
sold and released a tract of land lying in this Dist. containing 400
acres. Lying on waters of Cane Creek waters of Keowee River, where said
Prewit now lives (here Fields Prewet is Junr.) Wit: James Hendrix
and Hannah X Hendrix. Attested by James Hendrix before J. B. Earle,
Clk. this 26 Jan. 1796. Recd. 26 Jan. 1796.

WHORTON, BENJAMIN Deed Book G, Page 196. Clerk of Court Office.
Anderson, S. C. I Benjamin Whorton of Pendleton Dist. in consideration
of $200 to me paid by Phillip Cox of the same Dist. have granted, sold,
bargained, and released all the part of that tract of land which lies
on the North Fork of Cain Creek and on the East side. Containing
150 acres, originally granted to Job Lawrence on the 2 July 1787.
Wit: Elijah Floyd, John Beazley. Signed: Benjamin Whorton. Attested
on oath of John Beazley before Joseph Reid. This 30 Oct. 1802. Recorded 23 Nov. 1802.

WHORTON, JOHN Deed Book K, Page 157. Clerk of Court Office.
Greenville, S. C. I John Whorton of Spartanburg Dist. in consideration of $200 to me paid by Vardry Camp of the same Dist. have granted,
sold, released the tract of land lying in the Dist. of Greenville on
both sides of Mill Creek waters of South Pacolet. Containing 100
acres, originally granted to Wm. Jamison by patent dated 5 April 1790
from him to John Gowen from Gowen to John Townsend from Townsend to
me. Dated 11 Dec. 1817. Wit: Thomas Wharton,, Wm. D X Thomas.
Signed: John X Wharton.

WHORTON, WILLIAM Deed Book G, Page 377. Clerk of Court Office.
Greenville, S. C. This indenture made 18 Feb. 1806. Between William
Whorton of Greenville Dist. and William Chandler of the same Dist.
In consideration of $30 to me paid by William Chandler, have bargained,
sold, and convey a tract of land lying in Greenville Dist. on both
sides of Mountain Creek of Enoree River. Containing 100 acres, being
part of a three hundred acres tract granted to Wardsworth. Wit:
Robert McAfee, Ann McAfee. Signed: William X Whorton. Attested by
Robert McAfee before D. Goodlett, J.P. this 14 March 1806.
Recorded 5 April 1806.

WHORTON, WILLIAM Deed Book G, Page 122. Clerk of Court Office.
Greenville, S. C. This indenture made the 25 Jan. 1804 between
William Whorton of Pendleton Dist. and Anthony and Joseph Griffin
both of Pendleton Dist. In consideration of $1000 to me paid, I have
bargain, sold, deliver, convey and confirm a tract of land containing
500 acres lying and being in Greenville Dist. on both sides of
Mountain Creek and Buckhorn Creek waters of Enoree River. Adj. land
of Robert McAfee, Wm. Chandlers line. Originally granted to Wadsworth
and Turpin on the 1 Jan. 1787. Wit: John Pound, Joseph X Worldam.
Signed: William X Whorton. Attested to by John Pounds, before
Jas. Starrett, J.P. this 27 Jan. 1804. Recd. 4 Feb. 1804.

WIDEMAN, SAMUEL Pack 403. Clerk of Court Office. Abbeville,
S. C. Abbeville Dist. In Equity, To the Honr. the Chancellors:
Your oratrix Frances E. Zimmerman sheweth that Samuel Wideman Jr. late
of this dist. departed this life intestate in 1849. Leaving as heirs
and distributees, his widow Margaret Wideman, chn. Your oratrix Mary
S. Wideman, Columbia A. Wideman, William H. Wideman, James A. Wideman,
and the chn. of decd. dtr. Emily, namely James A. Pennel, William H.
Pennal who represent their mother and whose father is dead. Your
oratrix sheweth that all the children are minors under the age of
twenty one. At his death their father was possessed with three tracts
of land, one tract known as the home tract, containing 497 acres,
bounded by land of Joseph J. Lee, Thomas P. Dowtin, William W. Belcher,
another tract, the Long Cane tract containing 354 acres, bounded by
land of Joshua Wideman, Vincent McCelvey, Uel Wideman, another tract the
Glasgow tract on waters of Bold Branch containing 211 acres, bounded
by land of Thomas Thomson, William W. Belcher. The personal property
is believed to be in value of sixteen thousand dollars, with only

Wideman, Samuel - Continued. about one hundred dollars of debts. The widow has applied for letter of admnr. Filed 20 Nov. 1849. In a deed dated 5 Feb. 1845 from Thomas M. Glasgow and wife Maryan to Samuel Wideman. Another deed in this pack. From James Glasgow to his dtr. Mary Ann McClelland, for love and good will, gives her a tract of land of 72 1/2 acres, lying on a branch of Long Cane, originally granted to Sarah Crozier. Dated 16 Nov. 1839. Wit: A. McKinney, George Cochran, John P. McCelland, Mary McCelland. Another deed from Martha McCelland of Case Co., Ga. in consideration of $140 paid by William Gallaugher have granter, sold and released a tract of land containing 72 1/4 acres on Long Cane and Bold Branch, bounded by James Glasgow, William Belcher, Samuel Wideman and William McKinney. Dated 9 June 1847. Wit: Thomas P. Fulton, William C. McKinney. Signed: Martha McCelland, per A. Kennedy agent.

WIGGINTON, DUDLEY W. Pack 634 #164. Clerk of Court Office. Pickens, S. C. On 18 March 1844 Dudley W. Wigginton was appointed a constable of Pickens Dist.

WIGINGTON, O. J. Deed Book A, Page 216. Probate Judge Office. Pickens, S. C. On 19 Feb. 1858 O. J. Wigington and his wife Ruth Chapman Wigington were heirs of Joshua Chapman decd. and his wife Elizabeth Chapman of Pickens Dist. Were living out of State on 19 Feb. 1858.

WILBANKS, NANCY Box 20 #246. Probate Judge Office. Pickens, S. C. Est. admnr. 26 Jan. 1849 by Joseph Powell of Greenville, S.C. Wm. Ellis who are bound unto Wm. D. Steele, Ord. in the sum of $425. Was a dtr. of Elijah Barnett decd. Sett: 4 April 1853 amt. recd. of John Bowen, 7 Oct. 1850 to be divided between Peggy Holland decd. and Wm. Wilson and wife Lucinda giving each $223.34.

WILES, EVEN Pack 109 #10. Clerk of Court Office. Pickens, S.C. Pickens Dist. Before me L. Hendricks an acting magistrate in this dist. Evin Wiles appeared and after being duly sworn as the law directs says that on the 24th Dec. at night that John Rackley, John Pinson, Thomas Galien, and Franklin Holcombe came to his house and came in friendly and after being there some small space of time the above named men went out of the house and then John Rackely called him out as he thought friendly he went out and afterwards took him by the collar and tore his vest off and he was loosened from him he went into the house and the door was shut and the crowd then broke the door down and came in the second time and caught him the second time in fighting possession, then they went off and came back again and entered the house the second time for force. Sworn this 1 Jan. 1859. Signed: E. Wyles before L. Hendricks, M.P.D.

WILKS, POLLY #266. Clerk of Court. Abbeville, S. C. Your orator John L. Wilks sheweth Samuel Cunningham of Laurens Dist. made a deed of gift of a negro girl named Sarah and her increase unto Thomas Cunningham his heirs, executors, admnr. for uses to wit. in turst for the use of the Samuel Cunningham dtr. Polly Wilks during her natural life, and after her death the property to be equally divided among the chn. of the said Polly Wilks. Your orator further sheweth that his mother departed this life, leaving your orator, his brother Samuel M. Wilks, Thomas C. Wilks, and Warren D. Wilks. Your orator desires partition of the woman and her increase to wit Allen and Lem. Filed 22 Sept. 1842. The deed of gift was dated 28 Dec. 1822.

WILLARD, FRENCH P. Pack 564 #1. Clerk of Court Office. Pickens, S. C. An inquest held over the body of French P. Willard the 30 May 1869. Thomas E. Willard the father sworn says that between one and two o'clock in the night he discovered his barn on fire. He called to the boys also Young Rampy was staying with them that night. Norman his son passed him and turned the mares and mules out. He stopped at the corn crib to try and save it when heard a shot, thinking it to be an alarm. Then there were more shots and found his son lying on the ground. Erastus M. Willard sworn says that he and Harleston Ramphey were sleeping together when his father yelled that the barn

Willard, French P. - Continued. was on fire. He and Harleston
took a pistol to the yard to sound an alarm, but the pistol would not
fire, and he threw it to the ground, then heard four or five shots
and saw Wallace Boggs and his brother Edward Boggs with the light from
the fire. He helped to tract the horses from the Willard house to the
Boggs barn.

WILLIAMS, ANN Box 92 #980. Probate Judge Office. Pickens, S.C.
Ann Williams on 1 Jan. 1877 mentioned as being a dtr. of William
Hester Sr. decd. Nancy Hester another dtr. was wife of Abraham
Williams. Nancy Williams resided in Georgia.

WILLIAMS, E. L. Box 113 #1091. Probate Judge Office. Pickens,
S.C. E. L. Williams an heir of George Hendricks decd. whose estate
was admnr. 14 Sept. 1881 in Pickens Dist.

WILLIAMS, JAMES FRANK Pack 359. #13. Affidavit, Clerk of Court
Office. Pickens, S. C. "Personally appeared before me James Frank
Williams and makes oath that he is over twenty one years of age, that
he is a graduate of the Southern Medical College of Atlanta, Georgia,
that his Diploma was granted on the 1st day of March 1888, and that
he intends to practice medicine in the County of Pickens and has
located at Pickens, C.H." Sworn to before me this 19 March 1888.
Signed: J. F. Williams before J. J. Lewis, Clk.

WILLIAMS, JOHN Deed Book S, Page 38. Mesne Conveyance. Greenville, S. C. I John Williams of Greenville Dist. in consideration of
$300 to me paid by Austin Williams of the same Dist. have granted,
sold, bargained and released a tract of land lying in said Dist. on
the Seader Shoal Creek waters of Saluda River. Originally granted to
Miles Jennings Junr. the heir at law of said Miles Jennings decd. at
fall term 1813. Dated this 4 May 1831. Wit: John Clark, James E.
Allen. Signed: John Williams, Proved on oath of John Clark before
A. Acker, J.Q. on the 18 Jan. 1836.

WILLIAMS, JOHN H. Pack 653. #2. Clerk of Court Office.
Pickens, S. C. John H. Williams was charged as being the father of
a male bastard child that was born to Margaret Hester a single woman
of Pickens Dist. on the 11 June 1858.

WILLIAMS, JOSEPH Will Book 1791-1803. Page 23. Probate Judge
Office. Elberton, Ga. I Joseph Williams of Elbert Co., Ga. being
weak and low in body and health, but of sound and perfect mind and
memory. I give to my son John Williams all the negroes which I let
him have many years ago, with their increase. I give to my son
Mathew Lovett Williams, all the negroes, I let him have many years
ago, with their increase. My will and desire that the following
negroes, Charles, Hannah, Tiller, Jenny, Samen, Bartlett, Jacob, Miles,
Clabourn, Lymns, Charles a boy, Caleb and Mannuel to continue in
possession of Matthew Williams until 1 Feb. 1796 at this time to be
divided between himself and brother John Williams. I give unto Matthew
Williams all stock, household furniture of every kind. I give to my
grandson Joseph Williams negro man named Edmond. I appoint my sons
John Williams and Matthew Lovett Williams executors. Dated 13 Sept.
1792. Wit: Wm. Hatacher, Wm. Lankester, Jenny X Freeman. Signed:
Joseph Williams. Proved on 15 Oct. 1792.

WILLIAMS, JOSEPH Box 9 #115. Probate Judge Office. Pickens,
S. C. I Joseph Williams of Pickens Dist. being weak in the flesh but
of sound and disposing mind and memory. I give to my wife $900 which
is now in the hands of Asap Hill, with the interest, also my wife to
have choice of plantation, with one mare, two cows and calves, also
all household and kitchen furniture. Rest of estate to be sold and
equally divided among my chn. My sons Zebulon and Isaac William shall
attend to the collection of the $900 and give it to my wife Rebeca
Williams. Sons Zebulon and Isaac William to be executors. Dated 14
Sept. 1840. Wit: Joseph B. Reid, Daniel Looper, Joseph D. Looper.
Signed: Joseph X Williams. Proved by Joseph D. Looper before James
H. Dendy, O.P.D. this 2 Nov. 1840. Paid each legatee in 1841.

Williams, Joseph - Continued. Margaret Williams heir $9.68 3/4.
Thomas Williams heir $69.18 3/4. Abel Williams heir $8.00. John
Williams heir $8.81 1/4. Henry Williams heir $17.87 1/2. Zebulon
Williams heir $14.37 1/2. Thomas Hester heir $11.37 1/2. Isaac
Williams heir $9.06 1/4. William Williams heir $15.00. Elizabeth
Williams heir $8.25. Signed: Isaac Willias, executor.

WILLIAMS, MARTHA A. Pack 604. #5. Clerk of Court Office.
Pickens, S. C. Martha A. Williams made oath that on the night of the
12th April 1865, that a negro man by the name of Dave the property
of Wm. Smith now in custody of Charles Thompson. At or near 12 p.m.
he entered her room and committed an assult and battery upon her
person (sufficient to cause her to believe with intent to rape.) Sworn
this 15 April 1865. She said Dave came into her sleeping rrom and put
his hand on her leg. She arose from her bed asked him what he was
doing in her room, he said that he was hunting something. Mrs. Frances
Hamilton, wit. for the State saith that Martha Williams came into her
room on the said night, and woke her up and said that Dave was or had
been in her room where she was sleeping, she seemed very much frightened.
Dave has always acted prudently and respectfully towards the ladies of
the family and neighborhood so far as she has knowledge. Charles
Thompson, saith that he was woke by his daughter Frances calling her
mother, he rose and immediately went to the room where Miss Williams
was sleeping, saw no one, went to the kitchen and found Dave in bed.
He has had Dave in his possession about 18 months and he has been very
obedient to him and his family, he believes that he will steal little
things, otherwise his character is good. The jury found him guilty
and sentenced him to receive 50 lashes reasonably laid on. Signed:
F. N. Garvin Foreman, J. D. Gassaway, Wm. Oliver, Joseph Philpot,
E. P. Boroughs.

WILLIAMS, S. N. Book B, Page 120. Probate Judge Office. Pickens,
S. C. On 19 Nov. 1866 S. N. Williams and wife Ann Williams were heirs
of John E. Archer decd. of Pickens Dist. Malinda Archer their mother.

WILLIAMS, WILLIAM S. Land Warrant #90. Clerk of Court Office.
Pickens, S. C. By W. L. Keith, Clk. to any lawful surveyor, you are
authorized to lay out unto W. S. Williams a tract of land not exceeding ten thousand acres, making a true platt thereof. Dated this 5 Jan.
1846. Executed for 24 acres this 26 Feb. 1846. Tho. D. Garvin, D.S.

WILLIAMSON, CHARLES Box 18 #229. Probate Judge Office. Pickens,
S. C. Est. admnr. 24 Sept. 1849 by W. S. Grisham, J. W. Nevill who
are bound unto W. D. Steele Ord. in the sum of $80.00. Left five
heirs, paid 25 June Chas. Williamson $3.80. Paid 31 Jan. A. E. Sitton
$3.80. Paid 17 Dec. Nancy Anthony $3.80.

WILLIAMSON, JOHN Box 53 #579. Probate Judge Office. Pickens,
S. C. John Williamson and wife recd. a legacy 24 Dec. 1863 of $263.06
from the est. of Thomas Hallum decd. whose will was proven 17 Feb.
1860 in Pickens Dist. (wife probably a dtr. of Thomas Hallum).

WILLIAMSON, JOHN & SARAH Box 2 #48. Probate Judge Office.
Pickens, S. C. On 17 Aug. 1855, R. E. Holcombe, Col. John A. Easley
Jr. are bound to W. J. Parsons Ord. in the sum of $200. R. E. Holcombe
gdn. for John and Sarah Williamson minors and grandchildren of H. T.
Arnold.

WILLIS, JOSHUA Pack 289. Clerk of Court Office. Abbeville, S.C.
Joshua Willis by his last will gave to his chn., Julia F., Martha W.
Mars, Milly Ann D., Thomas J., Mary E., and Sarah C. each their negro
by name, cow and calf, saddle and bridle valued at $100. He had one
tract of land lying in the fork of Little River and Savannah River
adj. land of Isaac Moragne, Peter Smith and others. Land to be sold
and proceeds equally divided among my children. After the death of
the testator his widow soon died, then Mary E. died under the age of
sixteen without issue, Milly Ann D. who intermarried with Winston N.
Taylor and died after Mary E. without issue. Filed 6 Jan. 1838.

WIMBISH, ALEXANDER #3343. Clerk of Court Office. Abbeville, S. C. To the Honr. the Chancellors: Your orator and oratrixs, Joseph Scott of Henry County, Ga. and Sarah his wife, Henry S. Oliver of Muscogee County, Ga. and Nancy his wife, Gilbert Greer of Merriwether County, Ga. and Nancy his wife, Peyton C. Wimbish of the state of Ga., James Wimbish of Elbert County, Ga., Thomas C. Wimbish and Charles A. Wimbish of Abbeville, S. C. and Susannah Wimbish of the State of Miss. widow of John M. Wimbish decd. That Alexander Wimbish departed this life leaving in full force his last will bearing date 16 Sept. 1817, and appointed his brother William Wimbish executor. The testator died possessed of a tract of land on Middleton Creek, waters of Rockey River containing 350 acres, bounded by land of John Mosley, Josiah Patterson, James Alston, Nathaniel Norwood. He devised to his widow Frances Wimbish for a home during her widowhood with sufficient support from the same. The chn. shall have support and education out of the est. In case of marriage of his widow his property to be sold divided among his chn. viz. Peyton C., Thomas C., James, Charles A., Nancy Oliver, Sarah Scott, Lucy Gr-er or Green? John M. who has since died leaving three infant chn. living in Miss. Susannah his widow and Alexander F. Wimbish of Abbeville Dist. The widow resided upon the land until her death on 13 Oct. 1845. William Wimbish the executor appointed has departed this life also, and Alexander F. Wimbish was appointed in his place. Filed 19 Nov. 1845.

WITHERS, B. P. Case 12 File 542. Probate Judge Office. York, S. C. John G. Withers, John Elms and wife Malinda, Archibald Cracket and wife Eleanor, Good A. Mitchell and wife Elizabeth, James Gloves and wife Martha C. and Joshua Glover and wife Phebe J. and Silas C. Cook and Thomas G. Cook minors by their guardian John G. Withers. Heirs of Benjamin P. Withers. 338 acres on the waters of Sugar Creek bounded by land of John Springs, Jeremiah Withers, Joseph Smith, John C. Withers, Rebecca Daniel and others. John G. Withers and James Glover and wife reside out of State.

WITHERS, ELIZABETH T. Box 74 #2657. Probate Judge Office. Camden, S. C. Kershaw Dist. I Elizabeth T. Withers of said Dist. make this my last will, I give to my son William R. Withers the sum of $5,000. I give unto my youngest granddaughter Elizabeth B. Kirkland, all my silver plate. I give unto my dtr. Mary M. Kirkland all the rest and residue of my est. both real and personal. I appoint my dtr. Mary M. Kirkland, sole executrix. Dated this 26 Jan. 1866. Wit: Priscilla B. Perkins, Mary C. Johnson, Amelia McCaa?. Signed: E. T. Withers, Seal. Filed 6 May 1876.

WITHERS, FRANCES Vol 39, Page 892. Probate Judge Office. Charleston, S. C. I Frances Withers of the Parish of Saint James Santee, widow, being in perfect health of body and sound mind and memory. First I give to my grandson John Wells when he shall arrive at the age of twenty one yrs. three negroes, Bobin a boy, Tom and a girl named Jenny and her increase. The above property given in trust with my son William, the rest and remainder of my property I give to my son William Henry Wells during his natural life and at his death to his lawful heirs. Should my brother John Dubois be alive at that time, I desire him to have an equal share. I appoint my son William Henry Wells and my friend Archibald McClellan, James Hibben and Samuel Warren executor. Dated 26 Dec. 1808. Wit: Elisha Rembert, Mary Ann Barton. Signed: Frances Withers. Proven 2 Nov. 1830.

WITHERS, BENJAMIN F. Box 36 #1536. Probate Judge Office. York, S. C. Est. admnr. 6 July 1857 by Isaac N. Withers, R. C. Withers, H. F. Adickes and S. C. Youngblood who are bound unto John M. Ross in the sum of $40,000.

WITHERS, BENJAMIN P. Case 8 File 348. Probate Judge Office. York, S. C. Est. admnr. 18 Oct. 1847 by John G. Withers, Isaac Spencer, Robert Mitchell who are bound unto John M. Ross, Ord. in the sum of $2500.

WITHERS, FRANCIS   Vol. 44 Page 268.   Probate Judge Office.
Charleston, S. C. I Francis Withers of Charleston, planter, being of
sound and disposing mind and memory. I give to my wife Sarah P.
Withers my house and lot of land whereon I now reside at the corner
of Meeting and John Streets with all household and kitchen furniture,
plate, linen, beds, bedding, books, wines and every other kind of
property for the family comfort, also my carriages and horses, also
my pew in St. Paul's Church Radcliffeborough, also the parcel of ground
in St. Paul's Church yard which I purchased from the Vestry as a family
burial ground, also 100 shares in the bank of Charleston, and $10,000
of my state 6% stock. I give to my beloved wife during the term of
her natural life the use of my Friendfield Estate, including the land
which I purchased from the trustee of my neice Elenor Wilkinson and
my Midway and Cannan plantations, containing about 400 acres of rice
with all the upland, also the use of 200 of my negro slaves called the
Friendfield gang, etc. Upon the death of my wife I devise the above
named property to my beloved stepdaughter Elizabeth Hunt Warham for
the term of her life. If said stepdaughter die without issue the
property to be equally divided among the chn. of my two neices (except
Mrs. Mary Memminger) Eleonora Wilkinson and Mary Read decd. I give to
my stepdaughter Elizabeth Hunt Warham my two lots in Charleston and my
pew in St. Peter's Church in Charleston and my pew in the Episcopal
Church in Georgetown also $5,000 in stock. I give to Mrs. Mary
Memminger my Springfield plantation with the farm on the seashore and
my land on Waccamaw Sandy Island, she being a legatee under my brother
Robert Withers will, she is to pay to Annabell Keith, Sarah A. Wilkinson the sum of five thousand dollars without interest within the next
seven years. She to pay Charlotte Nelson (a free mulatto left by my
brother Robert), the sum of fifty dollars during her life time. If
Mrs. Mary Memminger refuse the above devise, my executors to offer
the said land to my grand nephew Harleson Read Jr. upon the same terms.
If he refuse or decline it then go to grand nephew James W. Wilkinson
upon the same terms. Should he decline it then go to friend Allard H.
Belin and Dr. Edward T. Heriott, should they decline, my executors to
sell and divide the proceeds among Annabell Keith, Sarah A. Wilkinson,
Virginia Wilkinson, James W. Wilkinson and William W. Wilkinson. I
give to my grand nephews I Harleston Read Jr. and James W. Read, my
Harmony plantation on Sampit River with a tract of Pine Land adj. it
on Turkey Creek, also the sum of ten thousand dollars to enable them
purchase negroes for the cultivation, also negroes Frank and his wife
who now lives there, also the remainder of my Friendfield gang that my
wife leaves. I also give to my grand nephew fifty share of my stock in
the Bank of Charleston, that is James W. Wilkinson. I give to William
Withers of Charleston, bricklayer fifty shares in the Band of Charleston.
I give to Caroline and Cornelia Withers each forty shares in my stock
in the Bank of Charleston. I give to Mary E. Heriot dtr. of Dr.
Edward T. Heriot twenty shares in the bank of Charleston. I give unto
Francis W. Heriot thirty shares in my stock in Bank of Charleston.
I give to Mary Cordes, wife of Dr. Samuel Cordes twenty shares of my
stock in the Band of Charleston. I give to the Vestry and Wardens of
the Protestant Episcopal Church in Georgetown, fifty share of my stock
in the bank of Charleston, to apply the interest from time to time for
the repair of the Church. I give to Mrs. James S. Belin 100 shares in
the bank of S. C. I give to Mrs. Elonora Wilkinson the sum of ten
thousand dollars, also all my household and kitchen furniture, plates,
books at my "Farm" at Springfield Plantation. I give to Rosalver
Withers (sister of William Withers) the sum of three thousand dollars.
I give to Elizabeth Cheesborough widow the sum of two thousand dollars.
I give to Francis R. Shackelford of Darien Georgia the sum of two
thousand dollars. I give to Rebecca Kennerly wife of Mr. Kennerly of
Alabama the sum of two thousand dollars. I give to Dr. Edward T.
Heriot the sum of three thousand dollars. I order that three thousand
dollars be put on interest and same paid to Mrs. Ann Jacks during her
life and after her death the same to be transfered to Major William
Laval. I give to Daniel G. Wayne the sum of two thousand dollars.
I give to Dr. Charles Goldthwait Adams son of my decd. friend Dr.
Daniel Adams formerly of Lincoln Mass. the sum of one thousand
dollars. To my friend Mrs. Lawrence formerly Patty Adams of the same
sister of Dr. Adams the sum of one thousand dollars and to Joseph

Withers, Francis - Continued. Henry Willard son of her decd.
sister Lovey Adams the sum of two thousand dollars. I appoint my wife
Sarah P. Withers executrix and friend I. Harleston Read Senr., Dr.
Edward T. Heriot, Allard H. Belin and Alexander Robertson executors.
(Date, "this twenty sixth year of America Independence) (1802). Wit:
Paul Henry Dickson, Frans A. DeLiesseline, H. A. DeSaussure. Codicil:
Mrs. Mary Memminger to have an equal share with the other chn. of my
two neices, Eleonora Wilkinson and Mary Read. Dated 26 Nov. 1841.
Wit: James Elder, Thomas H. Mathews, Daniel G. Wayne. Signed:
Francis Withers. Proved 25 Nov. 1847 and on 6 Dec. 1847 qualified the
executors.

WITHERS, JAMES Vol. 7 Page 537. Probate Judge Office. Charleston, S. C. I James Withers of Charleston, S. C. bricklayer, being of
sound mind and memory. I will and order my funeral expenses and just
debts be paid. I give to my beloved wife Mary Withers all my household furniture and plate, two horses or mares, two chairs, also negroes,
Quaquo, Bacco, and Joe bricklayer. Nanny, Nancy, Binah and their
increase, with Smart George, Charles and his brother Ben. If my wife
has a mind to live on the plantation to bring up the chn. then negroes
Old Akabe his wife Parthena, Simon and Quash, Abah, Long, Jenny,
Cuffey and Scipio, London, Old Tom, Hager. I give to my son John
Withers 400 acres of land in the Parish of St. James Goose Creek, also
29 acres at Winyaw to the Eastward on a creek and Westward on Sampit
River, also my Chesnutt stallion. I give to my son Richard Withers
a tract containing 300 acres in Christ Church Parish, formerly belonging to Mr. Hendrake, also the Island known by the name of Hendrack
Island and seven negroes, Prince, Bram, Tom, Betty and all her increase.
I give to my son William Withers a tract of land at Goose Creek known
by the name of Spring Garden containing 500 acres, with all the land
between Mr. James Coachmans and the above land, and seven negroes,
Cesar, Cloe, Celia, Peter, Minda, Jenny and their increase. After
the death of my wife I give my plantation called Mount Pleasant with
600 acres unto my dtr. Ann Lintwhite one negro called Lady, which is
in consideration of 120 pounds left her by Hugh Cartwright decd. when
paid. I give to my dtr. Elizabeth Withers one negro girl named
Ameritta Winyaw Kates dtr. which is in consideration of 120 pounds
left her by Hugh Cartwright decd. when paid. I give to my son
Frances Withers one tract of land adj. John Withers at Wayaw, containing 600 acres, also seven negroes, David, Befs, Silvia and two
chn. Toney and Hager and their issue. I give to my dtr. Sarah Withers
one negro named Grace being in consideration of 120 pounds, left her
by Hugh Cartwright decd. when paid. I desire one thousand pounds be
put on interest for the use of my dtr. Ann Lintwhite until my granddaughter Eliner Lintwhite come of age. If Eliner should die, the
interest to be paid any other children, if none, then to be divided
between my dtr. Elizabeth and Sarah. I appoint my son John Withers
and William Withers both of St. James Parish Goose Creek to be
executors. Dated 17 Feb. 1756. Wit: Isaac Lesnne, Robert Hume,
Thomes Smith, Lambt. Lance. Signed: James Withers, seal. Proved 9
July 1756.

WITHERS, MARTHEY M. Box 79 #3718. Probate Judge Office. York,
S. C. I Marthey M. Withers being of sound mind and memory, etc. I
will that all my just debts and funeral expenses be paid. I will to
my son James A. Withers 100 acres of land known as the Ben Patterson
place to be taken off the North West end of the plantation with the
buildings. I will to my son Jefferson T. Withers the remainder of
this tract consisting of 146 acres, and all personal property I may
have, should Jefferson D. Withers die without heirs, then the property
is to go to James A. Withers and his heirs. I appoint Jefferson D.
Withers my executor. Dated 7 Aug. 1895. Wit: L. G. Gulp, J. T.
Shaw, L. E. Shaw. Signed: Marthey X M. Withers. (no probate date).

WITHERS, RANDOLPH Box 74 #2659. Probate Judge Office. Camden,
S. C. Est. admnr. 20 July 1877 by William M. Shannon, H. M. W.
Shannon, Nannie S. Withers who are bound unto James F. Sutherland Ord.
in the sum of $5,000. He died 15 June 1877.

WITHERS, RICHARD Vol. 23 Page 572. Probate Judge Office.
Charleston, S. C. I considering the uncertainty of this life and the
certainty of death. First I give the use of the following negroes with
their increase unto my wife Francis during her life, Buther, Thom,
Prifs, Sam, Bukey, Cate, and girl Sara, Simon, Betty, Tubby, Trabeller,
Sampson, Giny, January, Toby, Sesar, Fillifs, Molly, Fan boat Gimmay,
Smart Sambo and Andrew. I also give to my wife negro named Pender with
her increase for ever. I also give to my wife Francis one half of my
stock, cattle, sheep household and kitchen furniture, etc. I also
give to my wife during her life one half of the money arising from the
rent from my lot in Charleston. I also give my wife the use of my
plantation whereon M. Elias Vanderhorst now lives. Heirs were: John
Withers, Ann Calvert, Rebecka Calvert, William Shekelford, and Richard
Shakelford. I appoint Mr. Elias Vanderhorst and Mr. Joseph Legare my
executors. Dated this 14 Oct. 1789. Wit: Philip Moer, M.D., James
Halsey, Anthoney Murrell, Peter Murrell. Signed: Richard Withers.
Proved before Charles Linning Esq. O.D.T.D. this 8 Dec. 1789.

WITHERS, RICHARD JUNR. Vol. 22 Page 10. Probate Judge Office.
Charleston, S. C. I Richard Withers of the Parish of St. James,
Goose Creek being of perfect and sound memory. I give to my brother
John Withers and plantation whereon I now reside called Mount Pleasant
and after his death to go to his lawful heirs, it being my desire that
it should not be sold out of the family. Also I give to John Withers
a tract of land containing 250 acres adj. Red Bank tract, to be
retained in the family in the same manner. It is my desire that the
land on Sandy Island and that on Waccamaw should be sold to pay my
debts. I give to my brother John Withers my negroman Philander, Sarah,
Affy. I give to my mother, Linder, Cato and Cloe and her child during
her life time at her death to go to my brother John and my sister
Mary Ann Gray. I also give to my sister Mary Ann Gray, Quamy, Flora,
Argus, Cudjoe. I give to my sister Nancy, Tenah, Carolina. I give to
my sister Rebecka, Frank and Peggy. I give to my aunt Barret a girl
Tyrah and after her death to go to my sister Rebecka and her heirs.
I also give to my mother all my stock, cattle, with the remainder to
be given to my brother John and my sister Mary Ann Gray. I appoint
my brother John Withers and Henry Gray executors. Dated 6 May 1786.
Wit: Francis Villepontoux, John Calvert Junr., Richard Fowler.
Signed: Richard Withers Junr. seal. Proved 19 May 1786.

WITHERS, RUFUS J. Box 24 #1018. Probate Judge Office. York,
S. C. I Rufus J. Withers in feeble health and knowing the uncertainty
of life. I will my just debts be paid. I will and devise all my
estate and property of every kind to my brother Walter C. Withers.
Consisting of my interest in a tract of land in York Dist. about 7
miles East of Yorkville on the waters of Little Allison Creek purchased
for myself and said brother Walter from Alexander Mc___?. Also notes
and accounts on various persons in both North and South Carolina. I
appoint my brother Walter C. Withers my executor. Dated 12 June 1854.
Wit: Wm. Johnston, John C. Hardister, William B. Lay. Signed:
Rufus J. Withers. Filed 8 July 1854.

WITHERS, SARAH P. #454. Probate Judge Office. Georgetown, S.C.
Est. admnr. 17 March 1864 by Alexius M. Forster, John C. Porter, Allard
H. Belin who are bound unto Eleazer Waterman, Ord. in the sum of
$90,000. She a widow.

WITHERS, SARAH M. Box 4 #187. Probate Judge Office. York, S.C.
I Sarah M. Withers of York Dist. being of a sound mind but of feeble
health. I wish for my four youngest chn. Amanda C., Benjamin F., Wm.
Randolph and Isaac N. Withers to have my dwelling house with the tract
of land known as the Chriswell and Gallant tracts, farming tools,
stock, waggon, household and kitchen furniture. To be held in common
until Amanda marry or Isaac come of age. I give to Amanda a negro
woman called Reiny with her child Adelaide. To my granddaughter Sarah
R. Adicks I will a small negro girl called Caroline and my tea table.
I wish my son John B. Withers to hold the buildings he has erected
in which he now resides with one acre of land. I wish Amanda,
Franklin Randolph and Isaac to pay the negroes I bought at sale of my

Withers, Sarah M. - Continued. deceased husband Randolph Withers.
I wish the portion of my estate which my dtr. Roscinda Simms is
entitled be sold and if she wish, purchase a negro with it. I appoint
Jessee Brumfield Esq., Capt. Wm. Faris and Henning F. Adicks executors.
Dated 24 Aug. 1846. Wit: Alex. Fewell, W. N. Simrill, P. E. Bishop.
Signed: Sarah X Withers. Probated 19 Oct. 1846.

WITHERS, THOMAS J. Box 74 #2658. Probate Judge Office. Camden,
S. C. Est. admnr. 26 Dec. 1865 by Mrs. E. T. Withers, Mary Miller
Kirkland, W. E. Johnson, A. M. Kennedy who are bound unto A. L.
McDonald Ord. in the sum of $158,700. The real estate consist of
the plantation at Liberty Hill, S. C. known as "The Dixon place" of
1700 acres, formerly mortgaged for the security of the bond of William
Dixon to T. J. Withers. The house and lots situated upon Fair Street
in the town of Camden the late residence of W. W. Workman. The
house and lot in the village of Kirkwood, late the residence of Thomas
T. Withers. The house and lot situated in the North East of Kirkwood,
late residence of Rev. Paul Tràpier. The 222 acres situated North of
the Village of Kirkwood being the divided half of a tract of 844 acres
formerly held as tenants in common by Withers and Thomas Lang.
William R. Withers a brother to Mary Miller Kirkland.

WITHERS, THOMAS Vol. 25 Page 129. Probate Judge Office.
Charleston, S. C. I Thomas Withers of Thomas's Parish in Berkley
County do make this my last will. I desire that my body be buried
near the grave of my wife's Aunt in the Sasafrax[sic]. I appoint my
wife Mary Withers executrix and my faithful friend Benjamin Waller,
schoolmaster of Charleston, my executor. I leave to my wife Mary
all my estate both real and personal. The land I bought of Jacob Vault
be invested in Thomas Withers youngest son to Elizabeth Morrow of
Charleston. Dated 28 June 1780. (No wits.) Signed: Thomas Withers.
Proved 5 March 1794.

YARBOROUGH, AMBROSE Box 1 Pack 13. Probate Judge Office.
Union, S. C. I Ambrose Yarborough of Union County, being of sound and
disposing mind, memory and understanding. I will is that my executors
shall make conveyances to John Bailie, Thomas Scales and Jonathan Pinnell
for the several tracts of land agreeable to my bonds to each of them
severally and take up the said notes or bonds. It is my will that my
executors may sell and part of my estate, real or personal as they may
judge proper for paying my just debts or the support of my family.
After my debts and funeral expenses are paid, I give to my beloved
wife Mary all my estate, both real and personal for the support of
herself and my children. After her decease, the whole of my estate
to be divided into five equal part. One for Ann Pinnell, one for
Jeremiah Yarborough, Humphry Yarborough, John Yarborough and Mary
Yarborough. I appoint Stephen Layton and Peter Pinnell executors.
Dated this 27 Aug. 1788. Wit: William Kelley, Elija X Alverson,
Thomas Tod. Signed: Ambrose Yarborough, seal. (No probate date.)

YOUNG, ALEXANDER #805. Probate Judge Office. Anderson, S.C.
Pendleton Dist. To the Honr. the Court of Pendleton. To Joseph
McClusky, Andrew Young, White Nathan Lusk, Moses Carley freeholders.
These are to authorize you or any three of you to repair to all
places in this County as shall be directed by Andrew Young executor of
the will of James Turner late of this County decd. ti view and
appriase, being first sworn and make a true inventory. Dated 25 Jan.
1796. Signed: J. B. Earle, C.C.

YOUNG, ANDREW Pack 804. Probate Judge Office. Anderson, S. C.
Anderson Dist. 6 July 1832. I Andrew Young being old and infirm
in body but of perfect mind and memory. First I will and order all
my lawful debts be paid. I will to my dtr. Janat McCalley one dollar.
I will to my dtr. Caty Herring one dollar. I give to my son John
Young a tract of land containing 100 acres. I give and release the
remainder part of my land whereon I now live to my dtrs. Nancy Karr
and Jane Karr. The said Nancy and Jane to hold said land for the term

Young, Andrew - Continued. of fifteen years, then said land to
be sold and equally divided among all my children. I will to my dtr.
Jane Karr all my household and kitchen furniture. I will to my dtr.
Elanor Holms one dollar. I leave all my books to be divided amongst
all my children. I leave my wearing apparel to be divided among
all my grandchildren. I appoint Francis Beaty, Archable Simson and
Andrew Reid as executors. Wit: George Brown, Thomas Obriant, Andrew
J. Obriant. Signed: Andrew Young. Proved on oath of George Brown
before John Harris Esq. this 1 July 1833. Power of attorney from
Catherine W. Herring of Bibb Co., Ala. who appointed Samuel G. Earles
Esq. as her true and lawful attorney, to ask, sue, demand and receive
and receipt from Archibald Simpson and Andrew Reid executors of the
last will of Andrew Young late of Anderson Dist. Dated this 23 Sept.
1854. Wit: Felix Shropshur. Signed: Catherine X Herring.
Sale of Andrew Young Estate was held 29 June 1833 Buyers. David Karr,
Wm. Sherard, Ruben Haley, Wm. B. Patterson, Thomas Obriant, Robison
Smith, John S. Karr, John Young, Mathew Earp, Wm. Newton, John Patter-
son. Sett. L March 1849. Amount paid William Sherard as per receipt
for four shares (to wit). John W. Young, Mack Homes and wife Elener,
John S. Kerr and wife Nancy, David Karr and wife Jane amt. $96.00.
Leaving two shares in hand of exor to wit. Catherine Herring and Jenet
McCalley each $21.89.

YOUNG, FRANCIS #803. Probate Judge Office. Anderson, S. C.
Est. of Francis Young late of Anderson Dist. was admnr. 20 Sept. 1841
by James Turner, F. A. Young, John Watt, John N. Young who are bound
unto John Martin Ord. in the sum of $25,000. An inventory was made
15 Oct. 1841. Negroes named, negro man, May, Joe, boy George, Woman
Rose and child, Swinay, Sarah and child. Items advanced by intestate
in his life time. Elijah E. Turnbull $135.00. James L. Young $1114.49.
Francis A. Young $2350.17. Jno. N. Young $1275.48. James Turner $290.
00. James P. Pressly $326.79. E. E. Turnbull $400.00.

YOUNG, JOSIAH Pack 111 #4. Clerk of Court Office. Pickens,
S. C. 5 April 1860. Know all men tha t we Josiah Young and J. B.
Clayton have this day traded lands that is the place adj. land of
F. C. Parsons (as youngs place) for the Abel T. Stevens place (as the
J. B. Clayton place) the price of each we put at $150, and further I
J. B. Clayton am to move the said Josiah Young or hall(haul) as much
as two loads on to the place, and pay him six bushels of wheat for
taking care of and cutting the same. Dated 5 April 1860. Wit: N. L.
Cox. Signed: Josiah X Young and J. B. Clayton.

YOUNG, STEPHEN Box 1 #6. Probate Judge Office. Pickens Dist.
Pickens, S. C. I Stephen Young, being weak in body but of sound mind
and memory, do ordain this as my last will etc. I will all my
effects that I may be possessed of both real and personal to my wife
Rebecca to be herefore the support of my dear children, and to be
divided amon-st them as she can and wishes to share it. I will to
Gibson Porter the use of that part of my land that I have counted off
to him. I appoint my wife executrix and Bailey Barton executor.
Dated this 27 July 1829. Wit: Ambrose Petty, Wiley Petty, James
Porter. Signed: Stephen X Porter. Proved on oath of James Porter
before James H. Dendy, Ord. this 7 Sept. 1829.

YOUNG, VALENTINE #227. Clerk of Court Office; Abbeville, S.C.
Abbeville Dist. In Equity, To the Honr. the Chancellors: Your
orator and Oratrixes Mrs. Mary Young (widow) Thomas Young, William
Young, Valentine Young, Washington J. Young, Abram Burden and Elizabeth his wife, William Franklin and Nancy his wife, sheweth that
Valentine Young late of this Dist. departed this life in 1828, leaving
a will whereby he disposed of only a portion of his estate, but was
intestate as to the estate hereinafter described. Leaving as his
next of kin and destributees (Mrs. Mary Young his wife), James Graham
and Mary his wife, James Franklin and Margaret his wife, Isaac Young
all of whom now living, are over the age of twenty one. Since his
death, Mary Graham has died leaving her husband and two infant chn.
Cely M. Graham, and Valentine Graham also Margaret the wife of James
Franklin, leaving her husband and three infant children, Asa Franklin,

328

Young, Valentine - Continued. Valentine Franklin, Mary Ann
Franklin, also Isaac Young, leaving his wife Maria and one child of
tender age Sarah J. Young. At the time of the death of Valentine
Young was, beside his estate real and personal disposed of by his will,
possessed of the following tract of land, lying on the waters of
Mulberry Creek in said Dist. bounded by land of Mrs. Anna Swain, Robert
Moore, Richard Gains, Joseph Agnew. Filed 16 April 1844.

YOUNG, WILLIAM #802. Probate Judge Office. Anderson, S.C.
the est. of William Young was admnr. 13 March 1801 by William
Marchbanks, George Foster and Stephen Cantral are bound unto John
Harris ord. of Pendleton Dist. in the sum of $2,000. Recd. 6 Nov. 1803
of Benjamin Barton $5.00 which is to be accounted for by me when I
and William Marchbanks settle about the surveying I did for said Marchbanks admnr. of Wm. Young decd. est.

YOUNG, MISS WILLIE PAULINE Family chart found in her notes
(key to chart, double the number of a person will be the father, plus
one will be the mother. Example (11) Margaret Merrill = (22) William
Merrill, father + or (23) Elizabeth Ashworth, mother (1) Willie
Pauline Young, born 18 July 1912 at Pelzer, Anderson Co., S. C. (2)
Walter Harrison Young, born 3 April 1888, Buncombe Co., N. C. Married
11 Aug. 1907. (3) Annie Laura Saxon born 20 Aug. 1892 at Williamston,
Anderson Co., S. C. (4) William Harrison Young, born 1853 in Buncombe
Co., N.C. Married 1880, died 13 April 1906 at Pelzer, Anderson Co.,
S. C. (5) Mary Maundy Ashworth born 11 April 1847 in Buncombe Co.,
N. C. died 6 Nov. 1942. Greenville, S. C. (6) Lude A. Sacon, born
12 Aug. 1870 Laurens Co., S. C. married 1890. (7) Leathen Alsippie
Moore, no inf. (8) William Hale Young, no inf. (9) Matilda Rhodes,
born 1827, Buncombe Co., N.C. died 15 Feb. 1912. Pelzer, Anderson Co.,
S. C. (10) Jesse Ashworth born 1860 at Little River, Buncombe Co.,
N. C. died 1904 at Gable Rock, Saluda Hill, S. C. (11) Margaret
Merrill, born 16 June 1811 at Liile? River, Buncombe Co., N. C.
(12) Hugh Robert Saxon born 1845 in Pickens Co., S. C. died 13 Jan.
1913, Anderson Co., S. C. (13) Annie Campbell, died 26 Aug. 1886.
Possum Kingdom, Anderson, S. C. (14) John M-ore, died 4 Feb. 1863?
(15) Charlotte Ashley, born 4 Feb. 1825, died 25 July 1922. Anderson
Co., S. C. Baptised 5 Sept. 1862 Little River Church. (16) William
Harvey Young, no inf. (17) Polly Young, no inf. (18)   (19) Sally
_____. (20) Jackson Ashworth. (21) _____. (22) William Merrill.
(23) Elizabeth Ashworth. (24) John Jackson Saxon. (25) Martha Shirley.
(26) Wm. Campbell. (27) _____ Wright. (28) _____. (29)____ (30) Joshua
Ashley. (31) Frances Charlotte_____.

YOUNGBLOOK, J. T. Box 137 #11. Probate Judge Office. Pickens,
S. C. Est. admnr. 25 April 1901 by Elizabeth J. Youngblood, W. W.
Youngblood, W. T. McFall, J. McD. Bruce are bound unto J. B. Newberry
Ord. in the sum of $5,200. Dise? 2 April 1901. Paid 6 Feb. 1904.
Sarah M. Youngblood, W. W. Youngblood, Martha J. Mann, Zina L.
Breazeale. Mrs E. J. Youngblood the widow and guardian for Elishe
Youngblood, John Youngblood, Frances K. Youngblood minors each $100.

YOUNGBLOOD, MINORS. Box 144 #6. Probate Judge Office. Pickens,
S. C. On 12 Dec 1903. Elizabeth J. Youngblood, W. T. McFall,
Ernest Folger are bound unto J. B. Newberry Ord. in the sum of $593.40
E. J. Youngblood gdn. of Elisha, John and Frances Youngblood minors
under 21 yrs. and chn. of John T. Youngblood.

YOUNGBLOOD, NANCY JANE. Pack 227 #15. Clerk of Court Office.
Pickens, S. C. Personally came Nancy Jane Youngblood before me and
deposed on oath that the following is a true statement of the cause
which led to her assault on Sarah White and to which she has pleaded
guilty at the present term of Court. That her husband William A.
Youngblood was a carpenter employed by the contractor at the tunnel
in this district, that then indigence required her to labor with her
own hands to aid in the support of the family consisting of three small
chn. That she with the consent of her husband opened a boarding house
at the tunnel for the laborers on the work, That she did nearly all
the cooking and washing for from ten to twenty five boarders.

Youngblood, Nancy Jane - Continued.   That to and in her severe
labor she hired a woman who called herself Sarah Busclark, that after
the woman had been in her employ about two or three weeks she learned
that her true name was Sarah White and that she was a loose woman.
That at the expiration of her month she dismissed said Sarah.   That
the manner of her husband changed very much towards her very much about
the time the woman left and insisted that Sarah White should be
retained.   She would not assent to it and drove her off.   About two
weeks after Sarah White left, she learned that her husband was con-
stantly visiting Sarah White and on one occasion, he had joined her in
a fishing party.   This deponent had rendered in her board bill to the
contractors amounting to $124 for board and washing for laborers.
About the same time her husband left his own home, his wife and children
and as she learned engaged board for Sarah White at a house at Kuthans
Copper mines.   That the arrangement was for Sarah to remain there for
two weeks, as it was supposed it would take that time to enable him
to finish a job he had secured at Kuthmans and then he was to take
Sarah, steal away the oldest child of this depoenent? and go to South
America to work on a contract which it was said Humbird had there to
build a railroad.   In the meantime she sent to the office of the
contractors to get bread and meat for herself and family, she dismissed
all her boarders the day before (and the very day that Youngblood
left home) and instead of the messenger bringing bread and meat he
return saying that nothing was due this deponent.   This deponent did
not eat a mouthful from Sunday night till Thursday night, she borrowed
a little meat and a little flour in the meantime for the children all
of which she gave to them.   Was satisfied that Sarah White was the
cause of her want, shame and distribution she counnselled(sic) several
of her female friends all of whom advised her to give Sarah a good
whipping with the hickory.   The advise was in confirmity with this
deponents own feeling and judgment and she went to the house where
Sarah was staying and invited her to come and stay all night with her.
It is due candor to say that the purpose of this was to Sarah to come
to her house and the next morning she intended to whip her.   Sarah
came the little flour and meat she had borrowed she divided with
Sarah.   The next morning this deponent rose early and went into the
room where Sarah was sleeping, she hesitated as to her course, but
upon a careful review of all the facts, she concluded that she ought
to chastise the strumpet.   She had previously prepared some hickories
and commenced on her, she tried to release herself but this defendant
held to her and administered a good chastisement, when this deponent
had given her about as much as she thought she deserved and when she
was about desisting deponent said to her this is what you get for
going a fishing with a married man, you came into my house and have
parted me and him, Sarah then said damn you I di, I have not parted
you and him but can do it you damn bitch I intend to make you shed
blood and tears in drops as big as tea cups, I have the money you
worked for, damn you help yourself.   I intend to break you up.   Then
this deponent exasperated beyond all endurance commenced upon her again
and inflicted upon her a severe chastisement, using herself only as
a hickory switch.   This deponent offered Sarah another indignity and
she left the premises.   Since the occurence her husband has returned
to his home and has treated her with a tenderness, kindness and
consideration worthy of his duties and obligation.   This deponent is
aware that under ordinary circumstances her offence might be justly
considered of magnitude in a woman but she throws herself upon the
clemency of the court in the earnest conviction that her provation
greatly extenates, the offence.. Sworn to this 20 March 1860.   Signed:
Nancy Jane Youngblood.   Wit: James L. Orr, Not. Pub.   The affadavit
of Wesley Pitchford made oath that he has known Mrs Youngblood for
near seven years and during that time she has enjoyed the reputation
among her neighbors of being a chastise and virtous woman.   Ambrose
J. Smith states that he has known Mrs. Youngblood from her infancy and
that she herself has for many years past been a member of the Methodist
Church.   James Lawrence and F. N. Garvin made oath that Sarah A. White
formerly Busclark is reported to be a common prostitute.

YOUNGBLOOD, SIMEON. Deed Book B., Page 60. Probate Judge Office. Pickens, S. C. On 23 Nov. 1861. Simeon Youngblood and wife Milly Youngblood were heirs of John Cassell decd. of Pickens Dist. and his widow Fanny Cassell.

YOUNGBLOOD, WILLIAM A. Pack 269. #26. Clerk of Court Office. Pickens, S. C. On 17 Aug. 1857 William A. Youngblood made oath that James H. Reeder did on 16 Aug. at tunnel hill strike him several blows.

YOWELL, JAMES. Box 23 Pack 799. Probate Judge Office. Anderson, S. C. Pendleton Dist. I James Yowell of this Dist. having lived to a great age but blessed with perfect sound mind and memory. First pay my just debts. I give to my beloved wife the plantation whereon I now live, with all the negroes, stock, tools, household and kitchen furniture during her neutral life. I give to my son Joel one negro woman named Lucy, to be received after the death of his mother. The balance of my negroes, household and kitchen furniture after the decease of my wife to be equally divided between my son Joel and the chn. of my son Joshua, and my dtr. Martha. The portion left to the chn. of son Joshua for the use and benefit of their mother during her widowhood. The land I intended for my son Allen and which he sold to my son Joshua having never been conveyed by me, I therefore vest in the chn. of Joshua reserving the use of it to his widow during her widowhood. The title of the land on which my son in law Davis Jones now lives being still in my. I direct that it finally decend to the chn. of my dtr. Polly. I appoint my son Joel Yowell and son in law Davis Jones executors. Wit: O.B. Trimmier, Meander Shaw, Ephm. B. Osborn. Dated 21 July 1814. Mary Yowell the widow petition the Court to sell part of the estate left to her during her life time, keeping negroes, Britian, Hester, and Morgan. Dated 19 Oct. 1814.

ZIMMERMAN, PETER. Box 104 Pack 2563. Probate Judge Office. Abbeville, S. C. We Elizabeth Zimmerman widow, Capt. Patrick Gibson, and Stephen Mantz all of this Dist. are bound unto the Judge of Abbeville Dist. in the sum of 1,000 pounds sterling. Dated this 25 March 1796. Inventory was had on 24 May 1796. By William Dorris, Joseph Herst, James Stiefel. Sale held on the 29 Nov. 1796. Buyers: Joseph Sanders, Elizabeth Zimmerman, John Wideman, Nicholas Hambay, Stephen Mantz, Henry Dilbon, James Henderson, Samuel Carter, David Rush, John Hose, Geo. and Wm. Perrin, Abner Perrin, Wm. Wade, John Scoggins, Jesse Harris, James Yeldell, Thomas McBride, Wm. Harris, John Glover, Wm. Coughran, Wm. Thomas, Isaac Ramsay, Jno. Perry, Jeremiah Cobb, Wm. Watson, John Syvart, Wm. Dorris, Henry Cosper, John Lawson, Wm. Childs, Philip Stiefel, James and John Adams, Jacob Cosper, Mrs. Belcher, Mathew Raods (sic), Saml. Perrin, Henry Andoph.

ZIMMERMAN, PHILLIP. #184. Clerk of Court Office. Abbeville, S. C. In Equity, To the Chancellors: William W. Belcher of said Dist. has our consent to be appointed guardian of Mary Caroline Zimmerman, and Phillip L. Zimmerman minor children of Phillip Zimmerman decd. and of Frances E. Gray now the wife of Dr. John Gray and formerly the wife of said Phillip Zimmerman, and we waive our right to the guardianship to W. W. Belcher. Dated this 23 May 1855. Signed: F. E. Gray and John Gray

Casey, John 108
  Moses 167
  Thomas 283
Cash, Stephen 238
Caskin, John 306
Cason, J. F. 288
  James 96
  Jas. 97
  John 12
  Joseph 12,72
  Josiah 72
  Larkin 73
  Rebecca 12
  Reuben 180
  Sarah 12
Casper, G. Henry 143
  Harmon P. 249
Cass, Fanny 271
Cassell, Fanny 271,331
  John 271,331
Castellaw, Tom 263
Castlebury, Young 30
Cathey, George 311
  John 311
Catledge, Isiah 249
Cates, Thomas 13
Caudle, Hannah 39
Cauly, Jacob 70
Cauncell, Edward C. 309
Causby, C. S. 302
Caven, Alexander 253
Cavin, Eleseraur 95
  Peter 95
Center, Elizabeth 42
  John 42
  Martha 42
  Nathan 42
  Thomas R. 49
  William 42
Certain, James 98
Chadwick, John 249
Chalmers, James 76
  Martha 43
Chamberlain, Alexander 42
  Charles 42
  Hubbard 42
  James 42
  Margaret 42
  Robert 42
  Wm. 42
Chambers, Benj. 266
  Benjamin 40,41,222,260,
  261,264,306,309
  Stephen 43
  Wm. 75
Chamble, George 29
Chambler, Thomson 62
  William 62
Chambles, Henry 247
  Preston 247
Chamblin, J. T. 127
  Telitha J. 127
Chamness, John 299
  Martha 299
Chandler, Daniel H. 43
  Daniel J. 43
  Frances 43
  Henry F. 43
  Joel 43
  Mary 43
  Matthew 43
  Sarah 12
  William 319
  Wm. 319
Chaney, David 15
Chaneys, Simion 137
Chany, Henrie 84
  Peter 84
Chapel, Thomas 35
Chapman, A. D. 226
  G. J. 213
  M. R. 215
  W. H. 110,166

Chapman, cont'd:
  Benjamin 43
  Elizabeth 320
  George 213
  James 43,243
  John 1,2,3,15,16,19,
  21,127,243
  Joshua 320
  Mary 183
  Matilda 213
  Narcissa 15,16
  Rebecca 43
  Sophia 2
  Willis 226
  Wm. 21
Chappell, John 2
  Thomas H. 300
Charlton, L. 201,202
Chastain, J. J. 44
  L. J. 44
  M. M. 44
  M. R. 44
  W. P. 44
  Abner 43,44
  Abner B. 44
  Abner D. 44
  Alfred M. 44
  Anson M. 44
  Cleveland 44
  Edward 43,44
  Feeby 171
  Friendly 44
  James 44
  James M. 43
  Jemima 44
  John 44,171
  John A. 43,44
  John B. 44
  John C. 44
  John D. 44
  John Henry 44
  John J. 44
  John L. 44
  Joseph 44
  Joseph T. 44
  Joseph Tilman 44
  Little 44
  Littleton 44
  Lucinda 43,44
  Malinda 44
  Margaret A. 261
  Martha L. 44
  Mary 44
  Mary Emelissa 44
  Matilda 44
  Maxwell 44
  Mileyann 43
  Nancy E. 44
  Nancy Eviline 43
  Nancy R. 44
  Nelson 44
  Peter R. 44
  Rachael L. 44
  Roland 44
  Samuel D. 44
  Sarah 44
  Susan 44
  Temperance 43,44
  Tilmon 44
  Tilmon R. 43,44
  William 44,261
  William L. 43
  Wm. 44
Chatham, Robert 72
  Thomas 224
Chasteen, Richard 138
Cheatham, B. 18
  B. M. 18
  W. J. 240
  Agnes 45
  Barnett M. 18
  Bartlett M. 45,284
  Calvin 45

Cheatham, cont'd:
  Elizabeth 45
  Frances 45
  Jackson 45
  James 45
  James Hayne 45
  John 45
  John L. 45
  John R. 45
  John T. 45
  Jno. 118
  Lucy 45
  Mary M. 45
  Nancy 45
  Preston Augustus 45
  Peter 45,137
  Robert 70
  Robert Joseph 45
  Sarah Ann 45
  Sarah E. 45
  Sophronia 45
  Susan 45
  Susan Ann 45
  Westley 45
  William Jasper 45
Cheesborough, Elizabeth 324
  John W. 45,46
Cherry, David 71
  Mary Margaret 24
  Samuel 54,71
Chesly, ___ 228
Chevelette, Louisa 263
Cheves, John 73
Child, R. A. 23,106
  Ida 46
  Jas. W. 76
  Robert R. 46
Childers, Mary 46
  William 118
Childress, B. S. 47
  J. M. 47
  J. T. 47
  L. E. 46
  M. O. 46,47
  R. E. 46
  R. S. 47
  W. B. 47
  Abraham O. 46
  Anderson M. 46
  Bethany C. 46
  Charles 46,47
  Edward N. 46
  Emily 46
  James 46
  Jeese 46
  John A. 46
  John H. 46
  John T. 46
  Laurissa J. 46
  Lucinda 46
  Marshall 46
  Martha Emma 46
  Mary M. 46
  Nancy 46
  Obediah W. 46
  Perry 46
  Robert 46,47
  Sarah 46
  W. Berry 46
  William B. 46
Childs, Nathan 68
  Wm. 331
Chiles, M. 18
  Benj. 121
  Benjamin 191
  Elizabeth 47,48
  Eunice 48
  Fanny 47
  Ferr 47
  Garland 70
  James 168
  John 47,48,91,200
  Juda L. 241

Duncan, cont'd:
  Lisly 79
  Margaret 79
  Mary 79
  Nancy 75,79,80
  Nathaniel 26,139
  Polly 79
  Rebecca 79
  Robert 297
  Sally 79
  Sion Turner 79
  Thomas 297
  William 79,80
  William Elbert 79
  Wm. 75
Duncomb, Abigall 149
  Elizabeth 149
  James 149
Dunham, B. 286
Durham, G. W. 150
  J. G. 80
  M. M. 140
  W. R. 207
  Daniel 109
  Eliza 107
  Elizabeth 80
  Eliza R. 107
  Geo. G. 80
  George G. 80
  Isaac 150,160
  Jeptha Allen 107
  John 80
  Margaret A. E. 209
Dunkin, Wm. 217
Dunlap, James 41
  Robert 105
  Saml. 306
  William 276
  Wm. 96,170
Dunn, A. J. 102
  Ally Ann 80
  Charles 311
  Edmund 311
  Elizabeth J. 80
  James 18,80
  Jane 80
  Jane C. 80
  John 80,88
  John E. 311
  Margaret 80
  Polly 206
  Robert 309
  Samuel 206
  William 311
  Wm. 80
Dunnehoo, Abner 80
  David 80
  John 80
  Sarah 80
  Whitfield 80
  William 80
Dupre, Cornelius L. 49
DuPre, Cornelius P. 42
Dupre, Mary 49
Dupree, Benjamin D. 62
Duram, Danial 21
Durant, Olin L. 22,56,125,
  127,209,211
Durborow, John 234
Durent, John 90
Durisee, W. F. 202
Durisoe, F. 14
Durner, Durury 299
Durrum, Stephen 91
Dushworth, William 254
Duvall, J. A. M. 138
  Elizabeth 80
  Michael 80
Dyar, William 277
  Wm. 277
Dye, Ch. L. 153
Dyer, Elizabeth 80
  Joshua 21
  Samuel 80

Dyer, cont'd:
  Thomas 80
Dyre, John 302
Dyson, Aquilla 20
  Isaac 105

Eades, John 227
Eakin, Alexander 80
  Joseph 80
  Mary Ann 260
  Matilda 260
  Minors 81
  Thomas 97,228,260
  Tom 246
Eakins, Elizabeth S. 81
  George W. 81
  James 81
  Jane 81
  John 81
  Thomas 81
  William W. 81
Earl, John 135
Earle, ___ 153
  B. 53,81
  E. J. 215
  J. B. 181,318,319,327
  J. W. 232
  Baylas 177
  Baylis I. 60
  Elias 66,185
  Elias Drayton 81
  Elizabeth 81
  Geo. W. 185
  George Washington 81
  Sam G. 7
  Samuel 26
  Samuel G. 81
  Sarah Caroline 81
Earles, Samuel G. 328
Early, Eanoch 81
  James 81
  Lettice 81
  Mary 81
  Patrick 81
  Phebe 81
  Pheby 81
Earnest, Nancy 208
  William 22
Earp, Mathew 328
Easley, John 45
  John A. 322
Easterling, Enos 98
Easters, Richard 11
Eastland, Thomas 105
Eaton, ___ 299
  J. C. 169
  James 32
  John 32
  Rebecca 32
  Sarah 32
  Wm. 32
Echard, Geo. B. 311
Eddins, James 162
  William 99,236
Edens, Alexander 125,194
  John 127
Edge, Caroline 106
Edgar, John 81
  Judeth 81
Edison, John 13
Edmondson, John 55
  Wm. 136
Edmondston, Charles 309
Edmunds, A. 59
Edmunson, Thomas 19
Edward, John 81
  Lemuel B. 113
  R. L. 102,109
  Adonejah 32
  Andrew 18
  Daniel 29
  David 81
  Henrietta 81
  James 81,284

Edwards, cont'd:
  John 81
  John S. 19,200
  Joseph 81
  Mary 81
  Mary Ann 81
  Patience 32
  Rebecca 81
  Robert S. 164
  Sarah 81
  Thomas 58,81,87
  William 81
  Wm. 153
Efort, Thomas 10
Ekerman, Christina 7
  Jacob 7
Elbert, Samuel 222
Elder, James 325
Elford, C. J. 126,261
Elgin, Ann 82
  Catharine 82
  Elizabeth 82
  Robert 82,221
Eliot, Jeremiar 19
Elison, Onan 73
Eliza, John 6
Elkins, John 303
  Jonas 179
Elledge, Abraham 96
Elles, Robert 189
Elliet, Andrew 94
Ellington, Bedy 82
  John 66,82,143
  Mary 82
  Stephen 294,295
Elliot, Alpha 31
  Doreas 311
  Samuel 311
Elliott, Allen R. 70
  Hum 311
  Nancy 122
Ellis, J. R. 312
  P. C. 246
  S. F. 246
  W. N. 246
  Adaline 213
  Amaziah R. 82
  Augustus E. 82
  Belle 246
  Benjamin F. 82
  Christopher 52,82
  Ebenezer 82
  Ebenzer P. 82
  Elizabeth 82
  Essie 52
  Eula 246
  Felix 257
  Gideon 83,212,213,216,
  316
  Harriet 213
  James Lucien 82
  John 19
  John Calvin 82
  John E. 82
  John L. 82
  Joseph 82
  Joseph N. 82
  Louanna 82
  Lucy 83
  Lula 246
  Luther T. 82
  Mahala Elizabeth 82
  Margaret 82
  Matilda 82
  Memminger M. 82
  Permelia 82
  Polly 82
  Reuben 83,216
  Robert 82,207
  Robert M. 82
  Savannah Paratine 82
  Underhill 257,268
  William 82
  William T. 82

Ellis, Wm. 320
Ellison, H. M. 56
 Joel 56,217
 Joseph 132
 William 224
Elmore, J. L. 276
 S. B. 283
Elms, John 323
 Malinda 323
Elrod, G. E. 265
 William B. 297
England, Mary 177
English, Amanda 83
 Andrew 83,119,161
 Behaheba 83
 Daniel 83,108
 David Jackson 83
 Elizabeth 83
 Frances 83
 Hugh P. 83
 James 83
 James B. 83
 Jane 83
 John 86
 Lucinda 83
 Mary 83
 Rosely 83
 Sallie 298
 Sarah 83
 Wm. 170
Enloe, John G. 256
Erwin, Jim 246
 Julia 246
 Rob 122
 Wm. R. 266
Ervin, F. A. 265
 John 257
Eskridge, Richard 9,191
Essery, Jonathan 160
Etheredge, Sallie A. 256
Ethridge, Lott 73
 Mary 77
Eubands, Aaron 155
 Harriet 155
Eubanks, Aaron 155,156
 Harriet 156
 William 318
Evan, Simpson 196
Evans, Alexina 304
 Benj. 8
 Emma Pauline 316
 Ezekiel 179
 Garner 159,243
 George 67
 James 83
 John 36
 Kesiah 316
 Keziah 317
 Mary 87
 Samuel W. 304
 Sarah 36
 Thomas 83,84
 William 36,250,317
Evatt, J. A. 43
 Hundley 199
 Wm. A. 59
Evens, Cary 96
 Elizabeth 83
Eves, William 25
Evins, T. A. 130
 James R. 112
Eymerie, Angelica 84
 Elizabet 84
 Henrie 84
 John 84
Eymore, John 154
Eyton, William A. 283
Ezzard, William 280

Fair, R. A. 89
 John H. 9
 John W. 9
Fant, O. H. P. 70
 V. D. 66

Fant, cont'd:
 George 202
Fargason, David 189
Faris, Wm. 327
Farley, Elizabeth 153
Farly, Elizabeth 152
Farmer, J. H. 315
 J. J. 245
Farr, James 67
 Lucy 203
 Richd. 203
 Thomas 311
Farramore, Ezekiel 221
Farrar, Thomas 92,273
Farris, Thomas 307
Faulkner, John 4,267,281
 Mary 281
Fawcet, Giles 25
Fawler, Keziah 24
Feemster, Caroline 84
 James 84
 James B. 84
 Jane 84
 Joseph 84
 Lettitia 84
 Mary 84
 Nancy 84
 Prudence 84
 Samuel 149
 William 84
Fendly, Charles 249
Fendley, William 46,302
Fenley, Charles 248
 Moses 67,68
Fennell, Elizabeth 139
 Hardy J. 139,177
 William M. 139,177
Fergus, John 120
Ferguson, G. 105,216,217
 J. G. 171,216,217
 S. N. G. 117
 Dale 246
 Denifie 246
 Frances 117
 J. Riley 205,217
 James 199
 James Hugh 63
 James T. 138,139
 Jane 216
 Jane Miller 63
 John 143,216
 Jno. 143
 John Ross 63
 Louisa E. 214
 Mary 63
 Sarah Ann 63
 Thomas 302
 William 63
Ferry, Tillers 121
Fewell, Alex. 327
 Alexander 307
Field, W. T. 211
 John M. 46
 Joseph A. 32
 Wm. T. 210
 Wm. 125
Fields, Elizabeth 189
 Joseph 189
 Joseph A. 19
 Nelson 312
Fiendly, Thomas 199
File, Adam 253
Filed, W. T. 210
Files, Adam 29
Finch, Edward 157
Fincher, Mary 278
 Timothy 278
Findley, James 134
 John 46
 Morning Jane 124
 Moses 134
 Sarah 227
Finley, James 101
 Thos. 239

Finney, Benjamin 102
Fish, John 195
Fisher, ____ 145
 James 195
 Polly 195
Fitchett, Daniel T. 5
Fitzgerald, Eli 142
 Margaret 152
 Thomas 152
 Thos. 152
Fitzpatrick, Peter O. 317
Fleming, James 84,85
 John 120
Fletcher, Leah 22
Flinn, Christian J. 122
Flippo, William 86
Flowers, Andrew 112
 John 118
Floyd, Elijah 319
 Enoch 292
Folger, A. W. 31
 R. W. 169
 Alonzo M. 23,225
 Ernest 329
 Lena F. 133
Folsom, Tobias 121
Foord, Barrat 85
 Elizabeth 85
 Fanny 85
 Milly 85
 Mosey 85
 Richard 85
 Sally Ann 85
 Samuel 85
Fooshee, C. B. 99
 Casen 85
 Charles 241
 Charles B. 85,98
 Chas. 109
 James 85
 James W. 192
 Joel 85
 John 85
 Jno. 137
 Martha 85,241
 Mary 85
 Rebecca Ann 85
 Sarah 85
 Washington 85
 William 137,242
Forbes, Elizabeth 23,292
 George 165
 John 23
 Mary 293
 Nathaniel 292,293
 Robert 293
 William 292,293
Ford, Ann 86,87
 Arasmus 86
 Daniel 36
 Edw. E. 6
 Erasmus 282
 Isaac 86
 John 86,87
 Leah 86,87
 Levi 86
 Linna 86
 Robert 267
 Tressia 86
 William 86
Foreman, Charity 85
 F. N. Garvin 322
 George 85,185
 Isaac 85
 Jacob 85
 Judah 85
 Martha 85
 Mary 85
 Olive 85
 Sarah 85
 Verly 85
 Zilpha 85
Forest, Jeremiah 85
Forman, George 85

Graham, cont'd:
  John 136,137
  Margaret 111
  Mary 328
  Polly 100
  Sela M. 100
  Susan 136
  Thursey 220
  Valentine 100,328
  Will 220
  William 100
  Wm. 100
Grant, A. B. 41,120,171
  Della E. 240
  Robert 158
  Roland 93
  Rolen 82
  Willis G. 240
Grantt, William 99
Graveley, Waddy B. 200
Graves, T. 291
  Caroline L. 291
  George 291
  Obed W. 215
  Thomas 291
  Wm. 100,215
Gravley, John L. 44
Gravly, C. 214
Gray, A. D. 101,223,253
  F. E. 331
  G. J. 100
  J. A. 316
  J. D. 101
  Agnes D. 100,101
  Alexander 34,101
  Alexander D. 102,253
  Alexander R. 94
  Alexr. 218
  Amanda 103
  Amy 37
  Andrew 88,231
  Anna C. 147
  Anne 102
  Arthur 102
  Daniel 147
  Eliza 103
  Elizabeth 100,101,102
  Frances E. 331
  George 100,101,144
  George J. 100
  Hannah 103
  Henry 326
  James 100,101,102,103
  James A. 74,103
  James Edwin 45
  Jane 258
  Jesse 103
  Jinney 103
  Jno. 161
  John 18,88,89,93,102,
  103,144,147,156,
  200,267,331
  John G. 103
  John H. 103,258
  John James 45
  Jonathan 94
  Lucinda 103
  Margaret 101,102
  Margret M. 101
  Martha Ann 103
  Mary 101,102,147
  Mary A. 101
  Mary Ann 326
  Nancy Augustine 102
  Rebecca 102,147
  Robt. 191
  Robert D. 74,231,297
  Robert Douglas 101
  Rosannah 102
  Sarah 101,102
  Sarah Jane 45
  Susan Ann 45
  Thomas 84,101,102,169
  Thomas R. 101

Gray, cont'd:
  Thos. 101,102
  William 80,100,101,102,
  103,224,249,302
  William A. 103
  Wm. 102,103,149
  Zachariah 100,102
Graybill, Henry 118,119
Grayham, Alexander 301
Grayson, B. M. 263
Grayton, Thos. 79
Greah, Thomas 88
Grealey, Oliver 156
Great, Thomas 88
Green, Aquiller 47
  Elisha 26
  Jane 170
  John 65,170,189
  Leroy 67
  Lucy (Gr er) 323
  Robert 185
  Samuel 96
  Susan 146
  Susannah 259
  William 252
Greene, Isreal W. 78
Greenlee, Deborah 104
  Dully 104
  Elizabeth 104
  James 104
  John 104
  Marget 104
  Mary 104
  Milley 104
  Nancy 104
  Peter 104
  Shadrach 104
  William 104
  Willie 104
Greenwood, Anne 104
  Fleming 104
  John 104
Greer, Gilbert 323
  Jos. 28
  Joseph 28,103
  Nancy 323
Gregg, Bishop Alexander 298
  Thomas 103
Gregory, 184
  Isaac 103,104
  John 203
  Polly 231
Grenike, John F. 65
Grenshaw, Elesebeth 203
Greyham, 220
  Nancy 161
Grice, D. 211
  J. 149
Griffin, B. M. 111
  C. B. 109
  E. 140
  E. H. 106,107,108,109,
  110
  E. M. 106
  E. S. 110,125
  F. J. 109
  G. B. 110
  G. W. 106
  H. P. 104
  J. C. 107,111
  R. Y. H. 110,251
  Abner T. 105,106
  Ada 110
  Adaline R. 105
  Adine 105
  Adino 94
  Agness 284
  Alva 105,106,161,265
  Alvah 105,108,262
  Amelia 284
  Anderson 110
  Ann 106
  Anna 107
  Anna M. 107

Griffin, cont'd:
  Anne 105
  Annie May 109
  Anthony 105,319
  Augustus 75,109
  Avarilla 110
  Avarilla A. 110
  Bailey 110
  Bailey B. 109,110
  Barton 110
  Benj. 106
  Benjamin 91,106,109,110
  Benjamin M. 107
  Benjmain 112
  Betty J. 105
  Betty Jane 106
  Buckner 284,285
  Carrie J. 110
  Charles B. 220
  David 105,109
  David Y. 39
  Elender 106
  Elender M. 106
  Elihu 70,106,107,110,
  212,213,225
  Elihu H. 107,108,109,
  110
  Elihu M. 110
  Elihu S. 106
  Eliza 107,108
  Elizabeth 105,106,107,
  108,110,145
  Elizabeth J. 107
  Elizabeth Jane 106
  Eula E. 110
  Florence 107,111
  George W. 106
  Geo. W. 105
  Green 105
  Floria 107
  Henry 19,105,108,232
  Holman 285
  Ira 105,108,109,168,170
  J. Calhoun 106
  Jac. C. 105
  Jacob 106
  James 99,110
  James A. 107
  James C. 255
  Jas. F. 109
  James M. S. 109,110
  Jane 220,284
  Jane Smith 105
  Jemima 105
  John 105,107,108
  John B. 106
  John C. 105,107
  John L. 109,111
  John V. 108,109,110
  Joseph 105,108,319
  Larkins 75,87,105,108
  Leonard 285
  Letty 300
  Lewis B. 109
  Lewis Brown 109
  Lucinda 105,284
  Lucy 105
  Lucy J. 110
  Lula L. 110
  Lyda 107
  Margaret 105,109
  Margaret J. 109,110
  Martha 39,109
  Martha C. 59
  Martha F. D. 109,110
  Mary 105,109
  Mary E. 109,110
  Matilda 105
  Melissa 108
  Milley 99
  Nathan 284
  Nancy V. 110
  Nancy 105
  Owen 110

Griffin, cont'd:
Parthonia 105
Patsey 285
Peggy 284
Rebecca 105
R. Harrison 106
Richard 104,105,108,109,
119,189,191,192,284,285
Richard H. 110
Robert 108,109
Robert C. 110
Robert T. 105,106
Robert Virginia 109
Robert Y. H. 107,110
Rosanah M. 110
Ruben 105
Sallie 105,106
Sarah 105,106,109,285
Sarah E. 110
Sargent 21,106,108,110
Susan A. 107
Susan Allen 110,111
Susan Steinbach 105
Susannah 108
Susannah G. 105
Thomas 59,106,108,110,
285
Thomas J. 108
Vincent 108,109,111,168,
314
Walter 107,109
Walter H. 111
Warren A. 110
William 105,108,109,
110,111,285
West 106
Wm. E. 110
Wm. Washington 109
Griffith, Jos. 1
Wm. 1
Grignillat, H. J. 165
Grigsby, Benjamin 2
James 104
Uriah 189
Grimes, Elizabeth 290
Hugh 111
Hugh (Graham) 111
Sarah 289,290
Grimke, John F. 273
Grimsly, Elijah 111
John 111
Mary 111
Sarah 111
Grindal, John 129
Rachel 129
Grisham, W. S. 322
Harriet T. 28
John O. 28,55,140,172
Jos. 112
Joseph 14,48,65,69,71,
112,162,208
Reuben 33
William 33
William S. 112,148
Grissop, John 112
Grogan, Jane Fidele 315
Grones, Joseph 99
Grooms, Robert 162
Gros, Francis 84
Grosse, Shepperd 80
Grub, William 219
Grubbs, Elizabeth 112
George 195
Nancy 26
Polly Ann 195
Richard 112
William 112
Grumbles, Lindsay 246
Guearineau, Pierre 84
Guerin, Abigail 112
Greenberry L. 112
Jacob 112
Margaret 112
Margaret K. 112

Guerin, cont'd:
Mary C. 112
Nat. 112
Nathaniel 112
Guess, James 113
Sophia 113
Guest, Allen 113
Moses 47
William 28,47,113
Guffen, Thos. 83
Guilbeau, Andrew 95
Eliser 95
James 95
Jean 95
Peter 95
Guinn, R. H. 196
Culp, L. G. 325
Gunnien, Benj. 113
Benjamin 113
Hannah W. 113
Isabella 113
James 113
Jeal 113
Mary 113
Gunnin, Benjamin 113
Gunnins, James 274
Gunter, John A. 243
Mary 246
Thomas M. 212
Gurgnard, James S. 257
Gusham, John O. 113
Joseph 113
Mary L. 113
Guthrie, John 81
Guyton, Aaron 115
Abraham 113,114,115
Amey 114
Betsey 115
Elizabeth 114
Hann 115
Hannah 114,115
Isaac 114,115
Jacob 114,115
John 114,115
John L. 114
John W. 254
Joseph 113,114,115
Joseph W. 114
Mariah 114
Martha 114
Mary 114
Molley 114,115
Moses 115,292
Nancy 114
Nathaniel 114,115
Patsy 113
Salley 115
Sarah 114,115
Tabitha 115
Vilet 114
Gwynn, Thomas 115
Gyton, Guyton 154

Hacket, Anna 116
Elijah C. 116
Martin 75,109
Hackett, E. C. 224
America E. 116
Anna 116
Augusta C. 116
Elijah C. 116
Elizabeth 116
Ella C. 116
Martin 118
William Freeman 116
Hacklaman, Conrod 61
Hadden, W. M. 89
Abraham 48
Daniel 78
Lucy 66
Polly 82
Wilson 66
Wm. 179
Zachariah 82

Haddon, Abraham 48
Abram 189
Clarence 245
Hagewood, T. 92
Nancy 92
Haggan, Edward 207
Haggos, James E. 225
Hagood, H. 183
J. E. 106,112,164,171,
214,251,264
J. O. 266
L. W. 219
W. H. 139
W. M. 139,217
W. N. 225
Benjamin 23,28,108,208,
209
James 138,250
James E. 59,110,116,139,
140,144,145,146,171,184,
200,204,209,213,219,225,
240,242,251,256,261,262,
263,272,312
Jane 270
John 219
Johnson 263
Lydia 260,263
Osborne 260
Hagwood, Benjamin 19
Haige, George 90
Haile, Benjamin 234
Hairison, J. H. 300
Hairson, John 273
Hairston, John 161
Thomas 116
William 116
Wm. 116
Halbert, Joshua 143
Thomas 32
Haley, Ruben 328
Halford, William R. 265
Hall, A. M. 253
E. 223
S. B. 261
T. J. 153
Aaron 122
Armstead M. 178
Caroline 153
Daniel 153
David 297
Drewry 297
Edward M. 178
Ezekiel 116,223
Fanton 253
Fenton 34,102,297
Frances E. 116
John 103
Lent 34,297
Lenton J. 297
Robert 188
Ruth 153
Sarah 153
Thomas 12
Wm. 94,153
Wm. B. 178
Zachariah 153
Zacharian 116
Halland, B. F. 180
Halloway, John 73
Rebecah 5
Hallum, T. F. 181
T. J. 180,182
Catharine 180,181,182
Eliza A. 243
Jefferson 180
Richard 243
Thomas 322
Thos. 99
Halsey, James 326
Hambay, Nicholas 331
Hambleton, John 86
Hambree, Edward 116
Elizabeth 116
Hamelton, John M. 297

Hamelton, cont'd:
Luke 297
Hamilton, A. 43,149,161
A. C. 75
T. 82
Alexander 11,117
Alexander C. 75,116,
117,283
Andrew 48,58,67,80,89,
90,108,143,149,160,170,
179,191,274,283
Ann Augusta 117
Augustus M. 318
David 73
Elizabeth S. 81
Frances 322
Harriet Eugena Davis
117
James Carson 318
Jane 117
John 117,136
John A. 100
John M. 51
Joseph Augustus 117
Luke 34
Mary 136
Mary C. 51,52
Paul 306,308
Richard Andrew 117
Robert B. 117
Sallie F. 316
Samuel Shiels 117
Susan 117
Thomas 99,100,302
Thomas P. 81
Warren 177
William 56,124
Wm. 157,168,316
Hamlin, Mary A. 177
Hammett, Je_se 65
Jesse 67
Jessey 67
Nancy 67
Hammond, J. H. 174
M. 92,235
Charles 8
Chas. 4
Christopher C. 4
Eben 1
Ebenezer 157
Frances 4
Herbert 31,131,215,218,
223,253,296
Julian F. 4
Margaret P. 117
Mary C. 4
Susanna 4
Teresa C. 4
William J. 117
Wm. H. 4
Wm. J. 218
Hammonds, Wm. 270
Hampton, Ephraim 34
Hamrick, David 40
William 120
Hamton, Joseph 157
Hanady, Jinny 69
Hancock, Sarah 123
Thos. 279
Hand/Hann, ___ 263
Handly, Peter 117
Hanie, Mary 73
Hannah, James 193
Robert 28
Hansell, John W. 22
Hanvy, Wm. 138
Hanway, Katharine 49
Harbin, T. W. 127,232
Frances 43
Thomas W. 43,213
Thomas W. H. 219
Thos. W. 184
Harbour, Noah 143
Hardee, John 254

Hardee, cont'd:
Sarah 254
Hardin, John 155
Sarah 83
William 83
Hardister, John C. 326
Hardy, Covington 5,8
Gallant 303
Gallant H. 303
Jeramiah 249
Lucy 302
Lusinday 303
Miles J. 317
Richard 249
Hargrove, Benj. 4
Harington, Young C. 277
Harkens, James 30
Harkness, J. N. 253
L. P. 245
James 170
Nancy N. 244
Robert C. 176
Theodosia Amanda 215
Vessie 246
Harlan, Nathan 278
Harland, George 24
Harlen, George 309
Harleston, ___ 321
Harley, Betsey 64
Jacob R. 266
Harling, Ellis 35
Harly, James 108
Harmon, Anthony 117,317
Appleton G. 117
Cornelia 117
Emanuel 117
John 117
Luke 117
Mary 117
Pickens 117
Thomas 117
William 117,303
Wm. 2,117
Harper, Elizabeth 71
James C. 289
John 71
Lucinda 117
Nancy 164
William 164,238,294
Harralson, Abigal 118
Benjamin 118
Gillen 118
Isom 117
Jesse 118
Lewis 118
Moses 117,118
Paul 118
Rebeckah 117
Harrel, Bidey 53
S. Wesley 122
Harrigal, G. W. 8
Harrington, Y. J. 3
Jepthah 234
Harris, A. O. 296
Alexander 120,150
Alexr. 143
Andrew 303
Azle D. 61
Benjamin 118,273
Christopher 275,276
Drucella 299
Elizabeth 275,314
Eliza C. 118
Jemima 275
Jesse 331
John 9,21,29,30,31,34,
37,39,54,58,67,69,70,
96,101,102,104,131,164,
167,184,195,255,294,
328,329
John C. 66
Larkin 203
Martha 143
Mary 37

Harris, cont'd:
Mathias 24
Nathan 215
Nathaniel 224
Nathl. 43
Richard 62,144
Saml. 143
Sherwood 282
Thomas 24,93,148,152,
238,292
William 108,203,275
Wm. 96,331
Harrison, B. 6
J. W. 130,131,296
W. H. 88
Ann 316
Ann Virginia 316
Benjamin 202
Edmund 8
Edw. 5,11
Frances 316
Frances Gillam 316
James 36
James M. 5
James W. 113
James White 316
John 6
John S. 236
Martin 160
Mary 316,317
Mary Longmire 316
Polly 221
Robt. 250
Susan W. 271
Valentine M. 134
Harriss, C. 302
Christopher 276
Hart, Wm. T. 40
Hartsfield, Miriam 138
Hartstom, Joikim 15
Harty, Richard 225
Harvey, Michael 118
Wm. 119
Harvy, Benjamin 85
Hase, John 138
Haskell, Charles T. 18,196,
294
Hassey, James S. 102
Hasty, Nancy 165
Hatacher, Wm. 321
Hatcher, J. 302
Archibald 263
Jeremiah 3
Mary 263
Priscilla 118
William 118,226,295
Hatfield, Sarah Ann 138
Hathorn, Charles 95
Hatter, Belinda 118
Benjamin 72,118
Elizabeth 118
Mahaly 118
Milly 118
Polly 118
Richard 118
Susannah 118
William 109,118
Zery 118
Hawes, Isaac 302
Hawkins, G. W. 200
T. G. 225
Andrew W. 297
Elizabeth 119
Julia 146
Mathew 119
Peter 67
Pinketham 118,119
Samuel 118,119
Sarah 119
Stephen 119
Thomas 119
Wm. 146
Haworth, B. 89
Hawthorn, A.C. 87,207,252

Hendrix, cont'd:
  Duncan 127
  Geo. 129
  Hannah 319
  Henry 56,169,226
  James 318,319
  Larkin 127
  Lawrence A. 169
  Margaret 56,169
  Moses 127,129
  Moses S. 129,274
  Susan 127
Hendrake, ___ 325
Hendrickson, Diana Abigail
  25
  Jacob Wane 25
Henkel, Silas 290
Henkle, Elijah 181
Henning, D. 67
Henry, John 8
  Peter 82
  Polly 29
Henson, Charles 129
  Frankey 73
  Henry 129
  James 104,129
  Joseph 129
  Lucy 47
  Mary 5
  Polly 73
  Rachel 129
Herd, John F. 229
Hering, Edward 129
  Marian 129
  Morgan 129
Heriot, Edward T. 324,325
  Francis W. 324
  Mary E. 324
Heriott, Edward T. 324
Heron, E. 121
  S. 121
  Catharine 121
  Christian H. 129
  Daniel 129
  Frances P. 129
  Gilly 129
  Isaac 130
  James 129
  Mahala 129
  Margaret C. 129
  Manuel 121
  Mary 129
  Nancy 129
  Rebecca 121
  Samuel 121,129
  Sarah 129
  William 129
  Zinnamon 129
Herrens, James B. 18
Herren, John Stephen 130
  Martha Elizabeth 130
  Stephen 129,130
Herrin, E. 79
  J. C. 130
  Elisha 29
  Ephraim 29
  Jesse 130
  Jesse C. 130
  Jesse J. 130
  John 34
  John W. 130
  Martha C. 130
  William 130
Herring, F. A. 285
  J. M. 130
  Benjamin Randolph 130
  Catherine 328
  Catherine W. 328
  Caty 327
  Elijah 130,131
  Elisha 131
  Eliza 130
  Esther 130
  Francis A. 130,285

Herring, cont'd:
  Isaac 3,36,130
  James M. 130
  Laura N. 130
  Mary 130,131
  Matilda 131
  Obedience 130
  Ruthy Ann 130
  Sarah Ann 130
  William 130,131
Herrins, James B. 18
Herrod, Charles B. 302
Herron, Andrew 131
  Daniel 129,131
  David 132
  Frances 131
  George 131,132
  George W. 131
  James 18,131,297
  John 132,297
  John T. 131
  Mary 132
  Mary T. 131
  Penelope 140
  Robert 132
  Samuel 130,131,132
  Sarah 131
  Thomas 131
  Thomas D. 140
  William 132
  William H. 131,140
  Wm. H. 140
Herst, Joseph 47,331
Hester, A. 170
  J. B. 145,180
  L. C. 145,267
  M. F. 250
  M. W. 145
  W. A. 145
  W. H. 145
  Abraham 140,145
  Alfred 140,141
  Amanda 146
  Ann 321
  Baliss J. 141
  Baylis M. 141,142
  Bettie 145
  Carville 140,142
  Carwell 145
  Cartharine 146
  Eady 141
  Elijah 144
  Elizabeth 140,145,146
  Elizabeth E. 144,145
  Emily 145
  Emily C. 140
  Harriet 146
  Henry 144,145,146,237
  James 141,145,146
  James B. 141
  Janie 144
  Jeptha 144
  Jobbery 146
  John 146
  John B. 145
  John Butler 145
  John Henry 144
  Joseph 146
  Julia 146
  Louisa 144,145,146
  Louisa J. 145
  Lucy 140,145
  Lucy M. 145
  Lula 140,145
  Lula J. 145
  Margaret 145,146,321
  Martin 146
  Mary 145,146
  Mary Jane 144,145
  Michael 145,146
  Nancy 146,321
  Rebecca 144,146
  Richard A. 140,145
  Robert 144,146

Hester, cont'd:
  Sallie 145
  Samuel 144
  Samuel J. 140,144,145
  Samuel R. 146
  Sarah A. 140
  Sare 144
  Susan 145,146
  Taylor 146
  Thomas 144,146,322
  William 107,144,145,146,
  321
  William H. 140
  Wm. Anderson 145
Heter, John 29
Hiatt, Elihu 24
  Mary Caroline 24
Hibben, James 323
Hibbler, E. B. 10
Hickman, Barbara D. 132,133
  Clarissa 132,241
  Dave 132
  James 132
  Jesse 132,241
  Joseph 132,241
  Martha (Patsy) 132,241
  Mary Caroline 132
  Richard 132,133
  William 132
Hicks, Edw. I. 2
  Landon 154
  Tabitha 2
Hidden, Dave 86
Hiett, James 36
  Mary A. 133
  Mary Ann 133
Higans, George 220
  Geo. 220
Higgins, A. J. 133
  H. S. 133
  J. A. 133
  J. F. 133
  O. K. 133
  T. B. 133
Higgenbottom, S. 302
Higginbotham, W. 294
  William 278
  Wm. 278
Higgins, Augusta A. 133
  George 220
  John 216
  John A. 133
  Lanny B. 133
  Samuel G. 133
  Victor B. 133
Hightower, Alfred 133
  Elizabeth 133
  George 133,134
  Jane 133
  John 133,134
  Joseph 134
  Joseph J. C. 55
  Joseph J. G. 55
Hilburn, L. J. 134
Hillburn, James 138,139
Hilburn, Rebecca E. 134
  Susan D. 134
Hillen, John 139
  Lewis 139
  Mary 139
  Nathaniel 139
Hillhouse, W. C. 181
Hillis, John 29
Hillman, John 132
Hill, ___ 259
  A. B. 145
  J. H. 190
  L. H. 137
  R. 135,137
  S. A. 137
  W. P. 138
  Abel 19,134
  Adam 61,76,135,139
  Andw. M. 137

Hill, cont'd:
Ann 123,139
Anny 138
Armistead Burt 220
Asap 321
Asaph 134
Ashworth 134
Benjamin 134,185,220
Betsy 136
Birdwell 134,160
Bluford 136
Caroline 136
Charity 134
Christiana 134
Daniel 123,136
David 136
Eleanor 136
Elisha 123
Eliza M. 190
Elizabeth 72,134,136,
138,220
Eliza 136
Fanny 136
Frances 134,135,137
Frances E. 136,137
George 135
Hamilton 91,134,135
Hel 80
Helen 137
Henry H. 136
Isaac Mitchell 137
Jacob 135,136
James 135,136,138,139
James Warren 134
Jane 136
Jesse 136
Jincy 136
Joel 8
John 135,136,138,139
Jos. 137
Joseh 137
Joseph 118,136,137
Josey 137
Joshua 80,138
Joycey 136
Katharine 135,136
Keziah 134
Larsey 136
Lewis 125,216
Lewis Hamilton 134
Lucretia 134
Malinda 136
Manes 136
Margaret 135,136,139
Martha 263
Mary 220
Milton 137
Mollie 139
Molly 138,139
Nancy 118,136,138,139
Peggy 135,138
Polly 136
Rebecca 136
Reuben 135
Richard 100,134,135,137
Robert 63,138,139
Sally 136
Saml. 137
Samuel 91,134,135,136,
220
Samuel Albert 134
Saml. L. 135
Samuel L. 91,134,287
Saml. S. 134
Samuel S. 135
Sarah 138
Sarah Cathrine 134
Sarah J. 137
Squire 302
Susan 125,135
Susan J. 137
Susan Jane 136
Susannah 136,137
Theophulus 8

Hill, cont'd:
Thomas 117,118,136,263
Thos. 189
Thos. J. 176
Travis 248
Uel 72,138
Wiley 137
William 54,74,92,95,
124,136,137,139,196,
220,258,294
William C. 136
William P. 138,310
Wm. 1,52,70,139,196,199,
268,282,283,313
Hinckle, James Farrow 138
Hindman, Lucy 261
Hinkle, Ailcey Adaline 138
Elias 138
Elias H. 138
Hinton, J. A. 139
J. T. 126,139
R. O. 139
Ada 139
Elizabeth 139
Allen 118,134
Huldah 232
James 94
Jeremiah 135
John 6,18,209,310
Martha 232
Mary 11
Robert 11
Ruth 139
Thomas 139,287
Thos. 287
Hitt, Elendor 139
Elisha P. 139
Elizabeth 139
Henry 139
James 139
Jane 139
John 139
Joseph 139
Martha 140,260
Mary 139
Nancy 139
Peter 139
Robert 139
Susannah 139
Thomas 139,140,260
William 139
Hix, H. 121
Balus 148
Elizabeth 140
Jesse 25
John 140
Reuben 62
Hobby, William J. 94
Hodges, N. W. 18
Blassongim 137
Charles 259
Elizabeth 136
Elvira 136
Frederick B. 148
Gabrel 88
Gabriel 237
George W. 253
Harrison 205
James 123
John 31,111,123,133,300
Richard 111
Robt. 254
Robert H. W. 253,254
Samuel A. 253
Sarah 111
Susan C. 253
Susan L. 254
Thompson 123
William 111,136,259,289
Hogans, James 92
Hogg, Jane 262
Hoke, D. 263
Holladay, J. W. 257
Holland, B. F. 180,181,182

Holland, cont'd:
D. T. 27
Franklin 180
Jno. 21
John 75
Jacob 46,47
Moses 301
Penelope 180,181,182
Peggy 320
Silas K. 182
Hollaway, Dan 6
Holleman, Edmund Peyton
185,186
Sarah Ann 186
Hollewager, John 6
Holliday, Eli 98
Rebecca 37
Hollinghead, J. 123
Hollingsworth, C. L. 183,
225
Columbus L. 213
Elias C. 177
Elias H. 117
Enoch 19
John 227
Malinda 213
Hollon, Jacob 46
Milley 290
Hollond, Rebekah 85
Holloway, Calib 10
John 248
Martha 248
Perry 249
William 10
Willis 70
Hollweys, Helene Catharine
142
Henrich 142
Henrick 142
Holbert, B. F. 177
Eliza 177
William 193
Holbrook, Jesse 296
Holcom, Jesse 237
Holcomb, R. E. 57
W. E. 55,59
Holcombe, ____ 124
E. T. 233
R. E. 22,23,150,204,233,
274,322
W. E. 46,105,106,108,
109,110,125,126,127,138,
140,144,145,146,151,152,
161,165,168,175,177,183,
206,209,212,213,217,243,
251,263,316
Elvira 47
Franklin 320
Vester E. 178
William 28,286
Wm. 286,287
Holden, James 169
Jinnete 169
John 169
Joshua 142,206
Keziah 142
Wm. 129,180
Holder, David 77
William 145
Holkom, Catharine 29
Holmes, Amos 150
Elizabeth 255
Frances America 201,202
George L. 255
John 281
Lewis 150
Martin 202
Patie 202
Sarah 281
Holms, Eleanor 328
John 249
Willis 70
Holomon, E. P. 176
Holsombeke, John 249

Kennady, Elizabeth 114
Kennan, Joseph 87
Kenneday, Isaac 203
Kennedy, A. 87
  A. B. 313,314
  A. M. 327
  J. I. 87
  J. L. 141
  J. P. 87
  Andrew 100
  Archibald 87,97
  Archibald B. 314
  Benjamin 25
  Benjamin B. 25
  Edmund 172
  George 160
  Isaac 37,78,313
  James 119
  Jas. 17
  John 78,83,97,180,238
  Michael 42
  Sarah 89
  Thomas 25
  Wm. 25
  Wm. E. 83
Kennemore, F. C. 46
  L. M. 272
  N. R. 272
  Amanda 150
  Benson 173
  D. Harvey 173
  Elias 173
  Elizabeth 173
  John 173
  J. Harvey 173
  John S. 173
  Juda 173
  Judy 173
  Lewis H. 173
  Martha 173
  Noah 173
  Rial 173
  Riley 173
  William 173
Kennemur, D. H. 173,174
  Lewis 173
  Lewis H. 173,174
  Amanda 174
  Cynthia 173
  David Harvey 177
  Harvey 173,174
  Elias 174
  Elizabeth 173
  Jane 173
  Joab John Harvey 173
  Joab 173
  John 173,174
  John S. 173,174
  Mary 173,174
  Noah 173,174
  Noah R. 177
  Rebecca 173
  Syntha 174
Kennerly, Rebecca 324
Kennmur, John R. 173
  Sarah 173,174
Kensler, Michael 174,175
Keown, James A. 175
  Robert 175
  Thomas 88,89
  Thos. 75
  William 34
  Wm. 93
Kerber, G. H. 168
Kerksey, Jared 180
Kernon, James N. 288
Kerr, Andrew 170
  Catherine 170
  David 170
  Isebella 170
  Jenney 170
  John 170
  Lettice 170
  Mary 170

Kerr, cont'd:
  Nancy 328
  Ruth 170
  Samuel 170
  William 170
  Wm. 95,170
Kersey, Dilly 171
  Jane A. 171
  Nancy 171
  Polly 171
  Robert 170
  Stephen 171
  Thomas 170,171
  William 170
Kershaw, James 267
Key, Anne J. 13
  John G. 13
  Robert 108,109
Kidd(Kid), Archibald 97
  Geo. 310
  George 172
  John 307
Kilcrease, Abraham 249
  Rody E. 310
Kilkelly, Mary 266
Killgore(Kilgore), Benja-
  min 103
Killingsworth, M. 205
  James 176,309
  Mark 176
  Martha 176
  Nancy 176
  Sarah 176
  Susan 176
  Susan E. 176
  Wm. 176
Kilpatrick, F. W. 175
  J. C. 34,175,176
  R. C. 175
  Alexander 175
  Amanda 175
  Andrew 179
  Barbary 179,180
  Benjamin F. 175
  Clara 175,176
  Clarissa 175
  F. Whitner 175
  John C. 175,176,300
  Rebecca C. 175
  Rebecca Cammella 175
Kimble, Elijah 93
Kinard, Jno. A. 256
King, J. B. 178
  J. E. 177
  W. J. 178
  Alexander W. 88
  Arthur G. 178
  Benjamin 177,300
  Chas. S. 178
  Clarence 178
  David 177
  Elijah 177
  Elisha 177
  Elizabeth 177,178
  Elizabeth A. 88
  Flora M. 178
  Flora Margaret 178
  Geo. W. 177
  George W. 176,177
  Henry 302
  Isaac 177
  Jacob 177
  Jacob M. 177,178
  James 168,177
  James B. 178
  James N. 288
  Jeremiah 177
  Jesse 177
  John 177,260,261,283
  John B. 177
  John Milton 178
  J. Monroe 177,178
  Jonathan 177,300
  Joseph 300

King, cont'd:
  Lou M. 178
  Lucinda 177
  Lurena 177
  Margaret C. 177,178
  Mary 177,178
  Mitchell 305
  Nancy 177
  Narcissa 177
  Peter 101
  Polly 177
  Robert 177,178
  Ruth 178
  Sally 177
  Saml. 177
  Samuel 177,300
  Sarah 177
  Thomas J. 178
  Thos. 254
  Vester E. 178
  Warren M. 178
  William 165,177,178
  Wm. 138
Kingsmore, J. 100
Kingsley, Chester 178,179
  Erasmus R. 179
  Eugene T. 179
  Francis E. 179
Kinman, S. 205
Kinmon, Saml. 309
Kinshley, Edward T. 12
Kirby, Jesse 72
Kirkland, Ann 179
  Bethany 8
  Elizabeth B. 323
  Isaac 149
  Lydia 179
  Mary 179
  Mary M. 323
  Mary Miller 327
  Richard 179
  Tempey 179
  Warren 10
  William T. 179
Kirkpatrick, Hannah 179
  Elizabeth 179
  James 179
  Jane 179,180
  John 267
  Margaret 180
  Mary 180
  Rebecca C. 175
  Richard 179,180
  Thomas 179,180
  Wm. 21
Kirksey, E. W. 180,181,182
  J. K. 181,183
  S. 141
  W. S. 181
  Catherine 180
  Christopher 180,181,182
  Eady Catherine 180
  Edy C. 182
  Edy Catherine 180
  Elisha 21
  E. Winchester 182
  Fair 180,181,182
  Isaiah 21,180
  Isaiah A. 182
  Isaiah W. 182
  James K. 181
  Jared 182
  Jared E. F. 182
  Jas. J. 181
  J. Brown 164
  Jay 21
  Jerod 180
  Joseph 182
  Joseph Brown 180
  Mark 181
  Mary 180
  Mary L. P. 182
  Mary P. L. 182
  Nancy 180,182

McAdams, cont'd:
James 150
Jim 246
Lindsay 195
Mason R. 195
Rachel 195
Vira 246
William 212
McAfee, Abuham 247
Ann 319
Catsey 195
Hugh 195
James 195
Jordan 195
Joseph 195
Martha 195
Patsey 194,195
Robert 247,319
McAlister, ___ 18
T. 297
W. 57
Alex. 42
Andrew 79
John 238
Maggie A. 245
Maggie P. 244
Nathan 79,296,297,317
McAllister, A. H. 237
Andrew 75,253
James 235
McAlwain, Wm. 179
McAnn, R. T. 235
McAnts, David W. 87
McAphee, Joseph 252
McArter, John James 306
McBee, Vardry 195
McBeth, George 195
McBride, T. C. 267
Hugh 161
James 97,196
Jane 196,267
Jno. 90
John 196
John Andrew 196
Joshua 196
Josiah 196
Robert 200
Samuel 196
Thomas 80,97,196,267,
331
McCaa, Amelia 323
McCain, Mary 94
William 303
Wm. 124
McCalisters, David R. 18
McCall, W. P. 152
McCalla, Ellen 309
George R. 94
John 258
McCalley, Janat/Janet 327,
328
Jenet 328
McCallister, Andrew 191
Jane 97
Miles 301
Nathan 317
McCallum, James 15
McCann, Robert 19,252
Rt. 167
McCanns, Robert 190
McCants, N. 85
David 88
Nathaniel 257
McCarley, Jos. 26
Rachel 274
William 34,285
McCarter, P. 20
W. P. 245,246
Emma 245
James 149,161
John 224
Lillian 246
Wickliffe 245
McCarty, Dennis 1,4

McCarty, cont'd:
Robert 4
McCary, Richard 250
McCaskill, Alexander 121
McCaslam, Moses 96
McCaslem, Patrick 313
McCaslan, M. O. 76,196,
232
R. A. F. 76
Alexander 76
James 96,196
Moses 96
Oliver 76
Patrick 219
Robert 102,138
William 77
McCasland, Oliver 97
McCaslin, Robert 101,292
Wm. 77
McCaulay, George 305
McCaw, ___ 57
Alexander Barr 196
Elizabeth 196
Julia Carolina 196
Margaret 196
Margaret Frances 196
Samuel 308
William H. 196
William Henry 196
Wm. 22
McCay, J. R. 263
Archibald 133
McCellan, Charity 197
Jane 197
Robert 197
McCelland, John P. 320
Martha 320
Mary 320
McCelvey, H. M. 197
J. H. 197
J. L. 196,197
George W. 197
Hezekiah C. 197
Hugh M. 197
James 276
James L. 196,197,277
Mary J. 196,197
Vincent 319
William 196,197
McChany, John 265
W. John 265
McClain, D. 23
J. O. 246
James 73,95,219
McClanahan, ___ 41
Wm. 161
McClanihaw, John 81
McClannahan, F. R. 126
McClare, ___ 142
McClellan, Archibald 323
Elijah 197
John 197,198,283
Margaret 197
Mary 96,197
Mary Ann 320
Mary Jane 198
Robert 197
McClelland, John 197,198
Nancy 27
McClendon, Jesse 8
McCleskey, Isabella 14
James 14
William 29
Wm. 95
McClintock, Henry K. 198
Henry King 198
Joseph 257
McClinton, A. S. 198,199
J. R. 199
Alexander 198
Alexander S. 198,199,
274
Caroline 199
George M. 199

McClinton, cont'd:
Hannah 199,274
James 172,199
James R. 199
Jane 199
John 103,199
John H. 198
Rosannah 199
Samuel 199
Samuel B. 199
William 96,199
McClunkin, ___ 63
McClure, ___ 143
Charles 177
Edward J. 200
John 104
Sarah 184
McCluskey, Jane 21
McClusky, Joseph 327
McCollister, Edward 29
John 65
McCollough, Elinor 309
McCollum, David 6,144,199
Duncan 80
James 23
Samuel 19
William 14
McColough, Catherine 17
John T. 17
Mary C. 17
McComb, Andrew 292
John 23,91,200,292
Robert 23,96,97,101,102,
149,161
McCombs, John 200
McConnel, James 86
Reuben 308
McConnell, Sarah 208
Wiley 208
McCool, Gabriel 200
Isaac 109
John 203
Wm. 191
McCoole, Gabl. 200
McCord, James A. 171
John 75,116
John R. 100
Lemuel 285
Margaret 285
Sarah A. 171
Wm. 18
McCords, Wm. P. 18
McCormick, David C. 110
Elvira J. 201
Hugh 74,201
John C. 201
Mary 201
McCoy, W. B. 106
Martin 118
Sarah Ann 106
McCracken, Samuel A. 108
McCrady, James W. 200,280
Parthena 200
Permelia 280
McCrae, Elizabeth 9
McCrary, J. B. 200
W. J. 200
Alfred 200,215
Alfred M. 200
Andrew 68
Elizabeth 215
Mary M. 200
Moses 69
Sarah E. 200
William J. 200
McCraven, A. M. 138
McCrawn, Edward 156
McCreary, John C. 200
Joseph 200,201
Mary 200
Peggy 200
McCree, James 100
William 207
McCreless, Surles 149

Martin, cont'd:
  Margaret 302,303
  Margaret P. 218,219
  Mary 189
  Mary Ann 296
  Matt. 6
  Matthew 6
  Melissa 218
  Nancy 18,146,219
  Oliver 179
  Phares 237
  Pharis 302
  Pheby 218
  Philip 145
  Rebeckah 219
  Richard 218
  Richard A. 219
  Rosey L. 208
  Sally 155
  Sarah 218,219
  Stephen 208
  Terry C. 6
  Thomas 249,277
  Thomas P. 84,85,277
  William 219
  William P. 92
  William Q. 218
  Wm. 144
Massengale, Elizabeth A.
  214
  Green W. 214
Massey, Agnew 161
Masingill, ___ 228
  W. K. 167
  Deborah 219
  Dread 219
  Jane 219
  John 232
  Joseph 219
  Sindarilla 232
Mason, Charles W. 219
  Daniel 176
  Elias 270
  Elizabeth 219
  Frances 193,219
  Joel 193,219
  John 219
  Milly 219
Massy, Elizabeth 177
  John 282
Masters, John 44
Mathewes,Jno. 282
Mathews, Catherine 264
  George 146
  Isaac 103
  James 170
  Jos. C. 123,143,239
  Joseph C. 123
  Thomas H. 325
  Thos. F. 264
Mathis, Elford 220
  George 8
  Isabella 219,220
  Jane 12,220
  Jesse 129
  John 78,88
  Luke 10,168,170,219
  Mary 220
  Molley 9
  Samuel 264
  Sarah 220
  William 9,220
  Zebulon 12
Mathison, Deencein 292
Matin, William P. 193
Matterson, ___ 89
Matthew, J. W. 5
  James 154
Matthews, John 4,6,35
Mattison, G. M. 92,157
  Benj. 82
  Benjamin 92,215
  Daniel 51

Mattison, cont'd:
  Elizabeth 4
  Gabriel M. 92,157,180
  Geo. 178
  George 92
  Jane 92
  John 92
  William 4,112
  Wm. 30
Mattox, ___ 206
  Augustin 259
  Letty 259
  Peggy 259
  Richard 259
  Wm. 205
Mattuce, John 131
Maulden, J. 124
  Archibald 238
Mauldin, B. D. 248
  J. B. 211
  R. 265
  Allen 23,163,165
  Arch. 317
  Elias E. 22
  Frances 28
  Francis 28
  Gula E. 240
  Joab 46,107,124
  Jacob 213
  John 234
  John G. 116
  Lewis 265
  Rucker N. 50
  Samuel E. 28
  Saml. E. 28
  Tyre B. 177,213,272,313
Mauldins, Rucker 265
Maus, Nancy 28
Maverick, Saml. 181
  Samuel 56,199
Mavericks, F. S. 232
Maxey, E. H. 132
Maxwell, Charles 109
  Chas. 109
  Elizabeth 176
  Hugh 41
  James 90
  Jane 178
  John 79,175,176,178,283
  John C. 198
  Robert 2,116,268
  Robert A. 156,175
  Samuel 155
  William 302
May, Albert 130
  Alford 6
  James 292
  John 4
  John W. 5
  Lewis 6
  Stanford 6
  William 5
Mayberry, Rhuben 101
Maybury, D. 205
Mayes, Daniel 6
  John 4
  John P. 10,11
  William B. 6
Mayfield, Ephriam 30
  Israel 173,216
  John W. 25
  Pearson 216
Mayn, William 179
Maynard, James 1,2,3
Mays, Edward S. 8
  Henry 220
  James 40
  John Mathew 220
  John P. 8
  Larkin 220,237,302
  Lucretia Ann 220
  Mary E. 237
  Mary Elizabeth 220

Mays, cont'd:
  Meady 237
  Medy/Meedy 220
  Nancy 136
  Needy 220
  William 136
Mayson, A. 118
  C. C. 207
  S. 13
  W. L. 13
  Archey 47
  Charles C. 109,189
  James 109
  James L. 75
  John 47,90
  Willis 72
Maysons, James 47
Meaders, Thomas 315
Mealing, David 8
  Jos. 4
Mealy, Thomas 94
Mederman, Hermon 169
Medford, Isham 60
  Rhoda 60
Medlin, Catharine 154
  Michael 154
Medlock, ___ 151
Meek, Wm. 269
MeGee, Tilmon C. 176
Megehe, Dabney 186
Mellard, William 98
Melton, S. W. 308
  Mack 8
  Michael 8
Memminger, Mary 324,325
Mendenhall, M. T. 98
Mercer, Jesse 21
Meree, J. W. 130
Merewether, Jno. 89
  Thomas 59
Meriwether, ___ 89
  John 191
Merk, Henry 77
Meroney, Nolen L. 44
Merratt, Cleveland 186
Merrill, Margaret 329
  William 329
Merriman, L. D. 51
  Frank Clinkscales 52
  Eleanor Brownele 52
  Jane 52
  Lewis D. 52,53
  Loisa Jane 51,52
  Rowena Elizabeth 52
Merritt, E. W. 127
Merriwether, C. S. 227
  Charles S. 227
  John 90
  Joseph 90
  Milly T. 227
Meyers, Leonard 273
Mgee, M. 245
MGilld(?), Isabella 95
Michie, James 69
Middleton, Ainsworth 11
  Elizabeth 11
  Henry 305
  John 11,116,224
  Margaret 11
  Robert 68
Miles, James H. 218
Milford, G. W. 26
  Nancy Alkansa 26
  Robert 34
Mill, Hooper 283
Miller, L. 118
  W. C. 204
  Adelia 163
  Alax. 309
  Allen T. 288
  Andrew J. 163
  Ann 12,149
  Caroline 215

Posey, cont'd:
Price 206
Robt. V. 156
Wm. 63
Postell, Eliza 239
James 238
Rachel 238
Potter, Wm. T. 69
Potts, Jeremiah 289
John 222
Wm. 261
Pound, John 319
Powel, Allen 181
George Gabriel 149
Powell, B. N. 239
Almon 239
Angeline 239
Asel 239
Elizabeth 239
Harrison 239
Isham 267
Jeremiah 239
Joseph 320
Robert 30,55,239
Thomas 239
Thos. 239
Power, H. F. 192
J. G. 240
V. I. 240
Drury 240
Henry 133,192,239,240
John William 253
J. William 240
Louis R. 253
Louisa 192
Louisa R. 254
Mariah 240
Mary Lieuezer 240
Nathaniel 240
William 253
William K. 240
Zachariah 240
Powers, J. G. 240
M. L. 240
Aquilla 279
Della E. 240
Drewry 240
Drury 240
Emily C. 240
Emma 66
Harriet E. 240
Harriet O. 240
James G. 240
Jesse 66
Jno. 22
Mary L. 240
Pinckney 240
Robert K. 240
Thomas 6
Victoria I. 240
Wm. K. 240
Prater, J. B. 243
Aaron 242,243
Austin 243
Eliza 243
Eliza A. 243
Henry 243
Jeremiah 213,242,243
John 242,243
Joseph 242,243
Josiah 242,243
Margaret 243
Philip 242,243
Susan 243
Wm. 75
Prather, James W. 302
Pratt, E.___ 244
J. J. 24,114
J. P. 245,246
S. C. 243
W. W. 245
Annie 245,247
Burts B. 245
Caroline 244

Pratt, cont'd:
Charles M. 245
Charley 247
Claude A. 245
Cornelia 243
Daist(?) 245
Elizabeth 243,244
Emma 244
Flora 245
Frances 245
Gussie 245
James 243
James A. 244
James Alex 243
James L. 243
James W. L. 243
Jane 244
Jane A. 244
Jane B. 245
Jessie L. 245
Jesse P. 244
J. Marion 245
John 243,244
John J. 278
John Lawrence 243
John N. 244,245,246,247
Joseph 158,243,244
Joseph J. H. 244
Langden 243
L. Annie 245
Lilly 245
Livy E. 245
Louisa Jane 243
Maggie A. 245
Maggie P. 244
Maggie R. 245
Marion 246
Mary 243,244,245
Mary Z. 244
M. Elizabeth 245
Milton 244
Nancy N. 243,244
P. Hassie 244
P. Minerva 244
R. Lewis 244,245
Robert 82,245
Robert M. 244,245
Rosa E. 244,245
Rosa Lee 245
Sarah 243,244
S. Langdon 244
Sue A. 243
Thom 244
Thomas 243
T. Rufus 244
W. Cecil 245
William 243
William A. 244
William L. 244
Wm. L. 246
W. Walter 244
Predriau, Susannah 285
Presley, Farr 47
John 47,97,149
Pressley, David 89
Ebenezer 142
Jamie 246
Saml. 138
R. A. 316
Pressly,___ 78
J. 157___
Ann 247
Calvin 292
David 86,161,247,296
David A. 297
Ebenezer 122
Ebenezer E. 7
Elizabeth 7,296
George 200
Geo. W. 100,196
James P. 328
Jane 292
John 47,91,103,110,149
John S. 122

Pressly, cont'd:
John T. 97,122
Levi 27
Robert C. 296
Saml. 73
Samuel 95,122
Wm. 122
Preston, Ezekrel 247
Isaac 247
Jesse 207
Prewet, Fields 319
Prewit, Auset 247
Dudly 247
Field 252
John 247
Micajah 247
Stephen 247
Prewitt, Austin 247
Bennett 247
Dudly 247
John 247
Josiah 247
Micajah 247
Solomon 247
Stephen 247
Price,___ 245
T. R. 44
W. W. 247
Anny 250
Cader 247
Charlotte 247
Charner 247
Cutberth 302
Eleanor 247
Elizabeth 248
Elizar J. 248
Hannah 247
Hannah E. 223
Henry 250
Hopkin 249
Isaac 69
James 250
Jane 248,249
John 55,247,249,250
Joseph 247,248,249
Joseph S. H. 248
Joseph T. 248
Joseph W. 248
Judith 248,249
Judy 248
Martha 248
Mary 247
Matilda 248
Mattie S. M. E. 248
Nancy 250
Paten 21
Pen 249
Penuel 34
Rachel F. E. J. 248
Rebecca 235
Rice 248,249
Samuel 249,250
Sarah 247
Sarah Wilson 247
Thomas 249
Thomas S. 248
William 247,249,250
William N. 248
William R. 44
Wilson 247
Wily 249
Wm. C. 250
Prichard, W. L. 251
Mary A. 251
Prince, F. M. 250
H. M. 18
J. M. 251
R. M. 251
W. M. 250
Arrenia 251
Caroline 127,250
Charles 250,251
Edward 19,170,250,251
Edward S. 21

Reagan, Young 97
Reas, Absalom 19
Reaves, George 6
  Hiram 239
Rector, Daniel 181
  Tom 68
Red, George 231
Redden, Samuel 108,121
  Thomas 162
Reddin, Samuel 108
Redmond, Andrew 108,200
  Frederick 117
Reddrick, Ulbrick 13
Redrick, Saml. 8
  Undrick 13
Ree, T. S. 80
  Thomas S. 80
  Wellington 80
Reed, Samuel 21
  William 302
Reeder, B. F. 153
  James H. 331
Reese, ___ 46
  Elizabeth 263
  George 255
  James E. 198
  Thomas L. 69
Reeve, James W. 112
Reeves, Wiley 40
  William D. 207
Reice, John 228
Reid, H. 188
  J. B. 180
  M. H. 127
  S. 157
  S. C. 141
  Alexander 17
  Andrew 328
  Geo. M. 176
  George 17
  James M. 141
  John 30,40,310
  John H. 218
  Joseph 319
  Joseph B. 141,161,321
  Lettie J. 200
  Mary T. 217
  Samuel 17,89,109,110,
    144,166,181,204,209
  Sarah 141
  Stephen C. 141
  Thomas B. 62
  William 30
Reighley, William 153,255
Reightly, Wm. 63
Rembert, Andrew 255,302
  Elisha 323
  Harriet M. 255
  James 255,302
  James A. 255
  Lewellen 255
  Louisa 255
  Louisa R. 255
  Mary H. M. 255
  Rebecca 255
  Samuel 255
  Samuel S. 255
  William P. 255
Remington, John 249
Rend, Arabella Ann 69
Rennolds, John 297
  William 248
Reynolds, Agness W. 111
  Bennett 198,310,313
  John V. 97
  Larkin 89,111,121,191,
    198,231
  Wm. 74
Rhea, Rebacka 306
Rhodes, Collins 27
  Matilda 329
  Patience 27
  Raidford 27
  Rollin 27

Rice, ___ 116
  Hezekiah 61,253
  Leonard 255
  Sarah/Sary 255
  William 18,25,113,115
  Wm. 114,234
Rich, Lewis 78
Richard, Adam 108
  James 273
Richards, ___ 254
  Adam 160,255
  James 160
  Mary P. 160
  Thomas 255
Richardson, E. B. 110
  J. 8,10,155
  Abraham 134
  Benjamin 2
  David 12
  Dudley 192,242
  James 6,288
  James B. 308
  Jefferson 10
  John 75,207
  Joseph 154
  Jno. 89
  Richard 154
  Turner 201
  Walker 68,146,295
  William 39
Richeson, David 170
Richey, H. A. 209,228
  J. 18
  R. C. 194
  Andrew 207
  Benjamin A. 255
  Caroline 215
  Elizabeth 199
  Elizabeth Jane 254
  Emilly 169
  George W. 168,169
  Isaac 309
  Isaac C. 254
  James 169,200,201,259
  James W. 279
  Jane 259
  John 18
  Joseph 31,87,205,309
  Jno. R. 309
  Nancy 31,136
  Reuben 309
  Robert 18,80,105,133
  Robert C. 136
  Robt. 75
  Ruben 308
  Virginia C. 255
  William 205
  Wm. 309
Richman, F. 40
Richmond, John 273
Rickets, Sallie 261
Riddle, Mary J. 145
  Mary Jane 145
  Sally 120
Ridell, Thomas 258
Ridgway, James 301
Ridings, T. 67
  Tyre 68
Rievs, George 123
Riggs, Abram 250
Right, Robert 195
  William 185
Riley, ___ 284
  Henry 18
  John 306
  Thomas 81
Rillen, William 318
Rion, John 6
Riser, H. H. 256
  A. Picken 256
  J. Elbert 256
  Jas. H. 256
  Keerrenhappuck 256
  Marill E. 256

Riser, cont'd:
  Sallie A. 256
Risor, George 256
  Jacob 256
  Jacob Collins 256
  Jacob Commick 256
  John Lagrone 256
  John Lightse 256
Ritchey, W. H. 192
  William H. 192
Rivers, Joseph 281
  Robert 281
Roach, Edmund 288
  Henry 312
  Randel Lee 312
  William 256
Robbeson, John 238
Robbosson, Ephraim 165
Roberson, David 75
  Frederick 219
  Jane 24
  Jno. 156
  John 189
  Jonathan 261
  Saml. 75
Robeson, Abel B. 256
  Catherine 256
  Charles 256
  Elizabeth 257
  Elizabeth L. 257
  Iven 303
  James 256
  John 96,170,256,257
  John W. 256,257
  Jonas 256
  Joseph 257
  Lusey 256
  Marie 256
  Martha 257
  Mary 257
  Sarah 256
  Washington 256
  William 256
  Willis 257
Roberts, ___ 255
  B. F. 163
  T. B. 126
  W. R. 250
  Adeline 106
  Amos 88
  George 97,102
  James C. 251
  John 10,170
  Joseph M. 33
  Little Berry 46
  Nancy 163
  Reuben 103
  Thomas 126,127
  Willis 167
Robertson, A. V. 259
  B. S. 259
  F. P. 176
  J. 205
  M. A. 259
  R. 206,268
  W. S. 259,260
  Alexander 325
  Allan 259
  Allen 140,255
  Andrew 187,259
  Benjamin 258
  Benjamin E. 257
  Catharine 140,255
  Charles 256
  Charity 258
  Charrity 258
  David 93,97,264
  Dorcas 257
  Elihue 258
  George 258
  Hardy 249
  Hugh 257
  James 207,208,258,259
  James M. 258

Shirley, cont'd:
  Letta Masena 283
  Levi Thompson 283
  Louvenia Naomi 26
  Martha 329
  Mastin 283,309
  Nancy 283
  Nathaniel 283
  Polly Ann 283
  Richard 283
  William 91,283
Shirly, Benjamin 112
  Nathaniel 112
Shockley, John 67
  Mary 277
  Rachel 277
  Richard 277
Shoemaker, Hannah Eliza-
    beth 284
  Laban 284
  Martin 143
  Polly M. 284
  Thomas 284
  Tompson 203
Shropshur, Felix 328
Shurley, Easter 63
Shuler, George 318
Sibert, Jasper 262
Sibley, Stacy 86
Sigane, Silas 120
Silleman, John 40
Sillerman, John 40
  Mary 40
Simeril, H. H. 310
  James 310
  Jancy 310
Simkins, John 6,13,202
  Mary 12
Simmons, Ervin 44
  Francis 284
  James H. 206
  Lewis 108,109
  Lewis S. 152,168
  Mary Y. 284
Simms, Riscubda 327
Simon, Lewillen 8
Simpkins, Arthur 12
  John 14,202
Simpson, A. 171
  G. W. 171
  J. L. 227
  Archibald 142,328
  George 171
  Henry 157,284
  Hugh 81
  James 221,249,254
  Jane 45
  Jas. 316
  John 119,238
  Mary 105
  Rebecca 153
  Robert 317
  Thos. 253
  William 34,54,162,207,
    238
Sims, W. K. 202
  Alex 293
  Amelia 284
  Elizabeth 206
  Elizabeth S. 205
  George 285
  George W. 207
  James 291
  Johnston 207
  Leonard 285
  Lizzie 285
  Martin 11
  Nathan 241,284,285
  Susan 292
  William 103
Simrill, W. N. 327
Simson, Archable 328
Sinclair, Duncan 256

Singletemy, John I. 98
Singleton, ___ 151
  G. W. 161,163
  J. W. 42,232
  W. B. 250
  Garland 163
  John W. 46
  Miles 161,163,165,257
  Strete 19
  William 55
Sisson, Nancy 241
  Nick 241
Sitton, A. E. 322
  Arranah 216
  Elizabeth B. 216
  James Y. 199
  John B. 316
  Phillip 215
  William 227
Skelton, Archibal 29
  Jacob 74
  John 276
  Jonathan 58
  Solomon 274,285
  William 193,276,285
  William W. 74
Skinner, W. 121
  James 121
  John 121
  Mariah 121
  Wm. 121
Skipper, ___ 299
Skirving, William 42
  Wm. 42
Slann, Andrew 75
Slappy, Jacob 168
Slaughter, Arthur 93,258
  Sarah 95
Sligh, Jacob 297
Sloan, ___ 41,142
  B. F. 166,181
  J. B. E. 181
  T. M. 176
  W. D. 150
  Alexander 61
  Benjamin 181
  Benjamin F. 88
  Benj. F. 88
  Berry 181
  David 54,65,88,92,203,
    273,298
  Elizabeth 60
  George T. 315
  John 294
  John T. 227
  Nancy 298
  Sarah R. 294
  Susan A. 88
  William 252
  William D. 183
Smith, ___ 240
  A. J. 218
  A. M. 194
  J. A. 174
  J. F. 174
  J. P. 178
  M. A. 163
  N. K. 174
  P. R. 212
  R. F. 178
  R. W. 4
  W. 156
  W. A. 127
  W. J. 22
  Z. 226,227
  Alexander 279
  Ambrose J. 330
  Amelia 285
  Anderson B. 285
  Andrew N. 17
  Archer 193
  Augustus M. 277
  Augustus W. 277

Smith, cont'd:
  Bailey 279
  Bazel 29
  Beda 280
  Beershaba 277
  Benjamin 205,279,309
  Betsey 289
  Buckner 21
  Charles A. 279
  Chas. 137
  Christina 315
  Daniel 113
  David 277,278
  Deliah 277
  Dorcas 278
  Eady 173,174
  Elijah 29
  Eliza 137
  Elizabeth 228,278,279
  Fanny 277
  Fleet 278
  Flora M. 178
  Frances 53,279
  Frederick 279
  Gabrill 74
  George 279
  Giles N. 279
  Ginsey 279
  Hannah 279
  Hazel 279
  Henry 277,278
  Isaac 278,279
  Jacob 4,187,306
  James 88,89,119,221,267,
    277,278
  Jane 69,105,279
  J. Bolton 308
  J. Clayton 127
  Jemima 278
  Jesse 7
  Jewette 279
  Job F. 110
  Joel 87,88,157,288
  John 82,92,94,100,115,
    165,188,193,200,267,278
  John E. 23
  John H. 1
  John W. 5
  Jonathan 115
  Joseph 113,323
  Joseph Ebenezer 279
  Joshua 12,21,72,235
  Josiah 86
  Joshey 21
  Levi 278
  Lewis 74
  Lewis Wardlaw 277
  Margaret 271
  Martha 279
  Mary 225
  Miles 279
  Molly 115
  Moses 19,278,279
  Moses B. 279
  Nancy 20
  Nancy C. 171
  Newell 279
  Noah 174
  Pater 279
  Patsey 279
  Permelia 280
  Peter 302,303,322
  Philip 42
  Polly 12
  Pricillah 278
  Priscilla 187
  Ralph 133,167
  Richard 279
  Riley 19
  Robert 4,93,96,220,231,
    279,309
  Robert S. 266
  Robison 328

Center, Dick 42
  Ephrim 42
  Rouk 42
  Sam 42
  Sarah 42
  Tantzey 42
Chiles, Abrilla 47
  Alley 47
  Dafney 48
  Fill 47
  Mary 47
  Moses 48
Christopher, Lindy 255
  Reuben 255
Clark, Alexander 48
  Andrew 49
  Archey 48
  Charles 49
  Eliza 48
  Harriet 48
  Jack 49
  Jane 48
  Jesse 48
  Jinny 48
  Katharine 48
  Lucinda 48
  Martha 48
  Mary 48
  Sally 48
  Sarah 48
  Thomas 48
  Washington 49
  William 49
Clinkscales, Curda 51
  Cyrus 51
  Dinah 52
  Eliza 51
  Frank 51
  Gracy 52
  Haney 52
  Harvey 246
  Henry 52
  Lige 52
  Lucy 52
  Mack 52
  Mary 51
  May 51
  Phillis 52
  Rose 52
Cochram, Tom 53
Coffee, Minerva 53
Conner, Joe 54
Covington, Alfred 57
  Charles 57
  Cinda 57
  Creswell 57
  Davy 57
  Frances 57
  Henry 57
  Isham 57
  Jan 57
  Joe 57
  Levi 57
  Lewis 57
  Lucy 57
  Melissa 57
  Mill 57
  Millie 57
  Milly 57
  Mima 57
  Nancy 57
  Nanny 57
  Olive 57
  Reuben 57
  Sally 57
  Sam 57
  Smart 57
Cowan, Harry 58
  Kate 58
  Smart 58
Crayton, Abb 60
  Clara 60
  Curtis 60
  Henry 60

Crayton, cont'd:
  Jackson 60
  Kitty 60
  Middleton 60
  Milly 60,
  Tilda 60'
  Washington 61
Crow, Allin 63
  Bob 62
  Jack 63
  John 63
  Lewis 63
  Marak 63
  Sarah 62
Cruikshanks, Ann 63
  Betty 63
  Chairity 63
  Chloe 63
  Dinah 63
  Fanny 63
  George 63
  George Brown 63
  Toby 63
Dacus, Andrew 68
  Ben 68
  Caroline 68
  Clarissa 68
  Cloe 68
  Creecy 68
  Daniel 68
  Elias 68
  Eliza 68
  Frances 68
  Gilbert 68
  Hammett 68
  Isham 68
  Jack 68
  John 68
  Lancaster 68
  Liza 68
  Magor 68
  Martha 68
  Mary 68
  Merida 68
  Nappy 68
  Peggy 68
  Randal 68
  Ritter 68
  Sarah 68
  Silvia 68
  Tom 68
Darby, Charity 69
  Fanny 68
  Frederick 69
  Garland 68
  Hamilton 69
  Jim 68
  John 69
  Sarah 68
  Simon 68
Dart, Amos 69
  Ben 69
  Cora 69
  Fanny 69
  Franklin 69
  Luncinda 69
  Richard 69
Davis, Aron 67
  Ben 67
  Bob 67
  Dicy 67
  Dolly 67
  Frank 67
  George 67
  Leah 67
  Little Joe 67
  Marta 67
  Mary 67
  Moses 67
  Notty 67
  Reuben 67
  Rose 67
  Ted 67
Devall, Sarah 80

Dill, Mint 73
  Mops 73
  Rubin 73
  Zed 73
Divall, Billy 71
  Catherine 71
  Charles 71
  Milley 71
  Molly 71
  Pompey 71
Donald, Antony 74
  Dicy 74
Donaldson, Charlotte 74
  Derry 74
  Jean 74
Dowten, Elenans 76
Duvall, Charles 80
  Cumbogh 80
  Grace 80
  Hannah 80
  Jane 80
  Lucy 80
  Rebeca 80
English, Abram 83
  Chany 83
  Hampton 83
  Huldah 83
  Wesly 83
Feemster, Mariah 84
Foreman, Joe 85
  Patt 85
Foster, Cain 86
  Carolina 86
  Cole 86
  Kitt 86
  Lill 86
  Limbrick 86
  Sall 86
  Sam 86
  Sawyer 86
  Sheriff 86
  Silvia 86
Franklin, Aggy 87
  Alford 87
  Annica 87
  Dick 87
  Fillis 87
  George 87
  Ginny Ann 87
  Hagar 87
  Hiram 87
  Jack 87
  Jane 87
  Jim 87
  Miley 87
  Patty 87
  Polly 87
  Pompy 87
  Sary 87
  Sudy 87
  Willie 87
Frazier, Anne 88
  Anthony 88
  Augustus 88
  Caroline 88
  Clara 88
  Charles Bingley 88
  Charlotte 88
  Eliza 88
  Henry 88
  Hiram 88
  John 88
  John Lewis 88
  Julia 88
  Louisa 88
  Martha 88
  Oliver 88
  Peter 88
  Rebecca 88
  Violet 88
  Washington 88
Gaines, Clarissa 89
  Henry 89
  Sally 89

\#

CPSIA information can be obtained
at www.ICGtesting.com
Printed in the USA
BVHW04s1147050618
518255BV00001B/11/P